Mechanical Vibrations

April, 2001

Bram de Kraker & Dick H. van Campen

Eindhoven University of Technology
Department of Mechanical Engineering
Engineering Dynamics Section

E-mail: A.d.Kraker@tue.nl/D.H.v.Campen@tue.nl
www.wfw.wtb.tue.nl/dyna

Printed in The Netherlands.

ISBN 90-423-0165-1

Shaker Publishing BV
St. Maartenslaan 26
6221 AX Maastricht
Tel.: 043-3500424
Fax: 043-3255090
http:// www.shaker.nl

Contents

Preface

In these lecture notes the general methodology for the linear analysis of multi-degree-of-freedom dynamical systems will be presented. The presented theory and discussed phenomena can be seen as a logical extension of the theory for single-degree-of-freedom systems spanning topics as the derivation of the equation(s) of motion, free undamped and damped motion, forced vibrations with especially harmonic motion and, finally, some experimental topics.
The central theme will be focussed on analysing linear models for the dynamic behaviour of realistic, mechanical systems. Not only the analysis methods and their numerical implementation will be treated, but also specific attention will be paid to the evaluation of the results and to the possibilities of using these methods in a design environment.

The first part is dealing with *two-degree-of-freedom linear systems.* The advantage of first looking at these 2-dof systems and not directly switching to multi-degree-of-freedom systems is that on the one hand still some familiar 1-dof approaches can be applied but that on the other hand systematically some new concepts, relevant for multi-degree-of-freedom systems can be introduced. Topics which will be treated are the general structure of the equations of motion, eigenfrequencies and corresponding eigenmodes and the decoupling property of eigenmodes. A typical application will be the analysis respectively tuning of a so-called dynamic vibration absorber.

In the second part an appropriate alternative for the application of Newton's Laws for the derivation of the equations of motion of a system will be derived, namely *Lagrange's equations of motion*. With this procedure the nonlinear, coupled equations of motion for complex mechanical systems can be derived in a straightforward systematic way. Especially the practical application of this methodology will be emphasized.

It will be shown how static equilibrium positions of the nonlinear equations of motion can be determined and in which way the nonlinear equations of motion can be transformed into a set of linear equations of motion by assuming small motions around a stable equilibrium position. This linear set of equations of motion will be the basis for the remaining chapters.

First the special case of *undamped multi-degree-of-freedom linear systems* will be treated. The analysis of the undamped behaviour is still one of the most important sources of information for the design of mechanical systems. It will also be shown that in general the results from the analysis of the undamped system build up an important input for the analysis of mechanical systems with damping included, especially the modal superposition method. This undamped part will be concluded by the presentation of systematic procedures for the reduction of the number of degrees of freedom of extremely complex systems such as for example created by using a Finite Element Method.

In Chapter 4, *damped multi-degree-of-freedom linear systems* will be discussed. Attention will be paid to the special case of harmonic excitation and to the subclass of systems for which the undamped eigenvalue problem still applies such as weakly- and/or proportionally damped systems. Some important practical issues will be treated in the analysis of a hydro-elastic engine mount. Finally a short introduction for the analysis of systems with a general type of viscous damping will be presented. It will be shown that by switching to a state-space description again a simple systematic procedure can be developed.

In some cases the theoretical/numerical analysis of a mechanical component is very difficult or not so efficient such as for example the determination of the characteristics of a car tyre as input for a vehicle model. Also the theoretical evaluation of damping (the type as well as the level) will be difficult in many cases. In those cases an experimental approach will be the obvious procedure to tackle the problem. Some fundamental topics of up-to-date experimental procedures will be discussed in the final chapter.

Attention will be paid successively to Fourier analysis (DFT/FFT), the definition and calculation of auto- and crosspower spectra and finally the estimation of frequency response functions of linear dynamic systems.

Throughout all chapters, many specific problems are presented and solved in order to allow the reader to get familiar with the practical application of the theory. Additionally, in appendix A, a collection of more overall problems is given together with the answers. In many cases not only the answer is given but also some additional discussion related to the practical relevance of the associated problem. Some of these problems can be solved by hand, many of them however are too complex and for these some computer programme has to be used. All the solutions and elaborations in these lecture notes are derived with the computer programme *MATLAB*.

BRAM DE KRAKER & DICK H. VAN CAMPEN

Eindhoven, April 2001

1

Time-Invariant Two-Degree-of-Freedom Linear Systems

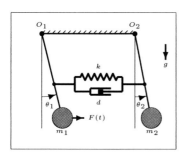

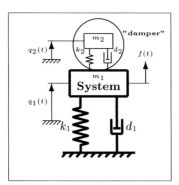

Dynamical systems that require two independent coordinates to describe their motion are called two-degree-of-freedom (2-dof) systems. They can be looked upon as a special case of the larger class of multi-degree-of-freedom linear systems. The top figure alongside shows a double pendulum system. A particular response of this system will contain the so-called beating effect. The bottom figure gives a simple model for a vibrating machine and an additional mechanical substructure serving as vibration damper

This chapter intends to give an elementary treatment of 2-dof linear systems but also is intended to introduce new concepts playing a role in the more general study of linear systems with an arbitrarily number of degrees of freedom, which is the subject of subsequent chapters.

1.1   INTRODUCTION

If we impose an arbitrary initial disturbance (excitation) to an undamped time-invariant single-degree-of-freedom linear system, then the ensuing so-called free motion can be phrased as free vibration or, alternatively, a natural vibration, which indicates that the system vibrates at a frequency depending on the system parameters, the *natural frequency*. Later, it will be shown that natural vibration of a time-invariant multi-degree-of-freedom linear system implies its arbitrary free motion to be composed of vibrations in a distinct number of *natural frequencies*, all depending on the system parameters. To each natural frequency corresponds a certain displacement configuration, or shape, for the system as a whole. For such a natural configuration, the ratio of any two time-dependent displacements taken at different locations in the system does not change during the vibration associated with that natural frequency. These natural configurations are known as *normal modes, principal modes*, or *natural modes of vibration*.

The mathematical formulation for a two-degree-of-freedom system results in two equations of motion. They are generally in the form of two *coupled* ordinary differential equations, that is, each equation involves both degrees of freedom. Hence, these equations cannot be solved independently. In the chapters on multi-degree-of-freedom linear systems, a general procedure will be discussed for uncoupling the equations of motion. We will elucidate the elementary treatment of two-degree-of-freedom linear systems in the following sections by taking a specific system as an accompaning example. In this way, we will successively discuss the general structure of the coupled differential equations, the free motions of the associated undamped system including the uncoupling of the equations, and the steady-state response to harmonic ex-citation. In the last two sections of this chapter we will treat two specific subjects, which can be looked upon as applications, namely, a phenomenon known as beating, as well as undamped dynamic vibration absorbers.

1.2   GENERAL STRUCTURE OF THE DIFFERENTIAL EQUATIONS

To elucidate the general structure of the coupled differential equations of motion for a two-degree-of-freedom linear system, we consider a system consisting of two pendulums connected by a linear spring and a linear viscous damper as shown in Fig. 1.1. Each pendulum consists of a concentrated mass (m_1,

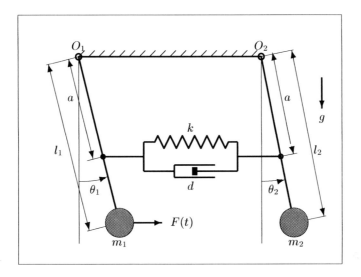

Fig. 1.1   Coupled pendulums

resp. m_2) attached to one end of a rigid massless bar (length l_1, resp. l_2), while the other end of the bar is fixed (at point O_1, resp. O_2). The linear spring (stiffness k) and the linear viscous damper (damping constant d) are connected to the bars l_1 and l_2 at a distance a from O_1, resp. O_2. On mass m_1 an external time-dependent force $F(t)$ is acting in horizontal direction. The pendulum system is moving in a vertical plane under the influence of gravity. During the motion the position of the bars l_1 and l_2 is described by means of the angles $\theta_1(t)$ and $\theta_2(t)$, as also shown in the figure.
It is assumed that $\theta_1(t)$ and $\theta_2(t)$ are small to such an extent that $\sin\theta_i$ may be replaced by $\theta_i (i = 1, 2)$, whereas $\cos\theta_i$ may be replaced by 1 ($i = 1, 2$). The free-body diagrams of the pendulums are shown in Fig. 1.2, in which the assumption of small angles θ_1 and θ_2 is implied. Because both pendulums act like rigid bodies moving in a plane about a fixed point, we can apply the angular momentum theorem for the left pendulum with respect to O_1 and for the right pendulum with respect to O_2. This yields the following differential equations of motion

$$m_1 l_1^2 \ddot{\theta}_1(t) - da^2 \left[\dot{\theta}_2(t) - \dot{\theta}_1(t)\right] - ka^2 \left[\theta_2(t) - \theta_1(t)\right]$$
$$+ m_1 g l_1 \theta_1(t) = l_1 F(t) \tag{1.1}$$

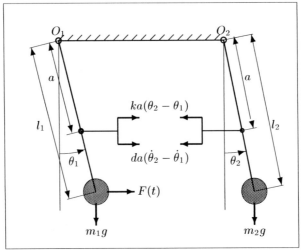

Fig. 1.2   Coupled pendulums

and

$$m_2 l_2^2 \ddot{\theta}_2(t) - da^2 \left[\dot{\theta}_1(t) - \dot{\theta}_2(t) \right] - ka^2 \left[\theta_1(t) - \theta_2(t) \right]$$
$$+ m_2 g l_2 \theta_2(t) = 0 \qquad (1.2)$$

We note that (1.1) for $\theta_1(t)$ contains terms involving $\theta_2(t)$, namely, $-da^2\dot{\theta}_2(t)$ and $-ka^2\theta_2(t)$. Also, (1.2) for $\theta_2(t)$ contains terms involving $\theta_1(t)$, namely, $-da^2\dot{\theta}_1(t)$ and $-ka^2\theta_1(t)$. Hence, (1.1) and (1.2) represent a system of two *coupled* differential equations. The terms rendering the equations dependent on one another are referred to as *coupling terms*. In the case of (1.1) and (1.2), the coupling terms are $-da^2\dot{\theta}_2(t)$ and $-ka^2\theta_2(t)$ in the first equation and $-da^2\dot{\theta}_1(t)$ and $-ka^2\theta_1(t)$ in the second equation. Hence, we must expect the motion of the right pendulum to influence the motion of the left pendulum, and vice versa, except for $d = k = 0$. In that case the equations of motion become independent of one another. The case $d = k = 0$ is of no interest for this chapter, however, because in this case we no longer have a two-degree-of-freedom system but two completely independent single-degree-of-freedom systems, as the bars l_1 and l_2 are not physically connected anymore. Equations (1.1) and (1.2) can be condensed in matrix form as

$$\underline{M} \, \ddot{\underline{q}}(t) + \underline{D} \, \dot{\underline{q}}(t) + \underline{K} \, \underline{q}(t) = \underline{f}(t) \qquad (1.3)$$

where the time-independent (2×2) matrices $\underline{M}$, $\underline{D}$, and $\underline{K}$ are known as the *mass matrix*, *viscous damping matrix*, and *stiffness matrix*, respectively, and are given by

$$\underline{M} = \begin{bmatrix} m_{cc} & m_{12} \\ m_{21} & m_{22} \end{bmatrix} = \begin{bmatrix} m_1 l_1^2 & 0 \\ 0 & m_2 l_2^2 \end{bmatrix} \qquad (1.4)$$

$$\underline{D} = \begin{bmatrix} d_{11} & d_{12} \\ d_{21} & d_{22} \end{bmatrix} = \begin{bmatrix} da^2 & -da^2 \\ -da^2 & da^2 \end{bmatrix} \tag{1.5}$$

$$\underline{K} = \begin{bmatrix} k_{11} & k_{12} \\ k_{21} & k_{22} \end{bmatrix} = \begin{bmatrix} (ka^2 + m_1 g l_1) & -ka^2 \\ -ka^2 & (ka^2 + m_2 g l_2) \end{bmatrix} \tag{1.6}$$

while the (2×1) column matrices $\underline{q}(t)$ and $\underline{f}(t)$ are called the *generalized displacement column* and *generalized force column*, and are given by

$$\underline{q}(t) = \begin{bmatrix} q_1(t) \\ q_2(t) \end{bmatrix} = \begin{bmatrix} \theta_1(t) \\ \theta_2(t) \end{bmatrix}, \quad \underline{f}(t) = \begin{bmatrix} f_1(t) \\ f_2(t) \end{bmatrix} = \begin{bmatrix} l_1 F(t) \\ 0 \end{bmatrix} \tag{1.7}$$

It is remarked that in literature often the terminology displacement *vector* and force *vector* is used instead of displacement *column* and force *column*. We prefer to use the latter terminology, because we want to distinguish explicitly between vector notation and matrix notation.

The elements of the matrices $\underline{M}$, $\underline{D}$ and $\underline{K}$ are known as the masses, viscous damping coefficients and stiffness coefficients of the system, respectively. They depend on the particular choice of the independent coordinates (often referred to as degrees of freedom) describing the system motion. It is easy to see from (1.4), (1.5) and (1.6) that the mass, damping and stiffness matrices are symmetric, as expressed by

$$\underline{M} = \underline{M}^T, \qquad \underline{D} = \underline{D}^T, \qquad \underline{K} = \underline{K}^T \tag{1.8}$$

where the superscript T denotes the transposed of the original matrix. The solution of the equations of motion (1.1) and (1.2) for an arbitary force $F(t)$ is difficult to obtain. This can be attributed predominantly to the fact that the two equations are coupled in the coordinates $q_1(t)$ and $q_2(t)$. We observe from (1.4)- (1.6) that this coupling manifests itself via the non-zero off-diagonal terms in the damping matrix and the stiffness matrix. In this particular example, the mass matrix is diagonal. Regularly, the mass matrix will also be non-diagonal, as we will see later.

1.3 FREE VIBRATION OF UNDAMPED SYSTEMS: NATURAL MODES AND GENERAL SOLUTION

In the absence of damping and the external force, the differential equations of motion for the two-degree-of-freedom system of Fig. 1.1 can be obtained from (1.1) and (1.2) by letting $d = 0$ and $F(t) = 0$. The resulting coupled *homogeneous* equations are

$$m_{11} \, \ddot{q}_1(t) + k_{11} \, q_1(t) + k_{12} \, q_2(t) = 0 \tag{1.9}$$

$$m_{22} \, \ddot{q}_2(t) + k_{21} \, q_1(t) + k_{22} \, q_2(t) = 0 \tag{1.10}$$

where the mass and stiffness coefficients are the elements of the mass matrix $\underline{M}$ and the stiffness matrix $\underline{K}$, respectively, which according to (1.4) and (1.6), for our system are given by

$$m_{11} = m_1 l_1^2, \; m_{22} = m_2 l_2^2 \tag{1.11}$$

$$k_{11} = ka^2 + m_1 g l_1, \; k_{12} = k_{21} = -ka^2, \; k_{22} = ka^2 + m_2 g l_2 \tag{1.12}$$

Now, we will discuss the structure of the general solution of (1.9) and (1.10). To this end, we first eliminate $q_2(t)$ from these equations. This can be done by differentiating (1.9) twice with respect to time, followed by the elimination of $\ddot{q}_2(t)$, using (1.10) and of $q_2(t)$, using (1.9). After dividing through by m_{11}, we obtain the following fourth-order linear ordinary differential equation for $q_1(t)$

$$q_1^{IV}(t) + \left(\frac{k_{11}}{m_{11}} + \frac{k_{22}}{m_{22}} \right) \ddot{q}_1(t) + \frac{1}{m_{11}m_{22}} \left(k_{11}k_{22} - k_{12}k_{21} \right) q_1(t) = 0 \tag{1.13}$$

It is remarked here that a similar differential equation can be obtained for $q_2(t)$. According to the general theory of homogeneous linear ordinary differential equations with constant coefficients, the general solution of (1.13) has the form

$$q_1(t) = \hat{C}_1 \, e^{\lambda t} \tag{1.14}$$

where λ is a characteristic exponent and $\hat{C}_1$ is a nonzero complex constant of integration. Inserting (1.14) into (1.13) and dividing through by $\hat{C}_1 \, e^{\lambda t}$, we obtain the characteristic equation for λ

$$\left(\lambda^2 \right)^2 + \left(\frac{k_{11}}{m_{11}} + \frac{k_{22}}{m_{22}} \right) \left(\lambda^2 \right) + \frac{1}{m_{11}m_{22}} \left(k_{11}k_{22} - k_{12}k_{21} \right) = 0 \tag{1.15}$$

This is a quadratic equation for $\mu = \lambda^2$, having the two roots

$$\mu_{1,2} = \lambda_{1,2}^2 = \frac{1}{2} \left[-\left(\frac{k_{11}}{m_{11}} + \frac{k_{22}}{m_{22}} \right) \right.$$

$$\left. \pm \sqrt{ \left(\frac{k_{11}}{m_{11}} + \frac{k_{22}}{m_{22}} \right)^2 - \frac{4}{m_{11}m_{22}} \left(k_{11}k_{22} - k_{12}k_{21} \right) } \; \right] \tag{1.16}$$

Elaborating the expression under the square-root sign, we can alternatively express the roots μ_1 and μ_2 as

$$\mu_{1,2} = \lambda_{1,2}^2 = \frac{1}{2} \left[-\left(\frac{k_{11}}{m_{11}} + \frac{k_{22}}{m_{22}} \right) \right.$$

$$\left. \pm \sqrt{ \left(\frac{k_{11}}{m_{11}} - \frac{k_{22}}{m_{22}} \right)^2 + \frac{4k_{12}k_{21}}{m_{11}m_{22}} } \; \right] \tag{1.17}$$

As follows from (1.6), for the two-degree-of-freedom system of Fig. 1.1 the stiffness matrix $\underline{K}$ is symmetric, so that for this system we have $k_{12} = k_{21}$. Later, in Chapter 2, we will evaluate systematically the system matrices for general multi-degree-of-freedom linear systems. There, we will show that a large class of linear systems exists with symmetric system matrices. In Chapters 3 and 4 a considerable simplification of the analysis will appear to be possible for those *symmetric linear systems*. Of course, this simplification will also affect the analysis of the undamped two-degree-of-freedom linear system considered in this chapter.

For the case that $k_{12} = k_{21}$ it can easily be seen that the discriminant

$$dis = \left(\frac{k_{11}}{m_{11}} - \frac{k_{22}}{m_{22}} \right)^2 + \frac{4k_{12}k_{21}}{m_{11}m_{22}} \tag{1.18}$$

under the square-root sign in (1.17) will always be positive or zero. In view of this, we conclude from (1.17) that both roots μ_1 and μ_2 are *real* in that case. If we also assume the determinant of the stiffness matrix $\underline{K}$ to be positive, implying that

$$k_{11}k_{22} - k_{12}k_{21} > 0 \tag{1.19}$$

then we conclude from (1.16) that both roots μ_1 and μ_2 are *negative*. Later, in Chapter 2, we shall see that the assumption underlying (1.19) is related to small motions with respect to a **locally stable equilibrium position**.

Intermezzo

It is left to the reader to verify from (1.12) that (1.19) is satisfied for the coupled pendulums of Fig 1.1, where $\theta_1 = \theta_2 = 0$ is a stable equilibrium position. Conversely, if we consider the coupled pendulums upside down, which is equivalent to replacing g by $-g$ in (1.12), it can easily be seen that (1.19) is not satisfied.

So, for small motions about a stable equilibrium position both roots $\mu_1 = \lambda_1^2$ and $\mu_2 = \lambda_2^2$ expressed by (1.16) or (1.17) are real and negative in sign. This means that the roots λ of (1.15) are purely imaginary, so that we can write

$$\lambda = \pm \sqrt{\mu} = \pm j\omega, \qquad j = \sqrt{-1} \tag{1.20}$$

where the quantities $\omega = \sqrt{-\mu}$ are real and positive in sign. Using (1.16) and (1.20), we obtain the following expressions for $\omega_1^2 = -\mu_1$ and $\omega_2^2 = -\mu_2$

$$\omega_{1,2}^2 = \frac{1}{2} \left[\frac{k_{11}}{m_{11}} + \frac{k_{22}}{m_{22}} \mp \sqrt{\left(\frac{k_{11}}{m_{11}} + \frac{k_{22}}{m_{22}} \right)^2 - \frac{4}{m_{11}m_{22}} (k_{11}k_{22} - k_{12}k_{21})} \right] \tag{1.21}$$

Inserting the roots $\lambda_1 = \pm j\omega_1$ and $\lambda_2 = \pm j\omega_2$ into (1.14), we can write the general solution of (1.13) as

$$q_1(t) = \hat{C}_1\, e^{j\omega_1 t} + \hat{C}_2\, e^{-j\omega_1 t} + \hat{C}_3\, e^{j\omega_2 t} + \hat{C}_4\, e^{-j\omega_2 t} \qquad (1.22)$$

where $\hat{C}_i,\ (i = 1, ..., 4)$ are complex constants of integration. Just as for single-degree-of-freedom linear systems, we can rewrite the general solution (1.22) as

$$q_1(t) = A_1^*\, \cos(\omega_1 t + \varphi_1) + A_2^*\, \cos(\omega_2 t + \varphi_2) \qquad (1.23)$$

where A_1^*, A_2^*, φ_1 and φ_2 are new constants of integration, which must be real on physical grounds. We observe that the solution (1.23) for $q_1(t)$ consists of two natural harmonic solutions $A_1^* \cos(\omega_1 t + \varphi_1)$ and $A_2^* \cos(\omega_2 t + \varphi_2)$, where the real quantities ω_1 and ω_2, determined by (1.21), appear to be characteristic frequencies of the system that are referred to as the *system natural frequencies*. Obviously our two-degree-of-freedom system posseses two natural frequencies, which we will denote ω_1 and ω_2 in rising magnitude

$$\omega_1 < \omega_2 \qquad (1.24)$$

In view of (1.21) the natural frequencies depend on the system parameters only. After having determined the general solution for $q_1(t)$, we determine the general solution for $q_2(t)$. To this end, we introduce (1.23) into (1.9) and obtain

$$q_2(t) = \frac{m_{11}\omega_1^2 - k_{11}}{k_{12}} A_1^* \cos(\omega_1 t + \varphi_1) + \frac{m_{11}\omega_2^2 - k_{11}}{k_{12}} A_2^* \cos(\omega_2 t + \varphi_2) \qquad (1.25)$$

We observe that the general solution for $q_2(t)$ also consists of two natural harmonic solutions with the same natural frequencies as those occurring in the general solution for $q_1(t)$, but with different amplitudes. If the system vibrates in one of the natural harmonic solutions, e.g. the solution associated with the natural frequency ω_1 with the constant A_2^* being zero, then the ratio between $q_2(t)$ and $q_1(t)$ remains constant during the motion. This ratio, which equals the ratio of the amplitudes of $q_2(t)$ and $q_1(t)$ of that natural harmonic solution, represents a specific *time-independent* configuration of the system. Such a configuration is called a *normal mode*, a *principal mode*, or a *natural mode of vibration*.   The general solutions (1.23) for $q_1(t)$ and (1.25) for $q_2(t)$ can be collected in the displacement column $\underline{q}(t)$ as follows

$$\underline{q}(t) = \begin{bmatrix} q_1(t) \\ q_2(t) \end{bmatrix} = \underline{u}_1^*\, A_1^* \cos(\omega_1 t + \varphi_1) + \underline{u}_2^*\, A_2^* \cos(\omega_2 t + \varphi_2) \qquad (1.26)$$

In (1.26) the natural modes of vibration are represented by the column matrices

$$\underline{u}_1^* = \begin{bmatrix} u_1^*\,[1] \\ u_1^*\,[2] \end{bmatrix} = \begin{bmatrix} 1 \\ (m_{11}\omega_1^2 - k_{11})/k_{12} \end{bmatrix} \qquad (1.27)$$

$$\underline{u}_2^* = \begin{bmatrix} u_2^*[1] \\ u_2^*[2] \end{bmatrix} = \begin{bmatrix} 1 \\ (m_{11}\omega_2^2 - k_{11})/k_{12} \end{bmatrix} \qquad (1.28)$$

The foregoing procedure for determining the *modal columns* $\underline{u}_1^*$ and $\underline{u}_2^*$ yields the first element $u_1^*[1]$ of $\underline{u}_1^*$ and the first element $u_2^*[1]$ of $\underline{u}_2^*$ both to be equal to unity. However, as has been stated before, for each of the natural harmonic solutions contained in (1.26) only the ratio of the amplitudes of $q_2(t)$ and $q_1(t)$ is fixed and determined by the system parameters. This implies that instead of the two sets of quantities $u_i^*[1]$, $u_i^*[2]$ and $A_i^*(i = 1, 2)$ in (1.26), we could select two different sets of quantities $u_i[1]$, $u_i[2]$ and $A_i(i = 1, 2)$, provided the ratios $u_i[2]/u_i[1]$ $(i = 1, 2)$ remain unchanged, i.e.

$$\frac{u_1[2]}{u_1[1]} = \frac{m_{11}\omega_1^2 - k_{11}}{k_{12}} = \frac{m_{11}}{k_{12}}\left(\omega_1^2 - \frac{k_{11}}{m_{11}}\right) \qquad (1.29)$$

$$\frac{u_2[2]}{u_2[1]} = \frac{m_{11}\omega_2^2 - k_{11}}{k_{12}} = \frac{m_{11}}{k_{12}}\left(\omega_2^2 - \frac{k_{11}}{m_{11}}\right) \qquad (1.30)$$

Because the constants $A_i(i = 1, 2)$ are undetermined and can be chosen arbitrarily, it is common practice to render the modal columns

$$\underline{u}_1 = \begin{bmatrix} u_1[1] \\ u_1[2] \end{bmatrix}, \qquad \underline{u}_2 = \begin{bmatrix} u_2[1] \\ u_2[2] \end{bmatrix} \qquad (1.31)$$

unique by using some *normalization condition*. In fact, the normalization condition used in (1.27) and (1.28) is that the first elements of the modal columns are put equal to unity. Alternatively, the elements of the modal columns with the largest absolute values could be put equal to unity. Another alternative normalization condition consists of putting the norms $(u_i^2[1] + u_i^2[2])$, $i = 1, 2$, equal to unity. In Chapter 3 we will discuss other general normalization conditions for undamped multi-degree-of-freedom linear systems.

In view of the above discussion, we will denote the general solution for the displacement column for undamped free vibrations of our two-degree-of-freedom linear system as

$$q(t) = \underline{u}_1\, A_1 \cos(\omega_1 t + \varphi_1) + \underline{u}_2\, A_2 \cos(\omega_2 t + \varphi_2) \qquad (1.32)$$

Equation (1.32) clearly expresses that the general solution of the homogeneous equations (1.9) and (1.10) can be written as a linear combination of the fundamental (harmonic) solutions corresponding to each of the natural frequencies. In (1.32) the ratios $u_1[2]/u_1[1]$ and $u_2[2]/u_2[1]$ of the elements of the modal columns $\underline{u}_1$ and $\underline{u}_2$ can be expressed in terms of the coefficients of the mass and stiffness matrices by inserting (1.21) into (1.29) and (1.30). Taking account of (1.24), this results in

$$\frac{u_1[2]}{u_1[1]} = \frac{1}{2}\frac{m_{11}}{k_{12}}\left[-\left(\frac{k_{11}}{m_{11}} - \frac{k_{22}}{m_{22}}\right) + \sqrt{\left(\frac{k_{11}}{m_{11}} - \frac{k_{22}}{m_{22}}\right)^2 + \frac{4k_{12}k_{21}}{m_{11}m_{22}}} \right]$$

$$(1.33)$$

$$\frac{u_2\,[2]}{u_2\,[1]} = \frac{1}{2}\frac{m_{11}}{k_{12}}\left[-\left(\frac{k_{11}}{m_{11}} - \frac{k_{22}}{m_{22}}\right) - \sqrt{\left(\frac{k_{11}}{m_{11}} - \frac{k_{22}}{m_{22}}\right)^2 + \frac{4k_{12}k_{21}}{m_{11}m_{22}}}\,\right]$$

$$(1.34)$$

It can easily be concluded that the expression between the brackets in (1.33) is always positive, whereas the expression between the brackets in (1.34) is always negative, independent of the sign of $(k_{11}/m_{11} - k_{22}/m_{22})$. Then, because for our undamped pendulum system $k_{21} = -ka^2 < 0$, see (1.12), we conclude from (1.33) that $u_1\,[2]/u_1\,[1]$ is positive, whereas we conclude from (1.34) that $u_2\,[2]/u\,[1]$ is negative. Because for the first natural vibration mode, corresponding to the lowest natural frequency ω_1, the modal elements $u_1\,[1]$ and $u_1\,[2]$ have the same sign, this mode is said to be an *in-phase* vibration mode.

Conversely, because for the second natural vibration mode, corresponding to the highest natural frequency ω_2, the modal elements $u_2\,[1]$ and $u_2\,[2]$ have opposite signs, this mode is said to be an *out-of-phase* vibration mode. The general solution (1.32) contains four constants, i.e. the amplitudes A_1 and A_2 as well as the phase angles φ_1 and φ_2. These constants are to be determined from the two initial displacements

$$q_1\,(0) = q_0\,[1]\,, \qquad q_2\,(0) = q_0\,[2] \tag{1.35}$$

and the two initial velocities

$$\dot{q}_1\,(0) = \dot{q}_0\,[1]\,, \qquad \dot{q}_2(0) = \dot{q}_0\,[2] \tag{1.36}$$

In Chapter 3 we will elucidate a simple general procedure to determine the constants A_i and φ_i $(i = 1, 2)$ from those initial conditions. Taking account of (1.32), it can already be anticipated that the general solution of the homogeneous equations of motion (1.9) and (1.10) satisfying arbitrary initial conditions (1.35) and (1.36) will always be composed of the two natural modes of vibration of the system.

The above procedure for determining the general solution of the homogeneous equations of motion is too complicated to apply for linear systems with more than two degrees of freedom and is only applied here to understand the basic structure of the solution. We will now illuminate a procedure which can be generalized easily to multi-degree-of-freedom linear systems. In this procedure we assume in advance the solution to have the structure

$$\underline{q}(t) = \begin{bmatrix} q_1(t) \\ q_2(t) \end{bmatrix} = \begin{bmatrix} u_1 \\ u_2 \end{bmatrix} A\cos\left(\omega t + \varphi\right) = \underline{u}\,A\cos\left(\omega t + \varphi\right) \tag{1.37}$$

with A and φ being unknown constants, while $u_1 = u\,[1]$, $u_2 = u\,[2]$ and ω representing characteristic parameters to be determined. The structure implied in (1.37) is consistent with the basic structure of the general solution found earlier in (1.32). Now, inserting (1.37) directly into (1.9) and (1.10), and dividing through by $A\cos\left(\omega t + \varphi\right)$, we obtain

$$\underline{Z}\,\left(\omega\right)\underline{u} = \underline{0} \tag{1.38}$$

with the matrix $\underline{Z}(\omega)$ being given by

$$\underline{Z}(\omega) = \begin{bmatrix} k_{11} - \omega^2 m_{11} & k_{12} \\ k_{21} & k_{22} - \omega^2 m_{22} \end{bmatrix} = \underline{K} - \omega^2 \, \underline{M} \qquad (1.39)$$

Equation (1.38) represents two simultaneous homogeneous *algebraic* equations in the unknowns u_1 and u_2, with ω^2 playing the role of parameter. The problem of determining the values of the parameter ω^2 for which (1.38) admits nontrivial solutions is known as the *characteristic-value problem*, or the *eigenvalue problem*. From linear algebra, (1.38) possess a non-zero solution only if the determinant of the matrix $\underline{Z}$ is zero, or

$$\det \begin{bmatrix} \left(k_{11} - \omega^2 m_{11}\right) & k_{12} \\ k_{21} & \left(k_{22} - \omega^2 m_{22}\right) \end{bmatrix} = 0 \qquad (1.40)$$

The resulting equation, known as the *characteristic equation* for ω^2, is a polynominal of second degree in ω^2, which is identical to (1.15) with $\left(\lambda^2\right)$ replaced by $\left(-\omega^2\right)$. The two positive roots ω^2 are again given by (1.21). It remains to determine the values of the elements $u\,[1]$ and $u\,[2]$ of the column matrix $\underline{u}$. As pointed out earlier, because the problem is homogeneous, only the ratio $u\,[2]\,/u\,[1]$ can be determined uniquely. To this end, we can use one of the two equations composing the eigenvalue problem (1.38), because the zero determinant will render these equations dependent. Taking the first equation of (1.38), we can write

$$\frac{u\,[2]}{u\,[1]} = \frac{m_{11}\omega^2 - k_{11}}{k_{12}} \qquad (1.41)$$

which is equivalent to (1.29) and (1.30) obtained earlier.

1.4   FREE VIBRATION OF THE SYMMETRIC COUPLED PENDULUM SYSTEM

We consider the undamped freely vibrating coupled pendulum system and let

$$m_1 = m_2 = m, \qquad l_1 = l_2 = l \qquad (1.42)$$

To simplify our expressions we define

$$ml^2 = m_0, \qquad mgl = k_0, \qquad ka^2 = k_c \qquad (1.43)$$

where m_0 and k_0 can be looked upon as a generalized mass and a generalized stiffness associated with each of the individual (uncoupled) pendulums, while k_c represents a generalized stiffness accounting for the coupling between the pendulums.

Using (1.12), we obtain the elements of the stiffness matrix in the form

$$k_{11} = k_{22} = k_0 + k_c, \qquad k_{12} = k_{21} = -k_c \qquad (1.44)$$

The resulting coupled pendulum system is said to be a *symmetric system*, because it has a point of symmetry in the middle of the coupling spring k. Using (1.21), we obtain the following natural frequencies of this system

$$\omega_1^2 = \frac{k_0}{m_0}, \qquad \omega_2^2 = \frac{k_0 + 2k_c}{m_0} \qquad (1.45)$$

The corresponding natural modes can be obtained from (1.33) and (1.34)

$$u_1\,[2]\,/u_1\,[1] = 1, \qquad u_2\,[2]\,/u_2\,[1] = -1 \qquad (1.46)$$

The resulting mode shapes are plotted in Fig 1.3. It can be observed that

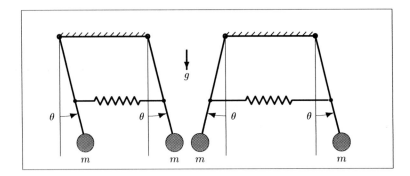

Fig. 1.3   Mode shapes for symmetric coupled pendulum system

for the first natural vibration mode the coupling spring remains unstretched, whereas for the second natural vibration mode the mid-point of the coupling spring does not move. Associated with this observation, we have for the first natural vibration mode $q_1(t) = q_2(t)$, whereas for the second natural vibration mode we have $q_1(t) = -q_2(t)$. Hence, the natural vibration modes possess symmetry or skew-symmetry characteristics with respect to the mid-point of the coupling spring. Although a different definition could have been used, it is common practice to refer to the natural vibration mode associated with the lowest eigenfrequency, i.e. the mode for which $q_1(t) = q_2(t)$, as a *symmetric* mode, and to call the other natural vibration mode, i.e. the mode for which $q_1(t) = -q_2(t)$, an *asymmetric*, an *anti-symmetric* or a *skew-symmetric* mode. Both natural vibration modes can be considered as free vibration modes for different single-degree-of-freedom linear systems, as shown in Fig. 1.4. For both modes we can consider only one half of the original coupled pendulum system. For the first natural mode, the coupling spring can be removed, whereas for the second natural mode the mid-point of the coupling spring is fixed. In Fig. 1.4 also the equation of motion associated with each of the single-degree-of-freedom systems is specified. In conclusion, the general free vibration of our symmetric mass-spring system is composed of

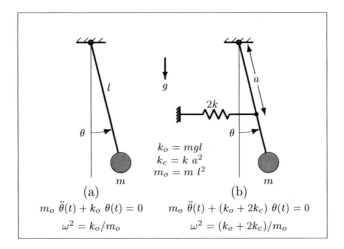

$$k_o = mgl$$
$$k_c = k\,a^2$$
$$m_o = m\,l^2$$

(a)   (b)

$$m_o\,\ddot{\theta}(t) + k_o\,\theta(t) = 0 \qquad m_o\,\ddot{\theta}(t) + (k_o + 2k_c)\,\theta(t) = 0$$

$$\omega^2 = k_o/m_o \qquad\qquad \omega^2 = (k_o + 2k_c)/m_o$$

Fig. 1.4 Single-degree-of-freedom systems for symmetric (a) and anti-symmetric (b) modes

a combination of a symmetric vibration and an anti-symmetric vibration with different frequencies. Taking the constants $u_1[1]$ and $u_2[1]$ in (1.46) arbitrarily to unity, we obtain the following expression for the general solution (1.32)

$$\underline{q}(t) = \begin{bmatrix} 1 \\ 1 \end{bmatrix} A_1 \cos\left(\omega_1 t + \varphi_1\right) + \begin{bmatrix} 1 \\ -1 \end{bmatrix} A_2 \cos\left(\omega_2 t + \varphi_2\right) \qquad (1.47)$$

All results of this section can be generalized to symmetric linear dynamic systems with more degrees of freedom.

1.5   UNCOUPLING OF THE EQUATIONS OF MOTION OF THE UNDAMPED SYMMETRIC SYSTEM

Let us return to the equations of motion in matrix form for the coupled pendulum system of Fig. 1.1, (1.3). As mentioned before, the two second-order scalar differential equations contained in (1.3) are coupled and, hence, these equations cannot be solved independently. In particular, for multi-degree-of-freedom linear systems the coupling of the equations of motion considerably complicates the direct analysis of these equations. Fortunately, it is possible to uncouple the equations of motion via a transformation utilizing the modal columns obtained during the analysis of the free motion. The general uncoupling procedure will be discussed in Chapter 3 for undamped multi-degree-of-freedom systems and in Chapter 4 for damped multi-degree-of-freedom systems. In the present section we will shed some physical light upon the uncoupling procedure and introduce its basic concept for the simple but illustrative case of the *undamped* symmetric coupled pendulum system. In that case, the equations of motion in matrix form, (1.3), simplify to

$$\underline{M}\,\ddot{\underline{q}}(t) + \underline{K}\,\underline{q}(t) = \underline{f}(t) \tag{1.48}$$

According to (1.7) and (1.42), for the symmetric pendulum system the generalized displacement column and the generalized force column are given by

$$\underline{q}(t) = \begin{bmatrix} q_1(t) \\ q_2(t) \end{bmatrix} = \begin{bmatrix} \theta_1(t) \\ \theta_2(t) \end{bmatrix}, \qquad \underline{f}(t) = \begin{bmatrix} f_1(t) \\ f_2(t) \end{bmatrix} = \begin{bmatrix} l\,F(t) \\ 0 \end{bmatrix} \tag{1.49}$$

whereas according to (1.4), (1.6), (1.42), (1.43) and (1.44) the mass matrix and the stiffness matrix are given by

$$\underline{M} = \begin{bmatrix} m_0 & 0 \\ 0 & m_0 \end{bmatrix}, \qquad \underline{K} = \begin{bmatrix} k_0 + k_c & -k_c \\ -k_c & k_0 + k_c \end{bmatrix} \tag{1.50}$$

At this point it is remarked that we have the freedom to describe the motion of the system in terms of any pair of *independent* generalized displacements, also referred to as *generalized coordinates*. Indeed, the generalized coordinates $\theta_1(t)$ and $\theta_2(t)$ are independent, because it can be observed from Fig. 1.1 that $\theta_1(t)$ and $\theta_2(t)$ can be assigned arbitrary values, independently from one another. Now, in the context of this section, the interest lies in selecting a pair of generalized coordinates offering the greatest simplification with respect to uncoupling of the equations of motion.

Let us first have a look at the freely vibrating symmetric coupled pendulum system whose general solution was discussed in the previous section, see (1.47). If we define a new set of generalized coordinates $\eta_1(t)$ and $\eta_2(t)$ such that

$$\underline{\eta}(t) = \begin{bmatrix} \eta_1(t) \\ \eta_2(t) \end{bmatrix} = \begin{bmatrix} A_1 \cos(\omega_1 t + \varphi_1) \\ A_2 \cos(\omega_2 t + \varphi_2) \end{bmatrix} \tag{1.51}$$

then, since $\eta_1(t)$ and $\eta_2(t)$ are harmonic functions, their corresponding equations of motion can be expressed as

$$\ddot{\eta}_1(t) + \omega_1^2\,\eta_1(t) = 0 \tag{1.52}$$

$$\ddot{\eta}_2(t) + \omega_2^2\,\eta_2(t) = 0 \tag{1.53}$$

These equations represent two uncoupled undamped single-degree-of-freedom linear systems. The general solutions of (1.52) and (1.53) can be written in the form of (1.51). From (1.47) and (1.51), we can write

$$\underline{q}(t) = \begin{bmatrix} \theta_1(t) \\ \theta_2(t) \end{bmatrix} = \begin{bmatrix} 1 \\ 1 \end{bmatrix} \eta_1(t) + \begin{bmatrix} 1 \\ -1 \end{bmatrix} \eta_2(t) \tag{1.54}$$

or

$$\underline{q}(t) = \underline{T}\,\underline{\eta}(t) \tag{1.55}$$

where the so-called *transformation matrix* $\underline{T}$ is given by

$$\underline{T} = \begin{bmatrix} 1 & 1 \\ 1 & -1 \end{bmatrix} \tag{1.56}$$

At this point it is of interest to give a geometrical interpretation of the new generalized coordinates $\eta_1(t)$ and $\eta_2(t)$. To this end, we express $\eta_1(t)$ and $\eta_2(t)$ in terms of $\theta_1(t)$ and $\theta_2(t)$ by inverting (1.54) and obtain

$$\underline{\eta}(t) = \begin{bmatrix} \eta_1(t) \\ \eta_2(t) \end{bmatrix} = \frac{1}{2} \begin{bmatrix} \theta_1(t) + \theta_2(t) \\ \theta_1(t) - \theta_2(t) \end{bmatrix} \tag{1.57}$$

In view of the geometry of the pendulum system given in Fig. 1.1 (with $l_1 = l_2 = l$), the generalized coordinate $\eta_1(t) = \frac{1}{2}\{\theta_1(t) + \theta_2(t)\}$ is related to the displacement of the mid-point of the coupling spring, whereas the generalized coordinate $\eta_2(t) = \frac{1}{2}\{\theta_1(t) - \theta_2(t)\}$ is related to the shortening of the coupling spring with respect to its mid-point. This is also illustrated in Fig. 1.5. Now, we return to the matrix equation of motion with external

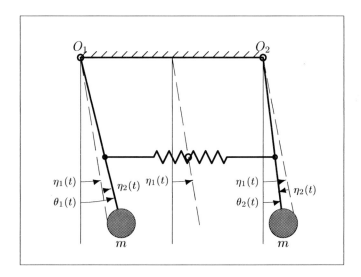

Fig. 1.5 Geometrical interpretation of $\eta_1(t)$ and $\eta_2(t)$

forces, (1.48). Again, we introduce a new set of generalized coordinates $\eta_1(t)$ and $\eta_2(t)$ and let those coordinates be related to the original generalized coordinates $\theta_1(t)$ and $\theta_2(t)$ by the same relationship as for the case in which $\underline{f}(t) = \underline{0}$, i.e. by (1.57). Then, because for the case that $\underline{f}(t) \neq \underline{0}$, $\theta_1(t)$ and $\theta_2(t)$ will differ from those for the case that $\underline{f}(t) = \underline{0}$, and, hence, $\eta_1(t)$ and $\eta_2(t)$ will differ from (1.51). But, because $\theta_1(t)$ and $\theta_2(t)$ are independent generalized coordinates, their sum $2\eta_1(t)$ and their difference $2\eta_2(t)$ are also independent.

To obtain the differential equations of motion corresponding to the new generalized coordinates $\eta_1(t)$ and $\eta_2(t)$, we could start from the free-body diagrams associated with $\eta_1(t)$ and $\eta_2(t)$. In fact, this would imply to account for the influence of $F(t)$ in Figs. 1.4 (a) and (b). However, we can alternatively start directly from the differential equations (1.48) for $\theta_1(t)$ and $\theta_2(t)$ and introduce the coordinate transformation defined by (1.55) and (1.56). Inserting (1.55) into (1.48), we obtain

$$\underline{M}\ \underline{T}\ \underline{\ddot{\eta}}(t) + \underline{K}\ \underline{T}\ \underline{\eta}(t) = \underline{f}(t) \tag{1.58}$$

or, using (1.50) and (1.57)

$$\begin{bmatrix} m_0 & m_0 \\ m_0 & -m_0 \end{bmatrix} \begin{bmatrix} \ddot{\eta}_1(t) \\ \ddot{\eta}_2(t) \end{bmatrix} + \begin{bmatrix} k_0 & k_0 + 2k_c \\ k_0 & -(k_0 + 2k_c) \end{bmatrix} \begin{bmatrix} \eta_1(t) \\ \eta_2(t) \end{bmatrix} = \begin{bmatrix} l\ F(t) \\ 0 \end{bmatrix}$$
$$\tag{1.59}$$

Taking first the sum of the two scalar differential equations contained in (1.59) and next the difference of these two equations, we arrive at the following two equations

$$2m_0\ \ddot{\eta}_1(t) + 2k_0\ \eta_1(t) = l\ F(t) \tag{1.60}$$

$$2m_0\ \ddot{\eta}_2(t) + 2\,(k_0 + 2k_c)\ \eta_2(t) = l\ F(t) \tag{1.61}$$

It is remarked here that (1.60) and (1.61) could equivalently be obtained by premultiplying (1.58), or (1.59), by the transposed of the matrix $\underline{T}$.

We observe that the two differential equations of motion (1.60) and (1.61) for $\eta_1(t)$ and $\eta_2(t)$ are *uncoupled*. The differential equation (1.60) only contains $\eta_1(t)$ and its second derivative, whereas the differential equation (1.61) only contains $\eta_2(t)$ and its second dervative. For $F(t) = 0$, (1.60) has the general solution $\eta_1(t) = A_1 \cos(\omega_1 t + \varphi_1)$ with the natural frequency $\omega_1^2 = k_0/m_0$, while (1.61) has the general solution $\eta_2(t) = A_2 \cos(\omega_2 t + \varphi_2)$ with the natural frequency $\omega_2^2 = (k_0 + 2k_c)/m_0$. These homogeneous solutions are completely consistent with (1.51), while the natural frequencies are identical to those obtained earlier for the original coupled pendulum system, see (1.45).

It can be easily understood that the new generalized coordinate $\eta_1(t)$ describes symmetric motions of the coupled symmetric pendulum system, with Fig. 1.4(a) for the free motions as a particular case. Conversely, the new generalized coordinate $\eta_2(t)$ describes anti-symmetric motions of the coupled symmetric pendulum system, with Fig. 1.4(b) for free motions as a particular case.

The above uncoupling procedure for the undamped symmetric coupled pendulum system can be generalized in a straightforward way to general undamped multi-degree-of-freedom linear systems. This is due to the fact that the columns of the transformation matrix $\underline{T}$, defined by (1.56) are proportional to the modal columns of the original coupled pendulum system, as becomes obvious from (1.46), (1.47), (1.54) and (1.55). Also, as a specific observation for the symmetric coupled pendulum system we conclude from (1.46) that

$$u_1\,[1]\,u_2\,[1] + u_1\,[2]\,u_2\,[2] = 0, \qquad \text{or} \qquad \underline{u}_1^T\ \underline{u}_2 = 0 \tag{1.62}$$

so that the modal columns $\underline{u}_1$ and $\underline{u}_2$ are really orthogonal in this case. This is due to the fact that for the symmetric coupled pendulum system the mass matrix is proportional to the identity matrix. In general the mass matrix is not proportional to the identity matrix so that (1.62) does not hold. However, it is possible to derive a generalized orthogonality property for the modal columns of the original coupled system that offers the basis for a generalization of the uncoupling procedure to general undamped multi-degree-of-freedom linear systems. This procedure will be discussed in Chapter 3.

1.6 STEADY-STATE RESPONSE TO HARMONIC EXCITATION

In this section we consider the damped coupled pendulum system with the original generalized coordinates $\theta_1(t)$ and $\theta_2(t)$ under the following harmonic excitation

$$F(t) = F_a \cos\left(\Omega t + \varphi\right) \qquad (1.63)$$

Here Ω is the excitation frequency, F_a is the amplitude of the external force $F(t)$, while φ is the phase angle of this excitation force. It is very convenient to rewrite the harmonic excitation in complex notation as follows

$$F(t) = F_a \cos(\Omega t + \varphi) = Re\left\{\hat{F}e^{j\Omega t}\right\} \qquad (1.64)$$

with the time-independent complex excitation amplitude $\hat{F}$ being given by

$$\hat{F} = F_a\, e^{j\varphi} \qquad (1.65)$$

We insert (1.64) into the matrix equation of motion (1.3), delete the $Re\{..\}$ notation, and obtain

$$\underline{M}\,\ddot{\underline{q}}(t) + \underline{D}\,\dot{\underline{q}}(t) + \underline{K}\,\underline{q}(t) = \hat{\underline{F}}\,e^{j\Omega t} \qquad (1.66)$$

where $\hat{\underline{F}}$ is the column of complex excitation amplitudes, which for this example is given by

$$\hat{\underline{F}} = \left[\begin{array}{c} l\,\hat{F} \\ 0 \end{array}\right] \qquad (1.67)$$

The mass matrix $\underline{M}$, the stiffness matrix $\underline{K}$ and the damping matrix $\underline{D}$ are given by (1.4), (1.6) and (1.5), respectively. Analogous to the familiar treatment for single-degree-of-freedom linear systems, we take the steady-state response of (1.66) to be harmonic and write it in complex notation as follows

$$\underline{q}(t) = \left[\begin{array}{c} q_1(t) \\ q_2(t) \end{array}\right] = \left[\begin{array}{c} \hat{q}_1 \\ \hat{q}_2 \end{array}\right] e^{j\Omega t} = \hat{\underline{q}}\,e^{j\Omega t} \qquad (1.68)$$

where the time-independent complex response amplitudes $\hat{q}_1$ and $\hat{q}_2$ can be written as

$$\hat{\underline{q}} = \left[\begin{array}{c} \hat{q}_1 \\ \hat{q}_2 \end{array}\right] = \left[\begin{array}{c} q_{1a}\,e^{j\psi_1} \\ q_{2a}\,e^{j\psi_2} \end{array}\right] \qquad (1.69)$$

Here q_{1a} and q_{2a} are the real amplitudes of the steady-state responses $q_1(t)$ and $q_2(t)$, while ψ_1 and ψ_2 are their phase angles. Inserting (1.68) into (1.66) and dividing through by $e^{j\Omega t}$, we obtain the following set of two algebraic equations for $\hat{q}_1$ and $\hat{q}_2$

$$\left[-\Omega^2 \underline{M} + j\Omega \underline{D} + \underline{K}\right] \hat{\underline{q}} = \hat{\underline{F}} \tag{1.70}$$

The matrix between the brackets in the left-hand side of (1.70) is sometimes referred to as the *dynamic stiffness matrix* $\underline{Z}(\Omega)$ and it is defined as

$$\underline{Z}(\Omega) = -\Omega^2 \underline{M} + j\Omega \underline{D} + \underline{K} = \left[\begin{array}{cc} Z_{11}(\Omega) & Z_{12}(\Omega) \\ Z_{21}(\Omega) & Z_{22}(\Omega) \end{array}\right] \tag{1.71}$$

Obviously, the elements $Z_{ij}(\Omega)$ of the dynamic stiffness matrix can be expressed in terms of the elements m_{ij}, d_{ij} and k_{ij} of the mass, damping and stiffness matrices as follows

$$Z_{11}(\Omega) = -\Omega^2 m_{11} + j\Omega d_{11} + k_{11} \tag{1.72}$$

$$Z_{22}(\Omega) = -\Omega^2 m_{22} + j\Omega d_{22} + k_{22} \tag{1.73}$$

$$Z_{12}(\Omega) = Z_{21}(\Omega) = j\Omega d_{12} + k_{12} \tag{1.74}$$

Here, use has been made of some features of our coupled pendulum system, namely, the symmetry of the damping and stiffness matrices, as well as the fact that the mass matrix is diagonal.

Now, the column of complex response amplitudes $\hat{\underline{q}}$ can be obtained by premultiplying (1.70) by the inverse of the dynamic stiffness matrix

$$\hat{\underline{q}} = \underline{Z}^{-1}(\Omega) \hat{\underline{F}} =: \underline{H}(\Omega) \hat{\underline{F}} \tag{1.75}$$

where $\underline{H}(\Omega) = \underline{Z}^{-1}(\Omega)$ is called the *matrix of complex frequency response functions*, or alternatively, the *frequency response function matrix* (often abbreviated as FRF-matrix). This matrix can be expressed in terms of the elements of the dynamic stiffness matrix as follows

$$\underline{H}(\Omega) = \underline{Z}^{-1}(\Omega) = \frac{1}{Z_{11}(\Omega)Z_{22}(\Omega) - Z_{12}(\Omega)Z_{21}(\Omega)} \left[\begin{array}{cc} Z_{22}(\Omega) & -Z_{12}(\Omega) \\ -Z_{21}(\Omega) & Z_{11}(\Omega) \end{array}\right] \tag{1.76}$$

The frequency response function matrix $\underline{H}(\Omega)$ can be considered as being the two-degree-of-freedom generalization of the frequency response function of a single-degree-of-freedom system. In fact, if we delete in our two-degree-of-freedom pendulum system the coupling spring k and the coupling damper d, then $Z_{12}(\Omega) = Z_{21}(\Omega) = 0$ and (1.76) degenerates to a diagonal matrix whose elements are the frequency response functions of two uncoupled single-degree-of-freedom pendulums.

Next, we return to the coupled two-degree-of-freedom pendulum system and delete the damper for reasons of simplicity, i.e. we consider the undamped

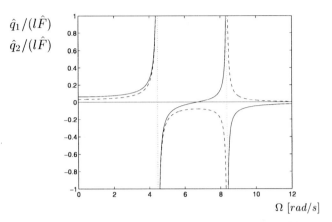

$\hat{q}_1/(l\hat{F})$
$\hat{q}_2/(l\hat{F})$

$\Omega \ [rad/s]$

Fig. 1.6 Frequency response curves for undamped two-degree-of-freedom system; left pendulum ($q_1(t)$) solid line, right pendulum ($q_2(t)$) dashed line

steady-state response. In that case, the elements $Z_{ij}(\Omega)$ of the dynamic stiffness matrix become real functions, see (1.72)- (1.74), and we obtain for the column of complex response amplitudes $\hat{\underline{q}}$, taking account of (1.75), (1.76) and (1.67)

$$\hat{\underline{q}} = \frac{l\ \hat{F}}{(k_{11} - \Omega^2 m_{11})(k_{22} - \Omega^2 m_{22}) - k_{12}^2} \begin{bmatrix} k_{22} - \Omega^2 m_{22} \\ -k_{12} \end{bmatrix} \tag{1.77}$$

The denominator of $\hat{\underline{q}}^T = [q_1 \quad q_2]$ is recognized as the characteristic determinant in the left-hand side of the characteristic equation (1.40) for the natural frequencies of the free vibration problem discussed in Section 1.3. Hence, the amplitudes q_{1a} and q_{2a} of $q_1(t)$ and $q_2(t)$ become infinite for $\Omega^2 = \omega_1^2$ and $\Omega^2 = \omega_2^2$, where ω_1 and ω_2 are the natural frequencies of the freely vibrating system. Thus there are two so-called *resonance frequencies of excitation* for the system: one at ω_1 and another one at ω_2. It can also be seen easily that the denominator of (1.77) is positive if $\Omega^2 < \omega_1^2$ or $\Omega^2 > \omega_2^2$ and negative if $\omega_1^2 < \Omega^2 < \omega_2^2$. For some arbitrary set of system parameters, the course of the frequency response curves $\hat{q}_1/\hat{F}$ versus Ω and $\hat{q}_2/\hat{F}$ versus Ω is shown in Fig. 1.6. For $\Omega = 0$, the static values of $\hat{q}_1/\hat{F}_1$ and $\hat{q}_2/\hat{F}_2$ can be found from $\underline{K}\ \hat{\underline{q}} = \hat{\underline{F}}$, giving

$$\left(\frac{\hat{q}_1}{l\hat{F}}\right)_{\Omega=0} =: k_{10} = \frac{k_{22}}{k_{11}k_{22} - k_{12}^2} = \frac{ka^2 + m_2 g l_2}{ka^2 g\,(m_1 l_1 + m_2 l_2) + g^2 m_1 l_1 m_2 l_2} \tag{1.78}$$

$$\left(\frac{\hat{q}_2}{l\hat{F}}\right)_{\Omega=0} =: k_{20} = \frac{-k_{12}}{k_{11}k_{22} - k_{12}^2} = \frac{ka^2}{ka^2 g\,(m_1 \ell_1 + m_2 l_2) + g^2 m_1 l_1 m_2 l_2} \tag{1.79}$$

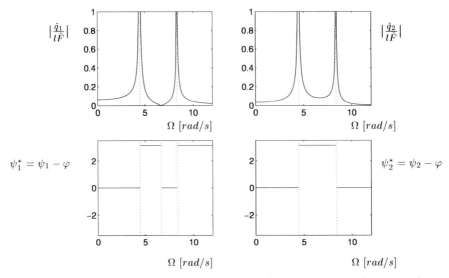

Fig. 1.7 Bode diagrams for $q_1 = \theta_1$ (left plots) and for $q_2 = \theta_2$ (right plots)

Except at the resonance frequencies ω_1 and ω_2, the vibration amplitudes are finite at all other values of the excitation frequency Ω. It can be observed from Fig. 1.6 that there is a particular value of Ω at which the vibration of the left pendulum (rotation $q_1 = \theta_1$), to which the force $F(t)$ is applied, is reduced to zero. From (1.77) this value of Ω can be concluded to be given by

$$\omega_{22}^2 = k_{22}/m_{22} \tag{1.80}$$

which appears to be the natural frequency of the system if the rotation of the left pendulum is suppressed. Using (1.21) and the inequality

$$0 < \frac{k_{12}k_{21}}{k_{11}k_{22}} = \frac{k^2 a^4}{(ka^2 + m_1 g l_1)(ka^2 + m_2 g l_2)} < 1$$

we can prove that

$$\omega_1^2 < \omega_{22}^2 < \omega_2^2 \tag{1.81}$$

The characteristic behaviour of the system at $\Omega^2 = \omega_{22}^2$ forms the basis of the dynamic vibration absorber discussed in Section 1.8. With respect to the curves in Fig. 1.6, it is remarked that for $\Omega < \omega_1$ the displacements $q_1(t)$ and $q_2(t)$ are both in phase with the force $F(t)$. For $\omega_1 < \Omega < \omega_{22}$ the displacements $q_1(t)$ and $q_2(t)$ are both out of phase with the force $F(t)$. For $\Omega > \omega_{22}$ one of the displacements is in phase with $F(t)$, whereas the other one is out of phase with $F(t)$. In Fig. 1.7 the Bode diagrams for q_1 and q_2 are shown.

1.7   BEATING AT THE FREELY VIBRATING SYMMETRIC PENDULUM SYSTEM

It can generally be shown that if the frequencies associated with any two (free or forced) harmonic vibration modes of an arbitrary complicated linear system are close to, but not exactly equal to one another, a so-called beating phenomenon can be encountered. To illustrate the phenomenon for two-degree-of-freedom systems, we consider free vibration of the symmetric coupled pendulum system of Section 1.4 and recall that its general solution can be expressed as (1.47)

$$\underline{q}(t) = \begin{bmatrix} 1 \\ 1 \end{bmatrix} A_1 \cos(\omega_1 t + \varphi_1) + \begin{bmatrix} 1 \\ -1 \end{bmatrix} A_2 \cos(\omega_2 t + \varphi_2) \qquad (1.82)$$

Letting the initial conditions be

$$\underline{q}(0) = \begin{bmatrix} q_0 \\ 0 \end{bmatrix}, \qquad \underline{\dot{q}}(0) = \begin{bmatrix} 0 \\ 0 \end{bmatrix} \qquad (1.83)$$

we obtain from (1.82) the following set of equations for the constants A_1, φ_1, A_2 and φ_2

$$q_0 = A_1 \cos \varphi_1 + A_2 \cos \varphi_2 \qquad (1.84)$$
$$0 = A_1 \cos \varphi_1 - A_2 \cos \varphi_2 \qquad (1.85)$$
$$0 = -\omega_1 A_1 \sin \varphi_1 - \omega_2 A_2 \sin \varphi_2 \qquad (1.86)$$
$$0 = -\omega_1 A_1 \sin \varphi_1 + \omega_2 A_2 \sin \varphi_2 \qquad (1.87)$$

From (1.86) and (1.87) we conclude that for nontrivial solutions ω_1, ω_2, A_1 and A_2 the phase angles φ_1 and φ_2 have to satisfy the following equations

$$\sin \varphi_1 = 0 \quad \text{and} \quad \sin \varphi_2 = 0 \qquad (1.88)$$

Without loss of generality, we put

$$\varphi_1 = \varphi_2 = 0 \qquad (1.89)$$

Inserting (1.89) into (1.84) and (1.85), we obtain for the constants A_1 and A_2

$$A_1 = A_2 = \frac{1}{2} q_0 \qquad (1.90)$$

Hence, the solution for free vibrations of our symmetric coupled pendulum system satisfying the initial condition (1.83) is

$$\underline{q}(t) = \begin{bmatrix} q_1(t) \\ q_2(t) \end{bmatrix} = \frac{1}{2} q_0 \begin{bmatrix} \cos \omega_1 t + \cos \omega_2 t \\ \cos \omega_1 t - \cos \omega_2 t \end{bmatrix} \qquad (1.91)$$

Using the trigonometric relations

$$
\cos\alpha + \cos\beta = 2\cos\tfrac{1}{2}(\alpha+\beta)\cos\tfrac{1}{2}(\alpha-\beta)
$$
$$
\cos\alpha - \cos\beta = -2\sin\tfrac{1}{2}(\alpha+\beta)\sin\tfrac{1}{2}(\alpha-\beta)
$$

(1.92)

we can rewrite (1.91) as

$$
\underline{q}(t) = \left[\begin{array}{c} q_1(t) \\ q_2(t) \end{array}\right] = q_0 \left[\begin{array}{c} \cos\left\{\tfrac{1}{2}(\omega_2-\omega_1)t\right\}\cos\left\{\tfrac{1}{2}(\omega_2+\omega_1)t\right\} \\ \sin\left\{\tfrac{1}{2}(\omega_2-\omega_1)t\right\}\sin\left\{\tfrac{1}{2}(\omega_2+\omega_1)t\right\} \end{array}\right]
$$

(1.93)

Now, let us consider the case in wich the coupling stiffness $k_c = ka^2$ is small in value compared to the direct stiffness $k_0 = mgl$. This statement is equivalent to saying that the coupling provided by the spring k is weak. Writing (1.93) in the form

$$
\underline{q}(t) = \left[\begin{array}{c} q_1(t) \\ q_2(t) \end{array}\right] = q_0 \left[\begin{array}{c} \cos(\tfrac{1}{2}\omega_B t)\ \cos(\omega_{AV} t) \\ \sin(\tfrac{1}{2}\omega_B t)\ \sin(\omega_{AV} t) \end{array}\right]
$$

(1.94)

with

$$
\omega_B = \omega_2 - \omega_1 = \sqrt{\frac{k_0}{m_0}(1+2\frac{k_c}{k_0})} - \sqrt{\frac{k_0}{m_0}}
$$

(1.95)

$$
\omega_{AV} = \frac{1}{2}(\omega_2+\omega_1) = \frac{1}{2}\left[\sqrt{\frac{k_0}{m_0}\left(1+2\frac{k_c}{k_0}\right)} + \sqrt{\frac{k_0}{m_0}}\right]
$$

(1.96)

we can approximate ω_B and ω_{AV} for $k_c/k_0 << 1$ by

$$
\omega_B \approx \left(1+\frac{k_c}{k_0}\right)\sqrt{\frac{k_0}{m_0}} - \sqrt{\frac{k_0}{m_0}} = \frac{k_c}{k_0}\sqrt{\frac{k_0}{m_0}} = \frac{k_c}{k_0}\omega_1
$$

(1.97)

$$
\omega_{AV} \approx \frac{1}{2}\left[\left(1+\frac{k_c}{k_0}\right)\sqrt{\frac{k_0}{m_0}} + \sqrt{\frac{k_0}{m_0}}\right] =
$$
$$
= \left(1+\frac{1}{2}\frac{k_c}{k_0}\right)\sqrt{\frac{k_0}{m_0}} = \left(1+\frac{k_c}{2k_0}\right)\omega_1
$$

(1.98)

Hence, $q_1(t)$ and $q_2(t)$ can be regarded as being harmonic functions with frequency ω_{AV} and with amplitudes varying slowly according to $q_0\cos(\tfrac{1}{2}\omega_B t)$ and $q_0\sin(\tfrac{1}{2}\omega_B t)$, respectively. The plots $q_1(t)$ versus t and $q_2(t)$ versus t are shown in Fig. 1.8, with the slowly varying amplitudes indicated by the dashed-line envelopes. Geometrically, Fig. 1.8 (a) implies that if two harmonic functions possessing equal amplitudes and nearly equal frequencies are added, then the resulting function is an *amplitude-modulated* harmonic function with a frequency equal to the average frequency ω_{AV}. At first, when the two harmonic functions reinforce each other, the amplitude is doubled, and later, as they cancel each other, the amplitude reduces to zero. The phenomenon is known as the *beat phenomenon*, The frequency of modulation ω_B, which

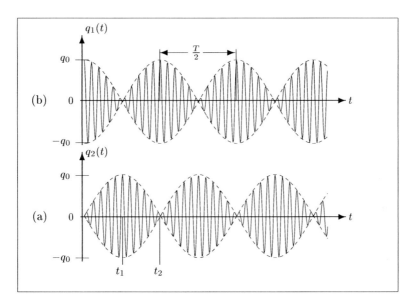

Fig. 1.8   Beating at two-degree-of-freedom system

in this particular case is given by (1.97), is called the *beat frequency*. From Fig. 1.8(a) we conclude that the period of the amplitude-modulated envelope is $T = 4\pi/\omega_B$.

Although in this section the beat phenomenon resulted from the weak coupling of two pendulum systems, the phenomenon is not exclusively associated with one- and two-degree-of-freedom systems. Indeed, the beat phenomenon is purely the result of adding two harmonic functions of equal amplitudes and nearly equal frequencies. For example, the phenomenon occurs in twin-engine propeller airplanes, in which the propeller noise grows and diminishes in intensity as the sound waves generated by the two propellors reinforce and cancel each other in turn. We observe from Fig. 1.8 that there is a 90° or $\pi/2$ rad phase angle between $q_1(t)$ and $q_2(t)$. At $t = 0$ the first pendulum (left pendulum in Fig. 1.1) begins to vibrate with the amplitude q_0 while the second pendulum is at rest. Soon thereafter the second pendulum is entrained, gaining amplitude while the amplitude of the first decreases. At $t_1 = \pi/\omega_B$ the amplitude of the first pendulum becomes zero, whereas the amplitude of the second reaches q_0. At $t_2 = 2\pi/\omega_B$ the amplitude of the first pendulum reaches q_0 once again and that of the second reduces to zero. The motion keeps repeating itself, so that at every interval of time $T/4 = \pi/\omega_B$ there is a complete transfer of energy from one pendulum to the other. Another well-known example of a two-degree-of-freedom system exhibiting the beat phenomenon is the "Wilberforce spring", consisting of a rigid mass of finite dimensions suspended by a massless helical spring such that the natural frequency of vertical translation and the natural frequency of torsional motion are close in value. In this example the coupling arises from the second-order interaction between extension and torsion of the helical spring (see e.g. [Den Hartog-56]). In this case, the kinetic energy changes from pure translational in the vertical direction to pure rotational about the vertical axis, as indicated in Fig. 1.9.

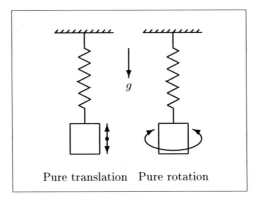

Fig. 1.9   Wilberforce spring

1.8   UNDAMPED DYNAMIC VIBRATION ABSORBERS

A machine or system may experience excessive vibration if it is acted upon by a force whose (constant) excitation frequency nearly coincides with one of the natural frequencies of the machine system. The reduction of the undesirable effects of such vibration is the subject of vibration isolation. In general, vibration reduction can be achieved by changing the mass, spring and damper characteristics of a system. In many cases however this will not be possible so an alternative strategy has to be followed to get an acceptable dynamic performance of the machine or the system.

In this section we will treat the case where an additional mass-spring-damper system is added to the original single-degree-of-freedom system under harmonic excitation. This second mass-spring-damper system, referred to as a *vibration neutralizer* or *dynamic vibration absorber*, is designed in such a way that the frequency response of the combined two-degree-of-freedom system is reduced at the excitation frequency. In the present section we will discuss the particular and simplest case in which both the main system and the dynamic vibration absorber are undamped, whereas the case of damped dynamic vibration absorber will be discussed in the following section.

Let us consider the system of Fig. 1.10, where the original single-degree-of-freedom system, referred to as the main system, consists of the mass m_1 and the spring k_1, while the added auxiliary linear system, referred to as the vibration absorber, consists of the mass m_2 and the spring k_2. The set of

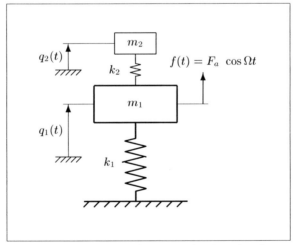

Fig. 1.10   Undamped dynamic vibration absorber

equations of motion of the combined two-degree-of-freedom system can easily be shown to be

$$\underline{M}\,\ddot{\underline{q}}(t) + \underline{K}\,\underline{q}(t) = \underline{f}(t) \tag{1.99}$$

where the displacement column and the force column are given by

$$q(t) = \left[\begin{array}{c} q_1(t) \\ q_2(t) \end{array} \right]$$

$$f(t) = \left[\begin{array}{c} f_1(t) \\ f_2(t) \end{array} \right] = \left[\begin{array}{c} F_a \sin \Omega t \\ 0 \end{array} \right] = \left[\begin{array}{c} F_a \\ 0 \end{array} \right] \sin \Omega t = \underline{F}_a \sin \Omega t$$

(1.100)

while the mass matrix and the stiffness matrix are given by

$$\underline{M} = \left[\begin{array}{cc} m_1 & 0 \\ 0 & m_2 \end{array} \right], \qquad \underline{K} = \left[\begin{array}{cc} k_1 + k_2 & -k_2 \\ -k_2 & k_2 \end{array} \right]$$

(1.101)

Letting in agreement with (1.68) and (1.69) the steady-state solution of (1.99) be

$$\underline{q}(t) = \left[\begin{array}{c} q_1(t) \\ q_2(t) \end{array} \right] = \left[\begin{array}{c} q_{1a} \sin \Omega t \\ q_{2a} \sin \Omega t \end{array} \right] = \left[\begin{array}{c} q_{1a} \\ q_{2a} \end{array} \right] \sin \Omega t = \underline{q}_a \sin \Omega t$$

(1.102)

we obtain a set of two algebraic equations for q_{1a} and q_{2a} having the matrix form

$$\left[-\Omega^2 \underline{M} + \underline{K} \right] \underline{q}_a = \underline{F}_a$$

(1.103)

The solution of (1.103) can be shown to be

$$\underline{q}_a = \left[-\Omega^2 \underline{M} + \underline{K} \right]^{-1} \underline{F}_a$$

$$= \frac{F_a}{(k_1 + k_2 - \Omega^2 m_1)(k_2 - \Omega^2 m_2) - k_2^2} \left[\begin{array}{c} k_2 - \Omega^2 m_2 \\ k_2 \end{array} \right]$$

(1.104)

It is remarked that this solution for the column of response amplitudes $\underline{q}_a$ has the same structure as (1.77) obtained in Section 1.6 for the steady-state response of the undamped coupled pendulum system. Hence, the denominator in the right side of (1.104), which equals the determinant of the matrix $\left[-\Omega^2 \underline{M} + \underline{K} \right]$, can be identified as the characteristic determinant of the eigenvalue problem for the natural frequencies $\omega_i (i = 1, 2)$ of free vibrations associated with (1.99). The characteristic equation resulting from this eigenvalue problem takes the form

$$\left(k_1 + k_2 - \omega_i^2 m_1 \right) \left(k_2 - \omega_i^2 m_2 \right) - k_2^2 = 0$$

(1.105)

So, the amplitudes q_{1a} and q_{2a} of $q_1(t)$ and $q_2(t)$ become infinite for $\Omega^2 = \omega_1^2$ and $\Omega^2 = \omega_2^2$, i.e. if the excitation frequency Ω equals each of the natural frequencies ω_1 and ω_2 of the two-degree-of-freedom system. Hence, $\Omega = \omega_1$ and $\Omega = \omega_2$ are resonance frequencies of excitation for the main system with vibration absorber. Also, we observe from (1.104) that the vibration amplitude q_{1a} of the main system will be zero for $\Omega^2 = k_2/m_2$, i.e. if the excitation frequency equals the eigenfrequency of the mass-spring absorber system if it is fixed to a motionless base.

It is customary to introduce the notation

$$\omega_n = \sqrt{k_1/m_1} = \text{ natural freq. of the main system} \qquad (1.106)$$

$$\omega_a = \sqrt{k_2/m_2} = \text{ natural freq. of the absorber system} \qquad (1.107)$$
$$\text{fixed to a motionless base}$$

$$q_{sta} = F_a/k_1 = \text{ static deflection of the main system due} \qquad (1.108)$$
$$\text{to the amplitude of the excitation force}$$

$$\mu = m_2/m_1 = \text{ ratio of the absorber mass to main mass} \qquad (1.109)$$

With this notation, (1.104) can be rewritten as

$$\underline{q}_a = \frac{q_{sta}}{\left[1 + \mu\left(\frac{\omega_a}{\omega_n}\right)^2 - \left(\frac{\Omega}{\omega_n}\right)^2\right]^2 \left[\left(\frac{\omega_a}{\omega_n}\right)^2 - \left(\frac{\Omega}{\omega_n}\right)^2\right] - \mu\left(\frac{\omega_a}{\omega_n}\right)^4}$$

$$(1.110)$$

$$\left[\frac{\left(\frac{\omega_a}{\omega_n}\right)^2 - \left(\frac{\Omega}{\omega_n}\right)^2}{\left(\frac{\omega_a}{\omega_n}\right)^2}\right]$$

We are primarily interested in reducing the vibration amplitude q_{1a} of the main system. From (1.110) we conclude that for $\Omega = \omega_a$, the amplitude q_{1a} reduces to zero which has already been found earlier. If the main system, before the addition of the dynamic vibration absorber, operates near its resonance, then $\Omega \cong \omega_n$. Hence the amplitude of vibration of the main system, while operating at its original resonance frequency $\Omega = \omega_n$, will become zero if the absorber is designed such that

$$\omega_a = \omega_n \qquad \text{or} \qquad \frac{k_2}{m_2} = \frac{k_1}{m_1} \qquad (1.111)$$

In the following we will restrict ourselves to vibration absorbers that are designed such that (1.111) is satisfied. First, we will consider the case in which the main system is operating at its original resonance frequency, i.e. $\Omega = \omega_n(= \omega_a)$. After that, we will investigate how the vibration absorber performs if the operating frequency Ω of the main system differs from ω_n. For $\Omega = \omega_n(= \omega_a)$ (1.110) simplifies to

$$\underline{q}_a = \begin{bmatrix} 0 \\ -q_{sta}/\mu \end{bmatrix} = \begin{bmatrix} 0 \\ -F_a/(k_1\mu) \end{bmatrix} \qquad (1.112)$$

For $\omega_n = \omega_a$, we obtain from (1.106), (1.107) and (1.109)

$$\mu = m_2/m_1 = k_2/k_1, \qquad or \qquad k_1\mu = k_2 \qquad (1.113)$$

so that (1.112) can be rewritten as

$$\underline{q}_a = \left[\begin{array}{c} 0 \\ -F_a/k_2 \end{array} \right] \tag{1.114}$$

Hence, in the case that $\Omega = \omega_n (= \omega_a)$, the vibration amplitude of the dynamic absorber will be F_a/k_2 (absolute value), whereas it vibrates 180° or π rad out of phase with the excitation force on the main mass. In this case, where the vibration amplitude q_a of the main system is zero, the force excerted on the main system by the absorber spring k_2 is

$$k_2 \, q_2(t) = k_2 \, q_{2a} \sin \Omega t = -F_a \, \sin \Omega t \tag{1.115}$$

This force *completely balances* the applied external force on the main mass, $F_a \sin \Omega t$. Within the design constraint (1.111), there is a wide choice of absorber parameters k_2 and m_2. The actual choice is generally dictated by limitations placed on the amplitude q_{2a} of the absorber motion.

Next, we investigate how the system consisting of the main mass and the vibration absorber behaves if Ω differs from ω_n, but still $\omega_n = \omega_a$. In that case, (1.110) simplifies to

$$\underline{q}_a = \frac{q_{sta}}{(1 + \mu - p)(1 - p) - \mu} \left[\begin{array}{c} 1 - p \\ 1 \end{array} \right] \tag{1.116}$$

where the dimensionless quantity p is defined to be

$$p = \Omega^2/\omega_n^2 \tag{1.117}$$

The denominator of the right-hand side of (1.116) will be zero if Ω equals one of the natural frequencies of the two-degree-of-freedom system. In that case, p satisfies the characteristic equation.

$$p^2 - (2 + \mu) \, p + 1 = 0 \tag{1.118}$$

The two roots of this equation are

$$p_{1,2} = 1 + \frac{\mu}{2} \mp \sqrt{\mu + \left(\frac{\mu}{2}\right)^2} \tag{1.119}$$

Because, these roots are related to the natural frequencies of the two-degree-of-freedom system, if p takes the value p_1 or p_2, the amplitude of both the main mass and the absorber mass will become infinite, and the associated excitation frequencies $\Omega_1 = \omega_n \sqrt{p_1}$ and $\Omega_2 = \omega_n \sqrt{p_2}$ are resonance frequencies. Hence, the vibration absorber, while eliminating vibration at the excitation frequency $\Omega = \omega_n$, introduces two resonance frequencies Ω_1 and Ω_2, at which the vibration amplitude of the main mass becomes infinite. In practice, the operating frequency Ω must therefore be kept away from the resonance frequencies Ω_1 and Ω_2. Fig. 1.11 shows the course of the resonance frequencies

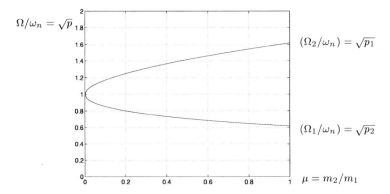

Fig. 1.11 Resonance frequencies Ω_1 and Ω_2 versus mass ratio m_2/m_1

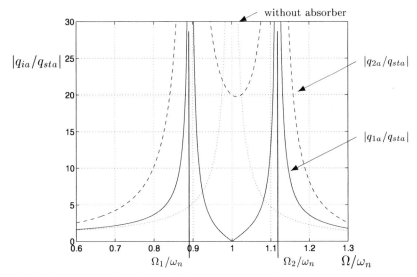

Fig. 1.12 Undamped vibration absorber: response of main mass and response of absorber mass, $m_2/m_1 = 0.05$, $\omega_a = \omega_n$

Ω_1 and Ω_2 as a function of the mass ratio m_2/m_1. It can be seen that the difference between Ω_1 and Ω_2 increases with increasing values of m_2/m_1.

To have a closer look at the response behaviour for varying excitation frequency, we consider the amplitude plots of $|q_{1a}/q_{sta}|$ and $|q_{2a}/q_{sta}|$ versus Ω/ω_n, shown in Fig. 1.12. These plots represent the variation of the amplitudes of vibration of the main system and of the absorber system with the excitation frequency of the main system. It is remarked that, if the main system is operating at the natural frequency $\Omega = \omega_n$, then Ω_1 is less than the operating speed and Ω_2 is greater than this speed. Thus, the main system must pass through Ω_1 during start-up and stopping. This can result in large amplitudes. To reduce the amplitude at the resonance frequencies damping can be added, but this results in an increase in amplitude in the neigbourhood of the operating frequency.

For more information on undamped dynamic vibration absorbers the reader is referred to [Den Hartog-56]. In the following section an introductory discussion will be given on damped dynamic vibration absorbers.

1.9   DAMPED DYNAMIC VIBRATION ABSORBERS

Let us consider the system of Fig. 1.13, where the original single-degree-of-freedom system consists of the mass m_1, the spring k_1 and the damper d_1, while the added absorber system consists of the mass m_2, the spring k_2 and the damper d_2. The set of equations of motion of the combined two-degree-

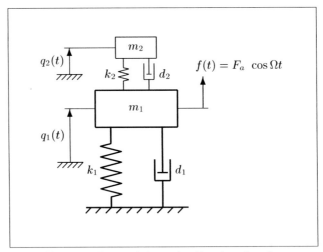

Fig. 1.13   Damped dynamic vibration absorber

of-freedom system can easily be shown to be

$$\underline{M}\,\ddot{q}(t) + \underline{D}\,\dot{q}(t) + \underline{K}\,q(t) = \underline{f}(t) \tag{1.120}$$

where the displacement column $q(t)$ and the force column $\underline{f}(t)$ are again given by (1.100), while the mass matrix $\underline{M}$ and the stiffness matrix $\underline{K}$ are given by (1.101). Finally, in (1.120) the damping matrix $\underline{D}$ is given by

$$\underline{D} = \begin{bmatrix} d_1 + d_2 & -d_2 \\ -d_2 & d_2 \end{bmatrix} \tag{1.121}$$

In agreement with (1.68) and (1.69) we express the steady-state solution of (1.120) as

$$\underline{q}(t) = \begin{bmatrix} q_1(t) \\ q_2(t) \end{bmatrix} = \begin{bmatrix} \hat{q}_1 \\ \hat{q}_2 \end{bmatrix} e^{j\Omega t} = \underline{\hat{q}} \, e^{j\Omega t} \tag{1.122}$$

where the time-independent complex response amplitudes $\hat{q}_1$ and $\hat{q}_2$ can be written as

$$\underline{\hat{q}} = \begin{bmatrix} \hat{q}_1 \\ \hat{q}_2 \end{bmatrix} = \begin{bmatrix} q_{1a} \, e^{j\psi_1} \\ q_{2a} \, e^{j\psi_2} \end{bmatrix} \tag{1.123}$$

Here q_{1a} and q_{2a} are the real amplitudes of the steady-state responses $q_1(t)$ and $q_2(t)$, while ψ_1 and ψ_2 are their phase angles. Inserting (1.122) into (1.120) and dividing through by $e^{j\Omega t}$, we obtain a set of two algebraic equations for q_{1a} and q_{2a} having the matrix form

$$\left[-\Omega^2 \underline{M} + j\Omega \underline{D} + \underline{K} \right] \underline{\hat{q}} = \underline{F}_a \tag{1.124}$$

Using (1.70)-(1.76), we express the solution of (1.124) in the form

$$\underline{\hat{q}} = \left[-\Omega^2 \underline{M} + j\Omega \underline{D} + \underline{K} \right]^{-1} \underline{F}_a = \frac{F_a}{det} \begin{bmatrix} -\Omega^2 m_2 + j\Omega d_2 + k_2 \\ j\Omega d_2 + k_2 \end{bmatrix} \tag{1.125}$$

where the determinant det of the matrix $\left(-\Omega^2 \underline{M} + j\Omega \underline{D} + \underline{K} \right)$ is given by

$$\begin{aligned} det &= \left\{ -\Omega^2 m_1 + j\Omega \left(d_1 + d_2 \right) + \left(k_1 + k_2 \right) \right\} \\ &\quad \left\{ -\Omega^2 m_2 + j\Omega d_2 + k_2 \right\} - \left(j\Omega d_2 + k_2 \right)^2 \\ &= \left(k_1 - \Omega^2 m_1 \right) \left(k_2 - \Omega^2 m_2 \right) - \left(k_2 m_2 + d_1 d_2 \right) \Omega^2 \\ &\quad + j\Omega \left[d_1 \left(k_2 - \Omega^2 m_2 \right) + d_2 \left\{ k_1 - \left(m_1 + m_2 \right) \Omega^2 \right\} \right] \end{aligned} \tag{1.126}$$

The expression (1.126) can be rewritten as

$$\begin{aligned} det &= k_1 m_2 \omega_n^2 \left[\left(1 - \frac{\Omega^2}{\omega_n^2} \right) \left(\frac{\omega_a^2}{\omega_n^2} - \frac{\Omega^2}{\omega_n^2} \right) - \left(\mu \frac{\omega_a^2}{\omega_n^2} + 4\xi_1\xi_2 \right) \frac{\Omega^2}{\omega_n^2} \right. \\ &\quad \left. + j\frac{\Omega}{\omega_n} \left\{ 2\xi_1 \left(\frac{\omega_a^2}{\omega_n^2} - \frac{\Omega^2}{\omega_n^2} \right) + 2\xi_2 \left(1 - (1 + \mu) \frac{\Omega^2}{\omega_n^2} \right) \right\} \right] \end{aligned} \tag{1.127}$$

where ω_a, ω_n and μ are again been given by (1.106), (1.107) and (1.109), respectively, while

$$\xi_1 = \frac{d_1}{2 m_1 \omega_n} = \text{dim. damping factor of the main system} \tag{1.128}$$

$$\xi_2 = \frac{d_2}{2 m_2 \omega_n} = \text{dim. damping factor of the absorber system} \tag{1.129}$$

Using the foregoing results, we can express the solution (1.125) as

$$\underline{\hat{q}} = \frac{q_{sta}}{ddet} \frac{1}{\omega_n^2} \begin{bmatrix} \omega_a^2 - \Omega^2 + 2j\Omega\omega_n\xi_2 \\ \omega_a^2 + 2j\Omega\omega_n\xi_2 \end{bmatrix} \tag{1.130}$$

where q_{sta} is again been given by (1.108), while

$$ddet = det/\left(k_1 m_2 \omega_n^2\right) = \left(1 - \frac{\Omega^2}{\omega_n^2}\right)\left(\frac{\omega_a^2}{\omega_n^2} - \frac{\Omega^2}{\omega_n^2}\right) - \left(\mu \frac{\omega_a^2}{\omega_n^2} + 4\xi_1\xi_2\right)\frac{\Omega^2}{\omega_n^2}$$

$$+j\frac{\Omega}{\omega_n}\left\{2\xi_1\left(\frac{\omega_a^2}{\omega_n^2} - \frac{\Omega^2}{\omega_n^2}\right) + 2\xi_2\left(1 - (1+\mu)\frac{\Omega^2}{\omega_n^2}\right)\right\}$$

(1.131)

We observe that for $\xi_1 = 0$, $\xi_2 = 0$, we obtain (1.110) from (1.130) as a particular case.

Our primary interest lies in the motion of the main system. We consider this motion for the particular case in which the damping of the main system without absorber can be neglected so that $\xi_1 = 0$. It can be concluded from (1.130) and (1.131) that in that case the vibration amplitude $|q_{1a}|$ of the main system can be written as follows

$$|q_{1a}| = \frac{q_{sta}}{den}\sqrt{\left(\frac{\omega_a^2}{\omega_n^2} - \frac{\Omega^2}{\omega_n^2}\right)^2 + 4\xi_2^2\frac{\Omega^2}{\omega_n^2}}$$

(1.132)

where the denominator den equals

$$den = \sqrt{\left\{\left(1 - \frac{\Omega^2}{\omega_n^2}\right)\left(\frac{\omega_a^2}{\omega_n^2} - \frac{\Omega^2}{\omega_n^2}\right) - \mu\frac{\omega_a^2}{\omega_n^2}\frac{\Omega^2}{\omega_n^2}\right\}^2 + 4\xi_2^2\frac{\Omega^2}{\omega_n^2}\left(1 - (1+\mu)\frac{\Omega^2}{\omega_n^2}\right)^2}$$

(1.133)

Fig. 1.14 shows the amplitude plot of $|q_{1a}/q_{sta}|$ versus Ω/ω_n for $\omega_a = \omega_n$, $\mu = 0.05$ and different values of the damping parameter ξ_2. For $\xi_2 = 0$ we obtain again the plot associated with the undamped system which was found earlier in Fig. 1.12. For $\xi_2 \to \infty$ both masses become rigidly connected to one another and we obtain a single-degree-of-freedom system with resonance frequency

$$\omega = \sqrt{\frac{k_1}{m_1 + m_2}} = \omega_n\sqrt{\frac{1}{1+\mu}}$$

(1.134)

For $0 < \xi_2 < \infty$ we wish to keep the vibration amplitudes of both masses m_1 and m_2 over the range of excitation frequencies of the main system as limited as possible. To achieve this goal, the parameters m_2, k_2 and d_2 of the absorber system have to be selected so as to minimize the maximum response amplitude over the considered frequency range. For a further discussion of this minimization problem the reader is referred to [Den Hartog-56, Rao-95]. In this discussion an important role is played by the so-called *invariant points* for which the value of $|q_{1a}/q_{sta}|$ does not depend on the value of ξ_2.

Nowadays for the optimal choice of the absorber parameters m_2, k_2 and d_2 advantageous use can be made of the developments in computer hard- and software technology. As an example Fig. 1.15 gives a three-dimensional representation of the amplitudes $|q_{ia}/q_{sta}|$ $(i = 1, 2)$ of the main system with absorber as a function of the mass ratio $\mu = m_2/m_1$ and the dimensionless

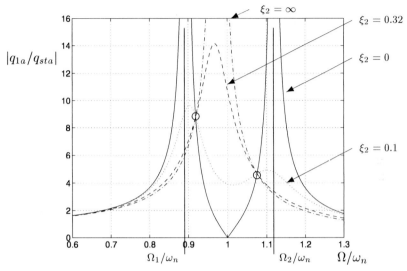

Fig. 1.14 Damped vibration absorber: amplitude plot of main mass, $\mu = 0.05$, $\omega_a = \omega_n$

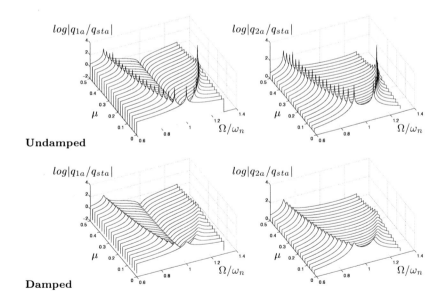

Fig. 1.15 Comparison of amplitude-frequency characteristics of damped and un-damped vibration absorbers as function of μ

excitation frequency Ω/ω_n for the case $\omega_a = \omega_n$. The top panels show the un-damped situation, whereas the bottom panels show the case where damping is added with dimensionless damping factors $\xi_1 = d_1/\left(2\sqrt{k_1 m_1}\right) = 0.01$ and $\xi_2^* = d_2/\left(2\sqrt{k_2 m_2}\right) = 0.01$. It can be observed that adding a footnotesize amount of damping does not affect too much the general picture. Only the high amplitudes near the resonance frequencies are reduced and the theoret-ical so-called anti-resonance point at $\mu = 0$, $\Omega/\omega_n = 1$ disappears. Pictures like those shown in Fig. 1.15 can assist the designer to select the parameters of the vibration absorber with respect to specific design criteria. For more in-formation on the subject of dynamic vibration absorbers the reader is referred to Rao (1995) and the references cited therein.

2

Lagrangian Mechanics

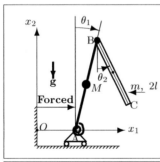

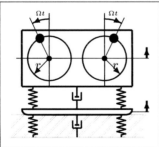

In this chapter the **Lagrange**'s equations will be derived and it will be shown that by using this approach (instead of Newton's Law directly), the differential equations of motion for complex systems can be generated systematically. Examples of such systems are the 2-dimensional forced pendulum system and the model for a soil compression machine driven by two counterrotating unbalances as shown alongside.

Procedures to find static equilibrium solutions and to evaluate their stability will be presented. This finally will lead to a linearized set of equations for small motions in the neighbourhood of equilibrium solutions.

2.1 INTRODUCTION

In general Newton's laws are formulated for a single particle and can be extended to systems of particles and rigid bodies. In describing the motion, physical coordinates and forces are employed, quantities that can be represented by vectors. The main drawback of this approach is that it considers the individual components of a system separately, thus necessitating the calculation of interacting forces resulting from connections between those components. Those connections result in so-called kinematical constraints. In many cases these interacting forces are of less interest and can be eliminated from the equations of motion. A different approach to dynamics considers the system as a whole rather than its individual components, thus eliminating the need to calculate interacting forces. This approach is attributed to Lagrange, and it formulates the problems in dynamics in terms of two scalar functions, the kinetic energy and the potential energy, and so-called generalized nonconservative forces. This formulation appears in a natural way from a *variational approach* to dynamics. In this approach, first the concept of coordinates is expanded to include the more abstract *generalized coordinates*, scalar coordinates not necessarily having physical meaning. Next, the concept of *virtual displacements* is introduced, which needs some basic rules of the calculus of variations. Then, the *principle of virtual work* permits a formulation of dynamics that is invariant to the coordinates used to describe the motion. This principle provides the basis for the simplest possible formulation of the equations of motion of complex mechanical systems, namely the *Lagrange's equations of motion*. In these equations the above mentioned kinetic energy, the potential energy and the generalized nonconservative forces appear in a straightforward way.

In this chapter the various concepts required for the variational approach in dynamics, outlined above, are introduced and elaborated. The resulting Lagrange's equations of motion are generalized to the case that still certain kinematical constraints and related interacting forces can be included in the formulation. The practical application of the Lagrange's equation of motion will be illustrated. Finally, the Lagrange's equations of motion are linearized for small motions in the neighbourhood of equilibrium configurations. The equations resulting from the linearization process are of particular interest for vibration analysis of multi-degree-of-freedom linear systems.

2.2 DEGREES OF FREEDOM; GENERALIZED COORDINATES

Let us consider a mechanical system consisting of a collection of cooperating parts. Examples of such systems are drive systems, machining tools and robots. It is assumed that in the modelling process the cooperating parts of the system may be approximated by particles or rigid bodies. The connections between the cooperating parts are being assumed to be massless. They may be springs, dampers, hinges, etc., and constrain the freedom of motion of the individual parts.

We will describe the motion of the individual parts and of the mechanical system as a whole with respect to an inertial frame, which is represented by the orthogonal axes x_1, x_2 and x_3 of a right turning Cartesian coordinate system, see Fig. 2.1. The origin of this coordinate system is O, whereas $\vec{e}_1$, $\vec{e}_2$ and $\vec{e}_3$ are the (time-independent) unit vectors along the axes x_1, x_2 and x_3, respectively.

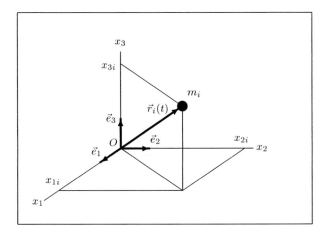

Fig. 2.1 Position vector $\vec{r}_i$ of mass m_i with respect to inertial coordinate frame

A mechanical system will be considered to consist of a collection or a system of material particles where discrete mass particles m_i and differential mass elements dm will be treated equivalently in the formulation. So, we consider the motion of a system of n_p particles of mass m_i $(i = 1, 2, \ldots n_p)$. If we express the motion of this system by means of the Cartesian coordinates x_{1i}, x_{2i} and x_{3i} of each particle m_i, then $3n_p$ coordinates would be required for n_p particles. However, in many problems the Cartesian coordinates x_{1i}, x_{2i} and x_{3i} $(i = 1, 2, \ldots, n_p)$ are not all independent due to connections between the mass particles. In general, the configuration of the assembled system of particles can be described uniquely by a finite number of independent (geometrical) parameters, say, $q_1, q_2, \ldots, q_n$. The total number n of those independent parameters is called the number of *degrees of freedom* of the system. The number of degrees of freedom of a system coincides with the minimum number of independent coordinates that are required to describe the system position uniquely. The n coordinates $q_1, q_2 \ldots, q_n$ are referred to as the *generalized coordinates*, with $n \le 3n_p$. They may not always have physical meaning, *nor are they unique*, which implies that there may be more than one set of generalized coordinates capable of describing the system position uniquely. However, the *number* of degrees of freedom of the system is unique.

The relation between the Cartesian coordinates x_{1i}, x_{2i}, x_{3i} $(i = 1, \ldots, n_p)$ and the generalized coordinates q_k $(k = 1, 2, \ldots, n)$ can be formally expressed as

$$\left. \begin{array}{l} x_{1i} = x_{1i}\,(q_1, q_2, \ldots, q_n) \\ x_{2i} = x_{2i}\,(q_1, q_2, \ldots, q_n) \\ x_{3i} = x_{3i}\,(q_1, q_2, \ldots, q_n) \end{array} \right\} i = 1, 2, \ldots n_p. \qquad (2.1)$$

Equations (2.1) represent a *coordinate transformation*. We will use this transformation to simplify the problem formulation.

Example 2.1

We consider the double pendulum system of Fig. 2.2. The system consists of two concentrated masses m_1 and m_2. The mass m_1 is attached to one end of an inextensible massless string with length ℓ_1, where the other end of the string is fixed at point O. The mass m_2 is attached to one end of another inextensible massless string with length ℓ_2, where the other end of this string is connected to the mass m_1. The double pendulum is moving in the vertical x_1, x_2 plane under the influence of gravity. The motions of the masses m_1 and m_2 can be described by means of the Cartesian coordinates $[x_{11},\ x_{21},\ x_{31}]$ and $[x_{12},\ x_{22},\ x_{32}]$ respectively. It is not difficult to see that these six coordinates are not independent, as they are related by the four equations

$$\begin{array}{l} x_{31} = x_{32} = 0 \\ x_{11}^2 + x_{21}^2 = l_1^2 = const. \\ (x_{12} - x_{11})^2 + (x_{22} - x_{21})^2 = l_2^2 = const. \end{array} \qquad (2.2)$$

Equations (2.2) can be regarded as constraint equations reflecting the two-dimensional motion and that the lengths ℓ_1 and ℓ_2 do not change. Rather than working with the Cartesian coordinates $[x_{11}, x_{21}, x_{31}]$ and $[x_{12}, x_{22}, x_{32}]$ subject to constraints, it is more convenient to describe the motion in terms of a smaller number of generalized coordinates. It

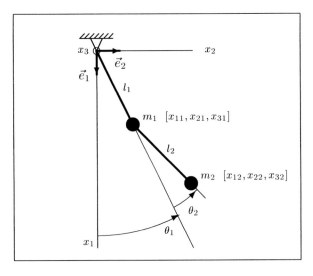

Fig. 2.2 Double pendulum (two masses)

is easy to see that the system has only two degrees of freedom and a convenient set of generalized coordinates is $q_1 = \theta_1$ and $q_2 = \theta_2$, where the angles θ_1 and θ_2 are shown in Fig. 2.2. In that case, the explicit version of (2.1) for the system at hand becomes

$$
\begin{bmatrix} x_{11} \\ x_{21} \\ x_{31} \end{bmatrix} = \begin{bmatrix} l_1 \cos \theta_1 \\ l_1 \sin \theta_1 \\ 0 \end{bmatrix}
$$

$$
\begin{bmatrix} x_{12} \\ x_{22} \\ x_{32} \end{bmatrix} = \begin{bmatrix} l_1 \cos \theta_1 + l_2 \cos(\theta_1 + \theta_2) \\ l_1 \sin \theta_1 + l_2 \sin(\theta_1 + \theta_2) \\ 0 \end{bmatrix}
$$

(2.3)

As remarked earlier, the generalized coordinates are not necessarily unique. For example, the motion of the double pendulum system of Fig. 2.2 can also be described uniquely by the two angles $q_1 = \theta_1$ and $q_2 = \varphi = \theta_1 + \theta_2$, where the second generalized coordinate represents the absolute rotation of the second pendulum.

For reasons of compactness of the formulation, the generalized coordinates q_1, q_2, ..., q_n will be stored in a column matrix $\underline{q}$, also shortly called column $\underline{q}$

$$
\underline{q} = \begin{bmatrix} q_1 \\ q_2 \\ \vdots \\ q_n \end{bmatrix}
\tag{2.4}
$$

The position of mass particle m_i of Fig. 2.1 can be described by means of the radius vector $\vec{r}_i$ of m_i relative to the origin O of the inertial frame. The description by means of the radius vector $\vec{r}_i$ has the advantage that it is independent of the specific coordinate system (Cartesian, cylindrical, etc.) chosen to quantify the motion. On the other hand, if we wish to quantify the motion with respect to a specific coordinate system, we replace the radius vector $\vec{r}_i$ by its column-matrix representation $\underline{r}_i$ with respect to the vector basis in that coordinate system. For example, the column-matrix representation of the radius vector $\vec{r}_i$ in Fig. 2.1 with respect to the Cartesian vector basis $\{\vec{e}_1, \vec{e}_2, \vec{e}_3\}$ is

$$
\underline{r}_i = \begin{bmatrix} x_{1i} \\ x_{2i} \\ x_{3i} \end{bmatrix}
\tag{2.5}
$$

Now, because the position of the system as a whole can be uniquely described by means of the generalized coordinates $q_1, q_2, \ldots, q_n$, the radius vector $\vec{r}_i$ can be considered to be a function of these coordinates. This dependency is formally expressed as

$$
\vec{r}_i = \vec{r}_i(\underline{q})
\tag{2.6}
$$

Similarly, the column-matrix representation $\underline{r}_i$ of the radius vector $\vec{r}_i$ with respect to a vector basis in a specific coordinate system can also be considered to be a function of the generalized coordinates $q_1, q_2, \ldots, q_n$. This dependency is formally expressed as

$$
\underline{r}_i = \underline{r}_i(\underline{q})
\tag{2.7}
$$

Example 2.2

We consider the double pendulum from example 2.1, page 38. If we make use of (2.3), the column-matrix representation of the radius vector of m_1 with respect to the Cartesian vector basis $\{\vec{e}_1, \vec{e}_2, \vec{e}_3\}$ becomes

$$
\underline{r}_1 = \begin{bmatrix} x_{11} \\ x_{21} \\ x_{31} \end{bmatrix} = \begin{bmatrix} l_1 \cos\theta_1 \\ l_1 \sin\theta_1 \\ 0 \end{bmatrix} = \underline{r}_1(\underline{q})
\tag{2.8}
$$

Analogously, the column-matrix representation of the radius vector of
m_2 with respect to the same Cartesian vector basis can be written as

$$\underline{r}_2 = \begin{bmatrix} x_{12} \\ x_{22} \\ x_{32} \end{bmatrix} = \begin{bmatrix} l_1 \cos\theta_1 + l_2 \cos(\theta_1 + \theta_2) \\ l_1 \sin\theta_1 + l_2 \sin(\theta_1 + \theta_2) \\ 0 \end{bmatrix} = \underline{r}_2(\underline{q}) \qquad (2.9)$$

Indeed it can be concluded from (2.8) and (2.9) that the radius vector
of mass m_1 and mass m_2 of the system generally depends on all the
generalized coordinates $\underline{q}^T = [\theta_1, \theta_2]$.

Example 2.3

We consider the double pendulum, sketched in Fig. 2.3. This system,
which differs slightly from the one in Fig. 2.2, is built from two ho-
mogenous rigid bars OA respectively AB with lengths l_1 respectively l_2,
and masses m_1 and m_2 . The rigid bars are connected to one another
and to the inertial space by frictionless hinges. The system moves in
the vertical x_1, x_2 plane under the influence of gravity. The position

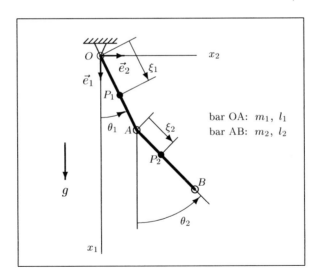

Fig. 2.3 Double pendulum (two rigid bars)

of the system can be described uniquely by means of two geometrical
parameters. Hence, the number of degrees of freedom for this system
equals two. As has been remarked previously, several choices for the
generalized coordinates are possible. For the system of Fig. 2.3 a con-
venient set of generalized coordinates consists of the angles θ_1 and θ_2

of bar OA and bar AB with respect to the vertical x_1 axis. So, for this system the generalized coordinates are $q_1 = \theta_1$ and $q_2 = \theta_2$. For this system the column of generalized coordinates $\underline{q}$ takes the form

$$\underline{q} = \begin{bmatrix} q_1 \\ q_2 \end{bmatrix} = \begin{bmatrix} \theta_1 \\ \theta_2 \end{bmatrix} \tag{2.10}$$

Now, we will specify (2.7) for an arbitrary point P_1 of bar OA and an arbitrary point P_2 of bar AB. To this end, the positions of P_1 and P_2 within these bars have to be specified. This can be done by means of body-fixed coordinates. Because the bars OA and AB can be considered to be one-dimensional bodies, we need only one body-fixed coordinate to specify the position of P_1 within OA, and also one body-fixed coordinate to specify the position of P_2 within AB. These body-fixed coordinates, ξ_1 and ξ_2, which do not change during the motion of the pendulum, are indicated in Fig. 2.3. The column-matrix representation of the radius vector of P_1 with respect to the Cartesian vector basis $\{\vec{e}_1, \vec{e}_2\}$ can be written as

$$\underline{r}_{P1} = \begin{bmatrix} x_1 \\ x_2 \end{bmatrix}_{P_1} = \begin{bmatrix} \xi_1 \cos\theta_1 \\ \xi_1 \sin\theta_1 \end{bmatrix} \tag{2.11}$$

Analogously, the column-matrix representation of the radius vector of P_2 with respect to the Cartesian vector basis $\{\vec{e}_1, \vec{e}_2\}$ can be written as

$$\underline{r}_{P2} = \begin{bmatrix} x_1 \\ x_2 \end{bmatrix}_{P_2} = \begin{bmatrix} l_1 \cos\theta_1 + \xi_2 \cos\theta_2 \\ l_1 \sin\theta_1 + \xi_2 \sin\theta_2 \end{bmatrix} \tag{2.12}$$

Again it can be concluded from (2.12) that the radius vector of an arbitrary point P of the system generally depends on all the generalized coordinates contained in the column $\underline{q}$, i.e. in this example on θ_1 and θ_2.

2.3   PRESCRIBED COORDINATES

Until sofar, we considered systems for which the motion can completely be expressed in terms of a set of generalized coordinates $q_1, q_2, \ldots, q_n$, collected in a column $\underline{q}$. However, additionally an important class of systems exists, for which the motion can be described by means of a set of generalized coordinates, but also depends on one or more geometrical parameters that are known *explicit* functions of time. In that case, we are dealing with "prescribed coordinates" or "drivers". Examples are met in cam mechanisms, prescribed road profiles in vehicle dynamics, and base excited vibrations of buildings. We denote the explicitly prescribed coordinates by $s_1(t), s_2(t), \ldots s_m(t)$ and they are stored in the column matrix $\underline{s}(t)$

$$\underline{s}(t) = \begin{bmatrix} s_1(t) \\ s_2(t) \\ \vdots \\ s_m(t) \end{bmatrix} \qquad (2.13)$$

For systems with prescribed coordinates, the motion depends on those coordinates (collected in the column $\underline{s}(t)$) and on the generalized coordinates (collected in the column $\underline{q}$). Hence, for these systems the radius vector $\vec{r}_i$ of mass particle m_i depends both on $\underline{q}$ and $\underline{s}(t)$. This dependency is formally expressed as

$$\vec{r}_i = \vec{r}_i\left(\underline{q}, \underline{s}(t)\right) \qquad (2.14)$$

which can be viewed upon as the generalization of (2.6) to systems with prescribed coordinates. Similarly, for systems with prescribed coordinates the column-matrix representation $\underline{r}_i$ of the radius vector $\vec{r}_i$ with respect to a vector basis in a specific coordinate system also depends both on $\underline{q}$ and $\underline{s}(t)$. This dependency is formally expressed as

$$\underline{r}_i = \underline{r}_i\left(\underline{q}, \underline{s}(t)\right) \qquad (2.15)$$

which can be viewed upon as the generalization of (2.7) to systems with prescribed coordinates.

Example 2.4

We consider the simple pendulum system with moving support of Fig. 2.4. The system consists of a rigid massless rod with length l and at the end the point mass m. The support of the rod is undergoing a vertical prescribed motion $s(t)$. For this system we have only one generalized coordinate for which we have chosen the angle θ between the rod and the vertical axis, so $\underline{q} = [\theta]$. The column of prescribed coordinates also contains only a single element $\underline{s}(t) = [s(t)]$.

The column-matrix representation $\underline{r}$ of the radius vector $\vec{r}(t)$ of mass m with respect to the shown vector basis $\{\vec{e}_1, \vec{e}_2\}$ becomes

$$\underline{r} = \begin{bmatrix} s(t) + l\cos\theta \\ l\sin\theta \end{bmatrix} = \underline{r}(\underline{q}, \underline{s}) = \underline{r}(\underline{q}, t) \qquad (2.16)$$

In writing such a column-matrix representation one should be aware of the lengths of the different column matrices, as in this case $\underline{r}$ is a (1×2)-matrix while $\underline{q}$ and $\underline{s}$ are scalar functions.

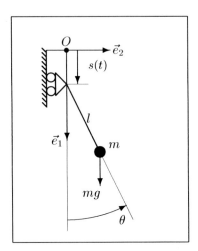

Fig. 2.4   Pendulum with moving support

The foregoing treatment elucidates that, in general, the position vector of a material particle m_i of a system can be considered to be an explicit function of the generalized coordinates and the time. We will express this through the compacted version of (2.14) and (2.15)

$$\vec{r}_i = \vec{r}_i(\underline{q}, \underline{s}(t)) = \vec{r}_i(\underline{q}, t) \qquad \text{and} \qquad \underline{r}_i = \underline{r}_i(\underline{q}, \underline{s}(t)) = \underline{r}_i(\underline{q}, t) \qquad (2.17)$$

It should be realized that the generalized coordinates themselves have to be considered of course as being *implicit* functions of time.

2.4 DIFFERENTIATION WITH RESPECT TO A COLUMN MATRIX; THE VELOCITY VECTOR

In order to create a compact formulation of the equations of motion, it appears to be useful to define an abbreviating notation for the derivatives of scalars, columns and vectors with respect to a column matrix. Let us first consider a *scalar function* $f(\underline{q}, \underline{\dot{q}}, t)$, which is an explicit function of the generalized coordinates $\underline{q}$, the generalized velocities $\underline{\dot{q}}$ and the time t. An illustrative example of such a function is the kinetic energy to be discussed later. We will define the partial derivatives of the scalar function f to the columns $\underline{q}$ and $\underline{\dot{q}}$ and the scalar t to be

$$f_{,\underline{q}} := \frac{\partial f}{\partial \underline{q}} := \begin{bmatrix} \dfrac{\partial f}{\partial q_1} & \dfrac{\partial f}{\partial q_2} & \cdots & \dfrac{\partial f}{\partial q_n} \end{bmatrix} \tag{2.18}$$

$$f_{,\underline{\dot{q}}} := \frac{\partial f}{\partial \underline{\dot{q}}} := \begin{bmatrix} \dfrac{\partial f}{\partial \dot{q}_1} & \dfrac{\partial f}{\partial \dot{q}_2} & \cdots & \dfrac{\partial f}{\partial \dot{q}_n} \end{bmatrix} \tag{2.19}$$

$$f_{,t} := \frac{\partial f}{\partial t} \tag{2.20}$$

In words, (2.18) and (2.19) imply that the partial derivative of a scalar function to a column matrix is a row matrix. Next, let us consider *the column matrix function* $\underline{f}(\underline{q}, t)$ of dimension m, which is an explicit function of the generalized coordinates $\underline{q}$ and time t.   An illustrative example of such a function is the column-matrix representation of the radius vector of a point P of a mechanical system with respect to a Cartesian vector basis. We will define the partial derivatives of the column-matrix function $\underline{f}$ to the column $\underline{q}$ and scalar t to be

$$\underline{f}_{,\underline{q}} := \frac{\partial \underline{f}}{\partial \underline{q}} := \begin{bmatrix} f_{1,q_1} & f_{1,q_2} & \cdots & f_{1,q_n} \\ f_{2,q_1} & f_{2,q_2} & \cdots & f_{2,q_n} \\ \vdots & \vdots & \ddots & \vdots \\ f_{m,q_1} & f_{m,q_2} & \cdots & f_{m,q_n} \end{bmatrix} ; \qquad f_{i,q_j} := \frac{\partial f_i}{\partial q_j} \tag{2.21}$$

$$\underline{f}_{,t} := \frac{\partial \underline{f}}{\partial t} := \begin{bmatrix} f_{1,t} \\ f_{2,t} \\ \vdots \\ f_{m,t} \end{bmatrix} ; \qquad f_{i,t} := \frac{\partial f_i}{\partial t} \tag{2.22}$$

Here $f_1, f_2, ..., f_m$ are the elements of the column matrix $\underline{f}$. In words, (2.21) implies that the derivative of a column matrix with dimension m to a column matrix with dimension n is an $m \times n$ matrix. Because in general $m \neq n$, this matrix is in general non-square and, hence, rectangular. The matrix $\underline{f}_{,\underline{q}}$ is also called a Jacobian matrix.   It can be seen easily that (2.18) can be considered to be a special case of (2.21) for $m = 1$.

The newly defined notation can, for example, be applied to write the **total** derivative of the scalar function $f(q, \dot{q}, t)$ with respect to time in a compact form

$$\dot{f} = \frac{df}{dt} = f_{,t} + f_{,q}\ \dot{q} + f_{,\dot{q}}\ \ddot{q} \qquad (2.23)$$

Another example applies to the column-matrix representation $\underline{v} = \underline{\dot{r}}$ of the velocity vector $\vec{v} = \vec{\dot{r}}$ of a point P of a mechanical system with respect to a Cartesian vector basis $\{\vec{e}_1, \vec{e}_2, \vec{e}_3\}$, which can be written in the following compact form

$$\underline{v} = \underline{\dot{r}} = \frac{d\underline{r}}{dt} = \underline{r}_{,t} + \underline{r}_{,q}\ \dot{q} \qquad (2.24)$$

Example 2.5

We consider the double pendulum system of example 2.1 on page 38 and specify the matrix $\underline{r}_{,q}$ for mass m_1 with respect to the Cartesian vector basis $\{\vec{e}_1, \vec{e}_2, \vec{e}_3\}$. Using (2.21) and (2.8), we obtain

$$\underline{r}_{1,q} = \begin{bmatrix} -l_1 \sin\theta_1 & 0 \\ l_1 \cos\theta_1 & 0 \\ 0 & 0 \end{bmatrix} \qquad (2.25)$$

Analogously, we can specify the matrix $\underline{r}_{,q}$ for the mass m_2 and obtain

$$\underline{r}_{2,q} = \begin{bmatrix} -l_1 \sin\theta_1 - l_2 \sin(\theta_1 + \theta_2) & -l_2 \sin(\theta_1 + \theta_2) \\ l_1 \cos\theta_1 + l_2 \cos(\theta_1 + \theta_2) & l_2 \cos(\theta_1 + \theta_2) \\ 0 & 0 \end{bmatrix} \qquad (2.26)$$

So, we can write directly

$$\underline{v}_1 = \underline{\dot{r}}_1 = \underline{r}_{1,q}\ \dot{q} \qquad \text{respectively} \qquad \underline{v}_2 = \underline{\dot{r}}_2 = \underline{r}_{2,q}\ \dot{q} \qquad (2.27)$$

Both matrices have dimension (3×2), because we are looking at a 3-dimensional problem with 2 generalized coordinates.

Example 2.6

We consider the double pendulum system consisting of two rigid bars as shown in example 2.3 on page 41. We specify the matrix $\underline{r}_{,q}$ for the point P_1 of the rigid bar OA with respect to the Cartesian vector basis $\{\vec{e}_1, \vec{e}_2\}$. Using (2.21) and (2.11), we obtain

$$\underline{r}_{P1,q} = \begin{bmatrix} -\xi_1 \sin\theta_1 & 0 \\ \xi_1 \cos\theta_1 & 0 \end{bmatrix} \qquad (2.28)$$

Analogously, we can specify the matrix $\underline{r}_{,q}$ for the point P_2 of the rigid bar AB. Using (2.21) and (2.12) we obtain

$$\underline{r}_{P2,\underline{q}} = \begin{bmatrix} -l_1 \sin \theta_1 & -\xi_2 \sin \theta_2 \\ l_1 \cos \theta_1 & \xi_2 \cos \theta_2 \end{bmatrix} \tag{2.29}$$

Example 2.7

For the 2-dimensional pendulum with moving support shown in example 2.4 on page 44, we are dealing with only one generalized coordinate and one prescribed displacement of the support. Then, using (2.16), we can write

$$\underline{r}_{,\underline{q}} = \begin{bmatrix} -l \sin \theta \\ l \cos \theta \end{bmatrix}; \qquad \underline{r}_{,t} = \begin{bmatrix} \dot{s}(t) \\ 0 \end{bmatrix} \tag{2.30}$$

So, again it is easy to see that

$$\underline{v} = \dot{\underline{r}} = \underline{r}_{,\underline{q}} \, \dot{\underline{q}} + \underline{r}_{,t} \tag{2.31}$$

As a final application of the newly defined notation we consider the second derivative of a scalar function $f(\underline{q})$ to the column $\underline{q}$ on which it depends. Applying (2.18) repeatedly, with f consecutively being replaced by $\partial f/\partial q_1, \partial f/\partial q_2, \ldots, \partial f/\partial q_n$, and utilizing additionally the definition for the derivative of a column with respect to another column, given by (2.21), we arrive at

$$(f_{,\underline{q}})^T{}_{,\underline{q}} = \begin{bmatrix} (f_{,q_1})_{,q_1} & (f_{,q_1})_{,q_2} & \cdots & (f_{,q_1})_{,q_n} \\ (f_{,q_2})_{,q_1} & (f_{,q_2})_{,q_2} & \cdots & (f_{,q_2})_{,q_n} \\ \vdots & & & \\ (f_{,q_n})_{,q_1} & (f_{,q_n})_{,q_2} & \cdots & (f_{,q_n})_{,q_n} \end{bmatrix} \tag{2.32}$$

$$\text{with} \quad (f_{,q_i})_{,q_j} := \frac{\partial}{\partial q_j}\left(\frac{\partial f}{\partial q_i}\right)$$

where the upper index T denotes the transposed of the corresponding column or matrix. We observe that the matrix in the right side of (2.32) is symmetric.

In the last part of this section, we will define an abbreviated notation for the derivatives of vector functions with respect to columns and scalars. To this end, let us consider a *vector function* $\vec{f}(\underline{q}, t)$, which means that the vector $\vec{f}$ explicitly depends on the generalized coordinates $\underline{q}$ and the time t. As a generalization of (2.18) and (2.20) the partial derivatives of the vector function $\vec{f}$ to the column $\underline{q}$ and scalar t will be defined to be

$$\vec{f}_{,\underline{q}} := \frac{\partial \vec{f}}{\partial \underline{q}} := \begin{bmatrix} \frac{\partial \vec{f}}{\partial q_1} & \frac{\partial \vec{f}}{\partial q_2} & \cdots & \frac{\partial \vec{f}}{\partial q_n} \end{bmatrix} \tag{2.33}$$

$$\vec{f}_{,t} := \frac{\partial \vec{f}}{\partial t} \tag{2.34}$$

In words, (2.33) implies that the derivative of a vector function to a column matrix is a row matrix of vectors. It should be noticed that (2.33) is useful in the sense that it is independent of the choice of the coordinate system needed to specify the motion of the mechanical system. In other words, it is said that the representation by means of (2.33) is basis independent. On the other hand, quantification of (2.33) requires representation with respect to a specific vector basis. In practice, this simply comes to deleting in (2.33) the arrows on top of the f symbols and introducing a representation by underlined symbols. As a generalization of (2.33) we need the partial derivatives of a *column of vector functions* $\vec{f}(\underline{q}, t)$ to the column $\underline{q}$ and scalar t. These derivatives are defined to be

$$\underline{\vec{f}}_{,q} = \frac{\partial \vec{f}}{\partial \underline{q}} := \begin{bmatrix} \vec{f}_{1,q_1} & \vec{f}_{1,q_2} & \cdots & \vec{f}_{1,q_n} \\ \vec{f}_{2,q_1} & \vec{f}_{2,q_2} & \cdots & \vec{f}_{2,q_n} \\ \vdots & \vdots & \ddots & \vdots \\ \vec{f}_{m,q_1} & \vec{f}_{m,q_2} & \cdots & \vec{f}_{m,q_n} \end{bmatrix} \quad ; \quad \vec{f}_{i,q_j} := \frac{\partial \vec{f}_i}{\partial q_j} \tag{2.35}$$

$$\underline{\vec{f}}_{,t} = \frac{\partial \vec{f}}{\partial t} := \begin{bmatrix} \vec{f}_{1,t} \\ \vec{f}_{2,t} \\ \vdots \\ \vec{f}_{m,t} \end{bmatrix} \quad ; \quad \vec{f}_{i,t} := \frac{\partial \vec{f}_i}{\partial t} \tag{2.36}$$

where $\vec{f}_1, \vec{f}_2, \cdots, \vec{f}_m$ are the vector elements of the column of vector functions $\underline{\vec{f}}$. As an example of the above definitions of derivatives of vectors, we can express the velocity vector $\vec{v} = \dot{\vec{r}}$ corresponding to the position vector (2.17) as follows

$$\vec{v} = \dot{\vec{r}} = \vec{r}_{,t} + \vec{r}_{,q} \ \dot{\underline{q}} = \vec{r}_{,t} + \dot{\underline{q}}^T (\vec{r}_{,q})^T \tag{2.37}$$

This is the basis-independent representation of (2.24). If we collect a set of radius vectors $\vec{r}_1, \vec{r}_2, \ldots, \vec{r}_m$ at different positions in a column of position vectors, $\underline{r}$, then the corresponding column of velocity vectors, $\underline{v}$, can be expressed as follows

$$\underline{\vec{v}} = \dot{\underline{\vec{r}}} = \underline{\vec{r}}_{,t} + \underline{\vec{r}}_{,q} \ \dot{\underline{q}} \tag{2.38}$$

2.5 VIRTUAL DISPLACEMENTS; SOME BASIC RULES OF THE CALCULUS OF VARIATIONS

In Section 2.6 the principle of virtual work will be presented, which needs the notion of virtual displacements and some basic rules of the calculus of variations. The principle of virtual work and Newton's second law of motion constitute the foundation for the systematic generation of the differential equations of motion for complex mechanical systems with a finite number of degrees of freedom. The starting point for the formulation of the principle of virtual work is the introduction of the notion of *virtual displacements*. Let us consider a mechanical system and let $\vec{r}$ be the position vector of mass particle m_i of the system with respect to the inertial Cartesian coordinate frame x_1, x_2, x_3, see Fig. 2.1. We take a movie of the motion of the mechanical system and in that movie we consider the (real or true) trajectory of mass particle m_i during the time interval $t \in [t_1, t_2]$. For the sake of brevity we denote this trajectory by $\vec{r}(t)$. This means that $\vec{r}(t)$ implicitly is time-dependent. Now, we stop the movie at the instant of time t and we change $\vec{r}(t)$ by the amount $\delta\vec{r}(t)$. Because the movie has been stopped, the change $\delta\vec{r}(t)$ has nothing to do with the real change of $\vec{r}(t)$ during the motion, and therefore it is called a *virtual displacement*. We repeat the above procedure for all instants of time over the whole time interval $t \in [t_1, t_2]$ and obtain in this way the course of the virtual displacement $\delta\vec{r}(t)$ over the time interval $t \in [t_1, t_2]$. Now, the *virtual trajectory* $\vec{r}_v(t)$ during the time interval $t \in [t_1, t_2]$ is defined to be

$$\vec{r}_v(t) = \vec{r}(t) + \delta\vec{r}(t) \tag{2.39}$$

Fig. 2.5 shows a schematic plot of the real trajectory $\vec{r}(t)$, the virtual trajectory $\vec{r}_v(t)$ and the virtual displacement $\delta\vec{r}(t)$ during the time interval $t \in [t_1, t_2]$. In mathematics, an entire branch is dealing with the change or variation in coordinates of a system, defined in the above sense. This branch, known as the *calculus of variations*, has mainly been developed for finding the stationary value of a function that depends on the system coordinates. In the calculus of variations, the following requirements are imposed on the virtual displacements

- they are taken on a *fixed point in time*.

- until further notice, they must be *consistent with the geometric or kinematic constraints* of the system. For the time being, only constraints are considered which impose kinematic restrictions on the coordinates and do not involve velocities. We will return to the subject of kinematic constraints in Sections 2.6 and 2.13.

- otherwise they are *arbitrary*, provided it should always be possible to take their values *infinitesimally small*.

In order to be able to use the notion of virtual displacements in dynamics, we need some basic rules from the calculus of variations.

The first rule states that the sequence of the differentiation and the variation operations can be interchanged. This follows directly from (2.39)

$$\frac{d}{dt}(\delta\vec{r}) = \frac{d}{dt}(\vec{r}_v - \vec{r}) = \dot{\vec{r}}_v - \dot{\vec{r}} = \delta\dot{\vec{r}} \tag{2.40}$$

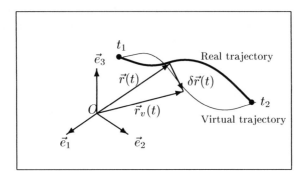

Fig. 2.5 Virtual displacements of mass particle m_i

Conversely, it can also be easily shown that this commutative property holds for the sequence of integration and variation operations as well.

In addition, we will need the change or variation of a function that depends itself on a number of changing generalized coordinates and/or velocities. For the sake of brevity, we consider the scalar function $f = f(\underline{q})$ of the generalized coordinates $\underline{q}$. The dependency on velocities could be added without any complication. For the generalized coordinates, it is easy to write an expression analogous to (2.39)

$$\underline{q}^v(t) = \underline{q}(t) + \delta\underline{q}(t) \qquad (2.41)$$

Here, $\underline{q}(t)$ are the real or true generalized coordinates, $\underline{q}^v(t)$ are the varied generalized coordinates and $\delta\underline{q}(t)$ are the changes or variations of the generalized coordinates, also called virtual displacements. Now, we investigate the value of the function f if $\underline{q}(t)$ is replaced by $\underline{q}^v(t)$. This value is denoted by $f^v(\underline{q}^v)$ and is called the varied function. Using (2.41), we can express the varied function as

$$f^v(\underline{q}^v, t) := f(\underline{q}^v, t) = f(\underline{q} + \delta\underline{q}, t) \qquad (2.42)$$

The function $f(\underline{q} + \delta\underline{q}, t)$ can be developed in a Taylor series of powers of $\delta\underline{q}$. Using the notation of (2.18) and (2.32), we obtain

$$
\begin{aligned}
f^v\left(\underline{q}^v, t\right) &= f\left(\underline{q}, t\right) + f_{,\underline{q}}\,\delta\underline{q} \\
&\quad + \frac{1}{2}\left[\sum_{i=1}^{n}\delta q_i \frac{\partial}{\partial q_i}\right]\left[\sum_{j=1}^{n}\delta q_j \frac{\partial}{\partial q_j}\right] f + O(\delta\underline{q}^3) \\
&= f(\underline{q}, t) + f_{,\underline{q}}\,\delta\underline{q} + \frac{1}{2}\delta\underline{q}^T\left[(f_{,\underline{q}})^T{}_{,\underline{q}}\right]\delta\underline{q} + O(\delta\underline{q}^3) \quad (2.43)
\end{aligned}
$$

where $O(\delta\underline{q}^3)$ denotes terms of third and higher powers of $\delta\underline{q}$. In the calculus of variations it is customary to define

$$f^v(\underline{q}^v, t) = f(\underline{q}, t) + \delta f + \delta^2 f + \delta^3 f + \cdots \qquad (2.44)$$

where δf is called the *first variation* of f, $\delta^2 f$ is called the *second variation* of f, etc. Comparing (2.43) and (2.44), we can express the first variation of the function $f(\underline{q}, t)$ in terms of the variations of $\underline{q}$ as follows

$$\delta f = f_{,\underline{q}} \; \delta \underline{q} = \delta \underline{q}^T \; (f_{,\underline{q}})^T \tag{2.45}$$

Because the virtual displacements $\delta \underline{q}$ can be taken infinitesimally small, δf represents a good approximation of the change of f at changing $\underline{q}$, provided the first derivative $f_{,\underline{q}}$ is not zero. If $f_{,\underline{q}}$ is zero, then the second variation has to be considered.

Equation (2.45) proves that the first variation of the function f can be expressed in terms of the variation of $\underline{q}$ by similar rules as in differential calculus. The above derivation can be repeated completely for a vector function of the generalized coordinates $\underline{q}$. Taking as an example the radius vector $\vec{r}(\underline{q}, t)$, we obtain for its first variation $\delta \vec{r}$

$$\delta \vec{r} = \vec{r}_{,\underline{q}} \; \delta \underline{q} = \delta \underline{q}^T \; (\vec{r}_{,\underline{q}})^T \tag{2.46}$$

2.6 PRINCIPLE OF VIRTUAL WORK; CONSTRAINT FORCES AND APPLIED FORCES

The principle of virtual work is basically a statement of the static equilibrium of a mechanical system and was formulated originally by Johann Bernoulli. One can extend it to the dynamic case and speak of dynamic equilibrium. In that case, the principle constitutes the foundation for the systematic generation of the differential equations of motion for complex mechanical systems with a finite number of degrees of freedom. The restriction made in this section to systems with a finite number of degrees of freedom is not a restriction to the generality of the principle. On the contrary, the principle of virtual work also appears to be a powerful tool in constructing approximate solutions for systems with continuous distributions of mass, stiffness and damping.

Let us consider a mass particle m_i of a mechanical system and let $\vec{r}_i$ be the position vector of m_i relative to the origin O of an inertial frame, see Fig. 2.1. If $\vec{F}_i^t$ is the total resulting force acting upon mass particle m_i, then Newton's second law of motion can be written for particle m_i in the following form[1]

$$\vec{F}_i^t - m_i \, \ddot{\vec{r}}_i = \vec{0} \tag{2.47}$$

Now, imagine that at a fixed time t, the radius vector $\vec{r}_i(t)$ is changed by the amount $\delta \vec{r}_i(t)$, being a virtual displacement in the sense of the preceding

---

[1] In (2.47) the term $-m_i \ddot{\vec{r}}_i$ can be regarded as an *inertia force* which is simply the negative of the rate of change of the momentum vector $\dot{\vec{p}}_i = m_i \ddot{\vec{r}}_i$. Equation (2.47) is often referred to as *d'Alembert's principle*, which states that the resultant force $\vec{F}_i^t$ is in equilibrium with the inertia force. This principle permits us to regard problems of dynamics as if they were problems of statics.

section. Because for a system in dynamic equilibrium (2.47) holds, the dot product of (2.47) and the virtual displacement vector $\delta \vec{r}_i$ vanishes, i.e.

$$\delta W_i = \left(\vec{F}_i^t - m_i \, \ddot{\vec{r}}_i \right) \cdot \delta \vec{r}_i = 0 \tag{2.48}$$

Here δW_i represents the virtual work performed by the resultant of $\vec{F}_i$ and $-m_i \ddot{\vec{r}}_i$ on particle m_i over the virtual displacement $\delta \vec{r}_i$. It follows from (2.48) that the virtual work for the entire system vanishes also

$$\delta W = \sum_{i=1}^{n_p} \delta W_i = \sum_{i=1}^{n_p} \left(\vec{F}_i^t - m_i \, \ddot{\vec{r}}_i \right) \cdot \delta \vec{r}_i = 0 \tag{2.49}$$

The total resulting force $\vec{F}^t$ acting upon mass particle m_i can be composed from forces of different nature. For systems with constraints, we distinquish between *applied forces* $\vec{F}_i^{appl}$ and *constraint forces* $\vec{F}_i^{constr}$, so that

$$\vec{F}_i^t = \vec{F}_i^{appl} + \vec{F}_i^{constr} \tag{2.50}$$

Constraint forces result from geometric or kinematic constraints in the motion of any part or particle of the system and are of a reactive nature. The most common ones are the forces that confine the motion of a system to a given path or surface, or the internal forces in a rigid body. For example, the forces in the two hinges, exerted during the motion of the double pendulum of example 2.1 on page 38, are constraint forces. *Applied forces* are all forces except constraint forces. Examples of applied forces are gravitational forces, aerodynamic lift and drag, magnetic forces, etc. Introducing (2.50) into (2.49), we have

$$\delta W = \sum_{i=1}^{n_p} \vec{F}_i^{appl} \cdot \delta \vec{r}_i + \sum_{i=1}^{n_p} \vec{F}_i^{constr} \cdot \delta \vec{r}_i - \sum_{i=1}^{n_p} m_i \, \ddot{\vec{r}}_i \cdot \delta \vec{r}_i = 0 \tag{2.51}$$

At this point we adopt the usual assumption that the work of the constraint forces through virtual displacements **compatible with the kinematic system constraints** is zero, implying that

$$\delta W^{constr} = \sum_{i=1}^{n_p} \vec{F}_i^{constr} \cdot \delta \vec{r}_i = 0 \tag{2.52}$$

One category of constraint forces satisfying (2.52) are constraint forces that are normal to the virtual displacements. As an example, we consider a particle constrained to a perfectly smooth surface, in which case the constraint force is normal to the surface and the virtual displacements, to be taken consistent with the constraints, must be parallel to the surface. Note that this rules out reaction forces due to friction, such as those caused by sliding on a rough surface, to belong to the above defined category of constraint forces. Hence, they must be necessarily taken in the category of applied forces. Another category of constraint forces satisfying (2.52) are forces exerted by mass particles in a rigid body on one another. This will be elucidated by the following example.

Example 2.8

We consider a so-called dumbbell as two mass particles m_1 and m_2 connected by a rigid massless rod, see Fig. 2.6. The constraint equation of the rigid link of length ℓ between the two particles reads

$$h\left(\vec{r}_1, \vec{r}_2\right) = \left(\vec{r}_2 - \vec{r}_1\right) \cdot \left(\vec{r}_2 - \vec{r}_1\right) - l^2 = 0 \qquad (2.53)$$

Variation of this relationship yields, using the rules for variation of a

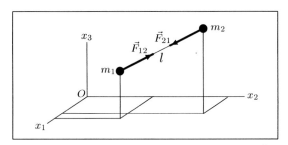

Fig. 2.6 Dumbbell

function as expressed by (2.45)

$$\left(\vec{r}_2 - \vec{r}_1\right) \cdot \left(\delta \vec{r}_2 - \delta \vec{r}_1\right) = 0 \qquad (2.54)$$

If $\vec{F}_{ij}$, is the force exerted by mass particle m_j on mass particle m_i, then we have according to Newton's third law

$$\vec{F}_{21} = -\vec{F}_{12} \qquad (2.55)$$

The force $\vec{F}_{12}$ acts along the connection line between m_1 and m_2. Hence, it can be expressed as

$$\vec{F}_{12} = \frac{F}{l}\left(\vec{r}_2 - \vec{r}_1\right) \qquad with \qquad F = \left\|\vec{F}_{12}\right\| \qquad (2.56)$$

The virtual work associated to the constraint forces is

$$\delta W^{constr} = \vec{F}_{12} \cdot \delta \vec{r}_1 + \vec{F}_{21} \cdot \delta \vec{r}_2 \qquad (2.57)$$

Using (2.55) and (2.56), we obtain

$$\delta W^{constr} = -\frac{F}{l}\left(\vec{r}_2 - \vec{r}_1\right) \cdot \left(\delta \vec{r}_2 - \delta \vec{r}_1\right) \qquad (2.58)$$

> *which shows that the virtual work of the constraint forces is zero if the*
> *virtual displacements $\delta\vec{r}_1$ and $\delta\vec{r}_2$ satisfy the constraint equation (2.54).*

Generally, if the kinematic constraint conditions of a system can be expressed in terms of coordinates of the system alone, and, for example, not in terms of time derivates of coordinates of the system (representing velocities), then (2.52) can be assumed to be valid. Confining ourselves to the case that (2.52) is satisfied, the expression (2.51) for the principle of virtual work reduces to

$$\delta W = \sum_{i=1}^{n_p} \left(\vec{F}_i^{appl} - m_i \ddot{\vec{r}}_i \right) \cdot \delta\vec{r}_i = 0 \qquad (2.59)$$

Stated in words, (2.59) expresses that the work performed by the applied forces (i.e. all forces except the constraint forces) plus the inertia forces through virtual displacements compatible with the kinematic system constraints is zero. Whereas the principle of virtual work in the form of (2.59) gives a complete formulation of the problems of dynamics, it is not very convenient for deriving the system equations of motion, because the problems are formulated in terms of position coordinates, which may not all be independent. The principle, however, is useful in providing the transition to a formulation in terms of generalized coordinates that does not suffer from this drawback.

2.7   TRANSITION FROM APPLIED FORCES TO GENERALIZED FORCES

In this section we will have a closer look at the virtual work of the applied forces $\vec{F}_i^{appl}$. According to (2.59), this virtual work is given by

$$\delta W^{appl} = \sum_{i=1}^{n_p} \vec{F}_i^{appl} \cdot \delta\vec{r}_i \qquad (2.60)$$

Our goal is to describe the motion of the system by means of the generalized coordinates $\underline{q}$ defined in Sections 2.2 and 2.3, i.e. in terms of the minimum number of independent coordinates. To this end we express $\delta\vec{r}_i$ in $\underline{q}$ and $\delta\underline{q}$ by means of (2.46) and insert this into (2.60). This yields

$$\delta W^{appl} = \left[\sum_{i=1}^{n_p} \vec{F}_i^{appl} \cdot \vec{r}_{i,\underline{q}} \right] \delta\underline{q} = \delta\underline{q}^T \left[\sum_{i=1}^{n_p} \left(\vec{r}_{i,\underline{q}} \right)^T \cdot \vec{F}_i^{appl} \right] \qquad (2.61)$$

The expression between the brackets in the right side of (2.61) can be interpreted as a column matrix of *generalized forces* $\underline{Q}$, related to the virtual changes $\delta\underline{q}$ of the generalized coordinates $\underline{q}$

$$\underline{Q} = \sum_{i=1}^{n_p} \left(\vec{r}_{i,\underline{q}}\right)^T \cdot \vec{F}_i^{appl} \qquad (2.62)$$

It is easy to see that this can also be written in matrix notation as

$$\underline{Q} = \sum_{i=1}^{n_p} \left(\underline{r}_{i,\underline{q}}\right)^T \underline{F}_i^{appl} \qquad (2.63)$$

Inserting (2.62) into (2.61), we can write the virtual work by the applied forces as

$$\delta W^{appl} = \underline{Q}^T \delta\underline{q} = \delta\underline{q}^T \underline{Q} \qquad (2.64)$$

Example 2.9

We consider again the double pendulum system of example 2.1 on page 38 under the influence of gravity. Additionally we assume that a horizontal external load $F(t)$ is acting on mass m_2 of the system. The relevant applied forces for this situation are shown in Fig. 2.7. So for

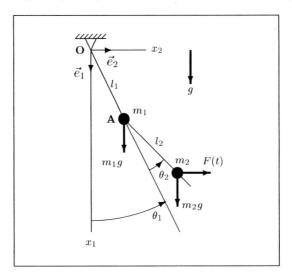

Fig. 2.7   Applied forces in double pendulum system with additional horizontal force $F(t)$

this system the applied forces are the external horizontal force $F(t)$ acting on mass m_2 and the gravitational forces $m_1 g$ and $m_2 g$. The forces acting in the hinges A and O are constraint forces, because they result from geometric constraints in the motion.

It is easy to see that the column-matrix representation $\underline{F}_1^{appl}$ of the applied forces $\vec{F}_1^{appl}$ acting on mass m_1 and the column-matrix representation $\underline{F}_2^{appl}$ of the applied forces $\vec{F}_2^{appl}$ acting on mass m_2 with respect to the Cartesian vector basis are

$$\underline{F}_1^{appl} = \begin{bmatrix} m_1 g \\ 0 \\ 0 \end{bmatrix} \; ; \qquad \underline{F}_2^{appl} = \begin{bmatrix} m_2 g \\ F(t) \\ 0 \end{bmatrix} \qquad (2.65)$$

In order to determine the contributions of the above applied forces $\underline{F}_i^{appl}$, $i = 1, 2$ to the column matrix of generalized forces, $\underline{Q}$, we need the quantities $(\underline{r}_{i,q})^T$, $i = 1, 2$ for this example as calculated before (see (2.25) and (2.26)). If we substitute these expressions in (2.63) we can obtain the following column-matrix of generalized forces

$$\underline{Q} = \begin{bmatrix} Q_1 \\ Q_2 \end{bmatrix} = \begin{bmatrix} -(m_1 + m_2)gl_1 \sin\theta_1 - m_2 gl_2 \sin(\theta_1 + \theta_2) \\ +F(t)[l_1 \cos\theta_1 + l_2 \cos(\theta_1 + \theta_2)] \\ \text{---------------------} \\ -m_2 gl_2 \sin(\theta_1 + \theta_2) + F(t)l_2 \cos(\theta_1 + \theta_2) \end{bmatrix}$$
$$(2.66)$$

It is remarked that the dimension of both generalized forces Q_1 and Q_2 contained in (2.66) is $[Nm]$, i.e. both generalized forces Q_1 and Q_2 have the dimension of a moment. This is also obvious from (2.64) because the corresponding generalized coordinates are rotation angles (dim [-]), while the product of the generalized forces $\underline{Q}$ and the virtual changes of these rotation angles, $\delta \underline{q}$, constitutes the virtual work (dim $[Nm]$).

2.8   HANDLING APPLIED MOMENTS

In practise it regularly happens that the resulting action of some of the applied forces is (at least partially) equivalent to the action of so-called *applied moments* being exerted at some or more distinct points of the system. To explore that situation we consider again the double pendulum system with two concentrated masses m_1 and m_2. Instead of the horizontal external force $F(t)$ acting on mass m_2 and the gravity forces $m_1 g$ and $m_2 g$, we consider two arbitrary external forces $\vec{F}_A$ and $\vec{F}_B$ of equal magnitude and opposite direction, acting in point A and point B as shown in Fig. 2.8. So we assume for the pair of forces that

$$\vec{F}_A = -\vec{F}_B \qquad (2.67)$$

The virtual work associated with these applied forces is

$$\delta W^{appl} = \vec{F}_A \cdot \delta \vec{r}_A + \vec{F}_B \cdot \delta \vec{r}_B \qquad (2.68)$$

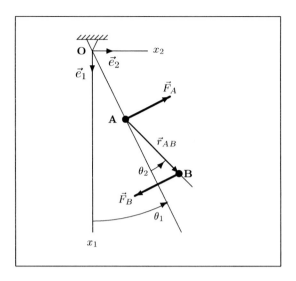

Fig. 2.8   Double pendulum system with a couple of external forces

where $\vec{r}_A$ and $\vec{r}_B$ are the radius vectors of A and B relative to O. Taking account of (2.67) and the relationship

$$\vec{r}_B = \vec{r}_A + \vec{r}_{AB} \tag{2.69}$$

where $\vec{r}_{AB}$ is the radius vector of B relative to A, we can rewrite (2.68) as

$$\delta W^{appl} = \vec{F}_A \cdot \delta \vec{r}_A - \vec{F}_A \cdot (\delta \vec{r}_A + \delta \vec{r}_{AB}) = -\vec{F}_A \cdot \delta \vec{r}_{AB} \tag{2.70}$$

As can be observed from Fig. 2.8, the rigid bar AB carries out a planar motion consisting of a translation in the x_1, x_2 plane and also a rotation about an axis perpendicular to that plane of motion. This rotation can be described by means of the angular rotational variational vector

$$\delta \vec{\theta} = (\delta \theta_1 + \delta \theta_2)\vec{e}_3 = \delta \vec{\theta}_1 + \delta \vec{\theta}_2 \tag{2.71}$$

where $(\delta \theta_1 + \delta \theta_2)$ is the absolute rotation of AB relative to the vertical x_2 axis (positive in counter-clockwise direction). In view of (2.71) and the geometrical picture of Fig. 2.8, the first variation of the vector $\vec{r}_{AB}$ can be expressed in terms of the first variation of the angular variational vector $\delta \vec{\theta}$ as follows[2]

$$\delta \vec{r}_{AB} = (\delta \vec{\theta}_1 + \delta \vec{\theta}_2) \times \vec{r}_{AB} \tag{2.72}$$

---

[2]In these expressions we will use the so-called vector product also called cross product of two vectors $\vec{a}$ and $\vec{b}$, written as $\vec{c} = \vec{a} \times \vec{b}$.
Further we will use the relation $\vec{a}.(\vec{b} \times \vec{c}) = \vec{b}.(\vec{c} \times \vec{a}) = \vec{c}.(\vec{a} \times \vec{b})$

Inserting (2.72) into (2.70), we obtain the following result for the virtual work of the applied forces $\vec{F}_A$ and $\vec{F}_B$

$$
\begin{aligned}
\delta W^{appl} &= -\vec{F}_A \cdot \left[\left(\delta\vec{\theta}_1 + \delta\vec{\theta}_2 \right) \times \vec{r}_{AB} \right] \\
&= -\left[\left(\delta\vec{\theta}_1 + \delta\vec{\theta}_2 \right) \times \vec{r}_{AB} \right] \cdot \vec{F}_A \\
&= -(\delta\vec{\theta}_1 + \delta\vec{\theta}_2) \cdot \left(\vec{r}_{AB} \times \vec{F}_A \right) := (\delta\vec{\theta}_1 + \delta\vec{\theta}_2) \cdot \vec{M}^{appl} \quad (2.73)
\end{aligned}
$$

where $\vec{M}^{appl}$ is the applied moment due to the pair of applied forces $\vec{F}_A$ and $\vec{F}_B$

$$
\vec{M}^{appl} = M^{appl} \vec{e}_3 = -\vec{r}_{AB} \times \vec{F}_A \qquad (2.74)
$$

The minus sign in the right side of (2.74) results from the fact that the moment due to $\vec{F}_A$ and $\vec{F}_B$ turns clockwise, whereas $\vec{M}^{appl}$ turns counter-clockwise. It follows from the above example, and in particular from (2.73), that the virtual work of an applied moment needs the absolute angular rotation vector at the point where the applied moment is exerted. Now, we can consider the case in which n_F applied forces $\vec{F}_i^{appl}$ $(i = 1, 2, \cdots, n_F)$ and n_M applied moments $\vec{M}_j^{appl}$ $(j = 1, 2, \cdots, n_M)$ are exerted on the system. The virtual work of those applied forces and moments is given by

$$
\delta W^{appl} = \sum_{i=1}^{n_F} \delta\vec{r}_i \cdot \vec{F}_i^{appl} + \sum_{j=1}^{n_M} \delta\vec{\theta}_j \cdot \vec{M}_j^{appl} \qquad (2.75)
$$

where $\vec{r}_i$ is the radius vector of the point at which $\vec{F}_i^{appl}$ is exerted, while $\vec{\theta}_j$ is the absolute angular rotation vector at the point where $\vec{M}^{appl}$ is exerted. As before, our goal is to describe the motion of the system in terms of the generalized coordinates. To this end, we use again (2.46) to express $\delta\vec{r}_i$ in $\underline{q}$ and $\delta\underline{q}$. Analogous to the discussion for the radius vector in Section 2.3, the angular rotation vectors $\vec{\theta}_j$ can also be considered to be an explicit function of the generalized coordinates $\underline{q}$ and the time t, i.e.

$$
\vec{\theta}_j = \vec{\theta}_j \left(\underline{q}, t \right) \qquad (2.76)
$$

This leads us analogously with (2.46) to the following expression for the first variation of the angular rotation vector

$$
\delta\vec{\theta}_j = \vec{\theta}_{j,\underline{q}} \, \delta\underline{q} = \delta\underline{q}^T \left(\vec{\theta}_{j,\underline{q}} \right)^T \qquad (2.77)
$$

Introducing (2.46) and (2.77) into (2.75), we obtain

$$
\delta W^{appl} = \delta\underline{q}^T \left[\sum_{i=1}^{n_F} \left(\vec{r}_{i,\underline{q}} \right)^T \cdot \vec{F}_i^{appl} + \sum_{j=1}^{n_M} \left(\vec{\theta}_{j,\underline{q}} \right)^T \cdot \vec{M}_j^{appl} \right] \qquad (2.78)
$$

Again, the expression between the brackets in the right side of (2.78) can be interpreted as a column matrix of generalized forces, $\underline{Q}$, related to the virtual changes $\delta\underline{q}$ of the generalized coordinates $\underline{q}$

$$\underline{Q} = \sum_{i=1}^{n_F} \left(\vec{r}_{i,\underline{q}}\right)^T \cdot \vec{F}_i^{appl} + \sum_{j=1}^{n_M} \left(\vec{\theta}_{j,\underline{q}}\right)^T \cdot \vec{M}_j^{appl} \qquad (2.79)$$

or in matrix-representation

$$\underline{Q} = \sum_{i=1}^{n_F} \left(\underline{r}_{i,\underline{q}}\right)^T \underline{F}_i^{appl} + \sum_{j=1}^{n_M} \left(\underline{\theta}_{j,\underline{q}}\right)^T \underline{M}_j^{appl} \qquad (2.80)$$

Inserting (2.80) into (2.78), we can write the virtual work of the applied forces again as (2.64).

Example 2.10

---

*As another variation of the double pendulum system we assume that in the hinge A some friction is present which will be modelled as a torsional damper with (torsion) damping constant d_A; see Fig. 2.9. The **forces** acting in this coupling hinge (A) between the two bars are constraint forces, because they result from geometric constraints in the motion. Therefore they will not have any contribution to the generalized forces. However, the moments acting in this hinge are applied moments, because they result from the action of the torsional damper in point A. So these moments will certainly have some contribution to the column matrix of generalized forces. We can express the applied moments M_{A1} and M_{A2} exerted on bars OA and AB due to the torsional damper (see Fig. 2.9) as*

$$M_{A1} = M_{A2} = d_A \dot{\theta}_2 \qquad (2.81)$$

because it is the relative angular velocity $\dot{\theta}_2$ which is responsible for the friction moment. The column-matrix representation $\underline{M}_{A1}^{appl}$ and $\underline{M}_{A2}^{appl}$ of the applied moments $\vec{M}_{A1}^{appl}$ and $\vec{M}_{A2}^{appl}$ acting on bars OA and AB in point A with respect to the Cartesian vector base $\{\vec{e}_1, \vec{e}_2, \vec{e}_3\}$ are

$$\underline{M}_{A1}^{appl} = \begin{bmatrix} 0 \\ 0 \\ d_A \dot{\theta}_2 \end{bmatrix}, \quad \underline{M}_{A2}^{appl} = \begin{bmatrix} 0 \\ 0 \\ -d_A \dot{\theta}_2 \end{bmatrix} \qquad (2.82)$$

In order to determine the contributions of the above applied moments $\underline{M}_{A1}^{appl}$ and $\underline{M}_{A2}^{appl}$ to the column matrix of generalized forces, $\underline{Q}$, we need to specify the quantities $(\underline{\theta}_{j,\underline{q}})^T$ of (2.80) for this example.

It is easy to see that the column-matrix representations $\underline{\psi}_1$ and $\underline{\psi}_2$ of the absolute angular rotation vectors $\vec{\psi}_1$ of bar OA and $\vec{\psi}_2$ of bar AB

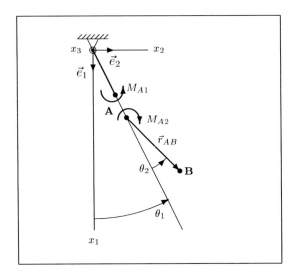

Fig. 2.9   Double pendulum system with coupling friction

with respect to the Cartesian vector basis $\{\vec{e}_1, \vec{e}_2, \vec{e}_3\}$ are

$$\underline{\psi}_1 = \begin{bmatrix} 0 \\ 0 \\ \theta_1 \end{bmatrix}, \qquad \underline{\psi}_2 = \begin{bmatrix} 0 \\ 0 \\ \theta_1 + \theta_2 \end{bmatrix} \qquad (2.83)$$

This leads us to the following matrix representations $(\underline{\psi}_{1,\underline{q}})^T$ and $(\underline{\psi}_{2,\underline{q}})^T$ of $(\vec{\psi}_{1,\underline{q}})^T$ and $(\vec{\psi}_{2,\underline{q}})^T$ with respect to the Cartesian vector basis $\{\vec{e}_1, \vec{e}_2, \vec{e}_3\}$

$$\left(\underline{\psi}_{1,\underline{q}}\right)^T = \begin{bmatrix} 0 & 0 & 1 \\ 0 & 0 & 0 \end{bmatrix}; \qquad \left(\underline{\psi}_{2,\underline{q}}\right)^T = \begin{bmatrix} 0 & 0 & 1 \\ 0 & 0 & 1 \end{bmatrix} \qquad (2.84)$$

Inserting (2.82) and (2.84) into the matrix representation of the right-hand side of (2.79), we obtain the following contribution of $\vec{M}_{A1}^{appl}$ and $\vec{M}_{A2}^{appl}$ to the column matrix of generalized forces

$$\begin{aligned} \underline{Q} &= \begin{bmatrix} 0 & 0 & 1 \\ 0 & 0 & 0 \end{bmatrix} \begin{bmatrix} 0 \\ 0 \\ d_A\dot{\theta}_2 \end{bmatrix} + \begin{bmatrix} 0 & 0 & 1 \\ 0 & 0 & 1 \end{bmatrix} \begin{bmatrix} 0 \\ 0 \\ -d_A\dot{\theta}_2 \end{bmatrix} \\ &= \begin{bmatrix} 0 \\ -d_A\dot{\theta}_2 \end{bmatrix} = -\begin{bmatrix} 0 & 0 \\ 0 & d_A \end{bmatrix} \begin{bmatrix} \dot{\theta}_1 \\ \dot{\theta}_2 \end{bmatrix} := -\underline{D}\,\underline{\dot{q}} \qquad (2.85) \end{aligned}$$

It is easy to see that the generalized force Q_1 has to be zero because the friction moment only depends on $\dot{\theta}_2$ and the virtual work for a virtual

rotation $\delta\theta_1$ is zero. It is remarked that the dimension of both generalized forces Q_1 and Q_2 contained in (2.85) is $[Nm]$, i.e. both generalized
forces Q_1 and Q_2 have the dimension of a moment. This is also obvious
from (2.64) because the corresponding generalized coordinates are rotation angles, while the product of the generalized forces $\underline{Q}$ and the virtual
changes of these rotation angles, $\delta\underline{q}$, constitutes the virtual work. Also,
as demonstrated in this example, the column of generalized forces due
to (viscous) damping in general can be written as $\underline{Q} = -\underline{D}\,\underline{\dot{q}}$ with $\underline{D}$
being the so-called viscous damping matrix.

It follows directly from (2.60) and (2.64) that a (often more) practical way
of finding the ith element Q_i of the column of generalized forces $\underline{Q}$ can be
obtained by putting $\delta q_i = 1$ and $\delta q_j = 0$ for $i \neq j$, and considering the virtual
work of all applied forces and moments. It should be remarked again that
when carrying out this variation procedure, the values of the applied forces
and/or moments should remain unchanged during this variation process.

Example 2.11

We consider again the double pendulum problem with two masses. In
particular we want to determine the generalized forces resulting from
the combined influence of the external horizontal force on bar 2 and
the (internal) moments due to the the frictional torsion damper in the
coupling point of the two bars as shown in the left part of Fig. 2.10.
First, we impose the special virtual displacement $\delta\underline{q}_1^T = [\delta\theta_1\,,\,0]$, where

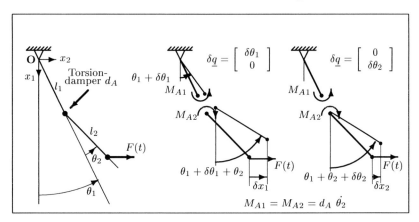

Fig. 2.10 Double pendulum system with hinge-friction and horizontal force

$\delta\theta_1$ is a (small) virtual change of the rotation angle θ_1. The virtual
displacement corresponding with this choice is also shown in Fig. 2.10

(middle part). The associated virtual work of $F(t)$, M_{A1} and M_{A2} can be written as

$$\delta W_1^{appl} = Q_1 \delta \theta_1 = F(t)\delta x_1 + M_{A1}\delta \theta_1 - M_{A2}\delta \theta_1$$
$$= F(t)\left[(l_1\delta\theta_1)\cos\theta_1 + (l_2\delta\theta_1)\cos(\theta_1 + \theta_2)\right]$$
$$+ (d_A\dot{\theta}_2)\delta\theta_1 - (d_A\dot{\theta}_2)\delta\theta_1 \tag{2.86}$$

So, we find the first generalized force Q_1 to be

$$Q_1 = F(t)\left[l_1\cos\theta_1 + l_2\cos(\theta_1 + \theta_2)\right] \tag{2.87}$$

For the second generalized force we superimpose the special virtual displacement $\delta q_2^T = [0 \ , \ \delta\theta_2]$, where $\delta\theta_2$ is a (small) virtual change of the rotation angle θ_2. The virtual displacement corresponding with this second choice is shown in Fig. 2.10 (right part). The virtual work of $F(t)$, M_{A1} and M_{A2} associated with the chosen virtual displacement can now be written as

$$\delta W_1^{appl} = Q_2 \delta\theta_2 = F(t)\delta x_2 - M_{A2}\delta\theta_2$$
$$= F(t)\left[l_2\delta\theta_2\cos(\theta_1 + \theta_2)\right] - (d_A\dot{\theta}_2)\delta\theta_2 \tag{2.88}$$

So, we find the second generalized force Q_2 to be

$$Q_2 = F(t)\left[l_2\cos(\theta_1 + \theta_2)\right] - d_A\dot{\theta}_2 \tag{2.89}$$

Indeed, the expressions for Q_1 and Q_2 resulting from (2.87) and (2.89) are consistent with the expressions obtained earlier in (2.85) and (2.66).

It is remarked that a different set of generalized coordinates, through the above procedure, automatically leads to a different set of generalized forces, because the product given by Q^T and δq in (2.64) represents the virtual work which should remain unchanged. It is left to the reader to calculate the generalized forces for the double pendulum system of example 2.11 on page page 61 if the generalized coordinates θ_1 and θ_2 are replaced by the generalized coordinates $\varphi_1 = \theta_1$ and $\varphi_2 = \theta_1 + \theta_2$ (the absolute rotation of beam 2).

2.9   GENERALIZED EXTERNAL AND INTERNAL FORCES; INTERNAL ENERGY

It will prove to be useful to split the applied force $\vec{F}_i^{appl}$, acting upon material particle m_i after subtracting the constraint force, into an *external force* $\vec{F}_i^{ex}$ and an *internal force* $\vec{F}_i^{in}$

$$\vec{F}_i^{appl} = \vec{F}_i^{ex} + \vec{F}_i^{in} \tag{2.90}$$

Similarly, it will appear to be useful to split the applied moment $\vec{M}_j^{appl}$ into an *external moment* $\vec{M}_j^{ex}$ and an *internal moment* $\vec{M}_j^{in}$

$$\vec{M}_j^{appl} = \vec{M}_j^{ex} + \vec{M}_j^{in} \tag{2.91}$$

Inserting (2.90) and (2.91) into (2.79), we obtain a partitioning of the generalized forces $\underline{Q}$ into generalized external forces $\underline{Q}^{ex}$ and generalized internal forces $\underline{Q}^{in}$

$$\underline{Q} = \underline{Q}^{ex} + \underline{Q}^{in} \tag{2.92}$$

with

$$\underline{Q}^{ex} = \sum_{i=1}^{n_F} \left(\vec{r}_{i,\underline{q}} \right)^T \cdot \vec{F}_i^{ex} + \sum_{j=1}^{n_M} \left(\vec{\theta}_{j,\underline{q}} \right)^T \cdot \vec{M}_j^{ex} \tag{2.93}$$

$$\underline{Q}^{in} = \sum_{i=1}^{n_M} \left(\vec{r}_{i,\underline{q}} \right)^T \cdot \vec{F}_i^{in} + \sum_{j=1}^{n_M} \left(\vec{\theta}_{j,\underline{q}} \right)^T \cdot \vec{M}_j^{in} \tag{2.94}$$

An example of generalized external forces are the forces due to $F(t)$ and the viscous damping moments M_{A1} and M_{A2} in the double pendulum of example 2.11 on page 61. Other practical examples of external forces are gravitational forces, aerodynamic lift and drag, magnetic forces, etc. We will *define* generalized *internal* forces to depend only on the generalized coordinates $\underline{q}$ and **not** on the generalized velocities $\underline{\dot{q}}$

$$\underline{Q}^{in} = \underline{Q}^{in}(\underline{q}) \tag{2.95}$$

The definition (2.95) implies that all damping forces and friction forces must be classified in the category external forces. Because (2.95) holds, the generalized internal forces $\underline{Q}^{in}$ can always be related to a state quantity $U^{in}(\underline{q})$ as follows

$$\underline{Q}^{in} = - \left(\frac{\partial U^{in}}{\partial \underline{q}} \right)^T = - \left(U^{in}{}_{,\underline{q}} \right)^T \tag{2.96}$$

Inserting (2.96) into (2.64), we obtain the virtual work by the internal forces, and moments, which can be expressed as

$$
\begin{aligned}
\delta W^{in} &= \delta \underline{q}^T \underline{Q}^{in} = -\delta \underline{q}^T \left(U^{in}{}_{,\underline{q}} \right)^T \\
&= - \left(U^{in}{}_{,\underline{q}} \right) \delta \underline{q} = -\delta U^{in}(\underline{q})
\end{aligned} \tag{2.97}
$$

Indeed, (2.97) implies that $\delta U^{in}(\underline{q})$ represents the first variation of a function. This function, U^{in}, is often called the *internal energy* of the system. A well-known example of internal energy is the elastic energy in a linear spring.

Example 2.12

We consider a system consisting of a cylinder with radius R, rolling

*without slip on a horizontal surface and connected to the world with
a linear spring with spring constant k. We record the motion of the
cylinder by the generalized coordinate φ which is the rotation of the
cylinder. For $\varphi = 0$ the spring is unloaded, see the left part of Fig.
2.11. The horizontal motion of the centre of the cylinder is indicated*

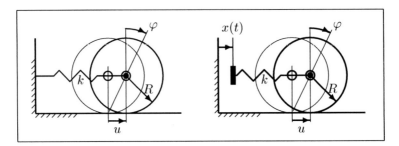

Fig. 2.11   Rolling cylinder with linear spring

*with u, where $u = \varphi R$. The elastic energy of the spring can be written
as*

$$U_{in}(\varphi) = \frac{1}{2}ku^2 = \frac{1}{2}kR^2\varphi^2 \tag{2.98}$$

*Applying (2.96) we obtain the following result for the column of gener-
alized internal forces (which has only one element)*

$$\underline{Q} = -(kR^2)\varphi \tag{2.99}$$

*Here we see again that the generalized force has the dimension of a mo-
ment $[Nm]$ which is obvious because the related generalized coordinate
is a rotation. One might also say that for this generalized coordinate
(φ), the effective spring constant is $k_{eff} = kR^2$ $[Nm]$.*

*It is remarked that for some applications time may appear explicitly in
the expression for the elastic energy, so that $U^{in} = U^{in}(\underline{q}, t)$. This happens for example if the system contains prescribed coordinates that are
influencing its internal energy. An example of a system for which this
occurs is the rolling cylinder problem where the left end of the spring is
not a fixed point but is undergoing a prescribed excitation as also shown
in Fig. 2.11 (right picture).*

*If we assume that the generalized coordinate φ has been chosen such
that the spring is unloaded for $\varphi = 0$ and $x(t) = 0$, then the elastic
energy can be written as*

$$U_{in}(\varphi, t) = \frac{1}{2}k\left(R\varphi - x(t)\right)^2$$

$$= \frac{1}{2}kx^2(t) - kRx(t)\,\varphi + \frac{1}{2}kR^2\,\varphi^2 \tag{2.100}$$

> *So, we can recognize a part which is independent of the generalized co-ordinates q, a part which is linear in q and a part which is quadratic in q.*

Inserting (2.93) into (2.64), we obtain the virtual work by the external forces and moments

$$\delta W^{ex} = (\underline{Q}^{ex})^T \delta \underline{q} = \delta \underline{q}^T \underline{Q}^{ex} \qquad (2.101)$$

Combining the foregoing results, we can express the virtual work by the applied forces and moments as

$$\begin{aligned} \delta W^{appl} &= \delta W^{ex} + \delta W^{in} \\ &= \delta \underline{q}^T \underline{Q}^{ex} - \delta U^{in} \end{aligned} \qquad (2.102)$$

2.10 CONSERVATIVE EXTERNAL FORCES; POTENTIAL ENERGY

Next, it will prove to be useful to divide the generalized external forces $\underline{Q}^{ex}$ into conservative generalized external forces, denoted by $\underline{Q}^{cons}$, and nonconservative generalized external forces, denoted by $\underline{Q}^{nc}$

$$\underline{Q}^{ex} = \underline{Q}^{cons} + \underline{Q}^{nc} \qquad (2.103)$$

It is remarked here that, by definition, all generalized internal forces are conservative, and, hence, there are no nonconservative generalized internal forces. An important category of conservative external forces are forces due to gravity. The conservative generalized external forces can be derived from a potential energy function $V^{ex}(\underline{q})$, which depends on the generalized coordinates only

$$\underline{Q}^{cons} = - \left(\frac{\partial V^{ex}}{\partial \underline{q}} \right)^T = - \left(V^{ex},\underline{q} \right)^T \qquad (2.104)$$

Using (2.103) and (2.104), we can transform (2.102) for the virtual work by the applied forces into

$$\delta W^{appl} = \delta \underline{q}^T \underline{Q}^{nc} - \delta V^{ex} - \delta U^{in} \qquad (2.105)$$

Now the *total potential energy function* of the mechanical system is defined to be the sum of the internal energy and the potential energy of the conservative external forces

$$V(\underline{q}) = U^{in}(\underline{q}) + V^{ex}(\underline{q}) \qquad (2.106)$$

Inserting (2.106) into (2.105), we obtain the following final expression for the virtual work by the applied forces and moments

$$\delta W^{appl} = \delta \underline{q}^T \underline{Q}^{nc} - \delta V = \left[\left(\underline{Q}^{nc} \right)^T - V,\underline{q} \right] \delta \underline{q} \qquad (2.107)$$

Example 2.13

We consider the potential energy function $V(q)$ of the double pendulum system with two masses of example 2.1, pages 38 and 55. In this case, the internal energy function $U^{in}(q)$ is zero, because there are no elastic elements in the system. The two gravity forces which are acting on the point masses are conservative external forces. Taking into account the coordinate notations of Fig. 2.2 (page 38), and taking the zero level of the potential energy at $x_1 = 0$, the potential energy of these gravity forces can be written as

$$V = -m_1 g[l_1 \cos\theta_1] - m_2 g[l_1 \cos\theta_1 + l_2 \cos(\theta_1 + \theta_2)] \qquad (2.108)$$

If we apply (2.104) we directly get the generalized forces corresponding to the gravity effect as already calculated in a different way in example 2.9 on page 55.

Example 2.14

We consider the potential energy function $V(q)$ of the double pendulum system with two rigid bars of example 2.3 on page 41. In this case, again the internal energy function $U^{in}(q)$ is zero, because there are no elastic elements in the system. The only external force acting upon the system is the gravity force, which is conservative. The potential energy of the gravity forces for these two rigid bar elements can be obtained by concentrating the mass of each of the bars in its centre of mass and computing the potential energy of the two resulting point masses. Taking into account the coordinate notations of Fig. 2.3 (page 41) and taking the zero level of the potential energy at $x_1 = 0$, we obtain

$$V = -m_1 g \frac{l_1}{2} \cos\theta_1 - m_2 g \{l_1 \cos\theta_1 + \frac{l_2}{2} \cos\theta_2\} \qquad (2.109)$$

2.11   KINETIC ENERGY; MASS MATRIX

In the preceding sections the virtual work of the applied forces has been elaborated. The coordinate transformation from $\vec{r}_i$ to q resulted in a natural way in the introduction of the potential energy. In addition, it will be shown in Section 2.12 that elaboration of the virtual work of the inertia forces will lead to the appearance of the kinetic energy. In this section we will first discuss the general structure of the kinetic energy of a mechanical system.

The kinetic energy of our mechanical system by definition has the form

$$T = \frac{1}{2} \sum_{i=1}^{n_p} m_i \, \dot{\vec{r}}_i \cdot \dot{\vec{r}}_i \tag{2.110}$$

Inserting (2.37) into (2.110), we obtain

$$T = \frac{1}{2} \sum_{i=1}^{n_p} m_i \, \left[\vec{r}_{i,t} + \underline{\dot{q}}^T \left(\vec{r}_{i,\underline{q}} \right)^T \right] \cdot \left[\vec{r}_{i,t} + \vec{r}_{i,\underline{q}} \, \underline{\dot{q}} \right] \tag{2.111}$$

After conversion, this expression can be rewritten as

$$T = T_0 + T_1 + T_2 = T_0 + \underline{m}^T \underline{\dot{q}} + \frac{1}{2} \, \underline{\dot{q}}^T \underline{M} \, \underline{\dot{q}} \tag{2.112}$$

In the right side of (2.112) the term

$$T_0 = T_0(\underline{q}, t) = \frac{1}{2} \sum_{i=1}^{n_p} m_i \, \vec{r}_{i,t} \cdot \vec{r}_{i,t} = \frac{1}{2} \sum_{i=1}^{n_p} m_i \, \underline{r}_{i,t}^T \, \underline{r}_{i,t} \tag{2.113}$$

represents the so-called *transport kinetic energy* of the system. It is the only term remaining if $\underline{\dot{q}} = 0$. Further, in the right side of (2.112) the second term

$$T_1 = T_1 \left(\underline{q}, \underline{\dot{q}}, t \right) = \underline{m}^T \underline{\dot{q}} \tag{2.114}$$

is the *mutual kinetic energy*, occuring in combination with the transport kinetic energy if prescribed motion is present, i.e. if $\vec{r}_{i,t} \neq \vec{0}$. It contains the row matrix $\underline{m}^T$, defined by

$$\underline{m}^T = \underline{m}^T \left(\underline{q}, t \right) = \sum_{i=1}^{n_p} m_i \, \vec{r}_{i,t} \cdot \vec{r}_{i,\underline{q}} = \sum_{i=1}^{n_p} m_i \, \underline{r}_{i,t}^T \, \underline{r}_{i,\underline{q}} \tag{2.115}$$

Finally, the last term

$$T_2 = T_2 \left(\underline{q}, \underline{\dot{q}}, t \right) = \frac{1}{2} \, \underline{\dot{q}}^T \underline{M} \, \underline{\dot{q}} \tag{2.116}$$

in the right side of (2.112) represents the kinetic energy if $\vec{r}_{,t} = \vec{0}$, i.e. if no drivers are active in the system. It contains the square matrix

$$\underline{M} = \underline{M}(\underline{q}) = \sum_{i=1}^{n_p} m_i \, \left(\vec{r}_{i,\underline{q}} \right)^T \cdot \vec{r}_{i,\underline{q}} = \sum_{i=1}^{n_p} m_i \, \left(\underline{r}_{i,\underline{q}} \right)^T \underline{r}_{i,\underline{q}} \tag{2.117}$$

which is called the *mass matrix* of the system. It can be seen easily that the mass matrix is *symmetric*, i.e.

$$\underline{M} = \underline{M}^T \tag{2.118}$$

Also, the mass matrix is *positive definite* if

$$2T_2 = \underline{\dot{q}}^T \underline{M} \, \underline{\dot{q}} > 0 \tag{2.119}$$

provided $\underline{\dot{q}}$ contains at least one non-zero element. A necessary but not sufficient condition for this to be true is that the main diagonal of the mass matrix does not contain zero or negative elements. At this point it is remarked that a different set of generalized coordinates, through (2.117) automatically results in a different mass matrix.

The above discussion of the kinetic energy demonstrates that the kinetic energy can be considered to depend explicitly on the generalized coordinates $\underline{q}$, the generalized velocities $\underline{\dot{q}}$ and time t

$$T = T\left(\underline{q}, \underline{\dot{q}}, t\right) \tag{2.120}$$

Example 2.15

We consider the kinetic energy of the double pendulum system with two masses of example 2.1 on page 38. In this case there are no prescribed coordinates and, hence, the transport kinetic energy T_0 and the mutual kinetic energy T_1 vanish. Consequently, only the third term in the right side of (2.112) is different from zero. We use the derivatives $\underline{r}_{i,\underline{q}}$ of the position vectors of the masses m_1 and m_2 with respect to the Cartesian vector basis $\{\vec{e}_1, \vec{e}_2, \vec{e}_3\}$ as calculated before in example 2.5 on page 46. It then follows that

$$\underline{M}_1 = m_1 \left(\underline{r}_{1,\underline{q}}\right)^T \left(\underline{r}_{1,\underline{q}}\right) = \begin{bmatrix} m_1 l_1^2 & 0 \\ 0 & 0 \end{bmatrix} \tag{2.121}$$

Hence, the kinetic energy of mass m_1 equals

$$T_{m_1} = \frac{1}{2} \, \underline{\dot{q}}^T \underline{M}_1 \, \underline{\dot{q}} = \frac{1}{2} \, m_1 \, l_1^2 \, \dot{\theta}_1^2 \tag{2.122}$$

Of course, this result can be obtained much easier by realizing that this represents the kinetic energy of mass m_1 due to rotation about the fixed point O.

Similarly, for the contribution of mass m_2 to the mass matrix of the system we get

$$\underline{M}_2 = m_2 \left(\underline{r}_{2,\underline{q}}\right)^T \left(\underline{r}_{2,\underline{q}}\right)$$
$$= m_2 \begin{bmatrix} l_1^2 + l_2^2 + 2l_1 l_2 \cos\theta_2 & l_2^2 + l_1 l_2 \cos\theta_2 \\ l_2^2 + l_1 l_2 \cos\theta_2 & l_2^2 \end{bmatrix} \tag{2.123}$$

Hence, the kinetic energy of mass m_2 equals

$$T_{m_2} = \frac{1}{2} \, \underline{\dot{q}}^T \underline{M}_2 \, \underline{\dot{q}} = \frac{1}{2} m_2 \left\{ \left(l_1^2 + l_2^2 + 2l_1 l_2 \cos\theta_2\right) \dot{\theta}_1^2 \right\}$$
$$+ m_2 \left\{ \left(l_2^2 + l_1 l_2 \cos\theta_2\right) \dot{\theta}_1 \dot{\theta}_2 + l_2^2 \dot{\theta}_2^2 \right\} \tag{2.124}$$

So, we find the following result for the (total) mass matrix of the system

$$\underline{M} = \underline{M}_1 + \underline{M}_2 \tag{2.125}$$

Just as a check we can look at a special situation, namely $\theta_2 = \dot{\theta}_2 = 0$, which means that we have only one rigid rod with length $(l_1 + l_2)$. If we substitute $\underline{\dot{q}}^T = [\dot{\theta}_1, 0]$ in $T_2 = \frac{1}{2}\underline{\dot{q}}^T \underline{M}_2 \underline{\dot{q}}$ we get

$$T_2 = \frac{1}{2}m_2 (l_1 + l_2)^2 \dot{\theta}_1^2$$

which is indeed the correct result.

This example demonstrates that the mass matrix generally depends on the generalized coordinates of the system. The total kinetic energy of the system can now simply be written as

$$T = \frac{1}{2}\underline{\dot{q}}^T \underline{M} \underline{\dot{q}} \tag{2.126}$$

Example 2.16

We consider the kinetic energy of the double pendulum system with two rigid bars of example 2.3 on page 41. In this case there are again no prescribed coordinates and, hence, the transport kinetic energy T_0 and the mutual kinetic energy T_1 vanish. Consequently, only the third term in the right side of (2.112) is different from zero. We specify the derivative $\vec{r}_{i,q}$ with respect to the Cartesian vector basis $\{\vec{e}_1, \vec{e}_2\}$ of Fig. 2.3 and obtain (2.28) for point P_1 of bar OA and (2.29) for point P_2 of bar AB. It follows from (2.28) that

$$
\left(\underline{r}_{P1,q}\right)^T \left(\underline{r}_{P1,q}\right) = \begin{bmatrix} -\xi_1 \sin\theta_1 & \xi_1 \cos\theta_1 \\ 0 & 0 \end{bmatrix} \begin{bmatrix} -\xi_1 \sin\theta_1 & 0 \\ \xi_1 \cos\theta_1 & 0 \end{bmatrix}
$$
$$
= \begin{bmatrix} \xi_1^2 & 0 \\ 0 & 0 \end{bmatrix} \tag{2.127}
$$

Inserting this result into (2.117) with m_i being replaced by $(m_1/l_1)\,d\xi_1$ and the summation by integration over ξ_1, we find the following contribution of bar OA to the mass matrix of the system

$$\underline{M}_1 = \int_{\xi_1=0}^{l_1} \begin{bmatrix} \xi_1^2 & 0 \\ 0 & 0 \end{bmatrix} \frac{m_1}{l_1} d\xi_1 = \begin{bmatrix} \frac{1}{3}m_1 l_1^2 & 0 \\ 0 & 0 \end{bmatrix} \tag{2.128}$$

Hence, the kinetic energy of bar OA equals

$$T_{OA} = \frac{1}{2}\underline{\dot{q}}^T \underline{M}_1 \underline{\dot{q}} = \frac{1}{2}\left(\frac{1}{3}m_1 l_1^2\right)\dot{\theta}_1^2 \tag{2.129}$$

Of course, this result can be obtained much easier by realizing that this represents the kinetic energy of bar OA due to rotation about the fixed point O. Next, we consider the kinetic energy of bar AB. It follows from (2.29) that

$$
\left(\underline{r}_{P2,\underline{q}}\right)^T \left(\underline{r}_{P2,\underline{q}}\right)
$$

$$
= \left[\begin{array}{cc} -l_1 \sin\theta_1 & l_1 \cos\theta_1 \\ -\xi_2 \sin\theta_2 & \xi_2 \cos\theta_2 \end{array} \right] \left[\begin{array}{cc} -l_1 \sin\theta_1 & -\xi_2 \sin\theta_1 \\ l_1 \cos\theta_2 & \xi_2 \cos\theta_2 \end{array} \right]
$$

$$
= \left[\begin{array}{cc} l_1^2 & l_1 \xi_2 \cos(\theta_1 - \theta_2) \\ l_1 \xi_2 \cos(\theta_1 - \theta_2) & \xi_2^2 \end{array} \right] \tag{2.130}
$$

Inserting this result into (2.117), with m_i being replaced by $(m_2/l_2)\, d\xi_2$ and the summation by integration over ξ_2, we find the following contribution of bar AB to the mass matrix of the system

$$
\underline{M}_2 = \int\limits_{\xi_2=0}^{l_2} \left[\begin{array}{cc} l_1^2 & l_1 \xi_2 \cos(\theta_1 - \theta_2) \\ l_1 \xi_2 \cos(\theta_1 - \theta_2) & \xi_2^2 \end{array} \right] \frac{m_2}{l_2} d\xi_2
$$

$$
= \left[\begin{array}{cc} m_2 l_1^2 & \frac{1}{2} m_2 l_1 l_2 \cos(\theta_1 - \theta_2) \\ \frac{1}{2} m_2 l_1 l_2 \cos(\theta_1 - \theta_2) & \frac{1}{3} m_2 l_2^2 \end{array} \right] \tag{2.131}
$$

Hence, the kinetic energy of bar AB equals

$$
T_{AB} = \frac{1}{2} \underline{\dot{q}}^T \underline{M}_2\, \underline{\dot{q}} \tag{2.132}
$$

$$
= \frac{1}{2} \left[m_2 l_1^2 \dot{\theta}_1^2 + m_2 l_1 l_2 \left\{ \cos(\theta_1 - \theta_2) \right\} \dot{\theta}_1 \dot{\theta}_2 + \frac{1}{3} m_2 l_2^2 \dot{\theta}_2^2 \right]
$$

It is left to the reader to verify that this kinetic energy is identical to the kinetic energy obtained by considering first the translational energy of the centre of mass and then adding the rotational energy of bar AB about this centre of mass. The total mass matrix of the system is

$$
\underline{M} = \underline{M}_1 + \underline{M}_2 = \left[\begin{array}{cc} \left(\frac{1}{3} m_1 l_1^2 + m_2 l_1^2\right) & \frac{1}{2} m_2 l_1 l_2 \cos(\theta_1 - \theta_2) \\ \frac{1}{2} m_2 l_1 l_2 \cos(\theta_1 - \theta_2) & \frac{1}{3} m_2 l_2^2 \end{array} \right] \tag{2.133}
$$

This result again demonstrates that the mass matrix generally depends on the generalized coordinates of the system. The total kinetic energy of the system is

$$
T = T_{OA} + T_{AB} = \frac{1}{2} \underline{\dot{q}}^T \underline{M}\, \underline{\dot{q}} \tag{2.134}
$$

$$
= \frac{1}{2} \left[\left(\frac{1}{3} m_1 l_1^2 + m_2 l_1^2\right) \dot{\theta}_1^2 + m_2 l_1 l_2 \left\{ \cos(\theta_1 - \theta_2) \right\} \dot{\theta}_1 \dot{\theta}_2 + \frac{1}{3} m_2 l_2^2 \dot{\theta}_2^2 \right]
$$

In the above example we were dealing with the kinetic energy of a system with a continuous distribution of mass. Because the system consists of rigid bodies, within each body a small volume element dV can be defined with mass density ρ. Then, the collection of volume elements can be treated as an infinite number of point masses $dm = \rho dV$ and the kinetic energy for the whole body can be determined by replacing the summation in (2.117) by an integration over the whole body volume V. However, as we demonstrated in the above example, for simple rigid bodies like bars, disks, cylinders, etc., the total kinetic energy can also be determined by taking the sum of the translational energy of the total mass concentrated in the centre of mass and the rotational energy of the body about its centre of mass. For the latter the relevant mass moment of inertia is needed which can often be found in standard text books.

We conclude this section with two examples for which prescribed motion is present.

Example 2.17

We consider the kinetic energy of the simple pendulum system with moving support of example 2.4 on page 43. We use the derivatives $\underline{r}_{,t}$ and $\underline{r}_{,q}$ of the position vectors of the mass with respect to the shown vector basis from page 46. It then follows that

$$T_0 = \frac{1}{2}m \begin{bmatrix} \dot{s}(t) & 0 \end{bmatrix} \begin{bmatrix} \dot{s}(t) \\ 0 \end{bmatrix} = \frac{1}{2}m\dot{s}^2(t) \tag{2.135}$$

$$\underline{m} = m \begin{bmatrix} \dot{s}(t) & 0 \end{bmatrix} \begin{bmatrix} -l\sin\theta \\ l\cos\theta \end{bmatrix} = -ml\dot{s}(t)\sin\theta \tag{2.136}$$

$$\underline{M} = m \begin{bmatrix} -l\sin\theta & l\cos\theta \end{bmatrix} \begin{bmatrix} -l\sin\theta \\ l\cos\theta \end{bmatrix} = ml^2 \tag{2.137}$$

So, the kinetic energy becomes

$$T = \frac{1}{2}m\,\dot{s}^2(t) - ml\,\dot{s}(t)\,\dot{\theta}\,\sin\theta + \frac{1}{2}ml^2\,\dot{\theta}^2 \tag{2.138}$$

Example 2.18

We consider a slight modification of the single pendulum system with moving support as shown in Fig. 2.12. The system consists of a rigid uniform beam with length $2l$ and mass m. The support of the beam is undergoing a vertical prescribed motion $s(t)$. For this system we have only one generalized coordinate for which we take the rotation θ of the beam with respect to the vertical axis, so $\underline{q} = [\theta]$. The column of prescribed coordinates also contains only a single element $\underline{s}(t) = [s(t)]$. The column-matrix representation $\underline{r}_C$ of the radius vector $\vec{r}_C(t)$

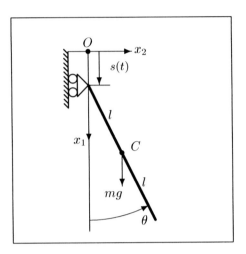

Fig. 2.12   Rigid-beam pendulum with moving support

of centre of gravity C of the beam with respect to the shown vector basis
$[x_1, x_2]$ *can be written as*

$$\underline{r}_C = \left[\begin{array}{c} s(t) + l \cos \theta \\ l \sin \theta \end{array} \right] \tag{2.139}$$

and for the column-matrix representation $\underline{v}_C = \dot{\underline{r}}_C$ *of the velocity vector*
$\vec{r}_C(t)$

$$\underline{v}_C = \left[\begin{array}{c} \dot{s}(t) - l\dot{\theta} \sin \theta \\ l\dot{\theta} \cos \theta \end{array} \right] \tag{2.140}$$

*The mass-moment of inertia of a uniform beam (mass m, length 2l)
with respect to the centre of gravity C can be found from standard textbooks to be*

$$J_C = \frac{1}{12}m \, (2l)^2 = \frac{1}{3}ml^2 \tag{2.141}$$

So, for the total kinetic energy we find

$$\begin{aligned}
T &= T(q, \dot{q}, t) = \frac{1}{2}m \, \underline{v}_C^T \underline{v}_C + \frac{1}{2}J_C \, \dot{\theta}^2 \\
&= \frac{1}{2}m[\dot{s}^2 - 2l\dot{s}\dot{\theta} \sin(\theta) + l^2\dot{\theta}^2] + \frac{1}{2}(\frac{1}{3}ml^2)\dot{\theta}^2 \\
&= [\frac{1}{2}m\dot{s}^2] - [ml\dot{s} \sin(\theta)] \, \dot{\theta} + [\frac{2}{3}ml^2] \, \dot{\theta}^2 \tag{2.142}
\end{aligned}$$

2.12 LAGRANGE'S EQUATIONS OF MOTION

In Section 2.2 we pointed out that the position vectors $\vec{r}_i$ may not all be independent and that it is often desirable to describe the motion of the system by means of a set of independent generalized coordinates $\underline{q}$. To this end, we used in Section 2.7 a coordinate transformation from $\vec{r}_i$ to $\underline{q}$, to obtain the virtual work of the applied forces in terms of the generalized coordinates $\underline{q}$. Now, we will apply the same coordinate transformation to the virtual work δW^{inert} of the inertia forces. Using (2.59) and (2.46), we can express this virtual work as

$$
\delta W^{inert} = -\sum_{i=1}^{n_p} m_i \, \ddot{\vec{r}}_i \cdot \delta \vec{r}_i = -\left[\sum_{i=1}^{n_p} m_i \, \ddot{\vec{r}}_i \cdot \frac{\partial \vec{r}_i}{\partial \underline{q}} \right] \delta \underline{q}
$$

$$
= -\left[\sum_{i=1}^{n_p} m_i \, \frac{d}{dt} \left(\dot{\vec{r}}_i \frac{\partial \vec{r}_i}{\partial \underline{q}} \right) - \sum_{i=1}^{n_p} m_i \, \dot{\vec{r}}_i \cdot \frac{d}{dt} \left(\frac{\partial \vec{r}_i}{\partial \underline{q}} \right) \right] \delta \underline{q} \quad (2.143)
$$

We will show that both sums in the right side of (2.143) are related to the kinetic energy, which has been discussed in the previous section. To this end, we need two lemma's.

The **first lemma** states that

$$
\sum_{i=1}^{n_p} m_i \, \dot{\vec{r}}_i \cdot \frac{\partial \vec{r}_i}{\partial \underline{q}} = \frac{\partial T}{\partial \dot{\underline{q}}} = T_{,\dot{\underline{q}}} \quad (2.144)
$$

To prove this lemma, we first determine the derivative of T with respect to $\dot{\underline{q}}$, using (2.110)

$$
T_{,\dot{\underline{q}}} = \sum_{i=1}^{n_p} m_i \, \dot{\vec{r}}_i \cdot \frac{\partial \dot{\vec{r}}_i}{\partial \dot{\underline{q}}} \quad (2.145)
$$

Next, we differentiate (2.37) for $\dot{\vec{r}}_i$ to $\dot{\underline{q}}$ and obtain

$$
\frac{\partial \dot{\vec{r}}_i}{\partial \dot{\underline{q}}} = \frac{\partial \vec{r}_i}{\partial \underline{q}} \quad (2.146)
$$

Inserting (2.146) into (2.145), we obtain (2.144) which completes the proof of the first lemma.

The **second lemma** states that

$$
\sum_{i=1}^{n_p} m_i \, \dot{\vec{r}}_i \cdot \frac{d}{dt} \left(\frac{\partial \vec{r}_i}{\partial \underline{q}} \right) = \frac{\partial T}{\partial \underline{q}} = T_{,\underline{q}} \quad (2.147)
$$

To prove this lemma, we first determine the derivative of T with respect to $\underline{q}$, using (2.110)

$$T_{,\underline{q}} = \sum_{i=1}^{n_p} m_i \, \dot{\vec{r}}_i \cdot \frac{\partial \dot{\vec{r}}_i}{\partial \underline{\dot{q}}} \tag{2.148}$$

Next, we differentiate (2.37) for $\dot{\vec{r}}_i$ to $\underline{q}$ and obtain

$$\begin{aligned}
\frac{\partial \dot{\vec{r}}_i}{\partial \underline{q}} &= \frac{\partial}{\partial \underline{q}} \left[\vec{r}_{i,t} + \frac{\partial \vec{r}_i}{\partial \underline{q}} \underline{\dot{q}} \right] \\
&= \frac{\partial}{\partial t} \left(\frac{\partial \vec{r}_i}{\partial \underline{q}} \right) + \frac{\partial}{\partial \underline{q}} \left(\frac{\partial \vec{r}_i}{\partial \underline{q}} \right) \underline{\dot{q}}
\end{aligned} \tag{2.149}$$

Because $\vec{r}_i$ depends on $\underline{q}$ and t only, see (2.17) the quantity $\vec{r}_{i,\underline{q}}$ will only depend on $\underline{q}$ and t. Therefore, the right side of (2.149) can be considered to be the total derivative with respect to time of the quantity $\vec{r}_{i,\underline{q}}$. Hence, we can write

$$\frac{\partial \dot{\vec{r}}_i}{\partial \underline{q}} = \frac{d}{dt} \left(\frac{\partial \vec{r}_i}{\partial \underline{q}} \right) \tag{2.150}$$

Inserting (2.150) into (2.148), we obtain (2.147), which completes the proof of the second lemma.

Using (2.144) and (2.147), we can express the right side of (2.143) in terms of the kinetic energy as follows

$$\delta W^{inert} = \left[-\frac{d}{dt} \left(T_{,\underline{\dot{q}}} \right) + T_{,\underline{q}} \right] \delta \underline{q} \tag{2.151}$$

Now, the transformation process for the principle of virtual work, (2.59), is completed. Introducing (2.107) and (2.151) into (2.59), we arrive at the following result for the transformed principle of virtual work

$$\begin{aligned}
\delta W &= \delta W^{appl} + \delta W^{inert} \\
&= -\left[\frac{d}{dt} \left(T_{,\underline{\dot{q}}} \right) - T_{,\underline{q}} + V_{,\underline{q}} - (\underline{Q}^{nc})^T \right] \delta \underline{q} = 0
\end{aligned} \tag{2.152}$$

Because the generalized coordinates in $\underline{q}$ are being defined to be completely independent, the elements in the virtual displacement column $\delta \underline{q}$ can be chosen completely independent from one another. This means that, if the principle of virtual work in the form of (2.152) holds for all possible values of $\delta \underline{q}$, the expression between the square brackets has to vanish, so that we obtain

Lagrange's equations of motion

$$\frac{d}{dt} \left(T_{,\underline{\dot{q}}} \right) - T_{,\underline{q}} + V_{,\underline{q}} = (\underline{Q}^{nc})^T \tag{2.153}$$

This matrix equation constitutes a set of scalar equations of motion, which are the famous *Lagrange's equations of motion*. In view of the way in which these equations have been obtained, the number of equations of motion is equal to the number of independent generalized coordinates. It follows from the procedure in Section 2.6 that the Lagrange's equations of motion will not provide any information about the constraint forces of the system, because the independent generalized coordinates have been selected for the constrained system. In Section 2.14 it will be discussed how the Lagrange's equations of motion can be modified to obtain information about the constraint forces.

It is possible to obtain the Lagrange's equations of motion in a more compact form by introducing the *function of Lagrange* or the *Lagrangian*, which is defined to be the difference between the kinetic energy and the potential energy

$$L\left(\underline{q}, \underline{\dot{q}}, t\right) = T\left(\underline{q}, \underline{\dot{q}}, t\right) - V\left(\underline{q}, t\right) \tag{2.154}$$

Taking into account that, by definition, the potential energy does not depend on the generalized velocities $\underline{\dot{q}}$, we have from (2.154)

$$T_{,\underline{\dot{q}}} = L_{,\underline{\dot{q}}} \tag{2.155}$$

Using (2.154) and (2.155), we can reduce (2.153) to the more compact form

$$\frac{d}{dt}\left(L_{,\underline{\dot{q}}}\right) - L_{,\underline{q}} = \left(\underline{Q}^{nc}\right)^{T} \tag{2.156}$$

The Lagrangian approach is quite efficient for deriving the system equations of motion, especially when the system gets a complicated structure, which happens for example if the number of degrees of freedom is large. All the differential equations of motion are derived from two scalar functions, namely, the kinetic energy T and the potential energy V, as well as the virtual work δW^{nc} associated with the nonconservative forces. The equations apply to linear as well as nonlinear systems. Although it appears that the identification of the generalized coordinates and generalized nonconservative forces is a major stumbling block in using this approach, this is actually not the case; in most physical systems this aspect presents no particular difficulty. As remarked earlier, a distinct feature of the Lagrangian approach is that it obviates the computation of constraint forces.

For pedagogic reasons, Fig. 2.13 depicts in a schematic overview the transition from the starting terms in the principle of virtual work to the final quantities $\left(T, V \text{ and } \underline{Q}^{nc}\right)$ needed for the Lagrange's equations of motion.

Example 2.19

We consider the Lagrange's equations of motion of the double pendulum system with rigid bars from Fig. 2.3 as discussed on the pages 41, 46 and 66. Using (2.134) for the kinetic energy of this system, the first

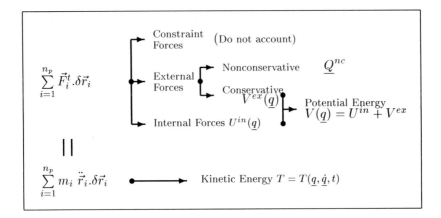

Fig. 2.13   Schematic transition from virtual work to Lagrangian quantities

term in (2.153) can be evaluated to be

$$
\left[\frac{d}{dt}\left(T_{,\dot{\underline{q}}}\right)\right]^{T} =
$$

$$
\left[
\begin{array}{c}
m^{*}l_{1}^{2}\ddot{\theta}_{1} + \frac{1}{2}m_{2}l_{1}l_{2}\left\{\ddot{\theta}_{2}\cos\left(\theta_{1}-\theta_{2}\right)\right. \\
\left. -\dot{\theta}_{2}\left(\dot{\theta}_{1}-\dot{\theta}_{2}\right)\sin\left(\theta_{1}-\theta_{2}\right)\right\} \\
\hline
\frac{1}{3}m_{2}l_{2}^{2}\ddot{\theta}_{2} + \frac{1}{2}m_{2}l_{1}l_{2}\left\{\ddot{\theta}_{1}\cos\left(\theta_{1}-\theta_{2}\right)\right. \\
\left. -\dot{\theta}_{1}\left(\dot{\theta}_{1}-\dot{\theta}_{2}\right)\sin\left(\theta_{1}-\theta_{2}\right)\right\}
\end{array}
\right]
$$

$$(2.157)$$

with $m^{*} = \frac{1}{3}m_{1} + m_{2}$. *The second term in (2.153) becomes*

$$
-T_{,\underline{q}} = \left[
\begin{array}{c}
\frac{1}{2}m_{2}l_{1}l_{2}\dot{\theta}_{1}\dot{\theta}_{2}\sin\left(\theta_{1}-\theta_{2}\right) \\
-\frac{1}{2}m_{2}l_{1}l_{2}\dot{\theta}_{1}\dot{\theta}_{2}\sin\left(\theta_{1}-\theta_{2}\right)
\end{array}
\right]^{T} \tag{2.158}
$$

The third term in (2.153) can be derived from the potential energy function, (2.109)

$$
V_{,\underline{q}} = \left[
\begin{array}{c}
(\frac{m_{1}}{2} + m_{2})gl_{1}\sin\theta_{1} \\
\frac{m_{2}}{2}gl_{2}\sin\theta_{2}
\end{array}
\right]^{T} \tag{2.159}
$$

In this example there are no nonconservative forces, and, hence, $Q^{nc} = \underline{0}$. *Substituting (2.157), (2.158) and (2.159) into (2.153), we obtain the Lagrange's equations of motion for this example. We observe that already for this seemingly simple example, the Lagrange's equations of motion take complicated appearance, although they have been derived in a fairly simple and straightforward way. The resulting coupled second-order differential equations of motion appear to contain a number of nonlinear terms.*

Example 2.20

We consider the single pendulum system consisting of a rigid bar with moving support from example 2.18 on page 71. This is an example of a system with only one degree of freedom but with an addditional prescribed displacement function $s(t)$.

Using (2.142) for the kinetic energy of this system, the first and second terms in (2.153) can be evaluated to be

$$\frac{\partial T}{\partial \dot{q}} = -ml\dot{s}\sin(\theta) + \frac{4}{3}ml^2\dot{\theta}$$

$$\frac{d}{dt}(\frac{\partial T}{\partial \dot{q}}) = -ml\dot{s}\cos(\theta)\dot{\theta} - ml\ddot{s}\sin(\theta) + \frac{4}{3}ml^2\ddot{\theta}$$

$$\frac{\partial T}{\partial q} = -ml\dot{s}\dot{\theta}\cos(\theta) \tag{2.160}$$

For the potential energy due to gravity we can write

$$V = -mg[s(t) + l\cos(\theta)] \tag{2.161}$$

which gives

$$\frac{\partial V}{\partial q} = mgl\sin(\theta) \tag{2.162}$$

In this example there are no nonconservative forces, and, hence, $Q^{nc} = 0$. Substituting (2.160), (2.161) and (2.162) into (2.153), we obtain the Lagrange's equation of motion for this example

$$\frac{4}{3}ml^2\ddot{\theta} - ml\ddot{s}\sin\theta + mgl\sin\theta = 0 \tag{2.163}$$

Because we have only one degree of freedom, we also have only one equation of motion. It is easy to see that this equation of motion has a time-dependent coefficient (the term $\ddot{s}$) and also is nonlinear due to the $\sin\theta$ terms. Both aspects will make the analytical solution of this equation of motion very difficult.

Example 2.21

In the following we will look at the two-degree-of-freedom mass-pendulum system as shown in Fig. 2.14. The system consists of a horizontally

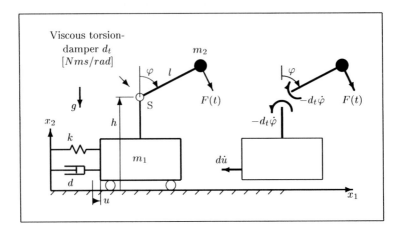

Fig. 2.14   Two-degree-of-freedom mass-pendulum system

*moving rigid block with mass m_1 which is connected to a rigid verti-
cal wall via a linear spring (spring constant k) and a viscous damper
(damper constant d). On top of the rigid block a rigid massless rod
with length l is connected to it via a hinge in which some friction is
present. This friction is modelled as a viscous torsional damper with
constant d_t. At the free end of the massless rod a concentrated mass m_2
is attached to it. This concentrated mass is subjected to a follower force
which acts in a direction that remains perpendicular to the rod during
its motion. The above system is moving in the vertical x_1, x_2 plane
under the influence of gravity. It is easy to see that this system has two
degrees of freedom. A convenient set of generalized coordinates consists
of the horizontal displacement u of mass m_1 from the unstretched spring
position and the rotation φ of the rod l with respect to the x_2 axis, so
that $\underline{q}^T = [u, \ \varphi]$.
After having selected a set of generalized coordinates, we express the
x_1 and x_2 coordinates of the centre of the rigid block m_1 and of m_2 in
terms of u and φ. The x_1 and x_2 coordinates of the centre of block m_1
are*

$$(x_1)_{m_1} = x_{10} + u, \qquad (x_2)_{m_1} = x_{20} \qquad (2.164)$$

*where x_{10} and x_{20} are time-independent reference positions. The x_1
and x_2 coordinates of the mass m_2 are*

$$(x_1)_{m_2} = x_{10} + u + l \sin \varphi, \qquad (x_2)_{m_2} = h + l \cos \varphi \qquad (2.165)$$

*where h is a time-independent reference position of the hinge. In order
to be able to compose the kinetic energy, we need the velocities of m_1*

and m_2. From (2.164) and (2.165) we obtain

$$(\dot{x}_1)_{m_1} = \dot{u}, \qquad (\dot{x}_2)_{m_1} = 0 \tag{2.166}$$

$$(\dot{x}_1)_{m_2} = \dot{u} + l\dot{\varphi}\cos\varphi, \qquad (\dot{x}_2)_{m_2} = -l\dot{\varphi}\sin\varphi \tag{2.167}$$

Now, the kinetic energy $T = T(\underline{q}, \underline{\dot{q}}, t)$ of the system becomes

$$T = \frac{1}{2}(m_1 + m_2)\dot{u}^2 + m_2 l\dot{u}\dot{\varphi}\cos\varphi + \frac{1}{2}m_2 l^2\dot{\varphi}^2 \tag{2.168}$$

The potential energy (in the spring k and due to gravity) takes the form

$$V = \frac{1}{2}ku^2 + m_2 g[h + l\cos\varphi] \tag{2.169}$$

The potential energy of mass m_1 does not change with a variation of the generalized coordinates, so that it can be neglected. To evaluate the generalized forces we isolate all the non-conservative forces and moments as shown in the right part of the figure. Next we apply the step-by-step approach to generate the nonconservative generalized forces $\underline{Q}^{nc} = [Q_u, Q_\varphi]^T$. First we impose $\delta\underline{q}^T = [\delta u, 0]$. The virtual work for this situation is

$$\delta W = -[d\dot{u}]\,\delta u + [F(t)\cos\varphi]\,\delta u = \underline{Q}^T\delta\underline{q} = Q_u\,\delta u \tag{2.170}$$

so that

$$Q_u = -d\dot{u} + F(t)\cos\varphi, \qquad dimension \ [N] \tag{2.171}$$

Next we apply $\delta\underline{q}^T = [0, \delta\varphi]$ which leads to

$$\delta W = [F(t)l]\,\delta\varphi + [-d_t\dot{\varphi}]\,\delta\varphi = Q_\varphi\,\delta\varphi \tag{2.172}$$

or

$$Q_\varphi = F(t)l - d_t\dot{\varphi}, \qquad dimension \ [Nm] \tag{2.173}$$

Hence, finally the column of nonconservative generalized forces becomes

$$\underline{Q}^{nc} = \begin{bmatrix} -d\dot{u} + F(t)\cos\varphi \\ F(t)l - d_t\dot{\varphi} \end{bmatrix} =$$

$$\begin{bmatrix} F(t)\cos\varphi \\ F(t)l \end{bmatrix} - \begin{bmatrix} d & 0 \\ 0 & d_t \end{bmatrix}\begin{bmatrix} \dot{u} \\ \dot{\varphi} \end{bmatrix} := \underline{f}(t) - \underline{D}\,\underline{\dot{q}} \tag{2.174}$$

Applying the methodology of Lagrange yields a set of two, coupled, non-linear differential equations

$$(m_1 + m_2)\ddot{u} + m_2 l\ddot{\varphi}\cos\varphi - m_2 l\dot{\varphi}^2\sin\varphi + k\,u + d\,\dot{u} = F(t)\cos\varphi$$

$$m_2 l^2\ddot{\varphi} + m_2 l\ddot{u}\cos\varphi - m_2 gl\sin\varphi + d_t\,\dot{\varphi} = F(t)\,l \tag{2.175}$$

So, we end up with two (nonlinear) equations of motion. All the terms in the first equation of motion have the dimension [N], which correlates with the first generalized coordinate being the translation u [m]. All the terms in the second equation have the dimension [Nm], which again correlates with the second generalized coordinate being the rotation φ [rad] of the swing-arm.

Example 2.22

We consider the two-dimensional pendulum system of Fig. 2.15. The system consists of two interconnected rigid bars AB and BC moving in the vertical x_1, x_2 plane under the influence of gravity, whereas a prescribed external force is acting in point C in the x_1 direction. The

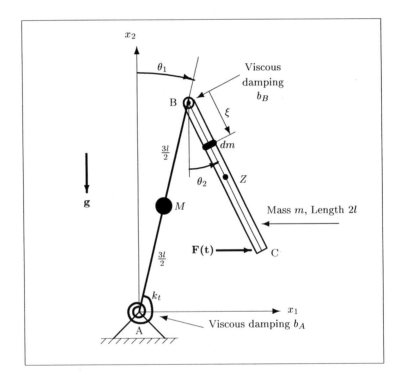

Fig. 2.15   Mixed Pendulum System

length of bar AB is 3l and its mass M is concentrated in the middle of the bar. The length of bar BC is 2l and its mass m is uniformly distributed over the length of the bar. Bar AB is connected to the support by a torsional spring with spring constant k_t. When this bar AB *is directed vertical upward, the spring is unloaded. The external force acting in point C in the horizontal x_1 direction is denoted by $F(t)$. In the coupling hinges between bar AB and the support and between this bar and bar BC some friction is present which will be modelled as torsional viscous dampers with torsional damping constants of b_A respectively b_B.*

It is easy to see that we need two geometrical parameters to define the position of the system completely. So, the number of degrees of freedom for this system equals two $(n = 2)$. We select as generalized coordinates the angles θ_1, and θ_2 of AB and BC with respect to the vertical x_2, axis. With $q_1 = \theta_1$ and $q_2 = \theta_2$ the column of generalized coordinates, q, takes the form

$$q = \begin{bmatrix} q_1 \\ q_2 \end{bmatrix} = \begin{bmatrix} \theta_1 \\ \theta_2 \end{bmatrix} \tag{2.176}$$

In this case there are no prescribed coordinates and/or a steady motion and, hence, the transport kinetic energy T_0 and the mutual kinetic energy T_1 will automatically be zero. So, we only will have to deal with the contribution $T_2 = \frac{1}{2}\, \dot{q}^T \underline{M}\, \dot{q}$. Considering first the bar AB, it is easy to see that the contribution of this bar $\underline{M}_{AB}$ can be expressed as

$$\underline{M}_{AB} = M\ (\underline{r}_{M,q})^T (\underline{r}_{M,q}) = M\ \begin{bmatrix} \frac{9}{4}l^2 & 0 \\ 0 & 0 \end{bmatrix} \tag{2.177}$$

Substituting this result in $T = \frac{1}{2}\, \dot{q}^T \underline{M}\, \dot{q}$, gives the following expression for the kinetic energy of bar AB

$$T_{AB} = \frac{9}{8}Ml^2\dot{\theta}_1^2 \tag{2.178}$$

Considering next bar BC, we first define an elementary mass dm of the bar, on a distance ξ from the hinge B, with the matrix representation of its position vector

$$\underline{r}_{dm}(q,t) = \begin{bmatrix} 3l\ \sin\theta_1 + \xi\ \sin\theta_2 \\ 3l\ \cos\theta_1 - \xi\ \cos\theta_2 \end{bmatrix} \tag{2.179}$$

so, this gives

$$\underline{r}_{dm,q} = \begin{bmatrix} 3l\cos\theta_1 & \xi\cos\theta_2 \\ -3l\sin\theta_1 & \xi\sin\theta_2 \end{bmatrix} \tag{2.180}$$

Now, we have to use the product

$$(\underline{r}_{dm,q})^T (\underline{r}_{dm,q}) =$$

$$\begin{bmatrix} 9l^2 & 3l\xi(\cos\theta_1\cos\theta_2 - \sin\theta_1\sin\theta_2) \\ 3l\xi(\cos\theta_1\cos\theta_2 - \sin\theta_1\sin\theta_2) & \xi^2 \end{bmatrix} =$$

$$\begin{bmatrix} 9l^2 & 3l\xi\cos(\theta_1 + \theta_2) \\ 3l\xi\cos(\theta_1 + \theta_2) & \xi^2 \end{bmatrix} \tag{2.181}$$

Using this result in the basic expression for $\underline{M}$, with m_i being replaced by $dm = \frac{m}{2l}d\xi$ and the summation over all the masses by an integration over ξ from zero to $2l$, we find the following contribution of bar BC to $\underline{M}$

$$\underline{M}_{BC} = \int_{\xi=0}^{2l} \begin{bmatrix} 9l^2 & 3l\xi\cos(\theta_1+\theta_2) \\ 3l\xi\cos(\theta_1+\theta_2) & \xi^2 \end{bmatrix} \frac{m}{2l} \, d\xi =$$

$$\begin{bmatrix} 9ml^2 & 3ml^2\cos(\theta_1+\theta_2) \\ 3ml^2\cos(\theta_1+\theta_2) & \frac{4}{3}ml^2 \end{bmatrix} \tag{2.182}$$

Using again $T = \frac{1}{2}\,\dot{q}^T\,\underline{M}\,\dot{q}$, we obtain for the kinetic energy of bar BC

$$T_{BC} = \frac{9}{2}ml^2\dot{\theta}_1^2 + 3ml^2\dot{\theta}_1\dot{\theta}_2\cos(\theta_1+\theta_2) + \frac{2}{3}ml^2\dot{\theta}_2^2 \tag{2.183}$$

Finally, the resulting expression for $\underline{M}$ of the complete system can be obtained by adding the individual contributions of the bars AB and BC. So, we arrive at the total mass matrix of the system

$$\underline{M} = \begin{bmatrix} \frac{9}{4}(M+4m)l^2 & 3ml^2\cos(\theta_1+\theta_2) \\ 3ml^2\cos(\theta_1+\theta_2) & \frac{4}{3}ml^2 \end{bmatrix} \tag{2.184}$$

Because we are dealing with a system, consisting of a point mass and a rigid body for which the mass moment of inertia is well known, the kinetic energy can also be expressed as follows

$$T = \frac{1}{2}\,M\,\underline{v}_M^T\underline{v}_M + \frac{1}{2}\,m\,\underline{v}_Z^T\underline{v}_Z + \frac{1}{2}J_Z\,\dot{\theta}_2^2 \tag{2.185}$$

giving directly

$$T = T_{AB} + T_{BC} = T_0 + T_1 + T_2 \qquad \text{with} \qquad T_0 = 0, \quad T_1 = 0$$

$$T_2 = \frac{1}{2}\left[\frac{9}{4}(M+4m)l^2\,\dot{\theta}_1^2 + 6ml^2\cos(\theta_1+\theta_2)\,\dot{\theta}_1\dot{\theta}_2 + \frac{4}{3}ml^2\,\dot{\theta}_2^2\right] \tag{2.186}$$

The moment exerted by the torsional spring in point A can be considered to be an internal moment. The associated internal energy equals the elastic energy of the torsional spring which can be expressed as

$$U^{in} = \frac{1}{2}\,k_t\,\theta_1^2 \tag{2.187}$$

Because the gravity forces are the only conservative external forces for this system, their potential energy represents $V^{ex}(\underline{q})$ of the system. The potential energy of the gravity forces acting upon the bar BC with uniform mass distribution can be obtained by concentrating the mass m of

*BC in its midpoint Z and computing the potential energy of the result-
ing point mass. For bar AB the mass M has already been concentrated
in its midpoint. This gives*

$$V^{ex} = Mg(x_2)_M + mg(x_2)_Z = Mg\frac{3}{2}l\cos\theta_1 + mg(3l\cos\theta_1 - l\cos\theta_2)$$

$$(2.188)$$

*The external horizontal force F(t) acting in point C will have to be
taken into account in the column of non-conservative generalized forces.
The forces acting in the coupling hinge between bar AB and bar BC as
well as the forces acting in the coupling hinge between bar AB and
the support are constraint forces, because they result from geometric
constraints in the motion. However, the moments acting in the hinges
A and B are applied moments. Hence, also these moments will lead to
a contribution in the non-conservative generalized force column. All the
applied forces and -moments leading to the non-conservative generalized
force column are shown in Fig. 2.16. We can easily see that*

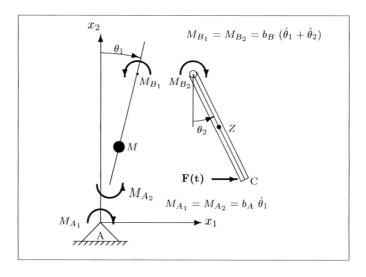

Fig. 2.16 Non-Conservative Loading Components

- *Force $\vec{F}$*

$$\underline{F} = \begin{bmatrix} F(t) \\ 0 \\ 0 \end{bmatrix}, \quad \underline{r}_C = \begin{bmatrix} 3l \sin\theta_1 + 2l \sin\theta_2 \\ 3l \cos\theta_1 - 2l \cos\theta_2 \\ 0 \end{bmatrix}$$

$$\underline{r}_{C,\underline{q}} = \begin{bmatrix} 3l \cos\theta_1 & 2l \cos\theta_2 \\ -3l \sin\theta_1 & 2l \sin\theta_2 \\ 0 & 0 \end{bmatrix} \qquad (2.189)$$

- *Hinge Moment $\vec{M}_{B_1}$*

$$\underline{M}_{B_1} = \begin{bmatrix} 0 \\ 0 \\ b_B(\dot{\theta}_1 + \dot{\theta}_2) \end{bmatrix}, \quad \underline{\theta}_{AB} = \begin{bmatrix} 0 \\ 0 \\ -\theta_1 \end{bmatrix}, \quad \underline{\theta}_{AB,\underline{q}} = \begin{bmatrix} 0 & 0 \\ 0 & 0 \\ -1 & 0 \end{bmatrix}$$

$$(2.190)$$

- *Hinge Moment $\vec{M}_{B_2}$*

$$\underline{M}_{B_2} = \begin{bmatrix} 0 \\ 0 \\ -b_B(\dot{\theta}_1 + \dot{\theta}_2) \end{bmatrix}, \quad \underline{\theta}_{BC} = \begin{bmatrix} 0 \\ 0 \\ \theta_2 \end{bmatrix}, \quad \underline{\theta}_{BC,\underline{q}} = \begin{bmatrix} 0 & 0 \\ 0 & 0 \\ 0 & 1 \end{bmatrix}$$

$$(2.191)$$

- *Hinge Moment $\vec{M}_{A_1}$*

$$\underline{M}_{A_1} = \begin{bmatrix} 0 \\ 0 \\ -b_A\dot{\theta}_1 \end{bmatrix}, \quad \underline{\theta}_{support} = \begin{bmatrix} 0 \\ 0 \\ 0 \end{bmatrix}, \quad \underline{\theta}_{support,\underline{q}} = \begin{bmatrix} 0 & 0 \\ 0 & 0 \\ 0 & 0 \end{bmatrix}$$

$$(2.192)$$

- *Hinge Moment $\vec{M}_{A_2}$*

$$\underline{M}_{A_2} = \begin{bmatrix} 0 \\ 0 \\ b_A\dot{\theta}_1 \end{bmatrix}, \quad \underline{\theta}_{AB} = \begin{bmatrix} 0 \\ 0 \\ -\theta_1 \end{bmatrix}, \quad \underline{\theta}_{AB,\underline{q}} = \begin{bmatrix} 0 & 0 \\ 0 & 0 \\ -1 & 0 \end{bmatrix}$$

$$(2.193)$$

So, for the (non-conservative) generalized force column we will get

$$\underline{Q}^{nc} = (\underline{r}_{C,\underline{q}})^T \underline{F} + (\underline{\theta}_{AB,\underline{q}})^T \underline{M}_{B_1} + (\underline{\theta}_{BC,\underline{q}})^T \underline{M}_{B_2}$$

$$+ (\underline{\theta}_{support,\underline{q}})^T \underline{M}_{A_1} + (\underline{\theta}_{AB,\underline{q}})^T \underline{M}_{A_2} \qquad (2.194)$$

$$= \begin{bmatrix} 3F(t)l \cos\theta_1 - b_B(\dot{\theta}_1 + \dot{\theta}_2) - b_A\dot{\theta}_1 \\ 2F(t)l \cos\theta_2 - b_B(\dot{\theta}_1 + \dot{\theta}_2) \end{bmatrix}$$

Both the generalized forces have dimension [Nm], which corresponds to the used generalized coordinates, both being rotations. As an alternative also the step-by-step appraoch can be followed to generate the column of generalized forces.

Next, we consider the Lagrange's equations of motion of this system. Using the expression for the kinetic energy of this system, the first term in the Lagrange's equations can be evaluated as follows

$$(T_{,\dot{\underline{q}}})^T = \left[\begin{array}{c} \frac{9}{4}(M+4m)\,l^2\dot{\theta}_1 + 3ml^2\dot{\theta}_2\cos(\theta_1+\theta_2) \\ m\dot{x}_A l\cos\theta_2 + 3ml^2\dot{\theta}_1\cos(\theta_1+\theta_2) + \frac{4}{3}ml^2\dot{\theta}_2 \end{array} \right] \quad (2.195)$$

$$\left[\frac{d}{dt}\left(T_{,\dot{\underline{q}}} \right) \right]^T$$

$$= \left[\begin{array}{c} \frac{9}{4}(M+4m)\,l^2\ddot{\theta}_1 + 3ml^2\ddot{\theta}_2\cos(\theta_1+\theta_2) \\ -3ml^2\dot{\theta}_2\left(\dot{\theta}_1+\dot{\theta}_2\right)\sin(\theta_1+\theta_2) \\ \hline \\ 3ml^2\ddot{\theta}_1\cos(\theta_1+\theta_2) \\ -3ml^2\dot{\theta}_1\left(\dot{\theta}_1+\dot{\theta}_2\right)\sin(\theta_1+\theta_2) + \frac{4}{3}ml^2\ddot{\theta}_2 \end{array} \right] \quad (2.196)$$

The second term becomes

$$(T_{,\underline{q}})^T = \left[\begin{array}{c} -3ml^2\dot{\theta}_1\dot{\theta}_2\sin(\theta_1+\theta_2) \\ -3ml^2\dot{\theta}_1\dot{\theta}_2\sin(\theta_1+\theta_2) \end{array} \right] \quad (2.197)$$

The third term can be derived from the potential energy function, resulting in

$$(V_{,\underline{q}})^T = \left[\begin{array}{c} k_t\theta_1 - \frac{3}{2}Mgl\sin\theta_1 - 3mgl\sin\theta_1 \\ mgl\sin\theta_2 \end{array} \right] \quad (2.198)$$

So, we obtain the Lagrange's equation of motion for this example in the form

$$\frac{9}{4}(M+4m)\,l^2\ddot{\theta}_1 + 3ml^2\ddot{\theta}_2\cos(\theta_1+\theta_2)$$

$$-3ml^2\dot{\theta}_2^2\sin(\theta_1+\theta_2) + k_t\theta_1 - \frac{3}{2}(M+2m)\,gl\sin\theta_1$$

$$-3F(t)l\cos\theta_1 + (b_A+b_B)\dot{\theta}_1 + b_B\dot{\theta}_2 = 0 \quad (2.199)$$

$$3ml^2\ddot{\theta}_1\cos(\theta_1+\theta_2) + \frac{4}{3}ml^2\ddot{\theta}_2 - 3ml^2\dot{\theta}_1^2\sin(\theta_1+\theta_2)$$

$$+mgl\sin\theta_2 - 2F(t)l\cos\theta_2 + b_B(\dot{\theta}_1+\dot{\theta}_2) = 0 \quad (2.200)$$

The coupled second-order differential equations of motion appear to contain a number of (strongly) **nonlinear** *terms.*

2.13 KINEMATIC CONSTRAINTS

2.13.1 Holonomic constraints

The derivation of the equations of motion in the preceeding sections has been based upon a choice of generalized coordinates q and virtual displacements δq that must be consistent with the kinematic constraints of the system. As a result, no information could be obtained about the corresponding forces. In Section 2.14 we will discuss a method which enables us to take into account the influence of kinematic constraints in the equations of motion. Before doing so, let us take a closer look at the problem of representing and classifying kinematic constraints. We consider a mechanical system for which we want to take into account the influence of a number of kinematic constraints in the equations of motion. Now, we tear off the (parts of the) system at the constraint positions and describe the position of the resulting system by n generalized coordinates $q_1, q_2, \ldots, q_n$. Next, we impose again the kinematic constraints at the above positions. This results in a number of kinematic constraint equations which generally contain the generalized coordinates $q_1, \ldots, q_n$, their time derivatives (generalized velocities) $\dot{q}_1, \ldots, \dot{q}_n$ and time t. In this subsection we consider the case that these kinematic constraint equations do not contain the velocities $\dot{q}_1, \ldots, \dot{q}_n$. In particular, we suppose that there are m independent kinematic constraint equations of the form

$$h_j (q_1, q_2, ..., q_n, t) = 0 \qquad (j = 1, 2, ..., m) \qquad (2.201)$$

Constraints of this form are known as *holonomic constraints*. In theory, one could use these equations to solve for m coordinates in terms of the $(n - m)$ remaining coordinates and time, thereby retaining only as many coordinates as there are degrees of freedom of the constrained system. Sometimes it is not feasible or even desirable to do this. In these instances one can use an approach such as the Lagrange's multipliers method, as we shall see in Section 2.14. More frequently, one searches for a set of generalized coordinates which can assume arbitrary values without violating the kinematic constraints, thereby permitting a complete description of the configuration of the system without the use of auxiliary equations of constraint. For a system having only holonomic constraints, it is always possible to find such a set of independent generalized coordinates. In fact, this is what we have done implicitly in the previous sections. The number of coordinates in this case is equal to the number of degrees of freedom.

Example 2.23

As an example of holonomic constraints, we consider the double pendulum system of example 2.3 on page 41, see Fig. 2.3. According to the foregoing procedure we tear off the system at the constraint positions O and A. We choose to represent the position of bar OA by the coordinates *of its centre of mass $[(x_1)_{C1}, (x_2)_{C1}]$ and the rotation θ_1 and the position of bar AB by the coordinates of its centre of mass $[(x_1)_{C2}, (x_2)_{C2}]$ and the rotation θ_2. Taking into account that the lengths of the bars remain unchanged, the kinematic constraint equations at O and A can be expressed as*

$$
\begin{aligned}
(x_1)_O &= (x_1)_{C1} - \tfrac{l_1}{2}\cos\theta_1 = 0 \\
(x_2)_O &= (x_2)_{C1} - \tfrac{l_1}{2}\sin\theta_1 = 0 \\
(x_1)_A &= (x_1)_{C1} + \tfrac{l_1}{2}\cos\theta_1 = (x_1)_{C2} - \tfrac{l_2}{2}\cos\theta_2 \\
(x_2)_A &= (x_2)_{C1} + \tfrac{l_1}{2}\sin\theta_1 = (x_2)_{C2} - \tfrac{l_2}{2}\sin\theta_2
\end{aligned}
\tag{2.202}
$$

Thus, the six position coordinates introduced for the unconstrained system have to satisfy four constraint equations, so that the system has only two degrees of freedom, as discussed already in example 2.3.

Example 2.24

As another example of holonomic constraints we consider the single pendulum system with moving support of example 2.18 on page 71, see Fig. 2.12. We choose to represent the position of the rigid bar by the coordinates $(x_1)_C$, $(x_2)_C$ and θ. Taking into account that the position of the support is prescribed, the kinematic constraint equations at the support can be expressed as

$$
\begin{aligned}
(x_1)_A &= (x_1)_C - l\cos\theta = s(t) \\
(x_2)_A &= (x_2)_C - l\sin\theta = 0
\end{aligned}
\tag{2.203}
$$

Thus, the three position coordinates introduced for the unconstrained system have to satisfy two constraint equations, so that the system has only one degree of freedom, as discussed already in example 2.18. We observe that for this example, the first of the constraint equations 2.203 contains the time explicitly.

Example 2.25

We consider the homogeneous rigid disc with radius R of example 2.12 on page 63, see Fig. 2.11. The disk is rolling without slip in the vertical plane as shown in the figure. The no-slip condition at the contact point P can be written as

$$
\dot{x}_P = \dot{u} - R\dot{\varphi} = 0
\tag{2.204}
$$

where u is the horizontal displacement of the centre of mass of the disk, while φ is its angle of rotation. At first sight, it looks as if the kinematic constraint (2.204) is not holonomic, because the velocities $\dot{u}$

and $\dot{\varphi}$ appear in (2.204). However, this equation can be integrated with respect to time, yielding the holonomic constraint equation

$$u \ - \ R \, \varphi = const. \tag{2.205}$$

Consequently, this system is a one-degree-of-freedom system.

Within the category of holonomic constraints two classes are being distinguished. Holonomic constraints which are explicitly depending upon time are known as *rheonomic constraints*. Holonomic constraints which do not depend explicitly upon time are called *scleronomic constraints*. In the examples 2.23 and 2.25 the kinematic constraints can easily be identified to be scleronomic, whereas in the example 2.24 they are rheonomic.

Finally, in view of the matrix notation used in this chapter, we collect the m holonomic constraint equations 2.201 in the column matrix

$$\underline{h}(\underline{q}, t) = \underline{0} \tag{2.206}$$

Later, in Section 2.13.2, we will need the first variation $\delta\underline{h}$ of $\underline{h}$ if q varies with δq. Using (2.45), we obtain

$$\delta\underline{h} = \underline{R} \, \delta\underline{q} = \underline{0} \tag{2.207}$$

where the $(m \times n)$ matrix $\underline{R}$ is given by

$$\underline{R} = \underline{R}\left(\underline{q}, t\right) = \underline{h}_{,q} \tag{2.208}$$

We conclude that for the derivation of (2.207) no distinction is needed between rheonomic and scleronomic constraints, because time remains constant during the variation process.

2.13.2 Nonholonomic constraints

Now, let us consider kinematic constraints which cannot be expressed in the form of (2.201). Constraints of this type are known as *nonholonomic constraints*. Nonholonomic kinematic constraints often appear in the form of linear combinations of the velocities

$$\sum_{i=1}^{n} r_{ji} \, \dot{q}_i = rh_j \qquad (j = 1, 2, ..., m) \tag{2.209}$$

where the coefficients r_{ji} $(j = 1, 2, \ldots, m;\ i = 1, 2, \ldots, n)$ and the right-hand sides rh_j $(j = 1, 2, \ldots, m)$ are, in general, functions of $\underline{q}$ and t

$$r_{ji} = r_{ji}\left(\underline{q}, t\right) \qquad , \qquad rh_j = rh_j\left(\underline{q}, t\right) \tag{2.210}$$

Furthermore, if the constraints are nonholonomic, the expressions (2.209) are characterized by being not integrable with respect to time. It can be seen that, if they were integrable with respect to time, the integrated forms of the constraint equations would be the same as those given in (2.201), and we have previously classed constraints of this type as holonomic. As a result of not being able to integrate (2.209), one cannot eliminate coordinates explicitly by using the equations of constraint. Therefore we find that systems containing nonholonomic constraints always require more coordinates for their description than there are degrees of freedom.

Example 2.26

We consider the motion of a rigid bar with centre of mass C in the horizontal x_1, x_2 plane, see Fig. 2.17. During the motion of the bar, its fixed point A (on a distance a from C), is constrained to have zero velocity in the direction perpendicular to the line CA. Describing the

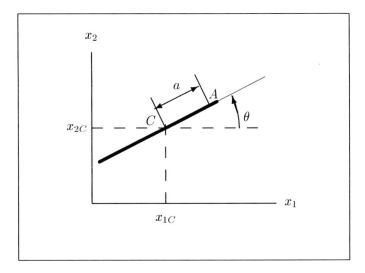

Fig. 2.17 Motion of rigid bar in x_1, x_2 plane

position of the bar by means of the coordinates x_{1C}, x_{2C} and the rotation θ, see Fig. 2.17, we can easily express the kinematic constraint equation resulting from this restriction as

$$-\dot{x}_{1C}\ \sin\theta + \dot{x}_{2C}\ \cos\theta + a\ \dot{\theta} = 0 \qquad (2.211)$$

We will now prove that this is a nonholonomic constraint. To this end, we write (2.211) in the form of a differential relationship

$$C_1\ dx_{1C} + C_2\ dx_{2C} + C_3\ d\theta = 0 \qquad (2.212)$$

with

$$\left.\begin{array}{l} C_1 = C_1\left(x_{1C}, x_{2C}, \theta\right) = -\sin\theta \\ C_2 = C_2\left(x_{1C}, x_{2C}, \theta\right) = \cos\theta \\ C_3 = C_3\left(x_{1C}, x_{2C}, \theta\right) = a \end{array}\right\} \qquad (2.213)$$

Integrability of (2.212), after multiplication with a factor
$\mu = \mu\left(x_{1C}, x_{2C}, \theta\right)$, *requires that*

$$\frac{\partial}{\partial x_{2C}}\left(\mu C_1\right) = \frac{\partial}{\partial x_{1C}}\left(\mu C_2\right) \qquad (2.214)$$

$$\frac{\partial}{\partial \theta}\left(\mu C_2\right) = \frac{\partial}{\partial x_{2C}}\left(\mu C_3\right) \qquad (2.215)$$

$$\frac{\partial}{\partial x_{1C}}\left(\mu C_3\right) = \frac{\partial}{\partial \theta}\left(\mu C_1\right) \qquad (2.216)$$

*Considering $C_3 \times (2.214) + A \times (2.215) + B \times (2.216)$ and dividing through
by μ, we obtain*

$$C_1\left(\frac{\partial C_2}{\partial \theta} - \frac{\partial C_3}{\partial x_{2C}}\right) + C_2\left(\frac{\partial C_3}{\partial x_{1C}} - \frac{\partial C_1}{\partial \theta}\right) + C_3\left(\frac{\partial C_1}{\partial x_{2C}} - \frac{\partial C_2}{\partial x_{1C}}\right) = 0 \qquad (2.217)$$

*Inserting (2.213) into (2.217), we can see that integrability of (2.212)
would require $\sin^2\theta + \cos^2\theta$ to be zero, which is not true. Hence, (2.212)
is not integrable and this constraint is nonholonomic. It is remarked
that the motion of the rigid bar with the above constraint can be considered to be a reasonable approximation for the motion of a sledge in
snow.*

As for holonomic constraints, we will express nonholonomic constraints in
matrix notation by collecting the m nonholonomic constraint equations (2.209
in the column matrix

$$\underline{R}\,\underline{\dot{q}} = \underline{rh} \qquad (2.218)$$

where the $(m \times n)$ matrix

$$\underline{R} = \underline{R}\left(\underline{q}, t\right) \qquad (2.219)$$

contains the elements $r_{ji}(\underline{q}, t)$ of (2.209), whereas the column

$$\underline{rh} = \underline{rh}\left(\underline{q}, t\right) \qquad (2.220)$$

contains the elements $rh_j\left(\underline{q}, t\right)$ of (2.209). Later, in Section 2.14, we will
need an expression of the constraint equations (2.209) in terms of virtual
displacements in stead of in terms of velocities. Rewriting (2.218) as

$$\underline{R}\,d\underline{q} = \underline{rh}\,dt \qquad (2.221)$$

taking for dq the virtual displacements δq and recalling that dt is zero in a virtual displacement, it can be seen easily that this expression takes the form

$$\underline{R}\,\delta\underline{q} = \underline{0} \tag{2.222}$$

Comparing (2.207) and (2.222), we conclude that if the kinematic constraints are expressed in terms of virtual displacements, no distinction appears between holonomic and nonholonomic constraints.

2.14   LAGRANGE'S EQUATIONS WITH CONSTRAINTS; LAGRANGE'S MULTIPLIERS

In the derivation of the Lagrange's equation of motion in Section 2.12 we found that there must be no more (generalized) coordinates used in the analysis than there are degrees of freedom if we are to be able to write the equations of motion in the standard form of (2.153) or (2.156). Also, we saw in the preceding subsection that the nonintegrable nature of the equations of constraint in the case of nonholonomic constraints makes it necessary to have more coordinates than degrees of freedom. In this section, we introduce the method of Lagrange's multipliers to allow us to take into account the influence of kinematic constraints in the Lagrange's equations of motion. To illustrate the method of Lagrange's multipliers, we first consider a system whose motion is described by two coordinates, q_1 and q_2. At any instant of time, the variations of q_1 and q_2 must meet the following kinematic constraint condition

$$r_{11}\,\delta q_1 + r_{12}\,\delta q_2 = 0 \tag{2.223}$$

This constraint equation results from (2.222) in case of two coordinates and one kinematic constraint. It is recalled that the kinematic constraint may be either holonomic or nonholonomic. We can repeat the elaboration of the principle of virtual work for this system identical to the treatment in Sections 2.6-2.7 and write the transformed principle of virtual work (2.152) for this system in the following abbreviated form

$$le_1\,\delta q_1 + le_2\,\delta q_2 = 0 \tag{2.224}$$

Here, le_1 and le_2 represent the first two elements of the column expression between the square brackets of the left-hand side of (2.152). In fact, le_1 and le_2 are the left-hand sides of the first two Lagrange's equation of motion contained in (2.153) or (2.156). Now, it cannot be concluded anymore from (2.224) that $le_1 = 0$ and $le_2 = 0$, yielding Lagrange's equations of motion in the standard form. This is because the virtual displacements δq_1 and δq_2 are not independent anymore as they have to satisfy the kinematic constraint condition (2.223). In fact, it results from (2.223) that

$$\delta q_2 = -\frac{r_{11}}{r_{12}}\,\delta q_1 \tag{2.225}$$

Substituting this dependency between δq_1 and δq_2 into the principle of virtual work (2.224), we obtain

$$\left(le_1 - le_2 \, \frac{r_{11}}{r_{12}}\right) \, \delta q_1 = 0 \tag{2.226}$$

Because this equation has to be satisfied for arbitrary values of δq_1, we conclude that

$$le_1 - le_2 \, \frac{r_{11}}{r_{12}} = 0 \tag{2.227}$$

or

$$\frac{le_1}{r_{11}} = \frac{le_2}{r_{12}} =: \lambda_1 \tag{2.228}$$

Here λ_1 is a newly defined unknown quantity, called a *Lagrange's multiplier*. By means of λ_1 the left equality in (2.228)can be replaced by the following two equations

$$le_1 = \lambda_1 \, r_{11} \tag{2.229}$$
$$le_2 = \lambda_1 \, r_{12} \tag{2.230}$$

The equations (2.229) and (2.230) can be interpreted as two modified Lagrange's equations of motion for the two coordinates q_1 and q_2. Of course, in (2.229) and (2.230) also the Lagrange's multiplier λ_1 is unknown, but it should be noticed that (2.229) and (2.230) have to be supplemented with the kinematic constraint condition (2.223). This results in three equations for the three unknowns q_1 and q_2 and λ_1. The modified Lagrange's equation of motion (2.229) and (2.230) can be related to a modified principle of virtual work as follows

$$(le_1 - \lambda_1 r_{11}) \, \delta q_1 + (le_2 - \lambda_2 r_{12}) \, \delta q_2 = 0 \tag{2.231}$$

If δq_1 and δq_2 can be considered to be completely independent, then the modified principle of virtual work (2.231) yields the independent modified Lagrange's equations of motion (2.229) and (2.230). Conversely, this implies that if the equations of Lagrange are modified according to the above procedure, then the virtual displacements δq_1 and δq_2 can be considered to be completely independent. This means that in that case q_1 and q_2 can be considered to be generalized coordinates of the system.

The above procedure for supplementing a kinematic constraint condition to the Lagrange's equations of motion for a system with two coordinates can be easily extended to supplementing a kinematic constraint condition to a system with n coordinates. Also, the generalization to supplementing m kinematic constraint conditions to a system with n coordinates is quite simple, because each of these constraint conditions can be supplemented separately. Let us denote the m kinematic constraint conditions as follows

$$\left. \begin{array}{l} r_{11} \, \delta q_1 + r_{12} \, \delta q_2 + \ldots + r_{1n} \, \delta q_n = 0 \\ r_{21} \, \delta q_1 + r_{22} \, \delta q_2 + \ldots + r_{2n} \, \delta q_n = 0 \\ \quad \vdots \qquad \quad \vdots \qquad \qquad \vdots \qquad \vdots \\ r_{m1} \, \delta q_1 + r_{m2} \, \delta q_2 + \ldots + r_{mn} \, \delta q_n = 0 \end{array} \right\} \tag{2.232}$$

These kinematic constraint conditions can be supplemented to the principle of virtual work (2.152) by multiplying the left-hand sides of (2.232) with independent Lagrange's multipliers $\lambda_1, \lambda_2, \ldots, \lambda_m$ and adding the resulting expressions to (2.152). Collecting the coefficients r_{ji} in (2.232) in the $(m \times n)$ matrix $\underline{R}$ defined in (2.222), and collecting the Lagrange's multipliers $\lambda_1, \lambda_2, \ldots, \lambda_m$ in the column matrix $\underline{\lambda}$, we can easily show that this modified principle of virtual work results in the following modified Lagrange's equation of motion

$$\frac{d}{dt}\left(L_{,\dot{q}}\right) - L_{,q} = \left(\underline{Q}^{nc}\right)^{T} + \left(\underline{R}^{T}\underline{\lambda}\right)^{T} \tag{2.233}$$

Considering the right-hand side of (2.233), we conclude that the term $\underline{R}^{T}\underline{\lambda}$ can be interpreted to be a column of generalized forces. In fact, this term represents the column of generalized forces due to the kinematic constraints. Consequently, the modified Lagrange's equations of motion (2.233) yield information about the magnitude of the constraint forces.

The modified Lagrange's equations of motion (2.233) constitute n second-order differential equations for $(n + m)$ unknowns, namely, the n q_i's and the m λ_j's. In order to be solvable, these equations have to be supplemented with the m algebraic constraint conditions contained in (2.222). Considering (2.233) and (2.222) together, we have replaced a system having originally n degrees of freedom by one with $(n + m)$ unknowns, considering the λ_j's as additional variables. This may not seem like progress, but quite often this procedure results in simpler equations. Also, the symmetry of the problem is preserved, since there are no preferred coordinates while others are eliminated. In addition, of course, one obtains the constraint forces in the process of obtaining the solution.

Example 2.27

We consider again the system shown in Fig 2.17 of example 2.26, p 89. The kinetic energy of the rigid bar is given by

$$T = \frac{1}{2}m\left(\dot{x}_{1C}^2 + \dot{x}_{2C}^2\right) + \frac{1}{2}J_C\,\dot{\theta}^2 \tag{2.234}$$

where m is the mass of the bar, while J_C is its mass moment of inertia with respect to C. Because the x_1, x_2 plane of motion is horizontal, the potential energy takes a constant value and hence, it disappears from the Lagrange's equations of motion. We assume that there are no nonconservative forces, except those imposing the kinematic constraint condition (2.211). In that case $\underline{Q}^{nc} = \underline{0}$ in (2.233). Because there is only one kinematic constraint equation, there is only one Lagrange's multiplier λ and the matrix $\underline{R}$ defined in (2.222) degenerates into a row matrix which takes the form

$$\underline{R} = [-\sin\theta \qquad \cos\theta \qquad a] \tag{2.235}$$

Inserting (2.234) and (2.235) into the modified Lagrange's equations of motion (2.233), we obtain the following differential equations of motion

$$\left.\begin{array}{c} m\,\ddot{x}_{1C} = -\lambda\sin\theta \\ m\,\ddot{x}_{2C} = \lambda\cos\theta \\ J\,\ddot{\theta} = \lambda a \end{array}\right\} \qquad (2.236)$$

It can be concluded immediately from these equations that the Lagrange's multiplier λ can be identified as a force acting in point A of the bar (see Fig. 2.17) in perpendicular direction. In fact, this is the resulting force which is required to impose the kinematic constraint condition in point A.

2.15   EQUILIBRIUM POSITIONS AND THEIR STABILITY

Let us return to Lagrange's equations as expressed by (2.153). These equations in general constitute a set of nonhomogeneous ordinary differential equations which generally are nonlinear and also can have time-dependent coefficients as shown in the last two examples of Section 2.12. Closed form solutions of such a set of nonlinear equations do not exist in general. However under particular circumstances (2.153) admit important special solutions.

In this section we will discuss special solutions which are of particular interest, namely, the constant or time-independent solutions for which $\underline{q} = \underline{q}_o =$ constant (i.e. time-independent) and $\dot{\underline{q}} = \dot{\underline{q}}_o = \underline{0}$. Such solutions are known as *equilibrium positions* in the configurations space spanned by the general coordinates $\underline{q}^T = [q_1, q_2, ..., q_n]$. It follows directly that for such solutions $\ddot{\underline{q}} = \ddot{\underline{q}}_o = \underline{0}$, which explains why these solutions are known as equilibrium positions in the configuration space. We will now address the question as to how to determine these equilibrium positions for a given dynamical system, corresponding to constant solutions $\underline{q}_o$ of the Lagrange's equations of motion. If we evaluate the first two terms in the left-hand side of these equations (2.153), i.e. the terms $\frac{d}{dt}(T_{,\dot{q}}) - T_{,q}$, for the general kinetic energy expression, (2.112), and for a constant solution $\underline{q}_o$, the only remaining terms appear to be $T_{o,q}$ and $-\underline{m}_{,t}^T$. Because we are searching for a time-independent solution, these parts are not allowed to depend explicitly on time. So, the influence of prescribed coordinates has to be removed. This generally will result in skipping the term $\underline{m}_{,t}^T$ and removing the influence of prescibed coordinates from T_o.

So, the only remaning terms from the left-hand side of Lagrange's equations will be $V_{,q} - T_{o,q}$. For $V_{,q}$ to be time-independent, the influence of prescribed coordinates has to be removed also from the potential energy. E.g. in example 2.12 of the rolling cylinder on page 63 this means that we have to accept the prescribed displacement $x(t)$ to be assigned an arbitrary constant value (for example zero).

The generalized nonconservative forces Q^{nc} in the Lagrange's equations of motion can be split into forces depending explicitly on time and forces not depending explicitly on time. The generalized forces depending explicitly on time, which are denoted by $Q(t)$, must be removed from the system in order to be able to determine a constant solution of equations (2.153). The remaining generalized nonconservative forces depend on the generalized velocities and, consequently, they are zero for constant solutions $\underline{q}_o$.

It can be concluded from the above discussion that for a constant solution $\underline{q}_o$ the Lagrange's equations of motion degenerate to

$$V^{*},_{\underline{q}} = V,_{\underline{q}} - T_o,_{\underline{q}} \; = \; \underline{0}^T \tag{2.237}$$

where the quantity

$$V^{*}(\underline{q}, t) \; = \; V(\underline{q}, t) \; - \; T_o(\underline{q}, t) \tag{2.238}$$

is called the *modified potential* or, alternatively the *effective potential*. Equations (2.237) represent the equilibrium equations, which imply that the modified potential V^{*} has a stationary value at an equilibrium position. In general (2.237) constitute a set of nonlinear **algebraic** equations for determining these equilibrium positions. The equations generally are nonlinear having more than one solution and, consequently, there may be several equilibrium positions.

In the particular case in which $T_o,_{\underline{q}}$ vanishes, the equilibrium position can be found from the familiar equilibrium equations

$$V,_{\underline{q}} \; = \; \underline{0}^T \tag{2.239}$$

which states that for systems with $T_o,_q = \underline{0}^T$ the potential energy V has a stationary value at an equilibrium position. An important category of systems for which this is the case consists of systems that *do not undergo overall motion and do not have prescribed coordinates.*

Example 2.28

We consider the double pendulum system with two masses of example 2.13 on page 66, for which the potential energy was derived as

$$V = -m_1 g[l_1 \cos\theta_1] - m_2 g[l_1 \cos\theta_1 + l_2 \cos(\theta_1 + \theta_2)] \tag{2.240}$$

Application of (2.239) yields the following two algebraic equilibrium equations

$$\begin{aligned} V,_{\theta_1} &= (m_1 + m_2)g l_1 \sin\theta_1 + m_2 g l_2 \sin(\theta_1 + \theta_2) = 0 \\ V,_{\theta_2} &= m_2 g l_2 \sin(\theta_1 + \theta_2) = 0 \end{aligned} \tag{2.241}$$

These equations possess four physically independent sets of solutions, namely

$$(A): \ \theta_1 = 0, \ \ \theta_2 = 0 \qquad (B): \ \theta_1 = 0, \ \ \theta_2 = \pi$$
$$(C): \ \theta_1 = \pi, \ \ \theta_2 = 0 \qquad (D): \ \theta_1 = \pi, \ \ \theta_2 = \pi \qquad (2.242)$$

These equilibrium positions are graphically shown in Fig. 2.18.

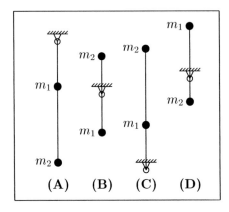

Fig. 2.18   Equilibrium positions for double pendulum system

Example 2.29

Next, we return to the two-dimensional, mixed pendulum system introduced in problem 2.22 on page 80. The potential energy for this problem appeared to be

$$V = \frac{1}{2} \, k_t \, \theta_1^2 + Mg\frac{3}{2}l \cos \theta_1 + mg(3l \cos \theta_1 - l \cos \theta_2) \qquad (2.243)$$

Application of $V,_q = \underline{0}$ yields the following algebraic equilibrium equations

$$k_t\theta_1 - \tfrac{3}{2}(M + 2m)gl \sin \theta_1 = 0$$

$$\qquad (2.244)$$

$$mgl \sin \theta_2 = 0$$

We will now analytically solve these equations. To get a simple solution we just choose some **specific value for the stiffness of the torsional spring** *at point A, namely*

$$k_t = \frac{3}{\pi}(M + 2m)gl \qquad (2.245)$$

In that case, we get

$$\sin \theta_1 = \frac{2}{\pi} \, \theta_1 \qquad and \qquad \sin \theta_2 = 0 \qquad (2.246)$$

We can easily see that the second possesses two physically independent solutions, namely

$$\theta_2 = 0 \quad and \quad \theta_2 = \pi \tag{2.247}$$

The solutions of the first equation can for example be found graphically by plotting $\sin\theta_1$ and $\frac{2}{\pi}\theta_1$ versus θ_1 and look for intersections as shown in Fig 2.19. It can be concluded from Fig. 2.19 that the solutions are

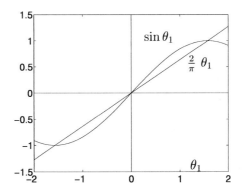

Fig. 2.19 Graphical determination equilibrium points

$$\theta_1 = -\frac{\pi}{2} \quad , \quad \theta_1 = 0 \quad , \quad \theta_1 = \frac{\pi}{2} \tag{2.248}$$

Because the equilibrium positions for $\theta_1 = -\pi/2$ do not differ physically from those for $\theta_1 = \pi/2$, we get the following four physically independent equilibrium positions

$$\begin{array}{llll} \theta_1 = 0 & , & \theta_2 = 0 & ; & \theta_1 = \frac{\pi}{2} & , & \theta_2 = 0 \\ \theta_1 = 0 & , & \theta_2 = \pi & ; & \theta_1 = \frac{\pi}{2} & , & \theta_2 = \pi \end{array} \tag{2.249}$$

These equilibrium positions are depicted schematically in Fig. 2.20.

In the final part of this section we will give an introductory discussion of the **stability** of the calculated equilibrium positions. The stability question of interest is whether a slight perturbation of a dynamical system from an equilibrium position will produce a motion remaining in the neighbourhood of that position or a motion tending to leave that position. We will address this question for the corresponding conservative system, i.e. the system for

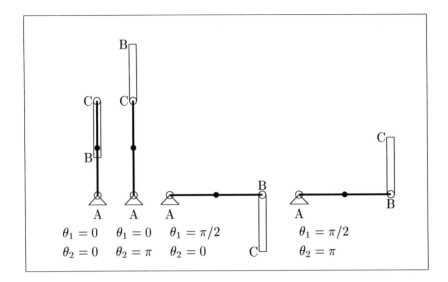

Fig. 2.20 Equilibrium positions

which also in the dynamic case all nonconservative forces are *not* taken into account in this introductory stability analysis.

Let us consider an equilibrium position $\underline{q} = \underline{q}_0$ of the conservative dynamical system defined above. We slightly perturb the system from its equilibrium position by imposing the initial generalized velocities $\underline{\dot{q}}_{in}$ to the system. This slight initial perturbation results in the kinetic energy $T = T(\underline{q}_o, \underline{\dot{q}}_{in})$. Now, if during the subsequent motion the kinetic energy increases, the equilibrium position is called **unstable**. If, during the subsequent motion, the kinetic energy decreases, then the equilibrium position is called **stable**. We elaborate the consequences of this stability definition by considering the **energy balance** for the **conservative** system.

Intermezzo

In the absence of prescribed coordinates we are dealing with the situation that $V = V(\underline{q})$ which means that

$$\frac{dV}{dt} = \underline{\dot{q}}^T \, (V,\underline{q})^T \tag{2.250}$$

It follows from (2.112) with $\vec{r}_{i,t} = \vec{0}$ that the kinetic energy becomes

$$T = \frac{1}{2} \, \underline{\dot{q}}^T \underline{M} \, \underline{\dot{q}} \tag{2.251}$$

For this function, which is quadratic in the generalize velocities, we can derive that

$$2\,T = \dot{\underline{q}}^T\,(T_{,\dot{\underline{q}}})^T \qquad (2.252)$$

leading to

$$2\,\frac{dT}{dt} = \dot{\underline{q}}^T\,\frac{d}{dt}(T_{,\dot{\underline{q}}})^T + \ddot{\underline{q}}^T\,(T_{,\dot{\underline{q}}})^T \qquad (2.253)$$

Because for a conservative system T does not depend explicitly on time, so that $T = T(\underline{q}, \dot{\underline{q}})$, we can also write

$$\frac{dT}{dt} = \dot{\underline{q}}^T\,(T_{,\underline{q}})^T + \ddot{\underline{q}}^T\,(T_{,\dot{\underline{q}}})^T \qquad (2.254)$$

If we next subtract (2.254) from (2.253), we get

$$\frac{dT}{dt} = \dot{\underline{q}}^T\,[\frac{d}{dt}(T_{,\dot{\underline{q}}})^T - (T_{,\underline{q}})^T] \qquad (2.255)$$

Now, premultiplying the transposed of the Lagrange's equations of motion (2.153) by $\dot{\underline{q}}^T$, and using (2.255) and (2.250), we conclude that

$$\frac{d}{dt}\,[T + V] = 0 \qquad (2.256)$$

This finally leads to the well known energy balance equation for conservative systems

$$T + V = \textbf{constant} \qquad (2.257)$$

So, for a conservative system we can use the fact that the sum of kinetic energy and potential energy will be constant for all t.

Denoting the generalized coordinates and the generalized velocities in a *slightly perturbed position* also by $\underline{q}$ and $\dot{\underline{q}}$ respectively, we can express the energy balance equation as follows

$$T(\underline{q}, \dot{\underline{q}}) + V(\underline{q}) = T(\underline{q}_o, \dot{\underline{q}}_{in}) + V(\underline{q}_o) \qquad (2.258)$$

Rewriting this equation as

$$V(\underline{q}) - V(\underline{q}_o) = T(\underline{q}_o, \dot{\underline{q}}_{in}) - T(\underline{q}, \dot{\underline{q}}) \qquad (2.259)$$

we arrive at the following *necessary* condition for the equilibrium position $\underline{q} = \underline{q}_o$ to be stable in the above sense

$$V(\underline{q}) - V(\underline{q}_o) > 0 \qquad (2.260)$$

for all possible *admissible small perturbations* $(\underline{q} - \underline{q}_o)$ from the equilibrium position. This shows that a stable equilibrium position corresponds to a local minimum of the potential energy. In order to specify the consequence of stability condition (2.260) we expand the potential energy in the form of a Taylor series in the neighbourhood of the equilibrium position. Using (2.32) we can write

$$V(\underline{q}) = V(\underline{q}_o) + (V,\underline{q})_{\underline{q}_o} \underline{q}_1 + \frac{1}{2} \underline{q}_1^T \left[(V,\underline{q})^T,\underline{q}\right]_{\underline{q}_o} \underline{q}_1 + \dots \qquad (2.261)$$

where the column $\underline{q}_1(t) = \underline{q}(t) - \underline{q}_o$ contains the perturbations of the generalized coordinates from the equilibrium position. Using the fact that according to (2.239), $(V,\underline{q})_{\underline{q}_o} = \underline{0}^T$, we can write this expression as

$$V(\underline{q}) = V(\underline{q}_o) + \frac{1}{2} \underline{q}_1^T \underline{K}_o \underline{q}_1 + \dots \qquad (2.262)$$

Here the matrix $\underline{K}_o$ with *stiffness coeffficients* k_{ij}

$$\underline{K}_o = [k_{ij}] = \left[(V,\underline{q})^T,\underline{q}\right]_{\underline{q}_o} \qquad (2.263)$$

is known as the **symmetric stiffness matrix** related to the equilibrium position $\underline{q} = \underline{q}_o$. Inserting (2.262) into the stability condition (2.260), we see that

$$V(\underline{q}) - V(\underline{q}_o) = \frac{1}{2} \underline{q}_1^T \underline{K}_o \underline{q}_1 + \dots > 0 \quad \text{for} \quad \underline{q}_1 \neq \underline{0} \qquad (2.264)$$

Because for sufficiently small values of $\|\underline{q}_1\|$, in the right side of the equality sign of (2.264) the quadratic term in $\underline{q}_1$ is dominating, we conclude from (2.260) that

$$\underline{q}_1^T \underline{K}_o \underline{q}_1 > 0 \quad \text{for} \quad \underline{q}_1 \neq \underline{0} \qquad (2.265)$$

Hence a necessary condition for an equilibrium position to be stable is that the symmetric stiffness matrix is **positive definite**. Here, it is recalled from linear algebra that a necessary and sufficient condition for a real symmetric matrix $\underline{K}_o$ to be positive definite is for all the principal minor determinants of $\underline{K}_o$ to be positive. Mathematically, these conditions can be written in the form

$$\det[k_{rs}] > 0, \quad r, s = 1, 2, \dots, m; \quad m = 1, 2, \dots, n \qquad (2.266)$$

This implies that at least all the diagonal terms should be positive but this is not sufficient. For a *diagonal matrix* however we conclude that if all diagonal terms are positive, then the stiffness matrix $\underline{K}_o$ must be positive definite. Another alternative statement of a necessary and sufficient condition for a real symmetric matrix to be positive definite is for all the eigenvalues to be positive. We will return to eigenvalues of a matrix in the next chapter.

We have seen before that for systems with some type of overall motion not the potential energy $V(q)$, but the modified potential $V^*(q) = V(q) - T_o(q)$ has to be used to determine the equilibrium positions of the system. So, it will not be surprising that for the evaluation of the stability of these equilibrium positions again the effective potential $V^*(q)$ has to be used. This means that we have to look whether the *effective stiffness matrix*, defined as

$$\underline{K}_o^* = \left[(V^*,\underline{q})^T,\underline{q} \right]_{\underline{q}_o} \qquad (2.267)$$

will be positive definite or not.

Example 2.30

We consider again the double pendulum system with two masses from example 2.28 on page 95, for which equilibrium positions have been obtained in (2.242). The second derivatives of the potential energy with respect to the generalized coordinates θ_1 and θ_2 can be obtained from (2.241)

$$V,\underline{qq} = \begin{bmatrix} V,_{\theta_1\theta_1} & V,_{\theta_1\theta_2} \\ V,_{\theta_2\theta_1} & V,_{\theta_2\theta_2} \end{bmatrix} \qquad \textit{with}$$

$$V,_{\theta_1\theta_1} = (m_1 + m_2)gl_1\cos\theta_1 + m_2gl_2\cos(\theta_1 + \theta_2)$$

$$V,_{\theta_2\theta_2} = m_2gl_2\cos(\theta_1 + \theta_2) \qquad\qquad (2.268)$$

$$V,_{\theta_1\theta_2} = V,_{\theta_2\theta_1} = m_2gl_2\cos(\theta_1 + \theta_2)$$

If we next calculate the stiffness matrix $\underline{K}_o$ for each of the four equilibrium positions given in (2.242), we get

$$(A): \quad \underline{K}_o = \begin{bmatrix} (m_1 + m_2)gl_1 + m_2gl_2 & ; & m_2gl_2 \\ m_2gl_2 & ; & m_2gl_2 \end{bmatrix}$$

$$(B): \quad \underline{K}_o = \begin{bmatrix} (m_1 + m_2)gl_1 - m_2g(l_1 - l_2) & ; & -m_2gl_2 \\ -m_2gl_2 & ; & -m_2gl_2 \end{bmatrix}$$

$$(C): \quad \underline{K}_o = \begin{bmatrix} -(m_1 + m_2)gl_1 - m_2gl_2 & ; & -m_2gl_2 \\ -m_2gl_2 & ; & -m_2gl_2 \end{bmatrix}$$

$$(D): \quad \underline{K}_o = \begin{bmatrix} -(m_1 + m_2)gl_1 + m_2gl_2 & ; & m_2gl_2 \\ m_2gl_2 & ; & m_2gl_2 \end{bmatrix}$$

$$(2.269)$$

The stiffness matrix $\underline{K}_o$ for situation (A) clearly is positive definite so this is a stable equilibrium position. Looking at the graphical representation shown in Fig. 2.18 this appears to be trivial. Both the stiffness *matrices for the situations (B) and (C) have at least one negative diagonal element ($\underline{K}_o[2,2]$) so that these equilibrium positions are unstable. This also seems to be obvious when looking at the corresponding representations in Fig. 2.18. For the last situation (D) both diagonal terms of the stiffness matrix will be positive if $m_2 l_2 > (m_1 + m_2) l_1$. However even then the determinant D of this stiffness matrix, which is $D = -(m_1 + m_2) m_2 g^2 l_1 l_2$, will always be negative for all realistic values of the system parameters. So also this equilibrium position is unstable. Hence, finally the only stable equilibrium position is the position indicated by situation (A).*

Example 2.31

Next we evaluate the stability of the equilibrium positions as found in example 2.29 (page 96) for the mixed pendulum problem as introduced in example 2.22 on page 80. The second derivatives of the potential energy with respect to the generalized coordinates can be obtained easily from (2.198)

$$V_{,\underline{qq}} = \begin{bmatrix} \frac{3}{2}(M + 2m)gl\left(\frac{2}{\pi} - \cos\theta_1\right) & 0 \\ 0 & mgl\cos\theta_2 \end{bmatrix} \quad (2.270)$$

*This is a diagonal matrix, so it can only be positive definite if both diagonal terms of $\underline{K}_0$ are positive. Hence, we conclude that **only** the equilibrium position $\theta_1 = \pi/2$, $\theta_2 = 0$ is a stable equilibrium position. Hence, for that position the stiffness matrix $\underline{K}_0$ becomes*

$$\underline{K}_0 = \begin{bmatrix} \frac{3}{2}(M + 2m)gl(\frac{2}{\pi}) & 0 \\ 0 & mgl \end{bmatrix} \quad (2.271)$$

Example 2.32

---

*In Fig. 2.21 the so-called speed regulator of **Proell** is shown schematically. Is is used as a mechanical device to control the rotational speed of a machine. It has a central rotation axis $A - B$ connected to a fictious plane rotating with a fixed rotational speed Ω around this axis. In the plane we have a mechanism, consisting of some massless rigid rods and friction-free joints with a central point mass M which can move up and down along the rotation axis $A - B$ and a couple of point masses m at the ends of rods with length 2l, rotating around the point C. As the (only) generalized coordinate we use the angle φ, the angle for measuring the position of the mechanism in the rotating plane.*

In this problem we are dealing with three points masses, moving in 3-D space. So, if we have their absolute velocities with respect to the given

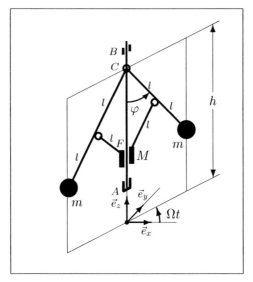

Fig. 2.21   Speed regulator

*inertial frame we can easily calculate the kinetic energy. The only gen-
eralized coordinate is the angle φ, so $\underline{q} = [\varphi]$.*
*For the positions of the point masses M and one of the (equal) masses
m we can write*

$$\underline{x}_M = \begin{bmatrix} 0 \\ 0 \\ h - 2l\cos\varphi \end{bmatrix} ; \qquad \underline{x}_m = \begin{bmatrix} 2l\sin\varphi\cos(\Omega t) \\ 2l\sin\varphi\sin(\Omega t) \\ h - 2l\cos\varphi \end{bmatrix} \qquad (2.272)$$

So, for the velocity columns we find

$$\underline{\dot{x}}_M = \begin{bmatrix} 0 \\ 0 \\ 2l\dot{\varphi}\sin\varphi \end{bmatrix} ; \qquad \underline{\dot{x}}_m = \begin{bmatrix} 2l\dot{\varphi}\cos\varphi\cos(\Omega t) - 2l\Omega\sin\varphi\sin(\Omega t) \\ 2l\dot{\varphi}\cos\varphi\sin(\Omega t) + 2l\Omega\sin\varphi\cos(\Omega t) \\ 2l\dot{\varphi}\sin\varphi \end{bmatrix}$$

$$(2.273)$$

If we substitute these expressions in

$$T = \frac{1}{2}M \ \underline{\dot{x}}_M^T \underline{\dot{x}}_M + 2 \left[\frac{1}{2}m \ \underline{\dot{x}}_m^T \underline{\dot{x}}_m\right] \qquad (2.274)$$

we get

$$T = 2Ml^2\dot{\varphi}^2\sin^2\varphi + 4ml^2(\dot{\varphi}^2 + \Omega^2 \ \sin^2\varphi) \qquad (2.275)$$

So, we find

$$\begin{aligned} T_0 &= 4ml^2\Omega^2\sin^2\varphi = T_0(\underline{q}) \\ \underline{m} &= 0 \\ \underline{M} &= (4Ml^2\sin^2\varphi \ + \ 8ml^2) = \underline{M}(\underline{q}) \end{aligned} \qquad (2.276)$$

For the potential energy due to gravity we can write

$$V = -2(M + 2m)gl \cos \varphi \qquad (2.277)$$

So, for the modified potential $V^*(\underline{q})$ we get

$$V^*(\underline{q}) = -2(M + 2m)gl \cos \varphi - 4ml^2\Omega^2 \sin^2 \varphi \qquad (2.278)$$

The equilibrium positions can be found from

$$V^*_{,\underline{q}} = \underline{0} = 2(M + 2m)gl \sin \varphi - 8ml^2\Omega^2 \sin \varphi \cos \varphi \qquad (2.279)$$

A trivial solution for this equation is $\varphi = \varphi_o = 0$. If we assume $\varphi \neq 0$, then we can devide the equation by $\sin \varphi$, giving

$$8ml^2\Omega^2 \cos \varphi = (2M + 4m)gl \qquad (2.280)$$

Next, we introduce

$$\Omega_c^2 := [1 + \frac{M}{2m}] \frac{g}{2l} \qquad (2.281)$$

where Ω_c is the (pendulum) eigenfrequency of this system in a non-rotating frame (can easily be checked). The solution for a non-zero equilibrium-position φ_o can then be written as

$$\cos \varphi_o = \left[\frac{\Omega_c}{\Omega}\right]^2 \qquad (2.282)$$

Because always $|\cos \varphi| \leq 1.0$, this equilibrium solution is only valid for $\Omega > \Omega_c$. So, resuming we have the two possible solutions

$$
\begin{array}{lll}
(A) & \varphi_o = 0 & 0 \leq \Omega < \infty \\
\\
(B) & \cos \varphi_o = (\Omega_c/\Omega)^2 & \Omega \geq \Omega_c
\end{array}
\qquad (2.283)
$$

Next, we investigate the stability of these equilibium positions. To do so, we look at the second derivative of the modified potential

$$
\begin{aligned}
(V^*_{,\underline{q}})^T_{,\underline{q}} &= [2(M + 2m)gl \cos \varphi - 8ml^2\Omega^2 \cos(2\varphi)] \\
&= [8ml^2\{\Omega_c^2 \cos \varphi - \Omega^2 \cos(2\varphi)\}]
\end{aligned}
\qquad (2.284)
$$

If we evaluate this expression for the two equilibrium solutions, we get the two stiffness matrices (scalar elements for this system with only one degree of freedom)

$$
\begin{array}{ll}
(A) & \underline{K}_o = [8ml^2(\Omega_c^2 - \Omega^2)] \\
\\
(B) & \underline{K}_o = [8ml^2(\frac{\Omega^4 - \Omega_c^4}{\Omega^2})]
\end{array}
\qquad (2.285)
$$

So, we may conclude that the trivial position $\varphi = 0$, which is valid for all values of Ω, will only be stable for (small) rotational frequencies $\Omega < \Omega_c$.

The nonzero equilibrium position, which only exists for (large) rotational frequencies $\Omega > \Omega_c$, will be stable. The different equilibrium positions are shown in Fig. 2.22 as function of the dimensionless rotational speed Ω/Ω_c. The stable equilibrium positions are marked by stars

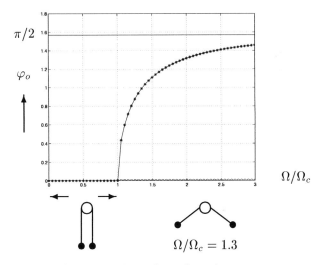

Fig. 2.22   Equilibrium positions of speed regulator

(*), whereas the unstable equilibrium positions are marked with circles (o). The asymptotic value for very high rotational speeds Ω is $\varphi_o = \frac{\pi}{2}$, which indicates a horizontal position of the pendulum arms.

2.16   LINEARIZATION ABOUT A STABLE EQUILIBRIUM POSITION

2.16.1   Preliminaries

As indicated in the previous section, general closed-form solutions of the non-linear Lagrange's equations of motion do not exist. On the other hand, special solutions do exist under particular circumstances. In the previous section we elaborated the most elementary type of special solution, namely the constant or time-independent solutions, $\underline{q} = \underline{q}_o =$ constant, representing equilibrium positions. In this section we will derive the Lagrange's equations of motion in a sufficiently small neighbourhood of a stable equilibrium position. By a sufficiently small neighbourhood we mean that in that neighbourhood the system behaves as if it were linear. This implies that the behaviour of the system in the neighbourhood of the equilibrium position $\underline{q} = \underline{q}_o$ is governed by a special version of the equations of motion, obtained by expanding the equations of motion (2.153) about $\underline{q} = \underline{q}_o$ and retaining the *linear* terms in $(\underline{q} - \underline{q}_o)$ alone. The resulting equations, known as the *linearized equations of motion*, play a very important role in linear vibrations of mechanical systems. To derive these linearized equations of motion, it is convenient to decompose the generalized coordinates $\underline{q}(t)$ as follows

$$\underline{q}(t) \;=\; \underline{q}_o \;+\; \underline{q}_1(t) \tag{2.286}$$

Here $\underline{q}_o$ is a constant or time-independent column matrix representing the equilibrium position under consideration, while $\underline{q}_1(t)$ is a time-dependent column matrix representing **small** perturbations of the generalized coordinates from the equilibrium position. In view of the fact that the position $\underline{q}_o$ is time-independent, we have

$$(\underline{\dot{q}})_{\underline{q}=\underline{q}_o} := \underline{\dot{q}}_o = \underline{0} \quad \text{and} \quad (\underline{\ddot{q}})_{\underline{q}=\underline{q}_o} := \underline{\ddot{q}}_o = \underline{0} \tag{2.287}$$

and, hence, we conclude from (2.286) that

$$\underline{\dot{q}}(t) \;=\; \underline{\dot{q}}_1(t) \quad \text{and} \quad \underline{\ddot{q}}(t) \;=\; \underline{\ddot{q}}_1(t) \tag{2.288}$$

It is recalled from the treatment in the previous section that two situations can be distinguished with respect to equilibrium positions. In the first and simplest situation the transport kinetic energy and mutual kinetic energy are zero. In the second and more involved situation prescribed motions and/or steady motions are present and the general expression for the kinetic energy has to be applied. Here we will first consider the simplest case. The more involved case will be considered in Section 2.17.

In the following subsections we will first successively consider the contributions of the kinetic and potential energies that are required for the linearized equations of motion. Next, we will linearize the generalized nonconservative forces and discuss the final linearized equations of motion about an equilibrium position.

2.16.2   Contribution of the kinetic energy to the linearized Lagrange's equations

In this case we can write for the kinetic energy

$$T(\underline{q},\underline{\dot{q}},t) = T_2(\underline{q},\underline{\dot{q}}) \;=\; \frac{1}{2}\, \underline{\dot{q}}^T \underline{M}(\underline{q})\, \underline{\dot{q}} \tag{2.289}$$

As follows from (2.153), the contribution of the kinetic energy to the Lagrange's equations of motion is

$$\frac{d}{dt}(T_{,\underline{\dot{q}}}) \;-\; T_{,\underline{q}} \tag{2.290}$$

Now, we evaluate the contribution of the quadratic kinetic energy term $T_2(q, \dot{q})$. Inserting T_2 from (2.289) into (2.290), we can express the quantity $T_{2,\dot{q}}$ as follows

$$T_{2,\dot{q}} = \dot{\underline{q}}_1^T \underline{M} \quad \text{with} \quad \underline{M} = \underline{M}(\underline{q}) = \underline{M}(\underline{q}_o + \underline{q}_1) \qquad (2.291)$$

It can easily be seen that the quantity $\dot{\underline{q}}_1^T \underline{M}$ can only induce linear terms in the equations of motion if $\underline{M}$ is taken to be independent of $\underline{q}_1$. Consequently, for linear systems the quadratic term T_2 has the form

$$T_2 = T_2(\dot{\underline{q}}_1) = \frac{1}{2} \dot{\underline{q}}_1^T \underline{M}_o \dot{\underline{q}}_1 \qquad (2.292)$$

in which

$$\underline{M}_o = \underline{M}(\underline{q}_o) = \underline{M}_o^T = \text{constant} \qquad (2.293)$$

So, the symmetric mass matrix only contains constant elements and is to be evaluated at the relevant static equilibrium position of the system.

In view of (2.292) and (2.293) the second term in (2.290) $(-T_{2,q})$ vanishes if we consider only motions in a small neighbourhood of the equilibrium position. Hence, inserting (2.292) into (2.290), we arrive at the following contribution of the kinetic energy to the linearized equations of motion for systems with $T_{o,\underline{q}} = \underline{0}^T$ and $\underline{m}(\underline{q}, t) = \underline{0}$

$$\left[\frac{d}{dt}(T_{,\dot{q}}) - T_{,\underline{q}} \right]^T = \underline{M}_o \ddot{\underline{q}}_1 \qquad (2.294)$$

Example 2.33

We consider again the double pendulum system with two masses. The kinetic energy for this system was derived earlier in example 2.15 on page 68. There are no prescribed coordinates so the transport- and mutual kinetic energy are zero. We also found the mass matrix for the given set of generalized coordinates to be

$$\underline{M} = \begin{bmatrix} m_1 l_1^2 + m_2(l_1^2 + l_2^2 + 2l_1 l_2 \cos\theta_2) & m_2(l_2^2 + l_1 l_2 \cos\theta_2) \\ m_2(l_2^2 + l_1 l_2 \cos\theta_2) & m_2 l_2^2 \end{bmatrix}$$

$$(2.295)$$

In example 2.28 on page 95 the only stable position of the system appeared to be $\theta_1 = \theta_2 = 0$ cf. Fig. 2.18,A. For this equilibrium position, the transposed form of (2.294) becomes

$$\left[\frac{d}{dt}(T_{,\dot{q}}) - T_{,\underline{q}} \right]^T =$$

$$\begin{bmatrix} m_1 l_1^2 + m_2(l_1^2 + l_2^2 + 2l_1 l_2) & m_2(l_2^2 + l_1 l_2) \\ m_2(l_2^2 + l_1 l_2) & m_2 l_2^2 \end{bmatrix} \begin{bmatrix} \ddot{\theta}_1 \\ \ddot{\theta}_2 \end{bmatrix} \qquad (2.296)$$

For this relatively simple problem we might also have started directly from the assumption of sufficiently small motions around the equilibrium position $\theta_1 = \theta_2 = 0$, implying that the velocities of the two point masses then can be written as

$$
\begin{array}{llll}
\text{mass } m_1: & v_1 = l_1\,\dot{\theta}_1 & \text{in } x_2 \text{ direction} \\
\text{mass } m_2: & v_2 = v_1 + l_2\,(\dot{\theta}_1 + \dot{\theta}_2) & \text{in } x_2 \text{ direction}
\end{array}
\tag{2.297}
$$

So, the kinetic energy can be written as $T = \frac{1}{2}m_1\,v_1^2 + \frac{1}{2}m_2\,v_2^2$. Inserting (2.297) into this expression and comparing the result with $T = \frac{1}{2}\,\dot{q}^T\,\underline{M}\,\dot{q}$ gives directly the mass matrix found above.

Example 2.34

Next, we look at the mixed pendulum system with torsional spring from example 2.22 on page 80 and its stable equilibrium position as derived in example 2.29 on page 96. Again, there are no prescribed coordinates so the transport- and mutual kinetic energy are zero. We also found the mass matrix for the given set of generalized coordinates to be

$$
\underline{M} = \begin{bmatrix} \frac{9}{4}(M + 4m)l^2 & 3ml^2\cos(\theta_1 + \theta_2) \\ 3ml^2\cos(\theta_1 + \theta_2) & \frac{4}{3}ml^2 \end{bmatrix}
\tag{2.298}
$$

The only stable equilibrium position for this system (with the specific choice for the torsional spring stiffness k_t) appeared to be $\theta_1 = \frac{\pi}{2}$ and $\theta_2 = 0$. If we substitute these values in (2.298) we get the mass matrix for the linearized equatuions of motion

$$
\underline{M}(\underline{q}_0) = \begin{bmatrix} \frac{9}{4}(M + 4m)l^2 & 0 \\ 0 & \frac{4}{3}ml^2 \end{bmatrix}
\tag{2.299}
$$

The first diagonal term can be recognized as the total mass moment of inertia with respect to the fixed point A of a system consisting of bar AB with point mass M in the middle and the mass m of the beam BC concentrated in point B. The second diagonal term is just the mass moment of inertia of beam BC with respect to point B.

2.16.3   Contribution of the potential energy to the linearized Lagrange's equations

Because the Lagrange's equations of motion (2.153) contain first derivatives of the potential energy V with respect to the generalized coordinates q, this potential energy has to be expanded up to terms which are quadratic in q, in order to arrive at equations of motion which are linear. The power series expansion of the potential energy up to terms which are quadratic in in q_1, has already been shown in Section 2.14 to take the form, see (2.261)

$$V(\underline{q}) \cong V(\underline{q}_o) + (V_{,\underline{q}})_{\underline{q}_o} q_1 + \frac{1}{2} \underline{q}_1^T \left[(V_{,\underline{q}})^T_{,\underline{q}} \right]_{\underline{q}_o} q_1 \qquad (2.300)$$

where the constant symmetric

$$\underline{K}_o = [k_{ij}] = \left[(V_{,\underline{q}})^T_{,\underline{q}} \right]_{\underline{q}_o} \qquad (2.301)$$

is referred to as the **stiffness matrix**. The equilibrium position $\underline{q}_o$ satisfies the algebraic equations $(V_{,\underline{q}})_{\underline{q}_o} = \underline{0}^T$. Then, the linear term in the right-hand side of (2.300) becomes zero and we can put the expansion (2.300) in the form

$$V(\underline{q}) \cong V(\underline{q}_o) + \frac{1}{2} \underline{q}_1^T \underline{K}_o \, q_1 \qquad (2.302)$$

Inserting (2.302) into (2.153), we arrive at the following contribution of the potential energy to the linearized equations of motion

$$(V_{,\underline{q}})^T = \underline{K}_o \, q_1 \qquad (2.303)$$

For example, for the double pendulum system with two masses the stiffness matrix $\underline{K}_o$ for the stable vertical position was derived in example 2.30 on page 101. For the mixed pendulum system the stiffness matrix for the only stable position was derived in example 2.31 on page 102.

2.16.4   Contribution of the generalized nonconservative forces

The remaining quantities to be considered for the linearization of Lagrange's equations of motion are the generalized nonconservative forces $\underline{Q}^{nc}$. In general, these forces will explicitly depend on $\underline{q}$, $\dot{\underline{q}}$ and t

$$\underline{Q}^{nc} = \underline{Q}^{nc}(\underline{q}, \dot{\underline{q}}, t) \qquad (2.304)$$

Forces depending on $\ddot{\underline{q}}$ are part of the inertia forces, which have already been accounted for in the Lagrange's equations of motion.

The Taylor's series expansion of the generalized nonconservative forces about the equilibrium position $\underline{q}_o$ up to terms which will be linear in $\underline{q}$ and $\dot{\underline{q}}$ can be written as

$$\underline{Q}^{nc}(\underline{q}, \dot{\underline{q}}, t) = \underline{Q}^{nc}(\underline{q}_o, \dot{\underline{q}}_o(=\underline{0}), t) +$$

$$\left[\underline{Q}^{nc}_{,\underline{q}} \right]_{\underline{q}_o, \dot{\underline{q}}_o(=\underline{0})} q_1 + \left[\underline{Q}^{nc}_{,\dot{\underline{q}}} \right]_{\underline{q}_o, \dot{\underline{q}}_o(=\underline{0})} \dot{q}_1 \qquad (2.305)$$

The first term in the right-hand side of (2.305) represents generalized nonconservative forces that depend explicitly on time alone. These forces are denoted by $\underline{Q}(t)$, so that

$$\underline{Q}(t) = \underline{Q}^{nc}(\underline{q}_o, \dot{\underline{q}}_o(=\underline{0}), t) \qquad (2.306)$$

The second term in the right-hand side is proportional to $\underline{q}_1$, which means that it can be seen as a stiffness term. It is denoted in abbreviated notation by

$$\underline{Q}^k = [\underline{Q}^{nc},q]_{\underline{q}_o,\dot{\underline{q}}_o=\underline{0}}\, \underline{q}_1 := -\underline{K}_o^Q\, \underline{q}_1 \qquad (2.307)$$

In general, the coefficients of the matrix $\underline{K}_o^Q$ can depend explicitly on time. In the special case where they do not depend explicitly on time, the term (2.307) represents a conservative force, which could (should) have been taken into acccount already earlier in the potential energy.

The third term in the right-hand side of (2.305) is proportional to $\dot{\underline{q}}_1$. It represents the well-known **viscous damping forces**, and is denoted by $\underline{Q}^d$, so that we can write

$$\underline{Q}^d = [\underline{Q}^{nc},\dot{q}]_{\underline{q}_o,\dot{\underline{q}}_o(=\underline{0})}\, \dot{\underline{q}}_1 \qquad (2.308)$$

The negative of the matrix in (2.308) that relates $\underline{Q}^d$ to $\dot{\underline{q}}_1$ is known as the **viscous damping matrix** $\underline{D}_o$, so that

$$\underline{Q}^d := -\underline{D}_o\, \dot{\underline{q}}_1 \qquad (2.309)$$

with

$$\underline{D}_0 = -\left(\underline{Q}^{nc},\dot{q}\right)_{\underline{q}_o,\dot{\underline{q}}_o=\underline{0}} = [d_{ij}] \qquad (2.310)$$

in which d_{ij} are *viscous damping coefficients*. The formulation expressed by (2.310) can be considered to be a generalization of the formulation for a two-degree-of-freedom linear system given in Chapter 1, see (1.5). Viscous damping forces are so-called *dissipative forces*, to which, by definition, a *non-positive* power is related

$$P^d = \dot{\underline{q}}_1^T \underline{Q}^d = -\dot{\underline{q}}_1^T \underline{D}_0\, \dot{\underline{q}}_1 \le 0 \quad \text{if} \quad \dot{\underline{q}}_1 \ne \underline{0} \qquad (2.311)$$

Moreover, if the influence of the damping forces affects all generalized coordinates in $\underline{q}_1$, then, again by definition, a *negative* power is related to those dissipative forces. The foregoing implies that the damping matrix is positive definite if its main diagonal does not contain zero elements, whereas it is semi-positive definite if this is not the case.

In literature, often the generalized viscous damping forces $\underline{Q}^d$ are derived from the so-called *Rayleigh's dissipation function* R^d which is defined to be

$$R^d = \frac{1}{2}\, \dot{\underline{q}}_1^T \underline{D}_0\, \dot{\underline{q}}_1 \qquad (2.312)$$

The obvious relationship between R^d and $\underline{Q}^d$ is

$$\underline{Q}^d = -\left(R^d,_{\dot{\underline{q}}_1}\right)^T = -\underline{D}_0^T\, \dot{\underline{q}}_1 \qquad (2.313)$$

If $\underline{Q}^d$ can be derived from R^d in a unique way, then the viscous damping matrix $\underline{D}_0$ has to be symmetric, so that

$$\underline{D}_0 = \underline{D}_0^T \tag{2.314}$$

This follows immediately from (2.312) by taking its transposed

$$\left(R^d\right)^T = R^d = \frac{1}{2}\,\dot{\underline{q}}_1^T\underline{D}_0^T\,\dot{\underline{q}}_1 \tag{2.315}$$

Then, if (2.314) would not hold, $\underline{Q}^d$ resulting from (2.312) would be different from $\underline{Q}^d$ resulting from (2.315). From now on, we will take the viscous damping matrix $\underline{D}_0$ to be symmetric.

We conclude from (2.312) and (2.311) and the accompanying text, that Rayleigh's dissipation function is positive definite if the main diagonal of the viscous damping matrix does not contain zero elements, whereas it is semi-positive definite if this is not the case.

The foregoing discussion results in the following decomposition of the generalized nonconservative forces $\underline{Q}^{nc}$ for linear systems

$$\underline{Q}^{nc} \;=\; \underline{Q}(t) \;+\; \underline{Q}^k \;+\; \underline{Q}^d \;=\; \underline{Q}(t) \;-\; \underline{K}_o^Q\,\underline{q}_1 \;-\; \underline{D}_o\,\dot{\underline{q}}_1 \tag{2.316}$$

It is recalled that the formulation expressed by (2.316) can be considered to be a generalization of the formulation for single- and two-degree-of-freedom linear systems.

Example 2.35

We consider again the mixed pendulum system with a point mass and a rigid beam from example 2.22 on page 80. The non-conservative forces originated from two viscous damping contributions in the hinges of the system and from an external horizontal forces $F(t)$ in the end point C of the beam. For the non-conservative force column we found

$$\underline{Q}^{nc} = \left[\begin{array}{c} 3F(t)l\cos\theta_1 - b_B(\dot{\theta}_1 + \dot{\theta}_2) - b_A\dot{\theta}_1 \\ 2F(t)l\cos\theta_2 - b_B(\dot{\theta}_1 + \dot{\theta}_2) \end{array} \right] \tag{2.317}$$

For the linearized version around the stable equilibrium position $\theta_1 = \pi/2$ and $\theta_2 = 0$, this gives

$$\underline{Q}(t) = \underline{Q}^{nc}(\underline{q}_0,\dot{\underline{q}}_0 = \underline{0}, t) = \left[\begin{array}{c} 0 \\ 2F(t)l \end{array} \right] \tag{2.318}$$

$$\underline{K}_o^Q = -[\underline{Q}^{nc},\underline{q}]_{\underline{q}_o,\dot{\underline{q}}_o} = \left[\begin{array}{cc} 3F(t)l & 0 \\ 0 & 0 \end{array} \right] \tag{2.319}$$

$$\underline{D}_o = -[\underline{Q}^{nc},\dot{\underline{q}}]_{\underline{q}_o,\dot{\underline{q}}_o} = \left[\begin{array}{cc} b_A + b_B & b_B \\ b_B & b_B \end{array} \right] \tag{2.320}$$

So we get a viscous damping matrix $\underline{D}_o$ due to the hinge-friction modelling and a time dependent excitation column $Q(t)$, with a zero contribution for the first generalized coordinate and a contribution $2F(t)l$ for the second generalized coordinate. But we also get a stiffness matrix contribution $\underline{K}_o^Q$ which might be surprising at first hand. We will come back to this point later in the discussion of the linearized equations of motion for this system.

2.16.5   The linearized Lagrange's equations of motion

Inserting (2.294), (2.303) and (2.316) into the Lagrange's equations of motion (2.153), we obtain the linearized Lagrange's equations of motion about an equilibrium position for systems with $T_{o,q} = \underline{0}^T$ and $\underline{m}(q,t) = \underline{0}$ in the form

$$\underline{M}_o \, \ddot{q}_1(t) \; + \; \underline{D}_o \, \dot{q}_1(t) \; + \; (\underline{K}_o \; + \; \underline{K}_o^Q) \, q_1(t) \; = \; Q(t) \qquad (2.321)$$

It is remarked that in this equation the constant matrices $\underline{M}_o$, $\underline{D}_o$ and $\underline{K}_o$ are symmetric.

Example 2.36

Looking again at the mixed pendulum problem, the only remaining thing to do for getting the linearized equations of motion is bringing together the results from example 2.31 (page 102), example 2.34 (page 108) and example 2.35 (page 111). This gives the linearized equations of motion with respect to the stable equilibrium position $\theta_1 = \pi/2, \theta_2 = 0$ for this example

$$\begin{bmatrix} \frac{9}{4}(M+4m)l^2 & 0 \\ 0 & \frac{4}{3}ml^2 \end{bmatrix} \begin{bmatrix} \ddot{\varphi}_1 \\ \ddot{\varphi}_2 \end{bmatrix} + \begin{bmatrix} b_A + b_B & b_B \\ b_B & b_B \end{bmatrix} \begin{bmatrix} \dot{\varphi}_1 \\ \dot{\varphi}_2 \end{bmatrix} +$$

$$\begin{bmatrix} \frac{3}{\pi}(M+2m)lg + 3lF(t) & 0 \\ 0 & mgl \end{bmatrix} \begin{bmatrix} \varphi_1 \\ \varphi_2 \end{bmatrix} = \begin{bmatrix} 0 \\ 2lF(t) \end{bmatrix}$$

$$(2.322)$$

*where φ_1 is the **small** rotation of bar AB, measured clockwise from the equilibrium position $\theta_1 = \pi/2$ and φ_2 the **small** rotation of beam BC, measured anti-clockwise from the equilibrium position $\theta_2 = 0$. The linearization was started with $q = q_o + q_1$ and $q_1^T := [\varphi_1, \; \varphi_2]$, the positive directions of these small rotations should be taken identical to the positive directions of the original generalized coordinates θ_1 and θ_2.*

Intermezzo

As an alternative, the nonlinear equations of motion as derived before ,see (2.199) and (2.200), can also be chosen to extract the linearized version with respect to the stable equilibrium directly. To this end we use again

$$\theta_1 = \frac{\pi}{2} + \varphi_1 \qquad \theta_2 = 0 + \varphi_2 \qquad (2.323)$$

and the first order Taylor series approximations

$$f(\theta) \approx f(\theta_o) + \left[\frac{df(\theta)}{d\theta}\right]_{\theta_o} \varphi \qquad (2.324)$$

giving

$$\cos\theta_1 \approx \cos(\tfrac{\pi}{2}) - \sin(\tfrac{\pi}{2})\,\varphi_1 = -\varphi_1$$
$$\sin\theta_1 \approx \sin(\tfrac{\pi}{2}) + \cos(\tfrac{\pi}{2})\,\varphi_1 = 1$$
$$\cos(\theta_1 + \theta_2) \approx \cos(\tfrac{\pi}{2} + 0) - \sin(\tfrac{\pi}{2} + 0)\,(\varphi_1 + \varphi_2) = -(\varphi_1 + \varphi_2)$$
$$\sin(\theta_1 + \theta_2) \approx \sin(\tfrac{\pi}{2} + 0) + \cos(\tfrac{\pi}{2} + 0)\,(\varphi_1 + \varphi_2) = 1$$
$$\cos\theta_2 \approx 1$$
$$\sin\theta_2 \approx \varphi_2$$

$$(2.325)$$

If we substitute these approximations in the nonlinear equations of motion, we get

$$\tfrac{9}{4}\,(M + 4m)\,l^2\ddot{\varphi}_1 - \underline{3ml^2\ddot{\varphi}_2(\varphi_1 + \varphi_2)} - \underline{3ml^2\dot{\varphi}_2^2} + k_t(\tfrac{\pi}{2} + \varphi_1)$$

$$-\tfrac{3}{2}\,(M + 2m)\,gl + \ 3F(t)l\varphi_1 + (b_A + b_B)\dot{\varphi}_1 + b_B\dot{\varphi}_2 = 0$$
$$(2.326)$$

$$\underline{3ml^2\ddot{\varphi}_1(\varphi_1 + \varphi_2)} + \tfrac{4}{3}ml^2\ddot{\varphi}_2 - \underline{3ml^2\dot{\varphi}_1^2}$$

$$(2.327)$$

$$+mgl\varphi_2 - 2F(t)l + b_B\dot{\varphi}_1 + b_B\dot{\varphi}_2 = 0$$

If we skip the underlined (higher order) terms, and remember the specific value for the torsional stiffness k_t, we get the same linear equations of motion.

To get some fysical interpretation of the terms in these linearized equations of motion, we look at the subsystems as shown in Fig. 2.23. The first equation of motion seems to represent a rotation of a rigid body around the fixed point A (left part of Fig. 2.23). The mass moment of inertia of the system with respect of this fixed point A (assuming the beam mass to be concentrated in point B), is $\frac{9}{4}(M + 4m)l^2$. The external force $F(t)$ has also been transferred to point B. The moment due to the force $F(t)$ gives a positive stiffness contribution in this equation. If we also take into account the more trivial contributions due to the torsional spring and the viscous damping terms, we can conclude that the first linearized equation can be seen as the moment equation of this system around the fixed point A.

For the second linearized equation of motion we look at the right part

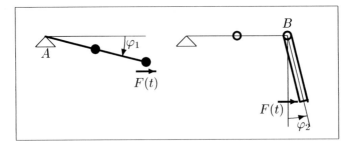

Fig. 2.23   Subsystem visualization

of Fig. 2.23. There we are dealing with the rotation of a rigid body around the fixed point B (with mass moment of inertia $J_B = \frac{4}{3}ml^2$). If we again take into account the more trivial terms due to gravity and viscous damping, this equation represents the moment equation for this degenerated system.

*For the particular case in which $b_A = b_B = 0$, we are dealing with undamped free motions of the system with respect to the fixed point A. In that case, the linearized equations degenerate into two **uncoupled equations of motion** with time-independent coefficients in the form*

$$\frac{9}{4}(M + 4m)l^2 \ \ddot{\varphi}_1 + \frac{3}{\pi}(M + 2m)gl \ \varphi_1 = 0$$

$$\frac{4}{3}ml^2 \ \ddot{\varphi}_2 + mgl \ \varphi_2 = 0$$

(2.328)

This means that we are dealing with a combination of two possible motions with the eigenfrequencies

$$\omega_1 = \sqrt{\frac{4(M + 2m)g}{3\pi(M + 4m)l}} \quad and \quad \omega_2 = \sqrt{\frac{3g}{4l}}$$

(2.329)

2.17   LINEARIZATION OF SYSTEMS WITH DRIVERS AND/OR STEADY MOTION

2.17.1   Preliminaries

In the previous section we derived the linearized Lagrange's equations for a motion in a sufficiently small neighbourhood of some stable equilibrium position for systems with no drivers and no steady motions. This mainly influenced the contributions of the kinetic energy, because we could simply state that the transport kinetic energy $T_0(\underline{q}, t)$ as well as the mutual kinetic energy $T_1(\underline{q}, \dot{\underline{q}}, t)$ could be taken to be zero. In the present section we will treat the more complex situation in which these terms are nonzero.

As for systems where these terms are missing and in agreement with Section 2.15, we can define an equilibrium position of a system with drivers and/or steady motions by a set of **time-independent** generalized coordinates $\underline{q} = \underline{q}_0 = constant$ for which (2.287) again holds. Also, for those systems the decomposition (2.286) of the generalized coordinates again appears to be convenient and, hence, (2.287) are again valid.

In the following subsections we will first consider the adaptations of the contributions of the kinetic and potential energies to the linearized Lagrange's equations of motion due to the fact that $T_{0,\underline{q}} \neq \underline{0}^T$ and $\underline{m}(\underline{q}, t) \neq \underline{0}$. Next, we will discuss the adaptation of the generalized nonconservative forces and compose the adapted linearized Lagrange's equations of motion.

2.17.2 Contribution of the kinetic energy to the linearized Lagrange's equations

In Section 2.11 the expression for the kinetic energy was found to be, see (2.112)

$$
\begin{aligned}
T(\underline{q}, \dot{\underline{q}}, t) &= T_0(\underline{q}, t) + T_1(\underline{q}, \dot{\underline{q}}, t) + T_2(\underline{q}, \dot{\underline{q}}) \\
&= T_0(\underline{q}, t) + \underline{m}^T(\underline{q}, t)\, \dot{\underline{q}} + \frac{1}{2}\, \dot{\underline{q}}^T \underline{M}(\underline{q})\, \dot{\underline{q}} \qquad (2.330)
\end{aligned}
$$

As follows from (2.153), the contribution of the kinetic energy to the Lagrange's equations of motion is

$$
\frac{d}{dt}(T_{,\dot{\underline{q}}}) - T_{,\underline{q}} \qquad (2.331)
$$

Now we will evaluate this contribution for each of the terms of the kinetic energy as given by (2.289).

It follows immediately from (2.331) and (2.113) that for systems with $T_{0,\underline{q}} \neq \underline{0}^T$ the contribution of the transport kinetic energy to the Lagrage's equations of motion can be expressed as

$$
\frac{d}{dt}\left(T_{0,\dot{\underline{q}}}\right) - T_{0,\underline{q}} = -T_{0,\underline{q}} \qquad (2.332)
$$

Expanding $T_{0,\underline{q}}$ in a Taylor series about the equilibrium position $\underline{q}_0$ up to linear terms in the perturbations $\underline{q}_1(t)$, we obtain the contribution of the transport kinetic energy to the linearized Lagrange's equations of motion in the form

$$
\left\{\frac{d}{dt}\left(T_{0,\dot{\underline{q}}}\right) - T_{0,\underline{q}}\right\}^T = -\left(T_{0,\underline{q}}\right)^T_{\underline{q}_0} - \left\{\left(T_{0,\underline{q}}\right)^T_{,\underline{q}}\right\}_{\underline{q}_0} \underline{q}_1 \qquad (2.333)
$$

$$:= - \left(T_{0,\underline{q}} \right)^T_0 \; - \; \underline{K}^g_0 \; q_1$$

with the symmetric matrix $\underline{K}^g_0$ being defined as

$$\underline{K}^g_0 = \left\{ \left(T_{0,\underline{q}} \right)^T_{,\underline{q}} \right\}_{\underline{q}_0} \tag{2.334}$$

In the following subsection we will combine the contribution (2.334) of the transport kinetic energy with the contribution of the potential energy.

Next, we evaluate the contribution of the mutual kinetic energy T_1 to the linearized equations of motion. Using (2.114), we conclude that the first term of (2.290) can be evaluated as follows

$$T_{1,\dot{\underline{q}}} \; = \; \underline{m}^T \quad \Longrightarrow \quad \frac{d}{dt} \{ T_{1,\dot{\underline{q}}} \} = \underline{m}^T_{,t} \; + \; \dot{\underline{q}}^T \, (\underline{m}_{,\underline{q}})^T \tag{2.335}$$

whereas the second term of (2.290) becomes

$$-T_{1,\underline{q}} \; = -\{ \dot{\underline{q}}^T \, \underline{m} \}_{,\underline{q}} \; = \; - \dot{\underline{q}}^T \, (\underline{m}_{,\underline{q}}) \tag{2.336}$$

Inserting (2.335) and (2.336) into (2.290), we conclude that the contribution of the mutual kinetic energy T_1 to the equations of motion amounts to

$$\left[\frac{d}{dt}(T_{1,\dot{\underline{q}}}) \; - \; T_{1,\underline{q}} \right]^T \; = \; \underline{m}_{,t} \; + \; \left[(\underline{m}_{,\underline{q}}) - (\underline{m}_{,\underline{q}})^T \right] \dot{\underline{q}}^T$$

$$:= \; \underline{m}_{,t} \; + \; \underline{G} \, \dot{q} \tag{2.337}$$

It is remarked that the matrix $\underline{G}$

$$\underline{G} = \underline{G}(\underline{q}, t) = (\underline{m}_{,\underline{q}}) - (\underline{m}_{,\underline{q}})^T \tag{2.338}$$

appearing as factor of $\dot{q}$ in the right hand side of (2.337) can be observed to be **skew-symmetric**, so that

$$\underline{G}(\underline{q}, t) \; = \; - \underline{G}^T(\underline{q}, t) \tag{2.339}$$

In the situation in which the matrix $\underline{G}(\underline{q}, t)$ does not vanish, the mutual kinetic energy T_1 is most commonly associated with motions relative to rotating reference frames. Hence the "forces" $\underline{G} \, \dot{q}$ arising from T_1 are called *gyroscopic forces*. It should be noticed here that, although gyroscopic forces are commonly associated with spinning bodies, they can for example also arise in elastic pipelines containing flowing liquid. We will not discuss here gyroscopic forces any further. Here we only remark that if we linearize the term $\underline{G} \, \dot{q}$ in the right side of (2.337) with respect to an equilibrium position $\underline{q}_o$, we should replace $\underline{G}(\underline{q}, t)$ by $\underline{G}(\underline{q}_o, t)$ in order to arrive at a linear term.

Next, we address the first term, $\underline{m}_{,t}$, in the right side of (2.337). If we want to linearize the equations of motion with respect to an equilibrium position $\underline{q}_o$, we will have to linearize this quantity $\underline{m}_{,t}(\underline{q}, t)$ with respect to $\underline{q}_o$. Therefore we write

$$\underline{m}_{,t}(\underline{q}_o + \underline{q}_1) \approx \underline{m}_{,t}(\underline{q}_o) + [(\underline{m}_{,t})_{,\underline{q}}]_{\underline{q}_o} \underline{q}_1 := (\underline{m}_{,t})_o + \underline{K}_o^m(t) \underline{q}_1 \qquad (2.340)$$

with

$$(\underline{m}_{,t})_o = \underline{m}_{,t}(\underline{q}_o) \qquad \text{and} \qquad \underline{K}_o^m(t) = [(\underline{m}_{,t})_{,\underline{q}}]_{\underline{q}_o} \qquad (2.341)$$

Finally we evaluate the contribution of the quadratic kinetic energy term $T_2(\underline{q}, \dot{\underline{q}})$. Inserting T_2 from (2.289) into (2.290), we can express the quantity $T_{2,\dot{\underline{q}}}$ as follows

$$T_{2,\dot{\underline{q}}} = \dot{\underline{q}}_1^T \underline{M} \qquad \text{with} \qquad \underline{M} = \underline{M}(\underline{q}_o + \underline{q}_1) \qquad (2.342)$$

It can easily be seen that the quantity $\dot{\underline{q}}_1^T \underline{M}$ can only induce linear terms in the equations of motion if $\underline{M}$ is taken to be independent of $\underline{q}_1$. Consequently, for linear systems the quadratic term T_2 has the form

$$T_2 = T_2(\dot{\underline{q}}_1) = \frac{1}{2} \dot{\underline{q}}_1^T \underline{M}_o \dot{\underline{q}}_1 \qquad (2.343)$$

in which

$$\underline{M}_o = \underline{M}(\underline{q}_o) = \underline{M}_o^T = \text{constant} \qquad (2.344)$$

So the symmetric mass matrix only contains constant elements and is to be evaluated at the relevant static equilibrium position of the system.

In view of (2.343) and (2.344) the second term in (2.290) $(-T_{2,\underline{q}})$ vanishes if we consider only motions in a small neighbourhood of the equilibrium position. Hence, inserting (2.343) into (2.290), we arrive at the following contribution of the kinetic energy term T_2 to the linearized equations of motion

$$\frac{d}{dt}(T_{2,\dot{\underline{q}}}) - T_{2,\underline{q}} = \ddot{\underline{q}}_1^T \underline{M}_o \qquad (2.345)$$

Adding (2.333), (2.337) and (2.345), we arrive at the following contribution of the kinetic energy to the linearized equations of motion for systems with drivers and/or steady motions

$$\left\{ \frac{d}{dt}(T_{,\dot{\underline{q}}}) - T_{,\underline{q}} \right\}^T =$$

$$\underline{M}_o \ddot{\underline{q}}_1 + \underline{G}_o \dot{\underline{q}}_1 + [\underline{K}_o^m - \underline{K}_o^g] \underline{q}_1 + (\underline{m}_{,t})_o - (T_{o,\underline{q}})_o^T \qquad (2.346)$$

Example 2.37

We consider a modification of the mixed two-dimensional pendulum *system from example 2.22 on page 80. The external force $F(t)$ and the viscous damping terms due to friction in the hinges will be skipped. Additionally, we now assume that the support point A undergoes a **prescribed motion** in the horizontal x_1 direction with the prescribed x_1 coordinate of point A being denoted by $x_A(t)$. The system is shown again in Fig. 2.24. It is easy to see that for given $x_A(t)$ we still need*

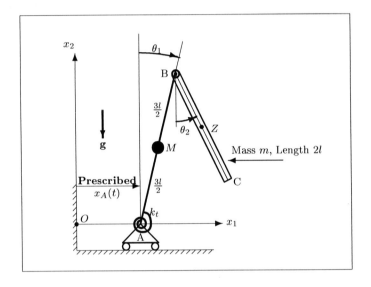

Fig. 2.24 Forced Mixed Pendulum System

two geometrical parameters to uniquely define the position of the system completely. So, the number of degrees of freedom for this system remains two ($n = 2$). Again, we select as generalized coordinates the angles θ_1, and θ_2 of AB and BC with respect to the vertical x_1, axis, so that

$$q = \begin{bmatrix} q_1 \\ q_2 \end{bmatrix} = \begin{bmatrix} \theta_1 \\ \theta_2 \end{bmatrix} \qquad (2.347)$$

whereas the column of prescribed coordinates, $\underline{s}(t)$, degenerates into a scalar, i.e.

$$\underline{s}(t) = x_A(t) \qquad (2.348)$$

Analogous to the procedure applied in example 2.22 we can calculate the kinetic energy to be

$$T = T_{AB} + T_{BC} = T_0 + T_1 + T_2 \qquad with$$

$$T_0 = \tfrac{1}{2}(M + m)\{\dot{x}_A(t)\}^2$$

$$T_1 = \tfrac{3}{2}(M + 2m)\{\dot{x}_A(t)\}\, l\cos\theta_1\ \dot{\theta}_1\ + m\{\dot{x}_A(t)\}\, l\cos\theta_2\ \dot{\theta}_2$$

$$T_2 = \tfrac{1}{2}\left[\tfrac{9}{4}(M + 4m)l^2\ \dot{\theta}_1^2 + 6ml^2\cos(\theta_1 + \theta_2)\ \dot{\theta}_1\dot{\theta}_2 + \tfrac{4}{3}ml^2\ \dot{\theta}_2^2\right]$$

$$(2.349)$$

So, in this case there is one prescribed coordinate and, hence, the transport kinetic energy T_0 and the mutual kinetic energy T_1 do not vanish. Using $T_1 = \underline{m}^T\dot{\underline{q}}$ respectively $T_2 = \tfrac{1}{2}\,\dot{\underline{q}}^T\,\underline{M}\,\dot{\underline{q}}$, we obtain

$$\underline{m}(\underline{q}, t) = \left[\begin{array}{c} \tfrac{3}{2}(M + 2m)\ \dot{x}_A(t)\ l\cos\theta_1 \\ m\ \dot{x}_A(t)\ l\cos\theta_2 \end{array}\right] \qquad (2.350)$$

and the total mass matrix of the system

$$\underline{M}(\underline{q}) = \left[\begin{array}{cc} \tfrac{9}{4}(M + 4m)l^2 & 3ml^2\cos(\theta_1 + \theta_2) \\ 3ml^2\cos(\theta_1 + \theta_2) & \tfrac{4}{3}ml^2 \end{array}\right] \qquad (2.351)$$

It is easy to see that in this forced vibration situation the transport kinetic energy does not depend on the generalized coordinates $\underline{q}$, so $T_{o,\underline{q}} = 0$. In Section 2.15 it was shown that for a constant solution $\underline{q}_o$ of the Lagrange's equations of motion we should demand $V^*_{,\underline{q}} = V_{,\underline{q}} - T_{o,\underline{q}} = \underline{0}^T$. So, the presence of this transport kinetic energy will not change the possible equilibrium positions of the system. Also on the second derivative $V^*_{,\underline{q}\underline{q}}$ this transport kinetic energy will have no effect, meaning that also the stability question is identical.

So, we will use the same stable equilibrium position as derived in example 2.29 on page 96, namely $\underline{q}_o^T = [\pi/2\ ,\ 0]$.

Next, we consider the Lagrange's equations of motion of this system. Using the expression for the kinetic energy of this system, the first term in the Lagrange's equations can be evaluated as follows

$$(T_{,\dot{\underline{q}}})^T = \left[\begin{array}{c} \tfrac{3}{2}(M + 2m)\,\dot{x}_A l\cos\theta_1 + \tfrac{9}{4}(M + 4m)\,l^2\dot{\theta}_1 \\ +3ml^2\dot{\theta}_2\cos(\theta_1 + \theta_2) \\ \hline \\ m\dot{x}_A l\cos\theta_2 + 3ml^2\dot{\theta}_1\cos(\theta_1 + \theta_2) + \tfrac{4}{3}ml^2\dot{\theta}_2 \end{array}\right] \qquad (2.352)$$

$$\left[\tfrac{d}{dt}\left(T_{,\dot{\underline{q}}}\right)\right]^{T} =$$

$$\begin{bmatrix} \tfrac{3}{2}\left(M+2m\right)\ddot{x}_{A}l\cos\theta_{1} - \tfrac{3}{2}\left(M+2m\right)\dot{x}_{A}l\dot{\theta}_{1}\sin\theta_{1} \\ +\tfrac{9}{4}\left(M+4m\right)l^{2}\ddot{\theta}_{1} + 3ml^{2}\ddot{\theta}_{2}\cos\left(\theta_{1}+\theta_{2}\right) \\ -3ml^{2}\dot{\theta}_{2}\left(\dot{\theta}_{1}+\dot{\theta}_{2}\right)\sin\left(\theta_{1}+\theta_{2}\right) \\ \hline m\ddot{x}_{A}l\cos\theta_{2} - m\dot{x}_{A}l\dot{\theta}_{2}\sin\theta_{2} + 3ml^{2}\ddot{\theta}_{1}\cos\left(\theta_{1}+\theta_{2}\right) \\ -3ml^{2}\dot{\theta}_{1}\left(\dot{\theta}_{1}+\dot{\theta}_{2}\right)\sin\left(\theta_{1}+\theta_{2}\right) + \tfrac{4}{3}ml^{2}\ddot{\theta}_{2} \end{bmatrix} \quad (2.353)$$

The second term becomes

$$\left(T_{,\underline{q}}\right)^{T} = \begin{bmatrix} -\tfrac{3}{2}\left(M+2m\right)\dot{x}_{A}l\dot{\theta}_{1}\sin\theta_{1} - 3ml^{2}\dot{\theta}_{1}\dot{\theta}_{2}\sin\left(\theta_{1}+\theta_{2}\right) \\ -m\dot{x}_{A}l\dot{\theta}_{2}\sin\theta_{2} - 3ml^{2}\dot{\theta}_{1}\dot{\theta}_{2}\sin\left(\theta_{1}+\theta_{2}\right) \end{bmatrix}$$
$$(2.354)$$

The third term can be derived from the (unchanged) potential energy function, resulting in

$$\left(V_{,\underline{q}}\right)^{T} = \begin{bmatrix} k_{t}\theta_{1} - \tfrac{3}{2}Mgl\sin\theta_{1} - 3mgl\sin\theta_{1} \\ mgl\sin\theta_{2} \end{bmatrix} \quad (2.355)$$

So, we obtain the Lagrange's equation of motion for this example in the form

$$\tfrac{3}{2}\left(M+2m\right)\ddot{x}_{A}l\cos\theta_{1} + \tfrac{9}{4}\left(M+4m\right)l^{2}\ddot{\theta}_{1} + 3ml^{2}\ddot{\theta}_{2}\cos\left(\theta_{1}+\theta_{2}\right)$$
$$- 3ml^{2}\dot{\theta}_{2}^{2}\sin\left(\theta_{1}+\theta_{2}\right) + k_{t}\theta_{1} - \tfrac{3}{2}\left(M+2m\right)gl\sin\theta_{1} = 0$$
$$(2.356)$$

$$m\ddot{x}_{A}l\cos\theta_{2} + 3ml^{2}\ddot{\theta}_{1}\cos\left(\theta_{1}+\theta_{2}\right) + \tfrac{4}{3}ml^{2}\ddot{\theta}_{2}$$
$$- 3ml^{2}\dot{\theta}_{1}^{2}\sin\left(\theta_{1}+\theta_{2}\right) + mgl\sin\theta_{2} = 0 \qquad (2.357)$$

We observe that already for this seemingly simple example, the Lagrange's equations of motion take an extremely complicated appearance, although they have been derived in a fairly simple and straightforward way. The coupled second-order differential equations of motion appear to contain a number of strongly nonlinear terms.

We have seen that the kinetic energy leads to the following contribution in the linearized equations of motion (see (2.255):

$$\left\{\tfrac{d}{dt}(T_{,\dot{\underline{q}}}) - T_{,\underline{q}}\right\}^{T} =$$

$$\underline{M}_{o}\,\ddot{\underline{q}}_{1} + \underline{G}_{o}\,\dot{\underline{q}}_{1} + [\underline{K}_{o}^{m} - \underline{K}_{o}^{g}]\,\underline{q}_{1} + (\underline{m}_{,t})_{o} - (T_{o,\underline{q}})_{o}^{T}$$
$$(2.358)$$

In this example the transport kinetic energy T_{0} appears to be independent of $\underline{q}$, so that

$$T_{0,\underline{q}} = \underline{0}^{T} \qquad (2.359)$$

This means that the terms $(T_o,q)_o^T$ and $\underline{K}_o^g \, \underline{q}_1$ which were the result of the linearization of the term $\overline{T}_{0,\underline{q}}$ around the equilibrium position $\underline{q}_o$ will be zero too.

It follows that the matrix $\underline{m}_{,q}$ for this example takes the form

$$\underline{m}_{,\underline{q}} = \begin{bmatrix} -\frac{3}{2}(M+2m)\dot{x}_A l \sin\theta_1 & 0 \\ 0 & -m\dot{x}_A l \sin\theta_2 \end{bmatrix} \tag{2.360}$$

This is a diagonal matrix, so we can conclude that for this example the gyroscopic matrix $\underline{G}(\underline{q}_0, t)$ vanishes, i.e.

$$\underline{G}(\underline{q}_0, t) = \underline{0} \tag{2.361}$$

For the part $\underline{m}_{,t}$ we can derive

$$\underline{m}_{,t} = \begin{bmatrix} \frac{3}{2}(M+2m)l\ddot{x}_A(t)\cos\theta_1 \\ ml\ddot{x}_A(t)\cos\theta_2 \end{bmatrix} \tag{2.362}$$

The linearized form of this term was shown to be

$$\underline{m}_{,t} \approx (\underline{m}_{,t})_o + \underline{K}_o^m \, \underline{q}_1 \tag{2.363}$$

with

$$(\underline{m}_{,t})_o = \begin{bmatrix} 0 \\ ml\ddot{x}_A(t) \end{bmatrix} \tag{2.364}$$

$$\underline{K}_o^m = [(\underline{m}_{,t}),\underline{q}]_{\underline{q}_o} = \begin{bmatrix} -\frac{3}{2}(M+2m)l\ddot{x}_A(t) & 0 \\ 0 & 0 \end{bmatrix}$$

The only term we still need is the mass matrix $\underline{M}$, evaluated for the equilibrium position $\underline{q}_0$, giving

$$\underline{M}(\underline{q}_0) = \begin{bmatrix} \frac{9}{4}(M+4m)l^2 & 0 \\ 0 & \frac{4}{3}ml^2 \end{bmatrix} \tag{2.365}$$

Using all the above results, the kinetic energy contribution to the linearized Lagrange's equations of motion can be expressed as follows

$$\begin{bmatrix} \frac{9}{4}(M+4m)l^2 & 0 \\ 0 & \frac{4}{3}ml_2 \end{bmatrix} \begin{bmatrix} \ddot{\varphi}_1 \\ \ddot{\varphi}_2 \end{bmatrix}$$

$$+ \begin{bmatrix} -\frac{3}{2}(M+2m)l\ddot{x}_A(t) & 0 \\ 0 & 0 \end{bmatrix} \begin{bmatrix} \varphi_1 \\ \varphi_2 \end{bmatrix} + \begin{bmatrix} 0 \\ ml\ddot{x}_A(t) \end{bmatrix} \tag{2.366}$$

Example 2.38

Next, we consider again the speed-regulator as introduced in example 2.32 on page 102. For the kinetic energy we have found

$$T = 2Ml^2\dot{\varphi}^2\sin^2\varphi + 4ml^2(\dot{\varphi}^2 + \Omega^2\sin^2\varphi) \tag{2.367}$$

Hence, the result for T_0, $\underline{m}$ and $\underline{M}$ becomes

$$T_0 = 4ml^2\Omega^2 \sin^2\varphi = T_0(\underline{q})$$
$$\underline{m} = 0 \tag{2.368}$$
$$\underline{M} = 4Ml^2 \sin^2\varphi + 8ml^2 = \underline{M}(\underline{q})$$

So, this is a situation where the transport kinetic energy T_o is a function of the (only) generalized coordinate φ.

In example 2.32 on page 102 we found two stable equilibrium positions, depending on the value for the constant rotational speed Ω

$$\begin{array}{lll} \varphi_o = 0 & for & 0 \leq \Omega \leq \Omega_c \\ \cos\varphi_o = (\Omega_c/\Omega)^2 & for & \Omega \geq \Omega_c \end{array} \tag{2.369}$$

with

$$\Omega_c^2 = \left[1 + \frac{M}{2m}\right]\frac{g}{2l} \tag{2.370}$$

The contribution of the kinetic energy to the linearized equations of motion was found to be

$$\left\{\tfrac{d}{dt}(T_{,\dot{q}}) - T_{,q}\right\}^T =$$

$$\underline{M}_o\,\ddot{\underline{q}}_1 + \underline{G}_o\,\dot{\underline{q}}_1 + [\underline{K}_o^m - \underline{K}_o^g]\,\underline{q}_1 + (\underline{m}_{,t})_o - (T_{o,\underline{q}})_o^T \tag{2.371}$$

If we define a dimensionless rotorspeed $\alpha := \frac{\Omega}{\Omega_c}$, we can write

- $\Omega \leq \Omega_c$ or $\alpha \leq 1.0$

$$\begin{aligned} \underline{M}_o &= [4Ml^2\sin^2\varphi + 8ml^2]_{\varphi=0} = 8ml^2 \\ \underline{G}_o &= 0 \\ \underline{K}_o^m &= 0 \\ \underline{K}_o^g &= [8ml^2\Omega^2\cos(2\varphi)]_{\varphi=0} = 8ml^2\Omega_c^2\alpha^2 \\ (\underline{m}_{,t})_o &= 0 \\ (T_{o,\underline{q}})_o^T &= [4ml^2\Omega^2\sin(2\varphi)]_{\varphi=0} = 0 \end{aligned} \tag{2.372}$$

So, for this equilibrium position the central mass M seems to be not relevant because it does not move for small rotations of the arms around this position. For $\Omega = 0$, the only remaining term is $\underline{M}_o = 8ml^2$, which is the total mass moment of inertia of the two arms with respect to their support C.

- $\Omega \geq \Omega_c$ or $\alpha \geq 1.0$

$$\begin{aligned} \underline{M}_o &= [4Ml^2\sin^2\varphi + 8ml^2]_{\varphi_0} = 8ml^2 + 4Ml^2[\tfrac{\alpha^4-1}{\alpha^4}] \\ \underline{G}_o &= 0 \\ \underline{K}_o^m &= 0 \\ \underline{K}_o^g &= [8ml^2\Omega^2\cos(2\varphi)]_{\varphi_0} = 8ml^2\Omega_c^2[\tfrac{2-\alpha^4}{\alpha^2}] \\ (\underline{m}_{,t})_o &= 0 \\ (T_{o,\underline{q}})_o^T &= [4ml^2\Omega^2\sin(2\varphi)]_{\varphi_0} = 8ml^2\Omega_c^2\tfrac{1}{\alpha^2}\sqrt{\alpha^4-1} \end{aligned} \tag{2.373}$$

For very high rotational speeds $\Omega \to \infty$, we get $\alpha \to \infty$, giving $\underline{M}_o \to (8ml^2 + 4Ml^2)$, $\underline{K}_o^g \to -8ml^2\Omega^2 \to \infty$ and $(T_o,\underline{q})_o^T \to 8ml^2\Omega_c^2$.

Example 2.39

Next, we consider again the beam-pendulum system with moving support of example 2.18 on page 71. The kinetic energy for this system was found to be

$$T = \frac{1}{2}m\dot{s}^2(t) - ml\dot{s}(t)\sin\theta\ \dot{\theta} + \frac{2}{3}ml^2\ \dot{\theta}^2 \qquad (2.374)$$

So, for this system the expressions for T_o, T_1 and T_2 become

$$\begin{aligned}
T_o &= T_o(t) &= \tfrac{1}{2}m\dot{s}^2(t)\\
T_1 &= T_1(\underline{q},\dot{\underline{q}},t) &= -ml\dot{s}(t)\sin\theta\ \dot{\theta}\\
T_2 &= T_2(\dot{\underline{q}}) &= \tfrac{2}{3}ml^2\ \dot{\theta}^2
\end{aligned} \qquad (2.375)$$

It is left to the reader to verify that the transport kinetic energy T_o for this example does not contribute to the linearized equations of motion. Because we only have a single degree of freedom (θ), the mass matrix degenerates to the scalar quantity

$$\underline{M} = \left[\frac{4}{3}ml^2\right] \qquad (2.376)$$

and the row matrix $\underline{m}^T$ also degenerates to a scalar quantity

$$\underline{m}^T = [-ml\dot{s}\sin\theta] \qquad (2.377)$$

depending explicitly on θ and t (via $\dot{s}$).
In example 2.32 on page 102 we derived that the only stable equilibrium position for this system is $\theta = 0$. For this equilibrium position the linearized version of $\underline{m}_{,t}$ becomes

$$\underline{m}_{,t} = -ml\ddot{s}\sin\theta \approx (\underline{m}_{,t})_o + \underline{K}_o^m(t)\ \theta_1 \qquad (2.378)$$

with $(\underline{m}_{,t})_o = 0$ and $\underline{K}_o^m(t) = -ml\ddot{s}(t)$. For the gyroscopic matrix $\underline{G}_o$ we get

$$\underline{G}_o = \left[(\underline{m}_{,\underline{q}}) - (\underline{m}_{,\underline{q}})^T\right]_{\underline{q}_o} = 0 \qquad (2.379)$$

This is trivial, because a skew-symmetric (1×1)-matrix can only be the scalar 0. Inserting (2.375) and (2.378) into (2.294), we obtain the contribution of the kinetic energy to the linearized equations of motion

$$\frac{d}{dt}(T_{,\dot{\underline{q}}}) - T_{,\underline{q}} = \left[\frac{4}{3}ml^2\ddot{\theta}_1 - ml\ddot{s}\theta_1\right] \qquad (2.380)$$

In this example the second term in the right-hand side of (2.380), which is linear in the perturbation $\theta_1(t)$, has a time-dependent coefficient $ml\ddot{s}(t)$. Linear systems with time-dependent coefficients will not be treated here any further.

Example 2.40

In the right part of Fig. 2.25, a so-called Laval-rotor has been drawn schematically. It consists of a shaft, supported by two bearings and a symmetrically positioned disk. If we assume a symmetrical motion, the disk (with mass m) will only move in the $[\vec{e}_X, \vec{e}_Y]$-plane and its position can be expressed by two displacements in this plane. The flexibility of the bearings and the shaft (two springs in series) can be modelled as a single linear spring with spring stiffness k_x respectively k_y, as shown in the left part of the figure. These springs connect the shaft to a fictive rigid ring which is assumed to rotate with constant angular velocity Ω in its plane about its centre, which is the origin of the inertial frame X, Y. These stiffnesses can be different for example in case of a non-rotational symmetric shaft (rectangular cross-section) or a shaft with a crack. We assume that in the shaft also some damping will be

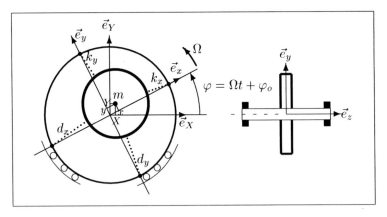

Fig. 2.25 Simple rotor model

*present which is modelled by the two viscous dampers d_x respectively d_y. This type of damping is often called **internal** damping because it is fixed to the rotating system. The springs k_x, k_y and dampers d_x, d_y are directed along the axes of the rotating orthogonal reference frame x, y which is embedded in the ring and whose origin coincides with the origin of the orthogonal inertial frame X, Y. Additionally, the mass m is subjected to **external** damping forces proportional to the absolute velocities $\dot{X}$ and $\dot{Y}$, where the proportionality constant is h in* *both directions. This is called external damping because it is due to a motion of the rotor with respect to the surrounding world (frequently a fluid-structure interaction).*

From Fig. 2.25, the position vector of m is given by

$$\vec{r} = x\vec{e}_x + y\vec{e}_y \tag{2.381}$$

where $\vec{e}_x$ and $\vec{e}_y$ are unit vectors along the rotating body axes x and y, respectively. These rotating coordinates x and y are selected as generalized coordinates, so that in this example

$$\underline{q} = \begin{bmatrix} x \\ y \end{bmatrix} \tag{2.382}$$

Moreover, the angular velocity vector of the system is

$$\vec{\omega} = \Omega \, \vec{e}_z \tag{2.383}$$

where $\vec{e}_z$ is a unit vector normal to $\vec{e}_x$ and $\vec{e}_y$. Taking the time derivative of (2.381) and recognizing that the unit vectors $\vec{e}_x$ and $\vec{e}_y$ rotate with angular velocity $\vec{\omega}$, we obtain the absolute velocity vector of the mass m

$$\begin{aligned} \vec{v} &= \dot{\vec{r}}_{rel} + \vec{\omega} \times \vec{r} \\ &= \dot{x} \, \vec{e}_x + \dot{y} \, \vec{e}_y + \Omega \, \vec{e}_z \times (x \, \vec{e}_x + y \, \vec{e}_y) \\ &= (\dot{x} - \Omega \, y) \vec{e}_x + (\dot{y} + \Omega \, x) \vec{e}_y \end{aligned} \tag{2.384}$$

where $\dot{\vec{r}}_{rel}$ is the velocity of m relative to the rotating body axes. Now, the kinetic energy of the mass m is

$$\begin{aligned} T &= \frac{1}{2} \, m \, \vec{v} \cdot \vec{v} = \frac{1}{2} \, m \, \left[(\dot{x} - \Omega \, y)^2 + (\dot{y} + \Omega \, x)^2 \right] \\ &= T_0 + T_1 + T_2 \end{aligned} \tag{2.385}$$

where

$$T_0 = \frac{1}{2} \, m \, \Omega^2 \left(x^2 + y^2 \right) = T_0 \left(\underline{q} \right) \tag{2.386}$$

$$T_1 = m\Omega \left(x\dot{y} - \dot{x}y \right) = \underline{m}^T \dot{\underline{q}} \tag{2.387}$$

$$\underline{m}^T = [-m\Omega y \quad m\Omega x] = \underline{m}^T \left(\underline{q} \right) \tag{2.388}$$

$$T_2 = \frac{1}{2} m \left(\dot{x}^2 + \dot{y}^2 \right) = \frac{1}{2} \, \dot{\underline{q}}^T \underline{M} \, \dot{\underline{q}} \tag{2.389}$$

$$\underline{M} = \begin{bmatrix} m & 0 \\ 0 & m \end{bmatrix} \tag{2.390}$$

Note that T_0 and $\underline{m}$ are not explicitly depending on time. In example 2.42, page 128, of the following subsection, we will show that the

origin $x = 0$, $y = 0$ is an equilibrium position of this system. We deter-
mine the quantities $\left(T_{0,\underline{q}}\right)_{\underline{q}_0}$, $\underline{m}_{,t}^T$, $\underline{K}_0^g$, $\underline{G}_0$ and $\underline{M}_0$ in the right-hand
side of (2.346) with respect to this equilibrium position and obtain

$$\left(T_{0,\underline{q}}\right)_{\underline{q}_0=\underline{0}} = \left[m\Omega^2 x \quad m\Omega^2 y\right]_{\underline{q}_0=\underline{0}} = [0 \quad 0] \qquad (2.391)$$

$$\underline{m}_{,t}^T = [0 \quad 0] \qquad (2.392)$$

$$\underline{K}_0^g = \left\{\left(T_{0,\underline{q}}\right)_{,\underline{q}}\right\}_{\underline{q}_0=\underline{0}} = \begin{bmatrix} m\Omega^2 & 0 \\ 0 & m\Omega^2 \end{bmatrix} \qquad (2.393)$$

$$\underline{G}_0 = \left[\left(\underline{m}_{,\underline{q}}\right) - \left(\underline{m}_{,\underline{q}}\right)^T\right]_{\underline{q}_0=\underline{0}} = \begin{bmatrix} 0 & -2m\Omega \\ 2m\Omega & 0 \end{bmatrix} (2.394)$$

$$\underline{M}_0 = \underline{M}\left(\underline{q}_0 = \underline{0}\right) = \begin{bmatrix} m & 0 \\ 0 & m \end{bmatrix} \qquad (2.395)$$

Hence, for this example (2.346) becomes

$$\frac{d}{dt}\left(T_{,\dot{\underline{q}}}\right)^T - \left(T_{,\underline{q}}\right)^T = \begin{bmatrix} m & 0 \\ 0 & m \end{bmatrix}\begin{bmatrix} \ddot{x} \\ \ddot{y} \end{bmatrix}$$
$$+ \begin{bmatrix} 0 & -2m\Omega \\ 2m\Omega & 0 \end{bmatrix}\begin{bmatrix} \dot{x} \\ \dot{y} \end{bmatrix} - \begin{bmatrix} m\Omega^2 & 0 \\ 0 & m\Omega^2 \end{bmatrix}\begin{bmatrix} x \\ y \end{bmatrix}(2.396)$$

2.17.3   Contribution of the potential energy; the effective stiffness matrix

In Subsection 2.16.3 the power series expansion of the potential energy about an equilibrium position has already been considered for systems with $T_{0,q} = \underline{0}^T$. For systems with $T_{0,q} \neq \underline{0}^T$ we can use again the quadratic expression (2.300), provided we allow the potential energy to depend under some circumstances explicitly on time. Hence, we slightly modify (2.300) as

$$V\left(\underline{q},t\right) \cong V\left(\underline{q}_0, t\right) + \left(V_{,\underline{q}}\right)_{\underline{q}_0} \underline{q}_1 + \frac{1}{2}\underline{q}_1^T \underline{K}_0 \, \underline{q}_1 \qquad (2.397)$$

with $\underline{K}_0$ being again the symmetric stiffness matrix

$$\underline{K}_0 = [k_{ij}] = \left[\frac{\partial^2 V}{\partial q_i \partial q_j}\right]_{\underline{q}=\underline{q}_0} = \left[\left(V_{,\underline{q}}\right)^T_{,\underline{q}}\right]_{\underline{q}_0} \qquad (2.398)$$

If $T_{0,q} \neq \underline{0}^T$ the equilibrium positions $\underline{q}_0$ satisfy the equations (see (2.237))

$$\left(V^*_{,\underline{q}}\right)_{\underline{q}_0} = \left(V_{,\underline{q}}\right)_{\underline{q}_0} - \left(T_{0,\underline{q}}\right)_{\underline{q}_0} = \underline{0}^T \qquad (2.399)$$

corresponding to equilibrium between restoring forces of potential-energy origin (the $V_{,q}$ term) and centrifugal forces (the $T_{0,q}$ term). Here, the modified or effective or dynamic potential $V^*\left(\underline{q}, t\right)$ was defined to be the difference between the potential energy $V\left(\underline{q}, t\right)$ and the transport kinetic energy $T_0\left(\underline{q}, t\right)$, see (2.238). It is recalled from the discussion in the previous subsection that the transport kinetic energy does not contribute to the first term in the left-hand side of the Lagrange's equations of motion (2.153), see (2.332). In view of this, the potential energy $V\left(\underline{q}, t\right)$ and the transport kinetic energy $T_0\left(\underline{q}, t\right)$ only contribute to the Lagrange's equations via the first derivative of their difference, i.e. in the form of

$$V_{,\underline{q}}^* = V_{,\underline{q}} - T_{0,\underline{q}} \tag{2.400}$$

Because of the above state of affairs, it is common practice to combine the expansion (2.397) for $V\left(\underline{q}, t\right)$ and the expansion for $T_0\left(\underline{q}, t\right)$ following from (2.333) to an expansion for $V^*\left(\underline{q}, t\right)$

$$V^*\left(\underline{q}, t\right) \cong V^*\left(\underline{q}_0, t\right) + \left(V_{,\underline{q}}^*\right)_{\underline{q}_0} \underline{q}_1 + \frac{1}{2}\, \underline{q}_1^T \underline{K}_0^* \, \underline{q}_1 \tag{2.401}$$

where the symmetric matrix

$$\underline{K}_0^* = \left[\left(V_{,\underline{q}}^*\right)^T_{,\underline{q}}\right]_{\underline{q}_0} = \left[\left(V_{,\underline{q}}\right)^T_{,\underline{q}}\right]_{\underline{q}_0} - \left[\left(T_{0,\underline{q}}\right)^T_{,\underline{q}}\right]_{\underline{q}_0}$$

$$= \underline{K}_0 - \underline{K}_0^g = \underline{K}_0^{*^T} \tag{2.402}$$

is called the *modified stiffness matrix*, the *effective stiffness matrix* or the *dynamic stiffness matrix*. The modified or effective stiffness coefficients are composed of the so-called *elastic stiffness coefficients* arising from the potential energy and the so-called *geometric stiffness coefficients* arising from the transport kinetic energy. Because the equilibrium position $\underline{q}_0$ satisfies (2.399), the linear term in the right side of (2.401) becomes zero, so that the expansion for $\underline{V}^*\left(\underline{q}, t\right)$ reduces to

$$V^*\left(\underline{q}, t\right) \cong V^*\left(\underline{q}_0, t\right) + \frac{1}{2}\, \underline{q}_1^T \underline{K}_0^* \, \underline{q}_1 \tag{2.403}$$

Example 2.41

For the speed regulator of **Proell** *the modified potential* $V^*(\underline{q})$ *was formulated in example 2.32 on page 102*

$$V^*(\underline{q}) = -2(M + 2m)gl\cos\varphi - 4ml^2\Omega^2\sin^2\varphi \tag{2.404}$$

This yielded the following equilibrium positions (see page 121)

$$\begin{array}{llll} (A) & \varphi_o = 0 & 0 \le \Omega < \infty \\ & & & (2.405) \\ (B) & \cos\varphi_o = (\Omega_c/\Omega)^2 & \Omega \ge \Omega_c \end{array}$$

and the corresponding effective stiffness matrices (scalar elements for this system with only one degree of freedom)

$$(A) \qquad \underline{K}_o = 8ml^2(\Omega_c^2 - \Omega^2)$$

$$(B) \qquad \underline{K}_o = 8ml^2(\tfrac{\Omega^4 - \Omega_c^4}{\Omega^2})$$

(2.406)

Example 2.42

We consider the rotor system of example 2.40 of the previous subsection, see Fig. 2.25. The linear springs k_x and k_y are characterized by the potential energy

$$V = \frac{1}{2}k_x x^2 + \frac{1}{2}k_y y^2 \qquad (2.407)$$

This equation implies that the origin of the reference frame x, y coincides with the unstretched spring position. The modified potential V^* follows from (2.407) and (2.386)

$$V^* = V - T_0 = \frac{1}{2}\left[\left(k_x - m\Omega^2\right)x^2 + \left(k_y - m\Omega^2\right)y^2\right] \qquad (2.408)$$

The equilibrium equations (2.399) become

$$\left.\begin{array}{l} V^*,_x = \left(k_x - m\Omega^2\right)x = 0 \\ V^*,_y = \left(k_y - m\Omega^2\right)y = 0 \end{array}\right\} \qquad (2.409)$$

These linear equations yield the only equilibrium position (for $k_x \neq k_y$)

$$x_0 = 0 \quad , \quad y_0 = 0 \qquad (2.410)$$

Using (2.398) and (2.407), we obtain the following stiffness matrix

$$\underline{K}_0 = \begin{bmatrix} k_x & 0 \\ 0 & k_y \end{bmatrix} \qquad (2.411)$$

Combining (2.334), (2.411) and (2.402), we can express the modified stiffness matrix as

$$\underline{K}_0^* = \begin{bmatrix} \left(k_x - m\Omega^2\right) & 0 \\ 0 & \left(k_y - m\Omega^2\right) \end{bmatrix} \qquad (2.412)$$

2.17.4   Power series expansion of the generalized nonconservative forces

The remaining quantities to be considered in the linearization process of the Lagrange's equations of motion are the generalized nonconservative forces

$\underline{Q}^{nc}$. In general, the generalized nonconservative forces will explicitly depend on $t, \underline{q}$ and $\underline{\dot{q}}$

$$\underline{Q}^{nc} = \underline{Q}^{nc}\left(\underline{q}, \underline{\dot{q}}, t\right) \tag{2.413}$$

This equation has the same appearance as the corresponding equation (2.304) for systems without prescribed coordinates. (2.413) can be evaluated in a similar way as (2.304), resulting again in (2.305)-(2.310). Hence, the resulting decomposition (2.316) of the generalized nonconservative forces for linear systems remains unchanged for systems with $T_{0,q} \neq \underline{0}^T$, so that

$$\underline{Q}^{nc} = \underline{Q}(t) + \underline{Q}^k(t) + \underline{Q}^d(t) = \underline{Q}(t) - \underline{K}_o^Q \, \underline{q}_1(t) - \underline{D}_0 \, \underline{\dot{q}}_1(t) \tag{2.414}$$

where the column $\underline{Q}(t)$ is given by (2.306), while the matrices $\underline{K}_o^Q$ and $\underline{D}_0$ are defined by (2.307) respectively (2.310).

Example 2.43

---

*We consider again the rotor system of examples 2.40 (page 124) and 2.42 (page 128). The linear (**internal**) dampers d_x and d_y are characterized by Rayleigh's dissipation function*

$$R^d = \frac{1}{2} \, d_x \, \dot{x}^2 + \frac{1}{2} \, d_y \, \dot{y}^2 \tag{2.415}$$

where d_x and d_y are coefficients of viscous damping. Comparing (2.415) and (2.312), we conclude that the (internal) damping matrix associated with d_x and d_y has the form

$$\underline{D}_0 = \begin{bmatrix} d_x & 0 \\ 0 & d_y \end{bmatrix} \tag{2.416}$$

*We will return to the **external** damping forces (also introduced in example 2.40) in the next example on page 130. In this example the first two terms in the right side of (2.414) vanish.*

Although the decomposition of the generalized nonconservative forces for linear systems given by (2.414) seems to cover all possible cases, this does not appear to be the case. For systems, whose motions are described with respect to rotating reference frames, another class of nonconservative forces can arise. In practice, such forces can occur in power-transmitting components such as cranks, shafts, etc., and they usually do not depend explicitly on time. They are referred to as *circulatory forces*, which often occur in tandem with viscous damping forces. For linear systems circulatory forces can be expressed as

$$\underline{Q}^{circ} = -\left(R^{circ}, \underline{\dot{q}}_1\right)^T \tag{2.417}$$

where the function

$$R^{circ} = \frac{1}{2}\,\underline{\dot{q}}_1^T \underline{D}'\,\underline{\dot{q}}_1 + \underline{\dot{q}}_1^T\,\underline{H}\,\left(\underline{q}_0 + \underline{q}_1\right) \tag{2.418}$$

is referred to as the *circulatory function*. In the above circulatory function the matrix $\underline{D}'$ appears to be symmetric, i.e. $\underline{D}' = \left(\underline{D}'\right)^T$, whereas the *circulatory matrix* $\underline{H}$ appears to be skew-symmetric, i.e. $\underline{H} = -\underline{H}^T$. For more information about circulatory forces the reader is referred to Bolotin (1964), Huseyn (1978) and Ziegler (1968). An example with circulatory forces will be discussed below. From (2.417) and (2.418), we conclude that the circulatory forces can be expressed as

$$\underline{Q}^{circ} = -\underline{D}'\,\underline{\dot{q}}_1 - \underline{H}\,\underline{q}_0 - \underline{H}\,\underline{q}_1 \tag{2.419}$$

Example 2.44

*We consider again the wheel system of examples 2.40, 2.42 and 2.43 on the pages 124, 128 and 129. No we will look at the **external** damping forces introduced in this problem. These forces, by definition acting in the directions X and Y, are associated with the dissipation function*

$$R^{circ} = \frac{1}{2}\,h\,\left(\dot{X}^2 + \dot{Y}^2\right) \tag{2.420}$$

where h is the proportionality constant for the external viscous damping forces defined in example 2.40. To express $\dot{X}$ and $\dot{Y}$ in terms of $x, y, \dot{x}$ and $\dot{y}$, we refer to Fig. 2.25 (page 124), and write

$$\begin{aligned} X &= x\cos\Omega t - y\sin\Omega t \\ Y &= x\sin\Omega t + y\cos\Omega t \end{aligned} \tag{2.421}$$

Taking time derivatives, we have

$$\begin{aligned} \dot{X} &= (\dot{x} - \Omega y)\cos\Omega t - (\dot{y} + \Omega x)\sin\Omega t \\ \dot{Y} &= (\dot{x} - \Omega y)\sin\Omega t + (\dot{y} + \Omega x)\cos\Omega t \end{aligned} \tag{2.422}$$

We observe that $\dot{X}$ and $\dot{Y}$ are merely the projections of $\vec{v}$ (see (2.384)) on the inertial axes X and Y, respectively. Inserting (2.422) into (2.420), we obtain

$$R^{circ} = \frac{1}{2}\,h\,\left[(\dot{x} - \Omega y)^2 + (\dot{y} + \Omega x)^2\right] \tag{2.423}$$

The circulatory function (2.423) leads to the circulatory forces

$$\underline{Q}^{circ} = -\left(R^{circ}_{,\underline{\dot{q}}}\right)^T = -\begin{bmatrix} h\,(\dot{x} - \Omega y) \\ h\,(\dot{y} + \Omega x) \end{bmatrix} \tag{2.424}$$

$$= -\begin{bmatrix} h & 0 \\ 0 & h \end{bmatrix}\begin{bmatrix} \dot{x} \\ \dot{y} \end{bmatrix} - \begin{bmatrix} 0 & -\Omega h \\ \Omega h & 0 \end{bmatrix}\begin{bmatrix} x \\ y \end{bmatrix}$$

Comparing (2.424) and (2.419), we obtain the matrix $\underline{D}'$

$$\underline{D}' = \begin{bmatrix} h & 0 \\ 0 & h \end{bmatrix} \tag{2.425}$$

as well as the circulatory matrix

$$\underline{H} = \begin{bmatrix} 0 & -\Omega h \\ \Omega h & 0 \end{bmatrix} \tag{2.426}$$

Adding (2.419) to the right side of (2.414), the total contribution of the generalized nonconservative forces to the linearized Lagrange's equations of motion can be written as

$$\underline{Q}^{nc} = \underline{Q}(t) + \underline{Q}^k + \underline{Q}^d + \underline{Q}^{circ} =$$

$$\underline{Q}(t) - \underline{D}_0^* \, \dot{\underline{q}}_1 - (\underline{H} + \underline{K}_o^Q) \, \underline{q}_1 - \underline{H} \, \underline{q}_0 \tag{2.427}$$

where

$$\underline{D}_0^* = \underline{D}_0 + \underline{D}' \tag{2.428}$$

is the total damping matrix of the system, which is symmetric as has been clarified earlier. It is recalled that the circulatory matrix $\underline{H}$ is skew-symmetric.

2.17.5 The resulting linearized Lagrange's equations of motion

The resulting linearized Lagrange's equations of motion can be obtained by inserting the approximations for the kinetic energy, the potential energy and the generalized nonconservative forces, derived in the preceding subsections, into the Lagrange's equations of motion (2.153). Introducing (2.346), (2.397) and (2.427) into (2.153) and using additionally, in stead of the potential energy V and the transport kinetic energy T_0, the effective potential $V^* = V - T_0$, see also (2.400), (2.401) and (2.402), we obtain the following set of linearized differential equations of motion

$$\underline{M}_0 \, \ddot{\underline{q}}_1(t) + (\underline{D}_0^* + \underline{G}_0) \, \dot{\underline{q}}_1(t) + [\underline{K}_0^* + \underline{H} + \underline{K}_o^m + \underline{K}_o^Q] \, \underline{q}_1(t) +$$

$$\left(V^*_{,\underline{q}} \right)_{\underline{q}_0}^T + \underline{H} \, \underline{q}_0 = \underline{Q}(t) - (\underline{m}_{,t})_0 := \underline{Q}^*(t) \tag{2.429}$$

According to the definition given in Section 2.15, the equilibrium configuration can be found from (2.429) by putting $\underline{q}_1(t) = \underline{0}$, $\underline{Q}(t) = \underline{0}$, $\underline{m}_{,t} = \underline{0}$ and deleting from $\left(V^*_{,\underline{q}} \right)_{\underline{q}_0}$ contributions that depend explicitly on time. This results in the set of equilibrium equations

$$\left(V^*_{,\underline{q}} \right)_{\underline{q}_0}^T + \underline{H} \, \underline{q}_0 = \underline{0} \tag{2.430}$$

which is a generalization of (2.237) obtained in Section 2.15 due to the presence of the term $\underline{H}\ \underline{q}_0$. Again, (2.430) constitute a set of algebraic generally nonlinear equations. Inserting (2.430) into (2.429) we obtain the linearized Lagrange's equations of motion in the form

$$\underline{M}_0\ \underline{\ddot{q}}_1(t) + (\underline{D}_0^* + \underline{G}_0)\ \underline{\dot{q}}_1(t) + \left[\underline{K}_0^* + \underline{H} + \underline{K}_o^m + \underline{K}_o^Q\right]\underline{q}_1(t)$$
$$= \underline{Q}(t) - \left(\underline{m}_{,t}\right)_0 := \underline{Q}^*(t) \tag{2.431}$$

In (2.431) the constant symmetric matrices $\underline{M}_0$, $\underline{D}_0^*$ and $\underline{K}_0^*$ are the mass, damping and modified stiffness matrix, respectively, whereas the skew-symmetric matrices $\underline{G}_0$ and $\underline{H}$ are the gyroscopic matrix and the circulatory matrix, respectively.
For systems for which $\underline{K}_o^m$ and $\underline{K}_o^Q$ vanish, (2.431) reduces to

$$\underline{M}_0\ \underline{\ddot{q}}_1(t) + (\underline{D}_0^* + \underline{G})\ \underline{\dot{q}}_1(t) + (\underline{K}_0^* + \underline{H})\ \underline{q}_1(t) = \underline{Q}^*(t) \tag{2.432}$$

Example 2.45

We consider the wheel system of examples 2.40, 2.42, 2.43, 2.44, see Fig. 2.25. Using (2.396), (2.412), (2.416), (2.425), (2.426), (2.427) and (2.428), the linearized equations of motion for this system take the form

$$\begin{bmatrix} m & 0 \\ 0 & 0 \end{bmatrix}\begin{bmatrix} \ddot{x} \\ \ddot{y} \end{bmatrix} + \begin{bmatrix} d_x + h & -2m\Omega \\ 2m\Omega & d_y + h \end{bmatrix}\begin{bmatrix} \dot{x} \\ \dot{y} \end{bmatrix} \tag{2.433}$$

$$\tag{2.434}$$

$$\begin{bmatrix} (k_x - m\Omega^2) & -\Omega h \\ \Omega h & (k_y - m\Omega^2) \end{bmatrix}\begin{bmatrix} x \\ y \end{bmatrix} = \begin{bmatrix} 0 \\ 0 \end{bmatrix} \tag{2.435}$$

From (2.435), the algebraic matrix equation for a (time-independent) equilibrium position x_0, y_0 becomes

$$\begin{bmatrix} (k_x - m\Omega^2) & -\Omega h \\ \Omega h & (k_y - m\Omega^2) \end{bmatrix}\begin{bmatrix} x_0 \\ y_0 \end{bmatrix} = \begin{bmatrix} 0 \\ 0 \end{bmatrix} \tag{2.436}$$

It is immediately obvious that the trivial solution $x_0 = 0$, $y_0 = 0$ represents an equilibrium point, regardless of the values of the system parameters. For a non-zero equilibrium position the determinant of the matrix should be zero. For a non-symmetric rotor (for example with a rectangular shaft cross section or a rotor with a crack) also nonzero equilibrium positions can be found for rotorspeeds in the range $\frac{k_x}{m} < \Omega^2 < \frac{k_y}{m}$. Here we assumed that $k_x < k_y$. We will not look at those solutions here, (see e.g. [Kraker-00]). It can be shown by means of stability analysis that the equilibrium point $x_0 = 0$, $y_0 = 0$ is stable if $m\Omega^2 \leq k_x$ and, also, $m\Omega^2 \leq k_y$ and unstable otherwise.

Example 2.46

For the speed regulator of **Proell**, *the effective stiffness matrices $\underline{K}_o^*$ for the two possible equilibrium positions have been derived in example 2.41 on page 127. The contribution of the kinetic energy to the linearized equations of motion has been evaluated in example 2.38 on page 121. For the latter we should keep in mind that the terms $\underline{K}_o^g$ and $(T_{0,q})_o^T$ (coming from the linearization of $T_{0,q}$), have already been taken into account when using the effective potential function V^*.*

So, we get the linearized equations of motion for the two situations (using the definition for the dimensionless rotorspeed $\alpha = \frac{\Omega}{\Omega_c}$)

- $\Omega \leq \Omega_c$ *or* $\alpha \leq 1.0$

$$\ddot{\varphi} + \Omega_c^2[1 - \alpha^2]\,\varphi = 0 \qquad (2.437)$$

This is the equation of motion of an undamped mass-spring system with an eigenfrequency ω which is dependent on the rotorspeed Ω (or α), namely

$$\omega = \Omega_c \sqrt{1 - \alpha^2} \qquad (2.438)$$

- $\Omega \geq \Omega_c$ *or* $\alpha \geq 1.0$

$$\{1 + \frac{M}{2m}\frac{\alpha^4 - 1}{\alpha^4}\}\,\ddot{\varphi} + \Omega_c^2\left(\frac{\alpha^4 - 1}{\alpha^2}\right)\,\varphi = 0 \qquad (2.439)$$

In this case the undamped eigenfrequency is

$$\omega = \frac{\alpha\,\Omega_c}{\sqrt{\frac{\alpha^4}{\alpha^4 - 1} + \frac{M}{2m}}} \qquad (2.440)$$

The results are illustrated in Fig. 2.46. The dashed line shows again the (stable) equilibrium position φ_o (zero for $\alpha \leq 1$). The solid line gives the eigenfrequency for small vibrations around this equilibrium position as function of the dimensionless rotorspeed.

From this figure we can see that for $\Omega > \Omega_c$ the angle φ_o directly is a measure for the rotational speed Ω of the device. So in this area it can serve as a rotational speed measurement instrument. For $\Omega \gg \Omega_c$ the eigenfrequency for small vibrations can be approximated by

$$\omega^2 \approx \Omega^2/(1 + \frac{M}{2m})$$

This asymptotic value is shown in the figure by a dotted line.

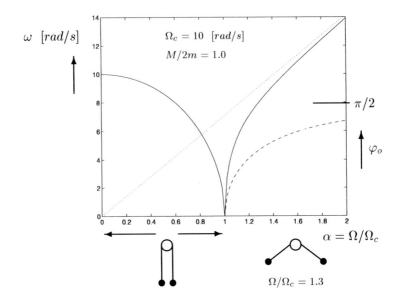

Fig. 2.26 Equilibrium positions and undamped eigenfrequencies

The class of systems covered by (2.432) will be discussed in Section 4.6. If the skew-symmetric matrices $\underline{G}_0$ and $\underline{H}$ disappear from the formulation, a system with symmetric matrices arises

$$\underline{M}_0 \, \underline{\ddot{q}}_1(t) + \underline{D}_0^* \, \underline{q}_1(t) + \underline{K}_0^* \, \underline{q}_1(t) = \underline{Q}^*(t) \qquad (2.441)$$

Systems with symmetric matrices will be treated in Chapter 3 (the undamped case) and in Sections 4.3 and 4.5 of Chapter 4 (the damped case).

2.18 A PRIORI LINEAR SYSTEMS

Using the methodology of Lagrange, the equations of motion of complex mechanical systems can be derived in a direct and systematic way. In general these equations of motion will be both coupled and nonlinear which will tend to make the solution process rather complicated. Then the procedures from the preceeding section can be applied to generate a set of linearized equations of motion which are valid in the neighbourhood of a stable equilibrium position.

In practice, however, we are frequently dealing with mechanical systems which are assumed to carry out small vibrations around some (trivial) equilibrium state and whose linearized equations of motion can be derived in a direct, simplified procedure. In this direct procedure the equations of motion for the linear system with a large number of degrees of freedom can be derived very systematically by means of a matrix formulation. It is recalled from (2.112) that the kinetic energy $T = T(q, \dot{q}, t)$ can be written in general as

$$T = T_o + \underline{m}^T \dot{q} + \frac{1}{2} \dot{q}^T \underline{M} \dot{q} \tag{2.442}$$

Example 2.18 on page 71 demonstrates the structure of (2.442) for a specific application. For linear systems with n degrees of freedom (generalized coordinates) the first term T_o and the factor $\underline{m}$ in the second term will only contain the explicit time-dependency and will not be a function of q and/or $\dot{q}$. The symmetric $(n \times n)$ mass matrix $\underline{M}$ will only contain constants.

The total potential energy $V = V(q)$ for a linear system will only contain up to quadratic terms in the elements of q, so that it can always be written as

$$V = V_o + \underline{k}^T q + \frac{1}{2} q^T \underline{K} q \tag{2.443}$$

with $\underline{K}$ being the so-called symmetric $(n \times n)$ stiffness matrix. Example 2.30 on page 101 shows an application of such a stiffness matrix.

In the presence of viscous damping terms the column matrix of non-conservative external forces $\underline{Q}^{nc}$ can be written as

$$\underline{Q}^{nc} = \underline{f}(t) - \underline{D} \dot{q} \tag{2.444}$$

where the column matrix $\underline{f}(t)$ contains the (external) loads, while the (symmetric, $(n \times n)$) matrix $\underline{D}$ is called the viscous damping matrix.

Applying now the methodology to derive Lagrange's equations from the above a priori linearized results, we obtain

$$[T_{,\dot{q}}]^T = \underline{m} + \underline{M}\dot{q}; \qquad \frac{d}{dt}[T_{,\dot{q}}]^T = \dot{\underline{m}} + \underline{M} \ddot{q}$$
$$[T_{,q}]^T = \underline{0}; \qquad [V_{,q}]^T = \underline{k} + \underline{K} q \tag{2.445}$$

In this way, we finally arrive at the following linear set of equations

$$\underline{M}\ddot{q}(t) + \underline{D}\dot{q}(t) + \underline{K}q(t) = \underline{Q}(t) = -\dot{\underline{m}}(t) - \underline{k}(t) + \underline{f}(t) \tag{2.446}$$

Example 2.47

To illustrate the above simplified procedure, which can often be applied when dealing with such an a priori linear system, we consider the simple two-dimensional, 2 degree-of-freedom model shown in Fig 2.27. It consists of a uniform beam with length 2l and mass M. The beam is supported at its right end (in point R) by a combination of a linear *spring with stiffness constant k_1 and a viscous damper with damping constant d. In the centre of gravity Z of the beam a second linear spring is mounted (with spring stiffness k_2). At the (upper) end of this spring a point mass m is connected. The vertical displacement of the left end of this beam (point L) is forced to follow a prescribed function s(t). The*

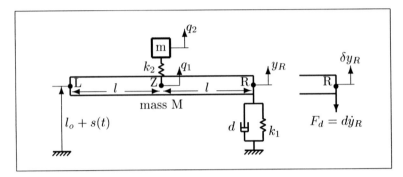

Fig. 2.27   Two-degree-of-freedom model

displacements of this system are measured from the static equilibrium position with s(t) = 0. This implies that the effect of gravity can be ignored. The constant l_o is chosen such that for s(t) = 0 the beam will have a horizontal position. As the generalized coordinates we choose the vertical displacement q_1 of the centre of gravity Z and the displacement q_2 of the point mass m, so that $\underline{q}^T = [q_1, q_2]$. The prescribed displacement s(t) will be small and therefore it seems to be correct to assume that the responses will be small too, at least sufficiently small to allow for the application of linear theory. The counter-clockwise rotation φ of the beam and the displacement y_R of the pont R of the beam can be expressed in terms of the generalized coordinates q_1 and q_2 as follows

$$\varphi(t) = \frac{q_1(t) - s(t)}{l}; \qquad y_R(t) = 2q_1(t) - s(t) \qquad (2.447)$$

Now, the kinetic energy can be written as

$$\begin{aligned} T &= \frac{1}{2}M\dot{q}_1^2 + \frac{1}{2}J_z\dot{\varphi}^2 + \frac{1}{2}m\dot{q}_2^2 \\ &= \frac{1}{2}[\frac{4}{3}M\dot{q}_1^2 + m\dot{q}_2^2] - \frac{1}{3}M\dot{q}_1\dot{s} + \frac{1}{6}M\dot{s}^2 \qquad (2.448) \end{aligned}$$

where we used the formula $J_Z = \frac{1}{3}Ml^2$ for the mass-moment of inertia of the beam around its centre of gravity. The kinetic energy can be rewritten in the standard form

$$T = \frac{1}{2}\dot{\underline{q}}^T \underline{M}\,\dot{\underline{q}} + \underline{m}^T\dot{\underline{q}} + T_o \qquad (2.449)$$

with

$$M = \begin{bmatrix} \frac{4}{3}M & 0 \\ 0 & m \end{bmatrix} ; \; \underline{m} = \begin{bmatrix} -\frac{1}{3}M\dot{s}(t) \\ 0 \end{bmatrix} ; \; T_o = \frac{1}{6}M\dot{s}^2(t) \quad (2.450)$$

The potential energy (here only the elastic energy) takes the form

$$V^{in} = \frac{1}{2}k_1 y_R^2 + \frac{1}{2}k_2(q_2 - q_1)^2 \quad (2.451)$$

This can also be rewritten in the standard form

$$V^{in} = \frac{1}{2}\underline{q}^T \underline{K} \; \underline{q} + \underline{k}^T \underline{q} + V_o \quad (2.452)$$

with

$$\underline{K} = \begin{bmatrix} 4k_1 + k_2 & -k_2 \\ -k_2 & k_2 \end{bmatrix} ; \; \underline{k} = \begin{bmatrix} -2k_1 s(t) \\ 0 \end{bmatrix} ; \; V_o = \frac{1}{2}k_1 s^2(t) \quad (2.453)$$

For the evaluation of the gegeneralized non-conservative forces we only have to look at the contribution due to viscous damping. The only viscous damping force is $F_d = d \; \dot{y}_R(t)$ shown in the right part of Fig. 2.27. From the virtual work of this force due to a virtual displacement $\delta y_R(t)$, the corresponding generalized forces can be calculated to be

$$\delta W = -F_d \; \delta y_R = -d(2\dot{q}_1 - \dot{s}) \; 2\delta q_1 := \underline{\dot{q}}^T \; \underline{Q}^{nc} \quad (2.454)$$

This directly yields the following column $\underline{Q}^{nc}(t)$ of generalized forces

$$\underline{Q}^{nc} = \begin{bmatrix} -4d\dot{q}_1 + 2d\dot{s} \\ 0 \end{bmatrix} = -\underline{D}\underline{\dot{q}} + \underline{f}(t) \quad (2.455)$$

From this result we conclude that the viscous damping matrix $\underline{D}$ and the column matrix of excitations $\underline{f}(t)$ become

$$\underline{D} = \begin{bmatrix} 4 \, d & 0 \\ 0 & 0 \end{bmatrix} ; \quad \underline{f}(t) = \begin{bmatrix} 2 \, d \, \dot{s} \\ 0 \end{bmatrix} \quad (2.456)$$

Application of the methodology to derive Lagrange's equations finally results in the following set of 2 coupled, linear equations of motion in matrix form

$$\underline{M} \; \underline{\ddot{q}} + \underline{D} \; \underline{\dot{q}} + \underline{K} \; \underline{q} = -\underline{\dot{m}}(t) - \underline{k}(t) + \underline{f}(t) \quad (2.457)$$

or

$$\begin{bmatrix} \frac{4}{3}M & 0 \\ 0 & m \end{bmatrix} \underline{\ddot{q}}(t) + \begin{bmatrix} 4d & 0 \\ 0 & 0 \end{bmatrix} \underline{\dot{q}}(t) + \begin{bmatrix} 4k_1 + k_2 & -k_2 \\ -k_2 & k_2 \end{bmatrix} \underline{q}(t) =$$

$$= \begin{bmatrix} \frac{1}{3}M\ddot{s} + 2d\dot{s} + 2k_1 s \\ 0 \end{bmatrix} \quad (2.458)$$

2.19   CHAPTER PROBLEMS

2.19.1   Offshore Crane

We will look at a deep-floating offshore crane vessel for mounting and dismounting of oil production platforms as shown schematically in Fig. 2.28. The main part is a large rigid structure consisting of the deck and the two driver sections and the crane. This part has a mass M, centre of gravity Z and mass moment of inertia J_Z with respect to Z. We only will look at planar

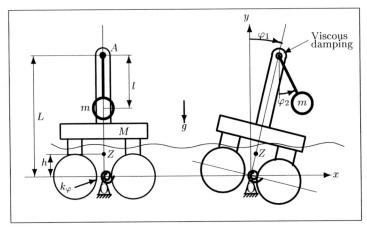

Fig. 2.28   Two-degree-of-freedom model of an offshore crane

rotations of the structure and assume that these rotations take place around a fictitious fixed point O. The hydrostatic effects which will drive the structure back to its vertical position are assumed to be represented by the torsional spring k_φ. The centre of mass Z is located at a distance h above this rotation point.

In a point A of the crane (at a distance L above the rotational point) a working load (modelled as a point mass m) is hanging on a massless, inextensible cable with length l. The whole system is operating in a gravitational field of strength g. All the friction effects in the combination of crane and load are taken into account by assuming that in the hinge A a viscous damping moment will be present with a magnitude which is proportional to the angular velocity difference between crane and cable with proportionality constant c.

So, we are dealing with a two-degree-of-freedom system. As generalised coordinates we choose the rotations φ_1 and φ_2 as shown in the figure, giving $\underline{q}^T = [\varphi_1 \, , \, \varphi_2]$.

First, we will derive the nonlinear equations of motion using the formalism of Lagrange. For the ship's kinetic energy we can write

$$T_s = \frac{1}{2}Mv_Z^2 + \frac{1}{2}J_Z\dot{\varphi}_1^2 \qquad (2.459)$$

where $\underline{v}_Z = \underline{\dot{x}}_Z$ is the velocity of the centre of gravity for which we can write

$$\underline{v}_Z = \underline{\dot{x}}_Z = \frac{d}{dt} \begin{bmatrix} h \sin\varphi_1 \\ h\cos\varphi_1 \end{bmatrix} = h\dot{\varphi}_1 \begin{bmatrix} \cos\varphi_1 \\ -\sin\varphi_1 \end{bmatrix} \qquad (2.460)$$

So we get

$$T_s = \frac{1}{2}Mh^2\dot{\varphi}_1^2 + \frac{1}{2}J_Z\dot{\varphi}_1^2 = \frac{1}{2}\{J_Z + Mh^2\}\dot{\varphi}_1^2 = \frac{1}{2}J_O\,\dot{\varphi}_1^2 \qquad (2.461)$$

Because we are dealing with a rotation of a rigid body around the fixed point O we might also write down directly the last equation which is based on the mass moment of inertia of the ship with respect of this fixed point O. Using Steiner's rule we can write $J_O = J_Z + Mh^2$.

The load in the crane can be treated as a point mass, so that the kinetic energy can be written as

$$T_m = \frac{1}{2}m\,\underline{v}_m^T\underline{v}_m \qquad (2.462)$$

with the absolute velocity $\underline{v}_m$ of mass m being

$$\underline{v}_m = \underline{\dot{x}}_m = \frac{d}{dt} \begin{bmatrix} L\sin\varphi_1 + l\sin\varphi_2 \\ L\cos\varphi_1 - l\cos\varphi_2 \end{bmatrix} = \begin{bmatrix} L\dot{\varphi}_1\cos\varphi_1 + l\dot{\varphi}_2\cos\varphi_2 \\ -L\dot{\varphi}_1\sin\varphi_1 + l\dot{\varphi}_2\sin\varphi_2 \end{bmatrix} \qquad (2.463)$$

This gives

$$
\begin{aligned}
T_m &= \frac{1}{2}m\{L^2\dot{\varphi}_1^2 + l^2\dot{\varphi}_2^2 + 2\,L\,l\,\dot{\varphi}_1\dot{\varphi}_2[\cos\varphi_1\cos\varphi_2 - \sin\varphi_1\sin\varphi_2]\} \\
&= \frac{1}{2}m\{L^2\dot{\varphi}_1^2 + l^2\dot{\varphi}_2^2 + 2\,L\,l\,\dot{\varphi}_1\dot{\varphi}_2\cos(\varphi_1 + \varphi_2)\} \qquad (2.464)
\end{aligned}
$$

For the potential energy we can write

$$V = \frac{1}{2}k_\varphi\varphi_1^2 + \{Mgh\cos\varphi_1 + mg[L\cos\varphi_1 - l\cos\varphi_2]\} \qquad (2.465)$$

where the first part is the elastic energy and the second part the potential energy due to gravity (zero level for $y = 0$).

The only part which has not yet been introduced into our model is the viscous damping in the hinge A. To derive the generalized force column $\underline{Q}^{nc}$ which will take account of this, we first separate the two parts and introduce the viscous damping moments as shown in Fig 2.29. If we choose the positive directions as shown in the figure (using action=reaction) we can write for both the damping moments $M_A = c(\dot{\varphi}_1 + \dot{\varphi}_2)$. If we next apply a virtual displacement (=rotation) $\delta\underline{q}^T = [\delta\varphi_1,\ 0]$, only the left moment is contributing to the virtual work

$$\delta W = -M_A\,\delta\varphi_1 = Q_1^{nc}\,\delta\varphi_1 \Longrightarrow Q_1^{nc} = -c\,(\dot{\varphi}_1 + \dot{\varphi}_2) \qquad (2.466)$$

If we next apply the virtual displacement $\delta\underline{q}^T = [0,\ \delta\varphi_2]$ we can write

$$\delta W = -M_A\,\delta\varphi_2 = Q_2^{nc}\,\delta\varphi_2 \Longrightarrow Q_2^{nc} = -c\,(\dot{\varphi}_1 + \dot{\varphi}_2) \qquad (2.467)$$

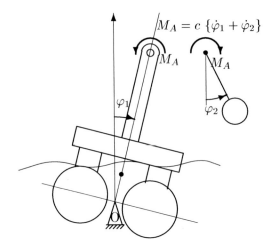

Fig. 2.29   Viscous damping mopment in hinge A

So we get

$$\underline{Q}^{nc} = -c \left[\begin{array}{c} (\dot{\varphi}_1 + \dot{\varphi}_2) \\ (\dot{\varphi}_1 + \dot{\varphi}_2) \end{array} \right] = -\underline{D}\,\dot{q} \tag{2.468}$$

where we introduced the viscous damping matrix $\underline{D}$

$$\underline{D}^{nc} = c \left[\begin{array}{cc} 1 & 1 \\ 1 & 1 \end{array} \right] \tag{2.469}$$

The final step in getting the set of differential equations will be the application of Lagrange's equations. For the kinetic energy we found

$$T = \frac{1}{2}\{J_o + mL^2\}\dot{\varphi}_1^2 + \frac{1}{2}ml^2\dot{\varphi}_2^2 + m\,L\,l\,\dot{\varphi}_1\dot{\varphi}_2\cos(\varphi_1 + \varphi_2) \tag{2.470}$$

This leads to

$$T_{,\dot{q}} = \left[\begin{array}{c} \{J_o + mL^2\}\dot{\varphi}_1 + mLl\dot{\varphi}_2\cos(\varphi_1 + \varphi_2) \\ ml^2\dot{\varphi}_2 + mLl\dot{\varphi}_1\cos(\varphi_1 + \varphi_2) \end{array} \right] \tag{2.471}$$

$$\frac{d}{dt}\{T_{,\dot{q}}\} = \left[\begin{array}{c} (J_o + mL^2)\ddot{\varphi}_1 + mLl\ddot{\varphi}_2\cos(\varphi_1 + \varphi_2) \\ - mLl\dot{\varphi}_2(\dot{\varphi}_1 + \dot{\varphi}_2)\sin(\varphi_1 + \varphi_2) \\ - \ - \ - \ - \ - \ - \ - \ - \\ ml^2\ddot{\varphi}_2 + mLl\ddot{\varphi}_1\cos(\varphi_1 + \varphi_2) \\ - mLl\dot{\varphi}_1(\dot{\varphi}_1 + \dot{\varphi}_2)\sin(\varphi_1 + \varphi_2) \end{array} \right] \tag{2.472}$$

$$T_{,q} = \left[\begin{array}{c} - mLl\dot{\varphi}_1\dot{\varphi}_2\sin(\varphi_1 + \varphi_2) \\ - mLl\dot{\varphi}_1\dot{\varphi}_2\sin(\varphi_1 + \varphi_2) \end{array} \right] \tag{2.473}$$

$$V_{,q} = \left[\begin{array}{c} -Mgh\sin\varphi_1 - mgl\sin\varphi_1 + k_\varphi\,\varphi_1 \\ mgl\sin\varphi_2 \end{array} \right] \tag{2.474}$$

Combining these expressions gives two coupled, strongly nonlinear differential equations

$$\{J_o + mL^2\}\ddot{\varphi}_1 + mLl\ddot{\varphi}_2 \cos(\varphi_1 + \varphi_2) - mLl\dot{\varphi}_2^2 \sin(\varphi_1 + \varphi_2)$$
$$-\{Mgh + mgl\} \sin\varphi_1 + k_\varphi \varphi_1 + c\{\dot{\varphi}_1 + \dot{\varphi}_2\} = 0$$
$$\text{and} \tag{2.475}$$
$$ml^2\ddot{\varphi}_2 + mLl\ddot{\varphi}_1 \cos(\varphi_1 + \varphi_2) - mLl\dot{\varphi}_1^2 \sin(\varphi_1 + \varphi_2)$$
$$+mgl \sin\varphi_2 + c\{\dot{\varphi}_1 + \dot{\varphi}_2\} = 0$$

We can see that the position $\varphi_1 = \varphi_2 = 0$ is an equilibrium solution of these equations. If we now assume the rotations φ_1 and φ_2 to be small enough, we can linearize the equations using $\sin\varphi_i = \varphi_i$ and $\cos\varphi_i = 1$. This first gives

$$\{J_o + mL^2\}\ddot{\varphi}_1 + mLl\ddot{\varphi}_2 - mLl\dot{\varphi}_2^2(\varphi_1 + \varphi_2)$$
$$-\{Mgh + mgl\}\varphi_1 + k_\varphi \varphi_1 + c\{\dot{\varphi}_1 + \dot{\varphi}_2\} = 0$$
$$\text{and} \tag{2.476}$$
$$ml^2\ddot{\varphi}_2 + mLl\ddot{\varphi}_1 - mLl\dot{\varphi}_1^2(\varphi_1 + \varphi_2) + mgl\varphi_2 + c\{\dot{\varphi}_1 + \dot{\varphi}_2\} = 0$$

In these equations the third terms in both the equations are higher-order terms (order φ_i^3), so that they may be neglected. This finally gives

$$\begin{bmatrix} J_o + mL^2 & mLl \\ mLl & ml^2 \end{bmatrix} \begin{bmatrix} \ddot{\varphi}_1 \\ \ddot{\varphi}_2 \end{bmatrix} + c \begin{bmatrix} 1 & 1 \\ 1 & 1 \end{bmatrix} \begin{bmatrix} \dot{\varphi}_1 \\ \dot{\varphi}_2 \end{bmatrix}$$
$$+ \begin{bmatrix} k_\varphi - (Mh + mL)g & 0 \\ 0 & mgl \end{bmatrix} \begin{bmatrix} \varphi_1 \\ \varphi_2 \end{bmatrix} = \begin{bmatrix} 0 \\ 0 \end{bmatrix} \tag{2.477}$$

We can see that the stiffness matrix is a diagonal matrix and that it will only be positive definite (so the solution will be stable) when both diagonal terms are positive. This means that for a stable solution the stiffness k_φ should fulfil

$$k_\varphi > (Mh + mL)g \tag{2.478}$$

In fact, this also directly follows from the evaluation of a static equilibrium position as shown in Fig 2.30.

2.19.2 Vibration Isolation

Very sophisticated equipment such as electron microscopes, measurement apparatus, etc. has to be isolated from its environment as much as possible. Especially, the transfer from ground vibrations to the equipment has to be eliminated. This can be done by mounting the equipment on very flexible elements such as air springs. Such an apparatus and its support is schematically shown in the left part of Fig. 2.31. The machine, modelled as a rigid body with mass m, centre of gravity Z and mass moment of inertia J_Z with respect to Z is supported by two identical air springs in vertical direction and two identical air springs in horizontal direction. The air springs are assumed to concentrate their action in two points of the main body, namely the points 1

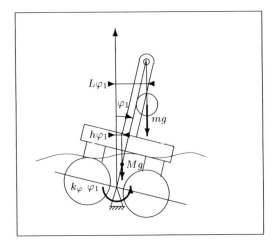

Fig. 2.30   Static equilibrium position

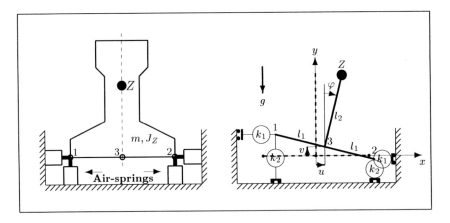

Fig. 2.31   A from its environment isolated measurement machine and the corresponding fysical model

(on the left) and 2 (on the right).

The fysical model is shown in the right part of the figuree. We will only look at (very small) planar motions and to characterise these motions we will use the 3 generalized coordinates u, v and φ, being the horizontal and vertical displacements of a fictitious point 3 and the rotation of the body, so $q^T = [u, \ v, \ \varphi]$. The system is operating in a gravitational field with strength g.

All the air springs are modelled as linear springs with spring stiffness k_1 for the horizontal springs and k_2 for the vertical springs. We also assume that the elastic energy in for example the left spring k_2 only depends on the vertical displacement of point 1. This assumption has been shown symbolically by allowing the bottom part of this spring to move freely in horizontal direction. An analogous assumption is valid for all the 4 air springs.

Additionally, we assume that all the dissipative effects (damping in the air springs due to cables coming from the machine, etc) can be represented by a single linear viscous damper acting in vertical direction in point 1 of the system. The damping constant is d and also for this damper we assume that only the vertical displacement of point 1 will be relevant. This is shown in Fig. 2.32. Finally, we assume that in the right point 2, an external force $F(t)$

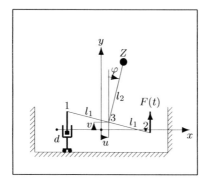

Fig. 2.32 Damping in the system and external excitation

is acting in vertical direction.

To evaluate the dynamical behaviour of this system we first will look at the nonlinear equations of motion. Next we will search for a stable equilibrium position and finally we will derive the linearized equations of motion for small motions around such an equilibrium position.

It is important to remember that $\underline{q}^T = [u\,,\,v\,,\,\varphi]$. For the rigid body kinetic energy we now can write

$$T_s = \frac{1}{2}m\,v_Z^2 + \frac{1}{2}J_Z\,\dot{\varphi}^2 \tag{2.479}$$

where $\underline{v}_Z = \underline{\dot{x}}_Z$ is the velocity of the centre of gravity for which we can write

$$\underline{v}_Z = \underline{\dot{x}}_Z = \frac{d}{dt}\begin{bmatrix} u + l_2\sin\varphi \\ v + l_2\cos\varphi \end{bmatrix} = \begin{bmatrix} \dot{u} + l_2\dot{\varphi}\cos\varphi \\ \dot{v} - l_2\dot{\varphi}\sin\varphi \end{bmatrix} \tag{2.480}$$

So we get

$$T_s = \frac{1}{2}m[\dot{u}^2 + l_2^2\dot{\varphi}^2 + \dot{v}^2 + 2l_2\dot{u}\dot{\varphi}\cos\varphi - 2l_2\dot{v}\dot{\varphi}\sin\varphi] + \frac{1}{2}J_z\dot{\varphi}^2 \tag{2.481}$$

giving

$$T_s = \frac{1}{2}m[\dot{u}^2 + \dot{v}^2] + ml_2\dot{\varphi}[\dot{u}\cos\varphi - \dot{v}\sin\varphi] + \frac{1}{2}[ml_2^2 + J_z]\dot{\varphi}^2 \quad (2.482)$$

If we call the horizontal and vertical displacement of point 1: δx_1 and δy_1 and of point 2: δx_2 and δy_2, we can write

$$\begin{aligned} \delta x_1 &= l_1(1 - \cos\varphi) + u & \delta y_1 &= l_1\sin\varphi + v \\ \delta x_2 &= u - l_1(1 - \cos\varphi) & \delta y_2 &= v - l_1\sin\varphi \end{aligned} \quad (2.483)$$

The elastic energy in the springs can then be expressed as

$$U^{el} = \frac{1}{2}k_1\delta x_1^2 + \frac{1}{2}k_1\delta x_2^2 + \frac{1}{2}k_2\delta y_1^2 + \frac{1}{2}k_2\delta y_2^2 \quad (2.484)$$

which gives

$$U^{el} = k_1[u^2 + l_1^2(1 - \cos\varphi)^2] + k_2[v^2 + l_1^2(\sin\varphi)^2] \quad (2.485)$$

For the position of the centre of mass in the inertial frame we can write

$$\underline{x}_z = \begin{bmatrix} u + l_2\sin\varphi \\ v + l_2\cos\varphi \end{bmatrix} \quad (2.486)$$

So the gravity potential reads

$$V^g = mg[v + l_2\cos\varphi] \quad (2.487)$$

Then the total potential energy becomes

$$V = k_1[u^2 + l_1^2(1 - \cos\varphi)^2] + k_2[v^2 + l_1^2(\sin\varphi)^2] + mg[v + l_2\cos\varphi] \quad (2.488)$$

The nonconservative forces which have to be transformed into the column of generalized forces are shown in Fig. 2.33. So, we have to take into account

- The external force $F(t)$

- The viscous damping force $F_d = d\,\dot{y}_1 = d\,(\dot{v} + l_1\dot{\varphi}\cos\varphi)$

For the transformation to generalized coordinates we first apply the virtual displacement $\delta q^T = [\delta u\ ,\ 0\ ,\ 0]$. This implies a horizontal shift of the system, so the virtual work of the two vertical forces will be zero and the first generalized force Q_u will be zero too.
Next we apply the virtual displacement $\delta q^T = [0\ ,\ \delta v\ ,\ 0\ ]$. For this purely virtual shift the work will be

$$\delta W = -F_d\,\delta v + F(t)\,\delta v := Q_v\,\delta v \quad (2.489)$$

This gives the second generalized force $Q_v = F(t) - d(\dot{v} + l_1\dot{\varphi}\cos\varphi)$, dimension $[N]$.

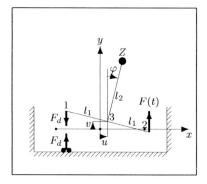

Fig. 2.33 Nonconservative forces

Finally we apply the virtual displacement $\delta \underline{q}^T = [0, 0, \delta\varphi]$ implying a rotation of the system around the point 3. For this virtual rotation the work will be

$$\delta W = -F_d \left(l_1 \delta\varphi \cos\varphi \right) - F(t) \left(l_1 \delta\varphi \cos\varphi \right) := Q_\varphi \, \delta\varphi \qquad (2.490)$$

So, the third generalized force reads $Q_\varphi = -F(t)l_1 \cos\varphi - d\dot{v}l_1 \cos\varphi - dl_1^2\dot{\varphi}\cos^2\varphi$, dimension $[Nm]$. This gives the following result for the column of generalized forces

$$\underline{Q}^{nc} = \begin{bmatrix} Q_u \\ Q_v \\ Q_\varphi \end{bmatrix} = \begin{bmatrix} 0 \\ F(t) - d(\dot{v} + l_1\dot{\varphi}\cos\varphi) \\ -F(t)l_1 \cos\varphi - d\dot{v}l_1 \cos\varphi - dl_1^2\dot{\varphi}\cos^2\varphi \end{bmatrix} \qquad (2.491)$$

Alternative

In the given coordinate system we can write

$$\underline{F}_1^{nc} = \begin{bmatrix} 0 \\ -F_d \end{bmatrix} \qquad \underline{F}_2^{nc} = \begin{bmatrix} 0 \\ F(t) \end{bmatrix} \qquad (2.492)$$

and also

$$\underline{x}_1 = \begin{bmatrix} u - l_1 \cos\varphi \\ v + l_1 \sin\varphi \end{bmatrix}; \qquad \underline{x}_2 = \begin{bmatrix} u + l_1 \cos\varphi \\ v - l_1 \sin\varphi \end{bmatrix} \qquad (2.493)$$

This leads to

$$\underline{x}_{1,\underline{q}} = \begin{bmatrix} 1 & 0 & l_1 \sin\varphi \\ 0 & 1 & l_1 \cos\varphi \end{bmatrix}; \qquad \underline{x}_{2,\underline{q}} = \begin{bmatrix} 1 & 0 & -l_1 \sin\varphi \\ 0 & 1 & -l_1 \cos\varphi \end{bmatrix} \qquad (2.494)$$

If we now use (2.64)

$$\underline{Q}^{nc} = \sum_{i=1}^{2} \left(x_{i,\underline{q}} \right)^T \underline{F}_i^{nc} \qquad (2.495)$$

we get the same expression.

Next we apply **Lagrange's equations**. The kinetic energy was found to be

$$T_s = \frac{1}{2}m[\dot{u}^2 + \dot{v}^2]ml_2\dot{u}\dot{\varphi}\cos\varphi - ml_2\dot{v}\dot{\varphi}\sin\varphi + \frac{1}{2}[ml_2^2 + J_z]\dot{\varphi}^2 \qquad (2.496)$$

We will use the following **abbreviations** $s := \sin\varphi$ and $c := \cos\varphi$. Then

$$T_{,\dot{\underline{q}}} = \begin{bmatrix} m\dot{u} + ml_2\dot{\varphi}\,c \\ m\dot{v} - ml_2\dot{\varphi}\,s \\ (ml_2^2 + J_Z)\dot{\varphi} + ml_2\dot{u}\,c - ml_2\dot{v}\,s \end{bmatrix} \qquad (2.497)$$

$$\frac{d}{dt}\{T_{,\dot{\underline{q}}}\} = \begin{bmatrix} m\ddot{u} + ml_2\ddot{\varphi}\,c - ml_2\dot{\varphi}^2\,s \\ m\ddot{v} - ml_2\ddot{\varphi}\,s - ml_2\dot{\varphi}^2\,c \\ (ml_2^2 + J_Z)\ddot{\varphi} + ml_2\ddot{u}\,c - ml_2\dot{u}\dot{\varphi}\,s - ml_2\ddot{v}\,s - ml_2\dot{v}\dot{\varphi}\,c \end{bmatrix} \qquad (2.498)$$

$$T_{,\underline{q}} = \begin{bmatrix} 0 \\ 0 \\ -ml_2\dot{u}\dot{\varphi}\,s - ml_2\dot{v}\dot{\varphi}\,c \end{bmatrix} \qquad (2.499)$$

$$V_{,\underline{q}} = \begin{bmatrix} 2k_1 u \\ 2k_2 v + mg \\ 2k_1l_1^2(1 - c)\,s + 2k_2l_1^2\,s\,c - mgl_2\,s \end{bmatrix} \qquad (2.500)$$

This finally leads us to the set of three coupled, strongly nonlinear differential-equations

$$m\ddot{u} + ml_2\ddot{\varphi}\cos\varphi - ml_2\dot{\varphi}^2\sin\varphi + 2k_1 u = 0$$

$$m\ddot{v} - ml_2\ddot{\varphi}\sin\varphi - ml_2\dot{\varphi}^2\cos\varphi + 2k_2 v + mg + d\dot{v} + dl_1\dot{\varphi}\cos\varphi = F(t)$$

$$(ml_2^2 + J_Z)\ddot{\varphi} + ml_2\ddot{u}\cos\varphi - ml_2\ddot{v}\sin\varphi + 2k_1l_1^2(1 - \cos\varphi)\sin\varphi \,+$$
$$2k_2l_1^2\sin\varphi\cos\varphi - mgl_2\sin\varphi + dl_1\dot{v}\cos\varphi + dl_1^2\dot{\varphi}\cos^2\varphi = -F(t)l_1\cos\varphi \qquad (2.501)$$

An equilibrium position can be found from

$$V_{,\underline{q}} = \begin{bmatrix} 2k_1 u \\ 2k_2 v + mg \\ \sin\varphi\,\{2k_1l_1^2(1 - \cos\varphi) + 2k_2l_1^2\cos\varphi - mgl_2\} \end{bmatrix} = \begin{bmatrix} 0 \\ 0 \\ 0 \end{bmatrix} \qquad (2.502)$$

So the (trivial) equilibrium position will be

$$\underline{q}_o = \begin{bmatrix} 0 \\ -mg/(2k_2) \\ 0 \end{bmatrix} \qquad (2.503)$$

To evaluate the stability we look at

$$V_{,\underline{qq}} = \begin{bmatrix} 2k_1 & 0 & 0 \\ 0 & 2k_2 & 0 \\ 0 & 0 & V_{33} \end{bmatrix} \qquad (2.504)$$

in which

$$V_{33} = [2k_1l_1^2(1- \cos\varphi) \cos\varphi + 2k_1l_1^2\sin^2\varphi + 2k_2l_1^2\cos^2\varphi - 2k_2l_1^2\sin^2\varphi - mgl_2\cos\varphi] \quad (2.505)$$

For the equilibrium state $\underline{q}_o$ this gives

$$\underline{K}_o = \begin{bmatrix} 2k_1 & 0 & 0 \\ 0 & 2k_2 & 0 \\ 0 & 0 & 2k_2l_1^2 - mgl_2 \end{bmatrix} \quad (2.506)$$

This stiffness matrix will only be positive definite (so the equilibrium $\underline{q}_o$ will only be stable), when

$$2k_2l_1^2 - mgl_2 > 0, \quad \text{or} \quad k_2 > \frac{mgl_2}{2l_1^2} \quad \text{or} \quad m < \frac{2k_2l_1^2}{gl_2} \quad (2.507)$$

To get the linearized equations of motion for small motions around the equilibrium position $\underline{q}_o$, we write

$$T = \frac{1}{2} \dot{\underline{q}}^T \underline{M} \dot{\underline{q}} \quad (2.508)$$

From (2.482) we can see that then the mass matrix $\underline{M}$ becomes

$$\underline{M} = \begin{bmatrix} m & 0 & ml_2\cos\varphi \\ 0 & m & -ml_2\sin\varphi \\ ml_2\cos\varphi & -ml_2\sin\varphi & (ml_2^2 + J_Z) \end{bmatrix} \quad (2.509)$$

If we evaluate this matrix for the equilibrium position, we obtain the (constant) mass matrix

$$\underline{M}_o = \begin{bmatrix} m & 0 & ml_2 \\ 0 & m & 0 \\ ml_2 & 0 & (ml_2^2 + J_Z) \end{bmatrix} \quad (2.510)$$

For the column of nonconservative forces $\underline{Q}^{nc}(\underline{q}, \dot{\underline{q}}, t)$ we can write the first order Taylor series approximation as follows

$$\underline{Q}^{nc}(\underline{q}, \dot{\underline{q}}, t) \approx \left[\underline{Q}^{nc}\right]_{\underline{q}_o, \dot{\underline{q}}=\underline{0}} + \left[\underline{Q}^{nc}_{,\underline{q}}\right]_{\underline{q}_o, \dot{\underline{q}}=\underline{0}} \underline{q}_1 + \left[\underline{Q}^{nc}_{,\dot{\underline{q}}}\right]_{\underline{q}_o, \dot{\underline{q}}=\underline{0}} \dot{\underline{q}}_1 \quad (2.511)$$

Using

$$\left[\underline{Q}^{nc}_{,\underline{q}}\right] = \begin{bmatrix} 0 & 0 & 0 \\ 0 & 0 & dl_1\dot{\varphi}\sin\varphi \\ 0 & 0 & 2dl_1^2\dot{\varphi}\cos\varphi\sin\varphi \end{bmatrix} \quad (2.512)$$

and

$$\left[\underline{Q}^{nc}_{,\dot{\underline{q}}}\right] = \begin{bmatrix} 0 & 0 & 0 \\ 0 & -d & -dl_1\cos\varphi \\ 0 & -dl_1\cos\varphi & -dl_1^2\cos^2\varphi \end{bmatrix} \quad (2.513)$$

we get the contribution of $\underline{Q}^{nc}$ to the linearized equations of motion

$$\underline{Q}^{nc} = \underline{f}(t) + \underline{D}_o \, \dot{\underline{q}}_1 \tag{2.514}$$

with

$$\underline{f}(t) = \begin{bmatrix} 0 \\ F(t) \\ -F(t)l_1 \end{bmatrix} \qquad \underline{D}_o = d \begin{bmatrix} 0 & 0 & 0 \\ 0 & 1 & l_1 \\ 0 & l_1 & l_1^2 \end{bmatrix} \tag{2.515}$$

So, finally the linearized equations of motion can be written as

$$\underline{M}_o \, \ddot{\underline{q}}_1(t) + \underline{D}_o \, \dot{\underline{q}}_1(t) + \underline{K}_o \, \underline{q}_1(t) = \underline{f}(t) \tag{2.516}$$

3

Undamped Multi-Degree-of-Freedom Linear Systems

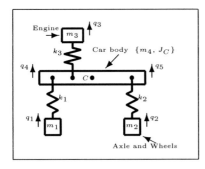

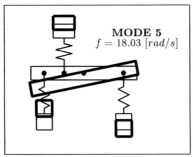

MODE 5
$f = 18.03 \ [rad/s]$

$\mathbf{T}$his chapter introduces the analysis needed to understand the vibrational behaviour of undamped systems. The important concept of a mode shape will be introduced. The left figure shows a simple 5 degree of freedom model for a half-car system and its 5th undamped normal mode. The mode shapes are the basis for the modal superposition or modal analysis method for studying the response of multiple degree of freedom systems systematically.

In design, large dynamical models can hardly be handled efficiently. Reduction methods will be presented which can systematically reduce the number of degrees of freedom.

3.1   INTRODUCTION

Vibration problems in engineering practice are still regularly investigated using approximations leading to single-degree-of-freedom linear systems with time-independent mass, stiffness and damping parameters. Although these systems are, in general, idealizations of real physical problems, they are frequently capable of capturing some essential dynamical characteristics of the system. Quite often, however, it is not possible to approximate the real physical system by a single-degree-of-freedom linear system and more refined multi-degree-of-freedom models are required. In this chapter we will elaborate the simplest class of multi-degree-of-freedom linear systems, namely the *undamped systems with time-independent symmetric matrices*. Linear systems with time-independent matrices are also referred to as *time-invariant linear systems*. . The analysis of undamped systems with symmetric matrices generally constitutes the first step in the analysis of more complex systems with damping and nonsymmetric matrices. It also enables a simple physical interpretation of the behaviour. Also, as will become clear later in Chapter 4, systems with weak damping, also called slightly damped systems, and systems with so-called proportional viscous damping can easily be analyzed using the results for undamped systems. It follows directly from (2.446) that the linearized Lagrange's equations of motion for undamped systems with time-independent symmetric matrices take the form

$$\underline{M}\ \underline{\ddot{q}}(t) + \underline{K}\ \underline{q}(t) = \underline{Q}(t) \tag{3.1}$$

In (3.1) $\underline{M}$ is the symmetric mass matrix of the system, $\underline{K}$ is the symmetric stiffness matrix and $\underline{Q}(t)$ is the column matrix with generalized forces depending explicitly on time. As we have seen in the previous chapter, the right-hand side $\underline{Q}(t)$ can also contain the influence of prescribed overall motions.

In the following sections we will first address the question whether the mass matrix and/or stiffness matrix will be positive definite or only semi-positive definite. This information will be very useful for the further evaluation of the dynamic behaviour of the system. Next we will consider the free motions of the undamped systems governed by (3.1) with $\underline{Q}(t) = \underline{0}$. Such systems belong to the class of *linear conservative natural systems*, which occupy a central position in vibrations. As we will see, these systems are capable of carrying out so-called *natural motions*, in which all the system coordinates execute harmonic oscillation at a particular frequency and with a specific displacement pattern, where the oscillation frequencies and displacement patterns are called *natural frequencies* and *natural modes*, respectively. The natural frequencies and modes represent an inherent characteristic of the system and they can be obtained by solving the so-called *algebraic eigenvalue problem* for the system, namely, a set of homogeneous algebraic equations. The solution consists of *real eigenvalues*, which are related to the natural frequencies, and *real orthogonal eigencolumns*, which represent the natural modes. The orthogonality property is very important, as it permits the transformation of the set of simultaneous (coupled) ordinary differential equations for forced motion, i.e. with $\underline{Q}(t) \neq \underline{0}$, to a set of independent (uncoupled) equations. Each of the independent equations is of second order and resembles entirely the equations of motion of un undamped single-degree-of-freedom linear system. This procedure of solving the inhomogeneous differential equations of motion is known as modal analysis or *modal decomposition* and it will be discussed in Section 3.4.

As can be concluded from the foregoing introduction, the algebraic eigenvalue problem plays a key role in the dynamic analysis of undamped multi-degree-of-freedom linear systems with symmetric matrices. The rapid rise in the ability of digital computers to process numerical solutions for systems of large order has stimulated an ever increasing interest in the development of computational algorithms for the eigenvalue problem. There are many algorithms for solving eigenvalue problems and in general two approaches can be distinguished. For systems with a moderate number of degrees of freedom (say < 100), the eigenvalue problem can be solved completely giving as many eigenfrequencies and eigenmodes as the number of degrees of freedom. An example of such an approach is the procedure *eig.m* of the *Matlab*-programme. For systems with a (very) large number of degrees of freedom (say $> 1000...300.000$) it is not only very difficult to calculate all the eigenfrequencies and modes but moreover also meaningless. For these problems an *iterative* approach has to be followed. In such an iterative method, we begin with a certain guessed solution for a (small) number of eigenmodes, corresponding to the smallest (practically relevant) eigenvalues and compute a sequence of improved guesses for this subset of eigenmodes. The iteration *converges* if, for every initial guessed solution, the subsequent sequence of guesses tends to the true solution for the subset, although the true solution itself is never reached exactly. One of the deciding factors in choosing a given interation method is the *rate of convergence*. We do not treat algorithms for solving the eigenvalue problem here. We only mention some advanced iteration methods, namely the Givens-Householder method, subspace iteration and the Lanczos method, and we refer to the literature for a comparative discussion of computational methods for the eigenvalue problem, see e.g. Géradin & Rixen (1997) and Meirovitch (1997).

3.2 SYSTEMS WITH SEMI-POSITIVE DEFINITE MATRICES; RIGID BODY MODES

In the previous chapter we have seen that the mass matrix M is directly coupled to the kinetic energy of the mechanical system and that the stiffness matrix K is coupled to the elastic energy. For many mechanical systems (except for example rotordynamic-type problems) this will result in *symmetric* matrices. Due to the fact that these matrices are coupled to energy expressions (energy will always be non-negative) both the mass matrix and the stiffness matrix will always be *semi-positive definite*. In many cases both the mass matrix and the stiffness matrix will even be *positive definite*. This can be a useful property for example if one wants to calculate the inverse of the mass matrix and/or stiffness matrix as we will see later. However, at times the property of both the mass matrix and the stiffness matrix to be positive definite can be lost. To illustrate this, we consider the simple case of a one-dimensional system consisting of a chain of two springs and two masses, as shown in Fig. 3.1. The right-hand side of the spring k_2 is loaded by a time-dependent horizontal

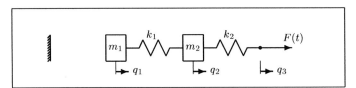

Fig. 3.1   One dimensional discrete mass-spring system

force $F(t)$. We only will look at one-dimensional (horizontal) motions and to prescibe these motions we will use the absolute displacements q_1, q_2 and q_3, measured with respect to the ground, $q^T = [q_1, q_2, q_3]$. These displacements are defined in such a way that the springs k_i ($i = 1, 2$) are unstretched if $q_i = 0$ ($i = 1, 2, 3$). Then, it is easy to derive a set of linear differential equations of motion for the system of Fig. 3.1. This set of differential equations can be expressed as follows

$$\underline{M}\,\ddot{q}(t) + \underline{K}\,q(t) = \underline{Q}(t) \tag{3.2}$$

with $\underline{M}$, $\underline{K}$ and $\underline{Q}(t)$ being the mass matrix, the stiffness matrix and the column of generalized forces. It is easy to show that

$$\underline{M} = \begin{bmatrix} m_1 & 0 & 0 \\ 0 & m_2 & 0 \\ 0 & 0 & 0 \end{bmatrix} \qquad \underline{K} = \begin{bmatrix} k_1 & -k_1 & 0 \\ -k_1 & k_1 + k_2 & -k_2 \\ 0 & -k_2 & k_2 \end{bmatrix} \tag{3.3}$$

It can be easily verified that the mass matrix $\underline{M}$ is only semi-positive definite. If we put, for example, the generalized velocities $\dot{q}_1$ and $\dot{q}_2$ equal to zero, i.e. if we take $\dot{\underline{q}}^T = [0, 0, \dot{q}_3]$ with $\dot{q}_3(t) \neq 0$, we conclude that

$$2T = \dot{\underline{q}}^T \, \underline{M} \, \dot{\underline{q}} = 0 \quad \text{for} \quad \dot{\underline{q}}^T = \begin{bmatrix} 0 & 0 & \dot{q}_3 \end{bmatrix} \neq \underline{0}^T \tag{3.4}$$

So we have a zero value of the kinetic energy for a nonzero velocity column. The physical background of this is that there is no mass associated to the specific generalized coordinate q_3. However, if we wish for the computational procedure the mass matrix $\underline{M}$ to be positive definite, this can be simply achieved by assigning a very small additional mass m_3 to the generalized coordinate q_3, for example $m_3 = 10^{-6} m_2$. From the point of view of computational accuracy, this will hardly influence the dynamic behaviour of the system, but it will create a positive-definite mass matrix $\underline{M}$. Also from a practical point of view where completely mass-less springs never will exist this approximation can be motivated.

After having discussed the mass matrix of the system, we will subsequently address the stiffness matrix of this system. We can easily verify from (3.3) that also the stiffness matrix $\underline{K}$ is only semi-positive definite. If we take, for example $\underline{q}^T = \alpha \begin{bmatrix} 1 & 1 & 1 \end{bmatrix}$ with α not equal to zero, we conclude that

$$\underline{K} \, \underline{q} = \underline{0} \quad \text{for} \quad \underline{q}^T = \alpha \begin{bmatrix} 1 & 1 & 1 \end{bmatrix} \neq \underline{0}^T \tag{3.5}$$

The physical background of this is that for $\underline{q}^T = \alpha \begin{bmatrix} 1 & 1 & 1 \end{bmatrix}$, the displacements q_1, q_2 and q_3 of the system do not differ from one another, so that the springs k_1 and k_2 remain unstretched. Hence, in view of $2U^{in} = \underline{q}^T \, \underline{K} \, \underline{q}$ the elastic energy of the system remains zero for $\underline{q}^T = \alpha \begin{bmatrix} 1 & 1 & 1 \end{bmatrix}$ being different from zero.

Generally, a displacement pattern for which a system does not undergo elastic deformation is called a **rigid-body mode** of that system. Denoting a rigid-body mode of a system by $\underline{q}^{rb}$, we have in view of (3.5)

$$\underline{K} \, \underline{q}^{rb} = \underline{0} \tag{3.6}$$

We conclude from the above discussion that rigid-body modes are the independent solutions $\underline{q} = \underline{q}^{rb} \neq \underline{0}$ of (3.6). Hence, for systems with rigid-body modes the stiffness matrix $\underline{K}$ is singular. The number of independent rigid-body modes of a certain system equals the degree of singularity of the stiffness matrix of that system. For example, it can easily be seen that the rigid-body mode $\underline{q}^T = \alpha \begin{bmatrix} 1 & 1 & 1 \end{bmatrix}$ of the system shown in Fig. 3.1 is the only independent rigid-body mode of that system. Examples of systems with rigid-body modes are

- rotor-bearing systems exhibiting torsional vibrations,

- airplanes exhibiting vibrations during flight,

- kinematically undetermined structures.

In many cases the rigid-body modes of a system can be easily identified by having a careful look at the geometrical structure of the model of that system. If this is not the case, we can apply the following more or less straightforward procedure. The key step in this procedure consists of selecting a generalized coordinate from which we know that it is an element of a certain (unknown) rigid-body mode. In the example of Fig. 3.1 we can select any generalized coordinate of the column q. Taking, for example, the generalized coordinate q_1 and assigning a special symbol to this generalized coordinate, namely $q_1 = \alpha$, we can write (3.6) for the system of Fig. 3.1 as

$$
\begin{bmatrix}
k_1 & -k_1 & 0 \\
-k_1 & k_1 + k_2 & -k_2 \\
0 & -k_2 & k_2
\end{bmatrix}
\begin{bmatrix}
\alpha \\
q_2 \\
q_3
\end{bmatrix}
=
\begin{bmatrix}
0 \\
0 \\
0
\end{bmatrix}
\tag{3.7}
$$

From the last two equations of the set (3.7) we obtain

$$
\begin{bmatrix}
k_1 + k_2 & -k_2 \\
-k_2 & k_2
\end{bmatrix}
\begin{bmatrix}
q_2 \\
q_3
\end{bmatrix}
=
\begin{bmatrix}
k_1 \\
0
\end{bmatrix}
\alpha
\tag{3.8}
$$

By means of (3.8) we can express q_2 and q_3 in terms of α as follows

$$
\begin{bmatrix}
q_2 \\
q_3
\end{bmatrix}
=
\begin{bmatrix}
k_1 + k_2 & -k_2 \\
-k_2 & k_2
\end{bmatrix}^{-1}
\begin{bmatrix}
k_1 \\
0
\end{bmatrix}
\alpha
=
\begin{bmatrix}
1 \\
1
\end{bmatrix}
\alpha
\tag{3.9}
$$

In this way, we obtain the rigid-body mode $q^T = \alpha \begin{bmatrix} 1 & 1 & 1 \end{bmatrix}$ which was already identified earlier. This procedure can be simply extended to the case of more than one rigid-body mode. In fact, by this procedure we consider the so-called null space of the matrix K.

When dealing with rigid-body modes, two strategies are available, at least in principle for the subsequent analysis

- The existence of rigid-body modes is noticed, as well as the semi-positive definiteness of the stiffness matrix, and the analysis is just continued.

- The rigid-body modes are de facto suppressed without influencing from a practical point of view the essential dynamics of the system. For example, we could also couple mass m_1 of the system to the ground by means of an additional spring k_0 with a very small stiffness (e.g. a spring with $k_0 = 10^{-6}k_1$). This again will hardly affect the essential dynamics of the system, but numerically the stiffness matrix will become positive definite. In fact, a similar procedure is followed when investigating a system with rigid-body modes experimentally. Commonly, real systems with rigid-body modes can not float free in space during an experiment. Usually, such systems are suspended on very flexible springs that just carry the weight of the system but do not add significant stiffness to the system, thereby not affecting its essential dynamic behaviour.

3.3   FREE VIBRATIONS OF UNDAMPED LINEAR SYSTEMS

3.3.1   The symmetric eigenvalue problem

For linear undamped, free vibrating systems we are dealing with

$$\underline{M}\,\underline{\ddot{q}}(t) + \underline{K}\,\underline{q}(t) = \underline{0} \tag{3.10}$$

where $\underline{M}$ and $\underline{K}$ are constant real symmetric matrices. Moreover $\underline{M}$ and $\underline{K}$ are at least semi-positive definite. We are interested in the special type of solution of (3.10) for which all the generalized coordinates $q_i(t)$, $i = 1, 2, ..., n$, contained in the column $\underline{q}(t)$, depend in a similar way on time. In this case, the system is said to execute *synchronous motion*. Physically, this implies a motion in which all generalized coordinates have the same time dependence, and the general configuration of the motion does not change, except for the amplitude, so that the ratio between any two coordinates $q_i(t)$ and $q_j(t)$, $i \neq j$, remains constant during the motion. Mathematically, this type of motion is expressed by

$$\underline{q}(t) = \underline{u}\,f(t) \quad , \quad \underline{u}^T = [u_1 \quad u_2 \cdots u_n] \tag{3.11}$$

where $u_i = u\,[i]$ $(i = 1, 2, ..., n)$ are constant amplitudes and $f(t)$ is an unknown *scalar* function of time that is the same for all the coordinates $q_i(t)$. Inserting (3.11) into (3.10), and dividing through by $f(t)$ (which should be non-zero) we obtain

$$\frac{\ddot{f}(t)}{f(t)}\,\underline{M}\,\underline{u} + \underline{K}\,\underline{u} = \underline{0} \tag{3.12}$$

The scalar equations contained in the set of equations (3.12) can be expressed as

$$-\frac{\ddot{f}(t)}{f(t)} = \frac{\sum\limits_{j=1}^{n} k_{ij}u_j}{\sum\limits_{j=1}^{n} m_{ij}u_j} \quad , \quad i = 1, 2, \cdots, n \tag{3.13}$$

where m_{ij} and k_{ij} represent the elements of the mass matrix and the stiffness matrix, respectively. We observe from those equations that the time dependence and the positional dependence are separated, which is akin to the separation of variables for partial differential equations. Using the standard argument, we observe that the left side of (3.13) does not depend on the index i, whereas the right side does not depend on time, so that the two ratios can only be a constant. Denoting the constant λ, (3.13) can be separated into a scalar time-dependent equation

$$\ddot{f}(t) + \lambda f(t) = 0 \tag{3.14}$$

and a set of positional dependent equations

$$[\underline{K} - \lambda\underline{M}]\,\underline{u} = \underline{0} \tag{3.15}$$

The solution of the second-order ordinary differential equation (3.14) can be written in the exponential form

$$f(t) = Ce^{st} \tag{3.16}$$

Introducing the solution (3.16) into (3.14), we conclude that the exponent s must satisfy the equation

$$s^2 + \lambda = 0 \tag{3.17}$$

which has two roots

$$s_{1,2} = \pm\sqrt{-\lambda} \tag{3.18}$$

In the following subsection we will prove that λ is a non-negative real number for real symmetric semi-positive definite mass and stiffness matrices. Letting $\lambda = \omega^2$, where ω is real, (3.18) yields

$$s_{1,2} = \pm j\omega \qquad \text{with} \qquad j^2 = -1 \tag{3.19}$$

In the case that $\lambda = 0$ (i.e. $s_{1,2} = 0$), the solution of (3.14) becomes

$$f(t) = C_1 + C_2 t \tag{3.20}$$

with C_1 and C_2 being arbitrary constants. This results in the same linear time dependence of each generalized coordinate $q_i(t)$, $i = 1, 2, \cdots, m$, and, hence, the associated velocities $\dot{q}_i(t), i = 1, 2, \cdots, n$, are constant.
In the case that $\lambda \neq 0$ (i.e. $s_{1,2} \neq 0$), the solution of (3.14) becomes

$$\begin{aligned} f(t) &= C_1 e^{j\omega t} + C_2 e^{-j\omega t} \\ &= B_1 \cos\omega t + B_2 \sin\omega t \\ &= A\cos(\omega t + \varphi) \end{aligned} \tag{3.21}$$

We conclude that for $\lambda \neq 0$ the time dependence is harmonic with ω the frequency of the harmonic motion. Further we have two arbitrary constants, φ (the phase angle) and A (the amplitude scaling) which will depend on the initial conditions. All three quantities (ω, φ, A) are the same for every coordinate $q_i(t)$ $(i = 1, 2, \cdots, n)$.
To complete the solution of (3.10), we must determine the frequency ω and the amplitudes u_j contained in the solution (3.11). To this end, we turn to (3.15), which constitute a set of n homogeneous algebraic equations in the unknowns $u_j = u[j]$, with $\lambda = \omega^2$ playing the role of a parameter. Only a specific set of values of ω^2 will permit a nontrivial solution of (3.15). The problem of determining the values of ω^2 for which a nontrivial solution $\underline{u}$ of (3.15) exists is known as the *characteristic-value* or (generalized) **eigenvalue problem**

$$\left[\underline{K} - \omega^2 \underline{M}\right]\underline{u} = \underline{0} \tag{3.22}$$

Equation (3.22) represents the (generalized) eigenvalue problem associated with the matrices $\underline{K}$ and $\underline{M}$ and it possesses a nontrivial solution if and only if the determinant of the matrix $\left[\underline{K} - \omega^2 \underline{M}\right]$ vanishes

$$\det\left(\underline{K} - \omega^2 \underline{M}\right) = 0 \tag{3.23}$$

where $\det \left(\underline{K} - \omega^2 \underline{M} \right)$ is called the *characteristic determinant*, with (3.23) itself being known as the *characteristic equation* or *frequency equation*. It is an equation in ω^2 of degree n, and it possesses in general n roots, referred to as *characteristic values* or *eigenvalues*. The n roots are denoted $\omega_1^2, \omega_2^2, ..., \omega_n^2$ and the (positive) square roots of these quantities are the system *natural frequencies* ω_r $(r = 1, 2, ..., n)$. The natural frequencies can be arranged in order of increasing magnitude, namely, $\omega_1 \leq \omega_2 \leq ... \leq \omega_n$. The lowest nonzero frequency is referred to as the *fundamental frequency*, and for many practical problems it is the most important one. In many cases all frequencies ω_r are nonzero and distinct, so that the equality sign does not hold. Exceptions arise in the case of rigid-body modes or in the *degenerate case*, as we will see later in Subsection 3.3.3.

Associated with any natural frequency ω_r there is a certain nontrivial column matrix $\underline{u}_r$ which is a solution of the eigenvalue problem, such that

$$\underline{K} \, \underline{u}_r = \omega_r^2 \, \underline{M} \, \underline{u}_r \qquad (3.24)$$

It will be shown in the following subsection that the elements $u_r[i]$ $(i = 1, 2, \ldots, n)$ of the column $\underline{u}_r$ are real numbers. The columns $\underline{u}_r$ $(r = 1, 2, ..., n)$ are referred to as *characteristic columns* or *eigencolumns*. The eigencolumns are also referred to as *modal columns* and represent physically the so-called *natural modes*. These columns are unique only in the sense that the *ratio* between any two elements $u_r[i]$ and $u_r[j]$ is constant. The value of the elements themselves is arbitrary, however, because (3.22) is homogeneous, so that if $\underline{u}_r$ is a solution of the equation, then $\alpha_r \underline{u}_r$ is also a solution, where α_r is an arbitrary constant, being at least theoretically even complex. Hence, we can say that the shape of the natural modes is unique, but the amplitude is not. If one of the elements of the eigencolumn $\underline{u}_r$ is assigned a certain value, then the eigencolumn is rendered unique in an absolute sense, because this automatically causes an adjustment in the values of the remaining $n - 1$ elements by virtue of the fact that the ratio between any two elements is constant. The process of adjusting the elements of the natural modes to render their amplitude unique is called *normalization*, and the resulting eigencolumns are referred to as *normal modes*. We will return to the normalization process in the following subsection.

Example 3.1

We consider the one-dimensional system shown in Fig. 3.2 which consists of three equal rigid masses m, connected by two equal linear springs with spring stiffness coefficient k and unstretched spring length ℓ_0. The masses can move without damping and friction along a straight horizontal line. The system represents a simple model describing the longitudinal dynamic behaviour of a three-carriage transport system. The motion of the system is described by means of the generalized coordinates $q_1(t)$, $q_2(t)$ and $q_3(t)$, with $q_1(t)$ being the position of the left

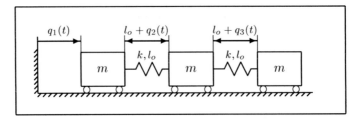

Fig. 3.2   Three-carriage railway vehicle model

mass with respect to the origin of an inertial frame, whereas $q_2(t)$ and $q_3(t)$ are the elongations of the left and right springs, respectively. The kinetic and potential energies of the system are

$$T = \frac{1}{2}m \; \dot{q}_1^2 + \frac{1}{2}m \; (\dot{q}_1 + \dot{q}_2)^2 + \frac{1}{2}m \; (\dot{q}_1 + \dot{q}_2 + \dot{q}_3)^2 \qquad (3.25)$$

$$V = \frac{1}{2}k \; q_2^2 + \frac{1}{2}k \; q_3^2 \qquad (3.26)$$

Hence, defining the column of generalized coordinates as

$$\underline{q}^T = [q_1 \; , \; q_2 \; , \; q_3] \qquad (3.27)$$

the mass and stiffness matrices for the system of Fig. 3.2 become

$$\underline{M} = m \begin{bmatrix} 3 & 2 & 1 \\ 2 & 2 & 1 \\ 1 & 1 & 1 \end{bmatrix} ; \qquad \underline{K} = k \begin{bmatrix} 0 & 0 & 0 \\ 0 & 1 & 0 \\ 0 & 0 & 1 \end{bmatrix} \qquad (3.28)$$

It is easy to see that in this example the stiffness matrix $\underline{K}$ is not positive definite. In this case the eigenvalue problem (3.22) takes the following form

$$\left[k \begin{bmatrix} 0 & 0 & 0 \\ 0 & 1 & 0 \\ 0 & 0 & 1 \end{bmatrix} - \omega^2 m \begin{bmatrix} 3 & 2 & 1 \\ 2 & 2 & 1 \\ 1 & 1 & 1 \end{bmatrix} \right] \underline{u} = \underline{0} \qquad (3.29)$$

or

$$\begin{bmatrix} -3\mu & -2\mu & -\mu \\ -2\mu & (1-2\mu) & -\mu \\ -\mu & -\mu & (1-\mu) \end{bmatrix} \underline{u} = \underline{0} \qquad (3.30)$$

where a dimensionless eigenvalue μ is introduced, defined by

$$\mu = \frac{\omega^2 m}{k} \qquad (3.31)$$

The (3rd-order) characteristic equation resulting from (3.30) is

$$\mu \left(\mu^2 - 4\mu + 3 \right) = 0 \qquad (3.32)$$

The roots of this characteristic equation are

$$\mu_1 = 0 \quad , \quad \mu_2 = 1 \quad and \quad \mu_3 = 3 \tag{3.33}$$

The corresponding natural frequencies are

$$\omega_1 = 0 \quad , \quad \omega_2 = \sqrt{\frac{k}{m}} \quad and \quad \omega_2 = \sqrt{\frac{3k}{m}} \tag{3.34}$$

We observe that in this example one of the eigenfrequencies is zero (which could be expected), whereas there are two nonzero eigenfrequencies ω_2 and ω_3.

Next, we determine the natural modes $\underline{u}_1$, $\underline{u}_2$ and $\underline{u}_3$ corresponding to these frequencies. To this end, we use (3.30). For $\mu_1 = 0$ (3.30) becomes

$$\begin{bmatrix} 0 & 0 & 0 \\ 0 & 1 & 0 \\ 0 & 0 & 1 \end{bmatrix} \underline{u}_1 = \underline{0} \tag{3.35}$$

which is equivalent to (3.6) of the preceding section. We notice that the determinant of the matrix in the left-hand side of (3.35) is indeed zero, whereas the solution for $\underline{u}_1$ of (3.35) can be written as

$$\underline{u}_1^T = \alpha\,[1\ ,\ 0\ ,\ 0] \tag{3.36}$$

with α being an arbitrary constant.
For $\mu_2 = 1$, (3.30) becomes

$$\begin{bmatrix} -3 & -2 & -1 \\ -2 & -1 & -1 \\ -1 & -1 & 0 \end{bmatrix} \underline{u}_2 = \underline{0} \tag{3.37}$$

Again, the determinant of the matrix in the left-hand side of this equation is zero. Now, we use two of the three scalar equations contained in (3.37). (A combination of all three equations has already been used to compose the characteristic equation (3.32)). Taking the second and third scalar equation contained in (3.37), we can write

$$\begin{bmatrix} -2 & -1 & -1 \\ -1 & -1 & 0 \end{bmatrix} \underline{u}_2 = \underline{0} \tag{3.38}$$

Assigning an arbitrary value to the first element $u_2\,[1]$ of $\underline{u}_2$, i.e. taking $u_2\,[1] = \beta$ with β being an arbitrary constant, we can rewrite (3.38) as

$$\begin{bmatrix} -1 & -1 \\ -1 & 0 \end{bmatrix} \begin{bmatrix} u_2\,[2] \\ u_2\,[3] \end{bmatrix} = \beta \begin{bmatrix} 2 \\ 1 \end{bmatrix} \tag{3.39}$$

The solution of this matrix equation is

$$\begin{bmatrix} u_2\,[2] \\ u_2\,[3] \end{bmatrix} = \beta \begin{bmatrix} -1 \\ -1 \end{bmatrix} \tag{3.40}$$

Together with $u_2 [1] = \beta$, this leads us to the following second natural mode or eigencolumn

$$\underline{u}_2^T = \beta [1 , -1 , -1] \qquad (3.41)$$

It is left to the reader to derive the third natural mode or eigencolumn by means of a similar procedure and to show that this eigencolumn takes the form

$$\underline{u}_3 = \gamma [1 , -3 , 3] \qquad (3.42)$$

with γ being an arbitrary constant. As can be seen from the basic expression for a free, undamped vibration as given in (3.11), the (time-independent) natural modes $\underline{u}_i$ are just the amplitude columns of the possible solutions. The variation of the motion in time is realized by the scalar time-function $f(t)$. This means that the natural modes can also be seen as the result of taken a picture of the real time-dependent vibration $\underline{q}(t)$ at an arbitrary time. The above three natural modes, $\underline{u}_1$,

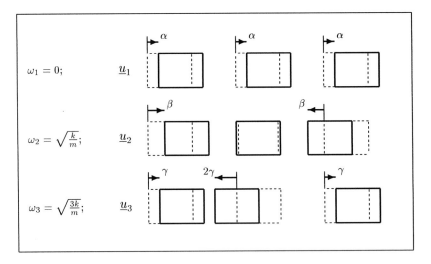

Fig. 3.3 Natural modes for freely moving three-mass system

$\underline{u}_2$ and $\underline{u}_3$ are depicted in Fig. 3.3, where the reference configuration (in which the springs are unstretched) is indicated by dashed lines, while the current configuration is indicated by solid lines. For the derivation of such a vibration display one should specially be aware of the definition of the generalized coordinates, as for this system shown in Fig. 3.3.

It can be concluded from the foregoing example that if the eigenvalue problem (3.22) possesses solutions for which $\omega_i = 0$, the corresponding eigencolumns

$\underline{u}_i$ satisfy the matrix equation

$$\underline{K}\,\underline{u}_i = \underline{0} \qquad\qquad (3.43)$$

This equation is completely equivalent to (3.6) of the previous section, defining the rigid-body modes of a system. Consequently, it can be stated that

> If a stiffness matrix of a system is not positive definite, then one or more rigid-body modes will be present, which are completely identical to the natural modes $\underline{u}_i$ associated with the eigenfrequencies $\omega_i = 0$ of the eigenvalue problem.

3.3.2   Characteristics of eigenvalues and eigencolumns; orthogonality and normalization

The natural modes possess a very important and useful property known as *orthogonality*. This is not orthogonality in the sense commonly used in mathematics ($\underline{u}_r^T\underline{u}_s = 0$ for $r \neq s$), but orthogonality with respect to the mass matrix $\underline{M}$ and also with respect to the stiffness matrix $\underline{K}$. Let us consider two distinct solutions $\{\omega_r^2,\ \underline{u}_r\}$ and $\{\omega_s^2,\ \underline{u}_s\}$ of the eigenvalue problem (3.22). We write the eigenvalue equations for these solutions in the form

$$\underline{K}\,\underline{u}_r = \omega_r^2\underline{M}\,\underline{u}_r \qquad\qquad (3.44)$$

$$\underline{K}\,\underline{u}_s = \omega_s^2\underline{M}\,\underline{u}_s \qquad\qquad (3.45)$$

Premultiplying both sides of (3.44) by $\underline{u}_s^T$ and both sides of (3.45) by $\underline{u}_r^T$, we obtain

$$\underline{u}_s^T\underline{K}\,\underline{u}_r = \omega_r^2\underline{u}_s^T\underline{M}\,\underline{u}_r \qquad\qquad (3.46)$$

$$\underline{u}_r^T\underline{K}\,\underline{u}_s = \omega_s^2\underline{u}_r^T\underline{M}\,\underline{u}_s \qquad\qquad (3.47)$$

Next, we transpose (3.47), recall from Sections 2.11 and 2.15 that the matrices $\underline{M}$ and $\underline{K}$ are symmetric, and subtract the result from (3.46). This yields the following equation

$$0 = \left(\omega_r^2 - \omega_s^2\right)\underline{u}_s^T\underline{M}\,\underline{u}_r \qquad\qquad (3.48)$$

In many cases, the natural frequencies are distinct, i.e. $\omega_r \neq \omega_s$. Then, it follows from (3.48) that

$$\underline{u}_s^T\underline{M}\,\underline{u}_r = 0 \qquad,\qquad r \neq s \qquad\qquad (3.49)$$

which is the statement of the *orthogonality condition* of the modal columns. We note that the orthogonality is with respect to the mass matrix $\underline{M}$ and it is said that the eigencolumns $\underline{u}_r$ and $\underline{u}_s$ are *mass orthogonal* or $\underline{M}$-orthogonal. Inserting (3.49) into (3.46), it is easy to see that the modal columns are also orthogonal with respect to the stiffness matrix $\underline{K}$

$$\underline{u}_s^T\underline{K}\,\underline{u}_r = 0 \qquad,\qquad r \neq s \qquad\qquad (3.50)$$

We stress again that the orthogonality relations (3.49) and (3.50) are valid only if $\underline{M}$ and $\underline{K}$ are symmetric. We will discuss the eigenvalue problem for non-symmetric matrices in the following chapter, where a generalized orthogonality property will be proven. Also, in deriving the orthogonality relation (3.49) from (3.48), it appeared to be necessary to require $\omega_r \neq \omega_s$, implying that the natural frequencies are distinct. We will discuss the case of multiple eigenvalues (including the case of a system with more than one rigid-body mode) later in this chapter.

In closing the treatment of orthogonality, we observe from (3.49) that if the mass matrix is proportional to the $(n \times n)$ identity matrix $\underline{I}$, then the modal columns are really orthogonal to one another in the commonly used mathematical sense, so that

$$\underline{u}_s^T \underline{u}_r = 0 \quad , \quad r \neq s \quad \text{if} \quad \underline{M} = m\underline{I} \tag{3.51}$$

At this point we come back to the item of normalization of eigencolumns. As pointed out in the preceding subsection, the eigencolumns are unique except for a single scalar scaling parameter, implying that the ratio between any two of their elements is completely determined by the eigenvalue problem. A possible normalization scheme consists of setting the value of the largest element of each modal column $\underline{u}_r$ equal to 1, which may be convenient for plotting the modes. Another very convenient and general normalization scheme consists of setting

$$\underline{u}_r^T \underline{M} \, \underline{u}_r = m_r \quad , \quad r = 1, 2, \cdots, n \tag{3.52}$$

where $m_r \ (r = 1, 2, ..., n)$ are *modal mass parameters* which can be chosen arbitrarily. An equivalent normalization scheme consist of setting

$$\underline{u}_r^T \underline{K} \, \underline{u}_r = k_r \quad , \quad r = 1, 2, \cdots, n \tag{3.53}$$

where $k_r \ (r = 1, 2, ..., n)$ are *modal stiffness parameters* which can again be selected arbitrarily. It is remarked that the parameters m_r and k_r depend on one another. In fact, taking in (3.46) the index s equal to the index r, we obtain in view of (3.52) and (3.53)

$$k_r = \omega_r^2 \, m_r \tag{3.54}$$

Hence, we can select either the mass parameters $m_r \ (r = 1, 2, ..., n)$ or the stiffness parameters $k_r \ (r = 1, 2, ..., n)$ as normalization parameters. If we select all mass parameters $m_r \ (r = 1, 2, ..., n)$ equal to 1, the eigencolumns are said to be *mass-matrix normalized* or $\underline{M}$-*normalized*

$$\underline{u}_r^T \underline{M} \, \underline{u}_r = 1 \quad , \quad r = 1, 2, \cdots, n \tag{3.55}$$

implying that

$$\underline{u}_r^T \underline{K} \, \underline{u}_r = \omega_r^2 \quad , \quad r = 1, 2, \cdots, n \tag{3.56}$$

Conversely, if we select all stiffness parameters k_r ($r = 1, 2, ..., n$) equal to 1, the eigencolumns are said to be *stiffness-matrix normalized* or $\underline{K}$-*normalized*

$$\underline{u}_r^T \underline{K} \, \underline{u}_r = 1 \quad , \quad r = 1, 2, \cdots, n \qquad (3.57)$$

implying that

$$\underline{u}_r^T \underline{M} \, \underline{u}_r = 1/\omega_r^2 \quad , \quad r = 1, 2, \cdots, n \qquad (3.58)$$

It should be clear from the above discussion that the normalization process is devoid of physical significance and should only be regarded as a mere (practical) convenience.

As we will see later, it can be convenient to arrange the modal columns in a square matrix of order n, known as the *modal matrix* or, alternatively, as the *matrix of eigencolumns*, and having the form

$$\underline{U} = [\underline{u}_1 \, , \, \underline{u}_2 \, , \, \cdots \, , \, \underline{u}_n] \qquad (3.59)$$

If the normal modes are normalized by means of the scheme contained in (3.52) then we can write

$$\underline{U}^T \underline{M} \, \underline{U} = \begin{bmatrix} m_1 & & 0 \\ & \ddots & \\ 0 & & m_n \end{bmatrix} := \lceil m_r \rfloor \qquad (3.60)$$

where the matrix in the right side is a diagonal matrix with the modal mass parameters $m_1, ..., m_n$ as diagonal elements. This matrix reflects both the orthogonality conditions (3.49) and the normalization scheme (3.52)

If the normal modes are normalized by means of the scheme contained in (3.53), then we can write

$$\underline{U}^T \underline{K} \, \underline{U} = \begin{bmatrix} k_1 & & 0 \\ & \ddots & \\ 0 & & k_n \end{bmatrix} := \lceil k_r \rfloor \qquad (3.61)$$

where the matrix in the right side is a diagonal matrix with the modal stiffness parameters $k_1, ..., k_n$ as diagonal elements. This matrix again reflects both the orthogonality conditions (3.50) and the normalization scheme (3.53). Taking account of (3.54), we have the following relationship between the diagonal matrices $\lceil k_r \rfloor$ and $\lceil m_r \rfloor$

$$\begin{bmatrix} k_1 & & 0 \\ & \ddots & \\ 0 & & k_n \end{bmatrix} = \begin{bmatrix} \omega_1^2 m_1 & & 0 \\ & \ddots & \\ 0 & & \omega_n^2 m_n \end{bmatrix}$$

$$= \begin{bmatrix} \omega_1^2 & & 0 \\ & \ddots & \\ 0 & & \omega_n^2 \end{bmatrix} \begin{bmatrix} m_1 & & 0 \\ & \ddots & \\ 0 & & m_n \end{bmatrix} \qquad (3.62)$$

or, in abbreviated notation

$$\lceil k_r \rfloor = \lceil \omega_r^2 \rfloor \lceil m_r \rfloor \tag{3.63}$$

Example 3.2

We consider the one-dimensional mass-spring system of example 3.1 on page 157. Using (3.36), (3.41) and (3.42), we can express the modal matrix $\underline{U}$ (defined by (3.59) for this example in the form

$$\underline{U} = \begin{bmatrix} \alpha & \beta & \gamma \\ 0 & -\beta & -3\gamma \\ 0 & -\beta & 3\gamma \end{bmatrix} \tag{3.64}$$

Inserting $\underline{M}$ from (3.28) and (3.64) into (3.60), we obtain

$$\lceil m_r \rfloor = \underline{U}^T \underline{M}\, \underline{U} = m \begin{bmatrix} 3\alpha^2 & 0 & 0 \\ 0 & 2\beta^2 & 0 \\ 0 & 0 & 6\gamma^2 \end{bmatrix} \tag{3.65}$$

Similarly, inserting $\underline{K}$ from (3.28) and (3.64) into (3.61), we obtain

$$\lceil k_r \rfloor = \underline{U}^T \underline{K}\, \underline{U} = k \begin{bmatrix} 0 & 0 & 0 \\ 0 & 2\beta^2 & 0 \\ 0 & 0 & 18\gamma^2 \end{bmatrix} \tag{3.66}$$

Inserting (3.65) and (3.66) into (3.63), and using the eigenfrequency values $\omega_1^2 = 0$, $\omega_2^2 = k/m$ and $\omega_3^2 = 3k/m$ determined earlier, we conclude that (3.63) is satisfied, as should be expected.
We observe from (3.66) that for this system, we cannot use the stiffness matrix for normalization, because the upper diagonal element of the matrix $\lceil k_r \rfloor$ is zero so that the parameter α cannot be identified. In fact, this is caused by the presence of a rigid-body mode.
If we select the eigencolumns to be mass-matrix normalized, we have in view of (3.55) and (3.65)

$$3m\alpha^2 = 1 \quad , \quad 2m\beta^2 = 1 \quad , \quad 6m\gamma^2 = 1 \tag{3.67}$$

This leads us to the following matrix of mass-matrix normalized eigencolumns

$$\underline{U} = \frac{1}{6\sqrt{m}} \begin{bmatrix} 2\sqrt{3} & 3\sqrt{2} & \sqrt{6} \\ 0 & -3\sqrt{2} & -3\sqrt{6} \\ 0 & -3\sqrt{2} & 3\sqrt{6} \end{bmatrix} \tag{3.68}$$

For systems without rigid-body modes, i.e. systems for which the stiffness matrix $\underline{K}$ is positive definite, (3.61) can be used to derive an expression for the inverse of the stiffness matrix which we will need later. Premultiplying (3.61) by $\underline{U}^{-T}$ $\left(= \left(\underline{U}^T\right)^{-1} = \left(\underline{U}^{-1}\right)^T\right)$ and postmultiplying by $\underline{U}^{-1}$, we obtain

$$\underline{K} = \underline{U}^{-T} \lceil k_r \rfloor \underline{U}^{-1} \tag{3.69}$$

From this result the following expression for the inverse of the stiffness matrix can be obtained

$$\underline{K}^{-1} = \underline{U} \lceil k_r \rfloor^{-1} \underline{U}^T = \underline{U} \lceil 1/k_r \rfloor \underline{U}^T \tag{3.70}$$

This result can also be written as

$$\underline{K}^{-1} = \sum_{r=1}^{n} \frac{1}{k_r} \underline{u}_r \underline{u}_r^T = \sum_{r=1}^{n} \frac{1}{\omega_r^2 m_r} \underline{u}_r \underline{u}_r^T \tag{3.71}$$

and it shows that the inverse of the stiffness matrix can be considered to be composed of contributions of the normal modes and that zero-eigenfrequencies may not be present. In literature this expression is often referred to as the *spectral decomposition of the stiffness matrix*. Following a similar procedure with respect to (3.60) the inverse of the mass matrix can be expressed in terms of the normal modes as follows

$$\underline{M}^{-1} = \sum_{r=1}^{n} \frac{1}{m_r} \underline{u}_r \underline{u}_r^T = \sum_{r=1}^{n} \frac{\omega_r^2}{k_r} \underline{u}_r \underline{u}_r^T \tag{3.72}$$

In the final part of this subsection we prove, as announced in the previous subsection, that the eigenvalues $\lambda = \omega^2$ of the eigenvalue problem matrix form, (3.22), are, indeed, non-negative real numbers, whereas, also, the eigencolumns contain real numbers. To this end, let us assume the eigencolumn $\underline{u}$ to be complex, i.e. $\underline{u} = \underline{a} + j\underline{b}$, where $\underline{a}$ and $\underline{b}$ contain real elements and $j^2 = -1$. Then, the eigenvalue problem (3.22) can be written as

$$\underline{K}\left(\underline{a} + j\underline{b}\right) = \omega^2 \underline{M}\left(\underline{a} + j\underline{b}\right) \tag{3.73}$$

We premultiply this equation by $\left(\underline{a} - j\underline{b}\right)^T$ and take into account that, owing to the symmetry of $\underline{K}$ and $\underline{M}$, the following relationships hold

$$\begin{aligned}
\underline{b}^T \underline{K}\, \underline{a} = \left(\underline{b}^T \underline{K}\, \underline{a}\right)^T = \underline{a}^T \underline{K}\, \underline{b} \\
\underline{b}^T \underline{M}\, \underline{a} = \left(\underline{b}^T \underline{M}\, \underline{a}\right)^T = \underline{a}^T \underline{M}\, \underline{b}
\end{aligned} \tag{3.74}$$

This yields the following expression for ω^2

$$\omega^2 = \frac{\underline{a}^T \underline{K}\, \underline{a} + \underline{b}^T \underline{K}\, \underline{b}}{\underline{a}^T \underline{M}\, \underline{a} + \underline{b}^T \underline{M}\, \underline{b}} \tag{3.75}$$

Because the elements of $\underline{K}, \underline{M}, \underline{a}$ and $\underline{b}$ are all real, we immediately may conclude that the eigenvalue $\lambda = \omega^2$ is a real number. Moreover, taking the mass matrix to be positive definite, the denominator in the right side of (3.75) is positive, unless $\underline{a} = \underline{b} = \underline{0}$, giving the unrelevant solution $\underline{u} = \underline{0}$. However, if the mass matrix is only semi-positive definite the denominator can become zero for a non-zero eigencolumn. In that case we will have one or more eigenvalues $\lambda = \omega^2 = \infty$. This happens for example if we are dealing with a massless degree of freedom. Then, from $\omega = \sqrt{k/m}$ we can conlude that the eigenfrequency will go to infinity. A semi-positive definite mass matrix should therefore be avoided.

If the stiffness matrix is also positive definite, then the numerator in the right side of (3.75) is always positive, unless (again) $\underline{a} = \underline{b} = \underline{0}$. In the case that we are dealing with a rigid-body mode $\underline{u}_r$, the stiffness matrix is semi-positive definite, and the numerator in the right side of (3.75) can be zero for nonzero columns $\underline{a}$ and $\underline{b}$. But then $\underline{a}$ and $\underline{b}$ should be proportional to the rigid-body mode, yielding $\underline{u} = \alpha\, \underline{u}_r$. Hence, we conclude that the eigenvalue $\lambda = \omega^2$ is always a non-negative real number.

Using the fact that ω^2 is real, we obtain from (3.73) the following two real eigenvalue problems

$$\underline{K}\,\underline{a} = \omega^2 \underline{M}\,\underline{a} \quad , \quad \underline{K}\,\underline{b} = \omega^2 \underline{M}\,\underline{b} \tag{3.76}$$

These eigenvalue problems are identical and, hence, the eigencolumns $\underline{a}$ and $\underline{b}$ are the same, apart from a real scaling factor α. So, the eigencolumn $\underline{u}$ becomes

$$\underline{u} = \underline{a} + j\underline{b} = \underline{a} + j\alpha\underline{a} = (1 + j\alpha)\,\underline{a} \tag{3.77}$$

This result implies that the eigencolumns $\underline{u}$ will always be real, or if they appear to be complex, they can be made real by introducing a single complex scaling factor (in (3.77) this is the factor $1 + j\alpha$). This is obvious, because when the real eigencolumn $\underline{u}$ satisfies the eigenvalue problem $\left(-\omega^2 \underline{M} + \underline{K}\right)\underline{u} = \underline{0}$, then also $c\,\underline{u}$ satisfies the same eigenvalue problem with c being an arbitrary complex constant.

3.3.3 Multiple eigenvalues

In deriving the orthogonality conditions (3.49) and (3.50), the eigenvalues have been assumed to be distinct. In this subsection we consider the case in which m natural frequencies ω_p are equal, when m is an integer such that $2 \le m \le n$. In this case the system is said to have a *multiple or repeated eigenvalue* $\lambda_p = \omega_p^2$, while m is called the *multiplicity* of the eigenvalue. A system with repeated eigenvalues is referred to as *degenerated*.

Example 3.3

We consider the four-body model of a passenger car shown in Fig. 3.4. The car body is considered to be rigid with mass m_4 and mass moment of inertia about its centre of mass equal to $I_C = \frac{1}{8}m_4\ell^2$. The *front and back axles together with the wheels are modelled as rigid bodies with masses m_1 and m_2. These masses are connected to the car body by means of the linear springs k_1 and k_2. The engine is modelled as a rigid body with mass m_3 that is connected to the car body by means of the linear spring k_3. Only small translational motions of m_1, m_2, m_3 and C are considered in the vertical direction. Moreover, the car body can have small rotations with respect to C. This model is capable of capturing*

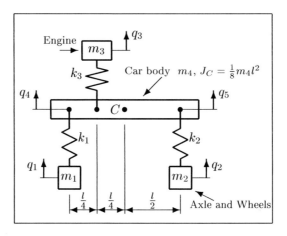

Fig. 3.4   Four-body model of a passenger car

some important dynamic characteristics of a passenger car for riding comfort and safety. It is remarked that often the elasticity of the tires is modelled by means of linear springs connecting the masses m_1 and m_2 to an (irregular) rigid base giving rise to prescribed displacements. We will not consider those springs here. In this example we will take the following specific values for the rigid-body masses and the spring stiffnesses

$$\left. \begin{array}{c} m_1 = m_2 = m \quad , \quad m_3 = 2m \quad , \quad m_4 = 5m \\ k_1 = k_2 = k \quad , \quad k_3 = 2k \end{array} \right\} \tag{3.78}$$

We select as generalized coordinates the vertical displacements $q_1, q_2, \ldots, q_5$ indicated in Fig. 3.4, so that the column of generalized coordinates becomes

$$\underline{q}^T = [q_1 \ , \ q_2 \ , \ q_3 \ , \ q_4 \ , \ q_5] \tag{3.79}$$

It is left to the reader to verify that the mass and stiffness matrices for this five-degree-of-freedom system can be written as

$$\underline{M} = \frac{m}{8} \begin{bmatrix} 8 & 0 & 0 & 0 & 0 \\ 0 & 8 & 0 & 0 & 0 \\ 0 & 0 & 16 & 0 & 0 \\ 0 & 0 & 0 & 15 & 5 \\ 0 & 0 & 0 & 5 & 15 \end{bmatrix} \tag{3.80}$$

$$\underline{K} = \frac{k}{16} \begin{bmatrix} 16 & 0 & 0 & -16 & 0 \\ 0 & 16 & 0 & 0 & -16 \\ 0 & 0 & 32 & -24 & -8 \\ -16 & 0 & -24 & 34 & 6 \\ 0 & -16 & -8 & 6 & 18 \end{bmatrix} \tag{3.81}$$

For reasons of simplicity, we take $m = 1$, $k = 1$. Computing with Matlab the eigenfrequencies and matrix of eigencolumns, we obtain

$$\omega_1 = 0, \quad \omega_2 = 0, \quad \omega_3 = 1, \quad \omega_4 = 1.2649, \quad \omega_5 = 1.4832 \tag{3.82}$$

$$\underline{U} = \begin{bmatrix} 0.16 & -0.61 & 0.80 & 0.00 & 0.56 \\ 0.66 & 0.20 & 0.27 & 0.84 & -0.19 \\ 0.28 & -0.41 & -0.53 & 0.21 & 0.38 \\ 0.16 & -0.61 & 0.00 & 0.00 & -0.68 \\ 0.66 & 0.20 & 0.00 & -0.50 & 0.23 \end{bmatrix} \tag{3.83}$$

We observe from (3.82) that the system of Fig. 3.4 has an eigenfrequency $\omega = 0$ with multiplicity 2. The two eigenfrequencies $\omega = 0$ correspond to the two rigid-body modes of this unconstrained system. The calculated natural modes are depicted in Fig. 3.5. The solid lines represent reference configurations, whereas the dotted lines represent modal shapes. For the modes 1 and 2 all the 3 linear springs in the system remain unstretched so that the elastic energy will be zero. So these modes indeed are rigid body modes although the numerical result might be somewhat surprising. We will come back to this later.
If we compute the matrix $\underline{U}^T \underline{M} \, \underline{U}$, with $\underline{U}$ and $\underline{M}$ according to (3.83) and (3.80), respectively, we obtain

$$\underline{U}^T \underline{M} \, \underline{U} = \left[\begin{array}{cc|ccc} 1.61 & -0.39 & 0.00 & 0.00 & 0.00 \\ -0.39 & 1.38 & 0.00 & 0.00 & 0.00 \\ \hline 0.00 & 0.00 & 1.29 & 0.00 & 0.00 \\ 0.00 & 0.00 & 0.00 & 1.27 & 0.00 \\ 0.00 & 0.00 & 0.00 & 0.00 & 1.40 \end{array} \right] \tag{3.84}$$

We observe from (3.84) that the orthogonality conditions are satisfied accurately, except for the numerically determined rigid-body modes $\underline{u}_1$

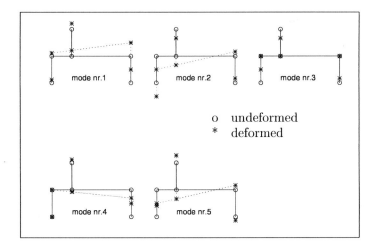

Fig. 3.5   Natural modes of four-body passenger car

and $\underline{u}_2$.

As we have seen in the foregoing example, if $\lambda_p = \omega_p^2$ is a repeated eigenvalue with multiplicity m, then, consistent with (3.49) the set of eigencolumns associated with the repeated eigenvalue are always orthogonal to the remaining $n - m$ eigencolumns, but at first glance they do not always automatically have to be orthogonal to one another, in general. However, due to the so-called *degeneracy theorem* it appears to be possible to construct an *orthogonal* basis of m eigencolumns spanning a subspace of dimension m which is orthogonal to the remaining $n - m$ eigencolumns. This orthogonal basis of eigencolumns is not unique because, for repeated eigenvalues, any linear combination of the associated eigencolumns is also an eigencolumn. However, the dimension, m, of the subspace mentioned above is unique and, hence, it contains only m mutually orthogonal eigencolumns, which, as mentioned before, are also orthogonal to the $n - m$ remaining eigencolumns. For a proof of the degeneracy theorem the reader is referred to Geradin & Rixen (1997).

Here, let us assume that in some way or another we have obtained a set of eigencolumns $\underline{u}_p$ $(p = 1, 2, \ldots, m)$ corresponding to an eigenvalue ω_p^2 with multiplicity m. So, $\underline{u}_p$ and ω_p^2 satisfy the eigenvalue equation

$$\underline{K}\,\underline{u}_p = \omega_p^2\,\underline{M}\,\underline{u}_p, \qquad \omega_1 = \omega_2 = \ldots \omega_m, \qquad p = 1, 2, \ldots, m \qquad (3.85)$$

whereas the matrix $\underline{U}_m^T \underline{M}\,\underline{U}_m$ is not diagonal with $\underline{U}_m$ being the matrix composed of only the m eigencolumns $\underline{u}_p$ $(p = 1, 2, \ldots, m)$. Then, we are faced with the problem to construct a new set of m eigencolumns in the subspace spanned by $\underline{U}_m$, which are not only orthogonal to the remaining $n - m$ eigencolumns but also to one another. The essential property which we will use in constructing this new set is that any linear combination of the (old) eigencolumns $\underline{u}_p$, $p = 1, \ldots, m$, will again be an eigencolumn corresponding to the eigenvalue ω_p^2. Here we will only introduce the basic idea to perform this orthogonalization by hand.

First, we look at the eigencolumns $\underline{u}_1$ and $\underline{u}_2$. We will not change the eigencolumn $\underline{u}_1$, but replace $\underline{u}_2$ by a new column $\underline{u}_2^*$ that lies in the plane spanned by $\underline{u}_1$ and $\underline{u}_2$, so that we can write

$$\underline{u}_2^* = \underline{u}_2 + \alpha \underline{u}_1 \tag{3.86}$$

with α being a constant. Now, we require $\underline{u}_2^*$ to be $\underline{M}$-orthogonal with respect to $\underline{u}_1$, so that

$$\underline{u}_1^T \underline{M} \, \underline{u}_2^* = 0 \tag{3.87}$$

Inserting (3.86) into (3.87), we obtain the following result for the constant α

$$\alpha = -\frac{\underline{u}_1^T \underline{M} \, \underline{u}_2}{\underline{u}_1^T \underline{M} \, \underline{u}_1} \tag{3.88}$$

Because $\underline{u}_1$ and $\underline{u}_2$ satisfy the eigenvalue problem (3.85), the new column $\underline{u}_2^*$ also satisfies the eigenvalue problem. Hence the old column $\underline{u}_2$ may be replaced by the new column $\underline{u}_2^*$. We repeat this process for all the remaining combinations $\{\underline{u}_1, \, \underline{u}_p\}$, $p = 3, \ldots, m$. At the end of this process we have constructed $(m - 1)$ new eigencolumns $\underline{u}_2^*, \underline{u}_3^*, \ldots, \underline{u}_m^*$ which all are $\underline{M}$-orthogonal with respect to $\underline{u}_1$, but which are not yet $\underline{M}$-orthogonal to one another, in general.

Next, we consider the $(m - 1)$ dimensional subspace spanned by $\underline{u}_2^*, \underline{u}_3^*, \ldots, \underline{u}_m^*$ and repeat the foregoing procedure. So, we create $(m - 2)$ new eigencolumns in this subspace which are $\underline{M}$-orthogonal with respect to the first column $\underline{u}_2^*$. This process can be continued and it finally yields a set of m mutually $\underline{M}$-orthogonal eigencolumns which still are $\underline{M}$-orthogonal with respect to the other $(n - m)$ eigencolumns of the problem. Hence, in this way we obtain a complete $\underline{M}$-orthogonal set of eigencolumns.

Example 3.4

We consider again the four-body five-degree-of-freedom model of a passenger car of example 3.3 on page 166, see Fig. 3.4. We carry out the above procedure with respect to the eigencolumns contained in the modal matrix given by (3.83). In this case, only the second eigencolumn has to be updated. Normalizing the eigencolumns with respect to the mass matrix, we obtain the following matrix of $\underline{M}$-orthogonal eigencolumns

$$\underline{U} = \begin{bmatrix} 0.12 & -0.51 & 0.71 & 0.00 & 0.48 \\ 0.52 & 0.30 & 0.24 & 0.75 & -0.16 \\ 0.22 & -0.30 & -0.47 & 0.19 & 0.32 \\ 0.12 & -0.51 & 0.00 & 0.000 & -0.57 \\ 0.52 & 0.30 & 0.00 & -0.45 & 0.19 \end{bmatrix} \tag{3.89}$$

Because the eigencolumns contained in (3.89) are not only $\underline{M}$-orthogonal, but also $\underline{M}$-normalized, the matrix $\underline{U}^T \underline{M} \underline{U}$ becomes equal to the identity matrix. The two orthogonal rigid-body modes obtained by means of the above procedure are depicted in the upper part of Fig. 3.6. For

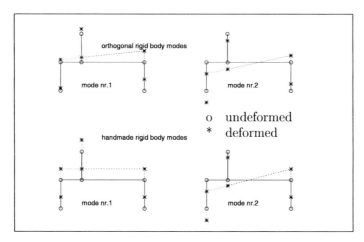

Fig. 3.6 Orthogonal- and handmade rigid body modes for four-body passenger car

this rather simple problem we can also generate two possible rigid-body modes by hand. The first rigid-body mode consists of only a vertical translation without spring elongation, whereas the second rigid-body mode consists of a rotation about the centre of mass C of the car body. These two rigid-body modes are also depicted in the lower part of Fig. 3.6.

However, it can be shown easily that the two handmade rigid-body modes do not satisfy the property of $\underline{M}$-orthogonality. Therefore, if we wish to have a complete set of five $\underline{M}$-orthogonal eigenmodes, we have to apply the previously discussed orthogonalization procedure to these two handmade rigid-body modes.

Resuming the foregoing discussion, we can say that due to the degeneracy theorem it is always possible to construct m linearly independent eigencolumns $\underline{u}_p$ $(p = 1, 2, \ldots, m)$ associated with the eigenvalue ω_p^2 of multiplicity m in such a way that they are orthogonal to one another and to the remaining eigencolumns. Hence, the orthogonality relationships (3.49) and (3.50) may be accepted in all generality.

3.3.4   General solution to initial conditions; natural coordinates

Let us consider the general solution of the undamped system

$$\underline{M}\ \underline{\ddot{q}}(t) + \underline{K}\ \underline{q}(t) = \underline{0} \tag{3.90}$$

to the given non-zero initial conditions

$$\underline{q}(0) = \underline{q}_0 \quad , \quad \underline{\dot{q}}(0) = \underline{\dot{q}}_0 \tag{3.91}$$

The eigencolumns $\underline{u}_r$ $(r = 1, 2, ..., n)$ associated with the eigenvalue problem (3.22) form a linearly independent set, implying that any n-dimensional column in the space spanned by the generalized coordinates q can be constructed as a linear combination of these eigencolumns. Physically this implies that any motion of the system can be regarded at any given time as a superposition of the natural modes multiplied by appropriate constants, where the constants are a measure of the degree of participation of each mode in the motion. By virtue of this so-called **modal expansion theorem** the solution $\underline{q}(t)$ of (3.90) can be regarded as a superposition of normal modes. Because the solution $\underline{q}(t)$ is time-dependent, the coefficients of the natural modes appearing in the superposition are also time-dependent. Denoting these coefficients by $\eta_r(t)$ $(r = 1, 2, ..., n)$, we can write

$$\underline{q}(t) = \eta_1(t)\ \underline{u}_1 + \eta_2(t)\ \underline{u}_2 + ... + \eta_n(t)\ \underline{u}_n \tag{3.92}$$

or

$$\underline{q}(t) = \sum_{r=1}^{n} \underline{u}_r\ \eta_r(t) = \underline{U}\ \underline{\eta}(t) \tag{3.93}$$

where $\underline{U}$ is recognized as the modal matrix defined earlier by (3.59), while $\underline{\eta}(t)$ is a column containing the **modal participation factors** $\eta_r(t)$ $(r = 1, 2, ..., n)$. Equation (3.93) can be regarded as a linear transformation relating the columns $\underline{q}(t)$ and $\underline{\eta}(t)$, where the transformation matrix $\underline{U}$ is constant. It follows immediately from (3.93) that

$$\underline{\dot{q}}(t) = \underline{U}\ \underline{\dot{\eta}}(t); \quad \underline{\ddot{q}}(t) = \underline{U}\ \underline{\ddot{\eta}}(t) \tag{3.94}$$

Inserting (3.93) and (3.94) into (3.90), the equations of motion become

$$\underline{M}\ \underline{U}\ \underline{\ddot{\eta}}(t) + \underline{K}\ \underline{U}\ \underline{\eta}(t) = \underline{0} \tag{3.95}$$

Premultiplying this set of equations by $\underline{U}^T$ and taking account of the orthogonality relationships and normalization schemes (3.60) and (3.61), and, additionally, of (3.63), we arrive at the following set of n *uncoupled* equations

$$\ddot{\eta}_r(t) + \omega_r^2\ \eta_r(t) = 0 \quad , \quad r = 1, 2, \cdots, n \tag{3.96}$$

The new variables $\eta_r(t)$ $(r = 1, 2, ..., n)$ can be considered as being a new set of generalized coordinates of the system. These coordinates are referred to as the **natural coordinates** or the *normal coordinates* because they decouple the original equations of motion. In solving (3.96) we will distinguish between the cases $\omega_r = 0$ and $\omega_r \neq 0$. It follows from the preceding subsections that if $\omega_r = 0$, we are dealing with rigid-body modes. If $\omega_r \neq 0$ we are dealing with so-called elastic eigenmodes.

In the case in which $\omega_r = 0$, (3.96) reduces to $\ddot{\eta}_r(t) = 0$, which has the solution

$$\eta_r(t) = B_{1r} + B_{2r}t \quad , \quad \omega_r = 0 \tag{3.97}$$

where B_{1r} and B_{2r} are constants of integration. In the case in which $\omega_r \neq 0$, by analogy with the free-vibration solution of an undamped single-degree-of-freedom system, the solution of (3.96) is

$$\eta_r(t) = B_{1r} \cos \omega_r t + B_{2r} \sin \omega_r t \quad , \quad \omega_r \neq 0 \tag{3.98}$$

where B_{1r} and B_{2r} are again constants of integration. We will assume that there are m zero eigenfrequencies $\omega_r = 0$ (corresponding to rigid-body modes) and $(n - m)$ nonzero eigenfrequencies $\omega_r \neq 0$ corresponding to elastic eigenmodes. Then, inserting (3.97) and (3.98) back into the transformation equation (3.93), we obtain

$$\underline{q}(t) = \sum_{r=1}^{n} \underline{u}_r \eta_r(t) = \sum_{r=1}^{m} \underline{u}_r \left(B_{1r} + B_{2r}t \right) \tag{3.99}$$

$$+ \sum_{r=m+1}^{n} \underline{u}_r \left(B_{1r} \cos \omega_r t + B_{2r} \sin \omega_r t \right)$$

so that the undamped free motion of a multi-degree-of-freedom linear system consists of a superposition of n modal columns multiplied by time-dependent functions. For the modal columns associated with the zero eigenfrequencies, these functions represent motions with constant velocities $\dot{\eta}_r(t)$, whereas for the modal columns associated with the nonzero eigenfrequencies, these functions represent harmonic motions with frequencies equal to the system natural frequencies. The constants B_{1r} and B_{2r} in the time-dependent functions $\eta_r(t)$ are to be determined from the initial conditions: $\underline{q}(0) = \underline{q}_0$ and $\dot{\underline{q}}(0) = \dot{\underline{q}}_0$. Then (3.99) leads to

$$\underline{q}_0 = \sum_{r=1}^{n} \underline{u}_r \eta_r(0) = \sum_{r=1}^{n} \underline{u}_r B_{1r} \tag{3.100}$$

$$\dot{\underline{q}}_0 = \sum_{r=1}^{n} \underline{u}_r \dot{\eta}_r(0) = \sum_{r=1}^{m} \underline{u}_r B_{2r} + \sum_{r=m+1}^{n} \underline{u}_r \omega_r B_{2r} \tag{3.101}$$

Premultiplying (3.100) by $\underline{u}_s^T \underline{M}$, and considering the orthonormality relations (3.60), we obtain

$$B_{1s} = \frac{1}{m_s} \underline{u}_s^T \underline{M} \, \underline{q}_0 \quad , \quad s = 1, 2, \ldots, n \tag{3.102}$$

Similarly, premultiplying (3.101) by $\underline{u}_s^T M$, and considering again the orthonormality relations, (3.60), we obtain

$$B_{2s} = \left\{ \begin{array}{ll} \frac{1}{m_s} \underline{u}_s^T M \underline{\dot{q}}_0 & , \quad s = 1, \ldots, m \\[2mm] \frac{1}{m_s \omega_s} \underline{u}_s^T M \underline{\dot{q}}_0 & , \quad s = m+1, \ldots, n \end{array} \right\} \tag{3.103}$$

Introducing (3.102) and (3.103) into (3.99), we obtain the general expression

$$\underline{q}(t) = \sum_{r=1}^{m} \frac{1}{m_r} \left[\underline{u}_r^T M \underline{q}_0 + \underline{u}_r^T M \underline{\dot{q}}_0 t \right] \underline{u}_r \tag{3.104}$$

$$+ \sum_{r=m+1}^{n} \frac{1}{m_r} \left[\underline{u}_r^T M \underline{q}_0 \cos \omega_r t + \underline{u}_r^T M \underline{\dot{q}}_0 \frac{1}{\omega_r} \sin \omega_r t \right] \underline{u}_r$$

which represents the response of the system to the initial displacement column $\underline{q}_0$ and the initial velocity column $\underline{\dot{q}}_0$. Now, let us assume that the initial displacement column resembles one of the normal modes, say $\underline{q}_0 = \alpha \, \underline{u}_s$, with α being an arbitrary constant, whereas the initial velocity column is zero, i.e. $\underline{\dot{q}}_0 = \underline{0}$. Introducing these initial conditions into (3.104), we obtain

$$\underline{q}(t) = \sum_{r=1}^{m} \left[\alpha \frac{1}{m_r} \underline{u}_r^T M \underline{u}_s \right] \underline{u}_r + \sum_{r=m+1}^{n} \left[\alpha \frac{1}{m_r} \underline{u}_r^T M \underline{u}_s \cos \omega_r t \right] \underline{u}_r \tag{3.105}$$

Taking account of the orthonormality relations (3.60), the response becomes

$$\underline{q}(t) = \left\{ \begin{array}{lll} \alpha \, \underline{u}_s & if & \omega_s = 0 \\[2mm] (\alpha \, \cos \omega_s t) \, \underline{u}_s & if & \omega_s \neq 0 \end{array} \right\} \tag{3.106}$$

For $\omega_s = 0$ the resulting motion will be nothing more than the given initial displacement. So, if a system with rigid body modes will be given a rigid-body-mode type of initial displacement, it will stay in that position, which is trivial. For $\omega_s \neq 0$ the response represents a synchronous harmonic oscillation at the particular natural frequency ω_s with the system configuration resembling the s-th mode at all times. This implies that the natural modes, represented by the pairs ω_r, $\underline{u}_r$ $(r = 1, 2, \ldots, n)$, can be excited independently of one another by applying the *appropriate initial conditions*. Finally, it is remarked that the general expression (3.104) for $\underline{q}(t)$ can be rearranged as follows

$$\underline{q}(t) = \left[\sum_{r=1}^{m} \frac{\underline{u}_r \underline{u}_r^T M}{m_r} + \sum_{r=m+1}^{n} \frac{\underline{u}_r \underline{u}_r^T M}{m_r} \cos \omega_r t \right] \underline{q}_0 \tag{3.107}$$

$$+ \left[\sum_{r=1}^{m} \frac{\underline{u}_r \underline{u}_r^T M}{m_r} t + \sum_{r=m+1}^{n} \frac{\underline{u}_r \underline{u}_r^T M}{m_r \, \omega_r} \sin \omega_r t \right] \underline{\dot{q}}_0$$

thus showing more straightforward the influence of q_0 and $\dot{q}_0$ on the solution. Finally, it should be remarked that the rigid-body-modes contributions (summations $r = (1, ..., m)$) can be viewed upon as the limiting case of the elastic-modes contributions (summations $r = (m + 1, ..., n)$) for $\omega_r \downarrow 0$.

3.4   GENERAL RESPONSE TO EXTERNAL EXCITATION

3.4.1   Decoupling of the equations of motion; natural coordinates

Until sofar, we have confined ourselves to the free vibrations of undamped multi-degree-of-freedom linear systems with symmetric matrices. In this section we consider the forced response of those systems. Recalling (3.1), we can represent the system differential equations of motion in the form

$$\underline{M}\ \ddot{\underline{q}}(t) + \underline{K}\ \underline{q}(t) = \underline{Q}(t) \tag{3.108}$$

where the column matrix $\underline{q}(t)$ contains the n generalized system coordinates with respect to a stable equilibrium position, while $\underline{M}$ and $\underline{K}$ are the $(n \times n)$ symmetric system mass and stiffness matrix, respectively, whereas the column matrix $\underline{Q}(t)$ contains the n generalized forces depending explicitly on time. The set (3.108) constitutes a system of n simultaneous or *coupled* ordinary linear differential equations with constant coefficients. At least in principle, a solution of (3.108) could be obtained by means of so-called Laplace transformation, which, in practice, requires elaborate computations, even for systems with a limited number of degrees of freedom. Therefore a different solution method is recommended, which is based upon a transformation of (3.108) to a set of independent or *uncoupled* equations of motion. In fact, the same transformation can be applied as used in Subsection 3.3.4 for the free response to arbitrary initial excitation. This implies that we expand the solution $\underline{q}(t)$ as a superposition of normal modes and write, identical to (3.93)

$$\underline{q}(t) = \sum_{r=1}^{n} \underline{u}_r\ \eta_r(t) = \underline{U}\ \underline{\eta}(t) \tag{3.109}$$

where $\underline{U}$ is the $(n \times n)$ modal matrix and the column matrix $\underline{\eta}(t)$ contains a new set of n generalized coordinates. To be able to write the solution of (3.108) in the form of (3.109), or, put in other words, to be able to apply the linear transformation defined by (3.109), we must first solve the eigenvalue problem associated with the matrices $\underline{M}$ and $\underline{K}$, which is expressed by the set of algebraic equations

$$\underline{M}\ \underline{U}\ \lceil \omega_r^2 \rfloor = \underline{K}\ \underline{U} \tag{3.110}$$

where $\lceil \omega_r^2 \rfloor$ is the diagonal matrix of the squared natural frequencies. We collect the orthogonality and normalization conditions for the modal columns in the expressions

$$\underline{U}^T \underline{M}\ \underline{U} = \lceil m_r \rfloor \quad , \quad \underline{U}^T \underline{K}\ \underline{U} = \lceil k_r \rfloor = \lceil \omega_r^2 \rfloor \lceil m_r \rfloor \tag{3.111}$$

where the diagonal matrices $\lceil m_r \rfloor$ and $\lceil k_r \rfloor$ contain the modal mass and stiffness parameters, respectively. Introducing the transformation (3.109) into the equations of motion (3.108), premultiplying the resulting equation by $\underline{U}^T$, and taking account of (3.111), we obtain

$$\lceil m_r \rfloor \left\{ \underline{\ddot{\eta}}(t) + \lceil \omega_r^2 \rfloor \ \underline{\eta}(t) \right\} = \underline{N}(t) \tag{3.112}$$

where

$$\underline{N}(t) = \underline{U}^T \underline{Q}(t) \tag{3.113}$$

is a column matrix of n generalized forces $N_i(t)$, $i = 1, 2, \cdots, n$, associated with the column of generalized coordinates $\underline{\eta}(t)$. Equation (3.112) represents a set of n independent or **uncoupled** equations of motion which can be written as

$$m_r \left\{ \ddot{\eta}_r(t) + \omega_r^2 \ \eta_r(t) \right\} = N_r(t) \quad , \quad r = 1, 2, \cdots, n \tag{3.114}$$

where, consistent with Subsection 3.3.4, the generalized coordinates $\eta_r(t)$ are referred to as the *normal coordinates* or the *modal coordinates* while the associated generalized forces $N_r(t)$ are given by

$$N_r(t) = \underline{u}_r^T \ \underline{Q}(t) \tag{3.115}$$

In fact, (3.115) implies that the generalized force $N_r(t)$ can be found by projecting the column of generalized forces $\underline{Q}(t)$ on the modal column $\underline{u}_r$. Equations (3.114) have the same structure as the differential equation of motion of an undamped single-degree-of-freedom time-invariant linear system with mass m_r, natural frequency ω_r, and external force $N_r(t)$. Hence, the general solution of (3.114) can be found in most introductory structural dynamics textbooks. Only the forced response to harmonic excitation will be discussed in the following subsection because of its importance.

Further it is remarked that the initial conditions for $\underline{q}(t)$, i.e. $\underline{q}(0) = \underline{q}_0$ and $\underline{\dot{q}}(0) = \underline{\dot{q}}_0$, can be transformed to initial conditions for $\underline{\eta}(t)$ by using $\underline{\eta}(t) = \underline{U}^{-1} \underline{q}(t)$ and $\underline{\dot{\eta}}(t) = \underline{U}^{-1} \underline{\dot{q}}(t)$. From (3.111) we can easily extract the matrix inverse $\underline{U}^{-1}$

$$\lceil m_r \rfloor^{-1} \underline{U}^T \underline{M} \ \underline{U} = \underline{I} = \underline{U}^{-1} \ \underline{U} \quad \text{so} \quad \underline{U}^{-1} = \lceil m_r \rfloor^{-1} \underline{U}^T \underline{M} \tag{3.116}$$

In this way we obtain the initial modal displacements

$$\eta_r(0) = \frac{1}{m_r} \underline{u}_r^T \underline{M} \ \underline{q}(0) \quad , \quad r = 1, 2, \cdots, n \tag{3.117}$$

and the initial modal velocities

$$\dot{\eta}_r(0) = \frac{1}{m_r} \underline{u}_r^T \underline{M} \ \underline{\dot{q}}(0) \quad , \quad r = 1, 2, \cdots, n \tag{3.118}$$

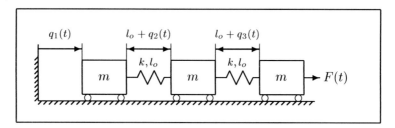

Fig. 3.7   Three-carriage railway vehicle model

Example 3.5

We again look at the one-dimensional three-carriage vehicle system of example 3.1 on page 157 and shown once more in Fig. 3.7. We now assume that a given external force $F(t)$ is acting on the right mass. The motion of the system is described by means of the generalized coordinates $q_1(t)$, $q_2(t)$ and $q_3(t)$, with $q_1(t)$ being the position of the left mass with respect to the origin of an inertial frame, whereas $q_2(t)$ respectively $q_3(t)$ are the elongation of the springs. The mass- and stiffness matrix for the system have been given before on page 157.

It is easy to check that the column $\underline{Q}(t)$ of generalized forces for this choice of generalized coordinates will be

$$\underline{Q}(t) = \begin{bmatrix} F(t) \\ F(t) \\ F(t) \end{bmatrix} \tag{3.119}$$

Solving the eigenvalue problem corresponding to undamped free vibrations yielded the following undamped eigenfrequencies

$$\begin{aligned} \omega_1 &= 0 \\ \omega_2 &= \sqrt{k/m} \\ \omega_2 &= \sqrt{3k/m} \end{aligned} \tag{3.120}$$

whereas the corresponding eigenmode matrix ($\underline{M}$-normalized) was calculated before in example 3.2 on page 164 to be

$$\underline{U} = \frac{1}{6\sqrt{m}} \begin{bmatrix} 2\sqrt{3} & 3\sqrt{2} & \sqrt{6} \\ 0 & -3\sqrt{2} & -3\sqrt{6} \\ 0 & -3\sqrt{2} & 3\sqrt{6} \end{bmatrix} \tag{3.121}$$

So we are dealing with one rigid-body mode and two elastic modes. Next, we apply the coordinate transformation $\underline{q}(t) = \underline{U}\,\underline{\eta}(t)$ giving the *uncoupled equations of motion*

$$\ddot{\eta}_1(t) = F(t)/\sqrt{3m}$$
$$\ddot{\eta}_2(t) + k/m\ \eta_2(t) = -F(t)/\sqrt{2m} \qquad (3.122)$$
$$\ddot{\eta}_3(t) + 3k/m\ \eta_3(t) = F(t)/\sqrt{6m}$$

We assume that at $t = 0$ a **constant** *force $F(t) = F_o$ is starting to act on the right mass and that for $t \leq 0$ the system is at rest, which means*

$$\begin{array}{ll} F(t) = 0 & t \leq 0 \\ F(t) = F_o & t > 0 \end{array} \qquad (3.123)$$

and

$$\underline{q}(t = 0) = \underline{0}; \qquad \underline{\dot{q}}(t = 0) = \underline{0} \qquad (3.124)$$

We can transform these initial conditions into initial conditions for the natural coordinates $\underline{\eta}(t)$, using

$$\underline{\eta}(0) = \underline{U}^{-1}\ \underline{q}(0) = \underline{0}$$
$$\underline{\dot{\eta}}(0) = \underline{U}^{-1}\ \underline{\dot{q}}(0) = \underline{0} \qquad (3.125)$$

Now, we will elaborate the respective solutions of each of the equations of the set (3.122).

- *Solution of $\ddot{\eta}_1(t) = F(t)/\sqrt{3m}$*
  The solution is

$$\eta_1(t) = (A_1 + A_2 t) + F_o\ t^2/\sqrt{12m} \qquad (3.126)$$

  where the first part is the homogeneous solution and the second part the particular solution. Using the initial conditions $\eta_1(0) = \dot{\eta}_1(0) = 0$, we obtain

$$\eta_1(t) = F_o\ t^2/\sqrt{12m} \qquad (3.127)$$

- *Solution of $\ddot{\eta}_2(t) + k/m\ \eta_2(t) = -F(t)/\sqrt{2m}$*
  The solution is

$$\eta_2(t) = [B_1 \cos(\sqrt{\frac{k}{m}}t) + B_2 \sin(\sqrt{\frac{k}{m}}t)] - \frac{\sqrt{m}}{k}F_o/\sqrt{2} \quad (3.128)$$

  where the first part again is the homogeneous solution and the second part the particular solution. Using the initial conditions $\eta_2(0) = \dot{\eta}_2(0) = 0$, we obtain

$$\eta_2(t) = \frac{F_o}{\sqrt{2}}\frac{\sqrt{m}}{k}[\cos(\sqrt{\frac{k}{m}}t) - 1] \qquad (3.129)$$

- *Solution of* $\ddot{\eta}_3(t) + 3k/m\ \eta_3(t) = F(t)/\sqrt{6m}$
  The solution is

$$\eta_3(t) = [B_1 \cos(\sqrt{\frac{3k}{m}}t) + B_2 \sin(\sqrt{\frac{3k}{m}}t)] + \frac{\sqrt{m}}{k}F_o/\sqrt{54} \quad (3.130)$$

where the first part again is the homogeneous solution and the second part the particular solution. Using the initial conditions $\eta_3(0) = \dot{\eta}_3(0) = 0$, *we obtain*

$$\eta_3(t) = \frac{F_o}{\sqrt{54}}\frac{\sqrt{m}}{k}[-\cos(\sqrt{\frac{3k}{m}}t) + 1] \quad (3.131)$$

So the resulting solution for the natural coordinates is

$$\underline{\eta}(t) = \frac{F_o}{\sqrt{12m}}\begin{bmatrix} t^2 \\ 0 \\ 0 \end{bmatrix} + \frac{F_o}{\sqrt{54}}\frac{\sqrt{m}}{k}\begin{bmatrix} 0 \\ -3\sqrt{3} \\ 1 \end{bmatrix} +$$

$$\frac{F_o}{\sqrt{54}}\frac{\sqrt{m}}{k}\begin{bmatrix} 0 \\ 3\sqrt{3}\cos(\sqrt{\frac{k}{m}}t) \\ -\cos(\sqrt{\frac{3k}{m}}t) \end{bmatrix} \quad (3.132)$$

We can transform this solution in the natural coordinates $\underline{\eta}(t)$ *back into the original coordinates* $\underline{q}(t)$ *by using* $\underline{q} = \underline{U}\ \underline{\eta}$, *giving*

$$\underline{q}(t) = \frac{F_o}{6m}\begin{bmatrix} t^2 \\ 0 \\ 0 \end{bmatrix} + \frac{F_o}{9k}\begin{bmatrix} -4 \\ 3 \\ 6 \end{bmatrix} +$$

$$\frac{F_o}{18k}\begin{bmatrix} 9\cos(\sqrt{\frac{k}{m}}t) - \cos(\sqrt{\frac{3k}{m}}t) \\ -9\cos(\sqrt{\frac{k}{m}}t) + 3\cos(\sqrt{\frac{3k}{m}}t) \\ -9\cos(\sqrt{\frac{k}{m}}t) - 3\cos(\sqrt{\frac{3k}{m}}t) \end{bmatrix} \quad (3.133)$$

To get some understanding we first look at the final response without the oscillating terms (first two terms of the solution). This non-oscillating part consists of a contribution $q_1 = \{F_o/(6m)\ t^2 - 4F_o/(9k)\}$ *and the contributions* $q_2 = F_o/(3k)$ *and* $q_3 = 2F_o/(3k)$. *Because* q_2 *and* q_3 *are constants this means that all the three masses are travelling with the same speed and acceleration (remember the definition of the generalized coordinates). This (constant) acceleration of the masses due to the (constant) force* F_o *is* $\ddot{q}_1 = F_o/(3m)$. *From Newton's law* $F = ma$, *we can conclude that in this case on each mass the same force* $F_o/3$ *should be acting which means that the force in the left spring will be* $F_o/3$ *and the force in the right spring will be* $2F_o/3$. *These forces devided by the spring constant* k *directly give the elongation of the springs*

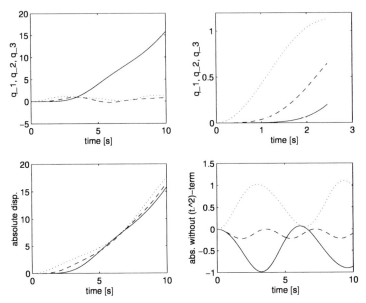

Fig. 3.8 Displacement-time plots, left mass (solid-line),
middle mass (dashed line) and right mass (dotted line)

$q_2 = F_o/(3k)$, respectively $q_3 = 2F_o/(3k)$.

For some further numerical evaluation we assume $m = 1$; $k = 1$; $F_o = 1$. *On this rigid-body-like acceleration of the train we have to superimpose the oscillating terms which are due to the fact that the train had to start suddenly from zero initial conditions. These total displacements are shown in Fig. 3.8. The upper left plot gives the original coordinates as function of time showing the **almost** quadratic function for* q_1 *and the oscillating functions for* q_2 *and* q_3. *The upper right part is a zoom-plot for small t showing the initial zero conditions. For small t first the right mass is starting to move (growing* q_3*), then the second mass is following (growing* q_2*) and after a while also the left mass (*q_1*) is starting to move.*

*The bottom left plot shows the **absolute** displacements* q_1, $(q_1 + q_2)$ *and* $(q_1 + q_2 + q_3)$ *for the masses. All the 3 displacements show the almost quadratic motion. The bottom right plot shows these absolute displacements with the quadratic part (the constant acceleration) removed. This plot shows that the distance between the three masses is changing harmonically with time. The two eigenfrequencies can clearly be distinguished.*

3.4.2   Steady-state response to harmonic excitation

First, we review some relevant aspects of the analysis procedure for single-degree-of-freedom systems under harmonic excitation. For systems with only a single degree of freedom $q(t)$ we have only one equation of motion which can be written as

$$m \ \ddot{q}(t) \ + \ d \ \dot{q}(t) \ + \ k \ q(t) = F(t) \tag{3.134}$$

In case of harmonic excitation the excitation $F(t)$ has the form

$$F(t) = F_a \ \cos(\Omega t + \varphi) \tag{3.135}$$

where Ω $[rad/s]$ is the excitation frequency , F_a is the excitation amplitude while φ is the phase angle of the excitation force. The response of (3.134) to harmonic excitation can be conveniently obtained by a notation using complex numbers. To this end (3.135) is rewritten as

$$F(t) = Re\{\hat{F} \ e^{j\Omega t}\} \tag{3.136}$$

where the time-independent complex quantity $\hat{F}$ is given by

$$\hat{F} = F_a \ e^{j\varphi} \tag{3.137}$$

Analogous to (3.135) and (3.136), we express the steady-state response $q(t)$ to harmonic excitation as

$$q(t) = q_a \ \cos(\Omega t + \psi) = Re\{\hat{q} \ e^{j\Omega t}\} \tag{3.138}$$

with

$$\hat{q} = q_a \ e^{j\psi} \tag{3.139}$$

where q_a is the amplitude of the response and ψ its phase angle. If we substitute (3.136) and (3.138) in the equation of motion (3.134), we get

$$Re\{[-m\Omega^2 \ + \ dj\Omega \ + \ k]\hat{q} \ e^{j\Omega t}\} = Re\{\hat{F} \ e^{j\Omega t}\} \tag{3.140}$$

This equation must be valid for all t, so that

$$\hat{q} = \frac{\hat{F}}{-m\Omega^2 \ + \ d \ j\Omega \ + \ k} \tag{3.141}$$

From this result the complex amplitude of the response $\hat{q}$ can easily be calculated. It is very important to note that in equation (3.141) the time t has disappeared and that we are dealing with the complex amplitudes of the excitation, $\hat{F}$, and of the response, $\hat{q}$. The latter now has become a function of the excitation frequency Ω

$$\hat{q} = \hat{q}(\Omega) \tag{3.142}$$

Of course, once this complex amplitude of the response has been determined, we can always calculate the time-dependent response $q(t)$ using (3.138). This means that we have moved from a representation in the **time domain** to a representation in the **frequency domain**. Finally it should be remarked that instead of looking at the real parts of the complex expressions, as done in (3.136) and (3.138), also the imaginairy parts could have been used.

For systems with multiple degrees of freedom under harmonic excitation the same procedure can be followed. Now the column matrix of generalized forces $\underline{Q}(t)$ in the right-hand side of the equations of motion (3.108) has the form

$$\underline{Q}(t) = \begin{bmatrix} Q_{1a} \ \cos(\Omega t + \varphi_1) \\ Q_{2a} \ \cos(\Omega t + \varphi_2) \\ ... \\ Q_{na} \ \cos(\Omega t + \varphi_n) \end{bmatrix} = Re\{\underline{\hat{Q}} \ e^{j\Omega t}\} \tag{3.143}$$

where Ω is the excitation frequency, Q_{ia} is the time-independent (known) amplitude of the generalized excitation force Q_i, while φ_i is the phase angle of this excitation force. The time-independent column of complex amplitudes, $\underline{\hat{Q}}$, can be written as

$$\underline{\hat{Q}} = \begin{bmatrix} Q_{1a} \ e^{j\varphi_1} \\ Q_{2a} \ e^{j\varphi_2} \\ ... \\ Q_{na} \ e^{j\varphi_n} \end{bmatrix} \tag{3.144}$$

It is remarked that (3.143) implies the excitation forces to act at only **one specific excitation frequency**. Because the system defined by (3.108) is linear, the case of excitation with multiple frequencies can be obtained by superposition of the responses at the individual harmonic functions. In agreement with the behaviour of single-degree-of-freedom linear systems, the forced response of our multi-degree-of-freedom system defined by (3.108) to the harmonic excitation defined by (3.143) can be found by taking the solution $\underline{q}(t)$ in the form

$$\underline{q}(t) = \begin{bmatrix} q_{1a} \ \cos(\Omega t + \psi_1) \\ q_{2a} \ \cos(\Omega t + \psi_2) \\ ... \\ q_{na} \ \cos(\Omega t + \psi_n) \end{bmatrix} = Re\{\underline{\hat{q}} \ e^{j\Omega t}\} \tag{3.145}$$

with $\hat{q}$ being the time-independent column of complex amplitudes of the response

$$\hat{\underline{q}} = \begin{bmatrix} q_{1a}\ e^{j\psi_1} \\ q_{2a}\ e^{j\psi_2} \\ ... \\ q_{na}\ e^{j\psi_n} \end{bmatrix} \qquad (3.146)$$

Inserting (3.143) and (3.145) into (3.108), we obtain the following solution for the complex amplitudes of the forced response

$$\hat{\underline{q}} = \left[\underline{K} - \Omega^2 \underline{M}\right]^{-1} \hat{\underline{Q}} \qquad (3.147)$$

The matrix $\underline{H}(\Omega) = \left[\underline{K} - \Omega^2 \underline{M}\right]^{-1}$ is commonly referred to as the **transfer function matrix** or the **matrix of frequency response functions** (in abbreviated terminology the **FRF matrix**). Because the determinant of the matrix $\left[\underline{K} - \Omega^2 \underline{M}\right]$ represents exactly the left-hand side of the characteristic equation (3.23) for the eigenvalue problem, this matrix will become singular (so the inverse will not exist) when Ω will be equal to one of the undamped eigenfrequencies of the system. This means that the response of the system tends to increase indefinitely if the excitation frequency Ω approaches one of these natural frequencies of the system. So, at least in principle, the harmonically excited system is at resonance at all the natural frequencies related to the free vibration problem.

If we wish to determine amplitude-frequency plots, we have to invert the matrix $\left[\underline{K} - \Omega^2 \underline{M}\right]$ over the practically relevant frequency range. Because of this, the above approach is suitable only for relatively low-order systems. For higher-order systems, it is more efficient to use a spectral representation using a decomposition into natural coordinates discussed in the previous subsection. To get this expression we write

$$\underline{H}^{-1} = \left[\underline{K} - \Omega^2 \underline{M}\right] \qquad (3.148)$$

Using the matrix $\underline{U}$ of eigencolumns of the undamped system we can rewrite (3.148) as

$$\underline{U}^T \underline{H}^{-1}\ \underline{U} = \underline{U}^T \left[\underline{K} - \Omega^2 \underline{M}\right]\ \underline{U} \qquad (3.149)$$

Next, we use the orthogonality properties of the eigencolumns, (3.60) and (3.61), so that we obtain

$$\underline{U}^T \underline{H}^{-1}\ \underline{U} = \lceil k_r \rfloor - \Omega^2 \lceil m_r \rfloor = \left[\lceil \omega_r^2 \rfloor - \Omega^2\ \underline{I}\right]\ \lceil m_r \rfloor \qquad (3.150)$$

Inverting this whole relationship, we obtain

$$\underline{U}^{-1}\underline{H}\ \underline{U}^{-T} = \lceil m_r \rfloor^{-1} \left[\lceil \omega_r^2 \rfloor - \Omega^2\ \underline{I}\right]^{-1} \qquad (3.151)$$

We premultiply this relation by $\underline{U}$ and post-multiply it by $\underline{U}^T$, yielding

$$\underline{H} = \underline{U}\ \lceil m_r \rfloor^{-1} \left[\lceil \omega_r^2 \rfloor - \Omega^2\ \underline{I}\right]^{-1}\ \underline{U}^T \qquad (3.152)$$

This result can also be written as

$$\underline{H}(\Omega) = \left[\underline{K} - \Omega^2\underline{M}\right]^{-1} = \sum_{r=1}^{n}\left[\frac{\underline{u}_r\underline{u}_r^T}{m_r\left(\omega_r^2 - \Omega^2\right)}\right] \qquad (3.153)$$

where the $(n \times n)$ matrix $\underline{H}(\Omega)$ again is the transfer function matrix. It can be considered as a generalization of the undamped single-degree-of-freedom frequency-response function to undamped multi-degree-of-freedom linear systems. The transfer function matrix relates the complex amplitudes of the excitation to the complex amplitudes of the response as follows

$$\hat{\underline{q}} = \underline{H}(\Omega)\,\hat{\underline{Q}} \qquad (3.154)$$

Combining (3.145), (3.153) and (3.154), we find the final solution of the generalized coordinates $\underline{q}(t)$ in terms of the eigencolumns to be

$$\underline{q}(t) = Re\left[\left\{\sum_{r=1}^{n}\frac{\underline{u}_r\underline{u}_r^T\,\hat{\underline{Q}}}{m_r\left(\omega_r^2 - \Omega^2\right)}\right\}e^{j\Omega t}\right] \qquad (3.155)$$

From this result some very important conclusions can be drawn. First, if the excitation frequency Ω approaches one of the natural frequencies ω_r, the response of the system tends to increase indefinitely and the system is at resonance, as stated earlier in this subsection. However, this is not true if Ω approaches ω_r and simultaneously $\underline{u}_r^T\,\hat{\underline{Q}} = 0$. In that case the column of generalized forces is said to be orthogonal to the eigencolumn $\underline{u}_r$, implying that the generalized forces produce no work on the eigenmode $\underline{u}_r$. The system is said to be in a situation of *apparent resonance* or *pseudo-resonance*.

Example 3.6

We consider the symmetric two-degree-of-freedom undamped mass-spring system shown in Fig. 3.9. The system consists of two equal masses m, both connected to the fixed world by a linear spring with spring stiffness k. Between the two masses a third spring with spring stiffness k_c is mounted. So we have a completely symmetric system. On the masses the forces $F_1(t) = F_{1a}\cos\Omega t$, respectively $F_2(t) = F_{2a}\cos\Omega t$ are acting. In this example the columns of generalized coordinates and of generalized forces are

$$\underline{q}(t) = \begin{bmatrix} q_1(t) \\ q_2(t) \end{bmatrix} \qquad (3.156)$$

$$\underline{Q}(t) = \begin{bmatrix} F_1(t) \\ F_2(t) \end{bmatrix} = \begin{bmatrix} F_{1a} \\ F_{2a} \end{bmatrix}\cos\Omega t \qquad (3.157)$$

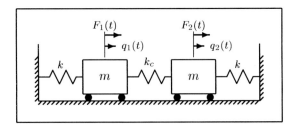

Fig. 3.9   Symmetric two-degree-of-freedom undamped
mass-spring system

*Here the two external forces $F_1(t)$ and $F_2(t)$ are assumed to be in phase,
which means that for the complex amplitude of the excitation we have
the simple expression*

$$\underline{\hat{Q}} = \begin{bmatrix} F_{1a} \\ F_{2a} \end{bmatrix} \tag{3.158}$$

The mass and stiffness matrices take the form

$$\underline{M} = \begin{bmatrix} m & 0 \\ 0 & m \end{bmatrix} \qquad \underline{K} = \begin{bmatrix} (k + k_c) & -k_c \\ -k_c & (k + k_c) \end{bmatrix} \tag{3.159}$$

*It is left to the reader to show that the squared eigenfrequencies for this
system are*

$$\omega_1^2 = \frac{k}{m} \quad , \quad \omega_2^2 = \frac{k + 2k_c}{m} \tag{3.160}$$

whereas the $\underline{M}$-normalized eigencolumns become

$$\underline{u}_1 = \frac{1}{\sqrt{m}} \begin{bmatrix} 1 \\ 1 \end{bmatrix} \quad , \quad \underline{u}_2 = \frac{1}{\sqrt{m}} \begin{bmatrix} 1 \\ -1 \end{bmatrix} \tag{3.161}$$

*So, the symmetric mass-spring system of Fig. 3.9 possesses a symmetric natural mode and an anti-symmetric natural mode. The frequency-response functions for this problem are plotted in Fig. 3.10, where the
system parameters have been assigned the specific values*

$$m = \frac{5}{6}, \quad k = m, \quad k_c = \frac{1}{2}k \tag{3.162}$$

Four different cases are distinguished, namely

(a) $F_{1a} = 1,\ F_{2a} = 0$

(b) $F_{1a} = 0,\ F_{2a} = 1$

(c) $F_{1a} = 1,\ F_{2a} = 1,$ *which is (a)+(b)*

(d) $F_{1a} = 1,\ F_{2a} = -1,$ *which is (a)-(b)*

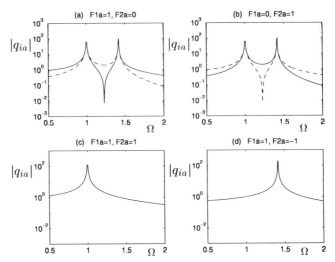

Fig. 3.10 System response amplitudes, q_{1a}: solid line,
q_{2a}: dashed line

From the two top figures we can clearly see the two resonances at
$\Omega = \omega_1 = 1.0$ *and* $\Omega = \omega_2 = \sqrt{2}$. *We observe from Fig. 3.10 (d)*
that if we excite the system harmonically in its lowest eigenfrequency
ω_1 *(for which the natural mode is symmetric, $\underline{u}_1^T = [1,1]$) with an anti-*
symmetric set of forces $F_1 = -F_2$ (so $\hat{\underline{Q}}^T = [1,-1]$), then there is no
resonance at ω_1 and the system is in pseudo-resonance. Similarly, we
observe from Fig. 3.10 (c) that if we excite the system harmonically
in its second eigenfrequency ω_2 (for which the natural mode is anti-
symmetric $\underline{u}_2^T = [1,-1]$) with the symmetric set of forces $F_1 = F_2$ (so
$\hat{\underline{Q}}^T = [1,1]$), *then there is no resonance at ω_2 and the system is again*
at pseudo-resonance. For arbitrary excitations in general all the reso-
nances will show up in such a frequency-response function.

The picture of the frequency-response functions with its resonances and
anti-resonances is a very important tool in understanding the dynamic
behaviour of a structure or machine. The interpretation of these frf's
can be very difficult. Therefore, the development of some practical ex-
perience can be very helpful to understand the underlying phenomena
in these frf's. To illustrate this, we look again at the symmetric two-
degree-of-freedom system of Fig. 3.9 and the frequency-response func-
tions corresponding to a unit harmonic excitation in the generalized
coordinate q_1, as depicted in Fig. 3.10(a).
In this figure we can recognize a so-called **anti-resonance** *at* $\Omega \approx$

1.2 [rad/s] where $|q_1|$ will tend to zero. This means that the left mass may be assumed to be fixed. So, in fact we have a system of a single (right) mass m in between a spring k and a spring k_c as shown in Fig. 3.11. This leads to an anti-resonance frequency for free vibrations of

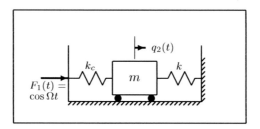

Fig. 3.11   Relevant system at anti-resonance

magnitude $\omega_{ar} = \sqrt{(k + k_c)/m}$. Using the chosen parameter values, ω_{ar} becomes equal to $\sqrt{1.5} \approx 1.2247$ [rad/s]. So, precisely at this frequency the right mass is vibrating with displacement $q_2 = q_{2a} \cos(\omega_{ar} t)$ and the force $[k_c \, q_2(t)]$ in the spring k_c is exactly balanced by the applied harmonic excitation force $F_1(t)$ with unit amplitude. Hence, the amplitude q_{2a} at $\Omega = \omega_{ar}$ must be $1/k_c = 2$. It can be verified from the plot that this indeed is the case.

Another conclusion to be drawn from (3.155) is related to the reduction of the number of degrees of freedom. Suppose a system with many degrees of freedom is excited harmonically in a certain frequency range which has an upper bound Ω_u. Now, if in the summation of (3.155) $\omega_r \gg \Omega_u$, then $(\omega_r^2 - \Omega^2)$ tends to become very large. Hence, starting from a certain cut-off frequency $\omega_c \gg \Omega_u$, the contributions of the modal columns $\underline{u}_r$ in the summation of (3.155) can be neglected and, consequently, only a limited number of eigencolumns $\underline{u}_r$ and eigenfrequencies ω_r have to be taken into account from a practical point of view. Thus, also the eigenvalue problem has to be solved only for a limited number of eigenvalues and eigencolumns, determined by the chosen cut-off frequency ω_c. The above observation forms the basis of reduction techniques for computational analysis of systems with a large number of degrees-of-freedom, which will be discussed in Section 3.5.

We will now have a closer look at the properties of the diagonal elements $h_{kk}(\Omega)$ of the transfer function matrix $\underline{H}(\Omega)$ defined by (3.153), also called the direct Frequency-Response Functions or, alternatively, the principal dynamic influence coefficients. In view of (3.153), these coefficients are given by

$$h_{kk}(\Omega) = \sum_{r=1}^{n} \frac{\{u_r\,[k]\}^2}{m_r\,(\omega_r^2 - \Omega^2)} \qquad (3.163)$$

The principal coefficients of the dynamic influence matrix, h_{kk}, possess the fundamental property

$$\frac{dh_{kk}}{d(\Omega^2)} = \sum_{r=1}^{n} \frac{\{u_r\,[k]\}^2}{m_r\,(\omega_r^2 - \Omega^2)^2} > 0 \qquad (3.164)$$

which implies that they always increase with increasing excitation frequency. This leads us to the frequency plot of the principal dynamic influence coefficient $h_{kk}(\Omega)$ sketched in Fig. 3.12 for the system show in Fig. 3.9. It should be remarked that due to the fact that the system in Fig. 3.9 is perfectly symmetric we will have $h_{11}(\Omega) = h_{22}(\Omega)$. In general however this will not be the case.

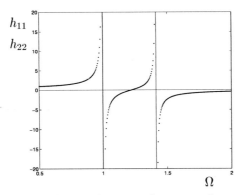

Fig. 3.12   Plot of $h_{11} = h_{22}$ terms for system shown in Fig. 3.9

It can be concluded from Fig. 3.12 that two subsequent resonance frequencies ω_r and ω_{r+1} are always separated by a so-called **anti-resonance** frequency at which $h_{kk} = 0$. Such a frequency is denoted by Ω_r^a and we have

$$\omega_r < \Omega_r^a < \omega_{r+1} \qquad (3.165)$$

Finally, we investigate the transfer function matrix if the excitation frequency tends to zero. In that case we conclude from (3.153) that

$$\underline{H}(0) = \underline{K}^{-1} = \sum_{r=1}^{n} \frac{u_r u_r^T}{m_r \omega_r^2} \qquad (3.166)$$

meaning that the transfer function matrix tends to approach the flexibility matrix $\underline{K}^{-1}$ of static influence coefficients if $\Omega \to 0$. The spectral expansion in the right side of (3.166) is identical to the expansion (3.71) for $\underline{K}^{-1}$ derived earlier.

Example 3.7

To illustrate some of the aspects which show up in the (practical) evaluation of the steady-state response to a harmonic excitation, we consider a simple two-dimensional passenger-car model as shown in Fig. 3.13. It

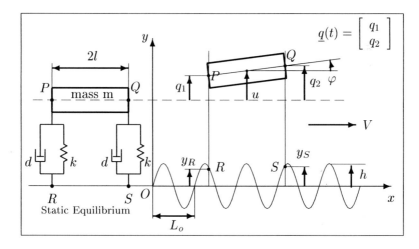

Fig. 3.13   Two-degree-of-freedom car model

consists of a car body which is modelled as a uniform beam with length 2l and mass m. The body is supported by the front wheel and rear wheel suspensions (including the tyres) which are both modelled as a combination of a linear spring with stiffness constant k and a viscous damper with damping constant d. The car is moving with a constant horizontal velocity V [m/s]. During riding, the tyre-contact points R respectively S follow a sinusoidal road profile with amplitude h [m] and wavelength L_o [m]. For the point S this implies $y_S(t) = h\ \sin(2\pi x/L_o)$. The motion of the car body is measured from the static equilibrium position with $y_R(t) = y_S(t) = 0$ (shown left in the figure). Hence, the effect of gravity can be ignored. As the generalized coordinates we choose the vertical displacements of the two points P and Q of the car body where the suspensions are mounted, so $q^T = [q_1, q_2]$. The corresponding vertical displacements $y_R(t)$ and $y_S(t)$ are considered to be prescribed displacements for the system and we only look at small displacements of the car model, so we will a priori use a linear approximation.
The kinetic energy can be written as

$$T = \frac{1}{2}m\dot{u}^2 + \frac{1}{2}J_z\dot{\varphi}^2 = \frac{1}{2}m(\frac{\dot{q}_1 + \dot{q}_2}{2})^2 + \frac{1}{6}ml^2(\frac{\dot{q}_2 - \dot{q}_1}{2l})^2$$

$$= \frac{m}{6}(\dot{q_1}^2 + \dot{q_2}^2 + \dot{q_1}\dot{q_2}) \tag{3.167}$$

where we used the formula $J_z = \frac{1}{3}ml^2$ for the mass-moment of inertia of the body around its centre of gravity. The kinetic energy can be rewritten as a quadratic form in $\dot{q}$

$$T = \frac{1}{2}\,\dot{q}^T \underline{M}\,\dot{q} \qquad \text{with} \qquad \underline{M} = \frac{m}{6}\begin{bmatrix} 2 & 1 \\ 1 & 2 \end{bmatrix} \tag{3.168}$$

The potential energy (here only the elastic energy) can be expressed as

$$V^{in} = \frac{1}{2}(q_1 - y_R)^2 + \frac{1}{2}(q_2 - y_S)^2 \tag{3.169}$$

or

$$V^{in} = \frac{1}{2}\underline{q}^T \underline{K}\,\underline{q} + \underline{k}^T \underline{q} + V_o \tag{3.170}$$

with

$$\underline{K} = \begin{bmatrix} k & 0 \\ 0 & k \end{bmatrix}; \quad \underline{k} = \begin{bmatrix} -k\ y_R \\ -k\ y_S \end{bmatrix}; \quad V_o = \frac{1}{2}k(y_R^2 + y_S^2) \tag{3.171}$$

For the evaluation of the generalized non-conservative forces we only have to look at the contribution due to viscous damping. The real damping forces f_{d1} respectively f_{d2} are shown in Fig. 3.14. To switch to gen-

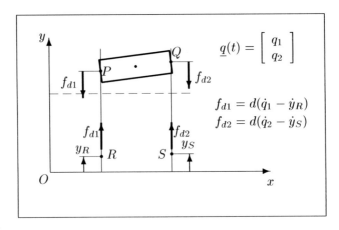

Fig. 3.14 Viscous damping forces in 2-dof car model

eralized forces, we first apply the virtual displacement $\delta \underline{q}^T = [\delta q_1 \ , \ 0]$. The virtual work for this situation can be written as

$$\delta W = Q_1 \delta q_1 = -f_{d1}\delta q_1 = -d(\dot{q_1} - \dot{y}_R)\delta q_1 \tag{3.172}$$

This equation directly yields the first generalized force Q_1. By apply-ing $\delta \underline{q}^T = [0, \ \delta q_2]$ we similarly can find Q_2. The resulting column $\underline{Q}$ becomes

$$\underline{Q} = \left[\begin{array}{c} -d \ (\dot{q}_1 - \dot{y}_R) \\ -d \ (\dot{q}_2 - \dot{y}_S) \end{array} \right] = -\underline{D}\dot{\underline{q}} + \underline{f}(t) \qquad (3.173)$$

yielding the following result for the viscous damping matrix $\underline{D}$ and the column matrix of excitations $\underline{f}(t)$

$$\underline{D} = \left[\begin{array}{cc} d & 0 \\ 0 & d \end{array} \right]; \qquad \underline{f}(t) = \left[\begin{array}{c} d \ \dot{y}_R \\ d \ \dot{y}_S \end{array} \right] \qquad (3.174)$$

Application of the methodology of Lagrange's equations finally results in a set of 2 coupled, linear equations of motion

$$\underline{M} \ \ddot{\underline{q}} + \underline{D} \ \dot{\underline{q}} + \underline{K} \ \underline{q} = \underline{Q}(t) = -\underline{k}(t) + \underline{f}(t) \qquad (3.175)$$

In this section we limit ourselves to the undamped behaviour. This means that we are dealing with

$$\underline{M} \ \ddot{\underline{q}} + \underline{K} \ \underline{q} = \underline{Q}(t) \qquad (3.176)$$

with

$$\underline{M} = \frac{m}{6} \left[\begin{array}{cc} 2 & 1 \\ 1 & 2 \end{array} \right]; \ \underline{K} = \left[\begin{array}{cc} k & 0 \\ 0 & k \end{array} \right]; \ \underline{Q}(t) = \left[\begin{array}{c} k \ y_R \\ k \ y_S \end{array} \right] \qquad (3.177)$$

For the further numerical evaluation we use the following specific pa-rameter values:
$m = 1200 \ [kg]$, $k = 10^5 \ [N/m]$, $l = 1.5 \ [m]$, road wavelength $L_o = 4 \ [m]$, road amplitude $h = 0.01 \ [m]$. The speed range will be taken to be $V = 0...30 \ [m/s]$. The undamped free vibrational behaviour is determined by the eigenfrequencies

$$\begin{array}{c} \omega_1 = 12.9099 \ [rad/s] \\ \omega_2 = 22.3607 \ [rad/s] \end{array} \qquad (3.178)$$

and corresponding eigenmode matrix ($\underline{M}$-normalized)

$$\underline{U} = \left[\begin{array}{cc} 0.0289 & -0.05 \\ 0.0289 & 0.05 \end{array} \right] \qquad (3.179)$$

In this result we can recognize a purely translational mode and a purely rotational mode.
Next, we will investigate the (undamped) forced harmonic response. In this case we do not have some external forces exciting the system but the excitation comes from the car driving with a certain speed V on a road with a (strongly) idealized harmonic wave profile as shown in the figure.

The road profile was given as $y_S(t) = h \sin(2\pi x/L_o)$ where x is the horizontal position of the tyre road contactpoint S. For a constant velocity V we can write $x = V t$ and for the contact point R we have to apply the position $(x - 2\ l)$ instead of x, which gives

$$y_S(t) = h \sin(\Omega t)$$
$$y_R(t) = h \sin(\Omega t + \psi)$$
(3.180)

where we introduced the excitation frequency $\Omega = 2\pi V/L_o$ [rad/s] and the phase shift $\psi = -4\pi l/L_o$ [rad]. We can write these harmonic functions in a notation using complex numbers as

$$y_S(t) = Im[\hat{y}_S\ e^{j\Omega t}]$$
$$y_R(t) = Im[\hat{y}_R\ e^{j\Omega t}]$$
(3.181)

with the complex amplitudes being $\hat{y}_S = h$ and $\hat{y}_R = he^{j\psi}$. For the time being we neglect that we have to take the imaginairy parts of these expressions (later we just can take the imaginairy parts of the complex responses to get the real response). Then, the excitation column becomes

$$\underline{Q}(t) = \hat{\underline{Q}}\ e^{j\Omega t} = \left[\begin{array}{c} hk\ e^{j\psi} \\ hk \end{array} \right] e^{j\Omega t}$$
(3.182)

It follows from this result that the column of complex amplitudes of the excitation takes the form

$$\hat{\underline{Q}} = hk \left[\begin{array}{c} e^{j\psi} \\ 1 \end{array} \right]$$
(3.183)

As we can see, this column of complex excitation amplitudes contains really complex elements due to the presence of the time shift between front wheel and rear wheel excitation. The steady-state response can now be written as

$$\underline{q}(t) = Im[\hat{\underline{q}}\ e^{j\Omega t}]$$
(3.184)

As shown earlier, the complex response amplitudes are related to the complex excitation amplitudes through

$$\hat{\underline{q}} = [-\Omega^2 \underline{M} + \underline{K}]^{-1} \hat{\underline{Q}}$$
(3.185)

The complex response $\hat{\underline{q}}$ has been calculated for a speed-range $V = 0...30$ [m/s], corresponding to a frequency-range $\Omega = 0...(60\pi)/L_o$ [rad/s] The result is shown in Fig 3.15. First of all the two magnitudes of the complex amplitudes $|\hat{q}_i|$ for this umdamped situation are equal for all speeds, so only one graph can be recognized.

The two undamped eigenfrequencies can be transformed into two critical speeds using $\Omega = 2\pi V/L_o$. This gives

$$V_1^{crit} = 8.2187\ [m/s]$$
$$V_2^{crit} = 14.2353\ [m/s]$$
(3.186)

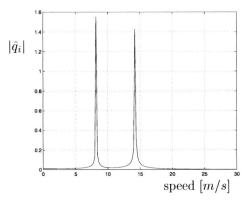

$|\hat{q}_i|$

speed $[m/s]$

Fig. 3.15   Magnitudes of complex amplitudes as a
function of speed variation

The corresponding two sharp resonance peaks can be clearly recognized
in the figure. In Fig. 3.16 the amplitudes are shown on a logarithmic
scale.

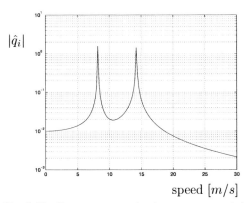

$|\hat{q}_i|$

speed $[m/s]$

Fig. 3.16   Response magnitudes versus speed, log scale

For very low speeds the magnitudes converge to the value 0.01. So, the
points P and Q simply follow the harmonic road profile without spring
deformation. For very high speeds we conclude from (3.185) that

$$-\Omega^2 \underline{M} \ \hat{\underline{q}} \approx \hat{\underline{Q}} \qquad (3.187)$$

so the amplitudes will quadratically go to zero for $\Omega \to \infty$.
In Fig. 3.17 the phase angles of the complex response amplitudes are
shown. For the interpretation we first calculate the excitation phase
shift $\psi = -4\pi l/L_o = -1.5\pi$ or $\psi = +\pi/2$ [rad]. So for the complex

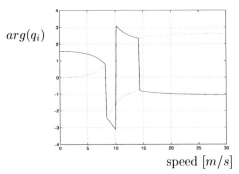

$arg(q_i)$

speed $[m/s]$

Fig. 3.17   Phase angles of $\hat{q}_1$ (solid line) and $\hat{q}_2$ (dotted line)
as function of speed

excitation column we get

$$\hat{Q} = hk \begin{bmatrix} j \\ 1 \end{bmatrix}$$ (3.188)

Using (3.185) and (3.187), we obtain for very low speeds

$$\hat{q} \approx \underline{K}^{-1}\hat{Q} = h \begin{bmatrix} j \\ 1 \end{bmatrix}$$ (3.189)

Hence, the phase angle for $\hat{q}_1$ will be $\pi/2$, whereas it is zero for $\hat{q}_2$.
Using (3.187) and (3.188), we obtain for very large speeds

$$\hat{q} \approx [-\Omega^2 \underline{M}]^{-1}\hat{Q} = -\frac{2\Omega^2}{m} \begin{bmatrix} 2 & -1 \\ -1 & 2 \end{bmatrix} \hat{Q} =$$

$$\frac{2kh\Omega^2}{m} \begin{bmatrix} 1 - 2j \\ -2 + j \end{bmatrix}$$ (3.190)

It is easy to check that this result leads to a phase shift for $\hat{q}_1$ of -
1.1 [rad] and for $\hat{q}_2$ of 2.7 [rad].
We can also see that the phases are only defined for the interval $[-\pi, \pi]$
and that at the critical speeds we are dealing with phase jumps of π [rad].
This is also known from the theory for single-degree-of-freedom undamped mass-spring systems or it follows directly from the spectral expansion of the transfer function matrix for an undamped system

$$\underline{H}(\Omega) = \sum_{r=1}^{n} \frac{\underline{u}_r \underline{u}_r^T}{m_r \left(\omega_r^2 - \Omega^2\right)}$$ (3.191)

For $\Omega \approx \omega_r$ only the rth term in this series is relevant and this term
will change sign when Ω passes ω_r leading to a phase jump of π [rad].

In Fig. 3.18 the complex response magnitudes are shown for a longer (American) car with length $2l = L_o = 4$ [m], so the car length in this case is equal to the road wavelength L_o. We can see that now only the translational mode is excited which is obvious.   Finally, in Fig. 3.19

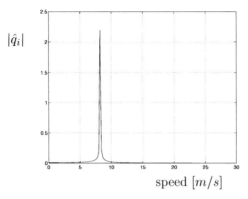

Fig. 3.18 Complex response magnitudes for
Car length = Road wavelength

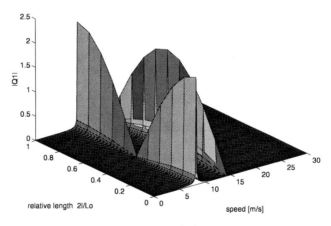

Fig. 3.19 Response magnitude $|\hat{q}_1|$ as a function of
speed range and relative car-length

the situation is shown for different values of the car length ranging from $l = 0$ up to $2l = L_o$. This figure shows that depending on the relative length $\frac{2l}{L_o}$, the translational and/or the rotational mode will play a dominant role in the response.

In the next chapter we will come back to this example and introduce

*some damping in the system. There we will see that this damping can
have a surprising influence on the complex responses of the system.*

3.5   REDUCTION AND SUBSTRUCTURING TECHNIQUES

3.5.1   Introductory remarks

The advent of digital computers has stimulated the development of increasingly powerful methods of analysis, such as the finite element method. But, for complex structures like airplanes, aerospace structures, ships and vehicles, application of the finite element method generally results in stiffness and mass matrices of extremely high dimension. This, in turn, can place severe strains on various computational algorithms, and on the available power and capacity of the digital computers. Because, in most cases, we are only interested in solutions with a frequency content upto a certain upper bound, it may prove to be advantageous to reduce the system matrices to a (much) smaller dimension. In this section we will discuss the most frequently used *reduction techniques*.

Another aspect of complex structures is that these structures are frequently divided into different parts, also referred to as substructures or components. A separate dynamical model is constructed for each part of the system and later these component models are assembled to a complete dynamical model for the original structure. Such a method is called a *substructuring technique* which is often utilized in the context of large projects where the analysis of the different substructures is regularly performed by distinct teams. In an aircraft model, for instance, wings, engine nacelles and landing gears are studied by different groups. Therefore, interconnecting surfaces or lines between the different components, also called *interfaces*, have to be defined carefully so as to ensure the compatibility between the different parts of the complete dynamical model.

In this section we will discuss the most frequently used substructuring techniques. They are referred to as *component mode synthesis* (abbreviated cms) techniques, and, usually, these techniques are combined with reduction techniques, where the reduction process is applied at component level.

Before discussing the most frequently used reduction and substructuring techniques in the following subsections, let us discuss the general principle of reducing the dimension of the system matrices, either at the level of a structure as a whole, or at component level. To this end, we repeat the linearized Lagrange's equation of motion, (3.1), for undamped systems with symmetric matrices

$$\underline{M}\,\ddot{\underline{q}}(t) + \underline{K}\,\underline{q}(t) = \underline{Q}(t) \tag{3.192}$$

In general, the dimension reduction of the system matrices can be achieved by expanding the n generalized coordinates contained in the column $\underline{q}(t)$ as a linear combination of a (much) smaller number n_p of new generalized coordinates, collected in a column $\underline{p}(t)$ by means of the linear transformation

$$\underline{q}(t) = \underline{R}\,\underline{p}(t) \tag{3.193}$$

where the $(n \times n_p)$ transformation matrix $\underline{R}$ is also called the *reduction matrix*, while, generally $n_p \ll n$. Introducing (3.193) into (3.192) and premultiplying the resulting set of equations by $\underline{R}^T$, we obtain the following reduced set of equations

$$\underline{M}^{red}\,\underline{\ddot{p}}(t) + \underline{K}^{red}\,\underline{p}(t) = \underline{Q}^{red}(t) \tag{3.194}$$

where

$$\underline{M}^{red} = \underline{R}^T\underline{M}\,\underline{R} \quad \text{and} \quad \underline{K}^{red} = \underline{R}^T\underline{K}\,\underline{R} \tag{3.195}$$

are the $(n_p \times n_p)$ reduced mass matrix and the $(n_p \times n_p)$ reduced stiffness matrix, respectively, while

$$\underline{Q}^{red}(t) = \underline{R}^T\underline{Q}(t) \tag{3.196}$$

is the reduced column of generalized forces depending explicitly on time. It is remarked that because $\underline{M}$ and $\underline{K}$ are symmetric matrices, the reduced matrices $\underline{M}^{red}$ and $\underline{K}^{red}$ are also symmetric.

In general, the transformation represented by (3.193) will result in deviations of the solution of the reduced set of equations (3.194) compared to the solution of the original unreduced set of (3.192). It is remarked that the better the subspace corresponding to the columns of the reduction matrix $\underline{R}$ represents the lowest natural modes of the original eigenvalue problem, the closer the solution of (3.194) is to that of the original unreduced problem. The various reduction and substructuring techniques differ from one another only by the choice of the reduction matrix $\underline{R}$.

3.5.2 Static condensation (Guyan-Irons reduction)

Let us consider the linearized Lagrange's equations of motion (3.192). To reduce the dimension of the matrices $\underline{M}$ and $\underline{K}$, we choose to eliminate a subset of generalized coordinates. These coordinates are called *local* or *condensed* coordinates, their number is assumed to be n_l, and the subset of local coordinates is denoted by $\underline{q}_l(t)$. The set of $n_m = n - n_l$ *master* or *remaining* coordinates is denoted by $\underline{q}_m(t)$, and, consequently, the set of n original generalized coordinates $\underline{q}(t)$ can be partitioned as follows

$$\underline{q}(t) = \left[\begin{array}{c} \underline{q}_m(t) \\ \underline{q}_l(t) \end{array} \right] \tag{3.197}$$

Of course, the elements of the column $\underline{q}_m(t)$ can be an arbitrary selection out of the elements of the original column $\underline{q}(t)$. Therefore it will be necessary in general to rearrange the sequence of the elements in the column $\underline{q}$ (and consequently also rearrange the matrices $\underline{M}$, $\underline{K}$ and column $\underline{Q}$) in order to make a partitioning as given by (3.197) possible. This can easily be done by defining a new column of generalized coordinates $\underline{q}_{new}^T = [\underline{q}_m^T, \underline{q}_l^T]$ (containing first the generalized coordinates selected as masters, and then the coordinates selected as locals). Using a perturbation matrix $\underline{P}$, this column can the be written as

$$\underline{q}_{new} = \underline{P}\,\underline{q} \quad \Longleftrightarrow \quad \underline{q} = \underline{P}^T\,\underline{q}_{new}$$

where the perturbation matrix only contains zeroes and ones. The matrices $\underline{M}$, $\underline{K}$ and column $\underline{Q}$, corresponding to this new coordinate sequence then directly follow from

$$\underline{M}_{new} = \underline{P}\,\underline{M}\,\underline{P}^T, \quad \underline{K}_{new} = \underline{P}\,\underline{K}\,\underline{P}^T, \quad \underline{Q}_{new} = \underline{P}\,\underline{Q}$$

We will assume that this re-ordering has been taken place.

The equations of motion (3.192) can be partioned accordingly (3.197)

$$\begin{bmatrix} \underline{M}_{mm} & \underline{M}_{ml} \\ \underline{M}_{lm} & \underline{M}_{ll} \end{bmatrix} \begin{bmatrix} \underline{\ddot{q}}_m(t) \\ \underline{\ddot{q}}_l(t) \end{bmatrix} + \begin{bmatrix} \underline{K}_{mm} & \underline{K}_{ml} \\ \underline{K}_{lm} & \underline{K}_{ll} \end{bmatrix} \begin{bmatrix} \underline{q}_m(t) \\ \underline{q}_l(t) \end{bmatrix} = \begin{bmatrix} \underline{Q}_m(t) \\ \underline{Q}_l(t) \end{bmatrix}$$

(3.198)

or

$$\underline{M}_{mm}\,\underline{\ddot{q}}_m + \underline{M}_{ml}\,\underline{\ddot{q}}_l + \underline{K}_{mm}\,\underline{q}_m + \underline{K}_{ml}\,\underline{q}_l = \underline{Q}_m \qquad (3.199)$$

$$\underline{M}_{lm}\,\underline{\ddot{q}}_m + \underline{M}_{ll}\,\underline{\ddot{q}}_l + \underline{K}_{lm}\,\underline{q}_m + \underline{K}_{ll}\,\underline{q}_l = \underline{Q}_l \qquad (3.200)$$

Now, in the condensation process the condensed coordinates $\underline{q}_l(t)$ are related to the remaining coordinates $\underline{q}_m(t)$ by making an assumption in the set of equations (3.200). In the *static condensation* process, as proposed independently by Guyan (1965) and Irons (1965), it is assumed that in (3.200) the contribution of the "dynamic" part $\left[\underline{M}_{lm}\,\underline{\ddot{q}}_m + \underline{M}_{ll}\,\underline{\ddot{q}}_l\right]$ and the contribution of $\underline{Q}_l(t)$ can be neglected with respect to **each of the separate terms** $\underline{K}_{lm}\,\underline{q}_m$ and $\underline{K}_{ll}\,\underline{q}_l$. In that case (3.200) reduces to the "static" equation

$$\underline{K}_{lm}\,\underline{q}_m + \underline{K}_{ll}\,\underline{q}_l = \underline{0} \qquad (3.201)$$

from which we obtain the following relationship between $\underline{q}_l(t)$ and $\underline{q}_m(t)$

$$\underline{q}_l(t) = -\underline{K}_{ll}^{-1}\,\underline{K}_{lm}\,\underline{q}_m(t) \qquad (3.202)$$

Introducing (3.202) into (3.197), we conclude that the static condensation process is governed by the following transformation

$$q(t) = \underline{R} \, \underline{q}_m(t) \tag{3.203}$$

where the $(n \times n_m)$ reduction matrix $\underline{R}$ for static condensation is given by

$$\underline{R} = \begin{bmatrix} \underline{I}_{mm} \\ -\underline{K}_{ll}^{-1} \, \underline{K}_{lm} \end{bmatrix} \tag{3.204}$$

with $\underline{I}_{mm}$ being the $(n_m \times n_m)$ identity matrix. The matrix $\underline{R}$ is often referred to as the *Guyan reduction matrix*. Substituting (3.204) into (3.195) and (3.196) and considering the fact that, due to the symmetry of the stiffness matrix $\underline{K}$, the transposed transformation matrix $\underline{R}^T$ is given by

$$\underline{R}^T = \begin{bmatrix} \underline{I}_{mm}^T & -\underline{K}_{lm}^T \, \underline{K}_{ll}^{-T} \end{bmatrix} = \begin{bmatrix} \underline{I}_{mm} & -\underline{K}_{ml} \, \underline{K}_{ll}^{-1} \end{bmatrix} \tag{3.205}$$

we obtain the following expressions for the reduced mass matrix

$$\begin{aligned} \underline{M}_{mm}^G = \underline{R}^T \underline{M} \, \underline{R} = \underline{M}_{mm} - \underline{M}_{ml}\underline{K}_{ll}^{-1}\underline{K}_{lm} \\ -\underline{K}_{ml}\underline{K}_{ll}^{-1}\underline{M}_{lm} + \underline{K}_{ml}\underline{K}_{ll}^{-1}\underline{M}_{ll}\underline{K}_{ll}^{-1}\underline{K}_{lm} \end{aligned} \tag{3.206}$$

the reduced stiffness matrix

$$\underline{K}_{mm}^G = \underline{R}^T \underline{K} \, \underline{R} = \underline{K}_{mm} - \underline{K}_{ml}\underline{K}_{ll}^{-1}\underline{K}_{lm} \tag{3.207}$$

and the reduced column of generalized forces

$$\underline{Q}_m^G(t) = \underline{R}^T \underline{Q}(t) = \underline{Q}_m(t) - \underline{K}_{ml}\underline{K}_{ll}^{-1} \, \underline{Q}_l(t) \tag{3.208}$$

For an error analysis of the eigenvalues corresponding to the eigenvalue problem for the reduced mass and stiffness matrices, the reader is referred to [Geradin/Rixen-97].

3.5.3 Component mode synthesis: general procedure

Let us consider a complete structure consisting of two substructures 1 and 2, as depicted schematically in Fig. 3.20. In this picture, the two substructures have been drawn separated at their interface. We write the equations of motion for a certain substructure in matrix form as

$$\underline{M} \, \ddot{q}(t) + \underline{K} \, q(t) = \underline{Q}(t) \tag{3.209}$$

Now, we split the n generalized coordinates of this substructure, collected in the column $q(t)$, into n_b boundary or interface coordinates, collected in the column $q_b(t)$ and n_i internal coordinates, collected in the column $q_i(t)$. The column $q_b(t)$ contains the generalized coordinates of the substructure at the

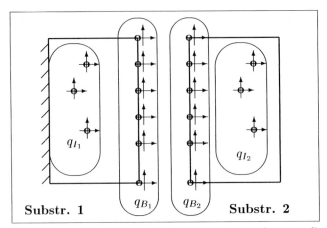

Fig. 3.20   Two substructures with internal and boundary coordinates

interface with other substructures. The column $\underline{q}_i(t)$ contains the remaining generalized coordinates of the substructure. However, if prescribed external forces or prescribed displacements are associated with generalized coordinates outside the interface, these generalized coordinates are, in general, also added to the column $\underline{q}_b(t)$. It is remarked that the boundary coordinates are often referred to as the boundary degrees of freedom, whereas the internal coordinates are often referred to as the internal degrees of freedom. In view of the above splitting of the set of generalized coordinates $\underline{q}(t)$ of the substructure, we can partition $\underline{q}(t)$ as follows, if necessary after rearranging

$$\underline{q}(t) = \left[\begin{array}{c} \underline{q}_b(t) \\ \underline{q}_i(t) \end{array} \right] \tag{3.210}$$

The substructure equations of motion (3.209) can be partitioned accordingly

$$\left[\begin{array}{cc} \underline{M}_{bb} & \underline{M}_{bi} \\ \underline{M}_{ib} & \underline{M}_{ii} \end{array} \right] \left[\begin{array}{c} \underline{\ddot{q}}_b(t) \\ \underline{\ddot{q}}_i(t) \end{array} \right] + \left[\begin{array}{cc} \underline{K}_{bb} & \underline{K}_{bi} \\ \underline{K}_{ib} & \underline{K}_{ii} \end{array} \right] \left[\begin{array}{c} \underline{q}_b(t) \\ \underline{q}_i(t) \end{array} \right] = \left[\begin{array}{c} \underline{Q}_b(t) \\ \underline{0}_i \end{array} \right] \tag{3.211}$$

Here it should be realized that, in view of the above discussion, by definition no generalized forces are associated with the set of internal coordinates $\underline{q}_i(t)$. Now, the different methods of component mode synthesis can be distinguished from one another by the specific choice or assumption for the boundary coordinates and the internal coordinates. The two most frequently used methods of component mode synthesis will be discussed in the following subsections, namely, the Craig-Bampton method and the Rubin method. After selecting a particular method of component mode synthesis and carrying out a dynamic analysis at substructure level, the different substructures have to be assembled and compatibility of the interface coordinates as well as continuity of the interface forces has to be imposed. To this end, commonly first a transformation of the interface coordinates and forces from a local component coordinate set to a global coordinate set at the level of the complete structure is required. We will express this transformation formally by

$$q_b(t) = \underline{T}^{lg} \, \underline{q}_b^g(t); \qquad \underline{Q}_b(t) = \underline{T}^{lg} \, \underline{Q}_b^g(t) \tag{3.212}$$

where $\underline{q}_b^g(t)$ and $\underline{Q}_b^g(t)$ denote the coordinates and forces of the substructure at the interface in terms of the global coordinate set, while $\underline{T}^{lg}$ is the transformation matrix from the local to the global coordinate set. Now, in the case of two substructures 1 and 2, the compatibility and equilibrium conditions at their interface take the form

$$\left(\underline{q}_b^g\right)_1 = \left(\underline{q}_b^g\right)_2 \tag{3.213}$$

$$\left(\underline{Q}_b^g\right)_1 + \left(\underline{Q}_b^g\right)_2 = \underline{0} \tag{3.214}$$

These equations enable a straightforward coupling of the different substructures. The elaboration to the resulting equations of motion for the complete structure depends on the specific method of component mode synthesis selected for the analysis.

3.5.4   The Craig-Bampton cms method

In the method of component mode synthesis proposed by Craig and Bampton (1968) the set of total generalized substructure coordinates $q(t)$ is written as a superposition of two independent sets of component modes. The first set of component modes is defined by imposing static condensation of the set of internal coordinates $q_i(t)$ by deleting the term $\left[\underline{M}_{ib} \, \ddot{\underline{q}}_b(t) + \underline{M}_{ii} \, \ddot{\underline{q}}_i(t)\right]$ from the second subset of (3.211). This leads us, analogous to (3.203) and (3.204), to the following set of so-called *static constraint modes* $q(t) := q^s(t)$

$$\underline{q}^s(t) = \left[\begin{array}{c} \underline{q}_b^s(t) \\[2mm] \underline{q}_i^s(t) \end{array} \right] = \left[\begin{array}{c} \underline{I}_{bb} \\[2mm] -\underline{K}_{ii}^{-1} \underline{K}_{ib} \end{array} \right] \underline{q}_b(t) \tag{3.215}$$

where $\underline{I}_{bb}$ is the $(n_b \times n_b)$ identity matrix. The second set of component modes is defined to be the set of eigenmodes related to (3.211) if all the boundary coordinates in the set $\underline{q}_b$ are suppressed. In that case the substructure is fixed on its interface, so that $\underline{q}_b = \underline{0}$ and $\ddot{\underline{q}}_b = \underline{0}$, and the second subset of (3.211) reduces to

$$\underline{M}_{ii} \, \ddot{\underline{q}}_i^d(t) + \underline{K}_{ii} \, \underline{q}_i^d(t) = \underline{0} \tag{3.216}$$

where the superindex d points at the fact that we consider dynamic component modes. These modes are referred to as *fixed-interface eigenmodes* and they are solutions of the algebraic eigenvalue problem

$$\left[\underline{K}_{ii} - \omega^2 \underline{M}_{ii}\right] \underline{u} = \underline{0} \tag{3.217}$$

The eigenfrequencies resulting from (3.217) are grouped in rising order, i.e. $\omega_1 \leq \omega_2 \leq \cdots \leq \omega_{n_i}$ and the corresponding modal columns $\underline{u}_1, \underline{u}_2, \cdots, \underline{u}_{n_i}$ are collected in the square $(n_i \times n_i)$ modal matrix

$$\underline{U}_{ii} = \begin{bmatrix} \underline{u}_1 & \underline{u}_2 & \cdots & \underline{u}_{n_i} \end{bmatrix} \qquad (3.218)$$

Now, reduction of the number of degrees of freedom at component level can be achieved by considering only a subset of the above free-interface eigenmodes. To be more specific, only those n_k eigenmodes are considered or kept which correspond to eigenfrequencies upto a certain selected upper bound $\omega_{\max}$. This implies that in stead of (3.218) we consider the non-square $(n_i \times n_k)$ matrix

$$\underline{U}_{ik} = \begin{bmatrix} \underline{u}_1 & \underline{u}_2 & \cdots & \underline{u}_{n_k} \end{bmatrix}, \qquad n_k < n_i \qquad (3.219)$$

The above reduction leads us to the following set of "dynamic" component modes $\underline{q}(t) := \underline{q}^d(t)$

$$\underline{q}^d(t) = \begin{bmatrix} \underline{q}_b^d(t) \\ \underline{q}_i^d(t) \end{bmatrix} = \begin{bmatrix} \underline{O}_{bk} \\ \underline{U}_{ik} \end{bmatrix} \underline{p}_k(t) \qquad (3.220)$$

where $\underline{p}_k(t)$ is a column containing the n_k modal coordinates related to the n_k fixed interface eigenmodes while $\underline{O}_{bk}$ is the $(n_b \times n_k)$ null matrix. For each combination of a static mode $\underline{q}^s$ and a dynamic mode $\underline{q}^d$ we can write

$$(\underline{q}^d)^T \underline{K} (\underline{q}^s) = \begin{bmatrix} \underline{0}_b^T, & \underline{u}_i^T \end{bmatrix} \begin{bmatrix} \underline{K}_{bb} & \underline{K}_{bi} \\ \underline{K}_{ib} & \underline{K}_{ii} \end{bmatrix} \begin{bmatrix} \underline{q}_b \\ -\underline{K}_{ii}^{-1}\underline{K}_{ib}\underline{q}_b \end{bmatrix} = 0 \qquad (3.221)$$

So, the "dynamic" component modes and the earlier defined static constraint modes appear to be orthogonal with respect to the stiffness matrix $\underline{K}$, and, hence, these two sets of component modes are independent, indeed. Combining (3.215) and (3.220), we obtain the following transformation of the generalized coordinates at component level

$$\underline{q}(t) = \underline{q}^s(t) + \underline{q}^d(t) = \underline{R}_{nc} \begin{bmatrix} \underline{q}_b(t) \\ \underline{p}_k(t) \end{bmatrix} \qquad (3.222)$$

where

$$\underline{R}_{nc} = \begin{bmatrix} \underline{I}_{bb} & \underline{O}_{bk} \\ -\underline{K}_{ii}^{-1}\underline{K}_{ib} & \underline{U}_{ik} \end{bmatrix} \qquad (3.223)$$

is the $(n \times n_c)$ reduction matrix at component level, n_c being given by $n_c = n_b + n_k$.

3.5.5   The that cms method

In the method of component mode synthesis proposed by Rubin (1975) the set of total generalized substructure coordinates $\underline{q}(t)$ is written as a superposition of three sets of component modes. The first set of component modes is only present if the component, separated from its neighbouring components, can undergo rigid-body motions. According to Subsection 3.3.1, *rigid-body modes* may be regarded as eigenmodes with zero eigenfrequency of the eigenvalue problem

$$\left[\underline{K} - \omega^2 \underline{M}\right] \underline{u} = \underline{0} \tag{3.224}$$

associated with (3.192). Hence, the rigid-body modes are the independent solutions of the algebraic equations

$$\underline{K} \, \underline{u}_i^{rb} = \underline{0} \tag{3.225}$$

The total number n_r of rigid-body modes $\underline{u}_i^{rb}$ will not exceed 6. We collect the columns $\underline{u}_i^{rb}$, $i = 1, 2, \cdots, n_r$, in the $(n \times n_r)$ matrix of rigid-body modes

$$\underline{U}_{nr} = \left[\underline{u}_1^{rb} \ \underline{u}_2^{rb} \ \cdots \ \underline{u}_{n_r}^{rb}\right] \tag{3.226}$$

We assume that the rigid body modes have been mass-matrix-normalized, so that

$$\underline{U}_{nr}^T \, \underline{M} \, \underline{U}_{nr} = \underline{I} \tag{3.227}$$

The second set of component modes is defined to be the set of eigenmodes related to (3.211) if all the boundary coordinates in the set $\underline{q}_b$ are left free. These modes are referred to as *free-interface elastic eigenmodes* and they are solutions corresponding to non-zero eigenfrequencies of the eigenvalue problem (3.224). We denote the free-interface elastic eigenmodes by $\underline{u}_j^{el}$, their total number n_e being given by $n_e = n - n_r$. We collect the columns $\underline{u}_j^{el}$, $j = 1, 2, \cdots, n_e$, in the $(n \times n_e)$ matrix of free-interface elastic eigenmodes

$$\underline{U}_{ne} = \left[\underline{u}_1^{el} \ \underline{u}_2^{el} \ \cdots \ \underline{u}_{n_e}^{el}\right] \tag{3.228}$$

and we assume that also these elastic eigenmodes have been mass-matrix normalized, so

$$\underline{U}_{ne}^T \, \underline{M} \, \underline{U}_{ne} = \underline{I}_{ee} \tag{3.229}$$

with $\underline{I}_{ee}$ the $(n_e \times n_e)$-unity matrix. The corresponding eigenfrequencies ω_j^{el}, $j = 1, 2, \cdots, n_e$ will be collected in the diagonal matrix $\lceil \Omega \rfloor_{ee}$

$$\lceil \Omega \rfloor_{ee} = \begin{bmatrix} \omega_1^{el} & & 0 \\ & \ddots & \\ 0 & & \omega_{n_e}^{el} \end{bmatrix} \tag{3.230}$$

Now, reduction of the number of degrees of freedom at component level can be achieved by considering only a subset of the above free-interface elastic eigenmodes. To be more specific, only those n_k eigenmodes are considered or kept which correspond to eigenfrequencies upto a certain selected upper bound $\omega_{\max}$. This implies that instead of (3.228) we consider the $(n \times n_k)$ matrix

$$\underline{U}_{nk} = \left[\underline{u}_1^{el}\ \underline{u}_2^{el}\ \cdots\ \underline{u}_{n_k}^{el} \right], \qquad n_k < n_e \tag{3.231}$$

and corresponding (nonzero) eigenfrequencies ω_j^{el}, building the $(n_k \times n_k)$ diagonal matrix

$$\lceil \Omega \rfloor_{kk} = \begin{bmatrix} \omega_1^{el} & & 0 \\ & \ddots & \\ 0 & & \omega_{n_k}^{el} \end{bmatrix} \tag{3.232}$$

In the cms method of Rubin a third set of component modes is used, referred to as *residual flexibility modes*. These modes originate from the spectral expansion (3.166) of the flexibility matrix $\underline{K}^{-1}$. The idea is that the n_k kept free-interface elastic eigenmodes "consume" a part of the flexibility matrix and that we are left with a residual flexibility matrix

$$\underline{G}^{res} = \underline{K}^{-1} - \sum_{j=1}^{n_k} \frac{\underline{u}_j^{el} \left(\underline{u}_j^{el} \right)^T}{(\omega_j^{el})^2} \tag{3.233}$$

$$= \underline{K}^{-1} - \underline{U}_{nk} \lceil \Omega \rfloor_{kk}^{-2} \underline{U}_{nk}^T$$

where

$$\lceil \Omega \rfloor_{kk}^{-2} = [\{ \lceil \Omega \rfloor_{kk} \}^2]^{-1} \tag{3.234}$$

We can see that the expression for the residual flexibility modes (3.233) can only be used in a situation where the relevant substructure will not contain any rigid body mode. In that case the stiffness matrix $\underline{K}$ will be positive definite and the inverse can be calculated. In the presence of rigid body modes the residual flexibility matrix has to be defined differently, namely

$$\underline{G}^{res} = \underline{G}_E - \underline{U}_{nk} \lceil \Omega \rfloor_{kk}^{-2} \underline{U}_{nk}^T \tag{3.235}$$

with $\underline{G}_E$ as the alternative for the nonexisting flexibility matrix $\underline{K}^{-1}$

$$\underline{G}^E = \underline{P}^T \underline{G}\ \underline{P} \tag{3.236}$$

with

$$\underline{P} = \underline{I} - \underline{M}\ \underline{U}_{nr}\ \underline{U}_{nr}^T \tag{3.237}$$

and

$$\underline{G} = \begin{bmatrix} \underline{K}_{ee}^{-1} & \underline{0}_{er} \\ \underline{0}_{re} & \underline{0}_{rr} \end{bmatrix} \tag{3.238}$$

In this matrix $\underline{G}$, the only nonzero submatrix is the matrix $\underline{K}_{ee}$. This matrix can be extracted from the (semi-positive definite) stiffness matrix $\underline{K}$ by suppressing a suitable set of n_r generalized coordinates in such a way that the remaining (partitioned) stiffness matrix $\underline{K}_{ee}$ becomes positive definite. For more details see [Kraker-00].

Now, the residual flexibility modes are defined by putting subsequently a unit force at each of the generalized boundary coordinates contained in the column $\underline{q}_b(t)$, and determining a "static" displacement field related to the residual flexibility matrix $\underline{G}^{res}$. If we partition the exerted unit forces consistent with the right-hand side of (3.211) and if we keep the internal generalized coordinates unloaded, then we can collect the resulting columns of exerted generalized external forces in the $(n \times n_b)$ matrix

$$\underline{F}_{nb} = \left[\begin{array}{c} \underline{I}_{bb} \\ \underline{O}_{ib} \end{array} \right] \qquad (3.239)$$

where $\underline{O}_{ib}$ is the $(n_i \times n_b)$ null matrix. In view of the above discussion, the $(n \times n_b)$ matrix of residual flexibility modes is defined to be

$$\underline{U}_{nb} = \underline{G}^{res} \, \underline{F}_{nb} \qquad (3.240)$$

It can be shown that the residual flexibility modes and the free-interface elastic eigenmodes are linearly independent, see e.g. Craig (1981). The component modes being the residual flexibility modes $\underline{U}_{nb}$, defined by (3.240), the rigid body modes $\underline{U}_{nr}$, defined by (3.226) and the kept elastic modes $\underline{U}_{nk}$ defined by (3.240) can now be collected to yield the resulting transformation of coordinates for the Rubin cms method

$$\underline{q}(t) = \underline{R}^*_{nc} \, \underline{p}^*(t) \qquad (3.241)$$

where $\underline{R}^*_{nc}$ is the $(n \times (n_c = n_b + n_r + n_k))$ reduction matrix at component level

$$\underline{R}^*_{nc} = [\underline{U}_{nb} \quad \underline{U}_{nr} \quad \underline{U}_{nk}] \qquad (3.242)$$

while $\underline{p}^*(t)$ is a column containing the n_c modal coordinates related to the modes collected in $\underline{R}^*_{nc}$. It is remarked that, in practice, the addition of residual flexibility modes appears to improve the accuracy of the computations up to the cut-off frequency $\omega_{\max}$ when coupling different substructures.

The last point to be addressed in the Rubin cms method is the final coordinate transformation needed for the coupling of substructures. The column of modal coordinates, $\underline{p}^*(t)$, does not contain the generalized coordinates at the interface, $\underline{q}_b(t)$. Therefore, an additional transformation is required, which can be obtained from (3.241) by re-arranging and partitioning

$$\left[\begin{array}{c} \underline{q}_b(t) \\ \underline{q}_i(t) \end{array} \right] = [\underline{U}_{nb} \, \underline{U}_{nr} \, \underline{U}_{nk}] \, \underline{p}^*(t) =: \left[\begin{array}{cc} \underline{U}_{bb} & \underline{U}_{bf} \\ \underline{U}_{ib} & \underline{U}_{if} \end{array} \right] \left[\begin{array}{c} \underline{p}_b(t) \\ \underline{p}_f(t) \end{array} \right] \qquad (3.243)$$

where the partitioned column $\underline{p}_f(t)$ contains the n_f modal coordinates related to the rigid-body modes and the free-interface elastic eigenmodes: $n_f = n_r +$

n_k. The first subset of (3.243) reads

$$\underline{q}_b(t) = \underline{U}_{bb}\, \underline{p}_b(t) + \underline{U}_{bf}\, \underline{p}_f(t) \tag{3.244}$$

From this equation we can express $\underline{p}_b(t)$ into $\underline{q}_b(t)$ and $\underline{p}_f(t)$ as follows

$$\underline{p}_b(t) = \underline{U}_{bb}^{-1}\, \underline{q}_b(t) - \underline{U}_{bb}^{-1}\, \underline{U}_{bf}\, \underline{p}_f(t) \tag{3.245}$$

This results in the following additional transformation

$$\underline{p}^*(t) = \left[\begin{array}{c} \underline{p}_b(t) \\ \underline{p}_f(t) \end{array} \right] = \underline{T}_2 \left[\begin{array}{c} \underline{q}_b(t) \\ \underline{p}_f(t) \end{array} \right] \tag{3.246}$$

with

$$\underline{T}_2 = \left[\begin{array}{cc} \underline{U}_{bb}^{-1} & -\underline{U}_{bb}^{-1}\underline{U}_{bf} \\ \underline{O}_{fb} & \underline{I}_{ff} \end{array} \right] \tag{3.247}$$

Inserting the transformation (3.246) into (3.241), we obtain the following final transformation

$$\underline{q}(t) = \left[\begin{array}{c} \underline{q}_b(t) \\ \underline{q}_i(t) \end{array} \right] = \underline{R}^*\, \underline{T}_2 \left[\begin{array}{c} \underline{q}_b(t) \\ \underline{p}_F(t) \end{array} \right] = \underline{R}_{nc}\, \underline{p}(t) \tag{3.248}$$

It is remarked that a particular advantage of the Rubin cms method can be obtained when coupling computational techniques with experimental techniques. In a number of practical situations the component modes are obtained from experimental investigations on the particular substructure under consideration. Then, it is much more easier to experimentally determine the free-interface eigenmodes than to experimentally determine the fixed-interface eigenmodes

Example 3.8

To illustrate the use of such a reduction method we look at the system shown in Fig. 3.21. The main part is a uniform bar with length l, cross section A, elasticity modulus E and density ρ. We only consider longitudinal vibrations. At the left side the bar is clamped in a rigid wall and the right side of the bar is connected to a linear spring with spring stiffness k. We will use the Finite Element Approach to create a numerical model for this bar. We will apply a simple element with two degrees of freedom, q_1 and q_2, as shown in the figure. If we define the column of degrees of freedom for the single element as $\underline{q}^{e^T} = [q_1, \; q_2]$, the mass matrix $\underline{M}^e$ and stiffness matrix $\underline{K}^e$ for the element with length l_e can be found in many textbooks as:

$$\underline{M}^e = \frac{\rho A l_e}{6} \left[\begin{array}{cc} 2 & 1 \\ 1 & 2 \end{array} \right] \qquad \underline{K}^e = \frac{AE}{l_e} \left[\begin{array}{cc} 1 & -1 \\ -1 & 1 \end{array} \right] \tag{3.249}$$

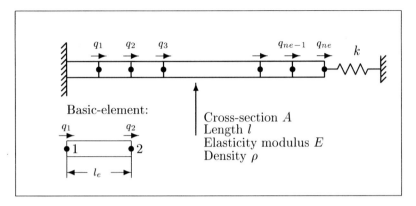

Fig. 3.21 Bar vibrating longitudinally with additional spring

For the numerical evaluation we use the following data:
$l = 1 \, [m]$, $A = 10^{-4} \, [m^2]$, $\rho = 8000 \, [kgm^{-3}]$, $E = 2 \, 10^{11} \, [Nm^{-2}]$, $k = 4 \, 10^7 \, [N \, m^{-1}]$. *The bar has been divided into $n_e = 40$ equal elements leading to a numerical model for the bar with also 40 degrees of freedom $q^T = [q_1, q_2, ..., q_{39}, q_{40}]$.*
First we calculate the (40) eigenfrequencies of the vibrating bar-model without additional spring and compare the results with theoretical values for this situation as given in [Blevins-95]. Both the results are shown in part A of Fig. 3.8 whereas part B gives the relative error. It can be seen that the 10-15 lowest eigenfrequencies of this 40-dof model are very accurate and that the higher eigenfrequencies are less accurate because of the simple linear element-interpolation function which is used for the finite element matrices.
Next we compare the numerical results of the situations with and without the additional spring (part C) and the relative difference (part D). From these two plots we can see that the additional spring has a large effect on the lower eigenfrequencies (the first eigenfrequency increases approximately 35%) but for the higher eigenfrequencies the spring appears not to be so important. Next we will apply the Craig-Bampton reduction method to get a model for the bar-spring system with (much) less degrees of freedom. We define two subsystems, namely the bar system with 40 dofs and the single spring with 1 dof. First the bar system will be reduced and then coupled to the spring system to compose the total reduced system. So, as the only boundary degree of freedom we have to choose q_{40} which is the displacement of the right end of the beam. Hence, we have only one static mode. It is easy to show that this static mode is a linear displacement from zero (left side) to 1.0 (right side) of the bar. Next, we calculate the constraint modes for the bar by suppressing also the right end of the system. The corresponding

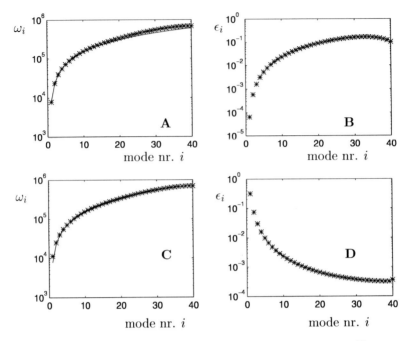

Fig. 3.8 Top-left plot: Eigenfrequencies of bar without spring (*)
compared with theoretical values (solid line);
bottom-left plot: eigenfrequencies with (*) and without spring (solid line).
The right plots give the corresponding relative errors

*eigenfrequencies are shown in Fig. 3.8 and are compared with those of
the original bar-with-spring system. We can see that for both situations
we get the same tendency, but that by suppressing the right end of the
bar the eigenfrequencies have been somewhat increased. The constraint
situation can also be seen as a bar-spring system with extremely high
spring stiffness k.*

Next, we will look at two situations:

- *Reduction based on the only static mode and additionally three
constraint modes leading to a 4-dof model*

- *Reduction based on one static mode and 10 constraint modes, giving a 11-dof model*

*The results for the two cases are shown in Fig. 3.22. The two top plots
show that for the 4-dof model the first 3 eigenfrequencies are (very) accurate. This means that for a frequency range up to 50.000 [rad/s] this
4-dof model will satisfy. If we want to have an accurate dynamic model
in a larger frequency range, for example up to 150.000 [rad/s], we can*

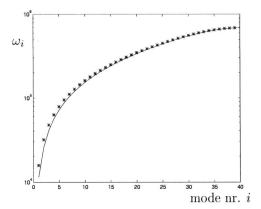

Fig. 3.8 Constraint eigenfrequencies of bar (*) compared
with eigenfrequencies for original bar-spring system (solid line)

conclude from the two bottom plots that the 11-dof model can be used.

3.6   CHAPTER PROBLEMS

3.6.1   Vibration Isolation

We return to the vibration isolation problem, introduced in Section 2.19.2 on
page 141. There we derived the linear equations of motion for small deviations
from the stable equilibrium position $\underline{q}_o^T = [0,\ v_o,\ 0]$. Here, v_o is the vertical
displacement of the mass m on the pair of springs k_2 due to the gravity effect.
We will use the following set of design values

- $l_1 = l_2 = 0.2\ [m]$
- $m = 20\ [kg],\quad J_Z = 0.3\ [kgm^2],\quad g = 10\ [m/s^2]$
- $k_1 = 250\ [N/m],\quad k_2 = 750\ [N/m]$
- $d = 10\ [Ns/m]$

The set of undamped, linearized equations of motion can be written as

$$\underline{M}\ \ddot{\underline{q}}(t) + \underline{K}\ \underline{q}(t) = \underline{Q}(t)$$

with $\underline{M}$, $\underline{K}$ and $\underline{Q}(t)$ being

$$\underline{M} = \begin{bmatrix} 20 & 0 & 4 \\ 0 & 20 & 0 \\ 4 & 0 & 1.1 \end{bmatrix} \quad \underline{K} = \begin{bmatrix} 2k_1 & 0 & 0 \\ 0 & 2k_2 & 0 \\ 0 & 0 & 2k_2 l_1^2 - mgl_2 \end{bmatrix} \quad \underline{Q}(t) = \begin{bmatrix} 0 \\ F(t) \\ -F(t)\, l_1 \end{bmatrix}$$

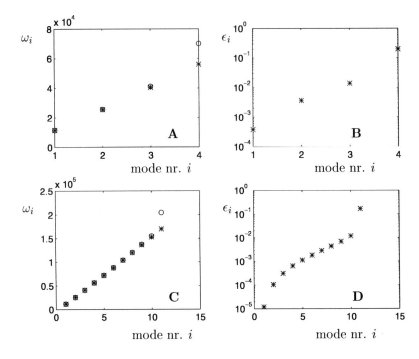

Fig. 3.22   Top plots: 4-dof model, bottom plots 11-dof model.
The left parts show the eigenfrequencies with (o) and without
reduction (*), the right parts show the relative errors

If we apply MATLAB to evaluate the free undamped behaviour, we get the
following results:

$$\begin{array}{ll} \omega_1 = 12.12 \ [rad/s] & f_1 = 1.93 \ [Hz] \\ \omega_2 = 3.36 \ [rad/s] & f_2 = 0.54 \ [Hz] \\ \omega_3 = 8.66 \ [rad/s] & f_3 = 1.38 \ [Hz] \end{array} \quad \underline{U} = \begin{bmatrix} 0.42 & -0.096 & 0 \\ 0 & 0 & 0.22 \\ -1.73 & -0.58 & 0 \end{bmatrix}$$

(3.250)

The eigencolumns have been **mass-normalized** and the modes are sorted in
arbitrary order.

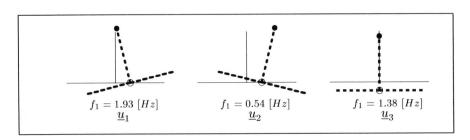

We can see that the first mode is a vibration mode without vertical v-displacement. The horizontal displacement seems to be compensated by a rotation, making the diplacement of the center of gravity small, leading to a high eigenfrequency.

The second mode also has no vertical v-component. Now the horizontal displacement looks to be in phase with the rotation, leading to large centre of gravity motions and a low eigenfrequency.

The third mode is a purely vertical mode, so it can be seen as being associated with a simple mass-spring system with mass m and stiffness $2\,k_2$. So, the eigenfrequency will be $\omega = \sqrt{2k_2/m} = 8.66\ [rad/s]$.

To optimize our isolation solution we can look at the effect of changing the support stiffness k_2 on the undamped eigenfrequencies. The result is shown in Fig. 3.23. If we reduce the spring stifness k_2, the following effects can be

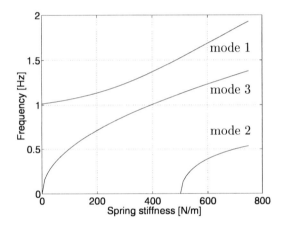

Fig. 3.23   Eigenfrequencies versus vertical stiffness k_2

seen

- The eigenfrequency corresponding to mode 1 will approach the asymptotic value $f_1 = 1\ [Hz]$. It can be shown that mainly some horizontal motion remains, specified by the springs k_1
- The eigenfrequency corresponding to mode 3 will always be the purely vertical mode with eigenfrequency $\omega_2 = \sqrt{2\,k_2/m}$. So, it will go to zero as a square-root function of k_2
- The eigenfrequency corresponding to mode 2 will already become zero for a spring stiffness value $k_2 = 500\ [N/m]$. This is exactly the value for which the trivial equilibrium position becomes **unstable** (see page 147). For lower values of k_2, the stiffness matrix $\underline{K}_o$ will be singular leading

to a purely imaginairy eigenfrequency. So for $0 \leq k_2 \leq 500 \ [N/m]$, our theory of small vibrations around a stable equilibrium position will not be valid anymore

For the forced, damped vibration we write the excitation $F(t) = \cos(2\pi f t)$ as $F(t) = Re \ [e^{2\pi j f t}]$, giving

$$\underline{Q}(t) = Re \ \left\{ \begin{bmatrix} 0 \\ 1 \\ -l_1 \end{bmatrix} e^{2\pi j f t} \right\} = Re \ \{ \hat{\underline{Q}} \ e^{2\pi j f t} \} \qquad (3.251)$$

with the column of complex amplitudes of the excitation being

$$\hat{\underline{Q}} = \begin{bmatrix} 0 \\ 1 \\ -l_1 \end{bmatrix} \qquad (3.252)$$

Now, we can determine the undamped harmonic response from:

$$\hat{\underline{q}} = \{(2\pi j f)^2 \underline{M} + \underline{K}\}^{-1} \ \hat{\underline{Q}} \qquad (3.253)$$

The complex responses $\hat{u}$, $\hat{v}$ and $\hat{\varphi}$ are shown in Fig. 3.24. Some remarks

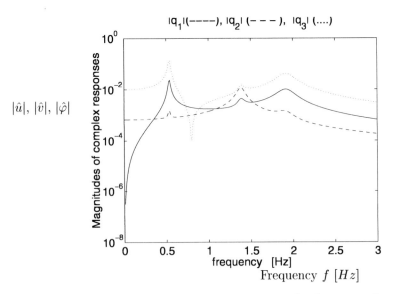

$|\hat{u}|, |\hat{v}|, |\hat{\varphi}|$

Fig. 3.24   Complex response magnitudes; u (solid), v (dashed) and φ (dash-dotted)

which can be made after looking at these responses are

• In the complex responses for the horizontal displacement u (solid line) and the rotation φ (dash-dotted line) only two resonance peaks can be distinguished. They correspond to the eigenfrequencies of respectively 0.54 and 1.93 [Hz]. The middle resonance is missing in these responses. On the other hand, the vertical coordinate v (dashed line) only shows a single peak at the middle eigenfrequency. To understand this we can look at the expression for the complex amplitude of the response, see (3.155)

$$\hat{\underline{q}} = \sum_{r=1}^{n} \frac{\underline{u}_r \, (\underline{u}_r^T \hat{\underline{Q}})}{m_r \, (\omega_r^2 - \Omega^2)} \tag{3.254}$$

In the case of pseudo-resonance, we have the situation that for one of the modes $\underline{u}_r$ the product $\underline{u}_r^T \, \hat{\underline{Q}}$ will be zero. Then the contribution of that mode to the total response will be zero for all excitation frequencies, even in the case that this excitation frequency Ω will approach the relevant eigenfrequency ω_r. So, one mode will be completely missing in the summation (3.254).

In this problem, however, we can easily check that this is not the case because for all three modes $\underline{u}_r^T \, \hat{\underline{Q}} \neq 0$. However, what is happening now is that for the modes 1 and 2 the vertical coordinate is zero whereas for the mode 3 the horizontal displacement and rotation both are zero. If a mode has one (or more) zeroes (also called nodes), it never can have a contribution to the corresponding generalized coordinate(s), not even in the case of resonance. So, if in one or more responses resonance peaks are missing, but they can be seen in all the other responses, we know that we are dealing with modes that do not contribute to the motion of certain degrees of freedom of the system (nodal points).

• At $f \approx 0.7 \, [Hz]$, the rotation φ shows an anti-resonance. The vertical motion v of the relevant structural point 3 is small and practically only the horizontal motion u is relevant, in spite of the fact that we are dealing with a vertical excitation force.

4

Damped Multi-Degree-of-Freedom Linear Systems

In any dynamical system energy dissipation (frequently modelled as viscous damping) is present. The consequences of damping can be small (material damping in aircraft fuselages, manipulators, etc.) where the main effects are that free vibration amplitudes always die out in time, while at resonance the maximum amplification factor will be limited.

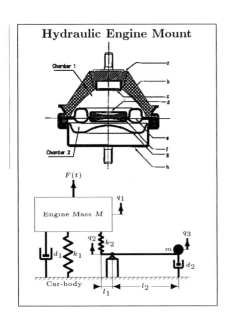

However, there are also many practical situations where damping effects can change the vibration picture completely. Examples are damping effects in rotor-bearing set ups and damping in car suspension systems. The picture on the left shows a so-called hydro-elastic engine mount, which is a device to reduce the vibration transmission from a car-engine to the car-body. It is designed to represent a frequency-dependent damping behaviour. In these situations a state-space approach can be followed to avaluate the dynamics of a system in a systematic way.

4.1 INTRODUCTION

In the previous chapter we elaborated the simplest class of multi-degree-of-freedom linear systems, namely the undamped systems with constant symmetric matrices. For such systems the eigenfrequencies ω resulting from the eigenvalue problem (3.22) for free vibrations are positive real numbers and the corresponding natural vibration modes, contained in the general solution for free motion, (3.99), represent synchronous motion with in-phase modes of vibration. These characteristics disappear, in general, for damped time-invariant multi-degree-of-freedom linear systems. Therefore, the treatment of such systems becomes generally more complicated, although a similar pattern can be followed as in the treatment of undamped systems with constant symmetric matrices. Before surveying the structure of this chapter, we recall from Subsection 2.18 the linearized Lagrange's equations of motion for time-invariant systems with viscous damping forces. According to (2.446) these equations take the form

$$\underline{M}\ \underline{\ddot{q}}(t) + \underline{D}\ \underline{\dot{q}}(t) + \underline{K}\ \underline{q}(t) = \underline{Q}(t) \tag{4.1}$$

where $\underline{M}$ is the symmetric mass matrix, $\underline{K}$ is the symmetric stiffness matrix, $\underline{D}$ is the symmetric damping matrix and $\underline{Q}(t)$ is the column of external, non-conservative loads.

First we will look at the special case of systems under harmonic excitation leading to a general expresssion for the transfer-function matrix for multi-degree-of-freedom systems with viscous damping. Among the systems described by (4.1) there are many systems of practical importance for which the damping characteristics are special in such a sense that the eigenvalue problem for the damped free motions reduces to the eigenvalue problem for the corresponding undamped free motions. These systems will be addressed next. To illustrate some aspects which might show up when dealing with a realistic design problem the dynamic behaviour of a hydro-elastic engine mount will be the third topic of this chapter. Next, the dynamic analysis of systems with a general type of viscous damping will be treated. For these systems a so-called state-space approach will be used to arrive at a straightforward procedure. Finally,some attention will be paid to systems with non-symmetric matrices.

These systems appear for example if gyroscopic effects are of importance. Also for these systems the state-space approach appears to be beneficial.

4.2   STEADY-STATE RESPONSE TO HARMONIC EXCITATION

In the case of harmonic excitation of damped systems the column matrix of generalized forces $Q(t)$ in the right-hand side of the equations of motion (4.1) can always be written as

$$Q(t) = Re\ \{\hat{Q}\ e^{j\Omega t}\} \tag{4.2}$$

where instead of the real part also the imaginary part might be chosen. In this expression, Ω is the excitation frequency and $\hat{Q}$ is the column containing the complex amplitudes of the excitation forces.

In agreement with the procedure for single-degree-of-freedom linear systems, the forced response of our multi-degree-of-freedom system defined by (4.1) to the harmonic excitation defined by (4.2) can be found by taking the solution $q(t)$ in the form

$$q(t) = Re\ [\ \hat{q}\ e^{j\Omega t}]   \text{respectively}   Im\ [\ \hat{q}\ e^{j\Omega t}] \tag{4.3}$$

where $\hat{q}^T = [\hat{q}_1, \hat{q}_2, ..., \hat{q}_n]$ now in general will be a complex column with the complex (unknown) amplitudes $\hat{q}_i$ of the generalized coordinates $q_i(t)$. Inserting (4.2) and (4.3) into (4.1), we obtain the following solution for the complex amplitudes of the forced response

$$\hat{q} = \left[-\Omega^2 M + j\Omega D + K\right]^{-1} \hat{Q} \tag{4.4}$$

The matrix $\left[-\Omega^2 M + j\Omega D + K\right]^{-1}$ is commonly referred to as the **transfer function matrix** or **matrix of frequency response functions** (in abbreviated terminology the **FRF matrix**). Once the complex amplitudes $\hat{q}$ of the response have been calculated the (real) physical response $q(t)$ can be calculated from (4.3). Before doing so, we express $\hat{q}$ as

$$\hat{q} = \begin{bmatrix} \hat{q}_1 \\ \cdot \\ \cdot \\ \hat{q}_n \end{bmatrix} = \begin{bmatrix} |\hat{q}_1|\ e^{j\psi_1} \\ \cdot \\ \cdot \\ |\hat{q}_n|\ e^{j\psi_n} \end{bmatrix} \tag{4.5}$$

where each complex amplitude $\hat{q}_r$ is defined by its modulus $|\hat{q}_r|$ and argument ψ_r. Now, if we want to know the real physical response we insert (4.5) into (4.3) and obtain

$$q(t) = \begin{bmatrix} |\hat{q}_1|\ \cos(\Omega t + \psi_1) \\ \cdot \\ \cdot \\ |\hat{q}_n|\ \cos(\Omega t + \psi_n) \end{bmatrix} \text{respectively} \begin{bmatrix} |\hat{q}_1|\ \sin(\Omega t + \psi_1) \\ \cdot \\ \cdot \\ |\hat{q}_n|\ \sin(\Omega t + \psi_n) \end{bmatrix} \tag{4.6}$$

So we arrive at a harmonic response $q(t)$, which for a specific excitation frequency Ω, is determined by the amplitudes $|\hat{q}_r|$ and the phase angles ψ_r.

To calculate the frequency response of a system, we have to evaluate the inverse of the (complex) matrix $\left[-\Omega_r^2 \underline{M} + j\Omega_r \underline{D} + \underline{K}\right]$ for a (broad) range of frequencies Ω_r. For systems with a (very) large number of degrees of freedom, say $n \geq 100 - 1000$ this can be a very time-consuming task. For such higher-order systems, it is more efficient to use some kind of decomposition into natural coordinates. However this will need the extension of the eigenvalue problem to complex eigenvalues and complex eigenmodes. This will be discussed in Section 4.5. For some specific types of damping the results obtained for the undamped system by means of the methods discussed in the previous chapter can also be used very efficiently for the damped case. In that case the modal decomposition will be simple as will be shown later in Section 4.3.

Example 4.1

Let us look again at the 2 degree-of-freedom car structure on a harmonic road profile for which we studied the undamped behaviour in example 3.7 on page 189. In addition to the mass- and stiffness data given there we use for the damping coefficients the numerical value $d = 2000\ [Ns/m]$. For the undamped eigenfrequencies we found before

$$
\begin{aligned}
\omega_1 &= 12.9099\ [rad/s] \Longrightarrow V_1^{crit} = 8.2187\ [m/s] \\
\omega_2 &= 22.3607\ [rad/s] \Longrightarrow V_2^{crit} = 14.2353\ [m/s]
\end{aligned}
\tag{4.7}
$$

If we now also include the viscous damping terms, the excitation column for this system becomes see (3.175)

$$
\underline{Q}(t) = \left[\begin{array}{c} k\ y_R(t)\ +\ d\ \dot{y}_R(t) \\ k\ y_S(t)\ +\ d\ \dot{y}_S(t) \end{array} \right]
\tag{4.8}
$$

Applying the simplified road-input from page 189, we can express $y_S(t)$ and $y_R(t)$ in complex numbers as, see (3.181)

$$
\begin{aligned}
y_S(t) &= Im\ [h\ e^{j\Omega t}] \\
y_R(t) &= Im\ [h\ e^{j\Omega t + \psi}] = Im\ [\{h\ e^{j\psi}\}\ e^{j\Omega t}]
\end{aligned}
\tag{4.9}
$$

Now, the velocity component $\dot{y}_S(t)$ in the excitation column $\underline{Q}(t)$ can be written as

$$
\begin{aligned}
\dot{y}_S(t) &= \tfrac{d}{dt}\{Im[h\ e^{j\Omega t}]\} = Im[\tfrac{d}{dt}\{h\ e^{j\Omega t}\}] \\
&= Im[\{j\Omega h\}\ e^{j\Omega t}]
\end{aligned}
\tag{4.10}
$$

Analogously $\dot{y}_R(t)$ can be written as

$$
\dot{y}_R(t) = Im[\{j\Omega h\ e^{j\psi}\}\ e^{j\Omega t}]
\tag{4.11}
$$

So, we see that a differentiation in the time domain corresponds to a multiplication with $j\Omega$ in the frequency domain. Inserting (4.9)-(4.11) into (4.8), we obtain the following results for the excitation column in complex numbers

$$\underline{Q}(t) = Im\ [\underline{\hat{Q}}\ e^{j\Omega t}] = Im\ \{ \begin{bmatrix} he^{j\psi}(k + bj\Omega) \\ h(k + bj\Omega) \end{bmatrix} e^{j\Omega t}\} \qquad (4.12)$$

As we can see, the column of complex amplitudes of the excitations $\underline{Q}$, contains truely complex elements due to the presence of a stiffness- and damping contribution and also due to the time shift between front wheel and rear wheel excitation. For a speed range $V = 0...30\ [m/s]$ we have to take a frequency-range $\Omega = 0...(60\pi)/L_o\ [rad/s]$ as derived for the undamped example on page 189. For this excitation range we calculate the complex response $\hat{\underline{q}}(V)$.

In Fig. 4.1 the moduli of the complex responses $\hat{q}_1$ and $\hat{q}_2$ are plotted as function of this speed range. Contrary to the undamped case we

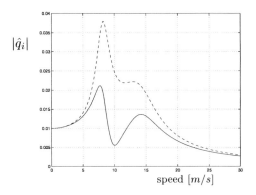

Fig. 4.1 Moduli of $\hat{q}_1$ (back wheel, solid) and $\hat{q}_2$ (front wheel, dashed)

now observe that the amplitudes of the front and back of the car model are different. The amplitudes at the front generally are two times as large as the amplitudes at the back. There still is some critical speed to see at approximately 8 [m/s], but the second critical speed at 14 [m/s] has become less clear. Also a typical situation occurs for a speed of 10 [m/s] where the back side behaves very calm but the front side is tilting strongly. For very low and very high speeds the damping effects appear to be small. In Fig. 4.2 the phase angles of the complex responses $\hat{q}_1$ and $\hat{q}_2$ are plotted. The values for low speeds are the same as those for the undamped case. The jumps at the critical speeds are now much more smooth then the stepwise jumps as seen in the undamped case (see Fig. 3.17).

Instead of being interested in the front- and/or back amplitudes of the

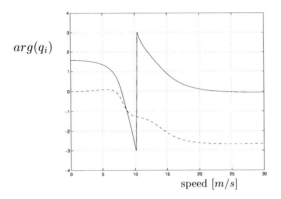

$arg(q_i)$

speed $[m/s]$

Fig. 4.2   Phases of $\hat{q}_1$ (back wheel, solid) and $\hat{q}_2$ (front wheel, dashed)

*car motion, one might also be interested in the motion of the centre of
the beam (where the passenger might be situated) or the rotation of the
car (tilting behaviour). The mid-point displacement q_m and rotation
φ can be expressed in terms of q_1 and q_2 via $q_m = (q_1 + q_2)/2$ and
$\varphi = (q_2 - q_1)/2l$. Now, we can determine the complex amplitudes for
these quantities directly from the complex amplitudes $\hat{q}_1$ and $\hat{q}_2$ by using*

$$\hat{q}_m = (\hat{q}_1 + \hat{q}_2)/2 \qquad and \qquad \hat{\varphi} = (\hat{q}_2 - \hat{q}_1)/2l \qquad (4.13)$$

*The magnitudes of these complex amplitudes are plotted in Fig 4.3.
Very typical is the fact that the midpoint-displacement plot only has*

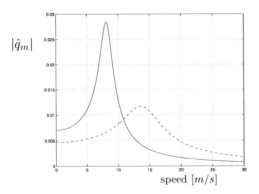

$|\hat{q}_m|$

speed $[m/s]$

Fig. 4.3   Moduli of $\hat{q}_m$ (mid-point displacement, solid)
and $\hat{\varphi}$ (tilting angle, dashed)

*one peak at the first critical speed and that the tilting plot also has only
one peak, but now at the second critical speed. It looks as if we are now*

dealing with two independent mass-spring-damper systems. In example 4.2 on page 223 we will see that this has to do with the fact that these two new generalized coordinates (q_m and φ) appear to be just the natural coordinates for this system and that they will decouple the equations of motion because we are dealing with proportional damping.

A next interesting point for the designer of a car might be to know not only the displacements and rotations but the acceleration of the midpoint as well and also the tilting acceleration, because the accelerations will determine the comfort of the car. Put in other words, these accelerations will make the driver feel happy or not. The complex amplitudes of these accelerations can be extracted directly from $\hat{q}_m$ and $\hat{\varphi}$, namely

$$a_m(t) = \ddot{q}_m(t) \Longrightarrow \hat{a}_m = (j\Omega)^2 \, \hat{q}_m$$
$$\alpha(t) = \ddot{\varphi}(t) \Longrightarrow \hat{\alpha} = (j\Omega)^2 \, \hat{\varphi} \tag{4.14}$$

The magnitudes of these accelerations are shown in Fig 4.4. Of course

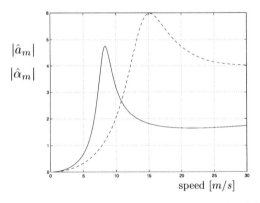

Fig. 4.4 Moduli of midpoint acceleration $|\hat{a}_m|$ (solid)
and rotational acceleration $|\hat{\alpha}|$ (dashed)

we again see the effect of two uncoupled systems. For low speeds the accelerations are small and for high speeds the acceleration magnitudes seem to approach the values 1.8 $[m/s^2]$, respectively 4.0 $[rad/s^2]$. This are misleading values. The complex amplitudes have been calculated from

$$\hat{q} = [-\Omega^2 \underline{M} + j\Omega \underline{D} + \underline{K}]^{-1} \left[\begin{array}{c} he^{j\psi}(k + dj\Omega) \\ h(k + dj\Omega) \end{array} \right] \tag{4.15}$$

For sufficiently large Ω we can apply the approximation

$$\hat{q} \approx -\frac{hjd}{\Omega} \, \underline{M}^{-1} \left[\begin{array}{c} e^{j\psi} \\ 1 \end{array} \right] \tag{4.16}$$

So, the complex amplitudes $\hat{q}$ will asymptotically go to zero ($1/\Omega$-behaviour). But the accelerations $-\Omega^2 \hat{q}$ will asymptotically go to ∞ (linearly in Ω).

This behaviour can also be observed when the accelerations will be plot for a much larger Ω-range. Hence, for high speeds the acceleration values can become unbounded high.

Finally in Fig. 4.5 the rear wheel displacement amplitude $|\hat{q}_1|$ is shown for different values of the car length (ranging from $l = 0$ up to $2l = L_o$. This figure shows that depending on the relative length $\frac{2l}{L_o}$, the translational and/or the rotational mode will play a dominant role in the response.

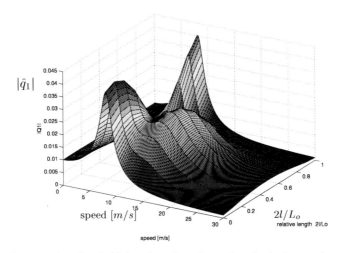

Fig. 4.5   Amplitude $|\hat{q}_1|$ as function of speed and relative car-length

4.3   DAMPED SYSTEMS FOR WHICH THE UNDAMPED EIGENVALUE PROBLEM APPLIES

4.3.1   Introductory remarks

As remarked previously, the treatment of damped multi-degree-of-freedom linear systems is more complicated, in general, than the treatment of the corresponding undamped systems. The increase in complexity can be attributed to the coupling introduced by damping. To explain this in more detail, let us consider the equations of motion (4.1) for damped systems with symmetric matrices and let us try to solve these equations via a modal expansion of $\underline{q}(t)$ in terms of the eigenmodes $\underline{u}_r$ of the associated *undamped* system. So, analogous to (3.109), we write

$$q(t) = \sum_{r=1}^{n} \underline{u}_r \, \eta_r(t) = \underline{U} \, \underline{\eta}(t) \tag{4.17}$$

This implies that again we apply a coordinate transformation from the (n) physical coordinates $\underline{q}(t)$ to (n) so-called natural coordinates $\underline{\eta}(t)$. If we can calculate these natural coordinates, the original solution $\underline{q}(t)$ can be found by taking a linear combination of the undamped eigenmodes $\underline{u}_r$, $r = 1, .., n$ with as factors the time-functions $\eta_r(t)$. This is a very frequently used procedure in Finite Element Programmes which is called the **modal superposition method**.

Introducing the transformation (4.17) into the equations of motion (4.1), pre-multiplying the resulting matrix equation by $\underline{U}^T$, and taking account of (3.60), (3.61) and (3.63) , we obtain

$$\lceil m_r \rfloor \ddot{\underline{\eta}}(t) + \underline{U}^T \underline{D} \, \underline{U} \, \dot{\underline{\eta}}(t) + \lceil k_r \rfloor \underline{\eta}(t) = \underline{N}(t) \tag{4.18}$$

where

$$\underline{N}(t) = \underline{U}^T \underline{Q}(t) \tag{4.19}$$

is a column matrix of generalized forces associated with the column of generalized coordinates $\underline{\eta}(t)$. If the matrix $\underline{U}^T \underline{D} \, \underline{U}$ from (4.18) will appear to be a diagonal matrix too we will end up with a system of uncoupled equations of motion. This particular cae of damping is called **proportional damping**.

However in general the matrix $\underline{U}^T \underline{D} \, \underline{U}$ will be non-diagonal. So, the analysis based on the eigenmodes of the associated undamped system does not lead to a system of decoupled differential equations of motion. In that case a formulation based on the undamped system properties will not be possible, but a so-called state-space approach should be followed. This will be treated in Section 4.5. In the present section we will consider situations in which the matrix $\underline{U}^T \underline{D} \, \underline{U}$ is diagonal, or at least it can be treated approximately as diagonal.

Example 4.2

To illustrate this decoupling possibility we analyse the two-degree-of-freedom car system discussed in the examples on the pages 189 and 218. For the undamped system we found the eigenfrequencies and mass-normalized eigenmodes to be

$$\begin{array}{ll} \omega_1 = 12.9099 \ [rad/s] \\ \omega_2 = 22.3607 \ [rad/s] \end{array} \qquad \underline{U} = \begin{bmatrix} 0.0289 & -0.05 \\ 0.0289 & 0.05 \end{bmatrix} \tag{4.20}$$

Then, the matrix $\underline{U}^T \underline{D} \, \underline{U}$ becomes

$$\underline{U}^T \underline{D} \, \underline{U} = \begin{bmatrix} 3.333 & 0 \\ 0 & 10 \end{bmatrix} \tag{4.21}$$

This matrix is perfectly diagonal. We might have drawn this conclusion also directly, because the damping matrix can be written as $\underline{D} = \alpha\underline{M} + \beta\underline{K}$ with $\alpha = 0$ and $\beta = b/k$. Because $\underline{U}^T\underline{K}\,\underline{U}$ is a diagonal matrix due to the orthogonality principle, $\beta\,\underline{U}^T\underline{K}\,\underline{U}$ will be a diagonal matrix too.

If we invert the coordinate transformation (4.17), i.e. if we put

$$\underline{\eta}(t) = \underline{U}^{-1}\,\underline{q}(t) \tag{4.22}$$

and utilize subsequently $\underline{U}^T\underline{M}\,\underline{U} = \underline{I} := \underline{U}^{-1}\underline{U}$, so that $\underline{U}^{-1} = \underline{U}^T\underline{M}$, we get

$$\underline{\eta}(t) = \begin{bmatrix} 17.3205 & 17.3205 \\ -10 & 10 \end{bmatrix}\underline{q}(t) \tag{4.23}$$

This means that the (new) natural coordinates $\underline{\eta}(t)$ (which obviously decouple the equations of motion) are related to the original physical coordinates $\underline{q}(t)$ via

$$\begin{aligned} \eta_1 &= 17.3205\,(q_1 + q_2) \\ \eta_2 &= 10\,(q_2 - q_1) \end{aligned} \tag{4.24}$$

We should keep in mind that q_1, respectively q_2 are the displacements of the left-end, respectively the right-end of the car-body beam. So, apart from some scaling parameter, the first natural coordinate η_1 equals the displacement of the mid-point of the beam $u = \frac{1}{2}(q_1 + q_2)$, whereas the second natural coordinate η_2 can be viewed upon seen as the unscaled rotation of the beam $\varphi = (q_2 - q_1)/2l$ (see also Fig. 3.13 in the example on page 189).

Is is left to the reader to repeat the analysis of this system, directly starting from this new coordinate definition (i.e. putting $\underline{q}^T = [u\,,\,\varphi]$) to check that indeed the equations of motion are decoupled in that case.

Hence, if not only the mass- and stiffness matrices but also the damping matrix $\underline{D}$ can be diagonalized by the matrix of undamped eigencolumns $\underline{U}$ we can switch from the set of (n) coupled equations of motion (4.1) to a set of (n) **decoupled** equations of motion, namely

$$m_r\,\ddot{\eta}_r(t)\,+\,d_r\,\dot{\eta}_r(t)\,+\,k_r\,\eta_r(t) = N_r(t), \qquad r = 1...n \tag{4.25}$$

For specific excitation functions $N_r(t) = \underline{u}_r^T\underline{Q}(t)$ and certain initial conditions (for example $\underline{q}(t = 0) = \underline{q}_o;\;\;\dot{\underline{q}}(t = 0) = \underline{v}_o$) first each separate solution $\eta_r(t)$ can be calculated using (standard) one-degree-of-freedom solutions, after which these solutions can be combined to generate the final solution $\underline{q}(t)$.

Example 4.3

We consider again the one-dimensional 3-vehicle train system from examples 3.1 and 3.5 on pages 157 and 177. Now, we additionally introduce two linear viscous dampers with damping factors d between the masses as shown in Fig. 4.6. Moreover, we assume that during the motion the rolling- and air resistance of the wagons can be modelled as three forces $c\,|v_i|$, whose magnitude is proportional to the absolute velocity $|v_i|$ of the relevant car (with a proportionality factor c), whereas they are acting in opposite direction of the velocity. For the mass matrix

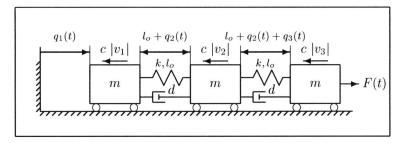

Fig. 4.6 Three-carriage railway vehicle model

and stiffness matrix we refer to example 3.1 on page 157. Te damping matrix can easily be shown to be

$$\underline{D} = \begin{bmatrix} 3c & 2c & c \\ 2c & 2c+d & c \\ c & c & c+d \end{bmatrix} = c \begin{bmatrix} 3 & 2 & 1 \\ 2 & 3 & 1 \\ 1 & 1 & 2 \end{bmatrix} \tag{4.26}$$

where we used the assumption $d = c$. Applying the matrix $\underline{U}$ of undamped, mass-normalized eigenmodes as calculated before on page 164,we get

$$\underline{U}^T \underline{D}\,\underline{U} = (c/m) \begin{bmatrix} 1 & 0 & 0 \\ 0 & 2 & 0 \\ 0 & 0 & 4 \end{bmatrix} \tag{4.27}$$

*This matrix is dagonal so that we are dealing with so-called proportional damping. This also follows directly from the observation that $\underline{D} = (c/m)\,\underline{M} + (c/k)\,\underline{K}$. Now, applying again the coordinate transformation to the natural coordinates using $\underline{q} = \underline{U}\,\underline{\eta}$, we arrive at the following set of 3 **uncoupled** equations of motion*

$$\underline{U}^T \underline{M}\,\underline{U}\,\ddot{\underline{\eta}} + \underline{U}^T \underline{D}\,\underline{U}\,\dot{\underline{\eta}} + \underline{U}^T \underline{K}\,\underline{U}\,\underline{\eta} = \underline{U}^T \underline{Q} \tag{4.28}$$

or

$$\ddot{\eta}_1 + c/m\,\dot{\eta}_1 \qquad\qquad = F(t)/\sqrt{3m}$$

$$\ddot{\eta}_2 + 2c/m\ \dot{\eta}_2 + k/m\ \eta_2 = -F(t)/\sqrt{2m}$$
$$\ddot{\eta}_3 + 4c/m\ \dot{\eta}_3 + 3k/m\ \eta_3 = F(t)/\sqrt{6m} \qquad (4.29)$$

Again, we assume the step-type excitation $F(t) = F_o$ for $t > 0$ and zero initial conditions for $\underline{q}(t)$ and elaborate the respective solution of each of the equations of the set (4.29).

- *Solution of $\ddot{\eta}_1(t) + (c/m)\ \dot{\eta}_1 = F(t)/\sqrt{3m}$*
  The solution is

$$\eta_1(t) = (A_1 + A_2\ e^{-c\ t/m}) + \frac{F_o\ \sqrt{m}}{c\sqrt{3}}\ t \qquad (4.30)$$

where the first part is the homogeneous solution and the second part the particular solution. Using the initial conditions $\eta_1 = \dot{\eta}_1 = 0$, we obtain

$$\eta_1(t) = \frac{F_o\sqrt{m}}{c\sqrt{3}}\ [\ t + \frac{m}{c}(e^{-c\ t/m} - 1)] \qquad (4.31)$$

- *Solution of $\ddot{\eta}_2(t) + (2c/m)\ \dot{\eta}_2 + (k/m)\ \eta_2 = -F(t)/\sqrt{2m}$*
  The solution is

$$\eta_2(t) = e^{-\xi_2\omega_{o2}t}[B_1\sin(\omega_{d2}t) + B_2\cos(\omega_{d2}t)] - \frac{\sqrt{m}}{k\sqrt{2}}F_o \qquad (4.32)$$

where the first part again is the homogeneous solution and the second part the particular solution. We also defined $\omega_{o2}^2 = k/m$; $\omega_{d2}^2 = \omega_{o2}^2\ (1 - \xi_2^2)$ and assumed that this system will be undercritically damped, which means

$$\xi_2 = (2c/m)/(2\sqrt{k/m}) = c/\sqrt{mk} < 1.0 \qquad (4.33)$$

Using the initial conditions $\eta_2 = \dot{\eta}_2 = 0$, we obtain

$$\eta_2(t) = \frac{F_o\sqrt{m}}{k\sqrt{2}}\left[-1 + e^{-\xi_2\omega_{o2}t}\left\{\frac{\xi_2\omega_{o2}}{\omega_{d2}}\sin(\omega_{d2}t) + \cos(\omega_{d2}t)\right\}\right] \qquad (4.34)$$

- *Solution of $\ddot{\eta}_3(t) + (4c/m)\ \dot{\eta}_3 + (3k/m)\ \eta_3 = F(t)/\sqrt{6m}$*
  Analogous to the solution for η_2 we find

$$\eta_3(t) = -\frac{F_o\sqrt{m}}{3k\sqrt{6}}\left[-1 + e^{-\xi_3\omega_{o3}t}\{\frac{\xi_3\omega_{o3}}{\omega_{d3}}\sin(\omega_{d3}t) + \cos(\omega_{d3}t)\}\right] \qquad (4.35)$$

with

$$\omega_{o3} = \sqrt{3k/m}$$
$$\xi_3 = 2(4c/m)/(2\sqrt{3k/m}) = 24c/\sqrt{3mk} < 1.0 \qquad (4.36)$$

So the resulting solution for the column of natural coordinates $\underline{\eta}(t)$ is

$$\underline{\eta}(t) = \frac{F_o\sqrt{m}}{c\sqrt{3}} \begin{bmatrix} t - m/c \\ -(c\sqrt{3})/(k\sqrt{2}) \\ c/(3k\sqrt{2}) \end{bmatrix} +$$

$$\frac{F_o\sqrt{m}}{3k\sqrt{6}} \begin{bmatrix} (3mk\sqrt{2})/(c^2) \ e^{-c\ t/m} \\ 3\sqrt{3}\ e^{-\xi_2\omega_{o2}t} \left[\frac{\xi_2\omega_{o2}}{\omega_{d2}} \sin(\omega_{d2}t) + \cos(\omega_{d2}t) \right] \\ -\ e^{-\xi_3\omega_{o3}t} \left[\frac{\xi_3\omega_{o3}}{\omega_{d3}} \sin(\omega_{d3}t) + \cos(\omega_{d3}t) \right] \end{bmatrix} \tag{4.37}$$

The first part of this solution represents a steady-state solution and the second part a transient solution. This latter part will damp out for large t. For large t therefore only the first part will be interesting. We can transform this part of the solution in the natural coordinates back into the original coordinates $\underline{q}$ by using $\underline{q} = \underline{U}\ \underline{\eta}$, giving

$$\underline{q}(t) = \frac{F_o}{3c} \begin{bmatrix} t - \frac{4c}{3k} \\ \frac{c}{k} \\ \frac{2c}{k} \end{bmatrix} = \frac{F_o}{3c} \begin{bmatrix} t \\ 0 \\ 0 \end{bmatrix} + \frac{F_o}{9k} \begin{bmatrix} -4 \\ 3 \\ 6 \end{bmatrix} \tag{4.38}$$

This means that for the steady-state part of the solution holds

$$q_1(t) = \frac{F_o t}{3c} - \frac{4F_o}{9k}; \quad \dot{q}_1 = \frac{F_o}{3}\frac{}{c} = v \quad (constant)$$

$$q_2(t) = \frac{F_o}{3}\frac{}{k}; \quad \dot{q}_2 = 0 \tag{4.39}$$

$$q_3(t) = \frac{2F_o}{3}\frac{}{k}; \quad \dot{q}_3 = 0$$

The above steady-state contribution consists of the time-dependent contribution $q_1(t)$ and the constant contributions $q_2(t)$ and $q_3(t)$. It can be concluded that all 3 masses are travelling with the same constant speed $v = F_o/(3\ c)$. This means that for large time t the train will have some constant speed while the force $F(t)$ will exactly be equal to the sum of the three air-resistance forces. Consequently, on each of the masses an air-resistance force is acting with a magnitude $c\ v = F_o/3$. So, the force in the left spring has to be $F_o/3$ and the force in the right spring $2F_o/3$. Therefore the extensions of the springs will be $F_o/(3k)$, respectively $2F_o/(3k)$ which are indeed the q_2-part respectively the q_3-part of the steady state solution.

On this constant-speed motion of the train we have to superimpose the transient terms which are due to the fact that the train had to start suddenly from zero initial conditions. To allow a numerical evaluation we assume $m = 1$; $k = 1$; $c = 0.2$. This leads to the dimensional modal damping factors $\xi_2 = 0.2$ and $\xi_3 = 0.23$. The total displacements are shown in Fig. 4.7. The left plot gives the original coordinates as

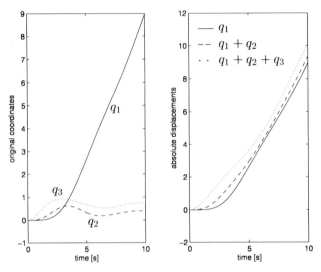

Fig. 4.7   Displacement-time plots

function of time showing the **almost** *linear function after some time for q_1 and the oscillating functions for q_2 and q_3.*

The right plot shows the **absolute** *displacements q_1, $(q_1 + q_2)$ and $(q_1 + q_2 + q_3)$ for the train parts. These displacements all exhibit the almost linear motion which remains after some time, whereas the extension of the right spring is shown to be twice the one of the left spring.*

4.3.2   Weakly damped systems

An important category of damping, which frequently is present in engineering structures, is refered to as *weak damping* or, alternatively, as light damping or small damping. To be able to analyse weakly damped systems by means of the expansion (4.17) in terms of undamped eigenmodes, an assumption has to be made. To show this, let us consider the free motions of the damped system which are solutions of the homogeneous set of equations

$$\underline{M}\,\underline{\ddot{q}}(t) + \underline{D}\,\underline{\dot{q}}(t) + \underline{K}\,\underline{q}(t) = \underline{0} \qquad (4.40)$$

Analogous to the general shape of the solution for undamped systems, discussed in Subsection 3.3.1, the solution of (4.40) can be written in the form

$$\underline{q}(t) = \underline{y}_r e^{s_r t} \qquad (4.41)$$

where the (generally complex) exponent s_r and the (generally complex) column $\underline{y}_r$ are solutions of the set of homogeneous algebraic equations

$$\left[s_r^2 \underline{M} + s_r \underline{D} + \underline{K}\right] \underline{y}_r = \underline{0} \tag{4.42}$$

If no damping were present, we would have $s_r = \pm j\, \omega_r$, $\underline{y}_r = \underline{u}_r$, with ω_r and $\underline{u}_r$ being the eigenfrequencies and eigencolumns associated with the undamped eigenvalue problem

$$\left[\underline{K} - \omega_r^2 \underline{M}\right] \underline{u}_r = \underline{0} \tag{4.43}$$

Now, it is assumed that for a weakly damped system s_r and $\underline{y}_r$ differ only slightly from $j\omega_r$ and $\underline{u}_r$, respectively, i.e. we write

$$s_r = \pm j\omega_r + \delta s_r \tag{4.44}$$

$$\underline{y}_r = \underline{u}_r + \delta \underline{y}_r \tag{4.45}$$

where δs_r and $\delta \underline{y}_r$ are small deviations from $j\omega_r$ and $\underline{u}_r$. In fact this means that the free vibrations of a damped system look very much like the free vibrations of the corresponding undamped system.

We insert (4.44) into (4.42), premultiply the resulting equation by $\underline{u}_r^T$ and obtain, taking account of the transposed form of (4.43)

$$\left\{\pm 2j\omega_r \delta s_r + (\delta s_r)^2\right\} \underline{u}_r^T \underline{M}\, \underline{y}_r + (\pm j\omega_r + \delta s_r)\, \underline{u}_r^T \underline{D}\, \underline{y}_r = 0 \tag{4.46}$$

At this point the damping is assumed to be small to such an extend that the second and fourth terms in the left-hand side of (4.46) may be neglected. This implies that

$$|\delta s_r| << \omega_r \tag{4.47}$$

and, in view of the fact that the fourth term in the left-hand side of (4.46) should be small compared to the first term, we also have

$$\left|\underline{u}_r^T \underline{D}\, \underline{y}_r\right| << \omega_r \left|\underline{u}_r^T \underline{M}\, \underline{y}_r\right| \tag{4.48}$$

Because $\underline{y}_r$ deviates only slightly from $\underline{u}_r$, the latter restriction may be replaced by

$$\underline{u}_r^T \underline{D}\, \underline{u}_r << \omega_r \left(\underline{u}_r^T \underline{M}\, \underline{u}_r\right) \tag{4.49}$$

If the restrictions imposed by Eqs. 4.47 and 4.49 are satisfied, we may approximate (4.46) by

$$\pm 2j\omega_r \delta s_r \left(\underline{u}_r^T \underline{M}\, \underline{y}_r\right) \pm j\omega_r \underline{u}_r^T \underline{D}\, \underline{y}_r = 0 \tag{4.50}$$

Again, because $\underline{y}_r$ deviates only slightly from $\underline{u}_r$, we may replace $\underline{y}_r$ in this equation by $\underline{u}_r$. This leads to the following (approximate) solution for δs_r

$$\delta s_r = -\frac{\underline{u}_r^T \underline{D}\, \underline{u}_r}{2\underline{u}_r^T \underline{M}\, \underline{u}_r} = -\frac{d_r}{2m_r} \tag{4.51}$$

with

$$d_r = \underline{u}_r^T \underline{D}\, \underline{u}_r \quad , \quad m_r = \underline{u}_r^T \underline{M}\, \underline{u}_r \qquad (4.52)$$

Inserting this result into (4.44), we arrive at the following (approximate) expression for the complex exponent s_r in the solution (4.41) for weakly damped systems

$$s_r = -\frac{d_r}{2m_r} \pm j\omega_r \qquad (4.53)$$

From this result some important conclusions can be drawn. The first conclusion is that for weakly damped systems the purely imaginary eigenvalues $s_r = j\omega_r$ of the associated undamped system are corrected by a purely (negative) real part depending on the modal damping coefficient $d_r = \underline{u}_r^T \underline{D}\, \underline{u}_r$ and the modal mass coefficient $m_r = \underline{u}_r^T \underline{M}\, \underline{u}_r$. The second conclusion is that in this correction only the diagonal terms of the matrix $\underline{U}^T \underline{D}\, \underline{U}$ occurring in (4.18) are involved and, hence, the influence of the non-diagonal terms in this matrix is of second order. The third conclusion is that in the above approximation for the modal solutions for weakly damped systems the eigencolumns may be assumed to remain unchanged compared to the eigencolumns of the associated undamped system. So, the presence of a small amount of damping will not significantly change the vibration modes of a system. The only effect will be that the free vibrations will not last for ever but decrease in amplitude with an exponential power-law, controlled by the **negative** real part of the exponents s_r, just as for undercritically damped single-degree-of-freedom systems.

Inserting the above results into (4.41), we can express the modal solution for a weakly damped system as follows

$$\underline{q}_r(t) = A_r\, e^{-\xi_r \omega_r t}\, \cos\left(\omega_r t + \varphi_r\right)\, \underline{u}_r \qquad (4.54)$$

where A_r and φ_r are constants of integration, while ξ_r is the *dimensionless modal damping factor*, defined by

$$\xi_r = \frac{d_r}{2\omega_r m_r} = \frac{d_r}{2\sqrt{m_r k_r}} \qquad (4.55)$$

The solution (4.54) represents a damped free vibration, which is completely consistent with the solution for a single-degree-of-freedom linear system. It is remarked that for small values of the dimensionless damping factor the frequency of the damped free vibration given by (4.54) may be approximated by the natural frequency of the undamped system, indeed. Finally, a remark is made with respect to the restrictions for weakly damped systems, expressed by (4.47) and (4.49). In view of (4.49), the solution (4.51) statisfies automatically (4.47). This implies that for weakly damped systems, the damping matrix has to satisfy the restriction (4.49) and, in view of (4.55), the dimensionless modal damping factor ξ_r has to meet the condition

$$\xi_r \ll 1 \qquad (4.56)$$

If (4.56) is fullfilled we can try to reconstruct an approximate system by just ignoring eventually present non-diagonal terms of the matrix $\underline{U}^T \underline{D} \, \underline{U}$ and only using the diagonal terms d_r, $r = 1, .., n$. We then can compare the dynamics of this approximate system with the original system. So, we assume

$$\underline{U}^T \underline{D} \, \underline{U} \approx \begin{bmatrix} d_1 & & 0 \\ & \ddots & \\ 0 & & d_n \end{bmatrix} := \lceil d_r \rfloor \qquad (4.57)$$

Finally, we can reconstruct a representative new damping matrix from the inverse expression

$$\underline{D}^* = \underline{U}^{-T} \lceil d_r \rfloor \, \underline{U}^{-1} \qquad (4.58)$$

In this process we assumed that we have been able to model the damping in the system leading to some damping matrix. In many practical situations however, the damping cannot be modelled directly by assuming discrete viscous damper elements in the system, for example in case of material damping in a longitudinally vibrating beam. However, if the damping can be assumed to be weak and if some type of experimental data is available, then also in this situation a representative damping matrix might be constructed. In that case estimates for the dimensionless modal damping factors should be extracted from the available experimental data.

4.3.3   Rayleigh damping

For the weakly damped systems considered in the previous subsection the matrix $\underline{U}^T \underline{D} \, \underline{U}$ in (4.18) is diagonalized in an approximate way. An exact diagonalization of this matrix will take place in the special case in which the damping matrix is a linear combination of the mass matrix and the stiffness matrix of the form

$$\underline{D} = \alpha \underline{M} + \beta \underline{K} \qquad (4.59)$$

where α and β are real constant scalars. This hypothetical type of damping can be visualized in the way shown in Fig 4.8. For this type of damping matrix the matrix $\underline{U}^T \underline{D} \, \underline{U}$ directly reduces to a diagonal matrix

$$\underline{U}^T \underline{D} \, \underline{U} := \lceil d_r \rfloor = \alpha \lceil m_r \rfloor + \beta \lceil k_r \rfloor = \lceil m_r \rfloor \{ \alpha + \beta \lceil \omega_r^2 \rfloor \} \qquad (4.60)$$

where account has been taken of (3.60), (3.61) and (3.63). Viscous damping characterized by a matrix of the form given by (4.59) is known as **Rayleigh damping**. In fact, the damping formulation according to (4.59) is only one example of the more general class of proportionally damped systems with the general condition $\underline{U}^T \underline{D} \, \underline{U} = \lceil d_r \rfloor$, so leading to a diagonal matrix. Hence, the eigenmodes $\underline{u}_r$ of the associated undamped system are capable of decoupling systems with proportional damping. To obtain the response, it is convenient to introduce the notation

$$\underline{U}^T \underline{D} \, \underline{U} = \lceil d_r \rfloor = \lceil m_r (\alpha + \beta \, \omega_r^2) \rfloor = \lceil 2\xi_r \omega_r m_r \rfloor \qquad (4.61)$$

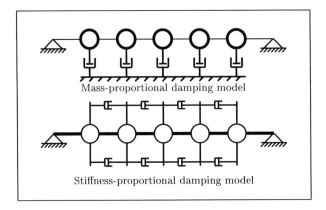

Fig. 4.8   Geometrical illustration of Rayleigh damping

where ξ_r is the *dimensionless modal damping factor* defined by

$$\xi_r = \frac{d_r}{2\omega_r m_r} = \frac{m_r\left(\alpha + \beta\omega_r^2\right)}{2\omega_r m_r} = \frac{\alpha m_r + \beta k_r}{2\sqrt{m_r k_r}} = \frac{1}{2}\left[\beta\omega_r + \frac{\alpha}{\omega_r}\right] \tag{4.62}$$

In Fig. 4.9 the dimensionless modal damping factor ξ_r has been plot as a function of the undamped eigenfrequentcy ω_{or} for some combinations of the tuning-parameters α and β. This figure shows that by tuning these parameters the damping level can be concentrated more or less in the low-frequency domain or if necessary in the high-frequency domain. The mass-matrix parameter α in particular creates damping for the low-frequency modes whereas the stiffness parameter β generates damping for the high-frequency modes. This also follows in some way from the geometrical illustration of this damping type as shown in Fig 4.8.

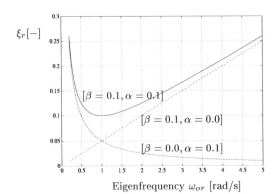

Fig. 4.9   Dimensionless modal damping factor

The assumption of proportional damping is made quite regularly in engineering, in particular in aerospace engineering. Due to the fact that each mode can have its own specific dimensionless modal damping factor value, the parameters for the assumed proportional damping model are to be determined or evaluated from experimental vibration testing whenever possible. Inserting (4.59) into (4.18), we obtain the n uncoupled equations

$$m_r \left\{ \ddot{\eta}_r(t) + 2\xi_r\omega_r\dot{\eta}_r(t) + \omega_r^2\eta_r(t) \right\} = N_r(t) \quad , \quad r = 1, 2, \cdots, n \qquad (4.63)$$

where $N_r(t)$ follows from (4.19). Note that (4.63) implies that there are no rigid-body modes. If rigid-body modes are present, then the solution procedure must be adapted in analogy with Subsection 3.3.4. Equations of the type (4.63) are discussed extensively in many elementary dynamic textbooks in conjunction with the response of second-order time-invariant single-degree-of-freedom linear systems. For example, for undercritically damped, single-degree-of-freedom systems we can write the free response simply as

$$\eta_r(t) = e^{-\xi_r\omega_r t} A_r \cos\left(\omega_{dr}t + \varphi_r\right) \qquad (4.64)$$

in which

$$\omega_{dr} = \omega_r \sqrt{1 - \xi_r^2} \qquad (4.65)$$

is the frequency of damped oscillation in the rth mode. For the response to arbitrary excitation the reader is referred to [Dimarogonas-92] and [Rao-95]. Below, we will consider the solution of the eigenvalue problem for systems with Rayleigh damping in a little more detail. To this end, we start from the general shape of the homogenuous solution of the uncoupled equations (4.63) which can be expressed as

$$\eta_r(t) = C \, e^{-st} \qquad (4.66)$$

Inserting (4.66) into (4.63), we obtain the (n) characteristic equations

$$s^2 + 2\xi_r\omega_r s + \omega_r^2 = 0 \qquad (4.67)$$

The roots of (4.67) are the eigenvalues

$$s_{1,2} = -\xi_r\omega_r \pm j\omega_{dr} \qquad (4.68)$$

with ω_{dr} being given by (4.65). This result was of course already reflected by the free response (4.64).
We can also start directly from the original equations

$$\underline{M}\,\ddot{\underline{q}}(t) + \underline{D}\,\dot{\underline{q}}(t) + \underline{K}\,\underline{q}(t) = \underline{0} \qquad (4.69)$$

Using the damping matrix $\underline{D} = \alpha\underline{M} + \beta\underline{K}$ and the general expression for the homogeneous solution

$$\underline{q}(t) = \underline{u}\,e^{st} \qquad (4.70)$$

we arrive at the eigenvalue problem in the quadratic form

$$[s^2 \underline{M} + s(\alpha\underline{M} + \beta\underline{K}) + \underline{K}] \underline{u} = \underline{0} \qquad (4.71)$$

which can be rewritten as

$$[(s^2 + \alpha s) \underline{M} + (\beta s + 1) \underline{K}] \underline{u} = \underline{0} \qquad (4.72)$$

or

$$[\{\frac{s^2 + \alpha s}{\beta s + 1}\} \underline{M} + \underline{K}] \underline{u} = \underline{0} \qquad (4.73)$$

This is exactly the same eigenvalue problem as used for undamped systems, namely $[-\omega_r^2 \underline{M} + \underline{K}]\underline{u}_r = \underline{0}$. Hence, for a system with Rayleigh damping the (complex) eigenvalues of the damped system can be extracted from the undamped eigenfrequencies by solving

$$\{\frac{s^2 + \alpha s}{\beta s + 1}\} = -\omega_r^2 \implies s^2 + (\alpha + \beta\omega_r^2) s + \omega_r^2 = 0 \qquad (4.74)$$

Obviously, the solutions of these equations have to be identical to the eigenvalues extracted directly from the decoupled equations (4.68). However, from the correspondence of (4.73) with the undamped eigenvalue problem we can also draw the important conclusion that the eigencolumns of both systems will be equal. So, the free vibrations of a proportional damped system are based on **real normal modes**. This means that when imposing a set of initial displacements equal to some scaled normal mode to a structure, then the structure will stay vibrating in this mode; only the amplitude will decrease in a way determined by the dimensionless damping factor for that mode.

It can be shown that in general for non-proportionally damped systems the eigenmodes will be **complex** leading to a much more complicated vibrational behaviour. This will be discussed in Section 4.5.

Example 4.4

To illustrate the treatment of weakly or proportionally damped systems in practice we look at the torsional system with 2 degrees-of-freedom and viscous damping shown in Fig. 4.10. The model consists of two rigid disks with mass-moments of inertia (J_1 respectively J_2) which can only rotate around a given straight axis. One of the disks is connected to the ground by a torsional spring with spring constant k_1 and the two disk are mutually connected by a second torsional spring with spring constant k_2. In the bearing of disk 2 we are dealing with a friction moment, the magnitude of which is proportional with the absolute rotational velocity of this disk. So, we can model this as a viscous torsion-damper with damping constant c_T

*As the generalised coordinates we choose the **absolute** rotation φ_1 of disk 1 and the **relative** rotation φ_2 of disk 2 with respect to disk 1, so*

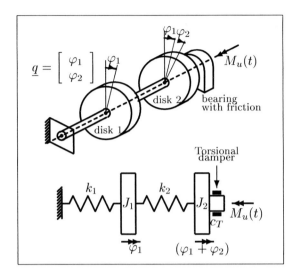

Fig. 4.10   2 degree-of-freedom torsional system with viscous damping

that $\underline{q}^T = [\varphi_1, \varphi_2]$. For $\varphi_1 = \varphi_2 = 0$ the springs are unloaded. On disk 2 also the (unit) external torsional moment $M_u(t) = \cos(\Omega t)$ is acting (see Fig.4.10). The application of Lagrange's equations will lead to the coupled set of differential equations

$$\underline{M} \, \underline{\ddot{q}}(t) \; + \; \underline{D} \, \underline{\dot{q}}(t) + \underline{K} \, \underline{q}(t) = \underline{Q}(t) \tag{4.75}$$

It is left to the reader to show that with the parameter values

$$J_1 = 3.0, \quad J_2 = 2.0 \; [kgm^2]$$
$$k_1 = 100, \quad k_2 = 100, \quad [Nm]$$
$$c_T = 5.0 \; [Nsm]$$

the mass-, damping- and stiffness matrices become

$$\underline{M} = \begin{bmatrix} 5 & 2 \\ 2 & 2 \end{bmatrix}; \;\; \underline{D} = \begin{bmatrix} 5 & 5 \\ 5 & 5 \end{bmatrix}; \;\; \underline{K} = 100 \begin{bmatrix} 1 & 0 \\ 0 & 1 \end{bmatrix} \tag{4.76}$$

First we analyse the undamped behaviour giving the following eigen-frequencies ([rad/s]) and corresponding eigenmodes (mass-matrix normalized)

$$\begin{matrix} \omega_1 = 4.0825 \\ \omega_2 = 10.0 \end{matrix} \quad \underline{u}_1 = \begin{bmatrix} 0.3651 \\ 0.1826 \end{bmatrix}; \;\; \underline{u}_1 = \begin{bmatrix} -0.4472 \\ 0.8944 \end{bmatrix} \tag{4.77}$$

Now, if we calculate the expression $\underline{U}^T\underline{D}\,\underline{U}$ using the damping matrix $\underline{D}$ from (4.76) we get

$$\underline{U}^T\underline{D}\,\underline{U} = \begin{bmatrix} 1.50 & 1.2247 \\ 1.2247 & 1.0 \end{bmatrix} \qquad (4.78)$$

We observe that this is certainly not a diagonal matrix, not even approximately.

Next, let us look whether a weak damping approach might be applicable. From the expression $\underline{U}^T\underline{D}\,\underline{U}$ (4.78) we can extract the diagonal terms d_r, giving $d_1 = 1.5$ and $d_2 = 1.0$. Due to the mass-matrix normalization the modal masses are $m_1 = m_2 = 1.0$ and, consequently, the modal stiffnesses are $k_1 = 16.6667$ (ω_1^2) and $k_2 = 100.0$ (ω_2^2). This leads to

$$\begin{aligned} \xi_1 &= 0.1837 & s_1 &= -0.75 \pm 4.0825\,j \\ \xi_2 &= 0.05 & s_2 &= -0.5 \pm 10.0\,j \end{aligned} \qquad (4.79)$$

So, both the dimensionless modal damping factors are not too large (18 % respectively 5 % dimensionless damping) and therefore we might assume this system to be weakly damped. Now, neglecting the non-diagonal terms of matrix $\underline{U}^T\underline{D}\,\underline{U}$, so, assuming

$$\underline{U}^T\underline{D}^*\,\underline{U} = \begin{bmatrix} d_1 & 0 \\ 0 & d_2 \end{bmatrix} \qquad (4.80)$$

we can reconstruct a representative damping matrix $\underline{D}^*$ from (4.58), giving

$$\underline{D}^* = \begin{bmatrix} 7.4 & 3.2 \\ 3.2 & 2.6 \end{bmatrix} \qquad (4.81)$$

Obviously, this matrix is different from the exact damping matrix given in (4.76). Nevertheless, it is interesting to look whether this will change the system dynamics drastically. To this end, we compute the complex

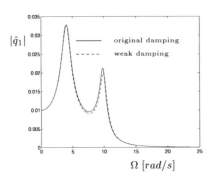 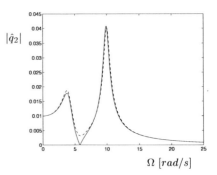

Fig. 4.11   Moduli of complex amplitudes

response amplitudes for a unit-harmonic excitation with the damping matrix given by (4.81) and compare the results with those obtained for the original damping matrix. The results are depicted in Fig. 4.11 and the differences appear to be small. Only in the anti-resonance area some

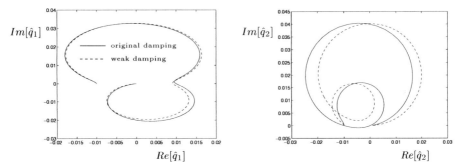

Fig. 4.12 Nyquist plots of complex amplitudes

small deviation can be noticed. In Fig. 4.12 the Nyquist plots for both the complex response amplitudes are given for the original damping case (solid lines) and the approximated damping (dashed lines). We can see that the damping approximation has some effect on the phase of the complex amplitudes but in general we still have a very satisfactory behaviour.

This means that in many practical situations in case of relatively weak damping a (representative) proportional damping model will be sufficiently accurate whereas the decoupling property of such a model can be used in the further analysis.

Next, we will try to generate a Rayleigh damping matrix of the form (4.59) and see whether also this approximation of the damping matrix can represent the real system dynamics sufficiently accurate. Taking, for example, $\alpha = 1.5$ and $\beta = -0.004$, we get the (automatically proportional) damping matrix $\underline{D}^{new}$

$$\underline{D}^{new} = \begin{bmatrix} 7.1 & 3 \\ 3 & 2.6 \end{bmatrix} \quad instead \ of \quad \underline{D} = \begin{bmatrix} 5 & 5 \\ 5 & 5 \end{bmatrix} \quad (4.82)$$

which lookes like the original damping matrix $\underline{D}$. Now, calculating the dimensionless dampings factors, we get

$$\xi_1^{new} = 0.1755; \qquad \xi_2^{new} = 0.0550 \qquad (4.83)$$

These values correspond so well with those found earlier for the weak damping model, see (4.79). This means that a reconstruction of the transfer-function matrix will show a very good fit and can be omitted here.

In the former we manipulated a damping matrix which followed from our modelling process. However, in many practical situations a damping matrix will not be available, for example when modelling the dynamical behaviour of a car body or machine frame. In that case we can use certain experimental data and if we think that the damping in the system will not be too large we can again try to generate a representative (proportional) damping matrix.

For a one-degree-of-freedom system we can use the so-called **half-power bandwidth** to estimate the dimensionless damping factor. To do so, we first plot the amplitude of the frequency-response function $H(\Omega)$. We determine the maximum amplitude $|H|_{max}$ and from that the two frequencies Ω_1 and Ω_2 for which $|H(\Omega_i)|^2 = [|H_{max}|^2]/2$. These are the so-called half-power points. The bandwidth $|\Omega_2 - \Omega_1|$ now equals $2\xi\omega_o$ where ω_o is the undamped eigenfrequency of the 1-dof model. The latter can be approximated by the damped eigenfrequency (frequency for which the FRF takes the maximum value).

Now, if we have a multi-degree-of-freedom system with multiple (sufficiently separated) peaks in its frequency-response function we can consider each individual peak as being a single-degree-of-freedom FRF and use the half-power bandwidth to estimate the modal damping for that peak. If we do so for all the peaks we get a set of modal damping factors which then can be used to generate an effective damping matrix $\underline{D}$.

Example 4.5

To illustrate this procedure we look at the two-disk rotor system for which some zoom sections around the two peaks for the complex amplitudes are plot in Fig. 4.13 In these figures the horizontal line in each plot indicates the half-power level. The width of the peaks at this level is the half-power bandwidth. The (averaged for the 2-dofs) half-power bandwidth for the first peak (top figures) is 1.62 $[rad/s]$, whereas for the second peak(bottom figures) it is 1.0150 $[rad/s]$. Using the undamped eigenfrequencies given in (4.77), we can determine the following estimates for the nondimensional damping factors

$$\xi_1 = 0.1984; \qquad \xi_2 = 0.0507 \qquad (4.84)$$

These values correspond surprisingly well with the earlier estimates, based on the diagonal terms of the matrix $\underline{U}^T \underline{D} \, \underline{U}$, see (4.79). Therefore, a reconstruction of the damped FRF using these values can again be omitted here.

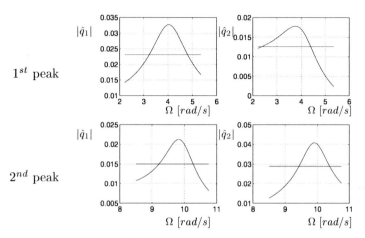

Fig. 4.13   Zoom plots of resonance peaks

4.3.4   Spectral representation of the transfer function matrix

It has been shown in the preceding subsections that for weakly damped systems and proportionally damped systems the linearized Lagrange's equations of motion can be decoupled via a modal expansion of $\underline{q}(t)$ in terms of the eigenmodes $\underline{u}_r$ of the associated undamped system. Introducing the transformation (4.17) into the equations of motion (4.1), we have shown that the matrix $\underline{U}^T \underline{D} \, \underline{U}$ in the transformed equations of motion (4.18) can be treated approximately as diagonal for weakly damped systems, whereas for proportionally damped systems it is exactly diagonal. The resulting uncoupled equations for the normal coordinates can be written as follows

$$m_r \left\{ \ddot{\eta}_r(t) + 2\xi_r\omega_r\dot{\eta}_r(t) + \omega_r^2\eta_r(t) \right\} = N_r(t) \quad , \quad r = 1, 2, \cdots, n \qquad (4.85)$$

where the dimensionless damping factor ξ_r is given by (4.55) for weakly damped systems and by (4.62) for proportionally damped systems. As remarked already in the previous subsection, equations of the type (4.85) are studied extensively in conjunction with second-order time-invariant single-degree-of-freedom linear systems. The free response has already been touched in the previous subsections, see (4.54) and (4.64), and will not be discussed here again. Because of its fundamental importance, we will adress the steady-state response to harmonic excitation. Referring to Section 4.2, we express the excitation and the response in terms of complex numbers and write

$$\underline{Q}(t) = Re\left\{ \hat{\underline{Q}} \, e^{j\Omega t} \right\} \qquad (4.86)$$

$$\underline{q}(t) = Re\left\{ \hat{\underline{q}} \, e^{j\Omega t} \right\} \qquad (4.87)$$

where ω is the frequency of the excitation, $\hat{Q}$ is the (known) column with the complex amplitudes of the excitation and $\hat{q}$ is the column with the complex amplitudes of the response which has to be determined. The (complex) transfer function matrix $\underline{H}(\Omega)$ relates $\hat{Q}$ to $\hat{q}$

$$\hat{q} = [-\Omega^2 \underline{M} + j\Omega \underline{D} + \underline{K}]^{-1} \hat{Q} = \underline{H}(\Omega) \hat{Q} \qquad (4.88)$$

Inserting (4.86) into (4.19), we can write the generalized forces $N_r(t), r = 1, \cdots, n$, as

$$N_r(t) = Re\left\{\hat{N}_r e^{j\Omega t}\right\} \qquad (4.89)$$

with

$$\hat{N}_r = \underline{u}_r^T \hat{Q} \qquad (4.90)$$

Inserting (4.87) into (4.17), we observe that the normal coordinates $\eta_r(t)$ have the form

$$\eta_r(t) = Re\left\{\hat{\eta}_r e^{j\Omega t}\right\} \qquad (4.91)$$

where $\hat{\eta}_r(r = 1, \cdots, n)$ are related to $\hat{q}$ by

$$\hat{q} = \sum_{r=1}^{n} \underline{u}_r \hat{\eta}_r = \underline{U} \hat{\eta} \qquad (4.92)$$

Now, $\hat{\eta}_r$ can be related to $\hat{N}_r$ by substituting (4.89) and (4.91) into (4.85). This yields

$$\hat{\eta}_r = \frac{\hat{N}_r}{m_r \left(\omega_r^2 - \Omega^2 + 2j\xi_r\omega_r\Omega\right)} \qquad (4.93)$$

which is completely equivalent with the transfer function of a single-degree-of-freedom, viscously damped system. Hence, the ratio between $\hat{\eta}_r$ and $\hat{N}_r$ represents the complex transfer function associated with (4.85). Inserting (4.90) into (4.93), substituting the resulting solution for $\hat{\eta}_r$ into (4.92), and comparing the solution for $\hat{q}$, obtained in this way, with (4.88), we conclude that the *transfer function matrix* $\underline{H}(\Omega)$ for weakly and proportionally damped systems can be expressed in terms of the undamped modal quantities ω_r and $\underline{u}_r$ as follows

$$\underline{H}(\Omega) = \sum_{r=1}^{n} \frac{\underline{u}_r \underline{u}_r^T}{m_r \left(\omega_r^2 - \Omega^2 + 2j\xi_r\omega_r\Omega\right)} \qquad (4.94)$$

This result can be considered as a straightforward generalization of the transfer function matrix for undamped multi-degree-of-freedom linear systems which has been derived in the previous chapter.

If we are not interested in all the elements of this matrix for a given frequency range but (as is usually the case in practical situations) only in one or more specific elements $H_{k,l}(\Omega)$, we can use

$$H_{k,l}(\Omega) = \sum_{r=1}^{n} \frac{\underline{u}_r[k] \, \underline{u}_r[l]}{m_r \left(\omega_r^2 - \Omega^2 + 2j\xi_r\omega_r\Omega\right)} \qquad (4.95)$$

where $\underline{u}_r[k]$ is the kth element of the eigencolumn $\underline{u}_r$.

So resuming, if we want to evaluate the transfer function matrix $\underline{H}(\Omega)$ for a certain frequency range $\Omega_{min} \leq \Omega \leq \Omega_{max}$ we can follow two strategies

- A direct approach:
    - Calculate for each excitation frequency Ω_p the matrix-inverse of the square and complex matrix $[-\Omega_p^2\underline{M} + j\Omega_p\underline{D} + \underline{K}]$ and take the relevant terms $H_{k,l}(\Omega_p)$.

- A spectral approach, consisting of the following consecutive steps:
    - Solve the undamped eigenvalue-problem $[-\omega^2\underline{M} + \underline{K}]\underline{u} = \underline{0}$, giving the eigenfrequencies ω_r and eigencolumns $\underline{U} = [\underline{u}_r, \ r = 1..n]$,
    - Calculate the modal masses (diagonal terms of $\underline{U}^T\underline{M}\,\underline{U}$), modal damping terms (diagonal terms of $\underline{U}^T\underline{D}\,\underline{U}$) and the modal stiffnesses (diagonal terms of $\underline{U}^T\underline{K}\,\underline{U}$),
    - Evaluate the relevant elements $H_{k,l}$ of the transfer function matrix for the given frequency range using (4.95).

In the preceeding sections a general procedure to analyse complex, multi-degree-of-freedom dynamical systems has been presented. This approach forms the basis for many of the advanced computer codes to analyze realistic dynamical problems, especially the programmes using so-called Finite Elements. These programmes can analyze realistic problems with a very large number of degrees of freedom (up to 300.000 or more, such as met in aircraft industry). One of the main limitations in these approaches is that the damping is assumed to be small or has to be modelled as proportional (Rayleigh) damping.

However, in many situations the necessary number of degrees of freedom is not soo large, but more importantly, an alternative damping formulation is necessary for a realistic description of the real dynamic behaviour of a machine. In that case a so-called *system analysis approach* using a **state-space formulation** can be used, combined with the application of a dedicated software tool such as for example the **MATLAB** -programme. This approach will be introduced in Section 4.5.

4.4 DESIGN PROBLEM: A HYDRO-ELASTIC ENGINE MOUNT

In modern cars and trucks sophistigated engine mounts are used. The purpose of these elements is on the one hand to create a comfortable dynamic road behaviour (mainly the large amplitude, low-frequency part for which damping is necessary) and on the other hand to create an acoustic isolation of the engine from the passenger part (mainly the small-amplitude, high-frequency part of the spectrum) where damping will have a negative effect. A schemat-

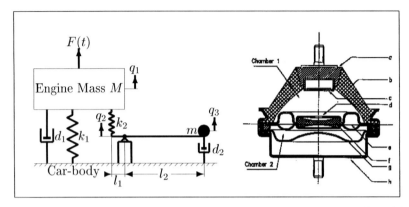

Fig. 4.14 Hydro-Elastic Engine Mount: picture and a simple mechanical model

ically plot of such an engine mount is shown in the right part of Fig. 4.14. A linear model very frequently used to study the effect of such a damper in a car model is shown in the left part (only the thick lines).

The engine mount roughly consists of a standard rubber support part (b) (modelled as the combination of the main spring k_1 and the damper d_1). Further it has two fluid-filled chambers connected by the circular channel (e). In the centre also some kind of short-circuit element (f) can be seen. For low-frequency, large-amplitude motions of the upper part the short-circuit will close and the fluid will be forced to flow through the circular channel from chamber (1) to chamber (2). The fluid mass in this channel is named m and the lever shown in the model has to represent the scaling between the acceleration ratio between the top part of the damper in vertical direction (q_1) and the much larger acceleration (q_3) of the fluid in the channel. The damper d_2 represents the resistance of the fluid in this channel. The spring k_2 finally originates from bulging out of the walls of chamber (1) due to the fluid pressure in this chamber.

The selected generalized coordinates for the model are the (visible) displacement of the top of the mount (q_1) and the scaled (invisible) displacement of the fluid in the channel of the mount (q_2), $\underline{q}^T = [q_1, q_2]$. The engine forces are introduced by the (harmonic) excitation force $F(t)$.

For the purpose of numerical evaluations we use the parameter values
$M = 100\ [kg]$; $m = 1\ [kg]$; $k_1 = 90000\ [N/m]$; $k_2 = 30000\ [N/m]$
$a = 5\ [-]$, $d_1 = 1000\ [Ns/m]$; $d_2 = 10\ [Ns/m]$.

The generalized coordinates chosen to describe the system are the displacements q_1 and q_2 as shown in the figure. All the displacements are defined referenced to the static equilibrium position, so that the effect of the gravity forces can be ignored. We have only translations, and, hence, the kinetic energy becomes

$$T = \frac{1}{2}M\dot{q}_1^2 + \frac{1}{2}m\dot{q}_3^2 \qquad (4.96)$$

Using the kinematic relationship $q_3 = -(l_2/l_1)q_2 = -aq_2$, with $a := l_2/l_1$, we can rewrite this expression as

$$T = \frac{1}{2}M\dot{q}_1^2 + \frac{1}{2}ma^2\dot{q}_2^2 = \frac{1}{2}\dot{\underline{q}}^T\underline{M}\,\dot{\underline{q}} \qquad (4.97)$$

with the mass matrix being given by

$$\underline{M} = \begin{bmatrix} M & 0 \\ 0 & ma^2 \end{bmatrix} \qquad (4.98)$$

The elastic energy takes the form

$$U = \frac{1}{2}k_1q_1^2 + \frac{1}{2}k_2(q_1 - q_2)^2 = \frac{1}{2}\underline{q}^T\underline{K}\,\underline{q} \qquad (4.99)$$

where the stiffness matrix equals

$$\underline{K} = \begin{bmatrix} k_1 + k_2 & -k_2 \\ -k_2 & k_2 \end{bmatrix} \qquad (4.100)$$

The generalized forces should represent the effect of the viscous dampers and the external force $F(t)$. Hence, the total virtual work can be written as

$$\delta W^{nc} = -F_{d1}\delta q_1 + F(t)\delta q_1 - F_{d2}\delta q_3 \qquad (4.101)$$

where

$$\begin{aligned} F_{d1} &= d_1\dot{q}_1; & F_{d2} &= d_2\dot{q}_3 \\ \dot{q}_3 &= -a\dot{q}_2; & \delta q_3 &= -a\delta q_2 \end{aligned} \qquad (4.102)$$

so

$$\delta W^{nc} = -d_1\dot{q}_1\delta q_1 + F(t)\delta q_1 - d_2a^2\dot{q}_2\delta q_2 := \underline{Q}^T\delta\underline{q} \qquad (4.103)$$

This gives the following result for $\underline{Q}$

$$\underline{Q} = \begin{bmatrix} -d_1\dot{q}_1 + F(t) \\ -a^2d_2\dot{q}_2 \end{bmatrix} := -\underline{D}\dot{\underline{q}} + \underline{f}(t) \qquad (4.104)$$

with

$$\underline{D} = \begin{bmatrix} d_1 & 0 \\ 0 & a^2d_2 \end{bmatrix}; \qquad \underline{f}(t) = \begin{bmatrix} F(t) \\ 0 \end{bmatrix} \qquad (4.105)$$

Solving the eigenvalue problem $[-\omega^2\underline{M} + \underline{K}]\underline{u} = \underline{0}$ yields the (undamped) eigenfrequencies ω_i and corresponding eigencolumns $\underline{u}_i$ which are building the matrix $\underline{U}$

$$\omega_1 = 24.5 \; [rad/s] \;\; (3.9 \; [Hz]), \qquad \omega_2 = 42.43 \; [rad/s] \;\; (6.75 \; [Hz]) \quad (4.106)$$

$$\underline{U} = \begin{bmatrix} 0.0707 & -0.0707 \\ 0.1414 & 0.1414 \end{bmatrix} \tag{4.107}$$

where the eigencolumns have been mass-normalized ($\underline{U}^T \underline{M} \, \underline{U} = \underline{I}$). The first eigenmode is an in-phase motion of q_1 and q_2 with a ratio of 1 : 2. This results in an out-of-phase motion of q_1 (the engine mass M) and q_3 (the fluid-mass m) with an amplitude ratio of approximately 1 : 10. The second eigenmode appears to be an in-phase motion of these two masses with the same amplitude ratio.

We are dealing with **proportional damping** because

$$\underline{U}^T \underline{D} \, \underline{U} = \underline{D} = \begin{bmatrix} 10 & 0 \\ 0 & 10 \end{bmatrix} \tag{4.108}$$

which is a diagonal matrix. Using the modal masses $m_i^* = 1.0$ (diagonal terms of $\underline{U}^T \underline{M} \, \underline{U}$), the modal damping d_i^* (diagonal terms of $\underline{U}^T \underline{D} \, \underline{U}$) and the modal stiffnesses k_i^* (diagonal terms of $\underline{U}^T \underline{K} \, \underline{U}$), we can calculate the dimensionless modal damping factors from $\xi_i = d_i^*/(2\sqrt{k_i^* m_i^*})$ to be

$$\xi_1 = 0.2041; \quad \xi_2 = 0.1179 \tag{4.109}$$

We conclude that the system is rather weakly damped.

Next, we assume a unit-excitation $F(t) = \cos(\Omega t)$ and calculate the response for the complex amplitudes of the generalized coordinates, using

$$\hat{\underline{q}} = \left[-\Omega^2 \underline{M} + j\Omega \underline{D} + \underline{K} \right]^{-1} \hat{\underline{F}} \tag{4.110}$$

with $\hat{\underline{F}}^T = [1, 0]$. The complex responses have been determined for a frequency range $0 \le \Omega \le 100$ [rad/s]. The results are plotted in Fig 4.15. The first peaks at ≈ 25 [rad/s] can more clearly be distinguished due to the smaller dimensionless modal damping factor. The second peaks are less pronounced (especially for q_2).

Next, we will investigate the possibility to replace the whole engine mount by a more simple spring-damper system. This might give more understanding about the practical relevance and design possibilities of such a complicated car component. We only look at the single engine mount so we will take the engine mass M to be zero. First we will try to generate some analytical expression for the dynamic equivalent of this mount. The complex amplitudes of the responses q_1 and q_2 can be obtained from

$$\begin{bmatrix} j\Omega d_1 + (k_1 + k_2) & -k_2 \\ -k_2 & -m_a\Omega^2 + jd_a\Omega + k_2 \end{bmatrix} \begin{bmatrix} \hat{q}_1 \\ \hat{q}_2 \end{bmatrix} = \begin{bmatrix} \hat{F} \\ 0 \end{bmatrix} \tag{4.111}$$

where we used the abbreviations $m_a := ma^2$; $d_a = d_2a^2$. Then, we can write the solution for the complex amplitudes of the response as

$$\begin{bmatrix} \hat{q}_1 \\ \hat{q}_2 \end{bmatrix} = \frac{1}{D} \begin{bmatrix} -m_a\Omega^2 + jd_a\Omega + k_2 & k_2 \\ k_2 & j\Omega d_1 + (k_1 + k_2) \end{bmatrix} \begin{bmatrix} \hat{F} \\ 0 \end{bmatrix}$$

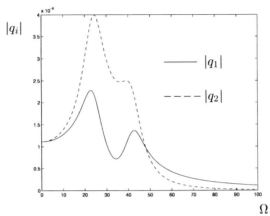

Fig. 4.15   Magnitude of the complex amplitudes of the responses

$$= \frac{1}{D} \left[\begin{array}{c} (-m_a\Omega^2 + jd_a\Omega + k_2)\hat{F} \\ k_2\hat{F} \end{array} \right] \tag{4.112}$$

with

$$D = [j\Omega d_1 + (k_1 + k_2)][-m_a\Omega^2 + jd_a\Omega + k_2] - k_2^2 \tag{4.113}$$

From (4.112) we obtain the following solution for the (external) response $\hat{q}_1$

$$\hat{q}_1 = [\frac{T}{N}] \, \hat{F} \tag{4.114}$$

with

$$\begin{aligned} T &= [k_2 - m_a\Omega^2] \; + \; j \, [\Omega d_a] \\ N &= [-(k_1 + k_2)m_a\Omega^2 - d_1 d_a\Omega^2 + k_1 k_2] \; + \\ &\quad j \, [-\Omega^3 d_1 m_a + \Omega d_1 k_2 + \Omega d_a(k_1 + k_2)] \end{aligned} \tag{4.115}$$

Defining the real quantities

$$\begin{aligned} T_r &= k_2 - m_a\Omega^2 \\ T_i &= \Omega d_a \\ N_r &= -(k_1 + k_2)m_a\Omega^2 - d_1 d_a\Omega^2 + k_1 k_2 \\ N_i &= -\Omega^3 d_1 m_a + \Omega d_1 k_2 + \Omega d_a(k_1 + k_2) \end{aligned} \tag{4.116}$$

we can rewrite (4.114) as

$$\hat{q}_1 = \frac{T_r \; + \; j \, T_i}{N_r \; + \; j \, N_i} \, \hat{F} \tag{4.117}$$

which can be abbreviated in the usual form

$$\hat{q}_1 = H_1(\Omega) \, \hat{F} \tag{4.118}$$

In this way, we have created a direct relationship between the complex amplitude of the excitation $\hat{F}$ and the complex amplitude of the (external) response $\hat{q}_1$. From this relationship we can easily extract the inverse relationship

$$\hat{F} = \frac{N_r + jN_i}{T_r + jT_i} = \frac{(N_r + jN_i)(T_r - jT_i)}{T_r^2 + T_i^2} \, \hat{q}_1 \qquad (4.119)$$

Further elaborating (4.119), we obtain

$$\left\{ \left[\frac{T_r N_r + T_i N_i}{T_r^2 + T_i^2} \right] + j \, \Omega \, \left[\frac{N_i T_r - N_r T_i}{\Omega(T_r^2 + T_i^2)} \right] \right\} \hat{q}_1 \; = \; \hat{F} \qquad (4.120)$$

or, simply

$$Z_1(\Omega) \, \hat{q}_1 \; = \; \hat{F} \qquad (4.121)$$

where the complex **dynamic stiffness** $Z_1(\Omega)$ is the inverse of the transfer function $H_1(\Omega)$. Next, we look at a simple alternative system consisting of a linear spring with stiffness coëfficient k^*, in parallel with a linear viscous damper with damping coëfficient d^* in parallel as shown in Fig. 4.16. It can

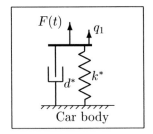

Fig. 4.16   Simple representative spring-damper model

easily be derived that the dynamic stiffness relation for this system yields

$$\{k^* + j\Omega \, d^*\} \, \hat{q}_1 \; = \; \hat{F} \qquad (4.122)$$

Now, if we want the two dynamic stiffness expressions (4.119) and (4.122) to be equivalent, we have to take the **frequency-dependent stiffness** $k^*(\Omega)$ in (4.122) equal to the real part of $Z_1(\Omega)$ and the **frequency-dependent damping** $b^*(\Omega)$ as the imaginary part of $Z_1(\Omega)$ devided by Ω. However, this leads to rather complex expressions, even for this simple 2-degree-of-freedom system.

Therefore we better can follow a numerical procedure consisting of three steps:

- Calculate numerically the complex responses for the unit excitation $\hat{F} = 1.0$ from

$$\left[\begin{array}{c} \hat{q}_1 \\ \hat{q}_2 \end{array} \right] = [-\Omega^2 \, \underline{M} + j\Omega\underline{D} + \underline{K}]^{-1} \left[\begin{array}{c} 1 \\ 0 \end{array} \right] \qquad (4.123)$$

From the numerical results we can extract $H_1(\Omega) = \hat{q}_1$.

- Calculate $Z_1(\Omega) = 1/H_1(\Omega)$.

- In the above complex function $Z_1(\Omega)$, the real part equals the representative stiffness $k^*(\Omega)$, whereas the imaginairy part devided by Ω equals the representative damping $d^*(\Omega)$.

In a practical situation the function $H_1(\Omega)$ can also be determined experimentally without first creating a model of the suspension. This can easily be done by generating a harmonic force acting on the damper and measuring the harmonic response (amplitude and phase) of the top-displacement for a specific range of excitation frequencies (see also Chapter 4).
In Fig. 4.17 the magnitude of $H_1(\omega) = \hat{q}_1(\Omega)$ is shown in the upper left plot, while the magnitude of $Z_1(\omega)$ is shown in the upper right plot. The resulting representative frequency-dependent stiffness $k^*(\Omega)$, respectively damping $d^*(\Omega)$ are shown in the bottom plots. Two typical aspect of these results are

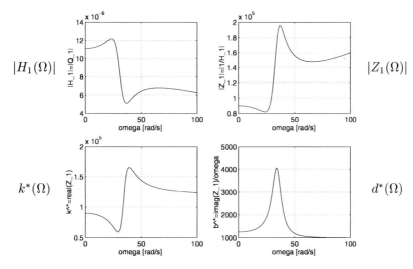

Fig. 4.17 Transfer function, dynamic stiffness and representative frequency-dependent stiffness and damping factors

- At some specific frequency (approximately 35 [rad/s]) the stiffness k^* is switching from a low value (only the spring k_1) to a higher value (k_1 and k_2 in parallel)

- The damping factor d^* is large in the range $30 \leq \Omega \leq 40$ [rad/s], but small outside this band.

Fig. 4.18 depicts the effect of changing the lever ratio $a = l_2/l_1$ on the value for the representative stiffness and damping. As can be seen this lever ratio a

can be used to create a situation where we have a lot of damping in a certain frequency band (for example to minimize engine suspension vibrations) but only little damping outside that band (which is important in order to stop high-frequency acoustic vibrations going from the engine to the car body.

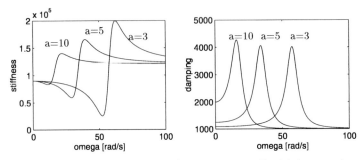

Fig. 4.18   Variation of stiffness k^* and damping d^* with lever ratio a

4.5   SYSTEMS WITH SYMMETRIC MATRICES AND GENERAL VISCOUS DAMPING

4.5.1   State-space formulation

In the previous section we considered damped systems for which knowledge of the solution of the undamped eigenvalue problem appears to be very beneficial for the analysis of the damped system. In the case of weak damping the undamped eigenmodes collected in the matrix $\underline{U} = [\underline{u}_1 \underline{u}_2 \dots \underline{u}_n]$ could be used to switch from a set of coupled equations of motion to a set of uncoupled equations of motion by neglecting the off-diagonal terms in the matrix $\underline{U}^T \underline{D} \, \underline{U}$. In the particular case of proportional damping this switching to a set of decoupled equations of motion could be carried out for any damping level without approximation. The use of a decoupling approach based on the undamped eigenmodes has a lot of advantages, the most important one of those being that solving the undamped eigenvalue problem generally is considerably easier and consumes less computational time than solving the damped eigenvalue problem. Even, in many complex engineering applications there will not be an alternative for this approach because the assumption of weak or proportional damping is the main (and often only) damping option in commercial finite element software codes.

In the present section we will treat multi-degree-of-freedom linear systems with symmetric system matrices and general viscous damping for which the equation of motion cannot be decoupled anymore using a transformation based on the eigenmodes of the associated undamped system. However, it still appears to be possible to decouple the set of second-order differential equations of motion by means of a suitably chosen transformation after reformulating these equations as a larger set of *first-order* differential equations of motion by introducing a set of new dependent variables. This is equivalent to putting the differential equations of motion in a so-called **state-space formulation**. According to Subsection 2.18, see (2.446), the linearized second-order Lagrange's equations of motion for systems with symmetric matrices are

$$\underline{M}\ \ddot{\underline{q}}(t) + \underline{D}\ \dot{\underline{q}}(t) + \underline{K}\ \underline{q}(t) = \underline{Q}(t) \tag{4.124}$$

where $\underline{M}$, $\underline{D}$ and $\underline{K}$ are the $(n \times n)$ symmetric mass, damping and stiffness matrices, $\underline{q}(t)$ is a column with n generalized coordinates, while $\underline{Q}(t)$ is the column with n generalized excitations depending explicitly on time. To recast the equations of motion (4.124) in the state form, we might introduce the following set of new dependent variables

$$\underline{z}^*(t) = \dot{\underline{q}}(t) \tag{4.125}$$

and rewrite (4.124) as a set of first-order differential equations

$$\underline{D}\ \dot{\underline{q}}(t) + \underline{M}\ \dot{\underline{z}}^*(t) + \underline{K}\ \underline{q}(t) = \underline{Q}(t) \tag{4.126}$$

Now, it is possible to combine (4.125) and (4.126) to a set of first-order differential equations of motion of the $2n$ variables $\underline{q}(t)$ and $\underline{z}^*(t)$, collected in the *state column* $\underline{x}(t)$

$$\underline{x}(t) = \left[\begin{array}{c} \underline{q}(t) \\ \underline{z}^*(t) \end{array} \right] = \left[\begin{array}{c} \underline{q}(t) \\ \dot{\underline{q}}(t) \end{array} \right] \tag{4.127}$$

However, if we use directly (4.125), as is commonly done in system analysis and control engineering, the resulting set of first-order differential equations appears to have non-symmetric system matrices. Because the symmetry of the system matrices in the resulting set of first-order equations of motion appears to be advantageous for the decoupling process of those equations (in a similar way as the symmetry of the system matrices in the set of second-order equations of motion for the undamped systems treated in Chapter 3), we have chosen in this section for a transformation resulting in a set of first-order equations with symmetric system matrices. It is remarked that for this transformation the symmetry of the system matrices $\underline{M}$, $\underline{D}$ and $\underline{K}$ in the original set of second-order equations (4.124) will appear to be essential.

We can obtain a set of first-order differential equations with symmetric system matrices by using in stead of (4.125) the equivalent set

$$\underline{M}\ \dot{\underline{q}}(t) - \underline{M}\ \underline{z}^*(t) = \underline{0} \tag{4.128}$$

Combining (4.126) and (4.128), we arrive at the following set of first-order differential equations of motion for the $2n$ variables $x_i(t)$ collected in the state column $\underline{x}(t)$

$$\underline{x} = \left[\begin{array}{c} \underline{q}(t) \\ \dot{\underline{q}}(t) \end{array} \right]$$

$$\underline{A}\ \dot{\underline{x}}(t) + \underline{B}\ \underline{x}(t) = \underline{r}(t) \tag{4.129}$$

where the $(2n \times 2n)$ real system matrices

$$\underline{A} = \begin{bmatrix} \underline{D} & \underline{M} \\ \underline{M} & \underline{0} \end{bmatrix}, \qquad \underline{B} = \begin{bmatrix} \underline{K} & \underline{0} \\ \underline{0} & -\underline{M} \end{bmatrix} \tag{4.130}$$

appear to be symmetric with $\underline{0}$ being the $(n \times n)$ null matrix. In (4.129) the column

$$\underline{r}(t) = \begin{bmatrix} \underline{Q}(t) \\ \underline{0} \end{bmatrix} \tag{4.131}$$

contains the $2n$ generalized forces related to the $2n$ generalized state coordinates contained in the column $\underline{x}(t)$. In view of the fact that the right-hand side of (4.128) is the null column, the last n elements of the column $\underline{r}(t)$ are zero.

At this point it is remarked that in system analysis and control engineering generally the state-space equations are written as

$$\dot{\underline{x}}(t) = \underline{\hat{A}}\ \underline{x}(t) + \underline{\hat{B}}\ \underline{u}(t) \tag{4.132}$$

This set of equations is equivalent with (4.129) if we take

$$\underline{\hat{A}} = -\underline{A}^{-1}\underline{B}; \qquad \underline{\hat{B}} = \underline{A}^{-1}\begin{bmatrix} \underline{I} \\ \underline{0} \end{bmatrix}; \qquad \underline{u}(t) = \underline{Q}(t) \tag{4.133}$$

We can easily express the system matrix $\underline{\hat{A}}$ and the column $\underline{\hat{B}}\underline{u}(t)$ in terms of the matrices $\underline{M}$, $\underline{D}$ and $\underline{K}$ and the column $\underline{Q}(t)$ of the original second-order system as follows

$$\underline{\hat{A}} = -\begin{bmatrix} \underline{0} & -\underline{I} \\ \underline{M}^{-1}\underline{K} & \underline{M}^{-1}\underline{D} \end{bmatrix}; \qquad \underline{\hat{B}} = \begin{bmatrix} \underline{0} \\ \underline{M}^{-1} \end{bmatrix} \tag{4.134}$$

Consequently, the mass matrix $\underline{M}$ should be non-singular (i.e. positive definite) to be able to determine $\underline{M}^{-1}$ and, hence to use the set of first-order equations (4.132). Moreover, consistent with the earlier announcement, the system matrix $\underline{\hat{A}}$ is not symmetric anymore and, hence, we will use the state-space formulation of the equations of motion in the form of (4.129).

Because the set of first-order differential equations of motion (4.129) contains two symmetric system matrices, it can be treated in a similar way as the set of second-order differential equations of motion (3.1) for undamped systems. Hence, in the following subsections we will first consider the free motions governed by (4.129) with $\underline{r}(t) = \underline{0}$. Again, inherent characteristics of the system can be obtained by solving the associated algebraic eigenvalue problem. The solution consists of *complex* eigenvalues and associated *complex* eigencolumns. These eigencolumns possess again the orthogonality property, for which derivation advantageous use can be made of the symmetry of the system matrices $\underline{A}$ and $\underline{B}$. Again, the orthogonality property permits the transformation of the set of simultaneous (coupled) first-order ordinary differential equations for forced motion, i.e. with $\underline{r}(t) \neq \underline{0}$, to a set of independent (uncoupled) equations of first order.

4.5.2 The eigenvalue problem

For free damped motions the set of linear first-order differential equations of motion (4.129) reduces to its homogeneous part

$$\underline{A}\ \underline{\dot{x}}(t) + \underline{B}\ \underline{x}(t) = \underline{0} \tag{4.135}$$

According to the theory of linear differential equations the solution of the above set of homogeneous ordinary differential equatons has the exponential form

$$\underline{x}(t) = \underline{v}\ e^{st} \tag{4.136}$$

where s is a constant scalar and the column $\underline{v}$ contains $2n$ constant elements $v_i = v\,[i]\,, i = 1, 2, ..., 2n$. Inserting (4.136) into (4.135) and dividing through by e^{st}, we obtain the *algebraic eigenvalue problem* for systems with general viscous damping and symmetric matrices

$$[s\underline{A} + \underline{B}]\,\underline{v} = \underline{0} \tag{4.137}$$

Equation (4.137) represents the eigenvalue problem associated with the matrices $\underline{A}$ and $\underline{B}$ and it can be solved numerically using commercially available software packages like **MATLAB** . In this text we will not elaborate computational procedures to numerically solve the eigenvalue problem, but confine ourselves to a discussion of the general characteristics of the solution.

Equation (4.137) possesses a nontrivial solution if and only if the determinant of the coefficients of $v\,[i]$ vanishes. This can be expressed in the form

$$\det\,(s\underline{A} + \underline{B}) = 0 \tag{4.138}$$

where $\det\,(s\underline{A} + \underline{B})$ is called the *characteristic determinant*, with (4.138) itself being known as the *characteristic equation*. This terminology is the same as for undamped systems, see Subsection 3.3.1. The characteristic equation (4.138) is of degree $2n$ in s and, hence, it possesses in general $2n$ distinct roots s_r, $r = 1, 2, \ldots, 2n$, referred to as *characteristic values* or *eigenvalues*. Associated with every one of the eigenvalues s_r there is a certain nontrivial column matrix $\underline{v}_r$ which is a solution of the eigenvalue problem, such that

$$s_r\,\underline{A}\,\underline{v}_r = -\underline{B}\,\underline{v}_r \tag{4.139}$$

It is remarked that, in general, the eigenvalues $s_r, r = 1, 2, \ldots, 2n$ resulting from (4.138) are complex. However, in the case of a moderately damped structure, some of the eigenvalues may become completely real, with the imaginary parts being zero and their real parts being negative. It follows immediately from (4.139) that if the eigenvalue s_r is complex, then also the associated eigencolumn $\underline{v}_r$ is complex. Moreover, it can be shown that if $(s_r, \underline{v}_r)$ is a complex solution of the eigenvalue problem, then its complex conjugate $(\bar{s}_r, \bar{\underline{v}}_r)$ is also a solution of the eigenvalue problem. To prove this, we take the complex conjugate of (4.139), utilize the theorem that the conjugate of a product is equal to the product of the conjugates, and obtain, in view of the fact that $\underline{A}$ and $\underline{B}$ are real matrices

$$\bar{s}_r \, \underline{A} \, \bar{\underline{v}}_r = -\underline{B} \, \bar{\underline{v}}_r \tag{4.140}$$

Hence, those solutions of the eigenvalue problem (4.137) that are complex can be grouped in n complex conjugate pairs which we write as

$$\left\{ \begin{array}{c} s_r = \mu_r + j\nu_r \\ \underline{v}_r \end{array} \right\} \qquad \left\{ \begin{array}{c} \bar{s}_r - \mu_r - j\nu_r \\ \bar{\underline{v}}_r \end{array} \right\} \tag{4.141}$$

where the real quantities μ_r and ν_r are referred to as the r-th *exponential damping factor* and the r-th *damped eigenfrequency*, respectively. Consistent with the situation for undamped systems, the above pairs of complex conjugate solutions are arranged in order of increasing magnitude of the damped eigenfrequencies, namely $\nu_1 < \nu_2 < \ldots < \nu_n$. In the case in which all the eigenvalues are distinct it follows that all the eigencolumns are independent. In the case in which some of the eigenvalues are completely real, it follows from the fact that both the dimension of the eigenvalue problem (4.137) and the number of complex eigenvalues are even that the number of completely real eigenvalues is also even. Hence, the latter eigenvalues could also be considered to show up in pairs of two, but there will not be any particular relationship between the two as for the case of complex eigenvalues.

In view of the special composition of the state column $\underline{x}(t)$, following from (4.127), the associated column $\underline{v}$, defined in (4.136), is also composed in a special way. Writing the (homogeneous) solution for $\underline{q}(t)$ as a subset of (4.136) in the form

$$\underline{q}(t) = \underline{u} \, e^{st} \tag{4.142}$$

where the column $\underline{u}$ contains the first n elements of the column $\underline{v}$, we obtain

$$\dot{\underline{q}}(t) = s \, \underline{u} \, e^{st} \tag{4.143}$$

Hence, the column $\underline{v}$, defined in (4.136), has the following special composition

$$\underline{v} = \left[\begin{array}{c} \underline{u} \\ s \, \underline{u} \end{array} \right] \tag{4.144}$$

and, accordingly, the eigencolumns $\underline{v}_r$, $r = 1, 2, \ldots, 2n$ have the following special composition

$$\underline{v}_r = \left[\begin{array}{c} \underline{u}_r \\ s_r \, \underline{u}_r \end{array} \right] \tag{4.145}$$

where the column $\underline{u}_r$ contains the first n elements of the eigencolumn $\underline{v}_r$. Consequently, only the upper half of each eigencolumn $\underline{v}_r$ contains the essential information about the free vibration characteristics.

Analogous to the situation for undamped systems, it can be convenient to arrange the columns $\underline{u}_1, \underline{u}_2, ...\underline{u}_{2n}$ in a $(n \times 2n)$ rectangular matrix having the form

$$\underline{U} = [\underline{u}_1 \quad \underline{u}_2 \quad ... \quad \underline{u}_{2n}] \tag{4.146}$$

Correspondingly, the eigencolumns $\underline{v}_1, \underline{v}_2, ..., \underline{v}_{2n}$, can be arranged in a square matrix of order $2n$ having the form

$$\underline{V} = [\underline{v}_1 \ \underline{v}_2 \ ... \ \underline{v}_{2n}] = \begin{bmatrix} \underline{u}_1 & \underline{u}_2 & \cdots & \underline{u}_{2n} \\ s_1\underline{u}_1 & s_2\underline{u}_2 & \cdots & s_{2n}\underline{u}_{2n} \end{bmatrix} \tag{4.147}$$

The matrix $\underline{V}$ can be rewritten in terms of the matrix $\underline{U}$ as follows

$$\underline{V} = \begin{bmatrix} \underline{U} \\ \underline{U} \lceil s_r \rfloor \end{bmatrix} \tag{4.148}$$

where the diagonal matrix $\lceil s_r \rfloor$ is defined by

$$\lceil s_r \rfloor = \begin{bmatrix} s_1 & & 0 \\ & \ddots & \\ 0 & & s_{2n} \end{bmatrix} \tag{4.149}$$

Example 4.6

To illustrate some of the above characteristics we look at the simple 2-dof system shown in Fig. 4.19. It is left to the reader to specify via Lagrange's equations the mass-, stiffness- and damping matrices for this system and to compute subsequently the matrices $\underline{A}$ and $\underline{B}$ of the associated first-order system using (4.130). Now, we will solve the

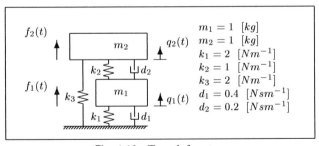

Fig. 4.19 Two-dof system

corresponding eigenvalue problem for two particular choices of the set of system parameters:

1. A general type of damping by taking the mass- and stiffness parameters as indicated in Fig. 4.19, whereas the damping parameters have been assigned the values $d_1 = 1.0 \ [Nsm^{-1}]$ and $d_2 = 0 \ [Nsm^{-1}]$.

2. *A proportionally damped system by taking the mass-, damping-
and stiffness parameters as assigned in Fig. 4.19, except for the
stiffness parameter $k_3 = 0$. It is easy to see that we are dealing
with proportional damping in this case.*

For both systems we can solve the eigenvalue problem, leading to

1. *General damping*

$$s_r : \; [-0.30 \pm 1.50j, -0.20 \mp 1.84j]$$

$$\underline{V} = \begin{bmatrix} 0.07 + 0.42j & 0.23 - 0.36j & 0.24 - 0.18j & 0.29 + 0.07j \\ -0.21 + 0.27j & -0.08 - 0.33j & -0.33 - 0.17j & -0.24 + 0.28j \\ -0.65 - 0.02j & -0.61 - 0.24j & -0.38 - 0.40j & -0.19 + 0.52j \\ -0.35 - 0.39j & -0.47 + 0.22j & -0.25 + 0.64j & -0.48 - 0.50j \end{bmatrix}$$
$$(4.150)$$

2. *Proportional damping*

$$s_r : \; [-0.06 \mp 0.76j, -0.34 \pm 1.82j]$$

$$\underline{V} = \begin{bmatrix} -0.30 + 0.01j & 0.03 - 0.30j & -0.08 - 0.43j & 0.44 + 0.06j \\ -0.73 + 0.02j & 0.07 - 0.73j & 0.03 + 0.18j & -0.18 - 0.02j \\ 0.03 + 0.23j & 0.23 + 0.04j & 0.81 - 0.00j & -0.04 - 0.81j \\ 0.06 + 0.56j & 0.55 + 0.09j & -0.34 + 0.00j & 0.02 + 0.34j \end{bmatrix}$$
$$(4.151)$$

These results exhibit the following typical characteristics:

- *All the eigenvalues appear in complex conjugate pairs.*

- *All the real parts of the eigenvalues are negative meaning that any
  free vibration will show a decreasing amplitude (which should be
  the case for a physically realistic modelling of damping). The fact
  that some of the eigenvalues are not so close to the imaginairy
  axis implies that the system is not extremely weakly damped.*

- *It seems that the eigencolumns do not show up in complex conjugate pairs as was predicted before. However, identical to the undamped eigenvalue problem, these complex eigencolumns are fully
  determined except for any arbitrary (possibly complex) scaling
  factor. So this situation might change if we choose some eigencolumn normalization. Let us choose the normalization where we
  make the first element of each eigencolumn equal to 1.0, just by
  deviding each column by its first element. If these first elements
  are real, they at least automatically fulfil the complex conjugate
  property. Then, this leads to the following eigencolumn matrices
  General damping*

$$\underline{V} = \begin{bmatrix} 1.00 & 1.00 & 1.00 & 1.00 \\ 0.55 + 0.59j & 0.55 - 0.59j & -0.55 - 1.12j & -0.55 + 1.12j \\ -0.30 + 1.50j & -0.30 - 1.50j & -0.20 - 1.84j & -0.20 + 1.84j \\ -1.04 + 0.64j & -1.04 - 0.64j & -1.96 + 1.23j & -1.96 - 1.23j \end{bmatrix}$$
$$(4.152)$$

Proportional damping

$$\underline{V} = \begin{bmatrix} 1.00 & 1.00 & 1.00 & 1.00 \\ 2.41 + 0.00j & 2.41 - 0.00j & -0.41 - 0.00j & -0.41 + 0.00j \\ -0.06 - 0.76j & -0.06 + 0.76j & -0.34 + 1.82j & -0.34 - 1.82j \\ -0.14 - 1.84j & -0.14 + 1.84j & 0.14 - 0.75j & 0.14 + 0.75j \end{bmatrix}$$

$$(4.153)$$

We observe that now the eigencolumns indeed show up in complex conjugate pairs. Also, we can clearly see that the bottom half of each eigencolumn is equal to the top half, multiplied by the corresponding eigenvalue.

- *The relevant top-parts of the eigencolumns for the proportionally damped case are all* **real columns**. *This has already been discussed before in section 4.3.3. It is easy to check that they are indeed identical to the (real) eigencolumns of the undamped system. However, the top-parts of eigencolumns for the generally damped system still are* **complex eigencolumns**. *This means that they cannot automatically be used to create a graphical picture of the free vibration of the system as we did for undamped systems (see for example the undamped three-car carriage system from example 3.1 on page 157).*

  In generally damped systems we will normally be dealing with fully complex eigenmodes which will make the interpretation much more difficult. If we want to illustrate the free vibrational behaviour of such a complex mode pair $\{s_r, \underline{v}_r\}$, we can go back to the fundamental solution

$$\underline{x}(t) = \underline{v}_r \, e^{s_r t} \qquad or \; better \qquad \underline{q}(t) = \underline{u}_r \, e^{s_r t} \qquad (4.154)$$

Hence, we only look at the first (n) elements of the eigencolumn. In reality of course, the displacements of a system should be real quantities, so we just can take and plot the real (or imaginairy) part of (4.154) as a function of time. We will return to this matter in Subsection 4.5.5. Fig. 4.20 shows plots of the real parts of the displacements q_1 and q_2 for the first and the third modes as a function of time for the two damping cases. From this figure we can see that for the proportionally damped system the two degrees of freedom always have an extreme value (or pass through zero) at the same points of time. Consequently, if we take a snapshot of the vibration at any time we will see the eigenmode except for some arbitrary scaling factor.

For the generally damped system this does not hold anymore. The masses do not reach their maximum displacement at the same points of time (and do not pass zero at the same points of time) which means that we will see some beating effect in the vibration. So, for the interpretation of complex eigencolumns we always will

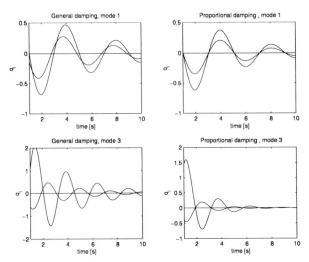

Fig. 4.20   Free vibrational behaviour in first
and third eigenmode

have to create some kind of time history of the free vibration.

*If we look again at the normalized eigenmodes for the generally
damped system, we can see that in this example the "order of being complex" is considerable. This means that also the vibration
of the masses m_1 and m_2 will be far from a synchronous motion
as we can observe in Fig. 4.20. Sometimes however, a representation of the real vibration mode is needed for some reason. This
might be done by just neglecting the imaginairy part of the eigencolumns but in general this is a tricky operation. (See for example
[Kraker-00]). In general however one should be careful in inter-
preting complex eigencolumns.*

Next, we will look at the evolution of the (complex) eigenvalues in the
complex plane (root-loci plot) if we change the overall damping level
by multiplying both viscous damping matrices with one single damping
scale factor α, in the range $0 \leq \alpha \leq 6$. This means that we look at the
variation of the complex eigenvalues if we slowly switch from an undamped system to a heavily damped system. The results are shown in
Fig 4.21. Let us first look at the generally damped system (top plots).
For $\alpha = 0$ we start with 4 eigenvalues on the imaginairy axes (undamped system) and for growing α they move into the left half-plane.
One pair of complex conjugate eigenvalues is going to the real axis for
larger α, becomes critically damped for approximately $\alpha = 3.2$ and then
changes into a pair of real (supercritically damped) eigenvalues. This
can also be seen from the right plot where at some α the imaginairy

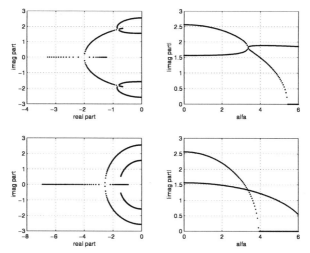

Fig. 4.21   Real(s) versus imag(s) (left plots) and $|imag(s|$
for changing damping scale factor α.
General damping (top) and proportional damping (bottom)

*part of a couple becomes zero. The other couple of complex conjugate
eigenvalues first moves away from the imaginairy axis but then bends
back to it. When α is increasing, the damping in the system will also increase (eigenvalues going to the left) but for larger α the (only) damper
in the system, d_1, will freeze and mass m_1 will become more and more
a fixed point. Then we end up with an undamped mass-spring system
$(m_2, k_2 + k_3)$ with two imaginairy eigenvalues $(\pm\sqrt{3}\ j)$. For generally damped systems these root-loci plots can show all kinds of strange
curves in the complex plane, curves can intersect, etc.*

*For the proportionally damped system we see a much more regular be-
haviour. We start with 4 eigenvalues on the imaginairy axis and with
increasing α they all move on a circle to the real axis. One pair becomes supercritically damped at approximately $\alpha = 5.4$ and subsequently
changes into a pair of real eigenvalues. The other pair still is undercritically damped. That they move on a circle can be explained by
realizing that increasing the damping scale factor α will increase all
dimensionless modal damping factors in the same way (and this proportionally damped system can be decoupled!). So we end up with (n)
decoupled mass-spring-damper systems with increasing modal damping
factor. For the eigenvalues s_i of a one-degree-of-freedom system with
undamped eigenfrequency ω_o and dimensionless damping factor ξ we
can write*

$$s_i = -\xi\omega_o \pm j\omega_o\sqrt{1-\xi^2}, \qquad |s_i| = \omega_o^2$$

Hence, the eigenvalues of a single degree-of-freedom mass-spring-damper system move on a circle when the damping is increased.
We conclude from the foregoing treatment that also the eigenvalues and corresponding eigenmodes of generally damped systems can be calculated in a simple and straightforward way, but that the interpretation of the results can be (much) more complex.

4.5.3   Orthogonality and normalization conditions

As announced already in Subsection 4.5.1, the eigencolumns $\underline{v}_r$, defined in the previous subsection possess the orthogonality property. Its derivation is completely similar to the derivation of the orthogonality property of the eigencolumns for undamped systems in Subsection 3.3.2. So, we consider two distinct solutions s_r, $\underline{v}_r$ and s_s, $\underline{v}_s$ of the eigenvalue problem (4.137) and write the eigenvalue equations for these solutions in the form

$$s_r \, \underline{A} \, \underline{v}_r = -\underline{B} \, \underline{v}_r \tag{4.155}$$

$$s_s \, \underline{A} \, \underline{v}_s = -\underline{B} \, \underline{v}_s \tag{4.156}$$

Premultiplying both sides of (4.155) by $\underline{v}_s^T$ and both sides of (4.156) by $\underline{v}_r^T$, we obtain

$$s_r \, \underline{v}_s^T \underline{A} \, \underline{v}_r = -\underline{v}_s^T \underline{B} \, \underline{v}_r \tag{4.157}$$

$$s_s \, \underline{v}_r^T \underline{A} \, \underline{v}_s = -\underline{v}_r^T \underline{B} \, \underline{v}_s \tag{4.158}$$

Next, we transpose (4.158), recall from Subsection 4.5.1 that the matrices $\underline{A}$ and $\underline{B}$ are symmetric, and subtract the result from (4.157). This yields the following equation

$$(s_r - s_s) \, \underline{v}_s^T \underline{A} \, \underline{v}_r = 0 \tag{4.159}$$

If the eigenvalues s_r and s_s are distinct, i.e. $s_r \neq s_s$, it follows from (4.159) that

$$\underline{v}_s^T \underline{A} \, \underline{v}_r = 0 \quad , \qquad r \neq s \tag{4.160}$$

which is the statement of the *orthogonality condition* of the eigencolumns. We note that the orthogonality is with respect to the system matrix $\underline{A}$. Inserting (4.160) into (4.157), it is easy to see that the eigencolumns are also orthogonal with respect to the system matrix $\underline{B}$

$$\underline{v}_s^T \underline{B} \, \underline{v}_r = 0 \quad , \qquad r \neq s \tag{4.161}$$

In the above discussion the eigenvalues s_r and s_s have been assumed to be distinct. In most practical situations the case of multiple eigenvalues can be treated analogously to the treatment for undamped systems in Subsection 3.3.3. An exception occurs if the so-called nullity does not equal the multiplicity for all the eigenvalues. The reader is referred to Müller & Schiehlen

(1985) for further discussion. The case of multiple eigenvalues will not be discussed here anymore.

Next, we address the *normalization* of the eigencolumns $\underline{v}_r$. It is recalled that in example 4.6 on page 253 we applied a normalization of the eigencolumns by putting the first element of each of those columns equal to one. However, similar to the treatment of normalization of undamped systems in Subsection 3.3.2, an alternative and more general normalization scheme consists of setting

$$\underline{v}_r^T \underline{A}\, \underline{v}_r = a_r \quad , \qquad r = 1, 2, ..., 2n \qquad (4.162)$$

where $a_r (r = 1, 2, ..., 2n)$ are normalization parameters to be selected as desired. In view of the fact that the eigencolumns $\underline{v}_r$ are in general complex, the parameters a_r are in general also complex. Hence, the above normalization scheme in general implies that the real parts of the parameters a_r have to be selected as well as their imaginary parts. An alternative and equally general normalization scheme consists of setting

$$\underline{v}_r^T \underline{B}\, \underline{v}_r = b_r \quad , \qquad r = 1, 2, ..., 2n \qquad (4.163)$$

where $b_r (r = 1, 2, ..., 2n)$ constitute another set of generally complex normalization parameters, whose real and imaginary parts can be selected. It is remarked that the parameters a_r and b_r depend on one another. In fact, taking in (4.157) the index s equal to the index r, we obtain in view of (4.162) and (4.163)

$$b_r = -s_r\, a_r \qquad (4.164)$$

Two frequently used normalization schemes in practice are

$$a_r = \underline{v}_r^T \underline{A}\, \underline{v}_r = 1 \quad \Longrightarrow b_r = -s_r \quad , \qquad r = 1, 2, ..., 2n \qquad (4.165)$$

or, alternatively

$$b_r = \underline{v}_r \underline{B}\, \underline{v}_r = 1 \quad \Longrightarrow a_r = -\frac{1}{s_r} \quad , \qquad r = 1, 2, ..., 2n \qquad (4.166)$$

These normalization schemes imply that all real parts of the complex parameters a_r or b_r have been selected equal to one, whereas their imaginary parts have been selected equal to zero.

Using the matrix of eigencolumns $\underline{V}$, defined by (4.147), we can combine the orthogonality conditions (4.160) and the normalization scheme (4.162) to

$$\underline{V}^T \underline{A}\, \underline{V} = \begin{bmatrix} a_1 & & 0 \\ & \ddots & \\ 0 & & a_{2n} \end{bmatrix} := \lceil a_r \rfloor \qquad (4.167)$$

where the matrix in the right side is a diagonal matrix with the parameters $a_1, \ldots, a_{2n}$ as diagonal elements. In a similar way, the orthogonality conditions (4.161) and the normalization scheme (4.163) can be combined to

$$
\underline{V}^T \underline{B} \, \underline{V} =
\begin{bmatrix}
b_1 & & 0 \\
& \ddots & \\
0 & & b_{2n}
\end{bmatrix}
:= \lceil b_r \rfloor
\tag{4.168}
$$

where the matrix in the right side is a diagonal matrix with the parameters $b_1, \ldots, b_{2n}$ as diagonal elements. Taking account of (4.164), we have the following relationship between the diagonal matrices $\lceil a_r \rfloor$ and $\lceil b_r \rfloor$

$$
\lceil b_r \rfloor = - \lceil s_r \rfloor \lceil a_r \rfloor = - \lceil a_r \rfloor \lceil s_r \rfloor
\tag{4.169}
$$

where the diagonal matrix $\lceil s_r \rfloor$ has been defined earlier in (4.149).

4.5.4   Elaboration of the orthogonality and normalization conditions for undercritically damped systems; stability of the solution

In this subsection the orthogonality and normalization conditions will be further elaborated for undercritically damped systems, resulting in a discussion of the stability of the solution. For undercritically damped systems the eigenvalues s_r are really complex, and together with the eigencolumns $\underline{v}_r$ they can be grouped in complex conjugate pairs, as indicated by (4.141). The stability of the solution is determined by the real parts of the eigenvalues s_r, and it can be concluded from the general shape of the solution, given by (4.136), that the solution is stable if the real parts μ_r of the eigenvalues s_r are all negative. We start the discussion by recalling (4.157), which was obtained from the eigenvalue equations (4.155) by premultiplying both sides by $\underline{v}_s^T$. First, we elaborate the quantity $\underline{v}_s^T \underline{A} \underline{v}_r$ after inserting (4.130) and (4.145) in it, and obtain

$$
\underline{v}_s^T \underline{A} \, \underline{v}_r = \underline{u}_s^T \underline{D} \, \underline{u}_r + (s_r + s_s) \, \underline{u}_s^T \underline{M} \, \underline{u}_r
\tag{4.170}
$$

Next, we insert (4.130) and (4.145) in the quantity $\underline{v}_s^T \underline{B} \, \underline{v}_r$, and obtain after elaboration

$$
\underline{v}_s^T \underline{B} \, \underline{v}_r = \underline{u}_s^T \underline{K} \, \underline{u}_r - s_r s_s \, \underline{u}_s^T \underline{M} \, \underline{u}_r
\tag{4.171}
$$

Now, two cases should be distinguished, namely, $r \neq s$ and $r = s$. In the first case we conclude from (4.170) in view of the orthogonality condition (4.160) that

$$
(s_r + s_s) \, \underline{u}_s^T \underline{M} \, \underline{u}_r = -\underline{u}_s^T \underline{D} \, \underline{u}_r \quad , \qquad r \neq s
\tag{4.172}
$$

and we conclude from (4.171) in view of the orthogonality condition (4.161) that

$$
s_r s_s \underline{u}_s^T \underline{M} \underline{u}_r = \underline{u}_s^T \underline{K} \underline{u}_r \quad , \qquad r \neq s
\tag{4.173}
$$

Considering for undercritically damped systems the particular case that $\underline{u}_s = \bar{\underline{u}}_r$, $s_s = \bar{s}_r$, we obtain from (4.172) and (4.173), using $s_r = \mu_r + j\nu_r$

$$
(s_r + \bar{s}_r) = 2 \, Re \, (s_r) = 2\mu_r = - \frac{\bar{\underline{u}}_r^T \underline{D} \, \underline{u}_r}{\bar{\underline{u}}_r^T \underline{M} \, \underline{u}_r}
\tag{4.174}
$$

$$s_r \bar{s}_r = |s_r|^2 = \mu_r^2 + \nu_r^2 = \frac{\bar{u}_r^T \underline{K} \underline{u}_r}{\bar{u}_r^T \underline{M} \underline{u}_r} \tag{4.175}$$

At this point we decompose $\underline{u}_r$ into its real and imaginary parts and write

$$\underline{u}_r = \underline{ur}_r + j \underline{ui}_r \tag{4.176}$$

where the columns $\underline{ur}_r$ and $\underline{ui}_r$ contain real elements. Inserting (4.176) into the quantity $\underline{u}_r^T \underline{D} \underline{u}_r$, we can write in view of the symmetry of the damping matrix

$$
\begin{aligned}
\bar{u}_r^T \underline{D} \underline{u}_r &= \left(\underline{ur}_r^T + j \underline{ui}_r^T \right) \underline{D} \left(\underline{ur}_r - j \underline{ui}_r \right) \\
&= \underline{ur}_r^T \underline{D} \underline{ur}_r + \underline{ui}_r^T \underline{D} \underline{ui}_r
\end{aligned} \tag{4.177}
$$

We consider *dissipative systems* for which the damping matrix $\underline{D}$ is positive definite and hence we have

$$\underline{ur}_r^T \underline{D} \underline{ur}_r > 0 \quad , \quad \underline{ui}_r^T \underline{D} \underline{ui}_r > 0 \tag{4.178}$$

so that

$$\bar{u}_r^T \underline{D} \underline{u}_r > 0 \tag{4.179}$$

Similarly, it is easy to prove that for systems with a positive-definite mass matrix we have

$$\bar{u}_r^T \underline{M} \underline{u}_r > 0 \tag{4.180}$$

Using (4.179) and (4.180), we conclude from (4.174) that for dissipative systems all exponential damping factors μ_r are negative

$$\mu_r = Re\left(s_r\right) = -\frac{\bar{u}_r^T \underline{D} \underline{u}_r}{2\bar{u}_r^T \underline{M} \underline{u}_r} < 0 \tag{4.181}$$

Hence, the free motions of undercritically damped dissipative systems about an equilibrium configuration are always stable.

Now, let us specify the conditions for generally viscously damped systems to be undercritically damped. To this end, it is convenient to return to the linearized second-order Lagrange's equations of motion, (4.124) with $Q^*(t) = \underline{0}$, and insert in those equations the solution (4.142) for $\underline{q}(t)$. This yields the following eigenvalue problem

$$\left[s_r^2 \underline{M} + s_r \underline{D} + \underline{K} \right] \underline{u}_r = \underline{0} \tag{4.182}$$

which can be shown to be completely equivalent to (4.137). Premultiplying this equation by $\bar{u}_r^T$, we obtain

$$s_r^2 m_r' + s_r d_r' + k_r' = 0 \tag{4.183}$$

with

$$m_r' = \bar{u}_r^T \underline{M} \underline{u}_r \tag{4.184}$$

$$d'_r = \underline{u}_r^T \underline{D}\, \underline{u}_r \tag{4.185}$$

$$k'_r = \underline{\bar{u}}_r^T \underline{K}\, \underline{u}_r \tag{4.186}$$

The quantities m'_r and d'_r have been shown to be real and positive for dissipative systems with a positive definite mass matrix. Similarly, the quantity k'_r can be shown to be real and positive semi-definite. The equation (4.183) can be viewed as the characteristic equation for a single-degree-of-freedom linear system with real mass m'_r, real damping coefficient d'_r and real stiffness coefficient k'_r. The undamped natural frequency of this system is given by

$$\omega_r = \sqrt{k'_r / m'_r} \tag{4.187}$$

while its dimensionless damping factor is

$$\xi_r = \frac{d'_r}{2\sqrt{k'_r m'_r}} \tag{4.188}$$

The roots of the characteristic equation (4.183) can be written as

$$\left\{ \begin{array}{c} (s_r)_1 \\ (s_r)_2 \end{array} \right\} = \left(-\xi_r \pm j\sqrt{1 - \xi_r^2} \right) \omega_r \tag{4.189}$$

and, hence, the system can be considered to be underdamped if $\xi_r < 1$, or, in view of (4.188), if

$$d'_r < 2\sqrt{k'_r m'_r} \quad , \qquad r = 1, 2, ..., n \tag{4.190}$$

After having considered the case $r \neq s$ in (4.170) and (4.171), we next consider the case $r = s$. Inserting (4.170) for $r = s$ into (4.162), we obtain

$$a_r = d_r + 2\, s_r m_r \tag{4.191}$$

where the complex quantity

$$m_r = \underline{u}_r^T \underline{M}\, \underline{u}_r \tag{4.192}$$

is referred to as the r-th *complex modal mass factor*,while the complex quantity

$$d_r = \underline{u}_r^T \underline{D}\, \underline{u}_r \tag{4.193}$$

is called the r-th *complex modal damping factor*. Inserting (4.171) for $s = r$ into (4.163), we obtain

$$b_r = k_r - s_r^2\, m_r \tag{4.194}$$

where the complex quantity

$$k_r = \underline{u}_r^T \underline{K}\, \underline{u}_r \tag{4.195}$$

is referred to as the r-th *complex modal stiffness factor*. The complex modal mass, damping and stiffness factors play an important role in modal analysis of systems with general viscous damping. As can be observed after inserting (4.191) and (4.194) into (4.164), the complex modal mass, damping and stiffness factors are related to one another by the relationship

$$s_r^2\, m_r + s_r\, d_r + k_r = 0 \qquad (4.196)$$

Again, this equation can be viewed as the characteristic equation for a single-degree-of-freedom linear system. However, the physical meaning of this viewpoint is rather limited, because the quantities m_r, d_r and k_r generally are complex. It is left to the reader to verify that the particular cases of weak damping and proportional viscous damping can be considered to be special cases of general viscous damping for which the modal mass, stiffness and damping factors become real quantities. In those cases m_r, d_r and k_r are identical to the quantities m'_r, d'_r and k'_r defined earlier and, hence, (4.196) is then identical to (4.183).

4.5.5   General solution of the free response

After having discussed and elaborated the eigenvalue problem for linear systems with general viscous damping in the preceding subsections, we wish to determine the associated general solution of the free damped motions. The $2n$ eigencolumns $\underline{v}_r (r = 1, 2, ..., 2n)$ associated with the eigenvalue problem (4.137) form a linearly independent set, implying that any $2n$-dimensional column in the state space spanned by the generalized coordinates q and the generalized velocities $\dot{q}$ can be constructed as a linear combination of these eigencolumns. Physically this implies that any motion $\underline{x}(t) = \left[\underline{q}^T(t)\, ,\, \underline{\dot{q}}^T(t) \right]^T$ of the system can be regarded at any given time as a superposition of the eigencolumns multiplied by appropriate constants, where the constants are a measure of the degree of participation of each eigencolumn in the motion. This corresponds completely to the general solution of the free undamped motions discussed in Subsection 3.4. Because the solution $\underline{x}(t)$ is time dependent, the coefficients of the eigencolumns appearing in the superposition are also time dependent. Denoting these coefficients $\eta_r(t)\,(r = 1, 2, \ldots, 2n)$, we can write

$$\underline{x}(t) = \eta_1(t)\, \underline{v}_1 + \eta_2(t)\, \underline{v}_2 + \ldots + \eta_{2n}(t)\, \underline{v}_{2n} \qquad (4.197)$$

or

$$\underline{x}(t) = \sum_{r=1}^{2n} \underline{v}_r\, \eta_r(t) = \underline{V}\, \underline{\eta}(t) \qquad (4.198)$$

where $\underline{V}$ is recognized as the square matrix of eigencolumns $\underline{v}_1, \underline{v}_2, ..., \underline{v}_{2n}$ defined earlier by (4.147), while $\underline{\eta}(t)$ is a column containing the functions $\eta_r(t)$ $(r = 1, 2, \ldots 2n)$. Equation (4.198) can be regarded as a linear transformation relating the columns $\underline{x}(t)$ and $\underline{\eta}(t)$ where the transformation matrix $\underline{V}$ is constant. Inserting (4.198) into (4.135) and premultiplying the resulting set of equations by $\underline{V}^T$, we obtain

$$\underline{V}^T \underline{A} \ \underline{V} \ \underline{\dot{\eta}}(t) + \underline{V}^T \underline{B} \ \underline{V} \ \underline{\eta}(t) = \underline{0} \tag{4.199}$$

Taking account of the orthogonality relationships and the normalization schemes, (4.167) and (4.168), and additionally of (4.169), we arrive at the following two sets of $2n$ *uncoupled* equations

$$\dot{\eta}_r(t) - s_r \ \eta_r(t) = 0 \quad , \quad r = 1, 2, ..., 2n \tag{4.200}$$

The new variables $\eta_r(t)$ $(r = 1, 2, ..., 2n)$ can be considered as being a new set of coordinates of the system in the state-space formulation. As for undamped system, these coordinates are referred to as the *natural coordinates* or the *normal coordinates* because they decouple the equations of motion (4.135). In this way, the above decoupling procedure for systems with general viscous camping can be considered to be a generalization of the decoupling procedure for undamped systems which was discussed in Subsection 3.3.4. The solutions of (4.200) can simply be written in exponential form as

$$\eta_r(t) = C_r \ e^{s_r t} \quad , \quad r = 1, 2, ..., 2n \tag{4.201}$$

where C_r $(r = 1, 2, ..., 2n)$ are complex constants of integration. Of course, the time-dependent parts of (4.201) are completely consistent with the exponential form appearing in (4.136). Inserting (4.201) back into the transformation equation (4.197), we obtain

$$\underline{x}(t) = \sum_{r=1}^{2n} \underline{v}_r \ \eta_r(t) = \sum_{r=1}^{2n} C_r \ \underline{v}_r \ e^{s_r t} \tag{4.202}$$

Utilizing the partitioning of $\underline{x}(t)$ defined in (4.127) and the associated partitioning of $\underline{v}_r$ defined in (4.144), we conclude that the solution for the original generalized coordinates $\underline{q}(t)$ can be written as follows

$$\underline{q}(t) = \sum_{r=1}^{2n} \underline{u}_r \ \eta_r(t) = \sum_{r=1}^{2n} C_r \ \underline{u}_r \ e^{s_r t} \tag{4.203}$$

Now, we will further elaborate the solution (4.203) for $\underline{q}(t)$ for the particular case of undercritically damped systems. For those systems the eigenvalues s_r are really complex quantities and together with the eigencolumns $\underline{v}_r$ they can be grouped in complex conjugate pairs, as indicated by (4.141). This means that in the case of undercritically damped systems the solution (4.203) for $\underline{q}(t)$ can be rewritten as

$$\underline{q}(t) = \sum_{r=1}^{n} \left(C_r \ \underline{u}_r \ e^{s_r t} + C_r^* \ \underline{\bar{u}}_r \ e^{\bar{s}_r t} \right) \tag{4.204}$$

where C_r^* $(r = 1, 2, \ldots, n)$ are new complex constants of integration which are related to the complex constants $C_{n+1}, \ldots .C_{2n}$ in (4.201) by

$$C_r^* = C_{n+r} \quad , \quad r = 1, 2, \ldots, n \tag{4.205}$$

Because all generalized coordinates contained in the column $\underline{q}(t)$ are real quantities, by definition, the column $\underline{q}(t)$ should be real for all possible values of t. This can only be achieved if in the right-hand side of (4.204) the term $\{C_r^* \bar{\underline{u}}_r \exp(\bar{s}_r t)\}$ is the complex conjugate of the term $\{C_r \underline{u}_r \exp(s_r t)\}$. Using repeatedly the theorem that the complex conjugated of a product is equal to the product of the complex conjugates, we conclude that C_r^* is the complex conjugate of C_r

$$C_r^* = \bar{C}_r \quad , \quad r = 1, 2, \ldots, n \tag{4.206}$$

Decomposing C_r into its real and imaginary parts as follows

$$C_r = A_r + jB_r \tag{4.207}$$

and utilizing the decompositions of $\underline{u}$ and s_r defined earlier in (4.176) and (4.141), we can express the solution (4.204) for $\underline{q}(t)$ in terms of real quantities after some elaboration as follows

$$\underline{q}(t) = \sum_{r=1}^{n} e^{\mu_r t} [\{A_r^* \cos(\nu_r t) + B_r^* \sin(\nu_r t)\} \underline{ur}_r \tag{4.208}$$

$$+ \{B_r^* \cos(\nu_r t) - A_r^* \sin(\nu_r t)\} \underline{ui}_r]$$

where A_r^* and B_r^* are new real constants, which are related to A_r and B_r by

$$A_r^* = 2A_r \quad , \quad B_r^* = -2B_r \tag{4.209}$$

The general solution (4.208) represents a superposition of damped free vibrations. In view of (4.189) the damped eigenfrequencies are given by

$$\nu_r = \omega_r \sqrt{1 - \xi_r^2} \quad , \quad r = 1, 2, ..., n \tag{4.210}$$

where $\omega_r (r = 1, 2, ..., n)$ are the corresponding undamped eigenfrequencies while $\xi_r (r = 1, 2, ..., n)$ are the dimensionless damping factors, defined by (4.188). The exponential damping factors μ_r are given by

$$\mu_r = -\xi_r \omega_r \tag{4.211}$$

The constants A_r^* and B_r^* in (4.208) can be determined from the initial conditions $\underline{q}(0) = \underline{q}_o$ and $\dot{\underline{q}}(0) = \dot{\underline{q}}_o$. The most convenient way to do this in to collect $\underline{q}_o$ and $\dot{\underline{q}}_o$ in the state column $\underline{x}(0) = \begin{bmatrix} \underline{q}_o^T , \dot{\underline{q}}_o^T \end{bmatrix}^T$ and to premultiply (4.202) for $t = 0$ by $\underline{v}_s^T \underline{A}$. Utilizing the orthogonality relationship (4.160) and the normalization scheme (4.162), we obtain

$$C_s = \frac{1}{a_s} \underline{v}_s^T \underline{A} \, \underline{x}(0) \quad , \quad s = 1, 2, ..., n \tag{4.212}$$

and, using (4.207) and (4.209)

$$A_s^* = 2\ Re\ (C_s) \quad , \quad B_s^* = 2\ Im\ (C_s) \tag{4.213}$$

As we have seen in Section 4.3, for systems with weak damping and proportional viscous damping the eigencolumns $\underline{u}_r$ are approximately or exactly real and, hence, for these systems $\underline{ui}_r = \underline{0}, r = 1, 2, ..., n$. Inserting this into (4.208), we conclude that for systems with weak damping and proportional viscous damping the general solution for the free response takes the form

$$\underline{q}(t) = \sum_{r=1}^{n} e^{\mu_r t}\ \underline{ur}_r \left\{ A_r^* \cos\left(\nu_r t\right) + B_r^* \sin\left(\nu_r t\right) \right\} \tag{4.214}$$

or

$$\underline{q}(t) = \sum_{r=1}^{n} e^{\mu_r t}\ \underline{ur}_r\ A_r' \cos\left(\nu_r t + \varphi_r\right) \tag{4.215}$$

where A_r' and φ_r are new real constants. Considering the solutions represented by (4.214) or (4.215) for one specific value of r, i.e. considering the solution associated with one specific eigenfrequency ν_r, this solution represents *synchronous motion*. This implies that if a system with weak damping or proportional viscous damping moves in an eigenvibration, there is no phase shift between the different generalized coordinates during the motion. This situations changes for systems with general viscous damping. To show this, we consider the solution (4.208) for one specific value of r and select the initial conditions in such a way that the value of the constant B_r^* in this vibration mode is zero. This yields the following modal solution

$$\underline{q}_r(t) = A_r^*\ e^{\mu_r t} \left\{ \underline{ur}_r \cos\left(\nu_r t\right) - \underline{ui}_r \sin\left(\nu_r t\right) \right\} \tag{4.216}$$

Now, the solution alternates between a solution which is completely proportional to $\underline{ur}_r$ at $(\nu_r t) = 0, \pi, 2\pi, ...$, and a solution which is completely proportional to $\underline{ui}_r$ at $(\nu_r t) = \frac{\pi}{2}, \frac{3\pi}{2}, \frac{5\pi}{2}, ...$. The corresponding motion does *not* represent synchronous motion anymore.

The above conclusions are completely consistent with the findings in example 4.6 from page 253.

4.5.6   Forced response via decoupling of the equations of motion

Until sofar, we have confined ourselves to the damped free vibrations of multidegree-of-freedom linear systems with general viscous damping and symmetric matrices. In this section we consider the forced response of those systems. Recalling (4.129), we can represent the system differential equations of motion in the state-space formulation as

$$\underline{A}\ \underline{\dot{x}}(t) + \underline{B}\ \underline{x}(t) = \underline{r}(t) \tag{4.217}$$

where the state column $\underline{x}(t)$ contains the original generalized coordinates $\underline{q}(t)$ and the associated generalized velocities $\underline{\dot{q}}(t)$, while $\underline{A}$ and $\underline{B}$ are $(2n \times 2n)$ symmetric system matrices composed of the mass, damping and stiffness matrices of the original system, whereas the column matrix $\underline{r}(t)$ contains the generalized forces $\underline{Q}(t)$ of the original system and is supplemented with zero elements. As for undamped, weakly damped, and proportionally damped systems, we determine the forced response by transforming the set of *simultaneous* or *coupled* equations (4.217) to a set of *independent* or *uncoupled* differential equations of motion. In fact, the same transformation can be applied as used in the previous subsection for the free response to arbitrary initial excitation. This implies that we expand the solution $\underline{x}(t)$ as a superposition of eigencolumns and write, identical to (4.198)

$$\underline{x}(t) = \sum_{r=1}^{2n} \underline{v}_r \ \eta_r \ (t) = \underline{V} \ \underline{\eta}(t) \tag{4.218}$$

where $\underline{V}$ is the square matrix of eigencolumns $\underline{v}_1, \underline{v}_2, ..., \underline{v}_{2n}$, while the column $\underline{\eta}(t)$ contains the functions $\eta_1(t)$, $\eta_2(t), ..., \eta_{2n}(t)$. These functions can be considered to constitute a new set of $2n$ state coordinates. To be able to write the solution of (4.217) in the form of (4.218), or, put in other words, to be able to apply the linear transformation defined by (4.218), we must first solve the eigenvalue problem associated with the matrices $\underline{A}$ and $\underline{B}$, which is expressed by the set of algebraic equations (4.137), where the eigencolums $\underline{v}_r$ satisfy the orthogonality and normalization conditions (4.160)-(4.164). Introducing the transformation (4.218) into the state equations of motion (4.217) and premultiplying the resulting set of equations by $\underline{V}^T$, we obtain

$$\underline{V}^T \underline{A} \ \underline{V} \ \underline{\dot{\eta}}(t) + \underline{V}^T \underline{B} \ \underline{V} \ \underline{\eta}(t) = \underline{V}^T \ \underline{r}(t) \tag{4.219}$$

Using the special composition of $\underline{V}$, defined in (4.148), and the partitioning of $\underline{r}(t)$, defined in (4.131), we can express the right-hand side of (4.219) as follows

$$\underline{V}^T \underline{r}(t) = \underline{U}^T \underline{Q} \ (t) \tag{4.220}$$

In Subsection 4.5.3, the matrices $\underline{V}^T \underline{A} \ \underline{V}$ and $\underline{V}^T \underline{B} \ \underline{V}$ have been proven to be diagonal, their composition being defined by (4.167) and (4.168). Consequently, the transformed equations of motion (4.219) appear to be independent. Substituting (4.167), (4.168) and (4.220) into (4.219) and taking account of (4.169), we arrive at the following set of $2n$ *uncoupled* equations

$$a_r \ \{\dot{\eta}_r(t) - s_r \ \eta_r(t)\} = N_r(t) \quad , \quad r = 1, 2, ..., 2n \tag{4.221}$$

where

$$N_r(t) = \underline{u}_r^T \ \underline{Q}(t) \quad , \quad r = 1, 2, ..., 2n \tag{4.222}$$

are the generalized forces in the decoupled state equations associated with the state coordinates $\eta_r(t)$. Because the new state coordinates $\eta_r(t)$ decouple the equations of motion, they are referred to as *natural coordinates* or as *normal coordinates* as in the preceding subsection. This terminology can also be understood to some extend by noticing that it follows from (4.221) and (4.222) that if $Q^*(t)$ acts "in the direction" of $\underline{u}_r$, i.e. $\underline{u}_s^T Q^*(t) = 0$ if $s \neq r$, then only the coordinate $\eta_r(t)$ contributes to the forced response. Because (4.221) has the same structure as the differential equation of motion of a single-degree-of-freedom first-order system, the general solution of (4.221) can be obtained quite easily. Only the steady-state response to harmonic excitation will be discussed in the following subsection because of its importance. Further it is remarked that the initial conditions for $\underline{x}(t)$, i.e. $\underline{x}(0) = \left[\underline{q}^T(0) , \dot{\underline{q}}^T(0)\right]^T = \underline{x}_0$, can be transformed to initial conditions for $\underline{\eta}(t)$ by premultiplying (4.218) by $\underline{V}^T \underline{A}$, and taking account of (4.167). In this way we obtain the initial modal state coordinates for nonzero a_r values in the form

$$\underline{\eta}(0) = \lceil 1/a_r \rfloor \ \underline{V}^T \underline{A} \ \underline{x}_0 \tag{4.223}$$

4.5.7 Steady-state response to harmonic excitation; the transfer function matrix

In the case of harmonic excitation the column matrix of generalized coordinates $\underline{Q}(t)$ in (4.222) has the form

$$\underline{Q}(t) = Re\left\{\hat{\underline{Q}} \ e^{j\Omega t}\right\} \tag{4.224}$$

where Ω is the excitation frequency and $\hat{\underline{Q}}$ is a column with constant known complex excitations amplitudes. Inserting (4.224) into (4.222), we can write the generalized forces $N_r(t)$ as

$$N_r(t) = Re\left\{\hat{N}_r e^{j\Omega t}\right\} \tag{4.225}$$

with

$$N_r(t) = \underline{u}_r^T \hat{\underline{Q}} \tag{4.226}$$

Inserting (4.225) into (4.221), we obtain the following steady-state solution for the modal state coordinates $\eta(t)$

$$\eta_r(t) = Re\left\{\hat{\eta}_r \ e^{j\Omega t}\right\} \tag{4.227}$$

with

$$\hat{\eta}_r = \frac{\hat{N}_r}{a_r\,(j\Omega - s_r)} = \frac{\underline{u}_r^T \ \hat{\underline{Q}}}{a_r\,(j\Omega - s_r)} \tag{4.228}$$

Now, the steady-state response of $\underline{q}(t)$ to harmonic excitation can be obtained by considering the first n elements of the column $\underline{x}(t)$. It is most convenient to consider the relevant subset of (4.218) and write

$$\underline{q}(t) = \sum_{r=1}^{2n} \underline{u}_r \ \eta_r(t) = \underline{U} \ \underline{\eta}(t) \tag{4.229}$$

Substituting (4.227) into (4.229) and using (4.228), we can write

$$\underline{q}(t) = Re\left\{\hat{\underline{q}}\ e^{j\Omega t}\right\} \tag{4.230}$$

with

$$\hat{\underline{q}} = \sum_{r=1}^{2n} \frac{\underline{u}_r\ \underline{u}_r^T}{a_r\ (j\Omega - s_r)}\ \hat{\underline{Q}} \tag{4.231}$$

As usual, the *(complex) transfer function matrix* $\underline{H}(\Omega)$ is defined to relate $\hat{\underline{Q}}$ to $\hat{\underline{q}}$

$$\hat{\underline{q}} = \underline{H}(\Omega)\ \hat{\underline{Q}} \tag{4.232}$$

By comparing (4.231) and (4.232) we conclude that the (complex) transfer function matrix $\underline{H}(\Omega)$ for systems with general viscous damping and symmetric system matrices is given by

$$\underline{H}(\Omega) = \sum_{r=1}^{2n} \frac{\underline{u}_r\ \underline{u}_r^T}{a_r\ (j\Omega - s_r)} \tag{4.233}$$

In this expression s_r is the $r-th$ complex eigenvalue resulting from the eigenvalue problem (4.137), $\underline{u}_r$ is the accompanying eigencolumn related to $\underline{q}(t)$, whereas a_r is the $r-th$ normalization parameter, which has been earlier defined by

$$a_r = \underline{v}_r^T \underline{A}\ \underline{v}_r \tag{4.234}$$

The (complex) transfer function matrix $\underline{H}(\Omega)$ is also referred to as the matrix of frequency-response functions (in abbreviated notation: FRF matrix). It is remarked that in stead of using (4.233), we can also determine the FRF matrix from

$$\underline{H}(\Omega) = \left[\underline{K} + j\ \Omega\ \underline{D} - \Omega^2\ \underline{M}\right]^{-1} \tag{4.235}$$

If we wish to determine amplitude-frequency plots using (4.235), we have to invert the matrix $\left[\underline{K} + j\Omega\underline{D} - \Omega^2\underline{M}\right]$ for a sufficiently large number of discrete frequencies Ω over the whole range of excitation frequencies Ω that is to be investigated.

If we use, alternatively, (4.233), we first have to solve the eigenvalue problem for generally damped systems and then compose (4.233) from the obtained results. For systems with a relatively large number of degrees of freedom (say, $n > 100$) this may result in a more efficient computational procedure.

Also, the expression (4.233) can be used as a basis for reduction of the number of generalized coordinates of a system. Suppose, a system with many degrees of freedom is excited harmonically in a certain frequency range which has an upper bound Ω_u. Now, if in the sum of (4.233) s_r is far outside this range (in the sense that $|s_r - j\Omega| \gg 0$), we expect that the associated modal contribution can be neglected. Hence, it is to be expected that from a practical point of view only a limited number of columns $\underline{u}_r$ and eigenvalues s_r need to be taken into account. We will not address the subject of reduction of the number of generalized coordinates of generally damped systems here, but refer to the literature, see [Kraker/Campen-96, Kraker/Campen-97].

The matrix of frequency-response functions $\underline{H}(\Omega)$ plays an important role in *experimental modal analysis*. Experimental modal analysis is concerned with obtaining knowledge about the modal characteristics of systems by means of experimental investigations that yield information about $\underline{H}(\Omega)$. In some modal analysis literature a so-called *residue matrix* $\underline{R}_r$ is introduced which is defined as

$$\underline{R}_r = \frac{\underline{u}_r \, \underline{u}_r^T}{a_r} \tag{4.236}$$

It is important to notice from (4.236) that the $l-th$ column $\underline{r}_{\ell,r}$ of the matrix of residues $\underline{R}_r$ is proportional to the associated eigencolumn $\underline{u}_r$

$$\underline{r}_{\ell,r} = \frac{\underline{u}_r \, u_r \, [\ell]}{a_r} := \alpha_\ell \underline{u}_r \tag{4.237}$$

where $\underline{u}_r \, [\ell]$ is the $\ell - th$ element of the eigencolumn $\underline{u}_r$ and α_ℓ can be considered to be a scaling factor. Using (4.236), we can express the matrix of frequency-response functions, given by (4.233), as

$$\underline{H}(\Omega) = \sum_{r=1}^{2n} \frac{\underline{R}_r}{(j\Omega - s_r)} \tag{4.238}$$

The elements $r\,[i,j]$ of the residue matrices $\underline{R}_r$, together with the eigenvalues s_r are sometimes referred to as the modal parameters of the system. For undercritically damped systems these parameters are usually being decomposed into their real and imaginary parts, i.e. we write

$$\underline{R}_r = \underline{R}_r^R + j \, \underline{R}_r^I \quad , \qquad s_r = \mu_r + j\nu_r \tag{4.239}$$

Inserting (4.239) into (4.238), we can express the matrix of frequency-response functions for undercritically damped systems in the well-known form

$$\underline{H}(\Omega) = \sum_{r=1}^{2n} \frac{\underline{R}_r^R + j \, \underline{R}_r^I}{-\mu_r + j\,(\Omega - \nu_r)} \tag{4.240}$$

We will not elaborate experimental modal analysis here any further and we will return to the subject of experimental determination of frequency-response functions in the following Chapter.

A final remark with respect to the matrix of frequency-response functions in this subsection is that the expression for the FRF matrix of weakly and proportionally damped systems, derived earlier in Subsection 4.3.3, see (4.95), should appear also as a special case of (4.233). For those special cases of damping the eigencolumns $\underline{u}_r$ have been shown to be real, implying that

$$\bar{\underline{u}}_r = \underline{u}_r \tag{4.241}$$

Considering (as in Subsection 4.3.4) undercritically damped systems, it then follows from (4.174) that for these special cases of damping we have

$$\underline{u}_r^T \underline{D} \, \underline{u}_r = -(s_r + \bar{s}_r) \, \underline{u}_r^T \underline{M} \, \underline{u}_r = -(s_r + \bar{s}_r) \, m_r \qquad (4.242)$$

Inserting this relationship into (4.170) and recalling that for undercritically damped systems s_r can be written as $s_r = \mu_r + j\nu_r$, we obtain

$$a_r = (s_r - \bar{s}_r) \, m_r = 2 \, j \, \nu_r \, m_r \qquad (4.243)$$

Because for undercritically damped systems the eigencolumns $\underline{u}_r$ and the eigenvalues s_r appear in complex conjugate pairs, (4.233) for the FRF matrix can be rewritten for those systems as

$$\underline{H}(\Omega) = \sum_{r=1}^{n} \left\{ \frac{\underline{u}_r \, \underline{u}_r^T}{a_r \, (j\Omega - s_r)} + \frac{\bar{\underline{u}}_r \bar{\underline{u}}_r^T}{a_r \, (j\Omega - \bar{s}_r)} \right\} \qquad (4.244)$$

Using (4.241) and (4.243), we can express the transfer function matrix $\underline{H}(\Omega)$, specified by (4.244), as follows

$$\underline{H}(\Omega) = \sum_{r=1}^{n} \frac{\underline{u}_r \, \underline{u}_r^T}{m_r \, (\omega_r^2 - \Omega^2 - 2j\mu_r\Omega)} \qquad (4.245)$$

with

$$\omega_r^2 = \nu_r^2 + \mu_r^2 \qquad (4.246)$$

Indeed, taking account of (4.210) and (4.211), (4.245) is completely identical to (4.95) obtained earlier for systems with weak damping and proportional viscous damping.

Example 4.7

It follows from the structure of the FRF matrix $\underline{H}(\Omega)$, given by (4.233) that, except for the frequency and amplitude of the external excitation, the (generally complex) eigenvalues s_r and the (generally complex) eigenmodes $\underline{u}_r$ fully determine the final response of the system. This can help us with the interpretation and understanding of calculated frequency-response functions. To illustrate this we calculate the FRF's for the system shown in Fig. 4.19 of example 4.6 on page 253). We assume a unit harmonic force $f_2(t) = \cos(\Omega t)$ acting in the generalized coordinate q_2, so that $f_1(t) = 0$. Fig. 4.22 depicts the computed frequency-response functions for both the more generally damped and the proportionally damped system. Some aspects to be observed from these plots are:

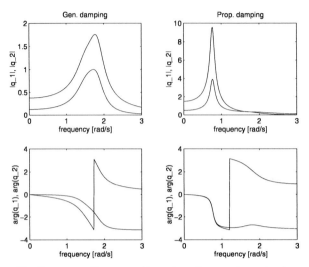

Fig. 4.22   Frequency Response Functions for a unit-excitation
in degree-of-freedom q_2

- *Both the more generally damped and the proportionally damped system possess two undercritically damped eigenvalues, but in the amplitude plots for both types of damping only one mode seems to be present.*

- *The skewness of the amplitude plot for the more generally damped system seems to indicate that we are dealing with two rather close modes.*

- *The relatively small bump in one of the phase curves for the proportionally damped system also suggests some mode to be present there.*

It is remarked that plots of frequency-response functions for moderately damped systems generally have to be handled with care.

4.5.8   Forced response evaluation by means of MATLAB

The state-space formulation of the differential equations of motion for multi-degree-of-freedom linear systems with general viscous damping, given in Subsection 4.5.1 cannot only be used advantageously for decoupling the equations of motion, but also for direct numerical computation of the forced response by means of a commercial software package like **MATLAB** . From a computational point of view the number of degrees of freedom of the systems for which the response is to be evaluated in this way should be sufficiently small, say, less than about 100.

In this subsection we will consider some aspects associated with the direct numerical computation of the forced response using the **MATLAB** software programme. In **MATLAB** a formulation of the state-space equations of motion is used that is common in system analysis and control engineering. This formulation of the equations of motion in first-order form has already been mentioned earlier in Subsection 4.5.1, and we simply recall (4.132)

$$\dot{\underline{x}}(t) = \hat{\underline{A}} \, \underline{x}(t) + \hat{\underline{B}} \, \underline{u}(t) \qquad (4.247)$$

In (4.247) $\underline{x}(t)$ is the column of state variables, defined by (4.127)

$$\underline{x}(t) = \left[\begin{array}{c} \underline{q}(t) \\ \dot{\underline{q}}(t) \end{array} \right] \qquad (4.248)$$

while the column $\underline{u}(t)$ contains the so-called inputs and is identical to the column of excitations $\underline{Q}(t)$, so that

$$\underline{u}(t) = \underline{Q}(t) \qquad (4.249)$$

Further, in (4.247) the matrices $\hat{\underline{A}}$ and $\hat{\underline{B}}$ are system matrices. It is remarked that in **MATLAB** for those matrices the notations $\underline{A}$ and $\underline{B}$ are used. However, we assigned the latter notations already to the symmetric system matrices of the alternative state-space formulation given in Subsection 4.5.1, see (4.129). We have seen before, see(4.134), that the system matrices $\hat{\underline{A}}$ and $\hat{\underline{B}}$ in the set of first-order equations (4.247) can be expressed directly in terms of the (standard) system matrices $\underline{M}, \quad \underline{D}$ and $\underline{K}$, as used in the original set of second-order equations (4.124), namely

$$\hat{\underline{A}} = \left[\begin{array}{cc} \underline{0} & \underline{I} \\ -\underline{M}^{-1}\underline{K} & -\underline{M}^{-1}\underline{D} \end{array} \right] ; \qquad \hat{\underline{B}} = \left[\begin{array}{c} \underline{0} \\ \underline{M}^{-1} \end{array} \right] \qquad (4.250)$$

In **MATLAB** the user has the freedom to select an arbitrary linear combination of the elements of the state column $\underline{x}(t)$ and the elements of the input- or excitation column $\underline{u}(t)$ as so-called *outputs*, denoted by the column $\underline{y}(t)$, so that

$$\underline{y}(t) = \hat{\underline{C}} \, \underline{x}(t) + \hat{\underline{D}} \, \underline{u}(t) \qquad (4.251)$$

In (4.251) the matrices $\hat{\underline{C}}$ and $\hat{\underline{D}}$ are additional system matrices for which in **MATLAB** the notations $\underline{C}$ and $\underline{D}$ are used. In order to avoid confusion, in particular with respect to the already used notation for the damping matrix, we assigned the former notations to those matrices.

It is remarked that in problems from the field of dynamics and vibrations very often the matrix $\hat{\underline{D}}$ is selected to contain only zeros, whereas the matrix $\hat{\underline{C}}$ is chosen to have a structure of zeros and ones, allowing for a selection of specific elements of the column $\underline{x}(t)$, i.e. a specific selection of responses, to be monitored.

Once the system matrices $\hat{A}$ and $\hat{B}$ have been determined and the matrices $\hat{C}$ and $\hat{D}$ have been defined, specific system characteristics can be evaluated by means of **MATLAB** , using a (large) number of available subroutines and starting from a given set of initial conditions $\underline{x}(0)^T = \left[\underline{q}(0)^T \ , \ \underline{\dot{q}}(0)^T\right]$. Examples of such system characteristics are:

- frequency response functions

- step response, impulse response

- response to external excitation

Example 4.8

To illustrate the above procedure in a forced vibration analysis of an arbitrarily damped system we look at the dynamical behaviour of a passenger car when passing a so-called traffic bump (this obstacle is also referred to as a Sleeping Policeman. In Fig. 4.23 a simple (2-dof) model is shown of the car engine system. It consists of mass m_1 (the car) and mass m_2 (the engine) connected to one another by the linear spring k_2 and the viscous damper d_2. Moreover, the connection between the car and the road has been modelled via a linear spring k_1 in parallel with a linear viscous damper d_1. The excitation exerted by the road has been modelled as the prescibed coordinate $q_o(t)$.

We use the numerical values $m_1 = 1000 \ [kg]$, $m_2 = 300 \ [kg]$, $k_1 = 2.0 \ 10^5 \ [Nm^{-1}]$, $k_2 = 5.0 \ 10^4 \ [Nm^{-1}]$, $d_1 = 1000 \ [Nsm^{-1}]$, $d_2 = 200 \ [Nsm^{-1}]$. The traffic bump has been modelled as

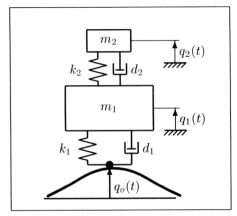

Fig. 4.23   Car model excited by Sleeping Policeman

$$q_o(t) = 0.05[1 - \cos(2\pi t/T_b)] \qquad 0 \leq t \leq T_b$$
$$q_o(t) = 0 \qquad\qquad\qquad\qquad t < 0 \quad and \quad t > T_b \qquad (4.252)$$

where the bump height is 5 [cm] and T_b [s] is the time duration of the bump. For a constant vehicle speed V this defines the length l_b of the bump and for a constant bump length this scales the speed of the vehicle, where $l_b = V T_b$. We can write the set of differential equations for the system as

$$\underline{M}\,\ddot{\underline{q}}(t) \; + \; \underline{D}\,\dot{\underline{q}}(t) \; + \; \underline{K}\,\underline{q}(t) \; = \; \underline{Q}(t) \qquad (4.253)$$

where

$$\underline{q}(t) = \left[\begin{array}{c} q_1(t) \\ q_2(t) \end{array} \right] \qquad (4.254)$$

while the system matrices $\underline{M}$, $\underline{D}$ and $\underline{K}$ are given by

$$\underline{M} = \left[\begin{array}{cc} m_1 & 0 \\ 0 & m_2 \end{array} \right]; \; \underline{D} = \left[\begin{array}{cc} d_1 + d_2 & -d_2 \\ -d_2 & d_2 \end{array} \right]; \; \underline{K} = \left[\begin{array}{cc} k_1 + k_2 & -k_2 \\ -k_2 & k_2 \end{array} \right] \qquad (4.255)$$

whereas the excitation column $\underline{Q}(t)$ can be expressed as

$$\underline{Q}(t) := \left[\begin{array}{c} f(t) \\ 0 \end{array} \right] = \left[\begin{array}{c} k_1\,q_o(t) + d_1\,\dot{q}_o(t) \\ 0 \end{array} \right] \qquad (4.256)$$

The bump (the prescribed displacement $q_o(t)$) has been modelled as given in (4.252), so that the excitation function $f(t)$ becomes

$$f(t) = k_1\,0.05[1 - \cos(2\pi t/T_b)] + d_1\,\frac{0.1\pi}{T_b}\sin(2\pi t/T_b) \qquad (4.257)$$

First, we study the undamped free vibrational behaviour, leading to

$$\begin{array}{ll} \omega_1 = 10.39\,[rad/s], & (f_1 = 1.65\,[Hz]) \\ \omega_2 = 17.57\,[rad/s], & (f_2 = 2.80\,[Hz]) \end{array}; \; \underline{U} = \left[\begin{array}{cc} 0.33 & 0.65 \\ 0.94 & -0.76 \end{array} \right] \qquad (4.258)$$

It is easy to see that the matrix $\underline{U}^T \underline{D}\,\underline{U}$ is not diagonal in this case, so we are not dealing with proportional damping. However, the matrix is diagonal dominant. Therefore we calculate estimates for the dimensionless modal damping factors from the diagonal terms, giving

$$\xi_1 = 2.4\,\%, \qquad \xi_2 = 3.9\,\% \qquad (4.259)$$

Hence, the system is only weakly damped.

For the calculation of the response we use the state-space formulation and also switch to the standard **MATLAB** *terminology. In this two-degree-of-freedom problem we have only a single excitation function $f(t)$ and $\underline{Q}^T(t) = [f(t)\ ,\ 0]$. So, we can define a column of excitation* *functions $\underline{u}(t)$ we have $\underline{u}(t) = [f(t)]$. Now, the following remarks can be made with respect to the excitation column, the system matrices and the output matrices*

- *The excitation column $\underline{u}(t)$ has only one element, namely the excitation function $f(t)$, so that $\underline{u}(t)$ is the (1×1) column $[f(t)]$.*

- *Because the (only) excitation is associated with the first generalized coordinate $\underline{x}[1] = q_1$, the matrix $\hat{\underline{B}}$ is just the first column of the matrix $\begin{bmatrix} O \\ M^{-1} \end{bmatrix}$.*

- *We want to plot all the elements of the state-space column (displacements as well as velocities). Hence, the matrix $\hat{\underline{C}}$ will be the (4×4) identity matrix.*

- *There is not a direct effect of the excitation $\underline{u}(t)$ on the chosen output $\underline{y}(t)$, so that the matrix $\hat{\underline{D}}$ will be a (4×1) null matrix.*

For the calculation of the response of this system to the given excitation and zero initial conditions $(\dot{\underline{x}}(t = 0) = \underline{x}(t = 0) = \underline{0})$ we take the following steps:

- *Select the total response time T (based on the period times corresponding to the eigenfrequencies) and choose the number of discrete time points, N, to evaluate the response.*

- *Make an array $\underline{t}$ of N discrete time points $t_k = k\delta T$, $k = 0...(N-1)$, with $\delta T = T/N$. In the calculations we used $N = 2000$; $T = 15$ [s]*

- *Generate the discrete input $\underline{u} = f(t_k)$ for $t_k \leq T_b$ and make $u(t_k) = 0$ for $T > T_b$.*

- *Calculate the response $\underline{y}$ using the MATLAB command*

$$y = lsim(A, B, C, D, u, t)$$

Next, we will look at the response for two situations, namely a short-duration bump (or high speed) with $T_b = 0.05$ [s] and a long-duration bump (low speed) with $T_b = 1.0$ [s]. For a bump-length of $l_b = 1$ [m] these times correspond with a car-speed of 72 [km/h], respectively 3.6 [km/h]. In Fig. 4.24 the car response for the short bump is shown. The top part of this figure depicts the relevant part of the effective (excitation) force on mass m_1 as defined by (4.257). In the middle and bottom plots the displacements respectively the velocities are shown for the generalized coordinates q_1 (solid lines) respectively q_2 (dotted lines). Fig. 4.25 gives the same data for the long bump. The following observations can be made:

- *For the long bump the effective excitation almost equals the bump itself (only $k_1 x_o(t)$ is important). For the short bump the damping*

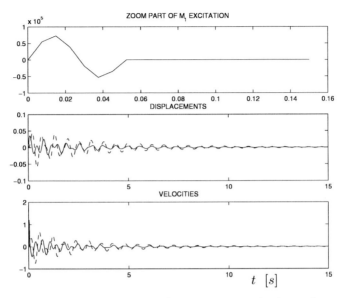

Fig. 4.24 Excitation and response (displacements and velocities)
for short bump or high speed

force transmission $b_1 \dot{x}_o(t)$ also seems to be important. For the
short bump this effective force even becomes negative. This is due
to the fact that we assume that the tyre will always be in contact
with the ground. (This is a necessary assumption in this linear
model). In reality a negative force will be impossible, so that we
are forced to introduce a loss of contact in our model for the high-
speed case. However, this will make our model nonlinear.

• In all the plots the response q_2 (dotted lines) is larger than q_1 (solid
lines).

• For the short bump, the displacement- and velocity plots show that
both the two eigenfrequencies can be recognized in the response.

• For the low-speed case, mainly a weakly damped, single harmonic
signal with a period time of ≈ 0.6 [s] can be recognized. This corresponds to the lowest eigenfrequency (1.65 [Hz]). For this situation
perhaps also a single-degree-of-freedom model (a single mass with
one spring and one damper) might have been used to model reality.

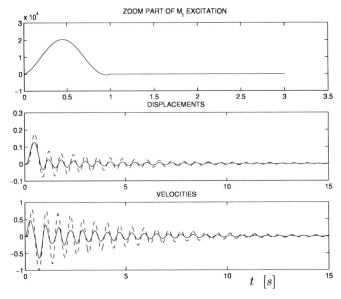

Fig. 4.25 Excitation and response (displacements and velocities)
for long bump or low speed

4.6 GENERAL NON-CONSERVATIVE SYSTEMS

4.6.1 State-space formulation

As for systems with general viscous damping and symmetric matrices it appears to be advantageous for general non-conservative systems with non-
symmetric matrices to reformulate the second-order linearized Lagrange's
equations of motion as a set of first-order differential equations of motion.
In view of the absence of symmetry characteristics of the system matrices,
no simplification of the associated eigenvalue problem can be achieved anymore and, also, the orthogonality relationships for the eigencolumns, which
provide the basis for the decoupling of the equations of motion, do not appear
in a straightforward way anymore. Hence, different transformations to a set
of first-order equations would be possible, all of which are equivalent. We
choose a transformation which renders the set of first-order equations (4.129)
for systems with general viscous damping and symmetric matrices, derived in
Subsection 4.5.1, as a particular case. So, we return to the system described
by (2.432)

$$\underline{M}\,\ddot{\underline{q}}(t) + (\underline{D}^* + \underline{G})\,\dot{\underline{q}}(t) + (\underline{K}^* + \underline{H})\,\underline{q}(t) = \underline{Q}^*(t) \tag{4.260}$$

introduce the set of new dependent variables

$$\underline{z}^*(t) = \dot{\underline{q}}(t) \tag{4.261}$$

and rewrite (4.260) as a set of first-order differential equations

$$(\underline{D}^* + \underline{G}) \; \underline{\dot{q}}(t) + \underline{M} \; \underline{\dot{z}}^*(t) + (\underline{K}^* + \underline{H}) \; \underline{q}(t) = \underline{Q}(t) \tag{4.262}$$

Again, it appears to be possible to combine (4.262) and (4.261) to a set of first-order differential equations of motion for the $2n$ variables $\underline{q}(t)$ and $\underline{z}^*(t)$, collected in the state column $\underline{x}(t)$

$$\underline{x}(t) = \left[\begin{array}{c} \underline{q}(t) \\ \underline{z}^*(t) \end{array} \right] = \left[\begin{array}{c} \underline{q}(t) \\ \underline{\dot{q}}(t) \end{array} \right] \tag{4.263}$$

In order to obtain a set of first-order differential equations which renders (4.129) for systems with symmetric matrices as a particular case, we use in stead of (4.261) the equivalent set

$$\underline{M} \; \underline{\dot{q}}(t) - \underline{M} \; \underline{z}^*(t) = \underline{0} \tag{4.264}$$

Combining (4.262) and (4.264), we arrive at the following set of first-order differential equations of motion for the $2n$ variables $x_i(t)$, $i = 1...2n$, collected in the state column $\underline{x}(t)$

$$\underline{A} \; \underline{\dot{x}}(t) + \underline{B} \; \underline{x}(t) = \underline{r}(t) \tag{4.265}$$

where the $(2n \times 2n)$ real matrices

$$\underline{A} = \left[\begin{array}{cc} (\underline{D}^* + \underline{G}) & \underline{M} \\ \underline{M} & \underline{0} \end{array} \right]; \qquad \underline{B} = \left[\begin{array}{cc} (\underline{K}^* + \underline{H}) & \underline{0} \\ \underline{0} & -\underline{M} \end{array} \right] \tag{4.266}$$

are not symmetric anymore, $\underline{0}$ being the $(n \times n)$ null matrix. In (4.265) the column

$$\underline{r}(t) = \left[\begin{array}{c} \underline{Q}^*(t) \\ \underline{0} \end{array} \right] \tag{4.267}$$

contains the $2n$ generalized forces related to the $2n$ generalized state coordinates contained in the column $\underline{x}(t)$. The column $\underline{r}(t)$ shows the same appearance as the associated column for systems with symmetric matrices defined in (4.131).

4.6.2   The non-symmetric eigenvalue problem

For free motions the set of linear first-order differential equations of motion (4.265) reduces to

$$\underline{A} \; \underline{\dot{x}}(t) + \underline{B} \; \underline{x}(t) = \underline{0} \tag{4.268}$$

Because (4.268) represents a linear homogeneous system with constant matrices, it admits a solution of the exponential form

$$\underline{x}(t) = \underline{v} \; e^{st} \tag{4.269}$$

where s is a constant scalar and $\underline{v}$ is a constant column, both in general complex. Inserting (4.269) into (4.268) and dividing through by e^{st}, we obtain the *general algebraic eigenvalue problem*

$$[s \, \underline{A} + \underline{B}] \, \underline{v} = \underline{0} \tag{4.270}$$

Equation (4.270) represents the eigenvalue problem associated with the non-symmetric matrices $\underline{A}$ and $\underline{B}$ and it possesses a nontrivial solution if and only if the determinant of the coefficients of the elements $v_i = v\,[i]\,(i = 1, 2, ..., 2n)$ contained in $\underline{v}$ vanishes, i.e. if

$$\det\,(s \, \underline{A} + \underline{B}) = 0 \tag{4.271}$$

The characteristic equation (4.271) of degree $2n$ in s possesses in general $2n$ roots $s_r(r = 1, 2, ..., 2n)$, referred to as eigenvalues. The associated eigen-columns $\underline{v}_r(r = 1, 2, ..., 2n)$ can be obtained from (4.270) and, hence, they satisfy the equations

$$s_r \, \underline{A} \, \underline{v}_r = -\underline{B} \, \underline{v}_r \tag{4.272}$$

The question arises naturally as to whether the eigencolumns are orthogonal in some sense and whether the solution for $\underline{x}(t)$ can be expanded in a series of eigencolumns, providing the basis for decoupling of the equations of motion. We confine ourselves to the case in which all the eigenvalues $s_r(r = 1, 2, ..., 2n)$ are distinct, from which it follows that all the eigencolumns $\underline{v}_r(r = 1, 2, ..., 2n)$ are independent. To serve as a basis for the problem at hand, the eigencolumns must be orthogonal with respect to the matrices $\underline{A}$ and $\underline{B}$. The eigencolumns cannot be orthogonal to $\underline{A}$ and $\underline{B}$, however, because $\underline{A}$ and $\underline{B}$ are not sym-metric anymore. But, whereas the eigencolumns are not orthogonal in the ordinary sense, they are orthogonal in some fashion. Before we explore the nature of the orthogonality, we recall from the theory of linear algebra that

$$\det\,(s \, \underline{A} + \underline{B})^T = \det\,(s \, \underline{A} + \underline{B}) \tag{4.273}$$

because the value of the determinant of a matrix is the same, regardless of whether the determinant is expanded by a row or a column. Hence, we con-clude from (4.273) that the characteristic equation (4.271) and the character-istic equation

$$\det\,(s \, \underline{A} + \underline{B})^T = 0 \tag{4.274}$$

possess the same eigenvalues. We can write the eigenvalue problem associated with the characteristic equation (4.274) in the form

$$[s \, \underline{A} + \underline{B}]^T \, \underline{w} = \underline{0} \tag{4.275}$$

This eigenvalue problem is referred to as the *adjoint eigenvalue problem* of (4.268). It admits solutions in the form of the eigenvalues $s_s(s = 1, 2, ..., 2n)$ and the eigencolumns $\underline{w}_s(s = 1, 2, ..., 2n)$, where $\underline{w}_s$ are called the *adjoint eigencolumns* of the eigencolumns $\underline{v}_r$. They satisfy the equations

$$s_s \, \underline{A}^T \, \underline{w}_s = -\underline{B}^T \, \underline{w}_s \qquad (s = 1, 2, ..., 2n) \tag{4.276}$$

Taking the transposed of (4.276), we obtain

$$s_s \; \underline{w}_s^T \; \underline{A} = \underline{w}_s^T \; \underline{B} \qquad (4.277)$$

Because of their position to the left of the matrices $\underline{A}$ and $\underline{B}$, the adjoint eigencolumns $\underline{w}_s$ are known as the *left eigencolumns* of the eigenvalue problem associated with (4.268). Consistent with this, the eigencolumns $\underline{v}_r$ are called the *right eigencolumns* of the eigenvalue problem associated with (4.268). It is of interest to note that when $\underline{A}$ and $\underline{B}$ are real symmetric matrices, i.e. $\underline{A} = \underline{A}^T$, $\underline{B} = \underline{B}^T$, then the adjoint eigencolumns $\underline{w}_s$ coincide with the eigencolumns $\underline{v}_s(s = 1, 2, ..., 2n)$ in which case the eigenvalue problem is said to be *self-adjoint*. Now, we premultiply (4.272) by $\underline{w}_s^T$ and postmultiply (4.277) by $\underline{v}_r$. Subtracting the second result from the first, we obtain

$$(s_r - s_s) \; \underline{w}_s^T \underline{A} \, \underline{v}_r = 0 \qquad (4.278)$$

Hence, because we have assumed all eigenvalues to be distinct, we must have

$$\underline{w}_s^T \underline{A} \, \underline{v}_r = 0 \quad , \quad s_r \neq s_s \quad , \quad r, s = 1, 2, ..., 2n \qquad (4.279)$$

Then, in view of (4.272), we must also have

$$\underline{w}_s^T \; \underline{B} \, \underline{v}_r = 0 \quad , \quad s_r \neq s_s \quad , \quad r, s = 1, 2, ..., 2n \qquad (4.280)$$

Equations (4.279) and (4.280) state that the right eigencolumns and the left eigencolumns of the real non-symmetric eigenvalue problem associated with (4.268) are so-called *bi-orthogonal* with respect to the matrices $\underline{A}$ and $\underline{B}$ if the related eigenvalues are distinct.

The pairs of right and left eigencolumns can be normalized by letting

$$\underline{w}_r^T \underline{A} \, \underline{v}_r = a_r \quad , \quad r = 1, 2, ..., 2n \qquad (4.281)$$

where $a_r(r = 1, 2, ..., 2n)$ are normalization parameters to be selected as desired and being generally complex. An alternative normalization scheme consists of setting

$$\underline{w}_r^T \underline{B} \, \underline{v}_r = b_r \quad , \quad r = 1, 2, ..., 2n \qquad (4.282)$$

where $b_r(r = 1, 2, ..., 2n)$ constitute another set of complex normalization parameters. It can be concluded from (4.272), (4.281) and (4.282) that the parameters a_r and b_r depend on one another via the relationship

$$b_r = -s_r \, a_r \qquad (4.283)$$

which is completely equivalent to (4.164), holding for systems with symmetric matrices.

The preceding bi-orthogonality conditions and normalization schemes can be expressed conveniently in a compact matrix form. To this end, we introduce the matrices of right and left eigencolumns

$$\underline{V} = [\underline{v}_1 \quad \underline{v}_2 \quad \cdots \quad \underline{v}_{2n}] \qquad (4.284)$$

$$\underline{W} = [\underline{w}_1 \quad \underline{w}_2 \quad \cdots \quad \underline{w}_{2n}] \tag{4.285}$$

Then, (4.279) and (4.281) can be written in terms of $\underline{V}$ and $\underline{W}$ as

$$\underline{W}^T \underline{A}\, \underline{V} = \begin{bmatrix} a_1 & & 0 \\ & \ddots & \\ 0 & & a_{2n} \end{bmatrix} := \lceil a_r \rfloor \tag{4.286}$$

whereas (4.280) and (4.282) can be written in terms of $\underline{V}$ and $\underline{W}$ as

$$\underline{W}^T \underline{B}\, \underline{V} = \begin{bmatrix} b_1 & & 0 \\ & \ddots & \\ 0 & & b_{2n} \end{bmatrix} := \lceil b_r \rfloor \tag{4.287}$$

In view of (4.283) we have

$$\begin{bmatrix} b_1 & & 0 \\ & \ddots & \\ 0 & & b_{2n} \end{bmatrix} = - \begin{bmatrix} s_1 & & 0 \\ & \ddots & \\ 0 & & s_{2n} \end{bmatrix} \begin{bmatrix} a_1 & & 0 \\ & \ddots & \\ 0 & & a_{2n} \end{bmatrix} \tag{4.288}$$

or, in abbreviated form

$$\lceil b_r \rfloor = - \lceil s_r \rfloor \lceil a_r \rfloor \tag{4.289}$$

It follows from (4.286) that

$$\underline{W}^T = \lceil a_r \rfloor (\underline{A}\, \underline{V})^{-1} \tag{4.290}$$

so that, in stead of solving the adjoint eigenvalue problem (4.275), it is possible to obtain the left eigencolumns by inverting the matrix $\underline{A}\, \underline{V}$ and premultiplying the resulting matrix by $\lceil a_r \rfloor$.

4.6.3   Decoupling of the equations of motion; the transfer function matrix

We return to the set of first-order differential equations of motion (4.265) for the generalized state coordinates contained in the column $\underline{x}(t)$. These equations can be decoupled by expanding $\underline{x}(t)$ in terms of the right eigencolumns $\underline{v}_r$ in the form

$$\underline{x}(t) = \sum_{r=1}^{2n} \underline{v}_r\, \eta_r(t) = \underline{V}\, \underline{\eta}(t) \tag{4.291}$$

where $\underline{V}$ is the square matrix of right eigencolumns defined by (4.284), while the column $\underline{\eta}(t)$ contains the functions $\eta_1(t), \eta_2(t), ..., \eta_{2n}(t)$

$$\underline{\eta}(t) = \begin{bmatrix} \eta_1(t) \\ \eta_2(t) \\ ... \\ \eta_{2n}(t) \end{bmatrix} \tag{4.292}$$

The functions contained in the column $\underline{\eta}(t)$ can be considered to constitute a new set of $2n$ state coordinates. Introducing the linear transformation (4.291) into the state equations of motion (4.265) and premultiplying the resulting set of equations by the transposed of the matrix of left eigencolumns, $\underline{W}^T$, we obtain

$$\underline{W}^T \underline{A} \, \underline{V} \, \dot{\underline{\eta}}(t) + \underline{W}^T \underline{B} \, \underline{V} \, \underline{\eta}(t) = \underline{W}^T \underline{r}(t) \tag{4.293}$$

Using (4.286), (4.287), (4.289) and (4.292), we arrive at the following set of uncoupled equations

$$a_r \{\dot{\eta}_r(t) - s_r \, \eta_r(t)\} = N_r(t) \quad , \quad r = 1, 2, ..., 2n \tag{4.294}$$

where

$$N_r(t) = \underline{w}_r^T \, \underline{r}(t) \tag{4.295}$$

are the generalized forces in the decoupled state equations associated with the state coordinates $\eta_r(t)$. The differential equations of motion (4.294) have to be supplemented with the initial conditions for $\eta_r(t)$. These can be obtained from the initial conditions for $\underline{x}(t)$, i.e. $\underline{x}(0) = \underline{x}_0 = \left[\underline{q}^T(0) \quad \dot{\underline{q}}^T(0)\right]^T$, by premultiplying (4.291) for $t = 0$ by $\underline{W}^T \underline{A}$ and utilizing the orthogonality conditions and normalization scheme (4.286). This results in

$$\eta_r(0) = \frac{1}{a_r} \underline{w}_r^T \, \underline{A} \, \underline{x}(0) \quad , \quad r = 1, 2, ..., 2n \tag{4.296}$$

The decoupled state equations of motion (4.294) for systems with non-symmetric matrices completely resemble the decoupled equations (4.221) for systems with symmetric matrices, the only difference being the appearance of the left eigencolumns $\underline{w}_r$ in the normalization parameters a_r and in the generalized forces $N_r(t)$. In view of this, the discussion of the free response is similar to the discussion carried out in Subsection 4.5.5 for systems with symmetric matrices and it will not be repeated here. Also, the solution of (4.294) for general external excitation can be obtained by the methods for single-degree-of-freedom linear systems. The transfer function matrix $\underline{H}(\Omega)$ for systems with symmetric matrices, given by (4.233) can be easily generalized to systems with non-symmetric matrices. Collecting the first n elements of the right eigencolumn $\underline{v}_r$ in the column $\underline{v}_r^u$

$$\underline{v}_r^u = \begin{bmatrix} v_{1r} & v_{2r} & .... & v_{nr} \end{bmatrix}^T \tag{4.297}$$

and collecting the first n elements of the left eigencolumn $\underline{w}_r$ in the column $\underline{w}_r^u$

$$\underline{w}_r^u = \begin{bmatrix} w_{1r} & w_{2r} & .... & w_{nr} \end{bmatrix}^T \tag{4.298}$$

we can express the transfer function matrix for systems with non-symmetric matrices as

$$\underline{H}(\Omega) = \sum_{r=1}^{2n} \frac{\underline{v}_r^u \left(\underline{w}_r^u\right)^T}{a_r \left(j\Omega - s_r\right)} \tag{4.299}$$

4.7   CHAPTER PROBLEMS

4.7.1   Mussel Shaking Machine

A mussel shaking machine can be seen as a large rigid riddle, experiencing
a harmonic motion to separate the mussels from all the other material. The
mussels have to be transported to the end of the machine and the rest has to
pass the holes in the riddle and fall down.

Such a machine might be modelled as a uniform rigid beam (representing
the riddle) with length $2l$, mass M_b and mass moment of inertia J_z with
respect to its centre of gravity Z. So we may assume that $J_z = M_b l^2/3$.
The beam is supposed to be supported by two linear-spring/viscous-damper
sets. The viscous damping constant is b, and this value is the same for left-
as well as right side of the machine. The spring constant for the left spring
is k_1, and this value will be different from the right spring value k_2 to make
a horizontal transportation mode possible. The left side of the machine is
connected to the fixed world by a very flexible leaf spring (bending stiffness
may be neglected), just to suppress any horizontal motion of that point of the
structure. On the right, a rotating unbalance device has been mounted. It

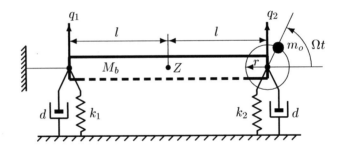

Fig. 4.26   Simple model of a mussel shaking machine

consists of an unbalance mass m rotating on a circle with radius r with a fixed
and prescribed rotational frequency Ω $[rad/s]$. As the generalised coordinates
we choose the end-displacements of the beam, q_1 and q_2, so $\underline{q}^T = [q_1, q_2]$.
These displacements are measured from the static equilibrium position, so the
effect of gravity can be ignored. We will only look at small vertical motions
of the beam. This means that we want to apply a linear theory.

For the numerical exercises we will use the following parameter values:
$M_b = 100$ $[kg]$, $k_1 = 60000$ $[N/m]$, $k_2 = 20000$ $[N/m]$, $d = 200$ $[Ns/m]$, $m = 1$ $[kg]$, $r = 0.02$ $[m]$.

- First we will derive the nonlinear and coupled set of differential equations
  using the formalism of Lagrange

- Next we look at the undamped free vibrations, test the normal mode orthogonality property and apply a mass-matrix normalization

- We concentrate on the lowest eigenfrequency ω_1 and corresponding vibration mode $\underline{u}_1 = [u_1, u_2]$. For an optimal transport of the mussels from the right to the left, we think that the amplitude ratio $\alpha = u_2/u_1 \approx 2$. This tuning should be done by changing the spring stiffness k_2. Therefore we will create a plot of this amplitude ratio for a stiffness range of $20000 \leq k_2 \leq 60000$ $[N.m]$. Then we can select a value for k_2 for which $\alpha \approx 2$.

- For the chosen value for k_2 we will check whether we are dealing with proportional damping or that the system may be assumed to be weakly damped. Then the dimensional model damping factors can be calculated to characterize the dynamics of the system.

- The main question deals with the analysis of the damped, forced response due to the rotating unbalances. This can be evaluated by looking at the complex amplitudes of the responses $\hat{q}$ of the response $\underline{q}(t)$. We will choose as excitation range $0 \leq \Omega \leq 120$ $[rad/s]$.

First we look at the main part, the rigid beam. The kinetic energy can be written as

$$T_b = \frac{1}{2}M_b v_Z^2 + \frac{1}{2}J_Z \dot{\varphi}^2 \tag{4.300}$$

where $\underline{v}_Z = \dot{q}_Z$ is the velocity of the centre of gravity and φ the rotation around this center of gravity. For very small displacements we can write:

$$q_Z = \frac{1}{2}\{q_1 + q_2\}; \qquad \varphi = \frac{1}{2l}\{q_2 - q_1\} \tag{4.301}$$

where we define the rotation φ to be positive in counterclockwise direction. Using $J_Z = M_b l^2/3$ we then get:

$$T_b = \frac{1}{6}M_b\{\dot{q}_1^2 + \dot{q}_2^2 + \dot{q}_1\dot{q}_2\} \tag{4.302}$$

The velocity associated to the absolute position $\underline{x}_m$ of the unbalance mass m is

$$\underline{v}_m = \dot{\underline{x}}_m = \frac{d}{dt}\begin{bmatrix} r\cos\Omega t \\ q_2 + r\sin\Omega t \end{bmatrix} = \begin{bmatrix} -r\Omega\sin\Omega t \\ \dot{q}_2 + r\Omega\cos\Omega t \end{bmatrix} \tag{4.303}$$

So, the kinetic energy of this component becomes

$$T_o = \frac{1}{2}m\{\dot{q}_2^2 + r^2\Omega^2 + 2r\dot{q}_2\Omega\cos\Omega t\} \tag{4.304}$$

This means that for the total kinetic energy we can write the general expression:

$$T = T_b + T_o = \frac{1}{2}\underline{\dot{q}}^T \underline{M}\ \underline{\dot{q}} + \underline{m}_o^T \underline{\dot{q}} + T_o \tag{4.305}$$

with:

$$\underline{M} = \frac{1}{12}\begin{bmatrix} 4M_b & 2M_b \\ 2M_b & 4M_b + 12m \end{bmatrix}; \quad \underline{m}_o = \begin{bmatrix} 0 \\ mr\Omega \cos \Omega t \end{bmatrix}; \quad T_o = \frac{1}{2}mr^2\Omega^2 \tag{4.306}$$

The elastic energy in the springs can be denoted as

$$U = \frac{1}{2}k_1 q_1^2 + \frac{1}{2}k_2 q_2^2 = \frac{1}{2}\underline{q}^T \underline{K}\underline{q} \tag{4.307}$$

with

$$\underline{K} = \begin{bmatrix} k_1 & 0 \\ 0 & k_2 \end{bmatrix} \tag{4.308}$$

The only elements which are still missing are the damping forces. We have to take these into account by the nonconservative (generalized) forces. To get these we first introduce the damping forces as shown in Fig. 4.27. If

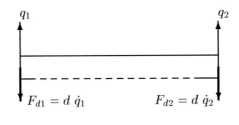

q_1 $\qquad\qquad$ q_2

$F_{d1} = d\ \dot{q}_1$ $\qquad\qquad$ $F_{d2} = d\ \dot{q}_2$

Fig. 4.27 Nonconservative forves

we now want to switch over to generalized forces, we assume first a virtual displacement column $\delta\underline{q} = [\delta q_1,\ 0]$. The virtual work of the two forces in this case is:

$$\delta W = -F_{d1}\ \delta q_1 := Q_1\ \delta q_1 \Longrightarrow Q_1 = -d\ \dot{q}_1 \tag{4.309}$$

and of course we find for the second generalized force: $Q_2 = -d\ \dot{q}_2$, so that

$$\underline{Q} = \begin{bmatrix} -d\ \dot{q}_1 \\ -d\ \dot{q}_2 \end{bmatrix} = -\underline{D}\ \underline{\dot{q}} \quad \text{with} \quad \underline{D} = \begin{bmatrix} d & 0 \\ 0 & d \end{bmatrix} \tag{4.310}$$

If we now apply Lagrange's equations we get:

$$\underline{M}\underline{\ddot{q}}(t) + \underline{D}\ \underline{\dot{q}}(t) + \underline{K}\ \underline{q}(t) = -\underline{\dot{m}}_o(t) = \begin{bmatrix} 0 \\ mr\Omega^2 \sin \Omega t \end{bmatrix} \tag{4.311}$$

with

$$\underline{M} = \frac{1}{12}\begin{bmatrix} 4M_b & 2M_b \\ 2M_b & 4M_b + 12m \end{bmatrix} \qquad \underline{D} = d\begin{bmatrix} 1 & 0 \\ 0 & 1 \end{bmatrix}$$

$$\underline{K} = \begin{bmatrix} k_1 & 0 \\ 0 & k_2 \end{bmatrix} \qquad \underline{f}(t) = \begin{bmatrix} 0 \\ mr\Omega^2 \sin(\Omega t) \end{bmatrix}$$

(4.312)

For the undamped, free vibrating system we take $\Omega = 0$. If we solve the eigenvalue problem with MATLAB, we get the following results:

$$\omega_1 = 23.0015 \ [rad/s] \quad f_1 = 3.66 \ [Hz]$$
$$\omega_2 = 51.1575 \ [rad/s] \quad f_1 = 8.14 \ [Hz]$$
$$\underline{U} = \begin{bmatrix} 0.0318 & 0.1965 \\ 0.1530 & -0.1227 \end{bmatrix}$$

(4.313)

where the eigenfrequencies have been sorted from small to large and the eigencolumns have been mass-matrix normalized. The eigencolumns are plotted in Fig 4.28. We can see that the first mode is an in-phase vibration where the

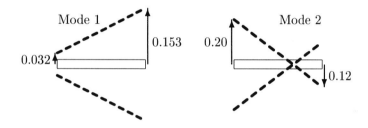

Fig. 4.28   Free vibration modes

right end has a 5 times as large amplitude as the left end. The second mode is an anti-phase mode. If we calculate the product $\underline{U}^T \underline{M} \, \underline{U}$ we can see that this is an identity matrix and the product $\underline{U}^T \underline{K} \, \underline{U}$ appears to be a diagonal matrix with ω_i^2 on its diagonal, which illustrates the mode-orthogonality property.

Part of the design of the machine is to change the spring stiffness k_2 such that the vibration amplitude u_2 is approximately twice as large as u_1 for the lowest vibration mode. For the default situation this quotient is $\alpha = u_2/u_1 = 4.8$. If the eigenvalue problem $[-\Omega^2 \underline{M} + \underline{K}]\underline{u} = \underline{0}$ is solved for a range of k_2-values and this quotient α is plotted for the lowest eigenmode we get the picture shown in Fig 4.29. We can see that increasing the stiffness k_2 will decrease the quotient $\alpha = u_2/u_1$. This means that the mode changes from a more or less rotational mode to a more translational mode. We want $\alpha \approx 2$, so we should take $k_2 \approx 38000$. For $k_2 = 38000 \ [N/m]$ we get the following eigenfrequencies and mass-normalized eigenmodes:

$$\omega_1 = 29.887 \ [rad/s] \quad f_1 = 4.76 \ [Hz]$$
$$\omega_2 = 54.2700 \ [rad/s] \quad f_1 = 8.64 \ [Hz]$$
$$\underline{U} = \begin{bmatrix} 0.0642 & 0.1884 \\ 0.1304 & -0.1465 \end{bmatrix}$$

(4.314)

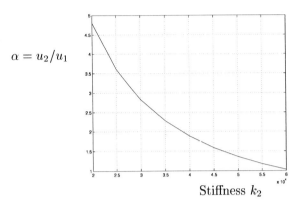

$$\alpha = u_2/u_1$$

Stiffness k_2

Fig. 4.29   Amplitude quotient $\alpha = u_2/u_1$ for different stiffness values k_2

So we see that the amplitude quotient $\alpha = u_2/u_1 = 0.1304/0.0642 = 2.03$ meaning that the design-goal has been reached. If we calculate the product $\underline{U}^T \underline{D} \, \underline{U}$ we get:

$$\underline{U}^T \underline{D} \, \underline{U} = \begin{bmatrix} 4.2238 & -1.4007 \\ -1.4007 & 11.3916 \end{bmatrix} \tag{4.315}$$

This is not a diagonal matrix which means that we are not dealing with proportional damping. The matrix however is diagonal dominant so if we calculate dimensionless modal damping factors using only these diagonal terms we at least have some idea about the damping level of this system. Using $\xi_r = d_r/(2\sqrt{k_r m_r})$ we get:

$$\xi_1 = 0.0707 \qquad \xi_2 = 0.1050 \tag{4.316}$$

So both modes are undercritically damped (7% respectively 11%). That mode 2 seems to be more heavily damped than mode 1 can be understood by looking at the modeshape. In mode 2, both degrees of freedom are equally active (so also both dampers are fully active) whereas in mode 1, degree of freedom q_1 does not move too much. So also the left damper will not be very active. The excitation column can be written as

$$\underline{Q}(t) = Im \left\{ \begin{bmatrix} 0 \\ m \, r \, \Omega^2 \, e^{\Omega t} \end{bmatrix} \right\} = Im \left\{ \begin{bmatrix} 0 \\ m \, r \, \Omega^2 \end{bmatrix} e^{\Omega t} \right\} = Im \, \{\underline{\hat{Q}} \, e^{\Omega t}\} \tag{4.317}$$

with the column of complex amplitudes of the excitation being

$$\underline{\hat{Q}} = \begin{bmatrix} 0 \\ m \, r \, \Omega^2 \end{bmatrix} \tag{4.318}$$

Now we can find the harmonic response from:

$$\underline{\hat{q}} = \{-\Omega^2 \underline{M} + j\Omega \underline{D} + \underline{K}\}^{-1} \, \underline{\hat{Q}} \tag{4.319}$$

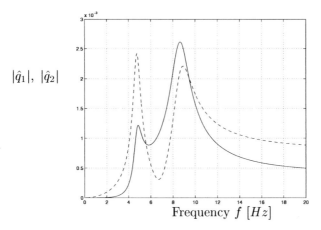

$|\hat{q}_1|, |\hat{q}_2|$

Frequency f [Hz]

Fig. 4.30   Complex response magnitudes; q_1 solid line, q_2 dashed

The magnitudes of these complex responses are plot in Fig 4.30. To this result the following remarks can be made:

1.   Both degrees of freedom show a peak at approximately 4.8 [Hz] and 8.6 [Hz]. These values are very close to the undamped eigenfrequencies.

2.   At $f \approx$ 4.8 [Hz] the amplitude quotient is close to 2.0. However, this only is the case in a rather small frequency range ($4 \leq f \leq 5$ [hz]). This can clearly be seen from Fig 4.31 where the amplitude quotient α for the damped, forced situation is shown for a frequency range around the first peaks. The optimum frequency for the driving motor should

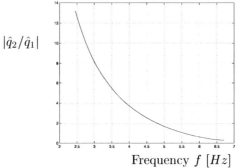

$|\hat{q}_2/\hat{q}_1|$

Frequency f [Hz]

Fig. 4.31   Amplitude quotient factor

be 4.7 [Hz] (280 [rev/min]). Adding mussels to the machine will somewhat decrease the eigenfrequencies, so if the unbalance will rotate with a fixed frequency this can easily destroy this optimised situation.

3. In general the magnitude of the right end displacement is larger than the magnitude of the left end displacement except for the frequency range $5.5 \leq f \leq 9.5 \ [Hz]$.

Finally we study the low- and high-frequency responses. For these we can write:

$$\Omega \ll \omega_1 \Longrightarrow \hat{\underline{q}} \approx \underline{K}^{-1} \begin{bmatrix} 0 \\ m \ r \ \Omega^2 \end{bmatrix} = \begin{bmatrix} 0 \\ m \ r \ \Omega^2/38000 \end{bmatrix}$$

$$\Omega \gg \omega_2 \Longrightarrow \hat{\underline{q}} \approx \{-\Omega^2 \underline{M}\}^{-1} \begin{bmatrix} 0 \\ m \ r \ \Omega^2 \end{bmatrix} \qquad (4.320)$$

$$= -\underline{M}^{-1} \begin{bmatrix} 0 \\ m \ r \end{bmatrix} = \begin{bmatrix} 0.3846 \\ -0.7692 \end{bmatrix} 10^{-3}$$

So for low frequencies both amplitudes go to zero but q_1 much faster which also was shown in Fig 4.30. For high frequencies both amplitudes go to a constant value (ratio 1:2). This high-frequency motion is illustrated in Fig 4.32.

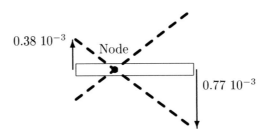

Fig. 4.32   High frequency vibration

4.7.2   Continuous Variable Transmission

In passenger cars a continuous variable transmission (CVT) can be used as central element in for example a hybrid drive (engine - flywheel system). In Fig. 4.33 such a CVT is schematically shown. The left part shows a side view where the two disk pairs and a part of the steel belt can be seen. The right part shows a cross-section of the CVT, seen from the same direction. The simplified dynamic model for this CVT consists of two rigid disks with mass moment of inertia J_1 for the left disk and J_2 for the right disk. These mass moments of inertia are not equal because they are not only based on the disks, but also take into account a part of the drive system connected to each disk. The distance between the shafts of the two disks is l. The steel belt will be modelled as an elastic uniform beam with cross-section A and elasticity modulus E. It allows

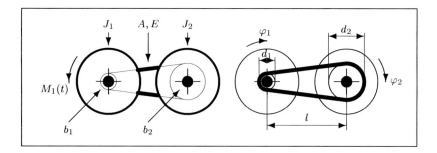

Fig. 4.33 Simple model of a CVT

the transfer of energy from the left disk (working at effective contact diameter d_1) to the right disk (working at effective contact diameter d_2). By variation of these contact diameters the variable transmission is created. Additionally, we make the following simplifying assumptions

- The contact between disks and belt is assumed to be ideal, so no slip is present
- The shaft distance l is assumed to be relatively large with respect to the effective diameters d_1 and d_2. Then we may conclude that for all transmission ratios, the free belt length (the two parts of the belt not in contact with the disks) will also have a constant length l. So, the two belt parts may both be modelled as a uniform beam with length l and (constant) spring stiffness $k = AE/l$.
- Approximately we may say that $d_1 + d_2$ will always be constant. In the nominal situation $d_1 = d_2 = 0.06$ $[m]$.
- The bearing friction for both disks will be modelled as two viscous rotation dampers with damping constant b_1, respectively b_2 $[Nms/rad]$.
- We will only study small (linear) vibrations around a globally non-rotating system. For the characterization of the motions we will use as generalised coordinates the (small) rotations of both disks φ_1, respectively φ_2, so $\underline{q}^T = [\varphi_1, \ \varphi_2]$
- The belt has such a high pre-load that it will always stay under tension (no free-hanging parts).
- On the left disk an external torsional moment $M_1(t)$ is acting.

We will use the following numerical data
$J_1 = 6.0 \ 10^{-3}$ $[kgm^2]$, $J_2 = 9.0 \ 10^{-3}$ $[kgm^2]$, $A = 1.0 \ 10^{-4}$ $[m^2]$, $l = 0.3$ $[m]$
$E = 1.0 \ 10^8$ $[Nm^{-2}]$, $b_1 = b_2 = 0.05$ $[Nms/rad]$.

The kinetic energy can simply be expressed as

$$T = \frac{1}{2}J_1\dot{\varphi}_1^2 + \frac{1}{2}J_2\dot{\varphi}_2^2 = \frac{1}{2}\underline{\dot{q}}^T \underline{M} \ \underline{\dot{q}} \tag{4.321}$$

with:

$$\underline{M} = \begin{bmatrix} J_1 & 0 \\ 0 & J_2 \end{bmatrix} \qquad (4.322)$$

The elastic energy in the two belt-parts takes the form

$$U = \frac{1}{2}k(r_2\varphi_2 - r_1\varphi_1)^2 + \frac{1}{2}k(r_1\varphi_1 - r_2\varphi_2)^2 = \frac{1}{2}\underline{q}^T \underline{K}\underline{q} \qquad (4.323)$$

with

$$\underline{K} = \frac{2AE}{l} \begin{bmatrix} r_1^2 & -r_1r_2 \\ -r_1r_2 & r_2^2 \end{bmatrix} \qquad (4.324)$$

The only elements which are still missing are the two damping moments and the external moment $M_1(t)$. These moments are depicted in Fig. 4.34. If we

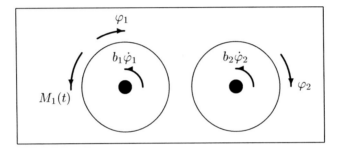

Fig. 4.34   Nonconservative "forces"

now want to switch over to the associated non-conservative generalized forces we assume first a virtual displacement column $\delta\underline{q} = [\delta\varphi_1, \ 0]$. The virtual .work of the three moments in this case is:

$$\delta W = \{-b_1\dot{\varphi}_1 - M_1(t)\} \, \delta\varphi_1 := Q_1 \, \delta\varphi_1 \Longrightarrow Q_1 = -b_1\dot{\varphi}_1 - M_1(t) \qquad (4.325)$$

and of course we find for the second generalized force: $Q_2 = -b_2 \, \dot{\varphi}_2$, so that

$$\underline{Q} = \begin{bmatrix} -b_1 \, \dot{\varphi}_1 - M_1(t) \\ -b_2 \, \dot{\varphi}_2 \end{bmatrix} = -\underline{D} \, \dot{\underline{q}} + \underline{f}(t) \qquad (4.326)$$

with

$$\underline{D} = \begin{bmatrix} b_1 & 0 \\ 0 & b_2 \end{bmatrix}; \quad \underline{f}(t) = \begin{bmatrix} -M_1(t) \\ 0 \end{bmatrix} \qquad (4.327)$$

If we now apply Lagrange's equations we get:

$$\underline{M} \, \ddot{\underline{q}}(t) + \underline{D} \, \dot{\underline{q}}(t) + \underline{K} \, \underline{q}(t) = \begin{bmatrix} -M_1(t) \\ 0 \end{bmatrix} \qquad (4.328)$$

We first will start from the nominal situation for which $r_1 = r_2 = 0.06 \ [m]$, giving a transmission ratio of 1.

If we evaluate the free undamped behaviour for this situation, we get the following results:

$$\begin{array}{ll} \omega_1 = 258.1989 \ [rad/s] & f_1 = 41.0936 \ [Hz] \\ \omega_2 = 0 \ [rad/s] & f_2 = 0 \ [Hz] \end{array} \qquad \underline{U} = \left[\begin{array}{cc} 10 & 8.165 \\ -6.6667 & 8.165 \end{array} \right]$$
(4.329)

where the eigencolumns have been mass-normalized.

We can see that the first mode corresponds to an out-of-phase vibration. This mode reflects that the amplitude of the left disk (with mass moment of inertia J_1) is 1.5 times as large as the amplitude of the right disk (with mass-moment of inertia $J_2 = 1.5 \ J_1$). The second eigenfrequency is zero and the corresponding eigenmode is a rigid body mode. This is due to the fact that the stiffness matrix is singular for all combinations of d_1 and d_2. For the default situation $d_1 = d_2$, the rotations of both disks should be equal for the elastic energy in the two belt-parts to be zero. Is is left to the reader to evaluate the eigenfrequencies and corresponding eigenmodes for situations where $d_1 \neq d_2$.

If we calculate the product $\underline{U}^T \underline{M} \ \underline{U}$ we see that this is an identity matrix, while the product $\underline{U}^T \underline{K} \ \underline{U}$ is also a diagonal matrix with ω_i^2 instead of ones on its diagonal. Because $\underline{U}^T \underline{K} \ \underline{U}$ always has a zero on its diagonal, a stiffness matrix normalization is impossible in this case.

Next we want to change the transmission ratio. Therefore we choose r_1 in the interval $0.02 \leq r_1 \leq 0.1$ and because $r_1 + r_2$ should remain constant, we have to take $r_2 = 0.12 - r_1$. We also define $\alpha = r_2/r_1$. For all transmission ratio values we can evaluate the undamped eigenvalue problem. This will each time give one zero eigenfrequency and one non-zero eigenfrequency. The non-zero eigenfrequencies are plotted against α in Fig 4.35. We can see that the nonzero eigenfrequency has a minimum value for $\alpha = r_2/r_1 \approx 1.5$. If we evaluate this situation ($r_1 = 0.048$, $r_2 = 1.5 r_1 = 0.072$) we will find an eigenfrequency of $f = 40.2634 \ [Hz]$ and a corresponding eigencolumn $\underline{u}^T = [10, \ 6.666]$. If we would like to avoid resonance problems we should advise only to use the CVT in the frequency range $0 \leq f \leq 40 \ [Hz]$. So the maximum speed of both disks should be less than 2400 rev/min.

Next we return to the default situation with $r_1 = r_2 = 0.06$.
If we then calculate the product $\underline{U}^T \underline{D} \ \underline{U}$ we get:

$$\underline{U}^T \underline{D} \ \underline{U} = \left[\begin{array}{cc} 7.2222 & 1.3608 \\ 1.3608 & 6.6667 \end{array} \right]$$
(4.330)

This is not a diagonal matrix which means that we are not dealing with proportional damping. If we anyhow want to calculate dimensionless modal damping factors we can use only the diagonal terms. Using $\xi_r = d_r/(2\sqrt{k_r m_r})$ we get:

$$\xi_1 = 0.014 \qquad \xi_2 = \infty$$
(4.331)

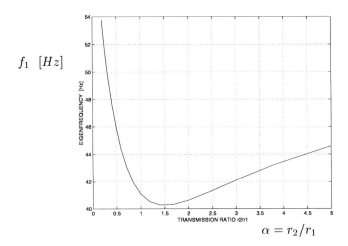

$f_1 \ [Hz]$

$\alpha = r_2/r_1$

Fig. 4.35   Non-zero eigenfrequency versus transmission ratio $\alpha = u_2/u_1$

So the rigid-body mode has a dimensionless damping $\xi_2 = \infty$ (it has no stiffness) and the elastic mode is undercritically damped (14%).

For the forced, damped vibration we write the excitation column as:

$$\underline{Q}(t) = Re \ \left\{ \begin{bmatrix} -e^{2\pi jft} \\ 0 \end{bmatrix} \right\} = Re \ \left\{ \begin{bmatrix} -1 \\ 0 \end{bmatrix} \ e^{2\pi jft} \right\} = Re \ \{\underline{\hat{Q}} \ e^{2\pi jft}\} \quad (4.332)$$

with the column of complex amplitudes of the excitation being

$$\underline{\hat{Q}} = \begin{bmatrix} -1 \\ 0 \end{bmatrix} \quad (4.333)$$

Now we can find the harmonic response from:

$$\underline{\hat{q}} = \{(2\pi jf)^2 \underline{M} + (2\pi jf)\underline{D} + \underline{K}\}^{-1} \ \underline{\hat{Q}} \quad (4.334)$$

The magnitudes of these complex responses are depicted in Fig 4.36. To this result the following remarks can be made:

- Both degrees of freedom show a peak at approximately 41 $[Hz]$, which is very close to the undamped eigenfrequency due to the small dimensionless damping factor for this mode
- For very small excitation frequencies (i.e. $f \to 0$) both amplitudes will go to ∞. For $f = 0$ we have a constant force on a system with a rigid-body mode, so both disks will start to rotate with an increasing (equal) rotational velocity
- For $f \to \infty$ we can write

$$\underline{\hat{q}} \approx \{(2\pi jf)^2 \underline{M}\}^{-1}\underline{\hat{Q}} = \begin{bmatrix} 1/(4\pi^2 f^2 J_1) \\ 0 \end{bmatrix} \quad (4.335)$$

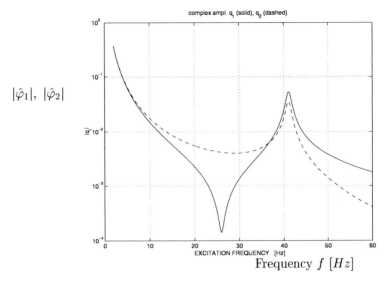

$|\hat{\varphi}_1|, \ |\hat{\varphi}_2|$

Frequency $f \ [Hz]$

Fig. 4.36   Complex response magnitudes; φ_1 solid line, φ_2 dashed

So both amplitudes will go to zero, but $\hat{\varphi}_2$ much faster. If we look at the rotational accelerations $\underline{\hat{a}} = (2\pi j f)^2 \ \underline{\hat{q}}$ we will see that for $f \to \infty$, $\hat{a}_2 \to 0$ and $\hat{a}_1 \to -1/J_1$

• At $f \approx 26 \ [Hz]$ the amplitude $\hat{\varphi}_1$ will become very small (anti-resonance). For that excitation frequency the left disk will hardly move and the oscillating right disk will create a moment on the left disk which will be cancelled exactly by the external moment $M_1(t)$. For this situation we can write

$$\frac{2AE}{l}(-r_1 r_2)\hat{\varphi}_2 \approx -1 \tag{4.336}$$

so $|\hat{\varphi}_2| \approx 4.17 \ 10^{-3}$. This can also be seen from the figure.

5

Experimental approach

This chapter gives a short introduction into techniques for experimental analysis. The basic idea is to excite a structure by a known harmonic force and to measure its (harmonic) response. An efficient procedure can be created by using digital- and Fast Fourier Transform techniques.

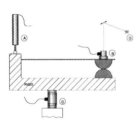

The accompanying figures show the test setup to study the dynamical behaviour of an impacting beam. The system is excited by a hydraulic shaker and the response is measured with a laser, some accelerometers and also a force transducer.

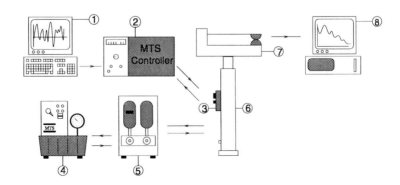

5.1   INTRODUCTION

It has been shown that the *frequency-response-function-matrix* $\underline{H}(\Omega)$ relates the (harmonic) system response to the (harmonic) system excitation. The resulting FRF-functions are an important tool in the analysis of the dynamic behaviour of structures. So the basic relation is:

$$\underline{f}(t) = \underline{\hat{f}} \, e^{j\Omega t}; \quad \underline{q}(t) = \underline{\hat{q}} \, e^{j\Omega t}; \quad \underline{\hat{q}} = \underline{H}(\Omega) \, \underline{\hat{f}} \tag{5.1}$$

The element $\underline{H}_{[i,j]}(\Omega)$ of this matrix is a function (complex, with as independent coordinate Ω) which relates the excitation in degree-of-freedom q_i and the response of degree-of-freedom q_j. The type of damping (viscous, structural, ..) is not relevant in this formulation and also the damping-level (weak or heavy) is not important.

Studying a systems's FRF can be very important for example to avoid resonanceproblems in structures or machines but it is also the fundamental dynamical property to develop an advanced experimental technique, the so-called *Experimental Modal Analysis*.

In the next sections some possibilities for the experimental determination of these FRF's will be presented.

5.2   HARMONIC EXCITATION

The far most trivial approach of course is to apply a harmonic excitation and monitor the corresponding harmonic response such as schematically shown for the 3-mass car-engine model in Fig 5.2. A (harmonic) force is exerted in vertical direction on the front wheel (corresponding to the degree of freedom q_1) for example by means of an electro-mechanical shaker. This shaker is driven by a signal generator coupled to a power amplifier. The real force going into the car system is measured by mounting a force transducer between the shaker and the front axle. The response of the system, for example the engine (degree of freedom q_3), to this excitation can be measured by mounting an accelerometer on the engine. Both the measurement signals (excitation and

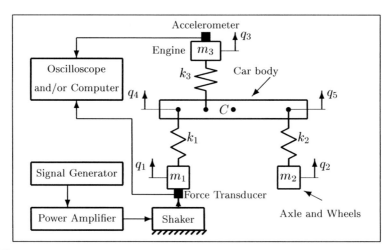

Fig. 5.1 Frequency Reponse Function determination by shaker-excitation

response) are fed to an oscilloscope or computer for further analysis. This combination of degrees of freedom (q_1 rsepectively q_3) can then be used to extract one element of the Frequency Response Function matrix, namely the element $H[1,3](\Omega) = H[3,1](\Omega)$.

In practise it is often easier to measure directly the acceleration of points of a structure instead of displacements. The complex amplitude of the acceleration ($\hat{a}$) is related to the complex amplitude of the displacement ($\hat{q}$) by:

$$\hat{a} = (j\ \Omega)^2\ \hat{q} \tag{5.2}$$

In this case we directly look at the relation between the complex amplitude of the excitation and the complex amplitude of the acceleration of (also called the *Inertance-FRF*), so:

$$\underline{a}(t) = \underline{\hat{a}}\ e^{j\Omega t};\quad \underline{\hat{a}} = \underline{H}_a(\Omega)\ \underline{\hat{f}};\quad \underline{H}_a(\Omega) = -\Omega^2\ \underline{H}(\Omega) \tag{5.3}$$

In case of measured velocities one often speaks of the *Mobility-FRF*. To avoid misunderstanding the type of FRF should be mentioned.
Next the following steps are taken:

- The structure is excited in some degree-of-freedom q_i by a harmonic force, written as:

$$f(t) = f_a \cos(\Omega_k t + \varphi_f) = Re[\{f_a e^{j\varphi_f}\}\ e^{j\Omega_k t}] = Re[\hat{f}\ e^{j\Omega_k t}]$$

with excitation frequency Ω_k, amplitude f_a and phase angle φ_f as schematically shown in Fig 5.2.

- The response is also measured and can be written as:

$$q(t) = q_a \cos(\Omega_k t + \varphi_q) = Re[\{q_a e^{j\varphi_q}\} \, e^{j\Omega_k t}] = Re[\hat{q} \, e^{j\Omega_k t}]$$

with the same excitation frequency Ω_k, but different amplitude q_a and phase angle φ_q as also shown in Fig 5.2). From the amplitudes and the

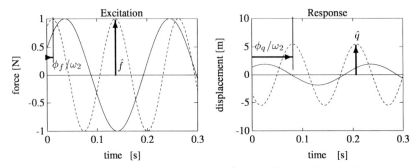

Fig. 5.2   Harmonic excitation and -response for two distinct frequencies
$\omega_1 = 30 \ [rad/s] \ (\text{—})$ en $\omega_2 = 50 \ [rad/s] (\text{- - -})$

phase-shift between complex amplitudes of response and excitation the corresponding FRF for this specific frequency Ω_k can be determined:

$$\underline{H}_{[i,j]}(\Omega_k) = A \, e^{j\varphi}, \qquad \text{where:} \qquad A = q_a/f_a; \quad \varphi = \varphi_q - \varphi_f \qquad (5.4)$$

- For a (large) number of discrete Ω_k-values (also called spectral-lines) this process should be repeated to get a discrete representation of the FRF-function $\underline{H}_{[i,j]}(\Omega)$. Because each frequency-line has to be handled seperately, it was a very time-consuming activity. A big advantage is that no special equipment is necessary.

5.3   PERIODIC EXCITATION

A procedure by which a discrete number of spectral-lines can be evaluated simultaneously is the application of a periodic excitation which automatically will give a periodic response. Examples are block-signals, saw-tooth signals, etc. Each periodic signal can be written as an (infinite) sum of harmonic signals by using the **Fourier series approach**. This can be written as:

$$x(t) = \sum_{n=-\infty}^{\infty} c_n \, e^{(\frac{2\pi n t}{T}j)}$$

$$(n = 0, \pm 1, \pm 2, ...) \qquad (5.5)$$

$$c_n = \tfrac{1}{T} \int_0^T x(t) \, e^{(\frac{-2\pi n t}{T}j)} \, dt$$

where $x(t)$ is the periodic signal with period T. For a physically real signal holds: $c_{-n} = c_n^*$ (complex conjugate of c_n).
We define $\omega_n := n(2\pi/T)$ so that we can also write:

$$x(t) = \sum_{n=-\infty}^{\infty} c_n\, e^{j\omega_n t}$$

$$(n = 0, \pm 1, \pm 2, ...) \qquad (5.6)$$

$$c_n = \tfrac{1}{T} \int_0^T x(t)\, e^{-j\omega_n t} dt$$

So we can write each periodic signal as a sum of harmonic signals with angular frequency $\omega_n = (2\pi n/T)$. If we want to measure a specific FRF for a range of discrete $\omega_n = n\Delta\omega$, $n = 0, 1, 2, ..m$ then we can apply the following procedure:

- Select a periodic excitation $f(t)$ with period time $T = 2\pi/\Delta\omega$

- Calculate the corresponding complex amplitudes $\hat{f}_n$ from:

$$\hat{f}_n = \frac{1}{T} \int_0^T f(t)\, e^{-j\omega_n t} dt$$

- Measure for this periodic excitation the periodic response $q(t)$

- Calculate the corresponding complex amplitudes of the response $\hat{q}_n$ from:

$$\hat{q}_n = \frac{1}{T} \int_0^T q(t)\, e^{-j\omega_n t} dt$$

- Determine the complex FRF $H(\omega_n)$ from $\hat{f}_n$ and $\hat{q}_n$ as shown in the section before.

For the experimental evaluation of a FRF in a selected frequency-band $[0, \omega_{max}]$ it is recommended that all the spectral contributions have more or less comparable amplitudes so that an optimal signal-to-noise ratio can be achieved. This means that all the complex excitation amplitudes $\hat{f}_n$ should have more or less equal moduli.
This can for example easily be achieved by starting from a set of discrete excitation frequencies ω_k, $k = 0, ..m$ with corresponding complex amplitudes $\hat{f}_k$ with uniform moduli and random phases: $\hat{f}_k = |\hat{f}|_k\, e^{j\varphi_k}$; $|\hat{f}|_k = 1.0$; $\varphi_0 = 0$; $\varphi_k =$ uniform random number from $[0, 2\pi]$ for k=1..m.
For this set the corresponding (real) periodic signal can be calculated from:

$$f(t) = \sum_{k=-m}^{m} \hat{f}_k\, e^{j\omega_k t}, \quad \hat{f}_{-k} = \hat{f}_k^* \qquad (5.7)$$

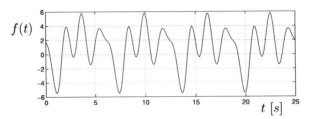

Fig. 5.3 Example of a periodic signal based on a
limited set of only 4 complex amplitudes

Example 5.1

As illustration we consider the following situation:

$$m = 4$$

$$\omega_0 = 0 \ , \omega_1 = 1 \ , \omega_2 = 2 \ , \omega_3 = 3 \ , \omega_4 = 4 \quad [rads^{-1}]$$

$$|\hat{f}_i| = 1.0$$

$$\varphi_0 = 0$$

$$\varphi_{i=1..m} = 2 * \pi * rand, \quad rand{=}uniform \ random \ number \ in \ [0,1]$$

The application of (5.7) gives a periodic signal with period time T_{max} where T_{max} is the least commom multiple of the period times of the contributing harmonic components, which of course should exist. In this case we get $T_{max} = 2\pi$ [s]. With a simple programme a result like shown in Fig. 5.3 can be calculated.

5.4 FOURIER ANALYSIS

In practice we will usually apply non-periodic signals or transient signals for example (hammer) impact-type signals, sine-sweeps, white noise etc.. In that case we use the *Fourier-integral* transformation which can be seen as the limit of the complex Fourier-series approach for a period time going to ∞. It is defined as:

$$X(f) \quad = \quad \mathcal{F}[x(t)] = \int\limits_{t=-\infty}^{\infty} x(t) \ e^{-2\pi jft} dt$$

$$x(t) \quad = \quad \mathcal{F}^{-1}[X(f)] = \int\limits_{f=-\infty}^{\infty} X(f) \ e^{2\pi jft} df \qquad (5.8)$$

We call such a combination of a forward transformation $(x(t) \Rightarrow X(f))$ and a backward transformation $(X(f) \Rightarrow x(t))$ a Fourier-transformation pair. To get a symmetric and unique pair of FFT transforms we used the frequency f $[Hz]$ as the independent variable instead of ω $[rad/s]$.

It is important to mention that in principle the function $x(t)$ should fulfill the Dirichlet condition:

$$\int_{t=-\infty}^{\infty} |x(t)|dt \text{ exists;} \quad x(t) \text{ piecewise smooth} \tag{5.9}$$

Many signals, especially all periodic signals do not fulfill this property which means that the Fourier-integral approach cannot be applied. A solution for this problem is the introduction of a so-called *generalised Fourier-transformation*. In practical situations, however we normally are using a signal which only is defined in a bounded time-interval $(0 \leq t \leq T)$, such as schematically shown in Fig 5.4. We will look at a signal $x(t)$, defined for $-\infty < t < \infty$ with its

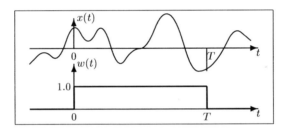

Fig. 5.4   Practical application Fourier-integral

theoretical Fourier-transform $X(f)$. We define a second signal $x_B(t)$ which inside the "window" $[0, T]$ is exactly the same as $x(t)$ but zero outside the window. So we can see this windowed signal $x_B(t)$ as being the result of the multiplication of the original signal $x(t)$ with the so-called boxcar window-function $w(t)$ as also indicated in the figure.

The signal $x_B(t)$ certainly fulfils the convergence property for the Fourier-integral with as result the Fourier-transform $X_B(f)$. Finally we make use of the assumption:

$$\lim_{T \to \infty} X_B(f) = X(f) \tag{5.10}$$

The application of the complex Fourier-series approach to a periodic signal will lead to a so-called discrete spectrum namely the coefficients c_n corresponding to the discrete frequencies $\omega_n = \frac{2\pi n}{T}$. It can be shown that the application of a Fourier-integral will lead to a continuous spectrum but in case of a periodic signal this will be a special type of continuous spectrum, namely a collection of δ-funktions.

The Fourier-transform $X(f)$ in general is a complex funktion so it can be visualised by amplitude and phase, or by real- and imaginairy part as function of the independent variable, the frequency f.

Example 5.2

As illustration we look at the Fourier-transform $W(f)$ of the window-function $w(t)$ as shown in Fig 5.4. So we are using:

$$w(t) = 1 \quad 0 \le t \le T, \qquad else \quad w(t) = 0$$

We then get:

$$W(f) = \int_{-\infty}^{\infty} w(t) \ e^{-2\pi j f t} dt = \int_{0}^{T} [\cos(2\pi f t) - j\sin(2\pi f t)]dt$$

$$= \frac{1}{2\pi f} [\sin(2\pi f T) + j\{\cos(2\pi f T) - 1\}]$$

$$= T \ \frac{\sin(\pi f T)}{\pi f T} \ e^{-\pi j f T} \tag{5.11}$$

In Fig 5.5 this Fourier-transform[1] is shown in different ways.

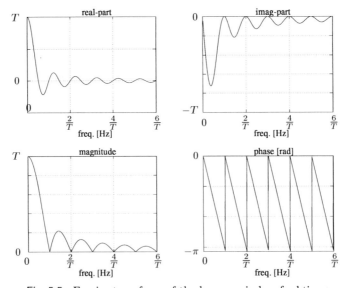

Fig. 5.5 Fourier-transform of the boxcar window-funktion

---

[1]It should be mentioned that this specific type of function in the limit for $T \to \infty$ can be seen as a so-called generalised δ-function.

5.4.1 Discrete Fourier Transform (DFT)

For the Fourier-transformation from time-domain to frequency-domain and vice-versa very efficient numerical procedures have been developed. Here we shall only look at the background of these procedures and discuss two important error-sources when applying these procdures in practical situations. We start from the signal $x(t)$ which in principle is defined for $-\infty < t < \infty$ but only the part $0 \le t \le T$ will be taken into account. The next important factor is that we will only use a discretised version of this part of the signal by applying an Analog to Digital (A-D) converter. This means that we only use the signal values at a limited number of equidistant points of time (with fixed timestep ΔT). This is called the *sampling* of the signal. The total measuring time (sampling time) is called T and we assume that this sampling time is devided in N equal time-intervals $\Delta T = T/N$. (see also Fig 5.6). In the

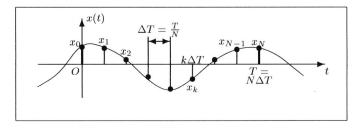

Fig. 5.6 Digital sampling of the signal $x(t)$

so-called *Discrete Fourier Transformation DFT* the Fourier-integral (5.8) will be approximated by:

$$X(f) \approx X_{DFT}(f) := \frac{1}{T} \sum_{k=0}^{N-1} x[k\Delta T] e^{-2\pi j f(k\Delta T)} \Delta T \qquad (5.12)$$

Where the factor $1/T$ is put for the summation to create an analogy with the complex Fourier series approach. By using this numerical approximation a first typical property can be recognised. The Fourier transform according to (5.12) can be evaluated for each arbitrary frequency f, $\infty < f < \infty$. If we have the result for a specific frequency f and then look at the expected result for $f = f + 1/\Delta T$ we get:

$$X_{DFT}(f + \frac{1}{\Delta T}) = \frac{1}{T} \sum_{k=0}^{N-1} x[k\Delta T] e^{-2\pi j (f + \frac{1}{\Delta T}) k\Delta T} \Delta T =$$

$$e^{-2\pi jk} [\frac{1}{T} \sum_{k=0}^{N-1} x[k\Delta T] e^{-2\pi j f(k\Delta T)} \Delta T] = X_{DFT}(f) \qquad (5.13)$$

This means that the DFT-result will be **periodic** with period frequency $f_N = 1/\Delta T$, whereas the theoretical Fourier transform in general will not be periodic at all. So we only should evaluate the DFT in a frequencyband $0 \leq f \leq f_N$ and if the DFT in that interval will be an accurate approximation for the theoretical Fourier transform we can live with this unexpected result. We still have the problem that also in this limited interval we have an infinite number of discrete frequencies for which the DFT should be evaluated in order to make the backtransformation possible.

In this backtransformation we only want to be able to represent the discrete values $x[k\Delta T]$ in the interval $[0, T]$. So it does not matter at all whether this (re-calculated) signal-part is a part of the original signal $x(t)$, $-\infty < t < \infty$ or a part of a **periodic** signal which inside the interval exactly equals $x(t)$ but outside the interval is just the periodic repetition of this intervalpart. From the complex Fourier series approach we know that for a periodic function with period time T we only have to consider the spectral lines $\omega_n = 2\pi n/T$ or in terms of frequency $f_n = n/T$.

Finally we see that in the interval $0 \leq f \leq f_N = N/T$ we only have to evaluate the DFT at the discrete frequencies $f = n/T$, $n = 0, 1, 2, ...N - 1$. So finally we get for the DFT:

$$\underline{X}_{DFT}[n] = \frac{1}{N} \sum_{k=0}^{N-1} \underline{x}[k] \, W^{kn}; \quad W = e^{-2\pi j/N}, \quad n = 0, 1, 2, ...N - 1 \quad (5.14)$$

In this expression $\underline{x}$ is the column of (usually real) discrete functionvalues of the sampled signal and $\underline{X}$ the column of complex discrete DFT values (both containing N elements).

Some additional remarks are:

- This DFT might also be applied directly to complex time-series

- In practice we normally are dealing with a sampled signal which only consists of real function values. In that case it can be shown easily that there is an additional property for the DFT which reads: $\underline{X}[\frac{N}{2} + p] = \underline{X}^*[\frac{N}{2} - p]$, $p \in \mathcal{N}$. (X^* is the complex conjugate of X). So in this case the DFT has a special symmetry (in complex conjugate sence) with respect to the frequency-line $f_{fold} = \frac{f_N}{2}$ also called the *folding frequency*. Consequently, of all the N complex numbers $\underline{X}$ only half contains essential information. One might also say that the set of N real numbers $\underline{x}$ has been transformed into a set of $N/2$ complex numbers $\underline{X}[0 : (N/2 - 1)]$.

- The inverse transformation corresponding with (5.14) reads:

$$\underline{x}[k] = \frac{1}{\Delta T} \sum_{i=0}^{N-1} \underline{X}[i] \, W^{-kn}, \quad k = 0, 1, 2, ...N - 1$$

- Sometimes also other definitions are used for the DFT. MATLAB for example is using the DFT-pair:

$$\underline{X}[n] = \sum_{k=0}^{N-1} \underline{x}[k] \, W^{kn}; \quad \underline{x}[k] = \frac{1}{T} \sum_{i=0}^{N-1} \underline{X}[i] \, W^{-kn}; \quad k, n = 0, 1..N-1$$

In the examples which will follow the DFT definition according to (5.14) will be used if not otherwise stated.

Example 5.3

To illustrate the use of the DFT algorithm we look again at the window-function $w(t)$ as shown in Fig. 5.7. So:

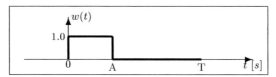

Fig. 5.7   Rectangular window function

$$w(t) = 1.0 \quad for \; 0 \le t \le A \; [s], \quad else \; w(t) = 0$$

We want to compare our results with the theoretical result as shown in Fig 5.5. So we choose our maximum frequentie $f_N = 20/(2A)$. We also apply:

- *$A = 10 \; [s]$, so f_N will be $f_N = 1 \; [Hz]$*
- *Number of time intervals $N = 200$*
- *Frequency-interval length $\Delta f = f_N/N = 0.005 \; [Hz]$*
- *Total sampling time T should be $T = 1/\Delta f = 200 \; [s]$*
- *Sampling time step becomes $\Delta T = T/N = 1 \; [s]$*

In Fig. 5.8 some results of the DFT are shown. The upper-left part gives the window-function $w(t)$. The upper-right part gives the amplitude $|X(f)|$ of the DFT as function of the frequency $0 \le f \le f_N$. The folding-frequency $f_{fold} = 0.5 \; [Hz]$ can be clearly recognized. The bottom figures give the real respectively imaginairy part of $X[n]$. These two also show the special folding property.
Finally the result from the DFT transform will be compared in Fig. 5.9 with the theoretical Fouriertransform as given in (5.11). (The DFT result has been scaled with the factor $N=200$ to get equal amplitude levels.) In Fig. 5.9 we only show the relevant part of the DFT up to the folding frequency. We see a good correspondence between DFT and theoretical

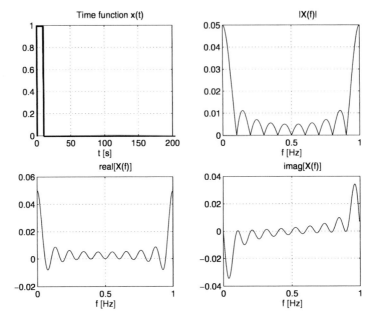

Fig. 5.8 Some results of the DFT of the boxcar window function

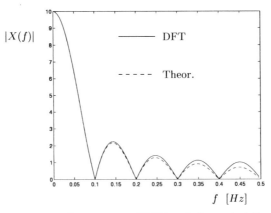

Fig. 5.9 Comparison of DFT and theoretical Fourier
Transform for the boxcar window function

*result exept for higher frequencies where some differences can be seen.
The reason for these deviations will be discussed later in section5.4.3.*

5.4.2   Fast Fourier Transformation (FFT)

In the derivation of the DFT algorithm the number of time-intervals and consequently also the number of frequency-intervals N could be selected free. Only for very large values for N ($N > 2000$) the computer time will be extremely large. By restriction of the choice for N to only powers of 2 ($N = 2^m$; $m \in \mathcal{N}$) and re-organisation of the calculations necessary for the DFT-algorithm the necessary CPU-time can be reduced enormously. This leads to a so-called Fast-Fourier-Transformation algorithm.

Here we will only look at the basic idea behind these algorithms. The problem is to calculate the DFT for the discretised function $x(t)$:

$$X[n] = \frac{1}{N} \sum_{k=0}^{N-1} x[k] \, e^{-2\pi jkn/N}, \qquad n = 0,1,2,...N-1 \qquad (5.15)$$

In principle this needs N^2 complex multiplications (which in numerical calculations are the dominant factors for the CPU-consumption). For large N ($N > x000$) this will lead to a very slow transformation from time- to frequency domain and vice-versa, especially because in practical situations this transformation has to be carried out a large number of times.

In the FFT-concept we do not take N to be arbitrary, but we only use $N = 2^m$, $m \in \mathcal{N}$. We start from the discrete time-series $x[k]$, $k = 0,1,..N-1$. This series can be splitted into two series of $N_2 = N/2$ elements each, namely:

$$y[l] = x[2l] \quad \text{and} \quad z[l] = x[2l+1]; \quad l = 0,1,...,N_2-1 \qquad (5.16)$$

We then get:

$$X[n] = \frac{1}{N} \sum_{l=0}^{N_2-1} y[l] \, e^{-2\pi jln/N_2} + \frac{1}{N} \sum_{l=0}^{N_2-1} z[l] \, e^{-\pi j(2l+1)n/N_2} = Y[n] + W[n]$$

$$(5.17)$$

For $W[n]$ we can write:

$$W[n] = e^{-\pi jn/N_2} \left[\frac{1}{N} \sum_{l=0}^{N_2-1} z[l] \, e^{-2\pi jln/N_2} \right] := e^{-\pi jn/N_2} Z[n] \qquad (5.18)$$

So we get:

$$X[n] = Y[n] + e^{-\pi jn/N_2} Z[n] \qquad (5.19)$$

It can easy be shown that both parts $Y[n]$ and $Z[n]$ are periodic with period N_2. So only half of these series has to be calculated, so only for $n = 0,1,..N_2 - 1$. The calculation of the wanted DFT using these two half time-series needs: $2 N_2^2$ multiplications for the series $Y[n]$ and $Z[n]$ and finally N_2 multiplications for the calcalution of $X[n]$ from $Y[n]$ and $Z[n]$. The total number of multiplications therefore becomes: $N_2(2N_2 + 1) = N(N+1)/2$. For the calculation of $Y[n]$ and $Z[n]$ however we can repeat the same tric.

We split the series $y[l]$ respectively $z[l]$ again in two equal parts (with the even and odd elements) and follow the same procedure. Due to the choice of $N = 2^m$ this time-series-splitting can be continued until we have N time-series of only a single element. The DFT of a single element is the element itself. It can be shown that following this procedure we now need $N \ log_2(N)$ complex multiplications for the calculation of the DFT $\underline{X}$ which implies a CPU-reduction-factor of:

$$\text{reduction-factor} = \frac{N^2}{N \ log_2(N)} = \frac{N}{m} \qquad (5.20)$$

If we take for example $N = 2048 = 2^{11}$ this wil lead to a CPU-reduction-factor of approximately 186. The result however is (numerically) exactly the same as by using the simple DFT-algoritm based on a single series of N elements. So, if possible it will be very attractive to use time-series of length $N = 2^m$.

Example 5.4

In this example we will use the FFT algorithm for the calculation of the spectral representation of some excitation signals which are frequently used for the FRF-evaluation of (mechanical) systems. First we will look at some impact-type excitations forms. In Fig. 5.10 in the upper left part two impact excitations are shown. To get a better indication of these two signals the upper right plot gives a zoom-part of the time axis. We can recognise a small-high impact (for example created by hitting a structure with a hammer with a steel head) and a lower-broader impact which might be the result of using a soft hammer head (rubber or plastic).

For the FFT we used $N = 1024$. The amplitude of the FFT of both signals is shown in the bottom part of Fig. 5.10. We can see that the hard-top hammer has a broader spectral contribution, so this excitation will also excite the higher harmonics of the structure. If we want to investigate only the lower modes of a system we can better use the soft hammer type, because this has a smaller spectral bandwidth. In real practice this tuning of the excitation in relation to the dynamics of the system or machine is a very important factor for getting accurate results.

Secondly we will look at two other types of excitation signals as shown in Fig. 5.11.

- *A sine sweep signal, (A)-plot, which is a harmonic signal with constant amplitude and in our case a frequency which is linearly growing in time from $f = 0...40 \ [Hz]$. So the signal has been created by:*

$$x(t) = \sin[2\pi(40\frac{t}{T})t]$$

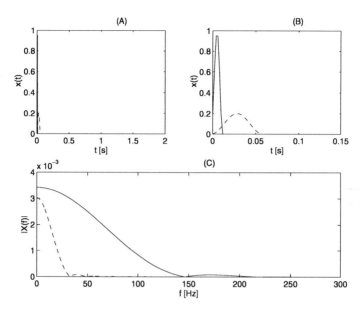

Fig. 5.10 FFT of two impact-type signals, *hard-top* hammer (solid)
and *soft-top* hammer (dashed)

with $T = 2[s]$ *the total measuring time and* $t = 0 : \Delta T : T$ *the discretised time-array.*

- *A type of random signal by generating random numbers from a normal distribution with mean value* $\mu = 0$ *and variance* $\sigma = 1$, *see plot(B)*

The plots (C) respectively (D) shows the amplitudes of the calculated FFT of the signals (A) respectively (B). It can be seen that with the sine-sweep signal very easily some kind of band-limited spectrum with uniform amplitude can be generated which makes it very attractive for practical application.

The noise-type signal gives a more or less uniform spectrum over the whole frequency range. Also this type of excitation is applied very frequently in the experimental modal analysis of structures.

5.4.3 Error sources in FFT-calculations

Looking at the formulation of the DFT/FFT algorithms in the preceeding sections it will be directly clear that in any case we will have two sources for errors in the numerical calculation of Fourier-transforms. Firstly we started

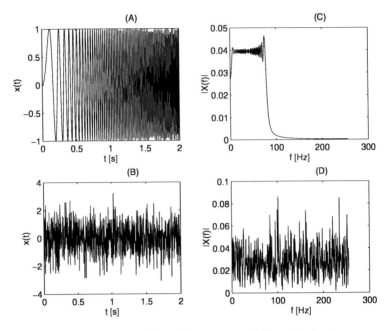

Fig. 5.11   Sine sweep signal (A) and its spectrum (C), and noise-type
signal (B) and its spectrum (D)

from a signal $x(t)$ which in principle is defined for $-\infty < t < \infty$ but we only
considered the (small) portion in the window $0 \leq t \leq T$. This can cause errors
in the digital result related to the so-called *Signal leakage*.

Secondly we used for the DFT calculation a discretised sample of this continu-
'ous signal part consisting of only a limited number of discrete function-values.
This source of errors is related to the so-called *Aliasing*. Both aspects will
not be treated in detail but only illustrated in the next paragraphs and also
some possible actions to reduce their negative effects will be illucidated.

5.4.3.1 Signal leakage   From the signal $x(t)$ defined for $-\infty < t < \infty$ we
only take into account the portion inside the window such as indicated before
in Fig 5.4. There are two situations where this in principle will not have any
consequence, namely:

- In case of a transient signal (for example an impulse response) which
  has been damped out before the window has been ended

- In case of a periodic signal for which the total measuring time T is
  exactly a multiple of the period time

Both cases are illustrated in Fig. 5.12.

   In general however the concentration on only a portion of a signal for the
FFT-evaluation will introduce some errors in the result. To illustrate this we

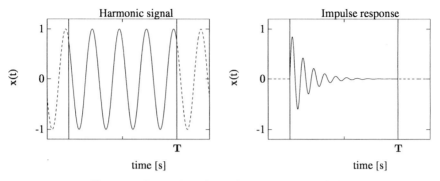

Fig. 5.12   Examples of signals without signal leakage

go back to a base-function $x(t)$ and the window-function $w(t)$ such as shown in Fig. 5.4. The windowed portion of the signal $x_B(t)$ (which is exactly equal to $x(t)$ inside the window but zero outside the window) can be written as $x_B(t) = x(t)w(t)$. Iw we apply the Fourier transformation on this relation we get:

$$X_B(f) = W(f) \otimes X(f) \tag{5.21}$$

where the symbol $\otimes$ stands for the convolution of two functions. So as a result we get the approximation $X_B(f)$ instead of the wanted Fourier transform $X(f)$.

For the Fourier transform $W(f)$ of the boxcar window-function $w(t)$ we have found before:

$$W(f) = T\frac{\sin(\pi fT)}{\pi fT}\, e^{-\pi jfT} \tag{5.22}$$

So the windowed Fourier Transform $X_B(f)$ can be seen as the convolution of the theoretical Fourier transform $X(f)$ with the window transform $W(f)$. This will lead to certain types of distortions in the calculated result.

It is very important to notice that if the window transform $W(f)$ should be a δ-function the convolution operation will not have any affect and we will get the theoretical result. This is the case for $T \to \infty$ which is obvious because we will not have any windowing effect.

Example 5.5

To illustrate the effect of this convolution effect we look at a harmonic signal with frequency $f_o = 0.125\ [Hz]$ so with a period time $T_o = 8\ [s]$:

$$x(t) = \cos(2\pi f_o t)$$

The theoretical Fourier transform of this function reads:

$$X(f) = \frac{1}{2}[\delta(f - f_o) + \delta(f + f_o)]$$

The convolution of these two δ-functions with the window function
$W(f)$ *will result in two of the functions* $W(f)$, *one shifted to* $f = f_o$
and another shifted to $f = -f_o$, *so:*

$$X_B(f) = \frac{1}{2}[W(f - f_o) + W(f + f_o)] \qquad (5.23)$$

So if we should calculate the analytical Fourier transform of the win-
dowed function we should get the result (5.23). If we however apply
a DFT/FFT procedure to calculate numerically the Fourier transform
we only evaluate this transform for discrete frequencies. We take for
example: $N = 32$ [s] *and* $T = 32$ [s], *so we sample exactly 4 pe-*
riods of the periodic signal. Then we only look at the spectral lines
$f_n = n/T$, $n = 0, 1, ..N - 1$. *If we evaluate the function (5.23) at these*
discrete frequencies then we only get zero-values except for $f = f_0$ *re-*
spectively $f = -f_0$ *(see also Fig 5.5).*
This numerical result is shown in Fig. 5.13, part (A). So, in fact we get

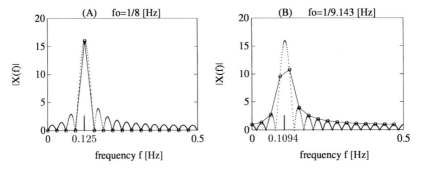

Fig. 5.13 DFT of $x(t) = \cos(2\pi f_o t)$, (A): $f_o = 1/8$ [Hz],
(B): $f_o = 1/9.143$ [Hz]; analytic result (dotted), numerical result (solid)

a perfect numerical result for the theoretical δ-function at $f = 1/8$ [Hz].
Secondly we look at a harmonic function with $f_o = 1/9.143$ [Hz] *which*
means that the window $[0, 32]$ *will cover only 3.5 period. The DFT*
parameters will be unchanged. First we have now a still correct ana-
lytical result which consists of two $W(f)$-*functions positioned at* $f_o = \pm1/9.143 = 0.1094$ [Hz]. *The spectral lines however do not coincide*
anymore with the zeroes of these $W(f)$-*functions. This leads to the re-*
sult shown in Fig. 5.13 (B).
The numerical representation gives the impression that energy of the
single harmonic component has been leaked to neighbouring spectral
lines (has been smeared out). This explains the name signal leakage.
One might also say that the discrimination of the transformation has
been decreased.

Sometimes the reason for signal leakage is illustrated by looking at the time domain. We only use the windowed part of the signal but in the DFT/FFT operation we did assume that this was one period of a periodic signal by just shifting this windowed part. If we are dealing with a periodic signal and if the window length is not exactly a multiple of the period time of this signal then we will get discontinuous jumps on the boundary of our window. This is shown in Fig. 5.14. So, resuming we can mention two causes for the presence

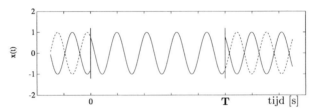

Fig. 5.14   Time domain illustration of signal-leakage

of signal leakage. In the frequency domain the main problem is that the window function $W(f)$ is not a perfect δ-function and in the time domain the problem is the presence of the discontinuities. These observations have led to the following actions to reduce the effect of this signal leakage:

- Instead of the boxcar window we should apply another window function with a Fourier transform which looks more like a real δ-function then the $W(f)$ function.

- Minimise the boundary discontinuities.

A number of window functions has been created to fulfill these demands such as the Hanning-window: $w(t) = \sqrt{\frac{8}{3}}[1 - \cos(2\pi t/T)]$, Blackman-, Hamming-, Kaiser-window etc.

The Mean-Square-Value (MSV) of the windowed signal can be written as:

$$MSV = \frac{1}{T} \int\limits_{0}^{T} w(t)^2 \, x(t)^2 \, dt \qquad (5.24)$$

The signal windowing might not change this MSV-value too much. One way to be sure that this will be the case is to normalise the window:

$$\alpha := \frac{1}{T} \int\limits_{0}^{T} w(t)^2 \, dt; \qquad w(t) = w(t)/\sqrt{\alpha} \qquad (5.25)$$

The former Hanning window has been normalized in this way.
Finally we investigate the effect of such an alternative window function on the

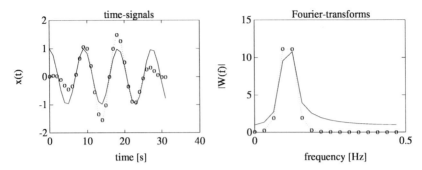

Fig. 5.15 Left: Harmonic signal without (solid) and with Hanning-window (dashed)
Right: Fourier transform without (solid) and with Hanning-window (dashed)

example of the single harmonic with the base-frequency of $f_o = 1/9.143 \, [Hz]$ (which was 3.5 periods in the window) and the FFT-parameters: $N = 32$ and $T = 32 \, [s]$. From Fig. 5.4.3.1 we may conclude that in this case the DFT/FFT result after using a Hanning window has been considerably improved. We still do not get the perfect δ-function which should be the case for this single harmonic, but the smearing-out effect due to the signal leakage has been reduced. In simulations where the frequency of the signals and also the sampling-time T can be controlled such a window function is not needed and the signal leakage effect very often can be avoided by choosing special parameter values. In practice however where we are dealing with arbitrary frequencies, including measurement noise, and sometimes also the sampling time cannot be choosen arbitrary, signal leakage will always be present and then such a window function can reduce the distortion considerably.

5.4.3.2 Aliasing Aliasing is an effect which is closely related to the digital sampling of the originally continuous signal on the discrete time points $t_i = n \, \Delta T$. We define the **sampling frequency** f_N:

$$f_N = \frac{1}{\Delta T} \, [Hz] \tag{5.26}$$

A digitally sampled signal $x_B(t)$ can also be seen as a socalled pulse-train with variable intensity:

$$x_B(t) = \sum_{n=-\infty}^{\infty} [\Delta T \, x(t)] \, \delta(t - n\Delta T) \tag{5.27}$$

So the discrete values are represented as an infinite sum of impulse functions at $t = n\Delta T$ with the intensity $\Delta T \, x(t = n\Delta T)$. The factor ΔT is introduced as a scaling parameter.

It can be shown that the analytical Fourier transform of this (continuous)

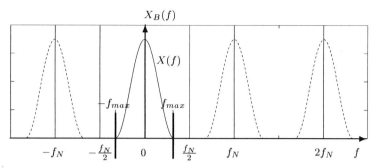

Fig. 5.16 Situation without Aliasing, $f_{max} \leq f_N/2$

signal is:

$$X_B(f) = X(f) \otimes \sum_{n=-\infty}^{\infty} \delta(f - nf_N) \tag{5.28}$$

which leads to:

$$X_B(f) = \sum_{n=-\infty}^{\infty} X(f - nf_N) \tag{5.29}$$

So the Fourier transform of the digitized signal consists of the infinite series of the exact Fourier transform but each time shifted over a multiple of f_N. To visualise the effect of this operation we consider an exact Fourier transform $X(f)$ for which holds that $|X(f)| = 0$ for $f > f_{max}$. So the signal has a finite bandwidth.

We can now distinguish two situations, namely $f_{max} \leq f_N/2$ and $f_{max} > f_N/2$.

Situation I: $f_{max} \leq f_N/2$. This situation is sketched in Fig 5.16. In this figure the theoretical Fourier transform $X(f)$ is plotted with the solid line and the shifted functions $X(f - nf_N)$ with a dotted line. The final result $X_B(f)$ according to (5.29) will be just the summation of the infinite set of these functions.

- $X_B(f)$ will be a periodic function with period f_N while the base function $X(f)$ is not periodic at all. This effect has already been mentioned before in the derivation of the DFT algorithm.

- In the interval $[-f_N/2 \leq f \leq f_N/2]$ the funktion $X_B(f)$ is **exactly equal** to $X(f)$. So if we only look at this interval we have a perfect result.

Situation II: $f_{max} > f_N/2$. This situation is sketched in Fig 5.17.

Again the theoretical Fourier transform is shown by the solid line, and the shifted functions $X(f - f_N)$ by a dotted line. The resulting summation of all

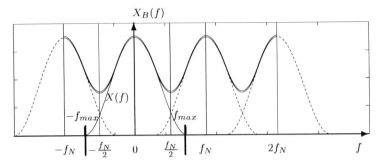

Fig. 5.17 Situation with Aliasing, $f_{max} > f_N/2$

these shifted functions is shown by the bold line. This final result $X_B(f)$ is of course again a periodic function but also in the interval $[-f_N/2 \leq f \leq f_N/2]$ is differs considerably from the searched function $X(f)$. Errors are introduced because the energy of the Fourier components with a frequency $f > f_N/2$ are folded back to the interval $[-f_N/2 \leq f \leq f_N/2]$. This also axplains the name Aliasing. To avoid this errorsource there is only one solution always to create a situation where:

$$f_{fold} = f_N/2 > f_{max}, \qquad \text{or} \quad \frac{1}{2\Delta T} > f_{max} \qquad (5.30)$$

The frequency $1/2\Delta T$ is also called the **Nyquist-frequency**. For a known f_{max} the FFT-parameteers must be chosen such that the criterion (5.30) is fulfilled.

Usually the maximum frequency f_{max} in a signal in not known or in principle it even can be infinitely large (think at noisy type measurement signals). The only solution then is to apply an analog/digital filtering technique and just remove all the frequency content in the signal above a selected folding frequency.

The background of Aliasing can also be illustrated by looking at the time-domain, for example the representation of a harmonic signal with different frequencies and fixed sampling frequncy. To illustrate this we look at a situation with $f_N = 12 \, [Hz]$ and so $\Delta T = 1/f_N = 0.08333 \, [s]$. We consider the harmonic functions $x(t) = \cos(2\pi f_i t)$ with $f_1 = 14 \, [Hz]$ and $f_2 = 22 \, [Hz]$. Both do **not** fulfill the Nyquist criterion. The signals will be discretised with the chosen ΔT as shown in Fig 5.18. In the figure we can see that the discrete representation of the signals with freq. $f_1 = 14 \, [Hz]$ and also freq. $f_2 = 22 \, [Hz]$ is exactly the same as the representation of a signal with a frequency of only $f = 2 \, [Hz]$. This means that in the FFT-spectrum the freq. of 14 [Hz] and 22 [Hz] are completly wrongly represented as a frequency of 2 [Hz]. So it is of vital importance always to use a signal filtering technique before an DFT/FFT algoritm will be applied.

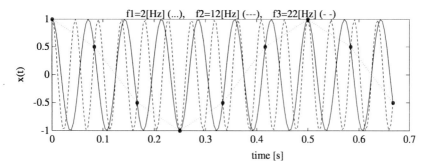

Fig. 5.18 Origin of seeming frequencies due to Aliasing

5.5 POWERSPECTRA

We start from a signal $x(t)$ and the corresponding windowed signal $x_B(t)$ with its Fourier transform $X_B(f)$:

$$x_B(t) = x(t) \quad \text{voor } 0 \le t \le T \quad \text{and} \quad x_B(t) = 0 \quad \text{else}$$

$$X_B(f) = \int_0^T x_B(t)e^{-2\pi jft}dt \tag{5.31}$$

The Mean Square Value (MSV) is defined as:

$$MSV = \frac{1}{T}\int_{t=0}^T x_B^2(t)\ dt = \frac{1}{T}\int_{t=-\infty}^\infty x_B^2(t)\ dt \tag{5.32}$$

We apply the inverse Fourier transform:

$$x_B(t) = \int_{f=-\infty}^\infty X_B(f)\ e^{2\pi jft}df \tag{5.33}$$

which leads to:

$$
\begin{aligned}
MSV &= \frac{1}{T}\int_{t=-\infty}^\infty \left[x_B(t)\int_{f=-\infty}^\infty X_B(f)e^{2\pi jft}df \right] dt \\
&= \frac{1}{T}\int_{f=-\infty}^\infty X_B(f)\left[\int_{t=-\infty}^\infty x_B(t)e^{2\pi jft}dt \right] df \\
&= \frac{1}{T}\int_{f=-\infty}^\infty X_B(f)X_B^*(f)df = \int_{f=-\infty}^\infty \frac{1}{T}|X_B(f)|^2)df \tag{5.34}
\end{aligned}
$$

If T is sufficiently large so that the windowed transform $X_B(f)$ is a good estimate for the real transform $X(f)$ we will get an accurate estimate of the total average power in the signal. In expression (5.34) the Fourier transform $X_B(f)$ is playing a central role.

We can also look only at that part of the total power which is due to frequencies in a frequency-band $[f, f + \Delta f]$:

$$\int_{f}^{f+\Delta f} \frac{1}{T}|X_B(f)|^2 df \tag{5.35}$$

For $\Delta f \to 0$ we can see $\frac{1}{T}|X_B(f)|^2)$ is the power-density of the signal for frequency f. So the **power spectral density or Auto-power spectrum** $S_{xx}(f)$ can be defined as:

$$S_{xx}(f) = \frac{1}{T}X_B^*(f)X_B(f) \tag{5.36}$$

which is always a **real** function !

About 15 years ago this auto-power spectrum was determined by feeding the analogue signal $x(t)$ to a (very small) bandfilter which resulted in almost a single harmonic compoment. The MSV value of such a harmonic component with amplitude A is simply $\frac{A^2}{2}$. By shifting the bandfilter the MSV-value as function of frequency could be determinded. Nowadays this power-spectrum is always calculated digitally by using efficient FFT-algorithms.

In practice measurement signals will always be distorted by the presence of measurement noise. This means that for getting an accurate estimate the autopower-spectrum should be calculated as the average of a (large) number of spectra calculated for choosen signaldiscretizations. So we assume that the noise will be statistically independent of the real signals and by taking an average the contribution of this noise will be cancelled out.

So we take M times the Fourier transform $X_B^k(f)$, $k = 1, 2..M$ of a part $x_k(t)$ of a long time-signal and calculate the autopower-spectrum estimate:

$$S_{xx}(f) = \frac{1}{M} \left[\sum_{k=1}^{M} \frac{1}{T}|X_B^k(f)|^2 \right] \tag{5.37}$$

Example 5.6

As illustration we look at a single harmonic function $x(t) = \sin(2\pi f_o t)$ with amplitude 1 and frequency $f_o = 5$ [Hz].

We assume to be dealing with a large contribution of measurement noise which can be modelled by a Gaussian probability density function with zero mean and standard deviation $\sigma = 3$. (This is 3 times as large as the original signal amplitude !!) For this combined signal we generate a sample of 4000 points with discretisation time-step $\Delta T = 1/40$ [s]. We

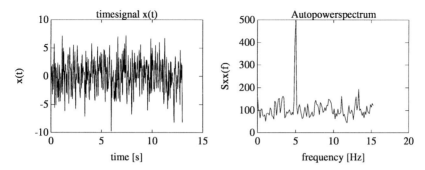

Fig. 5.19   Harmonic function with measurement noise and
estimated autopower spectrum

*assume this to be our measurement data. A piece of this signal is shown
in Fig. 5.6 (left). This figure clearly shows the enormous amount of
noise. The harmonic signal is completely invisible.*

*The discretisation time-step $\Delta t = 1/40$ [s] leads to a folding frequency
of 20 [Hz]. in this interval we want about 200 spectral lines which we
round off to N=256 because this is a power of two. From the sample of
4000 points we now take blocks of 256 points (which means 15 blocks),
calculate for each block (k) the FFT $X_B^k(f)$ and finally the average over
all the blocks. (to reduce the signal leakage we also applied a Hanning
window).*

*The final autopowerspectrum estimate is shown in Fig. 5.6 (right).
We can recognize a dominant sharp peak at 5 Hz indicating a harmonic
component with that frequency. Secondly we see a more or less constant-
level contribution of many harmonics with all the same magnitude and
if we should look at the spectral elements of a single Fourier transform
$X_B^k(f)$ we could see that they have a random phase ϕ, $0 \leq \phi \leq 2\pi$.
This also can be seen as a definition of white noise.*

*We have seen that the area under the autopowerspectrum-plot equals
the total power of the signal, see (5.34). If we compare the area under
the peak with the remaining area we again can see the large amount of
noise in the signal.*

*Concluding we can say that the autopowerspectrum is a powerfull tool
to calculate the frequency content of a signal fast and easy.*

Up to now we only considered a single signal $x(t)$. But we can also have
to deal with a second signal $y(t)$, for example the response of a system on the
input $x(t)$. In the same way as done for the autopower-spectrum function we
now define the so-called **Cross-power spectrum** without further derivation

as:

$$S_{xy}(f) = \frac{1}{T}X_B^*(f)Y_B(f) \tag{5.38}$$

Contrarary to the autopower-spectrum the crosspower-spectrum is a complex function, so it has amplitude- as well as phase-information. This crosspower-spectrum is a powerfull tool in the search for relations between signals such as the relation between output and input of a (linear) system. This will be the subject of one of the following paragraphs.

5.5.1 Linear Spectrum

In the beginning of this chapter we introduced the Fourier transformation as a tool to calculate the frequency content of arbitrary signals. For each harmonic component this Fourier transform (also called the linear spectrum) gives amplitude-information but also phase-information. After that the autopowerspectrum was introduced also to present the frequency content of a signal but this quantity only gives amplitude-information and no phase-information because it is a real quantity. So one might put the question of why to introduce a second prescribing function which has less information in it.

The main reason that in practice the autopowerspectrum in many cases will be preferred over the ordinary Fourier transform is that we usually are dealing with measurement noise. To reduce the influence of this measurement noice an avaraging procedure has to be followed. It is in this avaraging that the ordinary Fourier transform fails.

To illustrate this we look at a signal $x(t)$ with Fourier transform $X(f)$. It is easy to show that:

$$\text{if}\quad x(t) \overset{\mathcal{F}}{\Longrightarrow} X(f) \quad\text{then}\quad x(t - t_o) \overset{\mathcal{F}}{\Longrightarrow} X(f)\, e^{-2\pi j f t_o} \tag{5.39}$$

So if we introduce a time-shift t_o for a signal then each spectral component of the Fourier transform will be rotated in the complex plane over the angle $\phi(f) = -2\pi f t_o$. To understand the consequence of this fact we look again at the single harmonic function with measurement noise as discussed in the example on page 320. To eliminate the noise we take a number of realizations, calculate their Fourier transform and finally take the average value as the estimate.

Each realization however will contain an arbitrary part of the harmonic (and of course also the noise). The harmonic part will have a random fase. So if we look at all the Fourier transforms of only the harmonic part and plot them in the complex plane they will look like points evenly distributed over a circle around zero. (The amplitudes will be all equal, but their phase will be random). In the avaragingproces we will not only take the average of the noise contributions (which will go to zero for a large number of averages) but also the average of these points on a circle and this also wil go to zero. So finally we end up with nothing.

To illustrate it we look at the Fourier transform of a harmonic with 3 different phases:

$$x_k(t) = x(t - t_k) = \sin(2\pi f_o(t - t_k)); \qquad t_k = -\phi_k/(2\pi f_o)$$

with $f_o = 2.5 \ [Hz]$ and we take the arbitrary values $\phi_1 = \pi/4 \ [rad]$, $\phi_2 = 2\pi/3 \ [rad]$, $\phi_3 = 8\pi/7 \ [rad]$.

With FFT the Fourier transforms $X_k(f)$ are calculated and plotted in Fig. 5.20. In absence of signal-leakage the Fourier transforms are only nonzero for

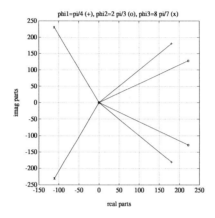

Fig. 5.20   Fourier transform of harmonic with 3 arbitrary time-shifts

$f = f_o$ and these values $X(f_o)$ are all on a circle in the complex plane with a phase-angle which is fully determined by the arbitrary time-shift t_k.

A solution for this problem should be to start all the realizations on a time that the harmonic has a fixed phase. This so-called *triggering* in general is very difficult. Sometimes a second signal can be used for this triggering proces. If one for example wants to study the noise production of a forging machine in a noisy room, the switch of that specific machine might be used for the start of each realization.

Transient type of signals such as with hammer excitation or sine-sweep signals can be used with some internal triggering which means that a specific measurement will be started as soon as the signal becomes nonzero.

Finally we should understand why the autopower spectrum does not need any triggering. If we take the Fourier Transform according to (5.39) with an arbitrary time shift: $X^k(f) = X(f) \ e^{-2\pi jft_o}$ then the autopowerspectrum will be:

$$S_{xx}(f) = \frac{1}{T} \ X^{k^*} \ X^k = \frac{1}{T} \ X^* \ X$$

So the phase shift does not have any effect on this autopowerspectrum.

5.6   FRF-ESTIMATION

We start from a linear system as symbolically shown in Fig 5.21. The exci-

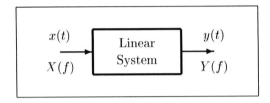

Fig. 5.21   Linear system with input and output

tation (or input) will be a signal $x(t)$ and the respons (output) a signal $y(t)$.
For this respons we can write:

$$y(t) = h(t) \otimes x(t) \tag{5.40}$$

with $h(t)$ the impulse-respons of the system and the symbol $\otimes$ the convolution-
integral. Transformation of this expression with Fourier transformation to the
frequency domain gives:

$$Y(f) = H(f) \, X(f) \tag{5.41}$$

The input $x(t)$ changes into its Fourier transform $X(f)$, the output $y(t)$ in its
Fourier transform $Y(f)$, and the impulse response $h(t)$ in its Fourier transform
$H(f)$ being the well-known frequency response function. The numerically
difficult convolution has been replaced by an ordinary multiplication.
So the frequency respons function $H(f)$ can be calculated very easy from $Y(f)$
and $X(f)$ using:

$$H(f) = \frac{Y(f)}{X(f)}, \quad \text{if } X(f) \neq 0 \tag{5.42}$$

As we mentioned before the calculation of an accurate estimate for the (linear)
transform $Y(f)$ and $X(f)$ can give some problems when dealing with non-
transient signals and the presence of noise.
It has been shown that the use of auto- and crosspower-spectra can be a
solution for that problem. Therefore we multiply numerator and denominator
of (5.42) with $\frac{1}{T}X_b^*(f)$ leading to:

$$H(f) = \frac{\frac{1}{T}X_b^*(f) \, Y(f)}{\frac{1}{T}X_b^*(f) \, X(f)} = \frac{S_{xy}(f)}{S_{xx}(f)} \tag{5.43}$$

So for the evaluation of the frequency respons funktion $H(f)$ we can also use
the crosspower-spectrum $S_{xy}(f)$ and the autopower spectrum $S_{xx}(f)$.

Example 5.7

To illustrate the presented procedures for FRF-estimation we consider a simulated experiment. In the experiment we use a simple two-degree-of-freedom system as shown in Fig. 5.22 We will use the data:

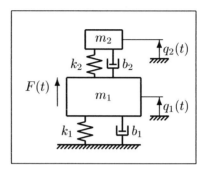

Fig. 5.22 Simple model for FRF-estimation from input-
and output Fourier Transfoms

$m_1 = 1 \ [kg]$, $m_2 = 0.3 \ [kg]$, $k_1 = 100 \ [Nm^{-1}]$, $k_2 = 50 \ [Nm^{-1}]$, $b_1 = 1.0 \ [Nsm^{-1}]$, $b_2 = 0.4 \ [Nsm^{-1}]$.

As excitation degree-of-freedom we choose $q_1(t)$ and as response degree-of-freedom also $q_1(t)$. (We might have choosen any other combination) First we look at a (simulated) impact excitation which has been modelled as a time-series of 512 elements with only one non-zero element, namely element nr. 2. The first part of this excitation is shown in Fig. 5.23 (left). The response of the system on this excitation has been determined numerically and is also shown in Fig. 5.23.

In the next step we forget the system and just take the input and output (blocks of 512 elements) to calculate the autopower-spectrum $S_{xx}(f)$ and the crosspower-spectrum $S_{xy}(f)$. They are both shown in Fig. 5.24. For S_{xx} we get a completely flat spectrum which was to be expected for a

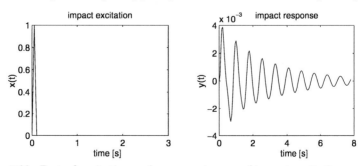

Fig. 5.23 Part of excitation and response in case of impact excitation

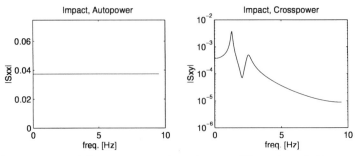

Fig. 5.24 Autopower- and Crosspower-spectrum in case of impact excitation

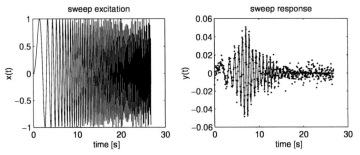

Fig. 5.25 Sine-sweep excitation (left) and the response
including measurement noise (right)

*δ-function. The autopower-spectrum and crosspower-spectrum directly
determine the Frequency-response function of the system. Because the
input spectrum is unity the crosspower-spectrum directly gives the FRF.*

*Another frequently used type of excitation is a sine-sweep excitation. It
consists of a constant-amplitude, harmonic excitation with a frequency
which is changing during the sampling time. Here we choose for a
frequency which will be growing linearly from zero up to a maximum
frequency $f_{max} = 3\,[Hz]$. So the excitation has been generated with:*

$$x_k = \sin[2\pi \frac{f_{max} t_k}{T} t_k], \quad t_k = 0...T$$

*This excitation is shown in Fig. 5.25 (left) and the corresponding re-
sponse is shown in the right part with a solid line. Next we will simulate
the situation that we are dealing with measurement noise in the output.
Therefore we add (Gaussian) random numbers with zero-mean and a
variance of 10% of the maximum output-amplitude to this output. The
output including noise is shown also in the right part of Fig. 5.25 with
dots. We can make the following remarks:*

- *The output without noise is growing to a maximum for approximately $t = 8\,[s]$ and then it is getting smaller again. Obviously*

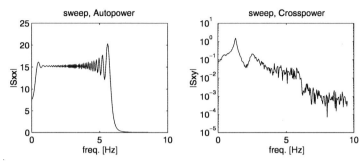

Fig. 5.26 Auto-power and Cross-power spectra for sine-sweep excitation

> *the sine-sweep has a momentary frequency in this neighbourhood which is almost equal to one of the two (weakly damped) eigenfrequencies of the system and resonance occurs. For the excitation frequencies at the beginning and at the end of the sampling window the system will act as a filter.*

- *It can be seen that the percentage measurement noise is (perhaps unrealistically) large in the second half of the window*

To show the averaging procedure we created 20 output blocks, consisting of the system-output, each time provided with a renewed noise contribution. The autopower-spectrum of the single input block $S_x x(f)$ and the average of the (20) crosspower-spectra $S_x y^k(f), k = 1, .., 20$, of the input block and each of the output blocks is shown in Fig. 5.26. It can be seen that we are dealing with an almost flat input-spectrum for a frequency-band which contains the main peaks of our system FRF. So, for this band we might expect a good FRF-estimation. The crosspower-spectrum looks like that of the impact-situation, but it has a more noisy character.

Finally the theoretical frequency response function together with the estimation result for impact- as well as sweep excitation are shown in Fig. 5.27. This last figure shows that both methods can estimate the system-behaviour very nice and that even in the case of a lot of measurement noise an avaraging procedure can eliminate this noise and given accurate results.

It should be remarked that in the preceeding discussion we only looked at the basic idea of FRF-estimation. In the application of these techniques in a real technical environment many more aspects will be important, especially the necessary soft- and hardware and the most important part: the signal monitoring and conditioning which will be vital for accurate results.

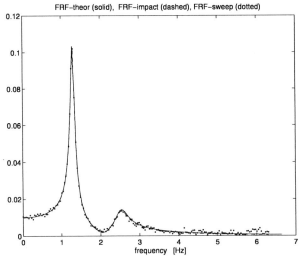

Fig. 5.27 Theoretical FRF (solid) and estimations from impact- (dashed) and sweep excitation (dotted)

Appendix A
Problems

A.1 PROBLEM OVERVIEW

A.2   PROBLEM DESCRIPTIONS

Problem 1   Torsional Gear Pair System

To study torsional vibrations we look at a model (see Fig. A.1) consisting of two interacting gears (mathing perfectly) with radius r_1 respectively r_2. The mass-moments of inertia of the two gears are J_1 and J_2. Gear 1 is connected

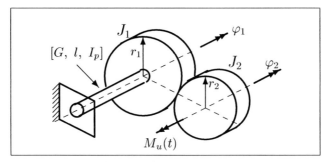

Fig. A.1   Gear pair system

to the ground with a torsion bar with a length l, shear modulus G and polar moment of inertia I_p. The absolute rotations of the gears are named φ_1 and φ_2. On one of the gears an external moment $M_u(t)$ is working (see figure). The system has only one generalized coordinate for which we choose the rotation φ_1. Give the differential equation of motion for this system.

Problem 2   Cylinder in Gutter

A small rigid cylinder is rolling without slip in a fixed cylindrical tube with radius R (see Fig. A.2) . The small cylinder has a mass m, radius r and a mass-moment of inertia $J_z = \frac{1}{2}mr^2$ with respect to the axis through the centre of mass Z. As the generalized coordinate we choose the rotation φ as shown

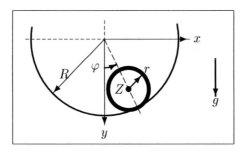

Fig. A.2   Cylinder in gutter

in the figure. The gravitational constant is g. Give the nonlinear differential equation of motion for this system. Show that the position $\varphi = 0$ is a stable equilibrium position is of the system. Derive the linearized equation of motion for small deviations around this equilibrium position. Calculate the eigenfrequency for free vibrations and plot this eigenfrequency for $0 \leq r/R \leq 1$.

Problem 3   Rotating Beam

The uniform beam from Fig. A.3 with length $2l$ and mass m and its massless rigid stay with length a can freely rotate around the fixed point O in a gravitational field with gravitational constant g. There is no friction in the point O. The describe the position of the beam we use the generalized coor-

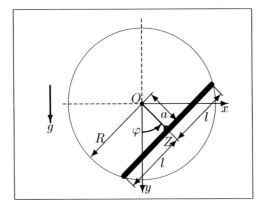

Fig. A.3   Rotating beam

dinate φ as shown in the figure. Derive the nonlinear differential equation(s) of motion for this system. Determine the equilibrium positions and evaluate their stability. Next, assume only small motions around $\varphi = 0$ and give the linearized equation of motion. Give the eigenfrequency for these small vibrations. Generate a picture of the variation of this eigenfrequency as a function of the offset parameter a, $0 \leq a < R$. Take R to be unchangedand update the beam length according to $l^2 = R^2 - a^2$.

Problem 4   Single Disk Hoist

A disk with mass M, radius R and mass-moment of inertia with respect to the centre $J = \frac{1}{2}MR^2$ can rotate without friction around a fixed point (see Fig. A.4) Around the disk an inextensional rope has been winded (no slip). One side of the rope has been connected to a mass m by a linear spring with spring constant k_2. The other end is connected to a second spring with spring constant k_1. The end of this spring has a prescribed motion $x_o(t)$. To rep-

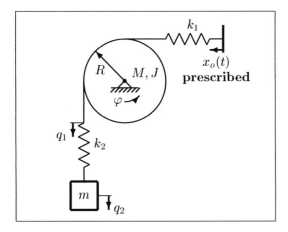

Fig. A.4 Single disk hoist

resent the motion of this system we use the generalized coordinates q_1 and q_2, so $\underline{q}^T = [q_1, q_2]$. These generalized coordinates are measured from the equilibrium position with $x_o(t) = 0$.

- Give the (linear) differential equations of motion for the system

- Take: $k_1 = 100$ $[N/m]$; $k_2 = 200$ $[N/m]$; $M = 3$ $[kg]$; $m = 4$ $[kg]$; $R = 0.2$ $[m]$; $x_o(t) = 0$.
  Determine the undamped eigenfrequencies and mode-shapes (give an interpretation).

- Assume $x_o(t) = cos(\Omega t)$. Evaluate the response for a well chosen frequency interval.

Problem 5 Sliding Pendulum

A rigid, massless rod with length l_1 can rotate without friction around the fixed point O. At its end the point mass m_1 is connected (see Fig. A.5). A second point mass m_2 can move along the rod (without friction) and is also connected to the fixed point by a linear spring with springstiffness k and initial length l_o. The gravity constant is g. To describe the motion of the system we use the angle θ between the rod and the vertical axis and the distance l between the mass m_2 and the fixed point O.

Derive the nonlinear differential equations of motion for the system. Give the equilibrium positions and evaluate their stability. Give a set of linearized equations of motion for small vibrations around the stable equilibrium position $\underline{q}^T = [\theta = 0, \; l = l_o + m_2 g/k]$.

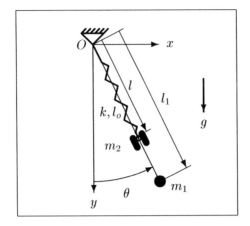

Fig. A.5   Sliding pendulum

Problem 6   Rotating Disk and Pendulum

A homogeneous disk shown in Fig. A.6 with mass M and radius R can rotate without friction around the z-axis as shown in the figure. The disk is con-

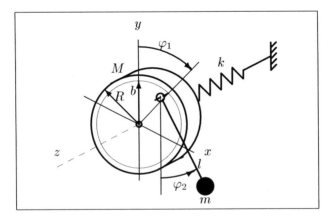

Fig. A.6   Rotating disk with pendulum

nected to the ground by a linear torsion-spring with torsional springstiffness k. At some point of the disk (at a distance b from the disk-centre) a massless rod with length l is connected with at the end the point mass m. This pendulum part can only move in a plane which is parallel to the plane of the disk. The gravity constant is g and as the generalized coordinates we choose the rotations φ_1 and φ_2. For $\varphi_1 = \varphi_2 = 0$ the spring is unloaded.

- Give the nonlinear equations of motion for this system using Lagrange.

- Evaluate the equilibrium positions of this system

- Determine the equilibrum position(s) and evaluate their stability for two situations: $k = 0.5\ mgb$ and $k = 4\ mgb$.

- For which value of the springstiffness k the equilibrium position with nonzero φ_1 will disappear.

- Take $k = 4\ mgb$. Assume very small rotations around the stable equilibrium position $\varphi_i = 0,\ \ i = 1, 2$ and derive the linearized equations of motion.

- Assume $m = 1\ [kg]$, $M = 12\ [kg]$, $b = R = 0.1\ [m]$, $l = 0.2\ [m], k = 4\ [Nm/rad]$, $g = 10\ [m/s^2]$. Calculate and interpretate the eigenfrequencies and corresponding eigencolumns according to the free vibration problem.

- Apply a mass-normalization and illustrate the orthogonality property of the eigenmodes.

Problem 7   Sliding Mass on Disk

A point mass m can move without friction in a slot of a rigid disk. It is connected to the disk by a linear spring with springstiffness k with unstretched length l_o. The disk is rotating in a horizontal plane with **constant** rotational velocity $\Omega\ [rad/s]$. The only generalized coordinate is the elongation of the spring u, (see Fig. A.7) .

- Give the (linear) equation of motion for the system.

- Define $\omega_o = \sqrt{k/m}$. Discuss the possible free vibrations for the situations $\Omega = 0$, $0 < \Omega < \omega_o$, $\Omega = \omega_o$ and finally $\Omega > \omega_o$.

Problem 8   Two-Disk Hoist

A system consists of two homogeneous disks with mass m and radius R (see Fig. A.8). One of the disks can rotate around a fixed point and the second disk is hanging in an inextensible, massless rope. One end of the rope is connected to a linear spring with springstiffness k and the other end of the

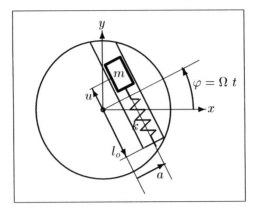

Fig. A.7 Sliding mass on disk

rope is connected to the ground. The free end of this spring is forced to follow the prescribed motion $x_o(t)$. In the centre of the moving disk a mass-spring system is connected (mass m, springstiffness also k). This subsystem and the moving disk can only move in a vertical direction and there is no slip between the rope and the disks. The gravity constant is g. As the zero

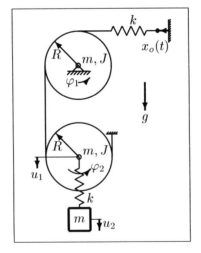

Fig. A.8 Two-disk hoist

position we define a situation with $x_o(t) = 0$ and both springs unloaded. As the generalized coordinates we choose the displacement u_1 of the moving disk centre and the displacement u_2 of the mass m, both measured from this zero position.

- Give the linear equations of motion in a matrix-representation

- Eliminate the offset due to the gravity forces by choosen new coordinates, measured from the static equilibrium position.

- Take $m = 1 \, [kg]$, $k = 100 \, [N/m]$. Solve the eigenvalue problem for free vibrations and give an interpretation of the eigenmodes.

- Assume the precribed motion to be $x_o(t) = \cos(\Omega t)$. Select an appropriate excitation range for Ω and plot the amplitudes of u_1 and u_2 as function of Ω.

- Discuss these results

Problem 9   Rolling Disk with Pendulum

A rigid disk with mass m and radius R can roll on a horizontal surface without slip. In the disk-centre (A) a homogeneous rod with mass m and length $2l$ is connected (no friction) and this centre-point is also connected to the ground by a linear spring with springstiffness k and unloaded length l_o (see Fig. A.9). There is only a motion in the $x - y$ plane and the gravity constant is g.

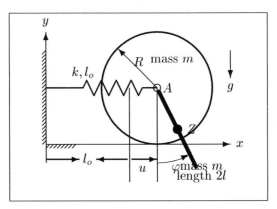

Fig. A.9   Rolling disk with pendulum

As the generalized coordinates we choose the horizontal displacement of the disk-centre u, measured from the unloaded spring position and the angle φ between the rod and the vertical. Give the nonlinear equations of motion and also the linearized version for small motions around the equilibrium position $u = \varphi = 0$.

Problem 10   Church-Bell

In Fig. A.10 a church bell is shown with fixed rotation point O, mass m_o, mass moment of inertia with respect to this rotation point J_o and centre of gravity Z at a distance S_o from O. At a point B (distance h from O), a clapper

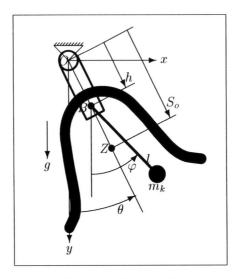

Fig. A.10   Church Bell

consisting of a massless rod with length l with at the end a point mass m_k can rotate without friction. We only look at (large) motions in the $x - y$ plane and for the description of the motions we use the generalized coordinates θ and φ. Give the nonlinear equations of motion using Lagrange.

Problem 11   Speed-regulator of Proell

In Fig. A.11 the so-called regulator of Proell is shown schematically. Is is used as a mechanical device to control the rotational speed of a machine. It has a central rotation axis $A - B$ connected to a fictious plane rotating around this axis. An external moment $\vec{M}^e(t)$ is acting on the axis $A - B$ and the friction in the bearings B and A can be modelled as a single viscous damping moment (magnitude proportional to the rotational velocity $\dot{\theta}$ with torsional damping constant γ). In the plane we have a mechanism, consisting of some massless rigid rods and friction-free joints with a central point mass M which can move up and down along the rotation axis $A - B$ and a couple of point masses m at the ends of rods with length $2l$, rotating around the point C. As the generalized coordinates we use the angles θ (angle to define the position of the plane in the fixed frame $[\vec{e}_x, \vec{e}_y, \vec{e}_z]$) and φ, the angle for measuring the position of the mechanism in that plane. Give the nonlinear equations of motion for this system.

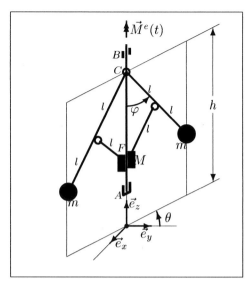

Fig. A.11   Speed regulator

Problem 12   Semicylinder Pair

A small rigid semicylinder with mass m and radius r can move without any slip over a larger fixed semicylinder with radius R as shown in Fig. A.12. The small cylinder has its centre of gravity Z at a distance $a = 0.424\,r$ from the flat side and the mass-moment of inertia of that part with respect to this centre of gravity is $J_z = 0.32\,mr^2$. We are dealing only with a motion in the $x - y$ plane. The gravity constant is g and for the description of the motion we use the angle θ which is the angle between the small-cylinder-flat surface and a horizontal line. For $\theta = 0$ the points C and D coincide, so the system then is in the symmetric position.

- Apply Lagrange's equations to derive the nonlinear equation of motion

- Determine the equilibrium position(s). For which value for r/R an equilibrium position with nonzero φ will be possible.

- Give the equilibrium positions for $r = R/2$ and evaluate their stability.

- Assume that the deviations from the (stable) equilibrium position $\theta = 0$ are small and give the linearized equation of motion

- Give the expression for the eigenfrequency for small free vibrations around this central position

- Present a plot of this eigenfrequency as function of the dimensionless radius $0 \le (r/R) \le 1.0$. Discuss your results.

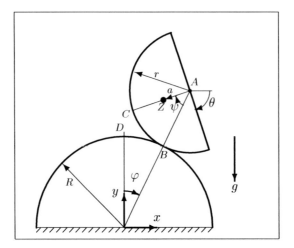

Fig. A.12 Cylinder on cylinder

Problem 13   Rotating Ring with Pendulum

A massless disk (radius R) is rolling without slip over a horizontal surface. In the friction-free joint A of this disk a massless rod with length l is connected with at its end the point mass m. The disk is connected to the fixed world by a linear spring with springstiffness k. The only motion is in the $x - y$

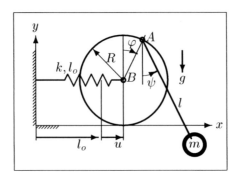

Fig. A.13 Rotating ring with pendulum

plane (see Fig. A.13). The gravity constant is g. We need two generalized coordinates for which we choose the rotation φ of the disk and the rotation ψ of the rod, measured from the vertical. For $\varphi = 0$ the spring is unloaded. The horizontal displacement of the cylinder centre measured from this position is called u.

- Give the nonlinear equations of motion

- We will distinguish between two different situations: I : $k = \frac{2mg}{R}$ and II : $k = \frac{2mg}{\pi R}$. Determine for both cases the equilibrium positions and check their stability.

- For the case $k = \frac{2mg}{R}$ we assume the rotations φ and ψ to be small. Give the corresponding linearized equations of motion.

- We assume $m = 1$ $[kg]$, $g = 10$ $[m/s^2]$, $R = 0.2$ $[m]$, $l = 0.4$ $[m]$, $k = 100$ $[N/m]$. Calculate the eigenfrequencies and eigenmodes for free vibrations. Give some discussion about your results.

Problem 14   Simple Rotor Model

In the right part of Fig. A.14, a so-called Laval-rotor has been drawn schematically. It consists of a shaft, supported by two bearings and a symmetrically positioned disk. If we assume a symmetrical motion the disk will only move in the $[\vec{e}_X, \vec{e}_Y]$-plane and its position can be expressed by two displacements in this plane. The flexibility of the bearings and the shaft (two springs in series) can be modelled as a single linear spring with spring-stiffness k_1 respectively k_2, see left part of the figure. These stiffnesses can be different for example in case of a non-rotational symmetric shaft (rectangular cross-section) or a shaft with a crack. The material damping in the shaft and in the shrink-fit

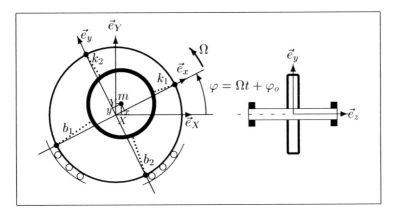

Fig. A.14   Rotor model

of the disk on the shaft is modelled as a linear viscous damper b_1 respectively

b_2. The mass of the disk including the moving part of the shaft is called m. The left part of the figure shows how this set of springs and dampers can be symbolically positioned between the shaft center and a fictious stiff rotating ring, rotating with the fixed rotorspeed Ω.

In this figure also two coordinate frames are shown. A fixed frame $(\vec{e}_X, \vec{e}_Y)$ with the coordinates (X, Y) to describe the disk-centre position and a rotating frame (fixed to the rotating shaft) with the shaft-centre coordinates (x, y).

- Give the (linear) differential equations of motion in the rotating coordinates (x, y) in matrix-representation. Discuss the result.

- The same for the non-rotating coordinates (X, Y).

Problem 15   Double-disk rotor

To illustrate the calculation and interpretation of frequency response functions for systems with damping we look at the torsional system with 2 degrees-of-freedom and viscous damping as shown in the next Fig. A.15. The model

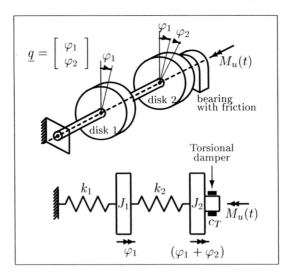

Fig. A.15   Two disk rotor

consists of two rigid disks with mass-moments of inertia (J_1 respectively J_2) which can only rotate around the given x-axis. One of the disks is connected to the ground by a torsional spring with springconstant k_1 and the two disk are mutually connected by a second torsional spring with springconstant k_2. In the bearing of disk 2 we are dealing with a friction-moment of which the magnitude is proportional to the absolute rotational velocity of this disk. So we can model this as a viscous torsion-damper with dampingconstant c_T

As the generalised coordinates we choose the **absolute** rotation φ_1 of disk 1 and the **relative** rotation φ_2 of disk 2 with respect to disk 1, so $q^T = [\varphi_1, \varphi_2]$. For $\varphi_1 = \varphi_2 = 0$ the springs are unloaded. On disk 2 also the (unit) external torsional moment $M_u(t) = \cos(\Omega t)$ is acting (see figure). We apply the parameter-values:

$J_1 = 1.0$, $J_2 = 2.0$ $[kgm^2]$, $k_1 = 100$, $k_2 = 100$, $[Nm]$, $c_T = 5.0$ $[Nsm]$.

- Derive the equations of motion.

- Investigate the undamped free vibration and calculate eigenfrequencies and mass-normalized eigenmodes.

- Take the forced, damped system. Plot magnitudes and phases of the complex amplitudes of the response for $0 \leq \Omega \leq 25$ $[rad/s]$. Discuss the results.

- Switch to a new set of generalized coordinates $q_1 = \varphi_1$, and $q_2 = \varphi_1 + \varphi_2$. These are the absolute rotations of the two disks. Plot again the magnitudes and phases of the complex amplitudes of the response and discuss the results.

- Finally look at the absolute accelerations instead of rotations and generate and discuss the magnitude-plots.

Problem 16   Soil Compression Machine

For the compression of soil or equalization of roads a vibrating machine can be used which can simply be modelled as shown in Fig. A.16. It consists of a machine part with mass M_1 which is resting on the actual suppression plate with mass M_2 and is supported by two linear springs k_1 and a viscous damper b_1. The (visco-elastic) behaviour of the soil can also be modelled as a combination of linear springs k_2 and a viscous damper b_2. In the machine part are two shafts, rotating in phase in opposite direction, each with an unbalance mass m at a radius r. The displacements q_1 and q_2 are measured from the equilibrium position which means that the effect of gravity might be ignored.

- Derive the linear set of equations of motion in matrix-notation.

- Assume: $M_1 = 50$ $[kg]$, $M_2 = 30$ $[kg]$, $k_1 = 25000$ $[N/m]$, $k_2 = 20000$ $[N/m]$
  $b_1 = 250$ $[Ns/m]$, $b_2 = 400$ $[Ns/m]$, $m = 1$ $[kg]$, $r = 0.05$ $[m]$. First look at the undamped free vibrations. Calculate the eigenfrequencies and corresponding eigenmodes (mass-normalized).

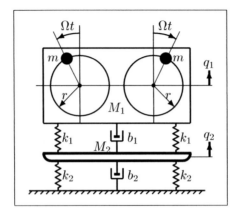

Fig. A.16   Soil compresor

- Check whether we are dealing with proportional damping.

- Select an effective range for the excitation frequency Ω. Calculate and plot the response amplitudes for the damped system.

- Evaluate the response for $\Omega \to \infty$.

Problem 17   Double Part Cross-Over

For the crossing of a valley a two-part cross-over structure has been designed as shown in Fig. A.17. It consists of two rigid bridge parts rotating around the fixed points O. The mass of each part is m and their mass-moment of

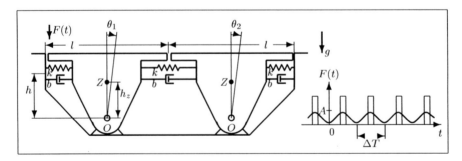

Fig. A.17   Cross-Over

inertia with respect to their centre of gravity (Z at a distance h_z above O) is

J_z. The parts are mutually and with the ground connected by sets of linear springs and dampers as shown in the figure. They may all be assumed to act on the same height h above the joints O. The gravity constant is g. Only very small rotations of the bridge parts are assumed and as the generalized coordinates we use the rotations θ_1 and θ_2.

Each time a heavy truck enters the structure from the left a more or less impulse-like excitation $F(t)$ will act on this part. A series of trucks with the same mutual distance therefore can be modelled as a *train* of pulse functions as shown in the right part of the figure. To simplify the calculations this train of pulses is replaced by a shifted sine-function with a specific amplitude and period as also shown in the figure.

- Give the linear equations of motion for the system

- Use: $m = 3.0\ 10^4\ [kg]$; $J_z = 3.0\ 10^6\ [kgm^2]$; $k = 4.0\ 10^6\ [N/m]$; $h_z = 20\ [m]$; $h = 25\ [m]$; $b = 8.0\ 10^4\ [Ns/m]$.
  Calculate the undamped eigenfrequencies and eigenmodes (<u>K</u>-normalized).

- Illustrate the orthogonality property of the eigenmodes and show the presence of proportional damping. Calculate the dimensionless modal damping factors.

- Assume a mutual truck distance of $S = 20\ [m]$. For which speed $[km/hr]$ resonance problems might be expected.

Problem 18   Cutting Tool Support

The cutting tool support of a turning lathe can be modelled as shown in Fig. A.18. The longitudinal support consists of the mass m_1, where the transversal stiffness of this support is modelled as a combination of a linear spring k_1 and viscous damper b_1. The transversal support is modelled as the mass m_2. The drive of this part is modelled by means of the linear spring k_2 and viscous damper b_2. The cutting tool is mounted on m_2, leading to the external cutting force $F(t)$. There are two generalized coordinates ($q^T = [q_1, q_2]$) , namely the (absolute) displacements of the masses m_1 and m_2, both measured from the equilibrium position (unloaded springs).

- Give the set of (linear) differential equations of motion.

- Assume:

$$m_1 = 50\ [kg] \qquad k_1 = 2.0\ 10^6\ [N/m] \qquad b_1 = 5.0\ 10^3\ [Ns/m]$$
$$m_2 = 25\ [kg] \qquad k_2 = 1.0\ 10^6\ [N/m] \qquad b_1 = 2.5\ 10^2\ [Ns/m]$$

Evaluate the undamped, free vibration. Check the eigenmode orthogonality property and apply a (stiffness matrix) <u>K</u>-normalization. Are we dealing with proportional damping?

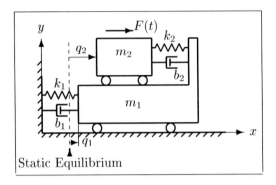

Fig. A.18   Cutting tool support

- The cutting force can be modelled as a random process. If we asume a white noise random process we as a matter of fact may look at an infinite sum of harmonic signals, each with the same amplitude but with random phases. Therefore we study the effect of a (unit)-harmonic excitation $F(t) = \cos(\Omega t)$. Select an interesting range for Ω and plot the response amplitudes for the mass-displacements. Comment your results.

- If we want to reduce the diplacement-amplitudes we might increase the damping in the system. Compare the two situations:

    - (A), b_1 unchanged, $b_2 = 4\, b_2$
    - (B), b_2 unchanged, $b_1 = 4\, b_1$

Which design modification seems to be the most effective.

Problem 19   Car-model on bump

In Fig. A.19 a simple (2-dof) car-engine model is shown, consisting of mass m_1 (the car) and mass m_2 (the engine). Further it consists of the linear springs k_1 and k_2 and the viscous dampers b_1 and b_2. (this model has been discussed before in the example on page 274.) The plots in Fig. A.20 show (simulated) measurement data for two situations

    - A short-duration bump (or high speed passage of the bump), which are the left plots

    - A long-duration bump (low speed passage of the bump) shown in the right part of the figure

The top plots show the relevant parts of the effective (suspension) force on the car body m_1, the middle plots show the body displacement q_1 (solid

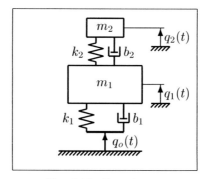

Fig. A.19   Bumping car

line) and engine displacement q_2 (dotted line) and finally the bottom plots show thee body velocity $\dot{q}_1$ (solid line) and engine velocity $\dot{q}_2$ (dotted line). These responses are stored in two MATLAB-data files **bumpcars.mat** and

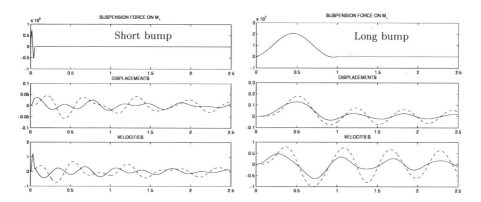

Fig. A.20   Bumping car measurement data

bumpcarl.mat each containing 6 arrays:

- t: discretized time for measured interval

- Feff: The effective suspension force on the car body, ($f(t)$ from (4.257)).

- q1: displacement q_1

- q2: displacement q_2

- q1dot: velocity $\dot{q}_1$

- q2dot: velocity $\dot{q}_2$

Calculate and plot the Fourier transforms for effective forces, displacements and velocities. Discuss the results. What do these plots tell us about the dynamics of the system.

Problem 20   Spindle on Air-bearings

In Fig. A.21 a simple rotor system is shown. It consists of a heavy and stiff foundation structure with mass m_1 supported by two rubber vibration isolators. The rotor (with mass m_2) which is also assumed to be very stiff is supported by two spiral groove air-bearings. We only will consider the sym-

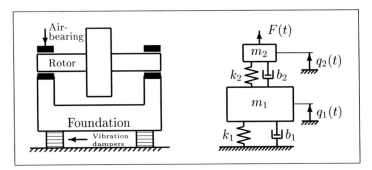

Fig. A.21   Air-bearing spindle

metrical motion which means that we have only 2 degrees of freedom, namely the foundation translation q_1 and the rotor translation q_2. For moderate shaft excentricities of the rotor in the bearings, these bearings can be modelled by a combination of a linear spring k_2 and a viscous damper b_2. Also the vibration isolators might be modelled by a linear spring (k_1) and viscous damper combination (b_1). Most of the parameters in the model can be measured or estimated sufficiently accurate, leading to:
$m_1 = 50$ [kg], $m_2 = 15$ [kg], $k_1 = 45000$ [N/m], $b_1 = 600$ [Ns/m]. The air bearing parameters however are unknown and difficult to calculate.
These parameters will be determined from an experiment. In that experiment the rotor has been excited by an impulse-type of force $F(t)$ and the rotor- and foundation response has been measured. The digital measurement signals are stored in the MATLAB data file airbear.mat. This file contains 4 arrays containing:

t : the discretized time.

excit : the discrete excitation $F(t)$.

resp1 : the response q_1.

resp2 : the response q_2.

- Calculate, plot and evaluate the autopowerspectra $S_{FF}(f)$ and $S_{q_1 q_1}(f)$ and the crosspowerspectrum $S_{Fq_1}(f)$.
  (For example by using the dedicated MATLAB function **adkspecs.m**

- Calculate, plot and evaluate the autopowerspectrum $S_{q_2 q_2}(f)$ and the crosspowerspectrum $S_{Fq_2}(f)$.

- Calculate and plot the transfer functions $H_{Fq_1}(f)$ and $H_{Fq_2}(f)$.

- Try to find parametervalues for the air bearing parameters k_2 and b_2 so that the numerical FRF's harmonize with the experimental data.

- Use the completed numerical model. Generate a different excitation $F(t)$ (for example a (white) noise excitation) and calculate the responses q_1 and q_2. Accept this input and two outputs as new experimental data and repeat the procedure.

A.3 ANSWERS AND DISCUSSIONS

Problem 1   Torsional Gear Pair System

$$[J_1 + (\frac{r_1}{r_2})^2 J_2]\ddot{\varphi}_1 + [\frac{GI_p}{l}]\varphi_1 = M_u(t)\frac{r_1}{r_2}$$

Problem 2   Cylinder in Gutter

$$\frac{3}{2}m(R-r)^2\ddot{\varphi} + mg(R-r)\sin\varphi = 0$$

Linearized:

$$\ddot{\varphi} + \frac{2g}{3(R-r)}\,\varphi = 0$$

Notice there is no mass m influence in this equation. The eigenfrequency for free vibrations is:

$$\omega_o^2 = \frac{2g}{3R}\frac{1}{1-\xi}$$

with dimensionless radius $\xi = r/R$. The variation of this eigenfrequency as a function of the parameter ξ is shown in the next figure.

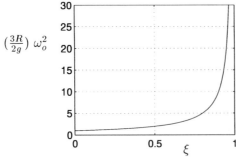

For $0 \leq \xi < 0.5$ the eigenfrequency is almost independent of the radius r and equal to $\frac{2g}{3R}$. For $r \to R$ the eigenfrequency will go to ∞.

Problem 3   Rotating Beam

$$m[a^2 + \frac{l^2}{3}]\ddot{\varphi} + mga\sin\varphi = 0.$$

Equilibrium positions: $\varphi = 0$ (stable), $\varphi = \pi$ (unstable). For $\varphi \approx 0$:

$$[a^2 + \frac{l^2}{3}]\ddot{\varphi} + ga\varphi = 0.$$

The eigenfrequency for free vibrations is:

$$\omega_o^2 = \frac{ga}{a^2 + l^2/3} = \frac{3ga}{2a^2 + R^2}$$

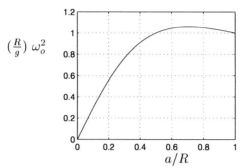

It is easy to show that the eigenfrequency will have a maximum value of $\omega_o^2 \approx 1.06 \, g/R$ for $a = l = R/\sqrt{2}$.

Problem 4   Single Disk Hoist

$$\underline{M} \, \underline{\ddot{q}} + \underline{K} \, \underline{q} = -\underline{k}_o$$

With the given values we get:

$$\underline{M} = \begin{bmatrix} 1.5 & 0 \\ 0 & 4 \end{bmatrix}; \quad \underline{K} = \begin{bmatrix} 300 & -200 \\ -200 & 200 \end{bmatrix}$$

$$\omega_1 = 3.7093 \, [rad/s]; \; \underline{u}_1 = \begin{bmatrix} 1.0 \\ 1.394 \end{bmatrix}; \; \omega_2 = 15.3580 \, [rad/s]; \; \underline{u}_2 = \begin{bmatrix} 1.0 \\ -0.2690 \end{bmatrix}$$

where the columns are normalized such that the first element=1.0. In the next picture these eigenmodes are illustrated by plotting $\underline{u}_1 \, \cos(\omega_1 t)$ left and $\underline{u}_2 \, \cos(\omega_2 t)$ on the right.

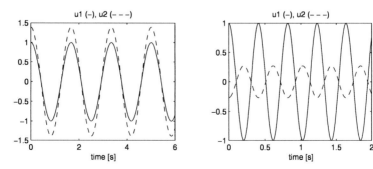

The next plot gives the frequency response.

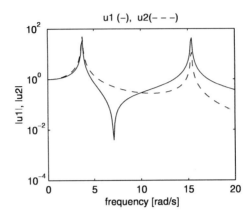

We can see two sharp peaks corresponding to the two undamped eigenfrequencies (resonance) but also one anti-resonance ($u_1 = 0$, meaning no disk rotation) at approximately $\Omega = 7$. This corresponds with an undamped vibration of only mass m with a fixed spring k_2, giving the eigenfrequencie of $\Omega_a = \sqrt{k_1/m_1} = \sqrt{50}$. At this specific frequency line the displacement $x_o(t)$ should now exactly balance the motion of u_2, so $k_1 x_o(t) = -k_2 u_2(t)$, which means that the amplitude of u_2 should be $k_1/k_2 = 0.5$ This can also be seen in the figure.

Problem 5   Sliding Pendulum

$$(m_1 l_1^2 + m_2 l^2)\ddot{\theta} + 2m_2 l \dot{l} \dot{\theta} + (m_1 l_1 + m_2 l)g \sin\theta = 0$$
$$m_2 \ddot{l} - m_2 l \dot{\theta}^2 + k(l - l_o) - m_2 g \cos\theta = 0$$

If we introduce all the relevant acceleration-vectors and external forces in the system as shown in the next figure we can see that the first equation is nothing more the result of the angular momentum theorem with respect to the fixed point O and the second equation the use of Newton's 2nd law in the direction of the rod l_1.

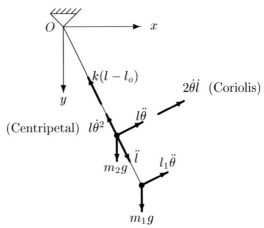

Equilibrium positions

$$(A): \quad \theta = 0; \ l = l_o + m_2 g/k \qquad (B): \quad \theta = \pi; \ l = l_o - m_2 g/k$$

Stability: (A) is unconditionally stable. Position (B) is only stable for $m_2^2 g/k > m_1 l_1 + m_2 l_o$ Linearized equations:

$$(m_1 l_1^2 + m_2 l_s^2)\ddot{\theta} + (m_1 l_1 + m_2 l_s)g\theta = 0$$
$$m_2 \ddot{u} + ku = 0$$

The first equation describes the rotation of a rigid pendulum (with mass m_2 fixed at $l = l_s$) around O and the second equation the vertical motion of mass m_2 under the action of spring k.

Problem 6   Rotating Disk and Pendulum

$$[\frac{1}{2}MR^2 + mb^2]\ddot{\varphi}_1 + mbl\ddot{\varphi}_2 \cos(\varphi_1 + \varphi_2) - mbl\dot{\varphi}_2^2 \sin(\varphi_1 + \varphi_2)$$
$$+ k\varphi_1 - mgb \sin \varphi_1 = 0$$
$$ml^2\ddot{\varphi}_2 + mbl\ddot{\varphi}_1 \cos(\varphi_1 + \varphi_2) - mbl\dot{\varphi}_1^2 \sin(\varphi_1 + \varphi_2) + mgl \sin \varphi_2 = 0$$

- $k = mgb/2$

  Stable equilibrium position $\varphi_1 \approx 1.895 \ [rad]; \quad \varphi_2 = 0$

$$\underline{K} = \begin{bmatrix} 0.1593 \ mgb & 0 \\ 0 & mgl \end{bmatrix}$$

- $k = 4 \ mgb$

  Stable equilibrium position $\varphi_1 = 0, \quad \varphi_2 = 0$

$$\underline{K} = \begin{bmatrix} 3mgb & 0 \\ 0 & mgl \end{bmatrix}$$

The nonzero equilibrium position only for $mgb/k > 1$.

Linearized equation of motion

$$[\frac{1}{2}MR^2 + mb^2]\ddot{\varphi}_1 + mbl\ddot{\varphi}_2 + (k - mgb)\varphi_1 = 0$$

$$ml^2\ddot{\varphi}_2 + mbl\ddot{\varphi}_1 + mgl\varphi_2 = 0$$

Finally it should be remarked that when $k < mgb$ the stifness-term in the first linear equation becomes negative which means that the equilibrium position $\varphi_1 = \varphi_2 = 0$ will be **unstable**.

$$\omega_1 = 5.7735\,[rad/s];\ \underline{u}_1 = \begin{bmatrix} 0.7071 \\ 0.7071 \end{bmatrix};\quad \omega_2 = 8.6603\,[rad/s];\ \underline{u}_2 = \begin{bmatrix} -0.5547 \\ 0.8321 \end{bmatrix}$$

We can see that the first mode is an in-phase vibration and the second mode an out-of-phase vibration as shown in the next figure.

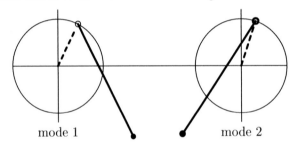

mode 1   mode 2

If we apply the mass-matrix normalize for the eigencolumns we get the matrix of eigencolumns:

$$\underline{U} = \begin{bmatrix} 2.5820 & -3.1623 \\ 2.5820 & 4.7434 \end{bmatrix}$$

It is easy to check that now $\underline{U}^T \underline{M}\, \underline{U}$ will be a unity matrix and $\underline{U}^T \underline{K}\, \underline{U}$ also a diagonal matrix (due to the orthogonality principle) with ω_i^2 on the diagonal.

Problem 7   Sliding Mass on Disk

$$\ddot{u} + (\omega_o^2 - \Omega^2)u = 0 \quad \text{with} \quad \omega_o^2 = k/m$$

If we give the mass at $t = 0$ a certain offset $u(t = 0) = u_0$, $\dot{u}(t = 0) = 0$ then we will get the following characteristic responses for different choices for the rotational velocity Ω (We used the arbitrary value $\omega_o = 1.0$).

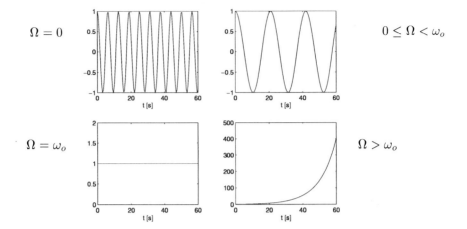

$\Omega = 0$

$0 \leq \Omega < \omega_o$

$\Omega = \omega_o$

$\Omega > \omega_o$

Problem 8   Two-Disk Hoist

$$m \begin{bmatrix} \frac{7}{2} & 0 \\ 0 & 1 \end{bmatrix} \ddot{\underline{q}} + k \begin{bmatrix} 5 & -1 \\ -1 & 1 \end{bmatrix} \underline{q} = \begin{bmatrix} 2kx_0 + mg \\ mg \end{bmatrix}$$

New set of generalized coordinates:

$$\underline{q} = \underline{q}_s + \underline{r}$$

$$\underline{q}_s = mg\underline{K}^{-1} \begin{bmatrix} 1 \\ 1 \end{bmatrix} = \frac{mg}{2k} \begin{bmatrix} 1 \\ 3 \end{bmatrix}$$

$$\underline{M}\,\ddot{\underline{r}} + \underline{K}\,\underline{r} = \begin{bmatrix} 2kx_0 \\ 0 \end{bmatrix}$$

$[-\omega^2 \underline{M} + \underline{K}]\underline{u} = \underline{0}$ gives:

$$\omega_1 = 7.9901\ [rad/s];\ \underline{u}_1 = \begin{bmatrix} 0.34 \\ 0.94 \end{bmatrix};\quad \omega_2 = 13.3797\ [rad/s];\ \underline{u}_2 = \begin{bmatrix} 0.62 \\ -0.78 \end{bmatrix}$$

where the columns are normalized such that the length of each column is 1.0. The eigencolumns are illustrated in the next figure. The equilibrium position is indicated by the thin lines whereas the deformed position is indicated by thick lines.

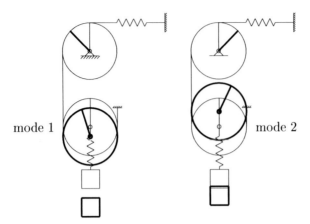

mode 1   mode 2

We can see that the first eigenmode is an in-phase motion of u_1 and u_2 with relatively large displacement for mass m, and the second mode an out-of-phase motion.

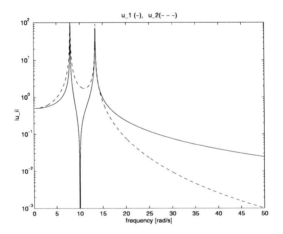

We can see two sharp peaks corresponding to the two undamped eigenfrequencies (resonance) but also one anti-resonance ($u_1 = 0$, meaning that the lower disk and consequently also the upper disk will not rotate) at $\Omega_a = 10$. This corresponds with an undamped vibration of only mass m with a fixed spring k, giving the eigenfrequencie of $\Omega_a = \sqrt{k/m}$. At this specific frequency line the force $kx_o(t)$ balances the spring force on the lower disk, so $2k|x_o(t)| = k|u_2|$, which means that the amplitude of u_2 should be 2.0 This can also be seen in the figure. The figure also clearly shows that for high frequencies $\Omega > 25\ [rad/s]$ both amplitudes will go to zero, but the amplitude $|u_2|$ of the mass m much faster.

Problem 9   Rolling Disk with Pendulum

$$\frac{5}{2}m\ddot{u} + ml\ddot{\varphi}\cos\varphi - ml\dot{\varphi}^2\sin\varphi + ku = 0$$

$$ml\ddot{u}\cos\varphi + \frac{4}{3}ml^2\ddot{\varphi} + mgl\sin\varphi = 0$$

Small motions around the equilibrium position $u = \varphi = 0$ we can linearize these equation giving:

$$\underline{M}\,\ddot{q} + \underline{K}q = 0$$

with the mass-matrix $\underline{M}$ and stiffness-matrix $\underline{K}$:

$$\underline{M} = \frac{m}{6}\begin{bmatrix} 15 & 6l \\ 6l & 8l^2 \end{bmatrix}; \quad \underline{K} = \begin{bmatrix} k & 0 \\ 0 & mgl \end{bmatrix}$$

Problem 10   Church-Bell

$$(J_o + m_k h^2)\ddot{\theta} + m_k hl\ddot{\varphi}\cos(\theta - \varphi) + m_k hl\dot{\varphi}^2\sin(\theta - \varphi) +$$
$$(m_o S_o\sin\theta + m_k h\sin\theta)g = 0$$
$$m_k l^2\ddot{\varphi} + m_k hl\ddot{\theta}\cos(\theta - \varphi) - m_k hl\dot{\theta}^2\sin(\theta - \varphi) + m_k gl\sin\theta = 0$$

Discussion

This churchbell will produce not any sound if after some initial excitation the following steady state situation will appear:

$$\theta(t) = \varphi(t) = \alpha(t)$$

for arbitrary $\alpha(t)$. If we assume this, we get:

$$(J_o + m_k h^2)\ddot{\alpha} + m_k hl\ddot{\alpha} + (m_o S_o + m_k h)g\sin\alpha = 0$$
$$m_k l^2\ddot{\alpha} + m_k hl\ddot{\alpha} + m_k gl\sin\alpha = 0$$

This can be written as:

$$\ddot{\alpha} + \frac{m_o S_o + m_k h}{(J_o + m_k h^2) + m_k hl}g\sin\alpha = 0$$

$$\ddot{\alpha} + \frac{m_k l}{m_k l^2 + m_k hl}g\sin\alpha = 0$$

With $r_o^2 := J_o/m_o$ (the radius of gyration of the bell) and $\beta := m_o/m_k$ (the bell-clapper mass ratio) these equations will be fulfilled for:

$$\frac{\beta S_o + h}{\beta r_o^2 + h^2 + hl} = \frac{l}{l^2 + hl}$$

So for the situation:

$$h = \frac{r_o^2}{S_o} - l$$

If we for the interpretation assume that also the bell might be modelled as a concentrated mass at point Z, so if $J_o = m_o S_o^2$; $r_o = S_o$. Then this condition becomes $h = S_o - l$ (the difference between bell-pendulum length and clapper pendulum length).

This particular condition was unintentionally approximately fulfilled for the so-called **Kaiserglocke** of the cathedral of Cologne. This was the reason that during the inauguration in 1876 this bell could not be brought to produce any sound.

Also the mediaeval so-called **Klokke Roelandt** from Gent in Belgium never produced any sound. In 1659 she was therefore melted and an new bell was recasted. (see: André Lehr: *De klokkengieters Francois en Pieter Hemony*, Eijsbouts, Asten 1959, p.54).

Problem 11   **Speed-regulator of Proell**

$$[4Ml^2 \sin^2 \varphi + 8ml^2]\ddot{\varphi} + 4Ml^2 \dot{\varphi}^2 \sin \varphi \cos \varphi - 8ml^2 \dot{\theta}^2 \sin \varphi \cos \varphi$$
$$+ (2M + 4m)gl \sin \varphi = 0$$

$$8ml^2 \ddot{\theta} \sin^2 \varphi + 16ml^2 \dot{\theta} \dot{\varphi} \sin \varphi \cos \varphi + \gamma \dot{\theta} = M^e(t)$$

Discussion

If we first assume φ=constant and $\dot{\theta} = \Omega$ =**constant**, then the second equation gives:

$$M(t) = \gamma \Omega$$

so in this time-independent situation the external moment $M(t)$ only has to compensate the viscous damping in the bearing B.

To find the equilibrium situation ($\ddot{\varphi} = \dot{\varphi} = 0$), the first equation gives:

$$-8ml^2 \Omega^2 \sin \varphi \cos \varphi + (2M + 4m)gl \sin \varphi = 0$$

One trivial solution for this equation is $\varphi = \varphi_o = 0$. If we assume $\varphi \neq 0$, then we can devide the equation by $\sin \varphi$, giving:

$$8ml^2 \Omega^2 \cos \varphi = (2M + 4m)gl$$

If we introduce:

$$\Omega_c^2 := [1 + \frac{M}{2m}] \frac{g}{2l}$$

the solution for the equilibrium-angle φ_o can be written as:

$$\cos \varphi_o = \left[\frac{\Omega_c}{\Omega}\right]^2$$

Because always $|\cos\varphi| \leq 1.0$ this equilibrium solution is only valid for $\Omega > \Omega_c$. So resuming we have the two possible solutions:

$$\varphi_o = 0 \qquad\qquad 0 \leq \Omega < \infty$$
$$\cos\varphi_o = (\Omega_c/\Omega)^2 \qquad \Omega \geq \Omega_c$$

Next we investigate the behaviour for small vibrations around these equilibrium positions.

- $\varphi_o = 0$.
  Then we may substitute: $\sin\varphi = \varphi$; $\cos\varphi = 1.0$; $\sin^2\varphi = 0$. This gives the linearized equation:

$$8ml^2\ddot{\varphi} + [(2M+4m)gl - 8ml^2\Omega^2]\varphi = 0$$

This is a standard mass-spring differential equation with a springstiffness:

$$k_{eff} = [(2M+4m)gl - 8ml^2\Omega^2] = 8ml^2[\Omega_c^2 - \Omega^2]$$

This stiffness will be negative (meaning that the equilibrium position φ_o is **unstable** when $\Omega \geq \Omega_c$ For $\Omega < \Omega_c$ we have stable equilibrium position with an eigenfrequency for small vibrations of:

$$\omega^2 = \Omega_c^2 - \Omega^2$$

- $\cos\varphi_o = (\Omega_c/\Omega)^2$.
  In this case we write $\varphi = \varphi_o + \delta$ with $\delta \ll 1$. Using goniometric expressions we can write:

$$\sin^2\varphi \approx \sin^2\varphi_o + 2\sin(2\varphi_o)\delta$$
$$\sin\varphi\cos\varphi \approx \cos(2\varphi_o)\delta + \tfrac{1}{2}\sin(2\varphi_o)$$
$$\sin\varphi \approx \sin\varphi_o + \cos\varphi_o\delta$$

This gives:

$$(4Ml^2\sin^2\varphi_o + 8ml^2)\ddot{\delta} + [(2M+4m)gl\cos\varphi_o - 8ml^2\Omega^2\cos(2\varphi_o)]\delta = 0$$

This can be written as:

$$[1 + \frac{M}{2m}\sin^2\varphi_o]\ddot{\delta} + \left[\frac{\Omega^4 - \Omega_c^4}{\Omega^2}\right]\delta = 0$$

This again is a standard mass-spring differential equation with a positive stiffness (**stable** equilibrium) for $\Omega > \Omega_c$. The eigenfrequency for small vibrations in this case is:

$$\omega^2 = \Omega^2 / \left[\frac{\Omega^4}{\Omega^4 - \Omega_c^4} + \frac{M}{2m}\right]$$

where we also used : $\sin^2 \varphi_o = 1 - \cos^2 \varphi_o = 1 - (\Omega_c/\Omega)^4$.

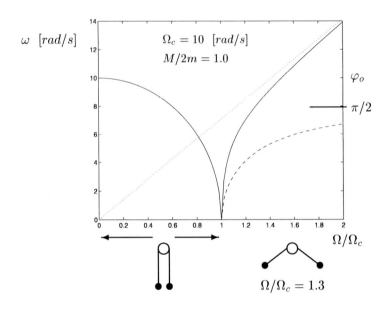

The results are illustrated in the figure above. The solid line gives the eigenfrequency dependence and the broken line the equilibrium angle φ_o.

From this figure we can see that for $\Omega > \Omega_c$ the angle φ directly is a measure for the rotational speed Ω of the device. So in this area it can serve as a rotational speed measurement instrument. For $\Omega \gg \Omega_c$ the eigenfrequency for small vibrations can be approximated by:

$$\omega^2 \approx \Omega^2/(1 + \frac{M}{2m})$$

This asymptotic value is shown in the figure by a dotted line.

Problem 12   Demi-Cylinder Pair

Nonlinear differential equation:

$$mr^2 \left[1.5 - 0.85 \cos\left(\frac{r\,\theta}{R+r} \right) \right] \ddot{\theta} + 0.425m \left(\frac{R\,r^2}{R+r} \right) \dot{\theta}^2 \sin\left(\frac{r\,\theta}{R+r} \right)$$
$$+ mgr \left[0.425 \sin\theta - \sin\left(\frac{r\,\theta}{R+r} \right) \right] = 0$$

Equilibrium position $\theta = 0$. A solution $\theta \neq 0$ only for $r < 0.74R$. For $r = R/2$ we get $\theta = 0$ and $\theta = 1.21\ [rad]$ giving $\varphi = 0.4\ [rad]$.
Only zero position is stable.

$$\underline{K}_{\theta=0} = mgr[0.425 - \frac{r}{R+r}]; \underline{M}_{\theta=0} = 0.65mr^2$$

Linearized equation of motion:

$$0.65 \, mr^2\ddot{\theta} + mgr \left[0.425 - \frac{r}{R+r}\right]\theta = 0$$

Eigenfrequency for $r < 0.74R$ is:

$$\omega^2 = mgr \left[0.425 - \frac{r}{R+r}\right] \bigg/ 0.65mr^2 = \frac{0.425 - 0.575 \frac{r}{R}}{0.65(1 + \frac{r}{R})}\left(\frac{g}{R}\right)$$

This eigenfrequency as a function of $\frac{r}{R}$ is shown in the next figure.

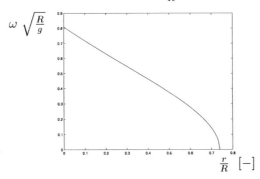

For $\frac{r}{R}$-values up to 0.5 we can recognize an almost linear relation between the eigenfrequency ω and the dimensionless cylinder radius $\frac{r}{R}$.

The stable-to-unstable switch of the system at $r = 0.74R$ can also be illustrated by looking at the potential energy of the system. This energy is shown in the next figure for $0.05 \leq r/R \leq 1.0$ and $-0.4 \leq \theta \leq 0.4$. The constant mgR is arbitrarely taken 1.0 and the potential energy nominal level has been chosen such that $V(\theta = 0) = 0$.

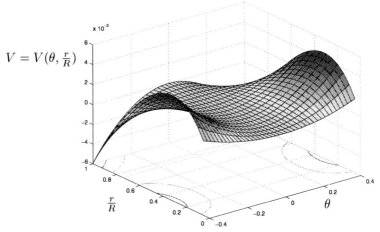

In the figure a 3-dimensional plot of the potential energy is shown and also on the bottom plane a plot of lines of constant potential energy. Now it is easy to see that for small r/R the energy has a concave shape (stable) and for large r/R the shape becomes convex (unstable). At $r/R = 0.74$ the potential energy does not change with changing angle θ which means that this is the transition value.

Problem 13   Rotating Ring with Pendulum

$$
\left[
\begin{array}{c}
2mR^2\ddot{\varphi}(1 + \cos\varphi) - mR^2\dot{\varphi}^2\sin\varphi + mRl\ddot{\psi}\cos\psi - mRl\dot{\psi}^2\sin\psi \\
+mRl\ddot{\psi}\cos(\varphi + \psi) - mRl\dot{\psi}^2\sin(\varphi + \psi) + kR^2\varphi - mgR\sin\varphi = 0 \\
\hline
mrl\ddot{\varphi}\cos\psi + ml^2\ddot{\psi} + mRl\ddot{\varphi}\cos(\varphi + \psi) \\
-mRl\dot{\varphi}^2\sin(\varphi + \psi) + mgl\sin\psi = 0
\end{array}
\right]
$$

$$
I: \quad k = \frac{2mg}{R} \quad \text{and} \quad II: \quad k = \frac{2mg}{\pi R}
$$

Solutions

Ia $\varphi = 0$; $\psi = 0$; stable

Ib $\varphi = 0$; $\psi = \pm\pi$; unstable

IIa $\varphi = 0$; $\psi = 0$; unstable

IIb $\varphi = 0$; $\psi = \pm\pi$; unstable

IIc $\varphi = \frac{\pi}{2}$; $\psi = 0$; stable

IId $\varphi = \frac{\pi}{2}$; $\psi = \pm\pi$; unstable

$$
(Ia)\ \underline{K} = \left[\begin{array}{cc} mgR & 0 \\ 0 & mgl \end{array} \right] \quad (IIc)\ \underline{K} = \left[\begin{array}{cc} \frac{2}{\pi}mgR & 0 \\ 0 & mgl \end{array} \right]
$$

$k = \frac{2mg}{R}$ and $\theta_o = 0$ gives the linearized equations of motion: $\underline{M}\,\ddot{\underline{q}} + \underline{K}\,\underline{q} = \underline{0}$, with

$$
\underline{M} = m \left[\begin{array}{cc} 4R^2 & 2Rl \\ 2Rl & l^2 \end{array} \right]; \quad \underline{K} = \left[\begin{array}{cc} mgR & 0 \\ 0 & mgl \end{array} \right]
$$

Free vibrations:

$$
\omega_1 = 2.89\ [rad/s]; \quad \underline{u}_1 = \left[\begin{array}{c} 0.89 \\ 0.45 \end{array} \right]; \quad \omega_2 = \infty\ [rad/s]; \quad \underline{u}_2 = \left[\begin{array}{c} -0.7 \\ 0.7 \end{array} \right]
$$

The first eigenmode is clear. It is an in-phase motion with $\varphi = 2\psi$. The second eigenfrequency appears to be ∞ with the given eigenmode. The reason for this is that the mass-matrix $\underline{M}$ is not positive-definite, namely:

$$
\underline{M} = \left[\begin{array}{cc} 0.16 & 0.16 \\ 0.16 & 0.16 \end{array} \right]
$$

For a velocity-column $\underline{v}^T = [1, -1]$ the kinetic energy $T = (1/2)\,\underline{v}^T\,\underline{M}\,\underline{v} = 0.0$. This means that for a situation $\varphi = -\psi$, and of course both very small, the point mass in this special case will not move (look at figure). It is easy to understand that such a special case will be present for each combination of R and l values, and for the eigencolumn then holds: $l\psi = -2R\varphi$.

Problem 14   Simple Rotor Model

First we will look at a rotating frame description

$$\underline{M}\,\ddot{\underline{q}} + \underline{D}\,\dot{\underline{q}} + \underline{K}\,\underline{q} = \underline{0}$$

with $\underline{q}^T := [x, y]$, and the system matrices $\underline{M}$, $\underline{D}$ and $\underline{K}$

$$\underline{M} = \begin{bmatrix} m & 0 \\ 0 & m \end{bmatrix}; \quad \underline{D} = \begin{bmatrix} b_1 & 0 \\ 0 & b_2 \end{bmatrix} + \Omega \begin{bmatrix} 0 & -2m \\ 2m & 0 \end{bmatrix}$$

$$\underline{K} = \begin{bmatrix} k_1 - m\Omega^2 & 0 \\ 0 & k_2 - m\Omega^2 \end{bmatrix}$$

Looking at these system matrices we can recognize three interesting phenomena, namely:

- The damping matrix $\underline{D}$ has a *skew-symmetric* contribution which is linearly in Ω

- Also when the dampers are not present $b_1 = b_2 = 0$, there is a damping-like term (linear in the velocities) in the equations of motion.

- The stiffnessmatrix $\underline{K}$ will not always be positive definite. For $m\Omega^2 < \min(k_1, k_2)$ the matrix will be positive definite. For $m\Omega^2 = k_1$ or k_2 the matrix will be singular (having "rigid-body modes").

If we look for **static** equilibrium positions and assume $k_1 \leq k_2$, we can distinguish the following situations:

- $m\Omega^2 < k_1$; The stiffnessmatrix is positive-definite. The static equilibrium is $\underline{q} = \underline{0}$. Then the point mass is in the origin of both frames.

- $\Omega^2 = \Omega_{c1}^2 = k_1/m$. The stiffnessmatrix is singular. Then we have the solution $\underline{q}^T = \alpha[1, 0]$, with arbitrary α. The mass m is somewhere on the rotating x-axis.

- $k_1 \leq m\Omega^2 \leq k_2$. The stiffnessmatrix is not positive definite. The only solution is $\underline{q} = \underline{0}$, but it is an unstable solution.

- $\Omega^2 = \Omega_{c2}^2 = k_2/m$. Stiffnessmatrix singular. Then we have the solution $\underline{q}^T = \beta[0, 1]$, with arbitrary β. The mass m is somewhere on the rotating y-axis.

- $m\Omega^2 > k_2$. Non positive definite stiffness matrix. The only solution is $\underline{q} = \underline{0}$, but it is an unstable solution.

Fixed-frame coordinates (X, Y):

$$\underline{M}_p \, \underline{\ddot{p}} + \underline{D}_p \, \underline{\dot{p}} + [\underline{K}_p + \underline{K}_p^*] \, \underline{p} = \underline{0}$$

$$\underline{M}_p = \begin{bmatrix} m & 0 \\ 0 & m \end{bmatrix}$$

$$\underline{D}_p = \begin{bmatrix} b_1 \cos^2 \varphi + b_2 \sin^2 \varphi & (b_1 - b_2) \sin \varphi \cos \varphi \\ (b_1 - b_2) \sin \varphi \cos \varphi & b_1 \sin^2 \varphi + b_2 \cos^2 \varphi \end{bmatrix}$$

$$\underline{K}_p^* = \Omega \begin{bmatrix} (-b_1 + b_2) \sin \varphi \cos \varphi & b_1 \cos^2 \varphi + b_2 \sin^2 \varphi \\ -b_1 \sin^2 \varphi - b_2 \cos^2 \varphi & (b_1 - b_2) \sin \varphi \cos \varphi \end{bmatrix}$$

To facilitate the interpretation of these results we choose $k_1 = k_2 = k$ and $b_1 = b_2 = b$ where $\underline{p}^T := [X, Y]$, and for the massmatrix $\underline{M}_p$, dampingmatrix $\underline{D}_p$ and stiffnessmatrices $\underline{K}_p$ and $\underline{K}_p^*$:

$$\underline{M}_p = \begin{bmatrix} m & 0 \\ 0 & m \end{bmatrix}; \quad \underline{K}_p = \begin{bmatrix} k & 0 \\ 0 & k \end{bmatrix}; \quad \underline{D}_p = \begin{bmatrix} b & 0 \\ 0 & b \end{bmatrix}; \quad \underline{K}_p^* = \Omega \begin{bmatrix} 0 & b \\ -b & 0 \end{bmatrix}$$

Now we can recognize the special a-asymmetric contribution of the damper elements b to the stiffness matrix. It is also worthwile to notice that this contribution is growing linearly with growing rotorspeed Ω.

Discussion

First we return to the formulation in the rotating reference frame. For $b_1 = b_2 = b$ and $k_1 = k_2 = k$ we found the set of equations:

$$m\ddot{x} + b\dot{x} - 2m\Omega\dot{y} + (k - m\Omega^2)x = 0$$
$$m\ddot{y} + b\dot{y} + 2m\Omega\dot{x} + (k - m\Omega^2)y = 0$$

We apply the special definition:

$$z := x + y \, j; \qquad j = \sqrt{-1}$$

Then we can combine the two differential-equations into one equation in the complex variable z:

$$m\ddot{z} + (b + 2m\Omega j)\dot{z} + (k - m\Omega^2)z = 0$$

The solution for this equation can be written as:

$$z = u \, e^{\lambda t}$$

So u is the modulus of the complex number $x + jy$ and $((\lambda t)/j$ the argument of that number.

This leads to the so-called characteristic equation:

$$\lambda^2 m + (b + 2m\Omega j)\lambda + (k - m\Omega^2) = 0$$

this equation has two solutions:

$$\lambda_{1,2} = \frac{1}{2m} \left[-(b + 2m\Omega j) \pm \sqrt{(b + 2m\Omega j)^2 - 4(k - m\Omega^2)m} \right]$$

If we also assume $b = 0$ we get:

$$\lambda_{1,2} = \frac{1}{2m} - \Omega j \pm \sqrt{\frac{k}{m}} = (-\Omega \pm \Omega_c) j$$

where $\Omega_c^2 = k/m$. The two possible solutions $z_1 = u_1 \, e^{\lambda_1 t}$ and $z_2 = u_2 \, e^{\lambda_2 t}$ are illustrated in the following figure.

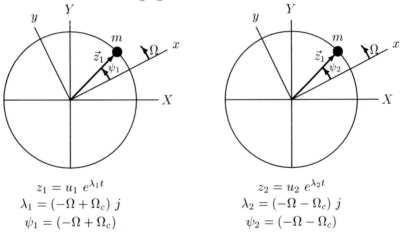

$$z_1 = u_1 \, e^{\lambda_1 t}$$
$$\lambda_1 = (-\Omega + \Omega_c) \, j$$
$$\psi_1 = (-\Omega + \Omega_c)$$

Forward Whirl

$$z_2 = u_2 \, e^{\lambda_2 t}$$
$$\lambda_2 = (-\Omega - \Omega_c) \, j$$
$$\psi_2 = (-\Omega - \Omega_c)$$

Backward Whirl

This shows the motions of the centre of the mass. The rotorspeed Ω was defined positive in counter-clockwise direction. In the first mode (left part) the center of mass is rotating with a rotational speed of $-\Omega + \Omega_c$ with respect to the rotating frame. This means that the effective rotational speed will be Ω_c in counterclock-wise direction, so in the same direction as the rotorspeed Ω. Therefore this is called a "forward whirl". For $\Omega = \Omega_c$ the position of the mass in the rotating frame will not change in time. This is one of the equilibrium positions discussed before.

In the second mode (right picture) the centre of mass is rotating with a rotational speed of $-\Omega - \Omega_c$ with respect to the rotating frame, leading to an effective rotational speed of Ω_c in clock-wise direction, so in the opposite direction as the rotorspeed Ω. Therefore this is called a "backward whirl".

We now step to the equations of motion with respect to the fixed frame:

$$\begin{bmatrix} m & 0 \\ 0 & m \end{bmatrix} \begin{bmatrix} \ddot{X} \\ \ddot{Y} \end{bmatrix} + \begin{bmatrix} b & 0 \\ 0 & b \end{bmatrix} \begin{bmatrix} \dot{X} \\ \dot{Y} \end{bmatrix} + \begin{bmatrix} k & b\Omega \\ -b\Omega & k \end{bmatrix} \begin{bmatrix} X \\ Y \end{bmatrix} = \begin{bmatrix} 0 \\ 0 \end{bmatrix}$$

We again investigate the free vibrational behaviour, so we substitute:

$$\begin{bmatrix} X \\ Y \end{bmatrix} = \underline{u}\, e^{\lambda t}$$

This gives the eigenvalue-problem:

$$\begin{bmatrix} \lambda^2 m + \lambda b + k & b\Omega \\ -b\Omega & \lambda^2 m + \lambda b + k \end{bmatrix} \underline{u} = \underline{0}$$

This eigenvalue problem leads to the characteristic equation:

$$\lambda^4 + a_3\lambda^3 + a_2\lambda^2 + a_1\lambda + a_0 = 0$$

with:

$$a_3 = 2b/m \qquad a_2 = 2k/m + b^2/m^2$$
$$a_1 = 2kb/m^2 \qquad a_0 = (k^2 + b^2\Omega^2)/m^2$$

The eigenvalues of this equation in general will be complex numbers. If the real part of one or more of these eigenvalues will be positive the solution will be unstable ($e^{\lambda t} \longrightarrow \infty$ for $t \longrightarrow \infty$). The equation however cannot be solved easily in general. However, for such a 4th order characteristic equation there exists a so-called **Routh-Hurwitz** criterion which garanties the stability if the following conditions are fulfilled:

$$1: \quad a_0,\ a_1,\ a_2,\ a_3 > 0$$
$$2: \quad a_1\, a_2\, a_3 - a_0\, a_3^2 - a_1^2 > 0$$

This leads to:

$$\frac{k}{m}\, b^2 - b^2\, \Omega^2 > 0$$

with $\Omega_c^2 := k/m$ this gives the stability-limit Ω_s:

$$\Omega_s^2 = \Omega_c^2$$

Therefore we must conclude that even in the presence of damping $b \neq 0$ the rotorsystem will be unstable for $\Omega > \Omega_c$. Although we used only a simple linear model in practice in such a situation the rotordesign will need a serious re-evalution.

In we resume the free vibrational results of the rotating frame- and fixed frame results we can conclude:

$$\Omega < \omega_c : \quad \begin{cases} \text{Stable Forward whirl} & +\Omega_c \\ \text{Stable Backward whirl} & -\Omega_c \end{cases}$$

$$\Omega = \Omega_c : \quad \text{Fixed point} \quad \begin{bmatrix} x \\ y \end{bmatrix} = \begin{bmatrix} \alpha \\ \beta \end{bmatrix}$$

$$\Omega > \omega_c : \quad \begin{cases} \text{Unstable Forward whirl} & +\Omega_c \\ \text{Unstable Backward whirl} & -\Omega_c \end{cases}$$

Problem 15   Double-disk rotor

$$\underline{M}\ \ddot{q}(t)\ +\ \underline{D}\ \dot{q}(t) + \underline{K}\ q(t) = \underline{Q}(t)$$

With the given parameter-values we get:

$$\underline{M} = \begin{bmatrix} 3 & 2 \\ 2 & 2 \end{bmatrix};\ \underline{D} = \begin{bmatrix} 5 & 5 \\ 5 & 5 \end{bmatrix};\ \underline{K} = 100 \begin{bmatrix} 1 & 0 \\ 0 & 1 \end{bmatrix};\ \underline{Q}(t) = \cos(\Omega t) \begin{bmatrix} -1 \\ -1 \end{bmatrix}$$

Undamped system:

$$\begin{array}{ll} \omega_1 = 4.6821 \\ \omega_2 = 15.1022 \end{array} [rad/s];\quad \underline{u}_1 = \begin{bmatrix} 0.3690 \\ 0.2881 \end{bmatrix};\quad \underline{u}_1 = \begin{bmatrix} -0.9294 \\ 1.1904 \end{bmatrix}$$

Complex amplitudes of the response $\hat{q}_i(\Omega)$.

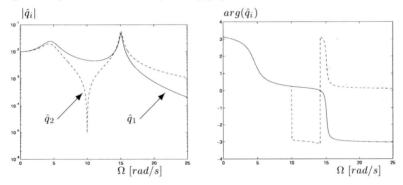

Next figures: the moduli of the complex amplitudes of the absolute rotations (left picture) and accelerations (right picture).

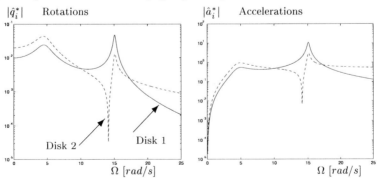

Problem 16   Soil Compression Machine

$$\underline{M} = \begin{bmatrix} M1 + 2m & 0 \\ 0 & M_2 \end{bmatrix}; \quad \underline{K} = 2 \begin{bmatrix} k_1 & -k_1 \\ -k_1 & k_1 + k_2 \end{bmatrix}; \quad \underline{D} = \begin{bmatrix} b_1 & -b_1 \\ -b_1 & b_1 + b_2 \end{bmatrix}$$

$$\underline{M}\,\ddot{\underline{q}} + \underline{D}\,\dot{\underline{q}} + \underline{K}\,\underline{q} = \underline{f}(t)$$

with

$$\underline{f}(t) = \begin{bmatrix} 2mr\Omega^2 \cos(\Omega t) \\ 0 \end{bmatrix}$$

$$\omega_1 = 18.8556 \ [rad/s] \qquad \underline{u}_1 = \begin{bmatrix} 0.1251 \\ 0.0788 \end{bmatrix}; \qquad \underline{u}_2 = \begin{bmatrix} -0.0599 \\ 0.1647 \end{bmatrix}$$
$$\omega_2 = 60.0500 \ [rad/s]$$

where the eigencolumns have been mass-normalized ($\underline{U}^T \underline{M}\,\underline{U} = \underline{I}$).
In the first eigenmode the masses M_1 and M_2 are moving in-phase with a largest displacement for the engine (mass M_1). In the second eigenmode we see an anti-phase motion with a dominant vibration for mass M_2 (the ground plate). At this moment we might conclude that running the machine with a frequency close to the second eigenfrequency might be preferred. Easily can be seen that we are not dealing with proportional damping, because

$$\underline{U}^T \underline{D}\,\underline{U} = \begin{bmatrix} 3.0206 & 2.5964 \\ 2.5964 & 23.4538 \end{bmatrix}$$

and this is not a diagonal matrix.
Just to get an idea of the damping-level of both modes we can calculate the dimensionless damping factors for both modes using the modal masses $m_i = \underline{U}^T \underline{M}\,\underline{U}[i,i] = 1.0$, the modal stiffnesses $k_i = \underline{U}^T \underline{K}\,\underline{U}[i,i] = \omega_i^2$ and a modal damping approximation $b_i = \underline{U}^T \underline{D}\,\underline{U}[i,i]$. Calculating the dimensionless damping ratios $\xi_i = b_i/(2\sqrt{k_i m_i})$. This gives:

$$\xi_1 = 0.0801, \qquad \xi_2 = 0.1953$$

which means that both modes are weakly damped.

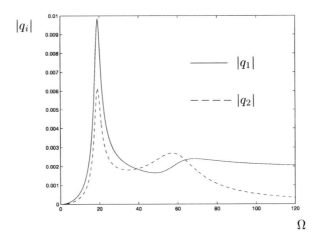

We can see two resonances corresponding to the undamped eigenfrequencies of the system. However the first resonance peak is much higher and sharper then the second, for both coordinates q_1 and q_2. The calculated estimates for the dimensionless modal damping factors already were an indication for this. For higher excitation frequencies ($\Omega > 80$) the response of the machine (q_1) is going to some constant level whereas the ground plate response is approaching zero very fast. For large enough Ω the term $-\Omega^2 \underline{M}$ in $\left[-\Omega^2 \underline{M} + j\Omega\underline{D} + \underline{K}\right]$ will dominate so the complex response $\hat{\underline{q}}$ can be approximated by:

$$\hat{\underline{q}} \approx [-\Omega^2 \underline{M}]^{-1} \hat{\underline{f}} = \left[\begin{array}{c} 2mr/(M+2m) \\ 0 \end{array} \right] = \left[\begin{array}{c} 0.0019 \\ 0 \end{array} \right]$$

This also shows the figure.

So resuming, the best way to use this machine is to choose the rotation frequency of the unbalance shafts close to the first eigenfrequency of ≈ 18 $[rad/s]$.

Problem 17   Double Part Cross-Over

Set of differential equations:

$$\underline{M}\,\ddot{\underline{q}} \;+\; \underline{D}\,\dot{\underline{q}} \;+\; \underline{K}\underline{q} = \underline{f}(t)$$

$$\begin{array}{ll} \omega_1 = 12.91\ [rad/s]\ (2.05\ [Hz]) \\ \omega_2 = 22.36\ [rad/s]\ (3.56\ [Hz]) \end{array} \qquad \underline{U} = \left[\begin{array}{cc} 0.7071 & -0.7071 \\ 0.7071 & 0.7071 \end{array} \right]$$

where the eigencolumns (collected in the matrix $\underline{U}$), are $\underline{K}$-normalized. It is easy to give a physical interpretation to these eigencolumns.

$$\underline{U}^T \underline{M}\,\underline{U} = \left[\begin{array}{cc} 0.0060 & 0 \\ 0 & 0.0020 \end{array} \right]; \;\; \underline{U}^T \underline{D}\,\underline{U} = 0.02 * \underline{I}; \;\; \underline{U}^T \underline{K}\,\underline{U} = \underline{I}$$

Dimensionless modal damping factors:

$$\xi_1 = 0.1291; \qquad \xi_2 = 0.2236$$

The harmonic term might introduce resonance problems for the first time when:

$$\frac{2\pi V}{S} \approx \omega_1 = 12.91 \; [rad/s]$$

For a minimum car distance of $S = 20 \; [m]$ this means a maximum speed limit of $V = 41 \; [m/s]$ or $V = 148 \; [km/h]$. This seams to be a practically safe limit.

Problem 18   Cutting Tool Support

$$\underline{M} = \left[\begin{array}{cc} m_1 & 0 \\ 0 & m_2 \end{array} \right]; \quad \underline{K} = \left[\begin{array}{cc} k_1 + k_2 & -k_2 \\ -k_2 & k_2 \end{array} \right]$$
$$\underline{D} = \left[\begin{array}{cc} b_1 + b_2 & -b_2 \\ -b_2 & b_2 \end{array} \right]; \quad \underline{f}(t) = \left[\begin{array}{c} 0 \\ F(t) \end{array} \right]$$

$$\begin{array}{ll} \omega_1 = 141.1 \; [rad/s] & (22.5 \; [Hz]) \\ \omega_2 = 282.8 \; [rad/s] & (45 \; [Hz]) \end{array} \qquad \underline{U} = \left[\begin{array}{cc} 0.447 & 0.707 \\ 0.894 & -0.707 \end{array} \right]$$

where the eigencolumns (collected in the matrix $\underline{U}$), are $\underline{K}$-normalized. The modes are illustrated in the following picture. The thin lines show the equilibrium position and the thick lines the deformed position.

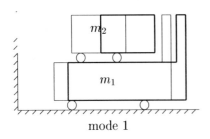

mode 1

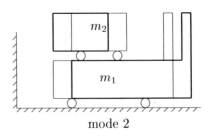

mode 2

$$\underline{U}^T \underline{M} \, \underline{U} = 1.0 \; 10^{-4} \left[\begin{array}{cc} 0.5 & 0 \\ 0 & 0.125 \end{array} \right]; \quad \underline{U}^T \underline{D} \, \underline{U} = 1.0 \; 10^{-2} \left[\begin{array}{cc} 0.18 & 0.11 \\ 0.11 & 0.10 \end{array} \right]$$

$$\underline{U}^T \underline{K} \, \underline{U} = \left[\begin{array}{cc} 1 & 0 \\ 0 & 1 \end{array} \right]$$

So, the orthogonality is OK but the dampingmatrix has not been diagonalized by $\underline{U}$, so we do not have proportional damping.

If we nevertheless calculate dimensionless modal damping factors using the diagonal terms of the matrix $\underline{U}^T \underline{D} \, \underline{U}$, we find:

$$\xi_1 = 0.12; \qquad \xi_2 = 0.14$$

so both modes seem to be weakly damped.

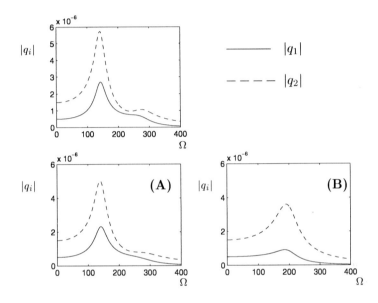

We can clearly recognize the first resonance peak. The second eigenfrequency however is hard to see. So it seems that the second mode has a (much) higher damping level then suggested by the dimensionless damping factors calculated before, ignoring the non-zero, non-diagonal elements of the modal damping matrix. So we see that in that case we can get somewhat misleading results. If we want to reduce the amplitude of the coordinate q_2, we can increase the dampingvalue b_1 and/or b_2. To study the effect two additional analysis have been carried out:

$$(A) \qquad b_1^* = b_1 \qquad\qquad b_2^* = 4 * b_2 = 1.0 \; 10^3$$
$$(B) \qquad b_1^* = 4 * b_1 = 2.0 \; 10^4 \qquad b_2^* = b_2$$

the results are shown in the bottom parts of the figure. From these we can conclude that increasing the damping-value b_2 by a factor of 4 just has a minor effect. The increase of the damping-value b_1 with a factor of 4 has not only a strong effect on q_1, but also reduces the amplitude $|q_2|$ by 50%.

Problem 19   Car-model on bump

$$\underline{M} = \begin{bmatrix} m_1 & 0 \\ 0 & m_2 \end{bmatrix}; \quad \underline{D} = \begin{bmatrix} b_1 + b_2 & -b_2 \\ -b_2 & b_2 \end{bmatrix}; \quad \underline{K} = \begin{bmatrix} k_1 + k_2 & -k_2 \\ -k_2 & k_2 \end{bmatrix}$$

$$\underline{Q}(t) = \begin{bmatrix} f(t) \\ 0 \end{bmatrix} = \begin{bmatrix} k_1 x_o(t) + b_1 \dot{x}_o(t) \\ 0 \end{bmatrix}$$

with $x_o(t) = 0.05[1 - \cos(2\pi t/T_b)]$ this gives:

$$f(t) = k_1 0.05[1 - \cos(2\pi t/T_b)] + b_1 \frac{0.1\pi}{T_b} \sin(2\pi t/T_b)$$

Undamped free vibrational behaviour:

$$\omega_1 = 10.39 \; [rad/s] \qquad f_1 = 1.65 \; [Hz]$$
$$\omega_2 = 17.57 \; [rad/s] \qquad f_2 = 2.80 \; [Hz]$$

$$\underline{U} = \begin{bmatrix} 0.33 & 0.65 \\ 0.94 & -0.76 \end{bmatrix}$$

If we calculate $\underline{U}^T \underline{D} \, \underline{U}$ we can see that this not leads to a diagonal matrix but the matrix certainly is diagonal dominant. Therefore we calculate the dimensionless modal damping factors from the diagonal terms, giving:

$$\xi_1 = 2.4\%, \qquad \xi_2 = 3.9\%$$

so the system is weakly damped.
Some remarks which respect to the given figures:

- For the long bump the effective excitation almost equals the bump itself (only $k_1 x_o(t)$ is important). For the short bump the damping force transmission $b_1 \dot{x}_o(t)$ seems to be dominating.

- In all the plots the response q_2 (solid lines) is larger then q_1 (dotted lines).

- For the short bump, the displacement- and velocity plots show that at least two eigenfrequencies can be recognized in the response.

- For the long bump, mainly a single harmonic with period-time of $\approx$ 0.6 $[s]$ can be recognized. For this situation maybe a single-degree-of-freedom might also be used to model reality.

Second part

Next plot shows the relevant parts of the Fourier-transforms (only the magnitudes) for the short and long bump.

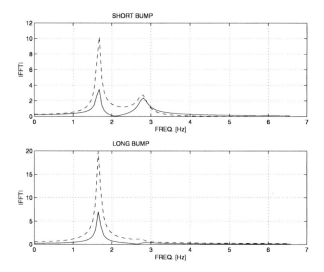

We can see that:

- The short-bump response indeed shows two frequencies, whereas the long-jump response only shows a single component. Apparently, the second eigenfrequency will not be excited by the (slow) excitation.

- From the upper plot we can estimate the eigenfrequencies to be 1.8 and 2.7 [Hz]. These fit very well with the theoretical ones before.

- A short bump excites the higher frequencies but a long bump leads to a larger displacement for q_2 (at least 2 times larger).

- For the long bump the displacement q_2 is 3 times larger then q_1. This is also reflected by the only (undamped) eigen-mode (see matrix $\underline{U}$) which is excited in this case.

Problem 20   Spindle on Air-bearings

Excitation and the two responses q_1 (solid line) and q_2 (dotted line). See next figure.

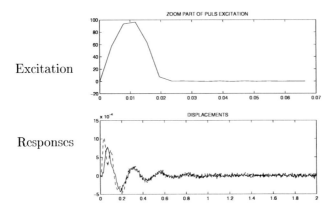

Excitation

Responses

We can see that we are dealing with a short-duration impulse (duration ≈ 0.02 [s]). The responses have some impulse-response-type of behaviour with at first sight only one dominant frequency.

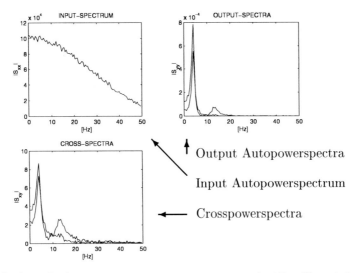

If we look at the input power spectrum we can see that it will contain spectral energy up to approximately 60 [Hz]. This means that input and consequently also the outputs will not contain higher frequencies than this 60 [Hz]. The transfer function therefore probably will show irregular results for frequencies higher the 60 [Hz] due to numerical abd measurement errors. If the transfer function should also be accurate for higher frequencies a sharper impulse (for example a hammer with a harder tip) should be applied.

If we look at the output autopower spectra and crosspower spectra we can recognize two peaks, a dominant low frequency peak ($\approx$ 4 [Hz]) and a smaller peak at $\approx$ 14 [Hz].

From autopower spectra and crosspower spectra the transfer functions between the excitation and the two response can be calculated. They are plot in the next figure. Only the interval up to 50 [Hz] is shown. For higher frequencies the FRF's show a very chaotic behaviour due to the lack of input power for these frequencies.

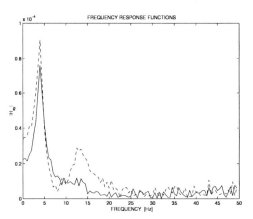

We can see very clear that we are dealing with two important eigenfrequencies at 4 and 13.5 [Hz]. Due to the damping in the system the second mode however is less visible for dof q_1 which is the foundation of the system.

Next we want to estimate the air bearing parameters k_2 and b_2. First we take $b_2 = 0$ because this damping will only influence the height of the peaks and only marginally their location. Then we evaluate the system for 3 values for k_2, namely $k_2 = 50000$, 100000, 150000 $[N/m]$. We will only look at the rotor displacement q_2 because the corresponding FRF did show also the second peak the most clearly. In the left part of the next plot the measured FRF is shown together with the 3 FRF's for the different values for k_2. Using some interpolation we estimate the optimal value for k_2 to be $k_2 = 80000$ $[N/m]$.

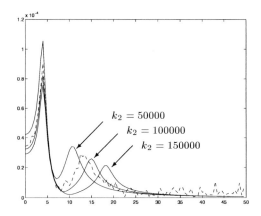

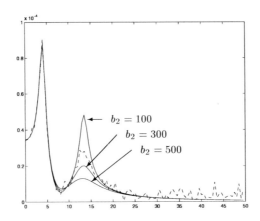

For the fixed value for k_2 we estimate 3 levels for b_2, namely $b_2 = 100, 300, 500\,[N$. The right part of the plot shows again the experimental FRF together with the 3 theoretical FRF's for the 3 damping estimations. It is surprising that a variation of this damper b_2 has hardly any influence on the damping of the first mode. The lowest undamped mode appears to be $\underline{u}_1^T = [0.66, 0.75]$ which means that both the masses move in phase with almost the same amplitude. So, it is obvious that a viscous damper between these two masses will not have much effect.

If we again use some interpolation the more or less optimal value (giving the best fit) seems to be $b_2 = 200\,[Ns/m]$. If we finally compare the two (for both degrees of freedom) experimental FRF's (non-smooth curves) with the corresponding theoretical FRF's (smooth curves) using these two optimal values we can see that we get a very good agreement as shown in the next plot.

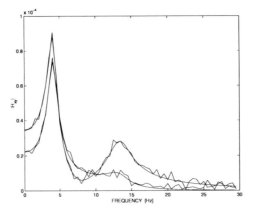

References

Argyris-91. Argyris, J., Mlejnek, H.P.; *Dynamics of Structures*, Elsevier Scientific Publishers B.V., 1991, ISBN 0-444-89045-9

Bendat/Piersol-80. Bendat, J.S., Piersol, A.G.; *Engineering Applications of Correlation and Spectral Analysis*, Wiley-Interscience, New-York, ISBN 0-471-05887-4, 1980

Blevins-95. Blevins, R.D.; *Formulas for Natural Frequency and Mode Shape*, Krieger Publishing Company, Florida, ISBN 0-89464-894-2, 1995

Bremer-88. Bremer,H.; *Dynamik und Regelung Mechanischer Systeme*, Teubner Stuttgart, 1988, ISBN 3-519-02369-5

Campen-97. Campen, D.H. van; *Engineering Dynamics, Part 1, Newtonian Mechanics & One- and Two-DOF Linear Systems*, TUE-dictaat 4.4777, Eindhoven, 1997

Childs-93. Childs, D.; *Turbomachinery Rotordynamics, Phenomena, Modelling and Analysis*, John Wiley & Sons, 1993, ISBN 0-471-53840-X

Close/Frederick-93.
Close, C.M. and Frederick, D.K. (1993). *Modelling and Analysis of Dynamic Systems.* Houghton Mifflin Co., Boston, Second Ed., ISBN 0-395-66158-7.

Craig/Bampton-68.
Craig Jr., R.R. and Bampton, M.C.C. (1968). *Coupling of substructures for dynamice analysis,* AIAA Journal, Vol. 6, No. 7, pp. 1313-1319

Craig-81.
Craig Jr., R.R. (1981). *Structural Dynamics, An introduction to Computer Methods,* Wiley, New York, ISBN 0-471-04499-7.

Dimarogonas-92.
Dimarogonas, A.D., Haddad, S.; *Vibration for Engineers,* Prentice Hall, ISBN 0-13-950841-4, 1992

Doebelin-83.
Doebelin, E.O.,: *Measurement Systems, Application and Design,* McGraw-Hill book co., ISBN 0-07-017337-0, 1983

Ewins-84.
Ewins,D.J.; *Modal Testing: Theory and Practice,* John Wiley & Sons, ISBN 0-471-90474-4, 1984

Geradin/Rixen-97.
Géradin, M. and Rixen, D. (1997). *Mechanical Vibrations: Theory and Application to Structural Dynamics,* Wiley/Masson, New York/Paris, Second Ed., ISBN 0-471-97524-9.

Guyan-65.
Guyan, R.J. (1965). *Reduction of stiffness and mass matrices,* AIAA Journal, Vol. 3, No. 2, p. 380.

Harrison/Nettleton-79.
Harrison, H.R., Nettleton, T,; *Principles of Engineering Mechanics,* Edward Arnold, 1979, ISBN 0-7131-3378-3

Den Hartog-56.
Den Hartog, J.P. (1985). *Mechanical Vibrations,* Mc Graw-Hill, Fourth Ed., 1956. Reprint, Dover Publ.

Heylen et al.-98.
Heylen, W., Lammens, S., Sas, P.; *Modal Analysis, Theory and Practice,* Katholieke Universiteit Leuven, ISBN 90-73802-61-X, Leuven, 1998

Hitchings-92.
Hitchings,D., *A Finite Element Dynamics Primer,* NAFEMS, Glasgow, 1992, ISBN 1-874376-05-0

Hughes-87.

Hughes, T.J.R. (1987). *The finite Element, Method: Linear Static and Dynamic Finite, Element analysis*, Prentice Hall, englewood Cliffs, New Jersey, ISBN 0-13-317017-9.

Irons-65.

Irons, B.M. (1965). *Structural Eigenvalue Problems: Elimination of Unwanted Variables*, AIAA Journal, Vol. 3, No. 5, pp. 961-962.

Kraker/Campen-96.

Kraker, A. de, Campen, D.H.van (1996). *Rubin's CMS reduction method for general state-space models*, Computers & Structures, Vol. 58, No. 3, pp 597-606

Kraker/Campen-97.

Kraker, A. de, Campen, D.H.van (1997). *Modification of the Craig-Bampton CMS procedure for general systems*, Proc. 1997 ASME Design Engineering Technical Conferences, Symposium on time-varying systems and structures, Sacramento, CA (USA), 14-17 Sept., 1997, Ed. by S.C. Sinha, J.P. Cusumano and O.M. o'Reilly, CD-Rom. paper DETC97/VIB-4030, 9pp.

Kraker-00.

Kraker, A. de. (2000). *A Numerical-Experimental Approach in Structural Dynamis*, Lecture Notes, University of Technology Eindhoven, Nr. 4.4784.

Kraker-00.

Kraker, A. de. (2000). *Rotordynamics*, Lecture Notes, University of Technology Eindhoven,

Meirovitch-97.

Meirovitch, L. (1997). *Principles and Techniques of Vibrations*, Prentice-Hall Inc., Upper Saddle River, New Jersey, ISBN 0-13-270430-7.

Meriam/Kraige-98.

Meriam, J.L., Kraige, L.G.; *Engineering Mechanics; Dynamics*, John Wiley & Sons Inc., 1998, ISBN 0-471-24167-9

Müller/Schiehlen-85.

Müller, P.C., Schiehlen, W.O.; *Linear Vibrations*, Martinus Nijhoff Publ., ISBN 90-247-2983-1, 1985

Newland-93.

Newland, D.E.; *Random Vibrations, Spectral & Wavelet Analysis*, Longman Scientific & Technical, ISBN 0582-21584-6, 1993

Rayleigh-45.

Rayleigh, Lord J.W.S. (1945). *Theory of Sound*, Vol. 1, Dover Publ. New York (first American edition of the 1894 edition).

Rao-95.   Rao, S.S. (1995). *Mechanical Vibrations*, Addison
                             Wesley, Third Ed., ISBN 0-201-52686-7.

Rubin-75.   Rubin, S. (1975). *Improved component mode
                             representation for structural dynamic analysis*,
                             AIAA Journal, Vol. 13, pp 995-1006

Weaver et al.-90.   Weaver Jr., W., Timoshenko, S., and Young, D.H.
                             (1990). *Vibration Problems in Engineering*, John
                             Wiley & Sons, Fifth Ed., ISBN 0-471-63228-7.

Zienkiewicz/Taylor-89.   Zienkiewicz, O.C. and Taylor, R.L. (1989). *The
                             Finite Element Method*, Mc Graw-Hill, London,
                             Fourth Ed.;
                             Vol. 1: Basic formulation and linear problems,
                             ISBN 0-07-08174-8.
                             Vol. 2: Solid and fluid mechanics, dynamics and
                             nonlinearity, ISBN 0-07-084175-6.

Index